ENDGAME
IN THE
BALKANS

ENDGAME
IN THE
BALKANS

*Regime Change,
European Style*

ELIZABETH POND

BROOKINGS INSTITUTION PRESS
Washington, D.C.

Copyright © 2006
THE BROOKINGS INSTITUTION
1775 Massachusetts Avenue, N.W., Washington, D.C. 20036
www.brookings.edu

Library of Congress Cataloging-in-Publication data
Pond, Elizabeth.
    Endgame in the Balkans : regime change, European style / Elizabeth Pond.
    p.   cm.
    Includes bibliographical references and index.
    ISBN-13: 978-0-8157-7160-9 (cloth : alk. paper)
    ISBN-10: 0-8157-7160-6 (cloth : alk. paper)
    1. Balkan Peninsula-Politics and government-1989–   2. European Union-Balkan Peninsula. I. Title.
    DR48.6.P66 2006
    949.6-dc22   2006025352

1 3 5 7 9 8 6 4 2

The paper used in this publication meets minimum requirements of the American National Standard for Information Sciences—Permanence of Paper for Printed Library Materials: ANSI Z39.48-1992.

Typeset in Minion

Composition by R. Lynn Rivenbark
Macon, Georgia

Printed by R. R. Donnelley
Harrisonburg, Virginia

TO HELEN

CONTENTS

PREFACE

As the last piece of the post-Yugoslav puzzle falls into place with settlement of Kosovo's status, it is time to hazard a contemporary analysis of the Balkans as a whole. Second-stage scholarship on the 1990s wars, incorporating in particular the legal truth established at the International Criminal Tribunal for the Former Yugoslavia, is now available. And the passing years have begun to distinguish underlying currents from surface froth. My contribution, I hope, will be an overview in which the quite distinctive dynamics of the eight lands I describe can shed light on each other, and on the overall impact on the Balkans of the European Union that each has chosen as its destiny.

To understand the Balkans today, it is essential to start with two foundation stones: the initial wars of the Yugoslav succession as they are perceived in retrospect and the drive for EU membership that is common to Central and to Southeast Europe. The former is presented in the survey of Yugoslavia's dissolution in chapter 1; the latter in chapters 2 on Bulgaria and 3 on Romania, the two countries that are farthest along the road to membership and that bridge Central and Southeast Europe. In particular, the Bulgarian chapter contains exerpts from a careful analysis by domestic actors who wanted to use EU pressure to help institute reforms at an early stage approximating the stage the Western Balkans are at now. The war in Kosovo and its aftermath are treated in chapter 4. In succeeding chapters, the tension between the heritage of the wars and the standards demanded of every new entrant to the European Union is then examined as it plays out quite differently in each country. I have not tried to describe the individual trajectories exhaustively in a book of this length, but seek rather to illuminate key turning points in each case.

Unexpectedly, I discovered in the writing that *Endgame in the Balkans* builds on my previous books, so much so that I now consider it the fourth in a linked quartet essaying a second draft of the history of post–cold war Europe. The first, *Beyond the Wall* (1993), tracks German unification. The second, *The Rebirth of Europe* (revised 2002), portrays the surprising emergence of the European Union (and monetary union) in the wake of German unity, despite widespread European malaise at the time. It is based on the crucial political interplay in Germany, in contrast to the more usual French orientation of popular American studies of the EU. The third, *Friendly Fire: The Near-Death of the Transatlantic Alliance* (2004), examines the clash between Old Europe and the Bush administration over the Iraq war. The present volume explores the daring premise that the Balkans belong to today's Europe, or can be brought to do so.

ACKNOWLEDGMENTS

MY THANKS GO first of all to the more than 380 persons in the Balkans, Germany, and the United States who generously shared their time and thoughts with me during the six-year gestation of this book. Even if I have not cited all of them individually in the text, I have benefited greatly from their ideas, ·directly and indirectly. I am also indebted to Tanjam Jacobson for her astute editing and to those who read and made helpful suggestions on one or more of my draft chapters: Robert Beecroft, Avis Bohlen, Shaun Byrnes, Mirza Hajric, Kathleen Imholz, Obrad Kesic, Kiril Nejkov, Stevan Niksic, J. D. Panitza, Brandusa Predescu, Dusan Reljic, Vjollca Shtylla, Elvana Thaci, Elisabeth Wendt, and three anonymous readers. Their willingness to render this service does not necessarily indicate agreement with my conclusions; two readers, indeed, took vehement exception to them. These judgments are my own, and I take sole responsibility for them.

I am grateful to the U.S. Institute of Peace for the grant that made this book possible. I thank the MIT Press for permission to use excerpts from four of my articles that appeared in the *Washington Quarterly*: "Reinventing Bulgaria" (vol. 22, no. 3, 1999); "Kosovo: Catalyst for Europe" (vol. 22, no. 4, 1999); "Romania: Better Late than Never" (vol. 24, no. 2, 2001); and "Kosovo and Serbia after the French Non" (vol. 28, no. 4, 2005). I thank the American Institute for Contemporary German Studies for permission to use a portion of an essay that I originally wrote for the AICGS in 2002, "Nation-Building in the Balkans."

Glossary of Abbreviations and Terms

AAK—Alliance for the Future of Kosova, party led by Ramush Haradinaj

ABiH—(Bosniak) Army of Bosnia and Herzegovina

Acquis communautaire (or just *acquis*)—the 93,000 pages of laws and regulations already adopted by the European Union that every new entrant must incorporate into its domestic law

Adriatic Charter—U.S.-sponsored group founded in 2003 to help prepare Croatia, Macedonia, and Albania for NATO membership

Althea—the EU-led operation that took over peacekeeping from NATO in Bosnia-Herzegovina in December 2004, with UN backing; 7,000 troops from thirty-three countries, including twenty-two EU member states

CARDS—Community Assistance for Reconstruction, Development and Stabilization, program of aid for the Western Balkans made available under the Stabilization and Association Process, beginning in 2001; see also IPA

CARPO—CARDS Regional Police Project

CEFTA—Central European Free Trade Agreement

CFSP—Common Foreign and Security Policy, the formal title of the EU's gradually increasing common foreign policy; see also ESDP

Concordia—first EU-led military operation, beginning in 2003 in Macedonia; succeeded NATO peacekeeping, involved 350 military personnel from twenty-seven countries, including thirteen of the then fifteen EU members)

Contact Group—the steering committee set up to deal with ex-Yugoslavia in 1994, composed of Germany, France, Britain, Italy, the United States, and Russia; see also Quint

Copenhagen criteria—democratic and market preconditions for EU accession, set in 1993

Dayton Accord—the 1995 American-brokered agreement that ended the fighting between ethnic Serbs, Croats, and Bosniaks in Bosnia

DOS—Democratic Opposition of Serbia, toppled Milosevic after he lost the 2000 elections in Serbia

DPA—Democratic Party of Albanians, ethnic Albanian party in Macedonia led by Arben Xhaferi

DS—Democratic Party (Serbia), originally led by Zoran Djindjic

DSS—Democratic Party of Serbia, led by Vojislav Kostunica

DUI—Democratic Union for Integration, ethnic Albanian party in Macedonia led by Ali Ahmeti

EBRD—European Bank for Reconstruction and Development, set up to help Central, East, and Southeast European economies

EC—European Community (until 1993); see also EU

EGF—European Gendarmerie Force, formally established in 2006 and based in Vicenza, Italy

Entities—the two subnational units in Bosnia-Herzegovina established by the Dayton Accord: the (Bosniak and Croat) Federation of Bosnia and Herzegovina and the Republika Srpska

ESDP—European Security and Defense Policy, the formal title of the EU's gradually increasing common security policy; see also CFSP

EU—European Union (after 1993); see also EC

EU-15—EU with fifteen Western European members, before 2004 enlargement

EU-25—EU with twenty-five members, after accession of ten Central European and Baltic countries in 2004

EUFOR—EU Forces in Bosnia-Herzegovina; see Althea

EUPM—EU Police Mission in Bosnia-Herzegovina, began in January 2003 with more than 500 police officers from thirty member and nonmember countries; the EU's first civil crisis management operation

EUPOL Proxima—the 200 EU police monitors and advisers who succeeded the Concordia operation in Macedonia from December 2003 through December 2005 to promote European policing standards and help fight organized crime

Europe Agreements—agreements between the EU and candidates who are close to promised membership

European Commission—the EU's supranational executive and legislation-initiating institution, consisting of a president, a collegium of commissioners, and the administrative bureacracy under them

European Council—the EU's intergovenmnental institution, which meets at least twice a year in summits of EU heads of government (and state, in the case of France)

EUSR—EU Special Representative in Bosnia, the successor, with reduced powers, to the OHR from 2007

Feasibility Study—EU evaluation of a country that is the first step toward a Stabilization and Association Agreement with the EU

FYROM—Former Yugoslav Republic of Macedonia, the official name that Greece finally agreed to for Macedonia

G17 Plus—small party of economist technocrats in Serbia that was a junior partner in Prime Minister Vojislav Kostunica's government

HDZ—Croatian Democratic Union (in both Croatia and Bosnia), nationalist political party founded by Franjo Tudjman

ICC—permanent International Criminal Court set up by the 1998 Rome Treaty and based in the Hague; opposed by the United States

ICTY—ad hoc International Criminal Tribunal for the Former Yugoslavia (in this book, often just "Hague Tribunal")

IFOR—Implementation Force, NATO-led peacekeepers in Bosnia-Herzegovina under a one-year UN mandate, beginning in December 1995; see also SFOR

IPA—Instrument for Pre-Accession Assistance, the single EU aid fund established for the 2007–13 budget term, consolidating earlier CARDS, ISPA, PHARE, and SAPARD programs

ISPA—Instrument for Structural Policies for Pre-Accession, giving large-scale EU environmental and transport investment support; see also IPA

JHA—EU bureaucratese for what used to be called domestic affairs within member states, short for Justice and Home Affairs; see JLS

JLS—new EU bureaucratese (Justice-Liberty-Security) for what used to be called JHA

JNA—Yugoslav People's Army

KFOR—Kosovo Force, NATO-led peacekeepers

KLA—Kosova Liberation Army, ethnic Albanian underground fighters against Serb rule in the late 1990s

KPC—Kosovo Protection Corps, set up by internationals to absorb veteran KLA fighters in a service to render disaster relief; regarded by Kosovar Albanians as their future army

KPS—Kosovo Police Service

LDK—Democratic League of Kosova, founded and led by Ibrahim Rugova

MAP—membership action plan, customized program of preparation for a nation's eventual membership in NATO or the EU

MAPE—the Multinational Advisory Police Element that began operating in Albania in 1997

MRF—Movement for Rights and Freedoms (Turkish and Pomak), junior coalition partner in both left and right governments in Bulgaria

NATO—North Atlantic Treaty Organization

Nice Treaty—EU treaty dating from 2000 that specifies current voting weights on the European Council and other operative arrangements; it is the default EU framework after French and Dutch referenda scotched the draft EU constitutional treaty in 2005

Nomenklatura—the party-vetted ruling elite in Communist times

OHR—Office of the High Representative, the international adminstrator in Bosnia-Herzegovina

Ohrid Agreement—the 2001 accord that ended the fighting between Slav Macedonians and ethnic Albanians in Macedonia

OSCE—Organization for Security and Cooperation in Europe; among its other watchdog democratic and human rights functions, it monitors elections in the Balkans

PDK—Democratic Party of Kosova, led by Hashim Thaci

People's VMRO—offshoot of Macedonian VMRO-DPMNE

PfP—Partnership for Peace, NATO's program of joint exercises and training for the armed forces of nonmember countries, either for joint peacekeeping operations or in preparation for these partners' eventual membership in the alliance

PHARE—Poland Hungary: Aid for the Reconstruction of Economies, pilot program for institution building and promotion of "economic and social cohesion" begun in 1989 for Poland and Hungary, then expanded to help prepare all Central European applicants for EU membership in the late 1990s, and later extended to future Balkan applicants; see also IPA

PIC—Peace Implementation Council, coordinates international civilian operations in Bosnia-Herzegovina

PISG—Provisional Institutions of Self-Government in Kosovo

PUR—Humanist Party of entrepreneurs in Romania that campaigned on a ticket with the Social Democrats but defected after 2004 to join the new center-right government, under the new name of Conservative Party

Quint—Western members of the Contact Group (that is, excluding Russia)

RCC—Regional Cooperation Council, the Balkan regional organization with a secretary general that is due to succeed the Stability Pact in 2008, with local ownership; see also SEECP

RS—Republika Srpska entity in Bosnia-Herzegovina

SAA—Stabilization and Association Agreement, the entry-level accord with the EU that promises eventual membership to Balkan lands

SAP—Stabilization and Association Process

SAPARD—EU's Special Accession Program for Agriculture and Rural Development; see also IPA

Schengen agreements—series of agreements from 1985 onward between an expanding inner EU core to scrap border controls

SDA—Party of Democratic Action, nationalist Bosniak party

SDB—State Security Service in Tito's and post-Communist Yugoslavia

SDS—Serbian Democratic Party, nationalist Serb party in Bosnia

SECI—Southeast European Cooperative Initiative, set up to fight regional crime and based in Bucharest

SEECP—Southeast European Cooperation Process, the locally run series of regional meetings at summit, ministerial, and ad hoc levels; see also RCC

SFOR—Stabilization Force, NATO-led peacekeepers in Bosnia; succeeded IFOR at the end of 1996

SHIK—National Intelligence Service in post-Communist Albania

SPAI—Stability Pact Initiative to Fight Corruption

SPC—Serbian Orthodox Church

SPOC—Stability Pact Initiative to Fight Organized Crime

Stability Pact for Southeastern Europe—loose coordinating umbrella for international civilian aid to the Balkans, led by the EU and based in Brussels; to be phased out shortly and replaced by the locally run RCC

Thessaloniki Council—meeting in 2003 at which the EU promised future membership to all Western Balkan countries that fulfill the stated prerequisites

TO—Territorial Defense Forces in Yugoslavia

UDF—Union of Democratic Forces, the center-right coalition that governed Bulgaria twice in the mid-1990s

UDMR—Hungarian Democratic Union of Romania, a junior partner in both left and right governments

UNPROFOR—UN Protection Force in Croatia and Bosnia, 1992–95

UNMIK—UN Mission in Kosovo, the UN administration pending Serb-Kosovar agreement on final status

VJ—Army of Yugoslavia, Milosevic's successor to the JNA, from 1993 on

VMRO-DPMNE—Internal Macedonian Revolutionary Organization–Democratic Party for Macedonian National Unity

VRS—Bosnian Serb Military, formally independent force formed in May 1992 out of the old JNA 2nd Military District Command

The Balkans and environs

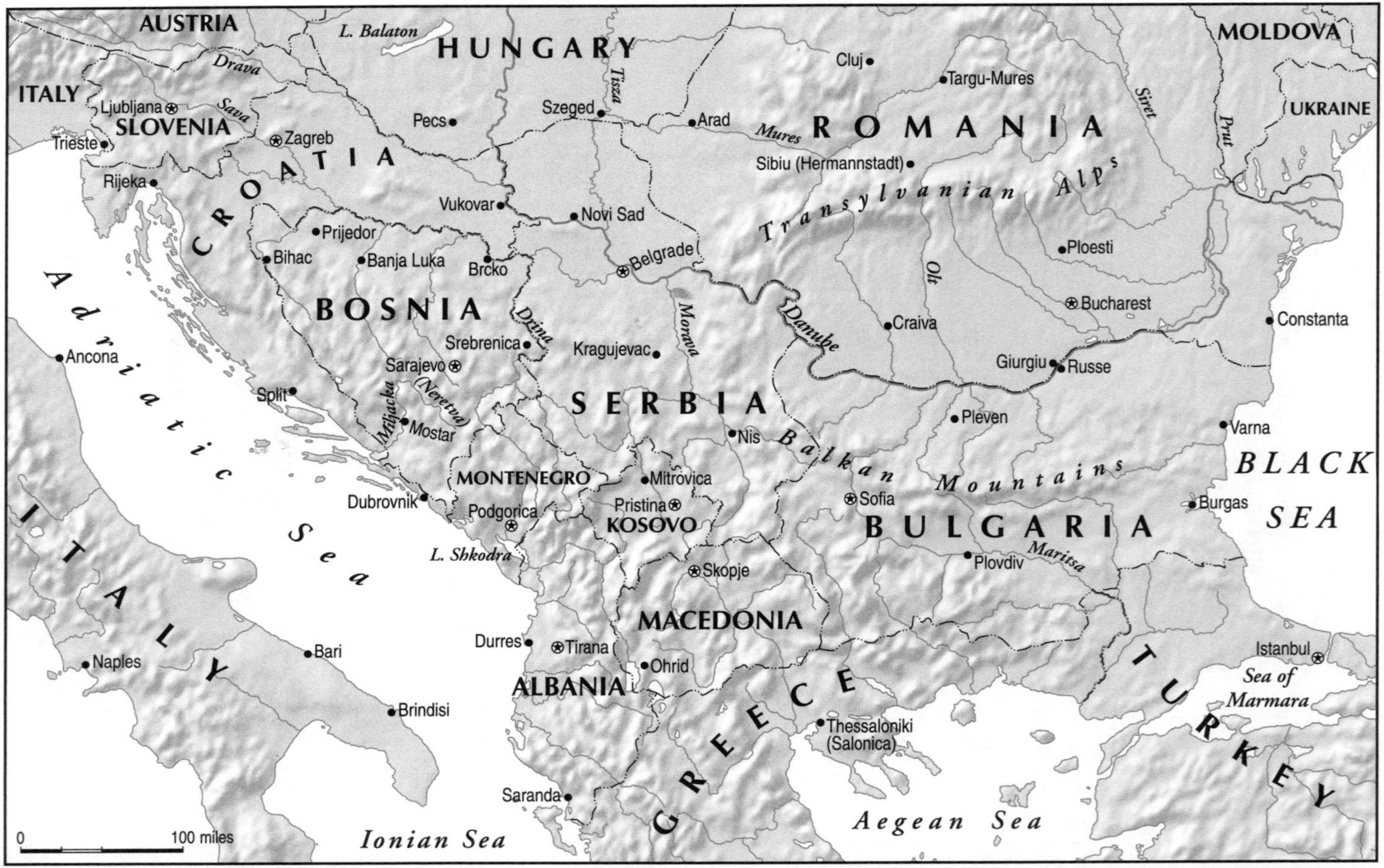

AUSTRIA

ITALY

Drava

HUNGARY

L. Balaton

Tisza

Ljubljana ⊗
SLOVENIA

Sava

⊗ Zagreb

Pecs ●

Szeged ●

Arad ●

Mures

Trieste ●

ROMANIA

Rijeka ●

C R O A T I A

Vukovar ●

Novi Sad ●

● Prijedor

Banja Luka ●

● Bihac

Brcko ●

⊗ Belgrade

B O S N I A

Drina

Morava

Danube

Ancona ●

Srebrenica ●

Kragujevac ●

Sarajevo ⊗

● Pale

Cacak ●

A
d
r
i
a
t
i
c

Split ●

Miljacka

(Neretva)

● Mostar

S E R B I A

● Nis

Trebinje ●

Ibar

Dubrovnik ●

MONTENEGRO

Mitrovica ●

Sofia ⊗

S
e
a

Podgorica ●

Vushtrri ●

Pristina ⊗

Cetinje ●

Tropoje ●

Gracanica ●

BULG.

I
T
A
L
Y

L. Shkodra

Shkodra ●

KOSOVO

Tetovo ●

Skopje ●

● Naples

Bari ●

Durres ●

⊗ Tirana

MACEDONIA

Ohrid ●

ALBANIA

Brindisi ●

G
R
E
E
C
E

Thessaloniki ●
(Salonica)

Saranda ●

0   100 miles

Ionian Sea

INTRODUCTION

It wasn't that the European Union deliberately conceived of the Balkans as the test of its nascent Common Foreign and Security Policy and Europol. Or that the United States conceived of "Southeastern Europe" as the proving ground of its twenty-first-century crusade for global democratic transformation. Or that the post-9/11 Bush administration thought of this as the pioneer region in the nation building that it first scorned, then reinvented in order to avert Afghanistan's reversion to a failing state that would invite recapture by al Qaeda. Or that social engineers resolved to compare and contrast postwar soft power in the Balkans—making others want what you want—with coercive regime change in Iraq. Or that the new ad hoc international criminal courts formed for Yugoslavia (as for Rwanda) deliberately set out to hand down the world's first convictions under the half-century-old Genocide Convention. Or that Japan, whose donated buses now provide essential transport in Sarajevo, saw the Balkans as a prime venue for demonstrating Tokyo's expanding engagement outside of Asia. It all just happened that way.

The European Community (EC), as it was still called in the early 1990s, was simply muddling through reactively, as was its wont with all those pan-European policies that were not purely economic. The United States, glad to turn the cantankerous Balkans over to European crisis management as the cold war ended and the mortal dangers on the old continent seemed to have been dispelled, focused instead on the Herculean tasks befitting the sole surviving superpower, especially in Saddam Hussein's Middle East.[1] And however much it criticized "Madeleine Albright's war" in the Balkans as frittering away American power on the remote fringes of any real national interest, the successor administration of George W. Bush eventually reconciled itself to finishing what the administration of Bill Clinton had begun there.

For the European Union, the Balkans, like most items on its agenda, were as much a domestic as a foreign policy issue. The same ambiguity attended "enlargement," aka "widening," the post–cold war improvisation for exporting to infant post-Communist governments both security and the democracy to underpin it. Though it was far less articulated than the drive for worldwide democratization that would become the declared organizing principle of U.S. policy after the disappointments of the 2003 Iraq war, democratic regime change became, de facto, the foreign policy of the EU in its own neighborhood.

This endeavor already had an honorable tradition. By the 1960s the EC had achieved its original goal of ending two millenniums of war in the bloody European heartland by reconciling the residual archenemies, France and Germany. Under NATO's protection, the EC devised a unique form of supranational cooperation that fell well short of federation but went far beyond a confederation in the unprecedented meddling in fellow members' internal affairs that it authorized.[2] In the 1970s the European Community expanded its political mission to embrace democratic transformation, through the integration of postdictatorship Spain, Portugal, and Greece. Inculcating this novel political culture in southern Europe was accomplished through tutelage in domestic governance, as rendered especially by the German political foundations that had played such an important role in democratizing post-Hitler West Germany—notably the Friedrich Ebert Foundation, which offered a robust social democratic alternative to the Communist and radical left utopias that U.S. Secretary of State Henry Kissinger so feared. Institutionally, the process was promoted by setting democratic as well as market criteria that the three Mediterranean states had to fulfill before they could be granted the privilege of EC membership.[3] By the time the Berlin Wall fell and the Soviet Union imploded in 1989–91, the system had already ensured the European heartland's longest period of peace in its history. "There is no precedent in world history for war being ruled out of forward calculations at such a high level," concluded the awestruck megahistorian Paul Johnson.[4]

After the collapse of the Soviet Union and its Warsaw Pact, the fledgling democracies in Central Europe, gazing wistfully at Western Europe's peace and prosperity, all yearned to join the European Community. The foreign policy of the EC toward the post-Soviet neighborhood quickly became a domestic EC policy of deciding who might be allowed into the exclusive club, and by what process. If liberalized Madrid, Lisbon, and Athens could accede, why not liberalized Warsaw, Prague, Budapest, Tallinn, Riga, and Vilnius, too? If impoverished Ireland, through EC membership, could leap in one generation from a residual potato-famine exporter of emigrants to become a high-tech importer of those lucky enough to have Irish grandparents, then why not let the Central Europeans follow the same trajectory? Germany and Britain became the chief promoters of European Union enlargement as both an economic and a security measure. In this advocacy, part of the British motivation was to ward off French-German desires to "deepen" the EC into some kind of political union, by confining the EU to a politically unwieldy, large free-trade zone. The motivation of the Federal Republic of Germany (by now incorporating the erstwhile Communist German Democratic Republic) was the desire to end its frontline status by surrounding itself with friendly democracies to the east as well as to the west.

With the end of the cold war, then, the earlier EC enlargement process was repeated for the new democracies that emerged as the Central Europeans were freed from Moscow's external empire. The iron curtain that on the one hand had ring-fenced Western Europe against Soviet meddling and allowed the EC to spread security and prosperity throughout the region had for decades, on the other hand, cut off "Eastern Europe" from Western Europe's golden age. Austria and Finland, which had not been much better off than neighboring Hungary and Latvia in 1945, were by 1989 viewed enviously by the latter. In the 1990s the Central Europeans clamored to "rejoin" Europe as both symbol and means to effect their belated modernization. "Rejoining" Europe may have been a myth for most of them, but it was a useful myth. On a popular level, the mantra of striving for EC accession perhaps signified little more than a hazy feeling that if Western European members of the EC were so unimaginably safe and rich, then newcomers to the club would magically partake of these qualities too. But a core of Central European elites saw the EC project precisely as a way to apply outside pressure to make up for their countries' lost half century. In the words of Polish finance minister Leszek Balcerowicz, reformers seized on the brief period of "extraordinary politics" afforded by the euphoria over release from the Soviet grip to raze old structures and start afresh.[5] On the whole, Polish, Czech, and Estonian nationalism worked positively, enhancing populations' solidarity in disavowing Russia's authoritarian urges and pressing for democratic self-determination.

The Central Europeans' mission of carrying out in one generation the political, social, and economic revolutions that the British, French, and Americans had completed in a more leisurely two centuries was a formidable one. Democratization had not proved durable in the 1980s in Latin America, the region where transitions to democracy had been studied the most intensively. Experts therefore tended to be pessimistic about its sustainability in Central Europe—or even to suggest that the Central Europeans were now more likely to go the way of the third than of the first world.[6] Nor had liberal economic transformation been an unalloyed success even in Europe. It was all very well that Ireland was on its way to surpassing the United Kingdom in per capita income, but Greece was still viewed by wary Polish economists in the early 1990s as an example of what to avoid.[7]

Under Central European badgering and German and British lobbying, enlargement proceeded—despite French fears that widening would only bring in low-wage Polish plumbers and a Trojan horse of admirers of that American superpower whose sense of its exceptionalism and civilizing mission so closely mirrored France's own self-image. The European Community signed ad hoc "Europe Agreements" with Poland, Hungary, and Czechoslovakia in 1991 and with Romania and Bulgaria in 1993, and at its 1993 Copenhagen summit regularized them with a formal promise to grant these partners membership as soon as they met the "Copenhagen criteria" of democratic and market standards.

Their challenge was even more daunting than that which the Spanish, Portuguese, and Greeks confronted twenty years earlier. While the southern Europeans may have been unfamiliar with an open political system, they were old hands at market economics. In Central Europe, by contrast, no one under the age of seventy had personally experienced a private-enterprise system. Balcerowicz and other Polish economists had managed to acquire a sophisticated theoretical understanding of the genre, and the occasional Bulgarian economist had begun the intellectual trek by learning Polish in order to wrestle with the professional literature from Warsaw. But basically the economic system was a greenfield undertaking. The Central Europeans had to learn not only how democracy works, but also how the market works. They did so with impressive speed. In particular, those that got the pain of "shock therapy" over with as fast as possible—Estonia above all, Poland with more ambiguity—set a solid foundation, began attracting foreign investment, and generated enough growth for a new prosperity to seep from the major cities into the countryside.

The future success of Central European transformation was by no means clear as Yugoslavia broke up in the early 1990s, however, and it was at first no model for the Balkans. A European Community that was groping to cope with the bewildering post–cold war world was slow to react to the Balkan bloodshed. It stretched credulity to believe that Yugoslavia, the liberal darling of the West during the cold war, could lapse into such barbarity when the post–cold war *zeitgeist* was so obviously the outbreak of peace. As the Serbs conquered 70 percent of Bosnia, the EC dithered and initially did no more than try to build a firewall to shield itself from any spillover of the Balkan violence. After half a century of configuring their troops to repulse a mass armored ground attack, EC members did not have the right kind or number of troops to intervene militarily, even if they had known, in the initial fog of war, which side to back. And after a half century of habitually deferring to U.S. leadership for their own defense, they certainly did not have the political will to intervene alone.

The 1995 Srebrenica massacre, the worst mass murder of civilians in Europe since the Holocaust, was the wake-up call. The United States responded first, strong-arming Serbia's Slobodan Milosevic, Croatia's Franjo Tudjman, and Bosnia's Alija Izetbegovic into a Dayton Accord that was flawed but ended the war. The European Union, reacting more slowly, then offered the "Western Balkans"—a neologism covering ex-Yugoslavia (minus Slovenia) and Albania—the same promise of eventual EU membership that it had extended to the Central Europeans. This became the incentive to deep reforms that, it was hoped, would mold the Balkan future. It moved the EU beyond firewall containment to the premise that a peninsula an hour's flight away from Vienna must be regarded as part of Europe—and that the only way to ensure European security was to adopt and transform the Balkans.[8] Once again, EU "foreign" policy was transformed into "domestic" policy.

Citizens of the new Western Balkan candidates-in-waiting were gratified by the prospect, above all, of visa-free travel to Munich and Paris if they became part of the European family.[9] But to qualify for EU membership they faced a third hurdle in addition to the dual task of democratization and marketization faced by the northern Central Europeans—as well as the Romanians and Bulgarians, who had failed to join the first accession but were better prepared than the Western Balkan states and were next in line for membership. Not only were the Western Balkan populations, with a standard of living a fifth of the Western European niveau, incomparably poorer than the Central Europeans—who had at least started out at a third of Western European levels—and proportionally less able to pay for social welfare to ease the pain of reform. Not only did most of the Balkans lack anything like Poland's defiantly pluralist civil society. Not only did their corruption far surpass Central European levels to approach Russian heights (if without the same mineral riches to plunder). The new states that emerged as Yugoslavia disintegrated (and as hermetic Albania rejoined the world) were also vastly less cohesive domestically than the Central European nations—or at least what cohesion there was tended to be dysfunctional, rabid chauvinism in a region of intermixed ethnicities.[10] The Poles, Hungarians, and Bulgarians all knew who they were and (for the most part) where their borders lay; the Macedonians and Bosnians did not. Nor did the Western Balkan nations share the Central Europeans' galvanizing myth of (Western) European identity. Theirs was not a positive nationalism that bolstered solidarity in the search for democracy, but a lethal authoritarian ultranationalism that stoked war passions. Like the Central Europeans, they sought the bliss of becoming "normal," which by definition meant like Western Europe.[11] But before they could become normal they had to do some elementary nation building of a sort that would accommodate rather than demonize the "other." And this in a region where 100,000 had just been butchered, often by known neighbors, in Bosnia alone.[12]

For its part, as the EU expanded its concept of enlargement to include the Balkans, it also shifted its rationale for the crucial conditionality that was helping to discipline the Central Europeans into building democratic institutions. Judgments about the readiness of candidate countries to withstand the rigors of membership were always as much subjective as objective, as recently attested by the EU's simultaneous admittance in 2004 of ten heterogeneous candidates who could not conceivably all be equally prepared. But with the starting level of the Western Balkan states so far below that of the Central Europeans, political encouragement of the candidates on their long road to membership took on more weight relative to robust fulfillment of the criteria set at Copenhagen in 1993. More (and tinier) steps of progress—like the new Stabilization and Association Agreements—were invented to give some interim rewards to the few politicians who began to glimpse the vision and nudge their countries toward a cooperative Europe in which the significance of fierce sovereignty, borders, and ethnicity would fade. Indeed, popular approval of the goal of EU membership in each of the eight Balkan candidates or prospective candidates rose and fell in clear correspondence with the attainment or failure to attain the various lesser stages en route to membership. This mattered. When citizen approval for EU accession increased, so did the capacity of pro-EU elites to implement essential but uncomfortable reforms. When approval decreased, the blocking power of the ultranationalist and often enough criminal resisters of reform was enhanced. In 2003, just after Croatia was accepted as a full candidate for quick entry into the club, some 82 percent of Croats favored the idea. In 2005, as the EU postponed the beginning of the real entry negotiations because of the country's failure to deliver war crimes indictee Ante Gotovina to the Hague, 57 percent of Croats opposed the idea.[13]

By the first anniversary of the "big bang" EU enlargement of 2004, the economic and political success of the new Central European members was already impressive.[14] Economic growth, projected at 4.5 percent in these new member states in 2005, was double that of sluggish Western Europe. Their exports, led by foodstuffs, were up 20 percent over pre-entry levels, while rural incomes were 50 percent higher, even though EU agricultural subsidies to the newcomers were only a quarter of Brussels's largesse to French farmers. Cumulative foreign direct investment in Poland was $73 billion. Estonia and the Czech Republic were beginning to rival India in data outsourcing.[15] "Social capital" (essentially, "trust" between strangers, as measured by participation in civil associations, networking, and the like) was growing toward Western European levels.[16] Moreover, in Kyiv in November 2004, Polish president Alexander Kwasniewski adroitly played his country's new membership to mobilize the weight of the EU to avert violent suppression of the Orange Revolution and ensure the peaceful succession of the elected Viktor Yushchenko to the Ukrainian presidency. By 2006, on the second anniversary of their accession, the new members had advanced from 44 percent of the average income of the fifteen old EU members to 55 percent—and they had also contributed to growth and trade in the EU-15 without swamping labor markets, increasing unemployment, or depressing wages.[17]

All this the Balkan onlookers know very well. Although many despair of their region's perpetual backwater status in Europe, others draw vicarious hope from the Central European success. Macedonia's vice premier Radmila Sekerinska spoke for all of her Southeast European colleagues when she told listeners in Austria that the EU's 2004 "enlargement round brought those countries democracy and economic development" and concluded, "We want more or less to use the same recipe for the Balkans."[18]

Here it is worth noting that the EU-Balkan interaction is not a one-way street. Even as the European Union is changing the Balkans, the Balkans are changing the European Union. The debacle of Europe's attempts at crisis management in the region in the early 1990s stimulated perception of a need to build more flexible European military capabilities, along with the political will to use these forces even outside the traditional NATO area for peacemaking by coercion. The outcome was European as well as U.S. approval of NATO's first-ever hot war, in Kosovo in 1999, in order to stop Milosevic's "ethnic cleansing" of a million Kosovar Albanians.[19] German foreign minister Joschka Fischer, who singlehandedly brought his pacifist Green Party around to elevate the precept of "no more genocide" above the precept of "no more war," insisted on adding to military intervention the civilian nation and state building encompassed in the Stability Pact for Southeastern Europe.[20] With this, the EU committed itself to an enormous outlay in money and manpower for a generation to come. It provided the bulk of the $4.5 billion in international assistance to the 4 million Bosnians in the country's first two postconflict years—a more generous package than the $4.1 billion the 75 million Japanese received in 1946–47. To tiny Kosovo, the EU and its member states bilaterally gave four times as much aid per capita ($800) as the victors of World War II gave West Germany in 1946–47.[21] The costs in the Balkans have been low only in comparison with the alternative costs of war.

Whether or not the EU's (and America's) huge investment in nation building, state building, and institution building in the Balkans over the past decade is actually working to transform the "crooked timber" in the Balkans is the question this book seeks to answer. Put another way: is the magnetic attraction of EU membership strong enough to pull the Balkans through the pain of reform to the democratic and market "normality" they long for?

CHAPTER ONE

THE WARS
OF THE YUGOSLAV SUCCESSION

UNDER OTHER CIRCUMSTANCES, it might have been the liberal Serbs and Croats (and Bosnians and Slovenians) and the growing middle classes who inherited Josip Broz Tito's relatively benign Communist Yugoslavia after the marshal's death in 1980. But by the time the cold war ended in 1989–91, stale socialist ideology provided no uniting myth for the two-alphabet, three-religion, four-language, five-nationality, six-republic country that had lasted for seven decades.[1] Tito contributed to the collapse of Yugoslavia by establishing a diffuse collective system with secret-police controls that prevented any lieutenant of his from usurping power prematurely—but at the same time built no orderly succession for when he was gone. The country lacked an integrated market and infrastructure, as well as any authoritative political center. Even pragmatic, incremental modernization failed to find any convincing champion as disintegration set in. Simmering nationalist hostility heated to fever pitch in the late 1980s and early 1990s. Slobodan Milosevic exploited these passions to become Yugoslavia's, and Serbia's, top leader.

The country's disintegration was a tragedy, both for Yugoslavia itself and for Europe. "Yugoslavia did not die a natural death; it was murdered, and Milosevic, more than any other single leader, is responsible," concludes Louis Sell, Milosevic's biographer.[2] The blue-ribbon Scholars' Initiative team of two dozen Yugoslav and Western academics that examined the rival Serb, Croat, Bosniak, Kosovar Albanian, Slovenian, and "cosmopolitan" historical narratives in 2000 agrees that no inherent dynamic predestined the contradictions in the multiple narratives to lead to war.[3] The team report blames the plunge into inhumanity in the 1990s on mismanagement or exploitation by "human agency" of Yugoslavia's economic deterioration, political illegitimacy, and institutional flaws—and on the Serb "revitalization movement," with its "territorial fantasies." Yet, "while the violent breakup of Yugoslavia was not inevitable, it was nonetheless overdetermined, so that it would have taken wise leadership, committed to the Yugoslav community as such and acting in good time, to pull the country back from the brink."[4] That wise leadership was lacking.

Blackbird Field

Milosevic, a rising young apparatchik in the 1980s, seems to have had neither convictions nor compunctions of his own. He began with pan-Yugoslav socialist orthodoxy and discovered the power of virulent chauvinism only in the latter part of the decade, as the attraction of socialism and Tito's third-worldism waned. In April 1987, apparently spontaneously, he pledged to aggrieved stone-throwing Serbs in the Serbian province of Kosovo, at the site of the epic Serb defeat by the Ottoman Turks in 1389, "No one will ever beat this people again," and heard the approving roar of the crowd.[5] Two years later, at the same Blackbird Field, on the six-hundreth anniversary of the defeat—against a backdrop of posters of himself and the fourteenth-century tsar Lazar and the fluttering banners of the Serbian Orthodox Church, which Milosevic had resurrected as a political actor after half a century of its being shut out of politics under Tito—he gambled on going further. The audience of a million Serbs greeted him with wild cheers when he threatened, for the first time, that future "armed battles . . . cannot be excluded."[6]

Those two appeals at the sacred cradle of Serbdom began what James Gow, delicately avoiding the more emotive phrase "Greater Serbia," calls Milosevic's "Serbian project." A professor at the Department of War Studies at King's College, London, Gow was the one Western expert on the Yugoslav military not of ethnic Yugoslav extraction who was available to the prosecution of the International Criminal Tribunal for the Former Yugoslavia (ICTY) at the Hague. It hired him to establish the factual military background to the wars of the Yugoslav succession on the basis of official military documentation, intercepts, interviews, and other sources, and to distinguish between legitimate war operations and war crimes of intended or indiscriminate violence against civilians. The case he made for detecting a deliberate Serbian "strategy of war crimes" from the outset of Milosevic's military campaigns laid the foundation for the court's conviction of General Radislav Krstic and other Serb leaders for genocide and war crimes.[7]

Milosevic's theatrical summons at Blackbird Field touched perfectly the chord of victimization that has long coexisted with the Serb superiority complex.[8] For two centuries, the Serbs have seen themselves as the most dynamic of the Balkan peoples and the natural leaders in the region. They outnumber other Slavs in the environs. In medieval times they ruled an empire, and in the less remote past they were the first Slavs to break out of the decaying Ottoman Empire, winning autonomy in 1830 and independence in 1878.[9] Their fierce nationalism, combined with the pan-Slav sentiments of the less numerous Croats and Slovenes in the Wilsonian aftermath of World War I, led to the birth of the first Yugoslavia, which was then dominated by the Serbs' King Aleksandar.

In the second Yugoslavia, after World War II, the deracinated Croat-Slovene Josip Broz Tito balanced off the Serbs against the other constituent national-ities. Once antifascism and communism had faded as political legitimation, however, Milosevic rediscovered on the hallowed soil of Kosovo the mobiliz-ing power of Serb grievance. At issue was the belated partial autonomy (not full autonomy as a Yugoslav republic) that Tito had granted Kosovo and its majority Albanians, along with Vojvodina and its large Hungarian minority, in the 1970s. Albanians had quickly supplanted Serbs in many senior posts in the Communist Party and the secret police, become prominent in the professional elite of teachers, managers, and professors at the new Pristina University—and stepped up the decade-old intimidation and harassment of local Serbs to try to make them move elsewhere. A new Albanian intelligentsia poured out of Pristina University and found no jobs. After Tito's death, students and young graduates demonstrated in 1981 against poor conditions in the university can-teen and the remaining Serb officials in Kosovo, and for an elevation of Kosovo's status to a full-fledged republic (with the nominal right to secede). Serb security forces cracked down and put thousands in jail, where they became radicalized and emerged to talk febrile politics in street cafes and form the leadership core of what would by the 1990s become the Kosova Liberation Army (KLA).

The roughly 13 percent Serb minority in Kosovo resented the loss of its positions of command through the expanded autonomy of the Kosovar Alba-nians and by the end of the 1980s hailed Milosevic as the savior who would reconstitute their rightful dominance.[10] Milosevic duly ended the autonomy of Kosovo and Vojvodina in 1989 and increasingly played the nationalist card in the province, expelling Albanian directors of hospitals, schools, state enter-prises, and the more lucrative stores in cities, firing the bulk of the Albanian workforce, and barring Albanian children from Serb-run schools in what became a kind of apartheid. A fifth of the Kosovar Albanians became depen-dent on humanitarian aid.[11] In the first few years of the 1990s the political and economic pressure induced some 400,000 Albanians to emigrate, in what

Albanians termed "silent cleansing." By late 1994, after he defeated domestic rivals and dissidents and expelled observers from the Organization for Security and Cooperation in Europe (OSCE) from Kosovo, Milosevic asserted to diplomats that the province was again fully under control. The Albanians in Kosovo went underground, running Albanian-language schools and holding a clandestine vote in which semiotician Ibrahim Rugova, preaching nonviolence and wearing his trademark Parisian ascot, was overwhelmingly elected shadow president.

Kosovo remained a thorn in the side of Milosevic, not only because of Albanian unrest, but also because as Yugoslavia broke up the Serb colonial rule there precluded any peaceful resolution of nationality problems elsewhere. Any readjustment of the republics' borders by local referendum that might have joined Serb villages in Croatia and Bosnia to the Serb motherland (and probably would have won international assent) would also have severed Blackbird Field from Serbia and delivered it to the local Albanian majority.[12] That Milosevic excluded as intolerable.

After some vacillation, he opted to fulfill by force what had quickly become his goal of establishing a Greater Serbia, if not as the dominant center of all of the old Yugoslavia, as he would have preferred, then as a new, expanded Serbia encompassing the territory of the third of Serbs who lived in Croatia, Bosnia, and Kosovo.[13] For Milosevic, and for Serb public opinion as a whole, it was unacceptable ever to have Serb minorities governed by non-Serb majorities. Yet few of the regions that Milosevic would ultimately claim were homogeneously Serb. Many were intermixed and intermarried; out of a total population of close to a million in the disputed districts that Serb forces overran in the early 1990s, some 51 percent were Croats, only some 30 percent Serbs.[14]

The downward spiral can be measured from January 1990, when the Slovenes—who, together with the Croats, wanted a much looser confederation—walked out of the Congress of the League of Communists of Yugoslavia and the LCY broke up. In March the inner Serbian party "coordinating committee" met secretly to prepare for the fallback plan of a new state with Serb areas carved out of Croatia and Bosnia and attached to the heartland. In April the first multiparty elections in Yugoslavia in half a century took place in Slovenia and Croatia. These two republics, which had in any case long resented their role as milch cows for the poorer Yugoslav regions to the south (including Kosovo), by now feared, too, that the new Serb assertiveness would soon deprive them of democratic self-rule, or indeed any self-rule at all.

In Croatia voters elected as president the old Yugoslav partisan and Croat nationalist Franjo Tudjman. Significantly, in the election the majority of ethnic Serbs in the republic, the culturally "Croatized" urban Serbs, backed the coalition that stood for civil democracy rather than the Serb nationalist party. Yet Tudjman never tried to appeal to the more cosmopolitan Serbs in Croatia as a counterweight to the ultranationalist Krajina Serbs, and he quickly alienated them.[15] Even before independence, his new Croatian Democratic Union (HDZ) practiced the "systematic" infringement of Serbs' civil, property, and employment rights, and Tudjman's "greed in seeking to annex Croatian areas of Bosnia" would prolong the war there.[16] In his election campaign he further offended all Serbs by glossing over the brutality against Serb Chetnik nationalist guerrillas practiced by the Ustasha puppet regime in World War II, even as both Ustasha and Chetniks fought Tito's partisans and both avoided fighting the Germans (the former explicitly, the latter tacitly).[17] The Ustasha regime was "not simply a quisling creation and a fascist crime; it was also an expression of the historical aspirations of the Croatian people," Tudjman asserted. Once he was elected, he renamed streets to honor members of the Ustasha regime and, more justifiably, stopped paying Serb policemen who had ceased obeying orders in 1990.[18] Unlike the ever-changing Milosevic, Tudjman "had a firm set of core beliefs that shaped his political behavior. These were a strong belief in Croatian nationhood and an almost messianic faith in himself as the symbol of the first independent Croatian state in one thousand years."[19] In spring 1990 President Tudjman did not yet want independence, however, given the clear signals that if Croatia seceded from Yugoslavia the Serbs in the Dalmatian hinterland of Krajina, mobilized and armed by Belgrade, would secede from Croatia. What Tudjman asked for instead was recognition of Croatia as a sovereign republic in a looser Yugoslav confederation.

In May 1990 Milosevic raised the stakes. He railed against the dangers of an "anti-Serb coalition," declared that "the interests of Serbia must be above all others," and presented a new Serbian constitution that allowed for breaking up Yugoslavia and, as he soon made clear, redrawing the old "administrative" republican borders to include all ethnic Serbs in a new Serbian state. Shortly thereafter, the Yugoslav People's Army (JNA) disarmed the non-Serb Territorial Defense Forces (TO) throughout the country—except in Slovenia, where local officers refused to relinquish their weapons. In June Mihaijlo Kertes, a senior Serb police official close to Milosevic, started funneling arms covertly to militant Serbs in Krajina, who began driving out Croats. In July 100,000 Serbs in the region founded a new Serb assembly, to the chant of "Kill the

Ustashe!" In August, as Krajina Serbs staged a referendum to form an autonomous area, the JNA ostentatiously blocked Croatian police from entering this Croatian region. Serb nationalist symbols were daubed onto Croat houses; some Croat-owned stores were looted; Croats prudently began moving away.[20] Hard-line Serb nationalist intellectuals in Belgrade began organizing their soulmates in Croatia and Bosnia in the radical Serbian Democratic Party (SDS); in Bosnia the psychiatrist and part-time poet Radovan Karadzic became the SDS leader.

At the same time, Milosevic began quietly building up paramilitary forces to be the shock troops in the forthcoming Serbian offensives and ethnic cleansing; to create the facts on the ground of "murder, mutilation, torture, rape and terrorization" that would maneuver the more hesitant JNA into supporting the militias; and—during the Bosnian offensive—to hide the chain of command leading to Milosevic and let him deny any responsibility for atrocities, blaming them instead on armed freelancers.[21] The most notorious and sadistic of the paramilitary commanders was Zeljko Raznatovic ("Arkan"), a convicted criminal who, along with many colleagues, was a veteran of the assassination squads of the old Communist state security service (SDB) that had murdered some sixty emigré Yugoslav dissidents in Western Europe in previous decades. In October Arkan began gathering and training his Tigers— a hard core of between 1,500 and 5,000 individuals—arming them with the kind of heavy weapons, tanks, and helicopters that he could obtain only from Yugoslav army stocks. A single Arkan, then Yugoslav interior minister Stane Dolanc pronounced as far back as 1981, was "worth more than the whole of the SDB." Milosevic clearly shared this evaluation, especially as he considered Arkan someone who would remain loyal to him and counteract less predictable militia chiefs.[22]

In November 1990 Arkan delivered some weapons to the enclave of the newly proclaimed Serbian Autonomous Region of Krajina to help Belgrade's Serbian Security Service and the JNA set up this "template for the Serbian strategic program" in creating a "no-go area for the official authorities in Croatia."[23] When he left Krajina to return to Belgrade, he was arrested by Croat police as he crossed the Bosnia-Croatia administrative border and was charged with gun-running and conspiracy to overthrow the Croatian state. Yet in mid-June 1991, in an odd episode after open Serb-Croat fighting had already erupted in Croatia, Arkan was suddenly freed from jail under mysterious circumstances that critics charged included a secret deal between Milosevic and Tudjman to later carve up Bosnia.[24]

As the Serbian preparations for takeover progressed in Croatia in 1990, the Slovenes worked methodically toward the secession that was their formal right as a republic under the Yugoslav constitution, and by October had annulled thirty major federal Yugoslav laws.[25] The clearer it became that Slovenia would break loose, the greater was the Croats' conviction that it would be folly to stay in a Serb-run federation without the Slovenes.

In Bosnia's first multiparty vote in December, Alija Izetbegovic was elected president. A practicing Muslim himself, he called for a dominant role for Bosnia's Muslims (who constituted a plurality but not a majority), without clarifying what role that would leave for Bosnia's Serbs, Croats, and others.[26] At that point he had, however, even less of a strategy for achieving this objective than Milosevic did for achieving his goals. Bosnia drifted as Slovenia and Croatia marched toward secession. Zagreb, which coveted Bosnia's ethnic Croat areas in Herzegovina and was planning on annexing them as soon as any war broke out, dragged Bosnia in its wake.

In Serbia in December Slobodan Milosevic, with a broad wink at chauvinist voters, veered temporarily toward moderation—in part by showcasing as a foil, on TV that he himself controlled, "a more rabid nationalist leader on his right," the "psychopathic racist" Vojislav Seselj.[27] Milosevic duly gained a brief centrist image and won the first multiparty elections in Serbia. Thereafter, his own renewed nationalism increasingly evoked more radical nationalism among both Croats and Bosnian Muslims.[28]

The War in Croatia

According to James Gow, the first Serb experiment with ethnic cleansing was conducted by forces under then colonel Ratko Mladic in April 1991 in the Croat village of Kijevo, which was surrounded by Serb villages in Croatia's Krajina region.[29] The first Serb paramilitary probe in Croatia was the massacre of a dozen Croat policemen in Borovo Selo in the eastern part of the country on May 2, 1991. By the yardstick of the next few years, this was only a small atrocity, but it set ugly precedents. The twelve had their throats slit, their noses sliced off, and/or their eyes gouged out.[30] The mutilations revived a centuries-old Balkan practice in warfare after a half-century hiatus during the Pax Yugoslavia. So swiftly had any idea of a broader Yugoslav citizenship evaporated that nationalist Serbs already viewed their Croat enemies anachronistically as Ustashe, while nationalist Croats conversely viewed their Serb enemies as Chetniks. In a referendum on May 15 a majority of Croats voted to declare independence if the ongoing constitutional question were not resolved. On

May 19 Milosevic blocked the routine rotation of Croat Stipe Mesic to head the Yugoslav collective presidency.

All-out war in Croatia was finally ignited in June by the well-prepared Slovene secession and the simultaneous ill-prepared Croatian secession, as Zagreb scrambled not to be left alone in Milosevic's Yugoslavia. Milosevic, who cared little about a Slovenia that had very few Serbs, had already told Slovene president Milan Kucan privately that he would not oppose their independence.[31] The JNA, which would not be fully Serbianized until 1992 and still saw itself as the defender of the Yugoslav state, had a different view, and fought to bring the northernmost republic back into the fold.[32] The Slovenes, however, having seized enough JNA weapons in the republic to hold off the far stronger force by the kind of territorial guerrilla defense that Tito had always envisaged, fought back and skillfully mobilized both political backing from the European Community (EC) and blanket Western media coverage of the surreal skirmishes in the pastoral Alpine landscape.[33] Within less than two weeks the EC brokered a deal that ended the phony war. The JNA retreated, the better to concentrate on Croatia.

As Serb forces spread out to attack targets on two-thirds of Croatia's territory in summer 1991, macho Croats and Serbs from the diaspora in Germany, Canada, and Australia "returned" to their homelands, spoiling for a fight.[34] It was not ancient hatreds but very new hatreds that fueled the chain reaction of revenge for the torture and death of comrades in arms, and increasingly of mothers, children, and old people. The Croats knew they were the victims of Serb aggression. Local Croatian Serbs knew they were the victims of illegitimate Croatian secession that would not allow them, in turn, to secede from the new Croatian state and join Serbia. The likes of Arkan's Tigers terrorized Croats into abandoning their homes to create homogeneous Serb villages—and also terrorized any local Serbs who were squeamish about killing their Croat neighbors.

In August the JNA laid seige to the Croatian town of Vukovar. The outgunned Croats held out for three months but were no match for the Serbs' daily artillery fire. The city fell in November, after some 90 percent of its buildings had been destroyed. Serb forces moved in, spirited two hundred patients out the back door of the Vukovar hospital (at the very moment former U.S. secretary of state Cyrus Vance was seeking assurances of humane conduct from the victors at the front door), transported them to the Ovcara farm, beat them, murdered them, and then dumped their corpses into mass graves.[35] Only a few weeks earlier, the JNA had begun a six-month seige of the all-but-undefended Dubrovnik from the Serb-held hills overlooking it, gratuitously shelling this fairytale Croatian city without ever occupying it.[36] Throughout the republic the Croats were beaten back. As stalemate set in on the front lines of a shrunken Croatia at the end of 1991, the two sides agreed on a cease-fire brokered by Vance. Refugees poured into Western Europe, and especially into Germany.

The West was appalled but paralyzed, as the JNA had assumed in explicitly calculating that it could wage its wars without triggering outside intervention.[37] The United States, preoccupied with its first Iraq war and the aftermath, was ostentatiously leaving European crisis management to the Europeans. NATO collectively had a wary respect for the JNA as the successor of the partisans, who had held off the Wehrmacht for years in the Balkan mountains, and was not eager to engage the army on its home territory. The Europeans, apart from the French and British, lacked expeditionary forces in any case and would not intervene without the United States. The British and French (and of course the Greeks) even favored the Serbs. The British position stemmed from residual camaraderie with Tito's partisans, alongside whom they had fought in World War II, and a *realpolitik* of letting the Balkan tribes fight among themselves long enough to establish a single (obviously Serb) hegemon whom the British could then deal with more efficiently.[38] The French harbored a certain nostalgia for the bygone years when Paris could upstage its great power continental rivals by championing the Serbs. All the Europeans shrank from new military commitments, since they were basking in the "peace dividend" from the end of the cold war by swiftly cutting their defense budgets and rechanneling money to domestic programs. And as the war progressed, enough atrocities were committed by Croats and Bosniaks for the morality of the wars to remain highly ambiguous to outsiders.[39] For its part, the Soviet Union—which, had it become an actor, would have intervened on behalf of the Serbs in any case—was in the process of disintegration and was fully occupied with completing the promised withdrawal of its military divisions from eastern Germany and Poland by 1994 and eliciting German funding for the construction of desperately needed housing so its troops would not be homeless on their return.

In the end, the only policy the West could agree on was a United Nations Security Council weapons embargo on all players in Yugoslavia in September 1991. On paper this was a neutral move, punishing all belligerents equally. In reality it hugely favored the Serbs, since they inherited the whole JNA structure and arsenal and had vastly more heavy weapons than the Croats or Bosniaks. Indeed, Gow calls the overwhelming Serb superiority in weapons one of the most striking aspects of the Yugoslav wars. In his analysis, the Serbs' "superabundance of weaponry" and the relative shortage of manpower in their overstretched military lines as they conquered or encircled more and more territory combined to produce a deliberately brutal "quasi-medieval" strategy. Siege, stand-off bombardment, murder, torture, and the terrorizing and ethnic cleansing of civilians became the chosen means of warfare.[40]

As the Balkan savagery escalated, however, Serb confidence in continued Western inaction failed to factor in the horror of the Europeans, whose proudest post–World War II accomplishment had been ending war on their continent. Catholics in Austria and Bavaria, in particular, identified with their fellow Catholics in underdog Croatia. All German TV viewers identified with the Croatian refugees who were pouring into Germany in greater numbers than anywhere else—and many thought that Germans could hardly deny to others the self-determination that had allowed East Germany to join West Germany in 1990 after half a century of German division. In the face of the Yugoslav carnage, Foreign Minister Hans-Dietrich Genscher especially sought to cut through the traditional ironclad ban on meddling in the sovereign affairs of others by getting international recognition for Croatia as a new sovereign state, entitled to ask the UN Security Council for help when it was being dismembered by Serb forces.[41] At the end of 1991 Germany did recognize the independence of beleaguered Croatia and pressed the EC to do the same in early 1992. The Serbs (and the French, and the British boulevard press) read into the campaign an illicit flexing of unified German muscle in asserting patronage of this one-time Nazi protégé. Conversely, Germans saw a throwback to the 1930s in incipient Italian and French mobilization of a Central European coalition including Serbia but excluding Germany.

Given the general murkiness of who was doing what to whom in ex-Yugoslavia and of Croatia's own latent claims to Herzegovina—along with U.S. refusal to put any American soldiers on the ground in the backwater Balkans, the French and British sympathies with the Serbs, and the four-decade-old German taboo on deploying the Bundeswehr outside NATO territory—recognition may have hastened the spread of war to Bosnia rather than triggering Western peacemaking on the ground.[42] Nonetheless, it set a marker. On June 4, 1992, NATO determined in its Oslo Declaration that in principle the alliance could intervene outside the territory of its member states on the demand of the UN or the Organization for Security and Cooperation in Europe.[43] By then, some 6,000 had already been killed, 15,000 wounded, and 550,000 displaced in the war between Serb and Croat.[44] Or perhaps the homeless numbered as many as 500,000 Croats and 230,000 Serbs.[45] Every seventh Croat was a refugee.[46] The JNA and Serb paramilitaries occupied a third of

Croatia, primarily in Krajina and a swath along the republic's eastern border with Serbia.

The War in Bosnia Begins

In mid-1991—half a year before EC recognition of independent Croatia and three-quarters of a year before EC recognition of independent Bosnia—the JNA began preparations to expand the war to Bosnia-Herzegovina.[47] It moved troops from Serbia and Montenegro into Bosnia, mobilized Bosnian Serbs into units that it immediately "demobilized" and spun off as putatively autonomous forces under the command of Bosnian Serb general Ratko Mladic, incorporated into its ranks Yugoslav Territorial Defense Forces in predominantly Serb localities, disarmed non-Serb TOs, and conducted continuous "peacekeeping" maneuvers in Bosnia. The mobilization, explained JNA commander in chief Veljko Kadijevic retrospectively in his memoirs, was of "vital significance," because "the Serb people in Bosnia and Herzegovina, by its geographical position and size, [is] one of the keystones for the formation of a common state for all Serb people."[48] These actions followed the Serb pattern in Croatia of declaring autonomous regions and then linking them up militarily.

In February–March 1992, at the EC's prodding, Bosnia conducted a referendum in which 90 percent of Bosniaks (Muslims) voted for independence; the Bosnian Serbs boycotted the exercise. In March Izetbegovic acted on the vote and proclaimed Bosnian independence. On April 1 Arkan's Tigers and Vojislav Seselj's Chetniks, ostensibly acting autonomously rather than under JNA command, attacked Bijeljina and Brcko in the northeast corner of Bosnia where it borders on Serbia and Croatia. There they carried out the "ethnic cleansing by terror" that they had perfected the previous year in Croatia's eastern Slavonia.[49]

On April 6 the EC recognized Bosnia. On April 7 Bosnian Serb leaders in Banja Luka declared the independence from Bosnia of the "Serbian Republic of Bosnia-Herzegovina" that would claim two-thirds of Bosnian territory and in August 1992 be renamed the Republika Srpska. On April 8 Arkan's Tigers and JNA units began shelling the Bosnian town of Zvornik (with a 60 percent Muslim population) in the Drina Valley, and on April 10 overran it. José Maria Mendiluce, the senior representative of the UN High Commission for Refugees in Yugoslavia, went directly to Zvornik after Milosevic told him in Belgrade that he had no control over the Bosnian Serbs. In Zvornik the local Serbs tried to keep out the unexpected and most unwelcome visitor, but finally let him through their checkpoints. "I could see trucks full of dead bodies. I could see militiamen taking more corpses of children, women and old people from their houses and putting them on trucks. I saw at least four or five trucks full of corpses. When I arrived the cleansing had been done. There were no people, no one on the streets. It was all finished. They were looting, cleaning up the city after the massacre. I was convinced they were going to kill me [too]," he told the BBC.[50]

The Serbs' ruthless ethnic cleansing along the Drina River left three besieged Bosniak enclaves: Gorazde, Zepa, and Srebrenica. Serb forces further began the three-year siege and constant bombardment of Sarajevo and swiftly conquered two-thirds of Bosnia, taking over not only primarily Serb villages, but also key economic, geographic, and military areas, along with corridors linking Serb-held regions. They established more than 400 detention centers in Bosnia, at least two of which, in the Prijedor area, would qualify as death camps. In the Prijedor area they razed mosques, Catholic churches, and 47,000 homes, and killed or expelled virtually all Muslims and more than half of the Croats.[51] The first ICTY verdict (apart from one earlier guilty plea) would find Dusko Tadic guilty of "killings, beatings, and forced transfer" at Prijedor. The appeals court would confirm, in John Hagan's summary, that there was a "close personal, organizational, and logistical interconnection between the Bosnian Serb army, paramilitary groups, and the Yugoslav military."[52] The Serbs' vicious serial rapes of captive Bosniak women and girls, some as young as twelve years old, was so systematized that this practice was for the first time added to the list of crimes against humanity in international law. In the land-mark Foca case, Dragoljub Kunarac and Radomir Kovac would be convicted by the ICTY in 2000 for enslavement, for using organized rape and expulsion as "instruments of terror," and for crimes against humanity.[53]

In July 1992 Bosnian Croats, imitating the Serb pattern in Krajina, pro-claimed their own separate Croatian Community of Herceg-Bosna in Herze-govina, as the first step to seceding from Bosnia and joining Croatia. Fighting broke out between Croats and Bosniaks in a sub-war that saw its own share of brutal ethnic cleansing.

The Hague Tribunal

As grisly details about atrocities in the Balkans began to reach the outside world, Europe and America both reacted slowly. Politicians were reluctant to spend blood and treasure on the nonstrategic Balkans. And the three-century-old taboo against violating national sovereignty that the Peace of Westphalia had established in ending the sanguinary Wars of Religion—and that deterred nuclear holocaust during the twentieth-century balance of ter-ror—still had a strong hold.[54] The West was only prepared to take three initiatives to—as critics charged—salve conscience without actually engaging to protect victims or end the fighting. First, the UN Security Council set up the International Tribunal for the Prosecution of Persons Responsible for Serious Violations of International Humanitarian Law Committed in the Territory of the Former Yugoslavia since 1991 (known as the ICTY) in February 1993.[55] Second, the United Nations sent UN Protection Forces (UNPROFOR) troops as peacekeepers to Croatia in 1992, with an unenforceable mandate to impound Serb heavy weapons. It subsequently established cruelly misnamed UN Safe Areas in Bosnia-Herzegovina in spring 1993, with UNPROFOR forces sufficient only to prolong the agony of the civilian victims, but neither to protect the victims nor to end the fighting.[56] Third, in April 1993 the UN imposed commercial sanctions on rump Yugoslavia, and in June 1993 authorized use of force by UNPROFOR and "regional organizations" (that is, NATO) to protect UNPROFOR from "any of the parties."

The ad hoc court that the UN established at the Hague was by no means a European institution. Initially it was an unwanted stepchild of both the European and the American governments, something forced on them by the "CNN effect" as the brutality in the Yugoslav wars escalated and appalled Western TV viewers in their living rooms.[57] As former U.S. secretary of state Madeleine Albright, herself an advocate of the tribunal, testified retrospectively in the court in 2002, "It was easy enough to take the first [Security Council] vote in February [1993] to get the Tribunal created, but nobody really believed that it would work. . . . [N]obody thought that there would ever be a court that actually functioned. . . . They said [there] would never be indictees, and then they said there would never be any trials, and then they said there would never be any convictions, and there would never be any sentencing."[58]

Those who lobbied to establish this first tribunal for mass murder since the Nuremberg and Tokyo war crimes trials and the agreement on the 1948 UN Genocide Convention hoped for several positive outcomes from the court. Beyond fixing individual guilt for individual crimes and thus weakening the destructive force of collective blame of "the other," they wished to give the victims at least symbolic justice. They wanted to record world condemnation of the Balkan savagery that especially horrified a Europe that thought it had banned such barbarity. And they intended to contribute to a "truth and reconciliation" process that could help the region find an antidote for the poisonous mutual accusations by ascertaining legal truth.

Arrayed against these noble aspirations there was resistance to the Hague Tribunal even on the part of its sponsoring nations. There were a number of reasons for this recalcitrance. The first was doubt that a legal, as distinct from a political, process could ever stop the terrible spirals of revenge murders and bestiality that were still gathering force in the Balkans. A second reason was the presumed need to avoid indicting Serbian president Slobodan Milosevic and preserve his legitimacy in order to have some Serbian authority to negotiate peace with; in this sense, justice was seen as a potential enemy of peace.[59] A third reason was the traditional sanctity of state sovereignty. And after the Dayton Accord in November 1995, a fourth reason, for those countries contributing soldiers to the NATO-led Implementation Force (IFOR, later Stabilization Force, or SFOR) in Bosnia, was to reject "mission creep" that might make peacekeeping troops responsible for the arrest of Bosnian Serb leaders Radovan Karadzic and General Ratko Mladic, with the attendant risk of loss of life.[60]

Whatever the reasons, at the beginning the court looked to critics rather more like tokenism than a serious attempt at international justice.[61] Its budget for the first year was a risible $276,000, and the judges initially had to rent their robes from a theatrical supplier.[62] With no police officers of its own, no way to arrest indictees or compel their extradition to the Hague, no capacity to enforce subpoenas, and certainly no military intelligence arm to help it reconstruct war crimes, the ICTY depended totally on the cooperation of the aloof sovereign states. It did not have crucial military analysts, trauma counselors, or even proper software to search databases. For an embarrassingly long time, for lack of any prisoners in the flesh, the court had to resort to *in absentia* hearings—actual *in absentia* trials were banned under the court's UN authorization—of charges against indictees who could flout this powerless forum with impunity. The ICTY was poorly funded, understaffed, and served by a sometimes incompatible mix of judges and prosecutors from different nations and legal traditions. There were disputes about conflicting rules of evidence, plea bargaining, proof of murder, interpretations of balancing fairness to the accused against the protection of witnesses (especially in the case of village witnesses who had lost family members under traumatic conditions and could hardly be given protective new identities short of wrenching them out of their communities and even countries). Not only were there major legal distinctions between the Anglo-Saxon common law and adversarial system and the continental Roman system. Even within the common law system there were dissimilarities. Senior ICTY trial attorney Minna Schrag cited as her favorite example counsel's preparation of witnesses for cross-questioning so that they could deal with the inevitable discrepancies in testimony. In Scotland such preparation is criminal; in Australia it is unethical, though not illegal; in the United States professional standards require it, and its omission would constitute malpractice![63]

After the original UN Security Council resolution, it took sixteen months even to name the tribunal's first chief prosecutor, South African justice Richard Goldstone. He had to spend much of his time fundraising. And even after he assumed office in 1994, it took several months for the court to issue its first indictment, of low-level police officer Dusko Tadic from Omarska, one of the notorious Serb-run concentration camps at Prijedor in northwestern Bosnia. It took several more months for Tadic to be extradited from Germany, where he had been arrested, to become the tribunal's first prisoner, in spring 1995.

When the tribunal did indict the highest-ranking Serbs short of Milosevic himself, Ratko Mladic (in July 1995) and Radovan Karadzic (in November 1995), the United Kingdom and France refused to let its prosecutors read their archives, to give the court evidence gathered by their blue helmets in Bosnia— or, of course, to order their forces on the ground to apprehend the pair. Both London and Paris were involved in peace negotiations with Karadzic and Mladic and feared that they might lose their interlocutors; the French, in addition, came to regard the ICTY as "an Anglo-American creation, aimed at producing show trials."[64] Goldstone, worried in turn that justice might fall victim to peace and that senior perpetrators of mass murder at Vukovar, Lasva Valley, and Srebrenica might be granted immunity, preemptively accelerated other indictments even as the Dayton negotiations proceeded in late 1995. Maybe the tactic worked; or maybe "the Balkan warlords felt so untouchable at the negotiating table in their new role as 'peacemakers' and 'pillars of the peace process' that they failed to bargain for guarantees for immunity against any future proceedings at the Tribunal," in the view of Mirko Klarin, the dogged chronicler of the tribunal in his South East News Service Europe and weekly Internet *Tribunal Update*.[65]

Despite all the court's tribulations, the bold idea of giving an international court potential jurisdiction over a head of state—Milosevic would indeed be brought before the Hague Tribunal in 2001—gradually seized the imagination of Europeans. The change began with Robin Cook, who became U.K. foreign secretary in the same year, 1997, as Madeleine Albright assumed direction of U.S. foreign policy; like her, he shifted his country's attitude toward the Hague Tribunal to positive support. The notion of an international court with real powers was in any case far more compatible with European supranationalism than with America's zealous defense of its own uniquely powerful sovereignty. In intra-EC relations in the post–World War II years, the European Court of

Justice (ECJ) had assumed a right to declare general principles of European law, to review national legislation, and to decide its own competences. By the 1990s Community members routinely obeyed its verdicts, even though the ECJ had no police or enforcement arm of its own, and indeed was not the court of any polity.[66] Europeans also overwhelmingly approved the establishment of the International Criminal Court (ICC) in the early twenty-first century as a permanent successor to the ICTY and other ad hoc tribunals and as an indispensable instrument for advancing civilized behavior in the world through international law. The Americans were more ambivalent. But the second Bush administration, while continuing to oppose the ICC, did bring its position on the ICTY more into line with EU policy in insisting unambiguously on Belgrade's cooperation with the tribunal, to the point of suspending economic aid to Serbia for four months in 2005 until indicted Serbian general Nebojsa Pavkovic appeared at the court in April 2005.[67]

Sarajevo, Srebrenica, and the Aftermath

The six Safe Areas that the UN created in Bosnia included Sarajevo, where UNPROFOR could not prevent the three-year Serb siege and strangling of the capital, and Srebrenica, where the tiny Dutch UNPROFOR battalion could not prevent the murder of close to 8,000 unarmed Muslim men and boys.[68] In spring 1993 UN members in general were not prepared to contribute the 35,000 troops estimated by the United States as the ground force needed to protect the Bosnian Safe Areas, and the United States in particular adamantly refused to contribute any soldiers at all to the operation. Members balked even at the 15,000 that UNPROFOR commanders asked for. In the end, the UN Security Council resolutions 819 and 824 authorized only the French light option of 7,500—without requiring either the Army of Bosnia and Herzegovina (ABiH) to disarm or Serb forces to allow inspections of compliance with pullbacks and the impounding of heavy weapons in depots.[69] This number did not suffice to give much relief to the inhabitants of Sarajevo, Tuzla, Bihac, and, in the Muslim majority Drina Valley, Srebrenica, Zepa, Gorazde, who were surrounded by besieging Serb forces that starved them of food, medicines, and other essentials and attacked convoys trying to deliver humanitarian aid.[70] Indeed, the Serb forces regularly fired on UNPROFOR patrols and several times brazenly seized and held peacekeepers themselves as hostages—a counterproductive act in the case of the French, who eventually soured on their erstwhile Serb protégés.

The main besieging force throughout Bosnia was the formally independent Bosnian Serb Military (VRS) of 50,000–80,000 that was formed in May 1992 out of the old JNA 2nd Military District Command. Its new commander as the VRS was also its old JNA commander, General Ratko Mladic. In eastern Bosnia the VRS was further backed up from across the Serbian border by the Army of Yugoslavia (VJ), as the JNA main force was now renamed.[71] The Serbs maintained that because of the pressure of the hastily improvised Army of Bosnia and Herzegovina, their military sieges of "the Turks" in the six Bosnian towns they had surrounded were essential to hold what were now the rear areas of their main Bosnian theaters. By December 1992 it seemed that the large majority of Serbs, angry at the West's sanctions on rump Yugoslavia, thought the Bosnian Serbs were fighting for their very survival against Muslim fundamentalists and Croat fascists.

Much of the contemporary Western media coverage presented the new Balkan wars as a natural consequence of ancient ethnic hatreds between Serbs, Croats, and Muslims—or at least of ancient Orthodox, Catholic, and Muslim hostilities.[72] The first thesis was surely semantically inappropriate, however, since all three came from the same Slavic stock and spoke the same language, with minor variations. More to the point, while the Serbs and Croats had strained relations in the first Yugoslavia—and Chetniks and Ustashe brutally murdered each other in World War II—Misha Glenny argues forcefully that these clashes reflected not so much ancient hostilities as instigation by outside European powers.[73] And the Muslims, though they got drawn into various confrontations, had made an art of accommodating rather than fighting their shifting hegemons.

The second, religious, thesis acknowledged valid cultural distinctions between the Greek-oriented Orthodox Serbs, the Hapsburg-oriented Catholic Croats, and the Bosniaks, many of whom had adjusted to four centuries of Ottoman rule by converting to Islam. Yet this second framework was anachronistic, not only because the Ottoman Empire was far more tolerant of its subjects' varied religious practices than medieval Europe was (and Bosnia still reflected this pluralism in the twentieth century), but also because Bosnia's "practical-magical" folk attitudes tended toward prudent eclecticism. Many Islamic and Christian festival days were fused. Orthodox neighbors visited Muslim friends during Ramazan Bajram. Muslims kissed icons, had amulets blessed by the Franciscans, and requested that Catholic masses be read to cure their illnesses, even if Ottoman officials were more suspicious of Hapsburg Catholicism than they were of the Orthodoxy that was already institutionalized within their empire.[74] Bosnia was highly secularized; Islam was widely understood more as a set of everyday cultural practices than an exclusive faith. The 1990s reporter whose name has been forgotten even though his inspired lead has not, was astute in explaining to novice readers: "The Serbs are the ones who don't attend the Orthodox Church, the Croats the ones who don't attend the Catholic Church, the Bosniaks the ones who don't visit the mosque."

The conspicuous bestiality of the Balkan wars of the 1990s must therefore have derived from something other than uncontrollable mythic drives. As the old Yugoslav cohesion came unglued, sadistic thugs on all sides were glad to conduct their own turf wars under the flag of their respective nationalisms. And once the butchery started, revenge and counterrevenge and the attendant shrill propaganda became self-perpetuating and smothered moderation. But there was no ethnic or religious or historical inevitability about the downward plunge of the war in Bosnia into "quasi-medieval" barbarity in Sarajevo and Srebrenica and the other alleged Safe Areas.

Throughout the encirclement of Sarajevo from spring 1992 through summer 1995—an even longer siege than Leningrad's 900 days in World War II—the plight of the Bosnian capital was far better known in the rest of the world than was that of any of the five other Safe Areas. Sarajevo had been famous for eight decades as the spot where the Bosnian Serb Gavrilo Princip assassinated Hapsburg crown prince Franz Ferdinand and ignited World War I. After World War II, Sarajevo had drawn tourists as yachters and sunbathers made sidetrips from Croatia's Adriatic beaches for a whiff of the exotic multiculturalism of a city where Muslims, Serbs, Croats (and until their extermination by the Nazis, a community of Ladino-speaking Jews expelled from Spain) had coexisted for half a millennium. Minarets, Eastern and Western rite crosses, synagogues, and dervish *tekkes* marked its skyline. The Islam practiced there was tolerant and not at all prohibitive of drinking *rakija*. Sarajevans, a high percentage of whom had interfaith marriages, tended to see themselves as the real Bosnians, proof that the parochial animosities that periodically erupted into bloodshed in Ivo Andric's *The Bridge on the Drina* were only provincial and obsolescent. Sarajevo was a microcosm of Bosnia, which was a microcosm of the Balkans, with 260,000 Muslims, 158,000 Serbs, and 36,000 Croats (before the war).[75] The arts and jazz flourished. The richly illustrated Sarajevo Haggadah was preserved there, along with texts from Ottoman Bosnia in Bosancica, Arabic, Turkish, Persian, and Aljamiado transcription of "Slavonic" into Arabic writing.[76] And many sports fans the world over were familiar with Sarajevo as the host of the 1984 winter Olympics.

In besieging Sarajevo, the tactics chosen by the VRS commander of the Sarajevo Romanija Corps, General Stanislav Galic, were to rain down artillery and mortar shells indiscriminately on civilian districts and deliberately hit public buildings "of no military significance," as the Hague Tribunal declared in finding him guilty of willfully inflicting terror on the civilian population.[77] Mladic himself, with "sadistic relish," personally specified such targets as the presidency building, the parliament, and Muslim neighborhoods.[78] Over the three years, an average of more than 300 rounds of artillery and mortars were fired each day. "Systematic targeting can be inferred from the shelling of hospitals and in particular the Sarajevo University Clinical Centre Kosevo which has constantly been under shell and sniper fire," stated the special UN Commission of Experts in its report completed halfway through the siege and made public on May 27, 1994.[79] "The sheer number of shells and the high percentage of direct hits on the complex indicates an intent by the besieging forces to hit this civilian target. Moreover, much of the shelling from the surrounding hillsides has taken place at midday, the time when the hospital is busiest with visitors."

Furthermore, against the rules of war, the report continued, Serb snipers "display an intent to hit civilian and non-combatant targets. . . . In many cases snipers with a clear view from high rise buildings and the surrounding hillsides have targeted the most vulnerable of civilians, including: children (even infants); persons carrying heavy plastic containers filled with water; persons in queues; pedestrians at intersections; and rescuers attempting to come to the aid of sniping and shelling victims." By fall 1993, 10,000 Sarajevans were dead and 56,000 wounded, of whom 15,000 were children. The total mortality figure would rise to 12,000. Some 430,000 people depended on food aid convoys that the Serbs periodically blocked or attacked. Malnutrition sunk to levels comparable to those in poorer developing nations. Electricity, gas, phone, and water connections in and to the city were severed early on; eighteen of the city's water technicians were killed while trying to repair water pipes. In the cold winters inhabitants had to burn furniture, books, and green wood they scavenged from city parks in order to keep warm. Sarajevo was denuded of trees, with the exception of the front line along the narrow Miljacka River running east-west and the long "Sniper's Alley" that paralleled the river, where it was too dangerous to linger long enough to collect wood.

Most of the buildings in the city were damaged and 35,000 dwellings were destroyed through September 1993, according to the UN account. Incendiary projectiles hit the library, apparently deliberately, burning up almost all of the 1.5 million volumes of Islamic literature. Another shell destroyed Sarajevo's Oriental Institute and its Ottoman-era archive of 5,000 codices.

The ABiH First Corps organized Sarajevo's defense force, which included some Serbs and about 2,000 Croats, even though Bosniaks and Croats were already fighting each other in Herzegovina, in the west of the country, and the

Croats would soon begin aggressive ethnic cleansing of Bosniaks in Herzegovina in preparation for outright annexation of territories by Croatia. The defense also relied on a dozen and a half criminal leaders and their gangs, who smuggled in sorely needed weapons but also preyed on the Sarajevans.[80] The defensive force approximately equaled the Serbs in manpower of about 30,000, but deployed vastly less firepower. Bosniak reservists on the north bank of the Miljacka front line huddled with little ammunition and sometimes even homemade rifles to face both Serb sharpshooters a few dozen meters away and the constant artillery and mortar fire from the hill on the south bank that dominates the city. After the first few months of the siege, the Serb forces grudgingly let UNPROFOR operate the airport, which lay on the flat southern edge of the city behind the Serb heights, within easy range of the Serb guns on the surrounding hills. On this terrain the Serb forces could in any case block airport deliveries of civilian humanitarian aid at will. The Bosniaks dug what was at first a secret tunnel from the city center to the airstrip under the Serb-held hill; most of the many VIP visitors who flew in during the siege ducked their heads and took the tunnel rather than entering town over ground by vehicle and running the risk of Serb strafing.

The siege of Sarajevo would be broken only after the massacre at Srebrenica.

Srebrenica

Srebrenica, though unknown to the outside world before the 1990s war, had been the fourth richest town in Bosnia, from its mines, silver artisanship, and tourist attraction of mineral baths. By spring 1993 its original mixed Muslim-Serb population of 6,000 was swollen by an additional 30,000 Muslim refugees who poured in after the VJ and Serb paramilitary assaults on Zvornik and other Drina Valley towns. Bosniaks in the villages surrounding Srebrenica were killed or driven out as the Serbs advanced. Serbs in the villages were killed or driven out as General Naser Oric and his ABiH 28th Division recaptured territory. General Oric welcomed the arrival of UNPROFOR troops but resisted surrendering to the peacekeepers the light weapons of his regulars, territorial forces, and irregulars.[81] Like many other Bosniaks who saw their only salvation in eliciting international help, he hoped that his periodic forays into the surrounding Serb-held territory might provoke the Serbs into retaliating with sufficiently publicized savagery to prod the West into intervening. For their part, the Serbs had no intention of letting their heavy weapons be impounded by the few hundred lightly armed UNPROFOR peacekeepers—or letting the peacekeepers enforce any pullback agreements or inspect Serb positions. The ill-fated Dutch battalion in Srebrenica had no heavy weapons of its own and could do little more than report, futilely, any violations of disengagement to superiors.

After numerous Serb feints over the two-year-plus siege that repeatedly turned into tactical maneuvering rather than some final assault on Srebrenica, the Dutch peacekeepers did not take the Serb artillery barrage that began at 3:15 a.m. on July 6, 1995, especially seriously.[82] But as the explosions came nearer and nearer to UNPROFOR observation posts and refugee centers, the Dutch commander, Colonel Thom Karremans, asked the regional UN headquarters for robust close air support to suppress the Serb fire. The VRS Drina Corps, under the direct command of Generals Radislav Krstic and Mladic himself, and with VJ support, paused, as so often before, to test the international reaction. When no airstrikes came, Drina Corps tanks breached the perimeter of the fifteen-square-kilometer Safe Area on July 9, capturing thirty Dutch soldiers and holding them hostage. One Dutch soldier was killed as Bosniak troops shot at the retreating peacekeepers. Thousands of alarmed refugees fled into the woods; 20,000 of them crowded into and around the main Dutch compound at Potocari.

At 2:30 p.m. on July 11 two Dutch F-16s finally dropped two less-than-robust bombs on Serb positions. Yet when the Serbs threatened to kill the Dutch hostages, the close air support ceased. An hour and a half later Srebrenica passed from rule by warlords and black-marketeers connected with the Bosniaks to rule by warlords and black marketeers connected with the Serbs.[83] A Belgrade journalist recorded the scene on video as a triumphant General Mladic entered the town, proclaimed that he was giving Srebrenica as a "present to the Serb nation," delivered the ultimatum that Muslim soldiers must surrender their weapons in order to save their lives, and assured the terrified Muslim refugees that no harm would come to them. On July 12, in a thoroughly prepared logistical operation, all boys and men between the ages of twelve and seventy-seven were separated from women and children, to be interrogated about "suspected war crimes." Over the next thirty hours some 23,000 women and children were transported to Tuzla and other Muslim areas in sixty waiting buses.

On July 13 Europe's worst massacre since the Nazi Holocaust began in a warehouse in nearby Kravica. The peacekeepers handed over some 5,000 Bosniaks in Potocari to the Serbs, got back the Dutch hostages, and were allowed to depart, leaving their weapons, food, and supplies behind. They took with them Hasan Nuhanovic, a bright young Bosniak refugee who two years earlier had taught himself enough English to become their interpreter.

Despite his frenzied importunings, however, the peacekeepers did not let his mother, father, and younger brother accompany them to safety. His brother and father were among the unarmed Bosniaks killed in the five-day slaughter. His mother, in prison, slit her wrists in preference to being raped by her Serb captors. Nuhanovic never saw them again. He married, named his first-born daughter after his mother, had guilty survivor's nightmares for years thereafter, and in 2005 joined Dutch activists in suing the Dutch government for its failure to protect those entrusted to its protection.[84]

As the scale of the atrocity slowly became known, the shock and shame in Western Europe was palpable. After half a century of vowing "never again Auschwitz," the Europeans, and the Americans, had looked the other way as genocide was committed in Europe. In the next few years, the horror of Srebrenica percolated with differing tempos through the Western institutions as they groped to adapt their old roles to the still amorphous post–cold war world. The first Clinton administration, focusing on domestic issues in an America that had only partly exorcised its Vietnam syndrome by repulsing Saddam Hussein's conquest of Kuwait, still regarded the Balkans as an annoying sideshow and certainly ruled out any controversial dispatch of U.S. footsoldiers to get bogged down there. With a few exceptions, administration officials still shared the pungent 1992 view of then secretary of state James Baker that the United States had "no dog in this fight."[85] And while American officials indulged in some *schadenfreude* in puncturing the proclamation by Luxembourg's foreign minister, Jacques Poos, that "the hour of Europe has dawned," their dominant attitude was probably exasperation that the Europeans couldn't manage even this much of a crisis on their own continent.[86]

President Clinton's secretary of state, Warren Christopher, had tried in vain to persuade America's European allies to approve a "lift and strike" policy— that is, to lift the onerous weapons embargo on Bosnia and strike concentrations of Serb heavy weapons from the air. The British and French, who had contributed the most UNPROFOR peacekeepers to the Balkans, however, adamantly opposed any change of policy that would leave their thinly stretched forces vulnerable to Serb retaliation; for some months U.S.-British relations were even frostier than U.S.-French relations. So conspicuous were the tensions that they gave rise to the popular theory that such rivalry was inevitable, now that Americans and Europeans were no longer compelled to stick together by a common Soviet threat. NATO learned the negative lesson that in any future intervention, the allies must go "in together, out together," if military logic was not to stoke political quarrels among them. The United

States came back into the Balkans game only slowly, after it joined a new Contact Group with Britain, France, Germany, and Russia in April 1994 to try to advance the general peace in the region that the Europeans had not managed to effect alone.[87]

Endgame in Sarajevo

Six weeks after the Srebrenica massacre, on August 28, 1995, the Bosnian Serb Romanija Corps lobbed five mortar shells into the Markale market in still-besieged Sarajevo, killing thirty-seven and wounding ninety. Both the Western Europeans and the Clinton administration reacted very differently than they had to the Srebrenica takeover. After a two-day pause to allow British peacekeepers to be extracted from their exposed positions in Gorazde, UN forces under British general Sir Rupert Smith, backed by NATO airpower, for the first time exercised serious coercion in Bosnia. Under an expanded interpretation of the Security Council mandate to protect Safe Areas, the alliance launched airstrikes—along with artillery barrages from the French-British-Dutch Rapid Reaction Force on Mount Igman—especially on the Serbs' heavy weapons and communications facilities ringing Sarajevo. Operation Deliberate Force continued for thirteen days, immobilizing the VRS by slowing communications time between its overstretched units from minutes to days and, not coincidentally, blowing up ammunition dumps close to General Mladic's home and the grave of his parents.

By then the officers of the Croatian army—with the help of American military advisers and arms smuggled in despite the embargo under the Americans' firmly closed eyes—had built their neophyte troops into an effective fighting force against the overextended Serb forces. The Croats' Operation Storm counteroffensive retook Krajina in less than a week and went on to restore some 49 percent of Bosnia-Herzegovina to Bosniak and Croat hands before the United States halted the march at an equilibrium that would permit diplomacy. In a mix of planned evacuation and ethnic cleansing, more than 200,000 new Serb refugees from the reconquered Krajina flooded into Republika Srpska territory or into a Serbia indifferent to their fate.[88] Ante Gotovina, the overall operations commander for Operation Storm in the UN Protected Area Sector South, would be indicted by the ICTY in June 2001 for individual and superior criminal responsibility for the largest single set of ethnic expulsions in the new Balkan wars until Kosovo in 1999, and for the murder of at least 150 Krajina Serbs. In a continuation of the half-century-old debate about the efficacy of air power versus ground troops, some analysts gave primary credit for the final defeat of the Serb conquest to NATO's two-week bombing of Serb positions around Sarajevo, in concert with British-French-Dutch artillery on top of Mt. Igman. Others gave primary credit to the Croat counteroffensive.[89]

Slobodan Milosevic, whose top priority had shifted to getting sanctions against Yugoslavia lifted, had apparently warned the VRS against the Srebrenica assault as too provocative toward the West. After the Bosnian Serb leadership proceeded anyway, the Serbian president distanced himself further from the leaders he had once empowered.[90] The way was prepared for peace talks, with Milosevic as the Serb negotiator whom the West could hold accountable. In November 1995 he, along with the Croatian and Bosnian presidents, duly agreed to the Dayton General Framework Agreement for Peace. The belligerents were not to resume the fighting that had killed at least 100,000 and made more than 2 million—out of Bosnia's population of 4.3 million—homeless.[91] The country of Bosnia and Herzegovina would henceforth consist of two "entities": the Bosniak-Croatian Federation, holding 51 percent of the territory, and the Republika Srpska, holding 49 percent. Multiple cantons at the subentity level within the Federation would accommodate different ethnic mixes, and a weak single national government would sit at the top, with a rotating triple presidency. NATO was commissioned to lead a 60,000-strong international Implementation Force to keep the peace.

The Dayton Accord, extracted by U.S. diplomat Richard Holbrooke from the three squabbling Balkan presidents (including Milosevic, who was drunk much of the time), was a twenty-one-day tour de force.[92] The U.S. participants deemed it further proof that American can-do, results-oriented flexing of power could accomplish what the timid, fissiparous, and process-oriented Europeans had failed to accomplish. The U.S. "approach had a patina of allied involvement and buy-in, but in the end it was largely unilateral, rejecting the United Nations and keeping allies at long arms-length," pointed out Derek Chollet, a member of Holbrooke's team who wrote a retrospective study of Dayton ten years after the event.[93] "The United States acted first and consulted later. And it was not only truly 'maximalist' in means, but also in ends. Rather than simply seeking a cease-fire between the parties (as most Europeans wanted), the United States sought to create the contours of a new Bosnian democratic state. Inaction in the name of consensus is not a virtue. And maximalism in the name of results is not a vice (especially when the results end conflicts)."[94]

Not surprisingly, the image of the Dayton Accord was less glowing in Europe. General Rupert Smith saw in it less Chollet's "contours of a new Bosnian democratic state" than "in effect . . . a very detailed peace agreement."[95]

Carl Bildt, Swedish prime minister in the early 1990s, formal European cochair at Dayton, and the first international high representative in Sarajevo, regarded the United States as too fixated on military issues, to the neglect of questions of civilian governance, in the accord. In his view, Dayton burdened Bosnia with dysfunctional, top-heavy, and costly government structures that constituted a formidable hurdle for the Europeans' assigned task of state and institution building in the fledgling country.[96] Similarly, Vladimir Gligorov, son of independent Macedonia's first president and an expert in Balkan economics at the Vienna Institute for International Economics Studies, concluded that the Dayton Accord left the weak Bosnian state level at the mercy of the real power vested in the Serb ethnic entity and the Federation's cantons. It was, he wrote, a typical example of the misplaced short-term approach and "politics of ambiguity" of the international community in the Balkans.[97] Paddy Ashdown, the most activist of the series of high representatives in Bosnia, saw the Dayton Accord as the birth defect he would have to cure if Bosnia were ever to attain real statehood.[98]

Impact on Transatlantic Relations

In the early and mid-1990s the European Union, like the Clinton administration, was preoccupied with domestic affairs. Scarcely had EC members decided in 1991 on the Maastricht Treaty's ambitious goals of transforming themselves into a European Union and pooling the major European currencies in a monetary union of unprecedented scale, than they fell into collective malaise. Italians were plunged into the Tangentopoli scandals. Germans discovered that uniting eastern and western compatriots after half a century of separation would be much harder—and, at an annual cost of $100 billion, much more expensive—than they had anticipated. Germany informed Brussels that it could no longer solve common problems as it had done over three decades by just conjuring up more money for Spanish fishermen or Italian vintners. And as Europe's long-heralded single European market came into force at the beginning of 1993, far from giving a boost to everyone, it failed to save the German economy from an absolute decline of 1.1 percent and the European economy as a whole from a decline of 0.3 percent. Europe sagged into its worst recession since the 1930s.

The French political class, too, was disgruntled over the dissolution of its half-century image of itself as the political rider steering a powerful German economic horse in a Paris-designed European Community. Unified Germany was once again much bigger than any of its allies, had shed its residual military restrictions from 1945 and regained full sovereignty, and had ended France's special status as a victorious World War II power with its own sector in Berlin. Moreover, once the cold war was over, France's cherished nuclear *force de frappe* seemed only expensive, and hardly politically fungible. Europe was not developing according to plan.

Nor was foreign policy much comfort. The many EU members who had cut their defense budgets and establishments after the Soviet Union disintegrated tended not to define power in military terms in any case. But they knew they no longer lived in a static balance of terror in which the two sole superpowers that could afford nuclear arsenals dwarfed all other players. They sensed that in a more fluid post–cold war constellation, they deserved a political voice that befitted their production of as much of the world's wealth as the United States generated. They therefore looked for a way to shape a more coherent and unified European foreign policy, to be called formally a European Security and Defense Identity (ESDI; later renamed the European Security and Defense Policy, ESDP). Yet, as the failure of their various efforts to broker an end to the Balkan violence suggested by default, the EU lacked a commensurate military instrument to leverage influence when needed. It tried—twice—to resuscitate the old, pre-NATO Western European Union as a way to coordinate the twelve armed forces (fifteen after the Swedes, Finns, and Austrians joined in 1995) and put these forces in the service of a common foreign policy. The attempts came to naught, however, because of European policy disarray, U.S. schizophrenia about whether a stronger Europe would help or hinder Washington, and the maverick French desire to use the ESDI to distance Europe from America.

Under these circumstances, European and American foreign policy practitioners tried to find some way to transform the transatlantic strife into synergy. It was a task NATO secretary general Javier Solana made his own. The simplest course was to get NATO and the EC/EU to cooperate and tear down the wall between the two institutions that both had assiduously preserved throughout the cold war. This was first achieved through the pragmatic coordination that was essential among the diverse IFOR peacekeepers in Bosnia, consisting of a third Americans, along with reassigned Western European UNPROFOR troops and volunteers from Egypt, Pakistan, Malaysia, and thirteen nations active in NATO's new Partnership for Peace program (the alliance's rough equivalent of the EU's outreach to the new Central European democracies—-but with no assurance of eventual membership for participants). So well did this improvisation succeed that the quip at NATO headquarters became: this works fine in practice, but will it ever work in theory?[99]

A partial answer to that rhetorical question was provided in 1996 as NATO and the EU agreed in principle—the details would still take years to work out—on Combined Joint Task Forces. The planned EU Rapid Reaction Force would be able to borrow "separable, but not separate" NATO assets for humanitarian, peacekeeping, or peacemaking operations in which the United States did not wish to participate directly. Solana stressed that this should strengthen transatlantic security links by giving Europe more muscle and letting it share more of the burden of common defense.[100]

Impact on the ICTY

The Hague Tribunal, which after two years of existence still had only one accused war criminal in custody, was also energized by Srebrenica. It had already indicted lower-level Serbs for inhumanity at the Prijedor concentration camps and it would shortly complete the indictment of the Serb Milan Martic, leader of secessionist Krajina, for rocket attacks on Zagreb the previous May. Now, as soon as they could gain access, ICTY investigators went personally to exhume bodies in the Srebrenica area and gather evidence not only of the original massacre, but also of the subsequent attempt, once the fortunes of war changed, to cover up the mass murder by bulldozing up Bosniak remains and transporting them en masse to dump into the earth in tightly guarded Serbian army compounds in Serbia proper. The hazards they encountered included land mines, the animosity of the Serbs who now populated the region, and the dearth of military protection for tribunal personnel.

In a few short months the inspectors nonetheless gathered enough evidence at the five main graves and thirty smaller reburial sites to indict both the president of the Republika Srpska, Radovan Karadzic, and VRS commander Ratko Mladic for genocide and complicity in genocide in Srebrenica.[101] As other investigations progressed, prosecutors also indicted more than twenty Croats at year's end, notably those accused of grave breaches of the 1949 Geneva Conventions in the Lasva Valley in west central Bosnia.[102] But there were still few indictees in custody, and certainly no high-ranking ones. In summer 1996 Chief Prosecutor Richard Goldstone, now frustrated both by the slow pace of the tribunal and by the conspicuous disinclination of NATO and of American, British, and other peacekeeping troops to arrest Karadzic or Mladic in Bosnia, opened *in absentia* hearings on these two most-wanted men. Goldstone's successor later summarized the testimony as "scenes from hell, written on the darkest pages of human history." Fifteen witnesses told of gang rapes and torture, "scenes of unimaginable savagery, thousands of men executed and buried in mass graves, hundreds of men buried alive, men and women mutilated and slaughtered, children killed before their mothers' eye, a grandfather forced to eat the liver of his own grandson."[103] Drazen Erdemovic, a (Croat) participant in the Srebrenica executions as a soldier in the 10th Sabotage Detachment of the Bosnian Serb VRS, told the court that he himself had shot seventy to one hundred men before he and three others refused to kill any more; and that, all told, his unit alone shot some 1,200 men.[104]

The ICTY hierarchy was further energized by the Canadian Louise Arbour when she became chief prosecutor in fall 1996. She backed the investigation teams to the hilt and, in a shift away from her previous avoidance of publicity as a Canadian judge, she successfully took on the task of popularizing the work of the tribunal. She went on a world tour to raise urgently needed money for their research, which, once major Western nations finally began cooperating with the tribunal, gradually expanded to include coordination with search and seizure of crucial logistical records in VRS headquarters by NATO-led Stabilization Forces. She utilized Secretary of State Madeleine Albright's new activism in bringing war criminals to the court, and in effect she shamed France, in her native French, into cooperating with the tribunal.

As John Hagan explains her role in his sociological analysis of court dynamics, she was the "norm enforcer" who used "esteem competition" to transform the game of the major state actors.[105] By the time the ICTY handed down its first verdict in May 1997 and sentenced Dusko Tadic to twenty years in prison, four years of the court's short life were gone.[106] And still, for all their rhetoric about the need for justice, none of the United States, Britain, or France had been willing thus far to risk the lives of its forces in Bosnia to apprehend indictees (or to risk voter disapproval should an operation go wrong in a region of such marginal importance to it).

A few weeks after the Tadic verdict, in June 1997, Arbour persuaded a willing Jacques Klein to help apprehend Slavko Dokmanovic, the one-time Serb mayor of Vukovar, whom the ICTY had charged under its new practice of issuing secret indictments to avoid driving suspects underground before they could be arrested. Klein, an independent-minded Alsace-born former American diplomat and polyglot raconteur who loathed injustice and bullies, headed the UN Authority in Croatia's eastern Slavonia. Dokmanovic had prudently moved across the border onto Serbian territory and now wished to see Klein about getting compensation for his unsold house in Vukovar. Klein's staff scheduled a meeting with Dokmanovic at a Polish base within Klein's jurisdiction; as soon as his vehicle entered the base, agents handcuffed, searched, and hooded the former mayor, who was then whisked off to the

Hague in a Belgian Air Force jet.[107] With this precedent to cite, Arbour found a receptive ear in the new British government of Tony Blair two weeks later and got British SFOR forces to send a SWAT team to arrest the secretly indicted Milan Kovacevic for his part in administering the Prijedor prison camps.

Flourishing this sudden new Anglo-Saxon cooperation, Arbour then turned to the more resistant French. As she attended an international conference in Paris, just after Defense Minister Alain Richard had publicly reiterated his refusal even to let French officers testify in "show trials" at the ICTY, she talked with reporters about the "total inertia" in the French sector in Bosnia, where "the vast majority" of war crimes suspects were to be found, and where they felt "absolutely secure." This conversion took longer, but by early 2000, the French, too, finally made their first arrest.[108]

In the public arena, Arbour, who had no budget even for a press spokesman, decided that she had to do something to rekindle the interest in the tribunal among reporters, who had drifted away over the years. Her most dramatic attempt to attract the attention of journalists and bring the prosecution from "historical time" into "real time," as she sometimes phrased it, would come in January 1999. When the corpses of forty-five ethnic Kosovar Albanians were discovered in Racak, near the Macedonian border—some with their hands tied behind their backs, some with gunshot holes in the backs of their necks—she immediately flew to Macedonia with three investigators, two bodyguards, and a legal adviser, to try to get to the town.[109] The Serb border guards' refusal to let her enter Kosovo over three successive days made TV news shows worldwide. Discouraged, she thought she had failed in her mission. Instead, she had put the Hague Tribunal firmly back on the media map.

Under Arbour and her Swiss successor, Carla Del Ponte, the investigations gradually matured into indictments, the trials into judgments. Following the world's first conviction under the 1948 Genocide Convention, handed down by the ICTY's twin, the ad hoc Rwanda Tribunal, in 1998, Radislav Krstic became the first defendant to be declared guilty of genocide in ex-Yugoslavia, in August 2001.[110] In February 2001 Dragoljub Kunarac, head of a special VRS volunteer unit in the Drina Valley town of Foca, made legal history as systematic rape for the first time was ruled to constitute a crime against humanity and a war crime. Women and girls who testified at the trial to being held captive and serially raped between April 1992 and February 1993 included one woman who reported being forced into sexual intercourse about 150 times over twenty days and one sixteen-year-old who was raped by a thirty-six-year-old former neighbor of the family who laughed as he deliberately humiliated her. These "Muslims, women and girls, mothers and daughters together, [were] robbed of their last vestiges of human dignity, women and girls treated like chattel," the judges summarized in their opinion.[111]

"Were it not for the tribunal, we would probably be very, very far from the truth and justice," commented Amor Masovic, an activist who has spent the last decade searching for the missing from the Yugoslav wars. "Were it not for the tribunal, we would perhaps still be discussing whether Srebrenica happened or not, whether the eight thousand people who were killed ever existed at all."[112]

CHAPTER TWO

REINVENTING BULGARIA

MENTION BULGARIA, and the rest of the world tends to picture wrestlers-turned-druglords who send contract killers to liquidate rivals in front of the Sofia McDonald's on Vitosha Boulevard or a diamond store on Amsterdam's Dam Square. Or Ian Fleming–type villains who stab critics of the regime with ricin-tipped umbrellas on Waterloo Bridge or narrowly fail to assassinate the pope (though even the new democrats who snooped around in the Bulgarian secret service archives never found proof of the latter hypothesis). Or they think of the cold war days, when Bulgaria was such a slavish follower of Moscow that its critics derided it as the sixteenth Soviet republic that it once tried to become. Or in a lighter vein, outsiders think, perhaps, of the attar of roses from the Valley of the Thracian Kings that gives Parisian perfume its staying power.

Neither end of the stereotypical spectrum does justice to today's Bulgarians, who are striving mightily to become "normal"—that is, European. Unlike the Poles, Czechs, and Hungarians, or even the neighboring Romanians, Bulgarians do not think they are Europeans by birthright, or that it is only accident and bad luck that heretofore barred them from their destiny.[1] "This is our first chance in 500 years to determine our own fate. Whatever we're doing to meet EU requirements is what we should be doing for ourselves anyway!" exclaimed one of the thirty-something workaholics who now populate the ministry of European integration in Bulgaria—as, indeed, in all the Balkan nations.[2]

The EU dream became operative at one clear turning point in 1996–97, when inertia and nostalgia for the poor but undemanding egalitarian Communist past yielded overnight to importunate modernization and Westernization. Ex-Communists who had proved unable to cope with the open new world and made a shambles of the economy were ousted in street protests. Liberals replaced them, instituted reforms, set up a depoliticized currency board that pegged the lev to the German mark, and freed prices. Society's many losers—teachers, pensioners, peasants, unskilled workers who got fired as behemoth socialist factories went bankrupt and lost their state subsidies— felt the pain and used the next election to take revenge. Exotically, though, they selected as their new savior in 2001 the king who had been forced to flee Bulgaria as a boy half a century earlier. But after years as a businessman in Spain, he of course followed the same liberal recipe as his predecessor when he became prime minister. And when society's losers soured on the ex-king, too, after four years, they turned in 2005 to the ex-Communist Socialists, who by then had sidelined the worst party hard-liners in favor of a younger generation of leaders, committed to pursuing that same liberal course.

All those fierce left-right clashes of the nineteenth and twentieth centuries, it seemed, had become relics of the past. Whatever the implications might be for the spectrum of democratic choice—and Ivan Krastev, chairman of the Center for Liberal Strategies in Sofia, one of Bulgaria's vigorous nongovern- mental organizations (NGOs), pointedly raised this question[3]—a neoliberal consensus soon reigned, with the minutely prescribed and contradictory details of its implementation enshrined in the 93,000 pages of the mandatory *acquis communautaire* of the European Union that everyone was clamoring to join.

Communist Legacies

In the immediate aftermath of the 1989 collapse of the Soviet system it was natural that the old Communists were the first to lead the post-Communist governments, in Bulgaria as elsewhere in Central Europe. They still held the levers of power, they inherited the only disciplined political structures in the old party and security apparats, and as part of the privileged *nomenklatura,* they had the prior education that enabled them to take initiative in the chaotic new world. A country like Poland, where virtually the whole population had been on strike against the system for a decade, was the exception in Central Europe—and even there, one of the most effective new democrats was the former Communist minister of sport who was elected president, Alexander Kwasniewski. But everywhere in Central Europe, the same taming of the ex- Communists occurred in the 1990s, so that by the time they had been out of power for four or eight years and then returned to office, they too were con- verts, with varying degrees of enthusiasm, to the need for more than just for mal democracy, for free markets, and for eventual membership in both the EU and NATO. In this respect Bulgaria followed the Central European pattern more closely than that of the war-riven Western Balkan states. Bulgaria was just slower and, along with Romania, missed out on the "big bang" EU accession that included eight of the post-Communist democracies in 2004. Both had to content themselves with the promise of accession in 2007—if they managed to make enough progress in reforming their judicial systems and combating corruption and organized crime.

Given the country's starting point, the lag was understandable. Apart from blood-curdling eruptions like the Balkan Wars of the early twentieth century, the Bulgarians' political default mode tended to be quiescence, whether under the half-millennium Ottoman rule or the half-century Communist rule. In the latter era, no Soviet troops needed to be stationed in the country to enforce allegiance. Even if the official propaganda grossly exaggerated Bulgarians' adulation of the Russians, ordinary people did feel comfortable with Russian influence. In Sofia the monument in the central square to the tsar liberator who rescued Bulgaria from the Turkish yoke never became an object of derision. And the marble mausoleum of founding father and Communist International official Georgi Dimitrov that repeated on a more bucolic scale the grandiose tomb of Lenin outside the Kremlin walls remained standing for a decade after the 1989 upheaval, long after such monuments were torn down elsewhere.

Bulgaria's foreign ministry was located on the outskirts of the capital, far away from government headquarters as distances were measured in the pre-1989 era, but conveniently near the Soviet embassy that dictated its policies. And until Communist authority began to erode throughout the bloc in the late 1980s, there were no Bulgarian dissidents of the sort that had long since agitated for change in Warsaw, Prague, and even Moscow itself. In 1987 Communist Party general secretary Todor Zhivkov did try, half-heartedly, to translate his long-standing loyalty to Moscow into support for the unwelcome new message of *glasnost* and *perestroika* issuing from President Mikhail Gorbachev. But after a few human rights activists took the cue to publicize Bulgarian violations of the Helsinki standards, the authorities again clamped down on such grass-roots meddling in politics. The real regime adaptation to the coming winds of change was not Zhivkov's fleeting nod to liberalization, but a nasty anti-Turk Bulgarian chauvinism that began in the mid-1980s, predating Milosevic's discovery of Serb chauvinism. The government forced ethnic Turks whose ancestors had lived in Bulgaria for generations to "slavicize" their names and made them scapegoats for popular discontent over poor living conditions. It shut down mosques. In 1989 it expelled 369,000 Turks, or about half of those living in Bulgaria at the time (and in the process hurt the country's lucrative tobacco exports, as the fields were left empty).[4]

When Russia's external empire vanished in 1989, the Bulgarians, too, dropped their own septuagenarian autocrat Zhivkov, who had ruled the country for thirty-five years, longer than any other Soviet bloc leader. What would replace the Communist Party's monopoly on power and truth, however, was less clear in Bulgaria than anywhere else in Central Europe. Bulgaria was the one country in which a European destiny was not necessarily taken for granted at the end of the cold war, and significant segments of the Communist elite saw a Russian orientation as a serious alternative to Euroatlantic integration. "With the Ottoman invasion, Bulgarians, as well as others, were torn apart from the European process of the Enlightenment and modernization," reflected Ognyan Minchev, executive director of the Institute for Regional and International Studies (IMIR) in Sofia. Like the other small states around it, Bulgaria had long seen a huge gap between itself and Europe and believed it could narrow the gap only "in opposition to its neighbors," he noted. "This inferiority complex, of course, deepened in Communist countries, because communism served as another isolation from the process in Europe after the Second World War. Now we are in a situation where we need to catch up."[5]

Solomon Passy, the founder of the Atlantic Club in 1991 (and future foreign minister), wanted to catch up faster than most and lobbied passionately for Bulgaria to join NATO from the day Zhivkov fell, but he was seen as an eccentric. Decades of anti-American indoctrination during the cold war had predisposed Bulgarian elites to be suspicious of Washington; the new Socialists seemed more in tune with the mood of the era in maintaining their opposition to the United States and NATO longer than any other ex-Communists in the region.

As in all of the improvisatory systems in the wake of Communist collapse, the first question was whether the old party elites could stay in control of the change, by overpowering or infiltrating opposition movements or by spawning mafias. And once the disparate opposition factions began to coalesce into parties, the next question was whether a point might come at which the fence-sitting elites, especially in the enforcer security services, would find it opportune to gamble their careers on leaving the familiar behind-the-scenes patronage networks to embrace instead an unfamiliar, more open politics and economics. And as a corollary, for anyone who thought that far ahead, once such a breakthrough occurred, would state institutions prove to be robust and flexible enough to support the shift or instead smother it, on the postsoviet pattern developing in Russia, Ukraine, and Central Asia?

In Sofia the turnaround did not come immediately. The umbrella opposition Union of Democratic Forces (UDF) that formed just a week before demonstrations helped topple Zhivkov in 1989 proved unable to unite on any positive agenda. Founded by philosopher Zhelyu Zhelev and poet Radoi Ralin, the UDF was a grab-bag of upstart environmentalists, human rights activists, and trade unionists, many of whom thought it immoral to want power. Personality clashes were rife. When general elections finally took place in June 1990, after half a year of roundtable talks between the Socialists and the new challengers, the far better organized Socialists won, only to succumb to further street protests in December. The 1991 successor coalition, led by the UDF, had difficulty reaching internal agreement and depended for parliamentary majorities on the small Turkish and Pomak (the Slavic Muslims in the mountains) Movement for Rights and Freedoms (MRF); it yielded to a Socialist-led government of technocrats in 1992. With a certain homesickness for the comfortable old torpor promised by the Socialists' opposition to unsettling market reforms, rural voters returned the old apparatchiks to office in 1994 with a majority of seats in the assembly.[6]

They had not yet really reformed themselves. What loomed was a continuation of the privileged rule of the old elite—this time around not in the form of a one-party monopoly of all political, economic, and social might, but in the form of a rudimentary illiberal democracy that threatened to become entrenched and resistant to real democratic reform.[7] Even as brash new politicians and entrepreneurs were cracking open the system and marginalizing the old clientelist networks in Poland and Hungary farther north, Bulgaria seemed to be stuck in a sham electoral choice between still-powerful old Communists who were liberalizing just enough to enrich themselves, and weak and ineffective challengers. The personification of this apparent consolidation was the young "Dostoyevskian" (as one Western diplomat described him) prime minister Zhan Videnov.

Accusing the government of trying to reestablish totalitarian control, Zhelyu Zhelev—who had been named Bulgarian president by the assembly in mid-1990 and confirmed in office by the first popular vote in 1992—vetoed or stopped the implementation of thirty-nine laws. Seconding the president, the independent constitutional court—the establishment of which was a major institutional accomplishment of the first UDF-led government—overruled Socialist legislation on land restitution, local elections, and the media, as it had overruled earlier UDF government legislation.[8] The ambivalent coupon privatization was carried out only sluggishly—but insider privatization and asset stripping by second-tier Communist apparatchiks and enterprise managers on the Russian and Ukrainian model led to "the biggest bank robbery in the history of national property," according to Vladimir Philipov, foreign policy adviser to President Petar Stoyanov in the late 1990s.[9] While the Socialists claimed to be championing workers and peasants in resisting Polish-style shock therapy, they were really defending these new mini-oligarchs at the expense of the subsistence stratum of the population. In 1996 GDP fell more than 10 percent, industrial production 11.8 percent. Inflation soared to 1,300 percent; average wages dropped from $120 to $30 as the lev was devalued; fifteen banks went bankrupt; foreign debt rose to 168 percent of GDP.[10] The decade's westward exodus of anywhere from 750,000 to a million young Bulgarians—there are no reliable statistics—was well under way. Bulgaria faced the gloomy prospect of being the only Central European state to be shut out of the race to join the Euroatlantic clubs. A foreign policy that the Zhan Videnov government termed "neutral" actually followed Russia's lead in encouraging Milosevic in his bloody attempt to create a greater Serbia—despite the legacy of the Serb-Bulgarian wars of 1885 and 1913, and despite discriminatory treatment of the 60,000-strong Bulgarian minority in Serbia.

The turning point finally came in the winter of 1996–97 and is worth examining in some detail because it was so revolutionary. Nothing in the seven years since the end of the cold war had prepared Bulgaria for the sharp turn it now made in setting an irrevocable course toward joining the EU by implementing the prerequisite reforms, however turbulent the domestic consequences might be. The shift began with six weeks of daily protests by young people in downtown Sofia against the bank collapse, hyperinflation, and the plunging standard of living. "They were fed up with the imitation of change," declared Philipov. They were disappointed with "imitation democracy, an imitation market economy—the companies which emerged came from the party and the secret services—and an imitation Western-oriented foreign policy, saying the government was for Euroatlanticism while playing games with Moscow."[11]

On January 10, 1997, the demonstrators besieged parliament and trapped Socialist deputies inside it in an attempt to compel them to dissolve the legislature and vote for early elections. The protest triggered a showdown within the Socialist government. According to eyewitnesses, a crucial argument over the use of force erupted between Prime Minister Videnov and his interior minister and designated successor, Nikolai Dobrev. Videnov wanted to use police and soldiers to disperse the crowds in an old-fashioned show of strength; Dobrev refused.

In the end, the Socialist members of parliament (MPs) were spirited out a back door and whisked away in buses, suffering no more than the scare of having stones thrown at them. Some of the demonstrators were less fortunate; in the one localized use of force by the police, several protesters were severely injured. The new president, Petar Stoyanov, a member of parliament who had won an upset election in fall 1996 and took office in late January—and the one official who seemed to grasp intuitively the issues that Western diplomats brought to his attention—persuaded Dobrev to waive his mandate to form a new government and to allow a fresh parliamentary vote. And this time the center-right UDF transformed itself from a grab-bag of political grouplets into a more coherent party, winning a clear majority.[12]

Sofia on the Cusp

So how can a late starter in a tough neighborhood possibly succeed? "With difficulty," sighed George Prohasky, a largely self-taught market economist, a government adviser, the chief executive officer of the nascent Bulgarian stock exchange, and one of the instigators of the currency board.[13] The reforms begun in 1997 had been under way for two years. And the reformers were discovering just how huge a task it would be to liberalize a poor, inertial economy that no longer had the comparative advantage of offering cheap labor to Western investors, since low wages, along with larger markets and much better business conditions had long since been on offer in Poland and elsewhere in northern Central Europe. As Prohasky and his colleagues saw it, though, there was no alternative. They had to institute tough shock therapy, or Bulgaria would never escape stagnation.

The UDF government put its financial house in order by establishing an independent currency board to stabilize the lev and remove any temptation to print more money. It got the hyperinflation down to 6 percent. It willingly adopted the macroeconomic austerity recommended by the International Monetary Fund (IMF) and the World Bank, complied with World Bank standards of budget transparency, cut subsidies to the old industrial white elephants, brought budget deficits down to a few percentage points of GDP, closed the failed banks, and set up stringent new banking and stock exchange codes. It freed prices. It liberalized internal and external trade and began reducing the burden of foreign debt. It passed legislation to create a functional land market. It cut the thicket of regulations (and their open invitation to bribes). It reduced taxes, and thus induced many to come out of the shadow economy and pay into state revenues. It also began serious privatization; by

1999, a still-modest 35 percent of assets were in the hands of nonstate owners, for a 65 percent share in gross domestic product, according to Deputy Prime Minister Alexander Bozhkov, the political driving force of the liberal reforms.[14] Notably, there was no popular backlash to the kind of tough policies that had set off street protests elsewhere in Central Europe; the economic collapse of 1996 had so traumatized ordinary Bulgarians that they were ready to accept radical measures. Unusually, the currency board and its concomitant austerity were actually popular, and remained so for years.

The government further began restraining the mafia conglomerates, removing their exemptions from sugar import tariffs, closing some of their bootleg compact disc factories—under American pressure—and cracking down on the new protection rackets thinly disguised as "insurance." Critics complained that the anticorruption campaign targeted opponents of rather than firms close to serving government officials, and they nicknamed one cabinet member "Mister Ten Percent" for his presumed rake-offs. But the drive did break up the most notorious corporation, Multigroup, which in the mid-1990s "may have been more powerful than the state," according to Philipov. And anecdotally, one start-up entrepreneur in downtown Sofia, Sylvia Perkova of the Two Sweety-pies, reported that her forty-three-person bakery was able to withstand pressure to buy "insurance" for a "scary" seven or eight months in the mid-1990s and was not bothered thereafter.[15]

Sociologically, the Bulgarians, with one of the world's highest rates of home-ownership, at 94–95 percent, were receptive to a system of private property. But as a very egalitarian people with no nobility—in the nineteenth century they had to import a German prince to rule over their newly autonomous state—they were at the same time offended by the excesses of the nouveaux riches. "Bulgaria was a land of middle peasants. That is the basis of everything. Bulgaria was much more egalitarian [than Romania]. Romania was a country of big estates, brilliant bourgeoisie, and brilliant intellectuals. But the median level in Bulgaria is much higher," pointed out historian Ekaterina Nikova of the Institute of Balkan Studies in the Bulgarian Academy of Sciences.[16]

For the UDF government, the corollaries to economic liberalization were reversing the 1980s persecution of ethnic Turks and repairing relations with neighbors—including even Bulgaria's century-and-a-quarter-old nemesis, Macedonia. Neither policy came easily. The similarities between Serbian and Bulgarian history might well have predisposed the Bulgarians to react to the new circumstances with the kind of xenophobia that Milosevic embraced. Like the Serbs, the Bulgarians had once ruled a great medieval empire and had a residual memory of grandeur. Like Milosevic, the Bulgarian Communists had sought popularity through ethnic cleansing in the 1980s. Yet in the end the new Bulgarians chose reconciliation over ultranationalism, in domestic as in foreign policy. The first Socialist government had already reversed the Communist course of expelling Turks and invited those who had been chased out to return to Bulgaria, readopt their old names, and reclaim their property. Many Bulgarians did not welcome this reversal, however. Demonstrations and passive resistance against the resettlement of the Turks and the mixing of Bulgarian and Turkish children in schools continued for some years, and still had to be overcome by the UDF government of the mid-1990s. Optional Turkish-language instruction was successfully reinstated in ethnically mixed schools. Mosques were reopened for the 9.5 percent of the population that was Turkish or Pomak.

Antonina Zhelyazkova, chairperson of the International Center for Minority Studies and Intercultural Relations in Sofia, recounted the difficulties she and other activists ran into in trying to persuade fellow Bulgarians to accept the return of their Turkish neighbors. "At the beginning of the 1990s there was a very strong nationalist backlash. When [the Turks'] human rights started to be restored and respected, it almost came to bloodshed against the Turks and Pomaks. The Communists were still very strong and had [earlier] involved Bulgarians from mixed regions in violence against Turks. So when rights were restored, Bulgarians thought there would be strong revenge against them and held rallies against the Turks."[17]

As tension grew, Zhelyazkova and allies founded the Committee on National Reconciliation. "People from the committee traveled throughout the country to calm people down. We managed to get onto Bulgarian television prime time and invite the best-known intellectuals to comment about reconciliation," and to set up telephone hotlines. The activists found themselves branded as traitors and even received death threats.

Pioneers of Bulgaria's civil society nevertheless persevered in appealing to a parallel Bulgarian tradition of generosity. They reminded critics that their country had saved its Jews in the Nazi era and given shelter to endangered Armenians who fled the Turkish massacres a half-century before that. Bulgarians should be proud of this history, they argued, and not squander their good reputation. At heart, Bulgarians are "tolerant people," Zhelyazkova maintained. "It is very difficult to get them involved or to go to fight for some kind of nationalist cause. They are very different from Serbs; they have a very different temperament. . . . It was enough just to talk softly and calmly in prime time and remind everyone that we should not lose the big capital [of good will] we had."

In the end the result was positive. The activists were not murdered. Socio-logical surveys "show that negative stereotypes are disappearing year by year. People are starting to regard these things more calmly. For the first time in the last ten years, Bulgarians are concluding that the Turks are part of the Bulgar-ian nation and are entitled to equality and participation in political and eco-nomic life," Zhelyazkova commented, and added as the inevitable after-thought, "This process of changing the mentality and way of thinking should sooner or later start among Serbs, too. Without that, they are lost."

Certainly Bulgaria's restitution of the rights of ethnic Turks in the 1990s laid the foundation for improved bilateral relations with Ankara. In 1997 Pres-ident Stoyanov publicly apologized in Turkey for Bulgarian conduct in the previous decade and promised to pay the pensions of those Turks who had been forced to leave his country. The two countries resolved border disputes and introduced bilateral free trade in 1999, agreeing to include Romania in the zone in 2000. Prime Minister Ivan Kostov struck up a friendship with his Turkish counterpart, effectively balancing the understanding his Socialist predecessor had established with Greece. The government willingly signed the International Pact on Civil and Political Rights, the International Pact on Social, Political and Cultural Rights, the European Human Rights Conven-tion, and the framework Convention for Protection of National Minorities.

"Whenever the scope of democracy expands in any part of the world, acceptable, civilized solutions are immediately possible," declared Deputy For-eign Minister Konstantin Dimitrov, praising the development. "They are pos-sible when schemes of cold war or the mechanisms of old-fashioned nine-teenth-century national thinking end, to be replaced by more Euroatlantic thinking. Then problems are overcome almost overnight. That happened in French-German relations after the Second World War. That happened with Bulgarian-Turkish relations."

It also happened even more dramatically in the 1990s reconciliation between Bulgaria and Macedonia—the first since Bulgaria had tried to seize Macedonia in the Balkan wars eight decades earlier, and had temporarily done so in World War II as an ally of Hitler. This rapprochement was the most dif-ficult of all, in part because Macedonia is as much the cradle of Bulgarian identity as Kosovo is of Serb identity. Yet the real stumbling block, Bulgarian officials insisted, was not innate ethnic hatred but the lingering effects of the ultranationalism stoked by previous Communist governments in both Skopje and Sofia. After Macedonians voted for independence from Yugoslavia at the end of 1991, Bulgaria was the first country to recognize the new country (if not its Macedonian language as anything other than a Bulgarian dialect), in

January 1992. President Zhelev persuaded Turkish prime minister Suleyman Demirel to recognize Macedonia shortly thereafter—and persuaded Russian president Boris Yeltsin to follow soon after Turkey. By the end of the 1990s Sofia and Skopje even agreed on compromise treaty wording that finessed the issue of the Macedonian language, and Skopje renounced any claim to speak for a Macedonian minority in Bulgaria. By 2004, as Bulgarian membership in the EU drew closer, many young Macedonians were choosing to get university degrees in Bulgaria and even to take on Bulgarian citizenship for the advantage this would give them in finding jobs.

"Bulgaria had to recognize the present, and Macedonia had to recognize the past," summed up Ognyan Minchev of the IMIR. "The Macedonian elite was bound to the Serbs" until the late 1990s and demonized Bulgaria. By contrast, he observed, Macedonia and Bulgaria were now marginalizing disputes and trying to "catch up" with pragmatic, modern thinking.[18] Symbolically, the Macedonians published a complimentary book about Bulgaria in 1999 after half a century of anti-Bulgarian propaganda. For their part, the Bulgarians gave their new partner several hundred decommissioned tanks and artillery pieces to replace weapons that the (Serbian) Yugoslav army had removed wholesale when Macedonia became independent a decade earlier. The two also began conducting joint military exercises.

This renunciation of populist appeals to nationalist claims and the attempt to establish an island of stability in a region dominated by the Yugoslav wars met with public acclaim in the new Bulgaria. After he signed multiple cooperation and open-border agreements with Macedonia, Prime Minister Kostov told an approving crowd of 2,000 in Sofia, "We have found a European solution to a Balkan problem." Minchev contrasted this escape from old-fashioned chauvinism with the powder keg next door. "Serbs are now witnessing the very bitter results of their centuries-old politics of trying to create a proto-empire at the expense of other nations and their interests" and therefore resent the prospect of losing Kosovo, he observed. "We know what that is like, for eighty years ago we, too, lost Macedonia, which was a kind of focus of mystical Bulgarian unity and a cause. It was very painful for us, and it will be hard for the Serbs, too, to give up primitive nationalism."[19]

"The Macedonian question" had plagued all of the Balkans in the 120 years after the Bulgarian Orthodox Church was founded in 1870 and claimed the allegiance of Skopje and Ohrid Christians. Its resolution in bilateral reconciliation "was probably the most important foreign policy move" of post-Communist Bulgaria and was a crucial development "in the whole Balkan history," commented J. D. (Dimitry) Panitza, a native of Sofia who lived in exile for forty-two years, was an editor at *Reader's Digest*, and returned to Sofia in 1990 as founder and chairman of the Free and Democratic Bulgaria Foundation. "They really buried the hatchet."[20]

Multilateral manifestations of Bulgaria's newfound cooperative foreign policy soon included the Central European Free Trade Agreement (CEFTA), collaboration between Black Sea littoral states on environmental and trade issues, and the "Balkan brigade" that was earmarked for peacekeeping operations abroad (though not in the Balkans). In becoming a member of CEFTA in 1998, Bulgaria joined Romania, Poland, Hungary, the Czech Republic, Slovakia, and Slovenia in agreeing to remove all tariffs on mutual trade as a preparatory step toward EU membership. Presidential adviser Philipov saw such economic cooperation exactly as EU sponsors saw it—as promising a "dramatic reduction of the importance of borders, reducing them to mere geographic impressions and eventually showing how to solve the security problem." The normalization of regional relations, agreed deputy foreign minister Dimitrov, was beginning to demonstrate that the Balkans, despite their odious reputation and the butchery in the former Yugoslavia, need not be "an accursed part of Europe" after all. It showed that Bulgaria was transforming itself to think in a "civilized," "European," or "transatlantic" way, he added, in the new vocabulary of leading circles in Sofia.[21]

Such a collaborative approach in the Balkans was innovative, Minchev pointed out, because "a substantial part of the political mentality in the region is based on zero-sum thinking: If I benefit, you lose." Deputy Foreign Minister Dimitrov made the same point in stressing the need to "demythologize the essence of Southeastern Europe" and to try "to be part of the solution, not part of the problem." Emil Mintchev of Bonn University's Center for European Integration wryly evaluated his home country's attainment after the first strenuous efforts of 1997–99: "We're the best of the losers."

The Quest to Join the EU—and NATO

In foreign policy, Bulgarians across the political spectrum wanted membership in the European Community (EC) from 1990 onward, even if this desire would not be translated into operational policy until 1997–98. Remarkably, for a decade and a half no anti-EU group comparable to Poland's nationalist peasant Self-Defense Movement formed among the 200 parties that materialized and vaporized in the new era of political experimentation.[22] Ordinary Bulgarians associated the EC with peace and prosperity (and visa-free travel in Western Europe), which they certainly wanted for themselves, and they had no idea how painful the qualifying market reforms would be. "At the beginning of the transition all of us were very naive. Our view was very romantic," reminisced Zhelyu Zhelev a decade after his presidency. One of his friends had thought that "in two years we would complete the transition. I was a little more realistic. I thought it would take five years. However, now it has been fifteen years, and we are still arguing about whether the transition is over or not. . . . The transition turned out to be much more complicated and difficult than we imagined." [23]

The slow road of transition to EU membership started in 1990, when Bulgaria signed a Trade and Economic Cooperation Agreement with the EC, began tapping into the EC's PHARE program of aid for Central Europe, and affirmed by parliamentary resolution its distant goal of EC membership.[24] In 1992 it passed the democratic test for the Council of Europe. In 1993—after the collapse of the Soviet Union in 1991 had led Brussels to speed up the integration of Central European states into the EC/EU and to devise ever tinier gradations in the precandidacy period as milestones to encourage countries that were far from qualifying for membership—Bulgaria signed the Europe Agreement for Association with the EC. In 1994 it joined the Partnership for Peace of that other premier Euroatlantic institution, NATO; although the North Atlantic alliance was still controversial in Bulgaria, its PfP program was not, since virtually all Europeans and even Central Asians were participating in some form and this entailed no commitment by either side to NATO membership. In 1995 the National Assembly approved Bulgaria's official application for membership in what had in the meantime become the European Union, and in its new 1997 constellation the assembly further adopted a Declaration for Simultaneous Launch of EU Accession Negotiations with the Associated Member States—that is, some degree of coordination with Romania, Hungary, and all the other hopefuls vis-à-vis Brussels.

At this point reforms began in earnest that would bring the country's economic, democratic, and legal system in line with European standards. In 1997 specialists published an essential trilingual (English-French-Bulgarian) dictionary of terms relating to European integration and began the laborious task of translating into Bulgarian the then 80,000 pages of the *acquis communautaire,* the cumulative body of EU law that all entrants have to accept and adopt in their own legal systems. In 1998 Bulgaria began screening its legislation to harmonize it with the *acquis* and prove that it was a stable democracy with a functioning market economy—as required by the 1993 "Copenhagen criteria" for membership. In December 1999 Bulgaria and Romania both graduated to become formal candidates for EU membership.

The contemporary view of the hurdles faced by a latecomer applicant for EU membership was set forth with unusual frankness in a 1999 analysis by

Sofia's Center for the Study of Democracy. It warrants citing at some length, since it remains valid for today's precandidates in the Western Balkans. The study is written from the point of view of elite activists who want to use EU conditionality to compel modernization of their country and need to persuade other elite actors that while the process will be tough, it will be worth the struggle. It begins by highlighting the moving target of a constantly changing EU and "the higher threshold for the new candidate countries [than for previous candidates] resulting from the completion of the [EC's 1992] single market and the launching [on January 1, 1999] of the Economic and Monetary Union," as well as the Amsterdam Treaty that entered into force in 1999—and, the writer would have added, had he published the study a year later, the Nice Treaty of 2000.

"Fundamental principles," the analysis notes bluntly, start with the fact that the "candidate countries must take on board the entire *acquis communautaire*. No permanent derogations [exceptions] are allowed." In the "screening" period, the EU examines applicants to set out a road map of what must be done to comply with existing EU treaties, "the instruments adopted in implementation of the Treaties and the case-law of the European Court of Justice; the declarations and resolutions adopted within the framework of the Union; the joint actions . . . and other measures adopted in the context of the common foreign and security policy; . . . co-operation in the field of justice and home affairs; [and] international treaties entered into by the Community." New members, the study warns, "join an already existing club," and any attempt to elicit special treatment is likely to backfire by upsetting internal EU politics of carefully balanced compromises made by the existing members. Negotiations about conditions of entry, therefore, are not negotiations in the usual sense of reaching compromises at some middle point between two distant opening positions, but instead "concentrate exclusively on the practical aspects of the adoption of the *acquis* by the applicant concerned." The only thing to negotiate is "transitional periods of limited duration" to let candidates meet the fixed standards the EU has set.

Furthermore, the "Community prefers to negotiate with blocks of countries which have already established close links among themselves," so cooperation among candidate countries (and in the Balkans) is advisable. And it is a political fact of life that existing member states use their veto over any new member to extract pet concessions from the EU for themselves. Candidate countries must therefore expect to import preexisting EU problems even as the EU imports their problems (though not their border disputes, which disqualify a candidate from the outset).

The domestic political impact of the long process of qualifying for EU membership will be huge, the report continues. The "national legal systems must absorb and integrate the entire *acquis* of the Community [and] put in place mechanisms for implementation." Yet there is compensation for loss of sovereignty in the representation that candidates win in EU councils even before they become members—and, the authors of the study would surely add today, in the financial assistance that even before accession amounts to more than 3 percent of Bulgaria's GDP, the EU's highest relative aid to any potential candidate. Moreover, in "all countries where the transition to democracy is relatively young, membership may be expected to exert a stabilising influence on the political parties and on the democratic process in the country." In participating in the larger whole of the EU, too, candidates "achieve a stronger influence in international relations." The trick here is to learn the art of the "linking of different issues and the building up of coalitions, both of them typical of the EU decision-making process;" this rolling coalition process will then become "typical of the decision-making process in the new Member-State" as well.

The economic impact of qualifying for EU membership will also be enormous. "The application of the *acquis communautaire* requres that large-scale economic reforms take place, . . . including deregulation in areas like public procurement, introduction of the principle of mutual recognition, foreign ownership of national companies and land, etc."[25]

In short, Bulgaria must give up the old Balkan zero-sum thinking. With the addition of a caution about the EU's own legitimacy crisis and its fears of enlargement after the French veto of the EU's draft constitution in 2005, this memo would hold good for any twenty-first-century modernizer in the Western Balkans.

Bulgaria's twin goal of membership in NATO did not become a consensus among the political elites until a decade after the EU consensus, in 2000. And before it did, the UDF reform government had to get through the severe test of the Kosovo war. The pro-Western government had tiptoed ever closer to the alliance. It had enforced the trade embargo on Serbia, at considerable economic cost to Bulgaria. And when NATO intervened militarily in Kosovo in 1999, the Bulgarian parliament granted the alliance overflight rights—despite the Socialists' strong objections to the airstrikes on Serbia and popular disapproval of the David-and-Goliath war and of the stray bombs that missed their targets and landed on Bulgarian soil. Since Bulgaria shares a border with southern Serbia, this offer of Bulgarian airspace was important for NATO planes; and conversely, the explicit extension of alliance protection to Bulgaria, as well as to Romania and others in the neighborhood, was important to Sofia.

In a striking turn of events, when Russian peacekeeping troops from Bosnia raced to occupy Kosovo's Pristina airport ahead of Western troops at the end of the eleven-week war, both Bulgaria and Romania refused to let their recent Warsaw Pact ally and hegemon use their airspace to reinforce or supply the errant troops. "The fight between Sofia and Moscow was a helluva big fight. The Russians threatened all kinds of retaliation. The Russian ambassador was in the [Bulgarian] Foreign Ministry banging on the table, saying people were dying in the Pristina airport because they did not have water and food," recalled Dimitry Panitza. Foreign Minister Nadezhda Mihailova immediaely phoned NATO commander Wesley Clark, explaining that the Russian ambassador in her office was worried about the survival of the Russian soldiers at the airport, and asking if NATO could help. Clark responded, "It's a done deal. We will give them everything they need." Bulgaria kept its airspace closed. "That is very important—the beginning, in fact, of the end of the Russian presence in the Balkans," concluded Panitza. "Two years later—it's still surprising—the Russians withdrew their troops from Kosovo and took away every instrument they had in the Balkans."

By 2000 the combination of Milosevic's defeat in Kosovo, a growing sense that only NATO could guarantee stability in volatile Macedonia next door, and the realization that the EU might not extend membership to an applicant that did not simultaneously want to join the military alliance induced a 180-degree turn at the party congress of the Bulgarian Socialists. Instead of passing the familiar resolutions condemning NATO as a fascist threat to peace, the Socialist Party endorsed a policy of seeking NATO membership. At about the same time, a scandal broke over a letter written by party head Georgi Parvanov to the Serb strongman with the salutation, "Dear Comrade Milosevic." "He denied this," recounted Academy of Sciences historian Ekaterina Nikova, "but journalists got hold of it and published it, and the alternative course of a close Serbian link was further discredited in political discourse."[26] By the time of the 2001 elections, the Socialists, like the other parties—and Parvanov, who in the meantime had been elected president of Bulgaria—were fully backing NATO as well as EU membership for their country.

The Western reorientation of the elites, along with the pro-European popular mood, gave the EU especially, and also NATO, extraordinary normative power in the country. The best examples of this effect are the shutting down of nuclear reactors and the reform of the judiciary. The *acquis*, say Bulgarian critics, required only such safety measures as retrofitting and not the full closure of the older four of the six Soviet-designed reactors at Kozloduy. Yet in its eagerness to please the EU and win official candidacy for EU membership, the Bulgarian government decommissioned two reactors early, in 2002, and promised to decommission the two other suspect reactors by 2007.[27]

Similarly, "judicial and home affairs" as such do not fall under the *acquis* in the EU's prevailing Amsterdam and Nice Treaties, but in practice one of the main EU issues that Bulgaria will have to resolve if it is to join as scheduled in 2007 is reform of its judiciary.[28] While the EU says that the important point is to institutionalize the rule of law and that it is up to the candidate countries to decide how best to do this, the reality is that the EU gets involved in micromanagement and the Bulgarians respond to this. The Bulgarians "still behave as if they need a big brother. Before, it was Russia. Now, it's Brussels who will tell them what to do," observed one senior European diplomat. He thought the overall process was beneficial for both sides in "exporting the EU's security and prosperity without military means." But he did worry about indigestion from Bulgaria's having to swallow in one gulp—at the insistence of the EU—all the "things we have adopted in Europe in the past thirty to forty years."[29]

By 2001, when it became the first post-Communist Bulgarian government to serve a full four-year term, the Kostov government had put the country irrevocably on the path to EU membership and Western identity.[30] It had begun the restructuring of the armed forces and brought them under civilian control. It had weathered the second "transformational recession" of 1996–97 that Bulgaria had shared with the transitional economies of Romania and Moldova; it had launched the country's first "real transition to competitive markets," under ferocious adverse conditions, and had begun second-generation reforms as well.[31] More than half of its trade was with the EU. The arrival of major Western investors was helping to squeeze out some of the worst mafia extortion and black economy and to introduce the concept of best practice. Bulgaria had started what would become its longest period of growth since the 1930s.

Moreover, Hewlett-Packard's Bulgarian chief, Sasha Bezuhanova, besides winning the contest with thirteen other countries to make Bulgaria the site of HP's new Global Delivery Center and being honored by selection for Western "manager of the year" lists, had imaginatively extended $50 million in Hewlett-Packard credits to the government to devise a nationwide system of secure, state-of-the-art, computer-readable identity cards and passports. As a result, from spring 2001 Bulgarians could travel in EU Schengen countries without visas. Not coincidentally, public support for Bulgaria's quest for EU membership continued high, ranging between two-thirds and three-quarters of the population.

Sofia on the Way

In June 2001 King Simeon II, having repossessed most of his property, though not his Bulgarian throne, became the first deposed monarch after Napoleon III to make a political comeback through elections. Peasant women kissed his hand reverentially as he campaigned for the Simeon II National Movement that he had founded only two months before the vote. His party swamped the UDF as he promised an 800-day economic miracle and an end to corruption. After four hard years, Balcerowicz's window of "extraordinary politics," it seemed, had finally ended. Prime Minister Kostov's economic austerity had hurt too many voters for the incumbents to win reelection.[32] Simeon Sakskoburggotski (Saxe-Coburg-Gotha) offered a fresh start, bringing in as his economics minister the thirty-one-year-old Nikolai Vassilev, formerly a Lazard analyst; and as his finance minister, the thirty-six-year-old Milen Velchev, formerly a Merrill Lynch investment banker. It was beginning to look as if Bulgaria might catch up with the other Central Europeans after all, not in the first admission of new members that would come in 2004, but in the second, alongside Romania. The transformation that remained to be accomplished before Bulgaria could reach even the starting point of candidate status was still daunting, but at least the cabinet ministers leading the further reforms had themselves lived and worked in the EU economic and political space, understood how it functioned, and could now build on the foundation laid by the UDF government.

So far advanced was the reconciliation with ethnic Turks by 2001 that for the first time in Bulgarian history the latter formally joined a governing coalition. Unusually for the Balkans, the small MRF, which had grown out of a 1980s underground network of resistance to ethnic persecution, joined the government on a platform not of collective minority rights but of individual civil rights. According to the Princeton-based Project on Ethnic Relations, this represented the preference of Bulgarian Turks for having their children integrate and attend Bulgarian-language schools, learning Turkish only as an extracurricular subject.[33] A less positive view was that, whatever its platform, the MRF "blackmailed" its coalition partners to gain financial advantages for itself and its Turkish clientele, as when it blocked privatization of the state tobacco monopoly.[34]

Sakskoburggotski's government accelerated Bulgaria's adaptation to EU norms, even as it acted on the new domestic security consensus to move closer to NATO. Economic recovery turned into regular 5 percent annual growth. Velchev balanced the budget, reduced the country's foreign debt further, to

17 percent of GDP, and introduced a flat 19 percent corporate tax rate. By October 2002—two years before Romania—Bulgaria could sign the EU document acknowledging that it had a functioning market economy and could now start on the long path to EU membership. It gradually opened up domestic energy markets. It followed International Monetary Fund advice and reduced domestic subsidies, curbed insider deals in privatization with more transparent auctions, and identified five priority economic sectors: energy, transport and communication, agriculture and forestry, high-tech, and tourism.

Even if many of the millions of dollars paid in privatization transactions leaked away before ever reaching government coffers, the share of the private sector rose to a healthy 77 percent of gross value added.[35] Per capita GDP income rose correspondingly and gradually began improving living conditions, but wages remained low enough—at half the Polish, Czech, and Hungarian levels and a tenth of the EU's average prior to the 2004 enlargement—to attract investors. Unemployment dropped to 11.5 percent. Meanwhile, whole villages of Bulgarians began working seasonally on Spanish farms, earning a net €1,000 or €2,000 per worker, or the equivalent of a year's wages at home. Remittances from Bulgarians working abroad made an increasingly important contribution to GDP, rising to some €1.3 billion by 2005. Some emigrés began trickling back to found small companies with skills they had learned and honed abroad. And university education remained more widespread in Bulgaria than in Germany, France, or Italy. Bulgaria completed bank privatization in 2003, with capitalization of the now overwhelmingly foreign-owned banks at 22 percent, or well above the Basel recommendation of 12 percent. Financial intermediation played an increasingly important role in the economy, and significant nonprivatization greenfield investment began to come in.

In various rankings Bulgaria climbed steadily upward. It reached a respectable fifty-fourth on Transparency International's 2004 Corruption Perception Index; sixteenth in the Bertelsmann Transformation Index, behind Slovenia (first) and Croatia (eleventh) but ahead of all other Balkan countries; and fifty-eighth in the World Economic Forum's 2005 ranking of economic competitiveness, behind Slovenia (thirty-second) but ahead of Croatia (sixty-second), Romania (sixty-seventh), Serbia and Montenegro (eightieth), Macedonia (eighty-fifth), Bosnia-Herzegovina (ninety-fifth), and Albania (one-hundredth).[36]

At the same time Solomon Passy, no longer a voice in the wilderness but foreign minister in the Sakskoburggotski cabinet, could put official weight behind his personal drive to get Bulgaria into NATO. The 9/11 terrorist strikes in New York and Washington gave him the opportunity. As first terrorism and then Saddam Hussein monopolized America's foreign attention, the Balkans as such became even less important for the United States, but every additional ally in Iraq became more important to the Bush administration—especially as "old Europe" refused to join in the Iraq war. Sofia quickly made itself useful to Washington by signing a bilateral agreement on cooperation in Operation Enduring Freedom in Afghanistan in November 2001 and letting the Burgas airport be used by air tankers refueling U.S. aircraft for the campaign. It deployed a company to protect UN Stabilization Force (SFOR) headquarters in Sarajevo in January 2002 and destroyed medium-range SS-23 missiles left by the Soviets in Bulgaria. It dramatically reduced the country's profitable export of small arms to African rebels and others to a tenth of its volume in its Communist heyday, or around $100 million. It cracked down on criminal rings running international forgery, credit card, and computer fraud and closed down counterfeiters who were second only to their Colombian rivals in their output of fake dollars. It facilitated a joint American-Russian raid to remove thirty-seven pounds of weapons-grade uranium from Bulgarian reactors to safeguard the material against terrorist theft. And in a climax in summer 2003 it sent 480 troops to serve alongside the United States in Iraq.[37]

The U.S. Congress got the message and—even though Bulgaria did not follow Romania in formally prohibiting the extradition of American personnel to the International Criminal Court that the Bush administration viewed as its nemesis—approved the accession of Bulgaria to NATO in March 2004, along with Romania, Slovenia, Slovakia, Estonia, Latvia, and Lithuania. En route there was one hiccup. When Prime Minister Sakskoburggotski, rather naively, Western diplomats thought, tried to appoint as his intelligence adviser a twenty-five-year veteran of the Bulgarian intelligence service, the United States, Britain, and NATO all objected strenuously. The candidate adviser duly withdrew, and Bulgaria joined the alliance as planned.

In parallel, by mid-2004 Bulgaria had successfully "closed" all thirty-one chapters that it had to agree on with Brussels in order to become a formal candidate for EU membership. In April 2005 it signed the accession treaty, vowing to enhance the rule of law, fix its system for disbursing agriculture subsidies, and enforce technical and environmental standards in time to be admitted with Romania in 2007.

Is Western conditionality working? "Absolutely. It's working," declared one American observer flatly. "Bulgaria has two overriding foreign policy objectives: membership in the two clubs, NATO and the European Union." Up until March 2003, when the U.S. Congress signaled its approval of Bulgarian entry into NATO, "pretty much any conditionality we set, official or unofficial, that is to say, things that weren't necessarily part of the formal requirements—dismantling of SS-23s, clamping down on international arms sales"—the Bulgarians met. "The EU right now has tremendous leverage." He acknowledged the huge remaining problems: "Bulgaria interdicts more narcotics than the rest of Europe combined"—five tons of cocaine in 2004—and "the rule of law issue is the biggest [problem]. The courts don't work. Organized crime is too big and influential. Police and prosecutors are ineffective, and everybody is pointing a finger at everybody else" for the failure to convict major criminals.

He did, however, praise the country's accomplishments and pace of change, as Bulgaria responds to the challenges. "In macroeconomics it's the darling of the international community. Low inflation. Stable currency. Five percent growth. . . . We Americans don't even grasp the depth of change, total change. Society, politics, economics, education—everything is in the process of change. It has only been fifteen years! We haven't had a change like this since maybe the end of the civil war in the South. Not the Great Depression. Not World War II. You have to go back to the 1860s for this kind of change. And because of information technology, the change is occurring at lightning speed. . . . All in all, when you look at the moderate political structure, the commitment to education, the very bright young people, the determintion to be a part of Europe and of Euroatlantic institutions, I am very upbeat on this place."

Not surprisingly, Bulgarian voters displayed a less charitable view of the government than outsiders did when they next got to express their opinion, in the mid-2005 elections. When the day of reckoning rolled around for the regally aloof Sakskoburggotski, it was his turn to pay for the austerity that after fifteen years was finally giving the Bulgarian economy a much sounder base. Just as the prime minister had been the agent for voters' revenge against the UDF four years earlier, so the Socialist Party became the agent for voters' revenge against him. Breakaway MPs from his Simeon II National Movement had already reduced his parliamentary plurality, and in 2005 he won only 20 percent to the Socialists' 31 percent, on a low turnout of 56 percent that apparently would have been even lower but for the lure of a special lottery for lethargic voters. A stalemate dragged on for two months before the thirty-nine-year-old Socialist leader, Sergei Stanishev, managed to form a coalition government with Sakskoburggotski and the MRF, which had won 11 percent. The new coalition thereby built up the two-thirds majority it would need to amend the constitution in the continued reforms required by the EU.[38]

The opposition consisted of the splintered UDF remnants and, in a major upset, the fourth-strongest party, the newcomer Ataka ("Attack") that with more than 8 percent of the vote for the first time brought a radically chauvinist, anti-Turk, anti-European, anti-American, anti-Roma, anti-political-parties voice into the National Assembly. Initial polls suggested that Ataka's message of "Bulgaria for the Bulgarians" could double the group's percentage of votes (on rapidly diminishing turnouts) in the next general election.[39] Especially noteworthy in the new party were "former generals from the security services, former military officers, and teachers, the once intelligent, responsible people who feel humiliated by their poverty," as Panitza analyzed it. Ataka was well-enough funded—in part, rumor had it, from sources in Moscow—to have its own TV station and its own newspaper, *Skat*. It quickly became the focus of opposition to EU membership for old apparatchiks and other losers in the social turmoil, and also for the mafias that profited from the relative disarray of transition and had no wish to see law enforcement strengthened through EU membership. It splintered within a year, however; after various fights, expulsions, and resignations, Ataka's parliamentary caucus shrank from twenty-one to fourteen.[40]

The new government picked up where the old government had left off. On taking office, Prime Minister Stanishev, a graduate of both Moscow State University and the London School of Economics and a quick learner, promptly confirmed his priorities of ensuring EU membership by 2007 and continuing macroeconomic and financial stability. He stated that Bulgarian troops would leave Iraq when their designated term finished at the end of 2005, but he noted that consultations were already under way with the United States on how Bulgaria could "commit itself to the stability in Iraq after the withdrawal."[41] Stanishev declared himself in favor of "modernization of the Socialist Party"—the code phrase for winning the final victory in his intramural wrestling with party hard-liners who still consider him a traitor for having endorsed NATO membership.

President Parvanov traveled to Washington in October 2005, met President Bush in the Oval Office, and sealed the deal on opening three American "lily pad" bases in Bulgaria, which the Simeon II National Movement had initiated, the Socialists had previously opposed, and the nationalist Ataka still opposed. The king's economic minister, Nikolai Vassilev, moved over to become minister of public administration, a key position if Bulgaria were to qualify for and use effectively all the financial aid the EU offers candidates for membership.

The outgoing interior minister and incoming justice minister, Georgi Petkanov, got parliament to pass the criminal procedures code that the Sakskoburggotski team had drafted and the Socialists had opposed before the election—some twenty minutes before European Commissioner for Enlargement Olli Rehn walked into the legislative chamber to take his last soundings before writing his October report approving Bulgarian entry into the EU.[42] The old, passive chief prosecutor was replaced by Boris Velchev, who quickly complained that he was getting more pressure from politicians to investigate their rivals than to investigate organized crime.[43] A similar objection came from squabbling coalition partners, who were all allotted their quotas of deputy minister slots—-as one Bulgarian observer put it, to "spy on each other."

Boyko Borisov, who had been promoted from his position as bodyguard of Communist boss Todor Zhivkov and then Simeon II to become the ex-king's anticorruption tsar, now moved on to become mayor of Sofia and found his own "movement" that everyone expected would become the next shooting-star party to steal protest votes from the existing parties and perhaps propel its founder into the presidency.[44] As for Simeon II, he stayed on as an ordinary member of parliament and expressed an interest in running for president in the next election.

Ruse

Back at the turn of the twentieth century, as Bulgaria emerged from Turkish rule, Ruse was the country's gateway to Europe, the cosmopolitan, multiethnic Danube port that introduced the latest Viennese fashions and intellectual trends to the southeastern Balkans. The rising bourgeoisie, including the parents of the future Nobel prize winner Elias Canetti, built villas in the town. The country's first bank, first insurance company, and first newspaper were born here. St. Paul's Church imported the first organ.

The golden era ended with World War II, however, and Russe never recovered. Even though it was Bulgaria's fifth-largest city, in the highly centralized Communist system it became a province, with little contact with the outside world, not even with Romanians across the wide Danube. Zhivkov made a show of fraternity by adding a special wing to his house in Ruse to host visits by Nicolae and Elena Ceausescu, should they drop in from Bucharest forty miles away. But neither that new wing nor the construction of the Friendship Bridge in the 1950s as the single land link along the 300-mile river border did much to advance bilateral communication. The one exception to this state of affairs came as living conditions worsened in Ceausescu's domain in the 1980s, and impoverished Romanians slipped across the bridge to buy food and gasoline.

In 1987 the city was awakened from its slumbers when small groups of environmentalists began protesting against the fumes from the new Romanian chlorine and sodium combine in Giurgiu across the Danube that prevailing winds brought to Ruse. Local doctors joined in as the incidence of lung disease and birth defects rose. The movement attracted support from a number of intellectuals, and in 1988 "Eco-Glasnost" staged the country's first sizable protest, gathering between 5,000 and 9,000 people outside the National Assembly to present an ecological petition.

Ruse's next claim on the nation's attention came a decade later, during the Kosovo war, when embargoes on Milosevic barred Bulgartrans trucks from plying their traditional route through Serbia to Vienna to carry Bulgaria's choice tomatoes to Austrian and German markets. The only alternative required an uneconomic two-day detour east over the Ruse bridge to drive through Hungary. In the years since then, Bulgaria has been pleading with Romania and the EU to construct a second bridge upriver. Bulgaria and Romania negotiated on the project for a decade, and the bridge was finally agreed on in principle. But it now looks as if it will not form part of the EU's grand Pan-European Corridor IV across southeastern Europe to Turkey. The latest EU plans for upgrading road, rail, and river transport in the region would bypass northern Bulgaria and southern Romania altogether and instead bring trunk routes south from Belgrade to Sofia, to then branch off southward to Greece and eastward to Turkey.[45]

In the twenty-first century there has been a bit of good news for Ruse. A consortium of German universities now sponsors a two-year graduate course in European studies for Bulgarian, Romanian, and other southeast European students, with classrooms on both sides of the river, on the pattern of the German-Polish Viadrina University on the Oder River. Local realtors are advertising Danube hideaways on the Internet, trying to tap into the new British and Japanese interest in buying second homes in Bulgaria (the Japanese, at least, inspired by Kotooshu, the Bulgarian who has become the only European sumo wrestler of ozeki rank). Local web designers are offering their services to international clients; cruise ships are scheduling stops at the city to visit Canetti's birthplace and the ruins of the palace of the Second Bulgarian Kingdom. The Ruse port should pick up more business as Danube freight traffic recovers from the five-year blockage of the river channel by the rubble of bridges bombed during the Kosovo war. Today Ruse, even with its many vacant buildings, has something of the feel of Sofia before its take-off a decade ago. New wastebaskets decorate lampposts to encourage European antilitter mores. Laborers work on Saturdays to lay gravel roadbeds. The heirs of grandparents who had their little shops or hotels nationalized in the 1940s are spending weekends and nights fixing up the premises they suddenly own after two generations of neglect. Family restaurants, cafes, and maybe even Hugo Boss boutiques should come next.

Politically, the city is also beginning to breathe. The centralized grip of Communist times is loosening. Bulgaria now has one of the best programs in the Balkans for invigorating local government—including a consensus on fiscal decentralization that will increasingly let local revenues fund municipal services and development and make towns less dependent on arbitrary transfers from Sofia. The National Association of Municipalities is learning the art of lobbying and is sometimes called Bulgaria's most powerful NGO (with *nongovernmental* here meaning non-central-government). At the same time, the modern bus system that Bulgaria has invested in for cheap domestic travel is bringing Ruse and dozens of district centers much closer to the capital. Every Friday night Sofia's pre-yuppies fan out from the capital's sleek airport-like bus terminal to their home villages, bearing Teflon frying pans, TV sets, and Chinese sweaters in new Samsonite suitcases.

Moreover, since 2001 Ruse and Giurgiu have been joined in one of the EU-sponsored "euroregions" designed to promote cross-border cooperation. To be sure, the euroregion and the common endeavor to qualify for EU membership have not pushed the two countries to cooperate as much as Brussels had hoped. Transport connections with Romania remain limited. The few daily trains to Bucharest are three-quarters empty, in part, perhaps, because of their very long pause in Giurgiu, which drags out the travel time. Bulgarian-Romanian contacts are still tentative not from any historical enmity, but from decades of noncommunication and mutual ignorance. Interpreters from Bucharest hesitate before accepting assignments in Bulgaria, half expecting to get shot by gangsters in the street—"Our criminals aren't as violent as the Bulgarians' criminals," explained one nervous Romanian. Bulgarians who attend introductory bilateral meetings of businessmen half expect to meet sheepherders in white felt trousers and capes.[46]

Nonetheless, trade between the two cities jumped sevenfold between 1998 and 2004. Businessmen do get together regularly and join local officials in designing common infrastructure plans. A common environmental and health commission meets quarterly to close down or upgrade industrial plants on both sides of the Danube in line with EU clean air and water standards. And more broadly, in the area of energy exports a new start is being made to look for ways to turn the past rivalry into collaboration. After Romanian NGOs demonstrated against Bulgaria's plans to build a modern nuclear reactor at

Belene near the Romanian border, a bilateral panel of experts was set up to review the plans, and the two sides have agreed to make their energy infrastructure mutually available, to liberalize their own internal energy markets, and to link the whole Balkan energy network with the EU grid that Romania already belongs to. Multilateral steps in this direction were taken with the "Athens process" that began with memoranda of understanding between EU and other donor countries and the Balkan countries on electricity in 2002 and on gas in 2003, the first connection of the grid systems in October 2004, and the first example of EU "sectoral enlargement" in the EU and South Eastern Europe Energy Community's coordinated plans for investment in power generation, transmission, and distribution in October 2005.[47]

Given the city's new role as the gateway to Bulgaria's twin newcomer to the EU, it is only fitting that every anniversary of the two countries' signing of EU accession treaties on April 25, 2005, is now celebrated by schoolchildren from Ruse and Giurgiu. They meet for festivities on their common bridge—and they will be joined in just a few years by those Bulgarian toddlers who were born on that auspicious date and have the specially minted gold coins saying "Europe Baby" to prove it.

Crime and Justice

Those dramatic mafia executions in Sofia and Amsterdam do not prove that crime is more rampant in Bulgaria than elsewhere in the Balkans.[48] Murders dropped from their peak of 490 a year in both 1993 and 1994 to an average annual rate of 240 between 1999 and 2004; in 2004 there were 225 murders among a population of 7.5 million, for a rate of 0.03 per thousand.[49] Romania (the only other Balkan country with equivalent UN crime statistics) has a lower rate—0.025 in the latest UN tally—but the United Statese has a higher rate, of 0.04.[50] What is more alarming, though, is that—unlike the Dutch, who promptly apprehended and convicted Edwin Bakker after he killed druglord Samokovetza in Amsterdam in December 2003—the Bulgarians have convicted few of the hitmen and even fewer of the senior crime bosses.[51] "No sane judge in this country, or prosecutor, would dare to touch organized crime bosses," observed one Bulgarian commentator, explaining the phenomenon.[52] The media periodically photograph known "godfathers" in the company of senior government officials. Researchers for the impressive empirical study of the Bulgarian narcotics trade compiled by Sofia's Center for the Study of Democracy were able to interview druglords directly, since the latter had no fear that they would be arrested and may even have enjoyed a chance to boast about their successes. And the reason for EU concern about criminal networks in Bulgaria was dramatized within twenty-four hours of the publication of the key Brussels report card on Bulgaria in October 2005 with the daylight assassination of Emil Kyulev, the owner of the DZI Bank and reputedly Bulgaria's second-richest man. This killing brought to 155 the number of execution-style murders in five years.[53] Victim number 156 was alleged crime boss Ivan ("Doctor") Todorov, who was shot in Sofia in broad daylight in February 2006.[54]

Bulgarian crime is instructive not as an exception, but as a conspicuous example of a common Balkan problem. It is also somewhat more apparent to outsiders than crime in other lands, because it—and its "symbiosis" with old security networks—has been well publicized in successive studies by the Center for the Study of Democracy think tank, operating in concert with some law enforcement officials. As recounted in the CSD's 2004 "Partners in Crime," the story properly begins with the dismantling and reform of the Communist Bulgarian state security services in successive steps in the early 1990s. Between 12,000 and 14,000 employees of the old services—about half the staff, most of them from the political police—were swiftly made redundant. The security services were brought under civilian control, and the centralized command of the various police and intelligence units was broken up to avoid any reconstitution of totalitarian control, with different functions assigned to the president, the Interior Ministry, and the Defense Ministry. The shakedown got rid of some of the worst political operatives, but also dismissed some of the best professionals, so that "regular enforcement functions were nearly paralyzed by this institutional collapse. . . . Thus, a large portion of laid-off or dissatisfied police officers joined the ranks of shadow economy structures. . . . The bond between present and former security officers and the criminal and quasi-criminal groups proliferating amid legal and institutional chaos (most pronounced at the start of the transition) has been one of the most ominous developments in post-1989 Bulgaria." The involvement of corrupt officers in the gray or black economy and "the formation of a corruption-breeding public sector . . . aided the formation of informal crime networks where political and economic interests intersect, and which . . . provide a political umbrella for the activities of criminal formations in post-communist states."[55]

The rate of reported crimes quadrupled between 1989 and 1992, to 2,646 per 100,000.[56] The appearance of a private sector in this period facilitated the rise of the extortion firms, often using as enforcers the world-class wrestlers, boxers, and martial arts athletes who became unemployed when the state no longer subsidized their sports. As a typical example, wrestler Samokovetza worked his way up to the top after first enforcing drug import deals at the Kapitan Andreevo border crossing with Turkey. Various former political intelligence and counterintelligence officers founded fifteen banks that seemed to have been deliberately designed to go bankrupt and allow millions of dollars in net "losses" to be clandestinely exported to private accounts abroad. Then, during the 1992–96 UN embargoes, high-profit smuggling rings developed to provide fuel and weapons for Serbia.[57] Further rackets included, through manipulation of the secret police files, the blackmailing of those among the half million former state security informers who might want to start new lives.

The CSD's "Partners in Crime" report further traces the same "symbiosis" between crime and security services in Serbia and other Western Balkan countries that built on the deliberate employment of criminals by Communist security services in the 1970s. Citing the popular jibe in the region, "Every country has a mafia, but only in ours does the mafia have a country," the study explains that "unlike in Western democracies or even in some other transition countries, organized crime in Southeast Europe developed through active . . . collaboration with the security sector and law-enforcement institutions. In other words, while in Western and Central Europe organized crime has operated despite the best efforts of law-enforcement bodies trying to curb it, in most of Southeast Europe it operated and, to a lesser extent, continues to operate through these institutions. . . . [C]orruption and common economic interests created a link between the respective security sectors and organized crime. Thus far, none of the reform attempts undertaken by the governments have been able to break this link."[58]

Under the circumstances, the EU reserved the right, should Sofia (and Bucharest) not make fast enough progress in their judicial reforms, and law enforcement in particular, to postpone accession of these candidates to 2008. The long-awaited EU report card on Bulgaria's readiness in October 2005 found no fundamental flaw with the country's economic restructuring; as a proof of growing competitiveness, exports were moving up the value added chain in electro-engineering products, machinery, furniture, and automotive parts, and there were growing foreign investments in the Bulgarian service sector.[59] The report repeated the EU's earlier basic finding that Bulgaria has a working democracy and a functioning market economy. And it noted that "progress has been made" in both Bulgaria and Romania in such areas as "freedom of expression," and in Bulgaria in "the fight against petty corruption." The EU assessment warned, however, that "immediate and decisive action" is needed in both countries in "public administration reform, the functioning of the justice system, the prosecution of high-level corruption, the fight against trafficking in human beings, ill-treatment in custody, the mental healthcare system and the integration of the Roma minority." And it identified as "areas of serious concern" such problems as "piracy and counterfeiting," especially in "intellectual property violations"; administration of EU "structural," farm, and other financial aid; "veterinary legislation"; external border controls; enforcement of motor vehicle insurance rules; and, of course, corruption.[60]

The mills of the EU grind slowly, yet they can on occasion grind exceeding small. The initial Bulgarian response to the criticism was yet another round of reforms of previous reforms that would shuffle the organizational charts but leave unaddressed one of the EU's main concerns: a prosecutorial and judicial system that seemed incapable of indicting, let alone convicting, major crime bosses or corrupt senior politicians, and at the same time denied timely justice in the backlog of mid- and low-level cases that dragged on for years without closure. Various EU member states let Sofia know informally that without more display of political will, both Bulgaria and Romania could expect the escape clause postponing their accession to be invoked.

Under this threat, the Bulgarian legislature in January 2006 finally scrapped as inadequate the constitutional amendments it had planned; in their stead, the Council of Ministers adopted a "National Strategy for Good Governance, Prevention and Counteraction of Corruption 2006–2008" that incorporated much of a painstakingly worked out public-private initiative generated by the anticrime, anticorruption Coalition 2000, especially in the areas of "political-level corruption, VAT fraud, a stricter system of implementation monitoring and a stronger mandate for the oversight government commission" and in limiting or lifting the immunity of members of parliament and magistrates under specified conditions.[61] As Maria Yordanova, a former professor of consitutional law and one of the movers and shakers of the initiative, put it, Bulgarians should not view the EU's constant nagging about the need for deeper reforms as outside pressure. Instead, they should themselves be insisting on the prerequisites for the rule of law and a real market economy.[62] In the judicial realm in particular, she continued, they must pull back from the post-Communist judicial independence that was established without concomitant accountability, thus leaving the judiciary "vulnerable to informal influences."[63]

The anticorruption badgering of Coalition 2000 offers one of the clearest examples in the Balkans of how the EU can empower local reformers who would otherwise lack the clout to contest the perpetuation of personal interests in executive, legislative, and judicial control.[64] The proof of the pudding, however, will be in the eating.

CHAPTER THREE

REINVENTING ROMANIA

MARIA TODOROVA IS surely right when she complains about the Western stereotype of the Balkans as the negative "other" of Europe, neatly encapsulated in the "imaginary Balkanoid principalities of homicidal atmosphere" that form the setting of one Agatha Christie murder-mystery: "one of the Balkan states. . . . Principal rivers, unknown. Principal mountains, also unknown, but fairly numerous. Capital, Ekarest. Population, chiefly brigands. Hobby, assassinating kings and having revolutions."[1] Or, Todorova might have added, as reflected in the setting of Tintin's *King Ottakar's Sceptre* in "Syldavia."

But the real problem is worse, as Todorova allows. It is not that outsiders have this malevolent image; it's that too many inhabitants of the Balkans believe the base calumny about themselves. How else can one explain the abhorrence of Slovenes and Romanians to being called "Balkan"? The Slovenes protest that they are really old Austro-Hungarians, after all; the Romanians, that they are descendants of the pre-Roman Dacians (the precursors of the Agathyrsians mentioned by Herodotus), and that the term *Balkans* applies only to countries south of the Danube. With the exception of the Serbs, perhaps, Balkan inhabitants sometimes seem to want nothing more than to escape being considered Balkan.

The problem in external perceptions is, if anything, exaggerated in the case of Romania, the largest country in Southeast Europe (and the second largest in Central Europe, after Poland). Western reporters, intent on beating out competing stories of suicide bombers and disasters from around the globe, tend to highlight such themes as the capital's wild dog packs, sewer children, the race between Bucharest and Budapest for the title of sleazy sex capital of Europe, maltreated orphans and the elite segment among them who were recruited for the dread Securitate secret police because they would not have inhibiting family loyalties.[2] And, of course, there is the precedent of Dracula, the victim of what was arguably the world's first character assassination, when German settlers in Transylvania sought to protect their charter privileges from Romanian interlopers.[3]

Romanian enthusiasm for the Dacian alternative to a Balkan identification goes back to the eighteenth- and nineteenth-century wave of nationalism and reimagined history in Europe. Through 2,000 years the Romanians had maintained their distinct identity but had been split between foreign rulers, latterly in the form of the Ottoman Turks, the Hungarians, the Russians, the Hapsburgs, and the Greek Phanariote administrators of the northern part of the Ottoman Empire.[4] In the late eighteenth century Transylvanian Romanians who went to Rome to study at Jesuit institutions discovered the column of Trajan, the emperor who had brought Dacia into the Roman Empire, and they "popularized the theory that they were the direct descendants of the Roman nobles, . . . a chosen people, an outpost of Latin culture in the surrounding sea of Slavic and Teutonic barbarism."[5] Accordingly, as they themselves became the ecclesiastical educators, they replaced Greek with Latinate Romanian as the language of instruction.

Subsequent efforts by clerics and intellectuals to spark a Romanian consciousness among the inert serfs who were spread among Russian, Austrian, and Hungarian landowners failed in 1848. But an unprecedented economic boom, as oil was discovered near Bucharest in the 1850s and the Iron Gate gorge at the Danube border with Serbia was dynamited in the 1890s to let large steamers sail far upriver, began to urbanize the Romanian upper classes and give them a self-confidence that was more amenable to national sentiment. When World War I unexpectedly united the scattered territories into a single Greater Romania, the seeds planted in the eighteenth century took root. Nationalism flourished as Bucharest became the sophisticated Paris of the east, its Athenée Palace the watering hole of aristocrats from around Europe. Rank chauvinism fed the fascism of the Iron Guards in the 1930s and, much later, Nicolae and Elena Ceausescu's megalomania in the country's Communist half century.

Hermannstadt and the Saxon Heritage

The mayor of Sibiu, Klaus Johannis, a former physics teacher and an ethnic German, was reelected in 2004 with 89 percent of his city's votes. Just as extraordinary as the size of his victory are the demographics, since today only 2 percent of the population of the city long known as Hermannstadt are themselves German. A visitor who asks Johannis how he earned such trust in a society renowned for its cynicism about politicians gets the genial answer that both Romanians and Germans serve on his team, without differentiation. But the citizens of Sibiu who voted for him (and for eleven ethnic Germans out of thirty-three on the city council) stress the mayor's honesty and efficiency at getting things done, identifying these qualities as Germanic traits. Implicitly, they justify the decision of the Democratic Forum of Germans in Romania—in contrast to that of Romania's Hungarian minority—to enter politics in a nonpartisan readiness to cooperate with any parties of good governance rather than as an ethnic lobby. Residents like Johannis because he put streetlights and flowers around the city and cleaned up the litter. They share the civic pride as the whole medieval Old Town is being dug up and renovated (in part by Franconian wayfaring apprentices in their distinctive black top hats, vests, and bell-bottoms). And, not least, they like him because he is attracting German and Austrian investors, who create jobs.[6]

When he first took office in 2000, Johannis started asking the obvious potential investors in Munich and Vienna why they were not flocking to an 850-year-old Germanic city with a well-educated labor force that demanded only a fraction of Western European wages. To his surprise, he found that the answer was not primitive infrastructure, but rather the evasiveness of would-be landlords who kept changing their terms like wily peasants instead of acting like long-term business partners. He solved the problem of the lack of city funds—decentralization has not yet gone far enough to let municipalities tax for the money they need—by trading unused city land until he could make a contiguous industrial park, extend electric cables and water mains to it, and offer businessmen fixed costs for leases through a single negotiator, who could also facilitate permits without delays or bribes.[7] Johannis's ingenuity and probity impressed his voters as well as investors like Krupp and Renault, and townsmen in Mediasch, fifty kilometers away, also elected a German mayor, Daniel Thellmann, a proselytizer of the democratic gospel of letting local communities make their own decisions.[8] Thus, in a sense the Germans are reclaiming the proto-democratic spirit of their Saxon forebears in the region; and as such it is no coincidence that Sibiu—along with Luxembourg, from whence came some of its original settlers—has been named European Cultural Capital for 2007.

It was in the twelfth century that the original Germanic settlers (in the Hermannstadt region they are called "Saxons" generically) came to Transylvania, once the heart of the Roman emperor Trajan's province of Dacia, later a part of Hungary for a millennium, and today the northwestern corner of Romania.[9] Hungarian king Geza II invited foreign settlers from western countries, especially tradesmen and advanced farmers, to come to the region to protect it from external (and sometimes internal) foes and to promote the economy. His invitation reflected the remarkable precept of Hungary's eleventh-century St. Steven that a kingdom of only one language and one set of customs is weak and frail, whereas a kingdom with a plurality of languages and customs is glorious. The Saxons had royal guarantees that they could elect freely their local (and later, even regional) superiors, called "judges," and in an exception from Roman Catholic canonical law, they could select their own priests and pay tithes to them rather than to the bishop who ordained them. In the thirteenth century these rights were "renewed" in written form in the Golden Letter of Freedoms. In the fourteenth century it was the Saxons (rather than the Hungarians or the region's other autonomous community, the Hungarian-speaking Szeklers), who built the medieval Transylvanian cities, constituted their guild craftsmen and patricians, and came to speak not only for the burghers but also for the free Saxon peasants.

In the process, the Saxons became "a more coherent community than were the Hungarians and the Romanians—and thus lived somehow nearer to a democratic inner structure." This structure survived three centuries of Turkish raids from 1396 on, a period in which the Saxons repeatedly had to shelter in the sanctuary of their distinctive walled churches. Under the Turkish threat, in the fifteenth century the three Transylvanian communities (Saxon, Hungarian, and Szekler) signed a pact that besides pledging common defense against sieges, bound the three groups to come to each other's aid should royalty try to curtail any of their privileges. (The Saxon chroniclers' smear campaign of Dracula, who as a Wallachian monarch was trying to extend his influence in Hungary and Transylvania, was a manifestation of such resistance.) After Sultan Suleiman defeated the Hungarian kingdom in 1526, Transylvania became an autonomous part of the Ottoman Empire and remained thus for the next century and a half, until it came de facto under direct rule by the Hapsburgs.

Under the relatively benign Ottoman suzerainty, Transylvania was spared the bloody religious wars in western Europe.[10] For their part, the Saxons immediately adopted Martin Luther's Reformation as more compatible with their "will to build the church from the basic congregational units."[11] To avoid internal battles, Transylvania set a European precedent in allowing religious freedom for the German Lutheran and the Hungarian Reformed (Calvinist) Churches, as well as for the Catholic and Unitarian faiths, and tolerated as well the Eastern Orthodox Church of the Romanians. Transylvania religious legislation in 1568 was thus less restrictive than the much later "toleration" proclaimed by Cromwell in England in 1653. The region, with its multiple religions and with "three political 'nations' in one parliament" developed "an inclination to plurality within a comprehending political unity." And lest this Latin-speaking parliament of noblemen shut out commoners, the "shoemakers and tailors" and other guilds of Hermannstadt insisted successfully on their own right to be represented in the legislature.[12] In the eighteenth century it was the young Transylvanian Romanian students of yet another church, the Uniate Church that reunited the Catholic and Orthodox clergy, who discovered Emperor Trajan anew and redefined Romanians as the oldest continuous inhabitants of Transylvania and thus the "Fourth Nation" in the region. The crucial word was *continuous*. Although there had been no Romanian nobility to articulate an ethnic identity in Transylvania in the thousand years of Hungarian rule, the rediscovery of their ancestral cradle fired the national imagination of educated Romanians in much the same way as the Serbs' nineteenth-century rediscovery of their ancestral Kosovo. The "notion of Daco-Roman continuity" became "the cornerstone of a national ideology."[13]

National consciousness also spread to the Hungarians in the early nineteenth century. The Szeklers came to be regarded "self-evidently" as Hungarians rather than as a Transylvanian political "nation" of their own. Transylvania was still formally a part of Hungary, and the new government in Budapest after the 1848 revolution—liberal in legislating a sweeping end to feudalism, but illiberal in its determination to Magyarize non-Hungarians—was intent on making the link a formal union. The Romanian serfs in Transylvania, who had accumulated grievances against the Hungarian landowners, revolted and helped the Hapsburgs and the Russians put down the Hungarian revolution. Yet by 1867 the Hapsburgs agreed to share their empire with the unruly Hungarians, and Transylvania came under the direct rule of Budapest. Magyarization followed. The 815,000 Hungarians (including Szeklers) in Transylvania compelled the 1.4 million Romanians to change surnames and place names and pressured them to enroll their children in Hungarian schools.[14]

Romanian peasants in Bessarabia faced equally stringent Russification. Those in Bukovina were better treated by the Austrians, who established an educational system and curbed the mismanagement of the huge estates by foreign-run monasteries. At the end of the nineteenth century "[t]he Rumanian motherland was as weak as the Hapsburg and Russian empires appeared to be invincible and everlasting." No one "could have foreseen that within four decades all Rumanians would be united for the first time in their history within the frontiers of a great Rumanian state," commented historian L. S. Stavrianos.[15] Yet in 1861 the principalities of Wallachia and Moldavia, under the patronage of Louis Napoleon and the Russians, had begun the consolidation by joining to become the Principality of Romania, then adding parts of Dobruja on the Black Sea coast in 1878 and 1913.

In World War I Romanian troops marched into Transylvania, which was then awarded to Bucharest in the Trianon Peace Treaty, increasing Romania's territory by two-thirds. The highly centralized "Greater Romania became an explicitly mono-national state." Romanian soldiers were given land expropriated from Hungarians and Saxons. These two groups were now demoted from their centuries-long status as constituent "nations" of Transylvania to become "minorities." This was especially hard for the Hungarians, "since for one thousand years Transylvania in one way or another was part of Hungarian self-assurance," and "[i]n the last 50 years (since 1867) they consciously were the ruling class in the country."[16] General Ion Antonescu and his xenophobic and antisemitic Iron Guard followed; in World War II Romania allied itself with Hitler. The old Saxon elite was no match for either Antonescu or the younger Saxon sympathizers of the German Reich; Romania sent more than 60,000 young ethnic Germans from Transylvania to join the German forces. Most of those who survived ended up in West Germany. They began an exodus of Romania's ethnic Germans that would continue through the 1980s, as Bonn ransomed tens of thousands of them at $5,000 a head from lives of poverty in Romania; and even into the 1990s, as the cold war ended, the borders opened, and thousands more fled to newly united Germany. The German population of 745,000 in Romania before World War II shrank to 385,000 after the war to some 200,000 in 1989 to 119,000 in 1990 and to a more or less stable 60,000 today.

Bucharest Politics

As a defeated ally of Germany, Romania was stripped of its industry by the Soviet Union after World War II and lost a fifth of its prewar territory. Although it regained Transylvania, which Hungary had reclaimed in 1940, Romania ceded Bessarabia and northern Bukovina (today's Moldova) to the Soviet Union and southern Dobruja to Bulgaria. There was chronic tension between the ruling Romanians and the 1.6 million Hungarians concentrated especially in Transylvania, over university instruction in the Hungarian language and other cultural issues. The strains only increased after the Hungarian uprising of 1956 was suppressed by the Soviet Union and Transylvanian Hungarian sympathies overwhelmingly flowed to Budapest.

Once Nicolae Ceausescu rose to become leader of the Romanian Communist Party in 1965 and head of state in 1967, he quickly distanced himself from

Moscow, to the initial accolades of the West. In the 1970s and 1980s, however, he and his wife, Elena, grew increasingly megalomaniac and remote from reality in their one-party authoritarian system. Ceausescu's strategy of industrialization and depopulation of half of the villages was disastrous for the country. Romania borrowed heavily from Western lenders in the 1970s to start up regional heavy industry, and Ceausescu forced peasants to leave the land and migrate to shoddy apartment blocks to provide labor in the resulting single-enterprise towns. Many villages were destroyed; others were consolidated into "agro-industrial complexes." Under the mismanagement of state monopolies and a dysfunctional autarky, the industrial firms quickly became obsolete. The damage was only compounded when Ceausescu insisted on paying the loans back fast in the 1980s. In the process, he exported fuel and food and anything else he could find, at the cost of growing hunger and malnutrition throughout the country and indoor winter temperatures even in Bucharest that gave rise to jokes about the high cost of refrigerators—several hundred thousand lei for one icebox with two bedrooms and one and a half baths. In this rich agricultural land food was rationed; for meat, Romanians without party connections ate chickens' feet and whatever they could scrape off pork bones, and they fought with each other over sacks of potatoes.

The deprivation was augmented by harsh political repression. Romania's Hungarians faced compulsory assimilation, by means that included the swamping of majority Hungarian localities with Romanians in the mass rural migrations to cities. Residents of Bucharest, one of the most densely populated cities in the world, were evicted from the 40,000 buildings Ceausescu razed in the 1980s in order to build a gargantuan People's Palace. Poverty grew, and combined with the lack of contraceptives to produce a surplus of babies whom parents could not support. One of the more horrifying results was a string of Dickensian overcrowded orphanages that came to be called "child gulags."

As awareness of the anti-Communist revolts in the other Central European states grew in Romania in 1989, street demonstrations broke out against Ceaucescu in December in Timisoara in Transylvania, and then in Bucharest. Securitate forces shot and killed more than a thousand demonstrators and bystanders.[17] Soldiers in Bucharest refused to fire on the demonstrators, and senior army commanders soon assisted a palace coup in which the Ceausescus were executed by firing squad. It was the only violent rout of a Communist leader in the 1989 *annus mirabilis* in Central Europe.

Romania's path since then may have been no more convoluted than that of any other Balkan country, but it is much harder for a Westerner to follow because of the exceptional disjunction in the 1990s between Romanian politics, economics, and society. Western analysts tend to assume a continuum between old Communist apparatchiks, old military officers, anti-Western attitudes, resistance to modernizing reforms, and proneness to corruption on the one hand, and anti-Communist politicians, pro-Western inclinations, zeal for market reform, and resistance to corruption on the other. Yet, counterintuitively, it was the foxy old apparatchik-turned-president, Ion Iliescu, who backed model depoliticization of the Romanian military—and who resisted the temptation of self-enrichment, if he can be judged by his modest lifestyle. It was the old apparatchik-turned-prime-minister, Adrian Nastase (whose flashy lifestyle and art collection did raise questions), who finally brought economic stability, administrative skills, and the beginnings of EU-compatible legislation in 2001. And it was under the decent but ineffectual outsider President Emil Constantinescu that an attempt was made to repoliticize the military. Under him the would-be center-right disintegrated in the late 1990s and would not regain the presidency or a working parliamentary majority until 2004. Yet through it all, among a people who continuously saw themselves as the only Latin Westerners in a sea of Slavs, all factions strove to join the Euroatlantic clubs of NATO and the EU.

Perhaps politics could not have developed otherwise in a land in which apparatchiks were supposed to become democrats overnight, with no intermediation even from a core of proto-democratic dissidents. There was no Vaclav Havel or Lech Walesa or even Zhelyu Zhelev in Bucharest. In this respect, Romania resembled Albania more than any other state in Southeast Europe. There was no transition period of preparation for change by a budding civil society, no obvious political alternatives as Romania leapt from Stalinist rigidity and atomization to electoral free fall.

Iliescu, an old factional adversary of Ceausescu in the Communist Party and the leader of the second- and third-echelon Communists in the new National Salvation Front that assumed power after the 1989 coup, set out to correct some of the worst party practices. The NSF program called for an end to "the leading role of a single party"; term limits for government officials; separation of legislative, executive, and judicial powers; an end to the export of food and oil; and an end to compulsory migration from villages to towns. It also broke with Ceausescu's stoking of nationalist anti-Hungarian emotions and condemned "hate-mongering based on a chauvinistic policy of forced assimilation as well as the successive attempts to defame neighboring Hungary and the Hungarians in Romania."[18] Budapest responded in kind and was the first capital to recognize the new Romanian government.

Hungarians in Cluj and Tirgu Mures in Transylvania promptly restored Hungarian as the dominant language of instruction in the secondary schools that Ceausescu had "Romanized" through the influx of Romanian peasants and party officials. Romanian pupils and their parents and teachers demonstrated against the changes, and were backed by new chauvinist Romanian cultural and political groups. Simultaneously, Hungarians took to the streets to demand the reinstatement of the Hungarian Babes-Bolyai University in Cluj. Iliescu then publicly condemned "separatist trends" in Transylvania.[19] Precisely what happened next in Tirgu Mures is still not clear, but fighting broke out in January 1990 between Romanians and Hungarians, with Gypsies joining in on the side of the latter. Security troops arrived and fired on the crowds, leaving three dead and almost 300 wounded, according to official figures. "This was the first time that young Hungarians [in Romania] came close to a huge explosion," commented a Westerner who witnessed the melee.[20]

In the same month, fledgling new parties organized street demonstrations in Bucharest against the National Salvation Front in protest against its declared intention to call new elections soon and run as a party in them before start-up political rivals could have a chance to select candidates and campaign properly. Iliescu, in the first of several such appeals, called on the 40,000 miners in the Jiu Valley, 200 miles west of the capital, to defend the government. The miners obliged, marching to Bucharest, beating up unarmed demonstrators, and ransacking the headquarters of the young opposition parties.[21]

Twenty weeks after the palace coup, the NSF indeed called the first multiparty elections in the country in half a century. As the only party that could draw on the residual Communist power structures, including the monopoly on state TV broadcasts, the NSF had a huge advantage. It surprised no one when Iliescu won the presidency with 85 percent of the votes and the NSF won close to a two-thirds majority in the Chamber of Deputies, over nascent parties that adopted prewar names like the Peasant Party or the Liberals or any of the other 200-odd personality-oriented groupings. More unexpected was the success of the hastily improvised Hungarian Democratic Union of Romania (UDMR), which attracted 7 percent of votes, corresponding to the 7 percent Hungarian minority.

A month later, in June 1990, Iliescu again broadcast an appeal to loyal Romanians to defend the new government against student sit-in demonstrations in University Square, which he termed a "legionary rebellion" in reference to the extreme right in the 1930s. In the view of the students, they were simply protesting peacefully against what they saw as unreformed neo-Communist rule. As police looked the other way, however, several thousand Jiu Valley miners who thought that reforms would rob them of the elite status they had enjoyed in Communist times again marched on Bucharest and defended their interests by beating up student demonstrators and trashing the headquarters and homes of critical newspaper editors and opposition politicians in a two-day binge of violence. The European Community immediately froze the economic assistance it had extended to Romania after Ceausescu was ousted. In September 1991 the miners repeated the exercise, this time occupying parliament. If things did not fall apart altogether in the chaos and instability of 1990–91, a Westerner who lived through it observed sardonically, the only reason was that the situation was so confused that no would-be usurper had any idea where the levers of power might be.[22]

In the next general election, in September 1992 the opposition parties were better prepared. At this point Iliescu, who had turned into something of a father figure, won a more moderate 61 percent in the presidential run-off vote, and his slightly renamed Democratic National Salvation Front won a far more modest plurality of 28 percent in the Chamber of Deputies.[23] Over the next three years this party governed with parliamentary support from the extreme nationalist Greater Romanian Party (PRM) and the Romanian National Unity Party (PUNR), and in the middle of its tenure, in July 1993, completed its own evolution in name, if not yet in mind-set, into a Social Democratic Party.[24]

In its first years of governing, the NSF decollectivized farmland, turning it over to peasants. It did not make essential credits, extension services, or modern rototillers and other machinery available to the 40 percent of the population who were subsistence farmers, however, as dislocated peasants swarmed from Ceausescu's towns back to their villages.[25] In the cities the government increased the supply of heating fuel and electric power and relaxed rationing. The government and President Iliescu, too, still viewed state-run industry as the natural economic order, however, and saw little need for thoroughgoing market reforms or privatization. The NSF began some institutional reforms on paper, but failed to implement them. It also started mass privatization through vouchers in 1994, but did nothing to restructure industry to salvage some profitability, try to attract strategic foreign investors, or protect enterprise plant from asset stripping by ex-Securitate operatives.

In foreign policy, both the ex-Communist government and all major parties proclaimed the goals of membership in the EU and NATO. In 1992–93 Romania was deemed sufficiently democratic to be admitted to the Council of Europe and enough of a market economy to regain most favored nation status with the United States (which Ceausescu had forfeited earlier). Its swift depoliticization and downsizing of the military also won it admission to

NATO's Partnership for Peace program in early 1994, despite American anger at rampant Romanian smuggling into Milosevic's Yugoslavia in violation of UN embargoes.

As an early signal of its ambition to join NATO, Bucharest sent a field hospital to support the U.S.-led Operation Desert Storm to repel the Iraqi attackers from Kuwait in 1991. Had the political atmosphere been warmer, Romania might have qualified for full NATO membership on purely military merit, since it swiftly instituted one of the most professional and thoroughgoing army reforms in the region.[26] Washington was still hesitating about whether to expand NATO at all, however, and even when it moved toward enlarging the alliance to take in the northern Central European states, it was suspicious of Iliescu as an old Communist. It did not take the president's requests for NATO membership seriously, nor did it credit Iliescu's professed desire to clean out the worst Romanian intelligence officials, given its confusion about who was really serving whom in the Romanian security community. Even though the West's original admiration of Ceausescu had shifted to distaste by the end of his days, the United States still wondered if Iliescu might have been opposing Ceausescu to please handlers in Moscow. The uncertainty and wariness about possible disinformation were only heightened when the station chief of the U.S. Central Intelligence Agency (CIA) in Bucharest from 1989 to 1992, Harold Nicholson, was himself outed as a Soviet agent and the very high-ranking Soviet mole in the CIA, Aldrich Ames, appeared at an intelligence conference in Bucharest in May 1993 and claimed—in what sounded like the opening of a James Bond tale—that his cipher case was tampered with while he was there.[27]

The Carnegie Endowment's specialist for democracy promotion, Thomas Carothers, attributes the subsequent U.S. "decision to stop treating Romania as the black sheep of the region" to the generally free and fair local elections in February 1992.[28] Other analysts suggest that NATO's show-me attitude toward Iliescu was not dispelled until 2001, when he again became president and he and the other ex-Communists rallied to Washington's side in the post-9/11 world. In a later overall assessment, having seen the weak and quarrelsome anti-Communists succeed Iliescu from 1996 to 2000, Carothers categorized Romania as a whole as "teetering" on the edge of Latin American–style "feckless pluralism," in which elections produce "alternation of power between genuinely different political groupings," but "democracy remains shallow and troubled."[29] Romania, like Bulgaria, looked as if it might consolidate its post-Communist system into an illiberal democracy impervious to fundamental reform.[30]

Certainly the ex-Communist politicians, managers, and trade union leaders resisted macroeconomic stabilization measures and the urgently needed restructuring of the industrial, agricultural, and financial sectors. The first post-Ceausescu governments piled up large fiscal deficits in continued subsidies to white elephant state enterprises that were covered by inflation, arrears in wages and payments, and international financial aid. Some Romanian economists and would-be Westernizers looked wistfully at Poland's take-off in the late 1990s after instituting shock therapy, and then at the shattering of half-hearted reform in favor of real reform in neighboring Bulgaria after the economic meltdown there.

Alina Mungiu-Pippidi, the premier Romanian analyst of democratization, drew a damning balance in her first broad evaluation of the early Iliescu years.[31] Romania started with no preparation whatever for the kind of individual initiative and responsibility that must underlie democratic and market systems, she charged. Overnight it emerged from being a Stalinist state—in which perhaps every seventh person was a secret-police informer—to become a democracy *manqué*. The regime may have changed in December 1989, but Romanian society and political habits did not. The country inherited a major problem from "the most terrible totalitarian regime in Eastern Europe: the disappearance of social identity and individual autonomy, which produces a psychological state of helplessness and chronic dependence on bureaucracy." On top of this came "oligarchization; corruption; poverty; the survival of the state economic sector that produces for non-existent markets and lives [parasitically] off . . . state subsidies; the rise and entrenchment of some private (personal) monopolies; . . . the lack of political will to establish a middle class; . . . the minimalization of citizen interest in political issues, along with a lack of trust in politicians; [and] the appearance of mafia-like ties between smugglers, officials, and corrupt policemen, etc."

Iliescu, Mungiu-Pippidi continued, was an intelligent man. He finally grasped that the Russian ability to project power was gone, and that help for Romania could come only from the West. But he and his coterie did not understand that the only dynamic that could lead to "integration" with Europe was "real economic reform and domestic democratization." They did not have the political will to respond to European demands for these reforms. Moreover, the Romanian government remained susceptible to the temptations of populism, nationalism, and repressive measures against the Hungarian minority.

Yet, she acknowledged, a great deal was accomplished in those first few years. "Despite the attitude of the leading class, which exploits the poor education of peasants, Romania's orientation to democracy and Europe is strong."

Autonomous media developed. Romania's universities finally started to be integrated with the network of European universities. "Workers' mentality shifted from a very collectivist one in 1990 to one favoring privatization. . . . Romania is by no means an ungovernable land. . . . Despite all the barriers, society is searching out the path to normality."

The proclaimed anti-Communists who defeated the Social Democrats in the 1996 election came in with high expectations that rejecting continuity with the past and ousting ex-Communists would suffice to put Romania at long last on the road to the European future. The center-right was quarrelsome and amateurish, though, with too many clashing egos; it never got its act together, and it finally fragmented.[32] With its drive against corruption, however—the second main point of its 1996 campaign, alongside denunciation of old Communists—it at least began to dent the customary deferential rural vote for existing power-holders and introduced a novel sense of choice in elections. The issue of corruption caught the attention of villagers who were slipping below the poverty line even as the conspicuous winners of the new era were showing off their flashy Mercedes on TV. Emil Constantinescu, a respected university professor who belonged to no party, won the presidency and enjoyed a brief honeymoon. The pro-market Romanian Democratic Convention, an umbrella for eighteen organizations under the leadership of the Christian Democrat and National Peasant Party (PNTCD), took over the government.

Once in office, the Democratic Convention did lay the groundwork for economic restructuring and liberal reforms that the Social Democrats had not laid. Largely by decree, thus bypassing the fractious parliament, it succeeded in producing an initial macroeconomic stabilization, abolished most price controls, and put Romania on Hollywood's map as it welcomed *Cold Mountain* and a string of other film productions. Its economic efforts, along with an upturn in EU markets, finally yielded growth of 1.5 percent in 2000, cut inflation to about 41 percent, and quadrupled the country's hard currency reserves to $3.7 billion. This was still the worst performance among the dozen candidates or pre-candidates for EU accession; it failed to reverse the slide in living standards; and it left Romania behind its little neighbor of Bulgaria in gaining visa-free entry to EU countries. But it was a start. And in the important area of strengthening local self-government, it passed legislation that for the first time in Romanian history prescribed a "system of resource-sharing based on automatic formulas, thus making the local budgetary process more autonomous, transparent and predictable."[33]

Before losing its nerve, the center-right government also tried to deal with the horrors of Ceausescu's secret police by letting victims see their own Securitate dossiers and perhaps thereby make some kind of peace with the cruelties of the past.[34] It further took the first steps on the long road to European integration by signing up to a four-year EU Membership Action Plan in spring 2000 and setting up the European Institute of Romania to train a core of young civil servants who would be able to deal with the bewildering European Union. With its unpopular decision to grant NATO overflight rights (and deny them to Russia) during the Kosovo war, the government also paved the way for Romanian membership in NATO.[35] If this did not suffice to win success for French lobbying to admit Romania into the 1999 tranche of NATO enlargement, the failure perhaps had more to do with Washington's quarrel with Paris over NATO's southern command than with the merits or flaws of Bucharest's qualifications.

The Democratic Convention government also stabilized ethnic relations as the Hungarian UDMR joined the cabinet for the first time—notably, with little backlash from ordinary Romanians. From then on, the Hungarian minority of 1.6 million pursued a strategy that diverged sharply from the approach of the far less numerous Saxons. When the next change of government came, in 2000, the UDMR shifted over to give parliamenty support to a minority coalition led by the Social Democrats, and when a more coherent center-right again unseated the Social Democrats in 2004, the UDMR shifted back to join the new constellation. This pattern is similar to that of the Turkish minority in Bulgaria, both in the tactics of permanent government participation and in the specific insistence by both "organizations" that their groupings are not "parties." The Democratic Convention–UDMR coalition also agreed to let Hungary open a consulate in Cluj, put up bilingual signs in areas with a large Hungarian population, and amend laws to ensure that children would be educated in their native tongue and that Hungarian as well as Romanian would be used in official dealings in courts and in the administration of local services.

In a land with Romania's mix of ethnicities and religions, such willingness to compromise did not solve all communal confrontations, of course. The resurgent Romanian Orthodox Church, released from Communist strictures, and the Greek Catholic (Uniate) Church, legal once more after spending a half century underground, quarreled over repossession of originally Uniate churches. In the most spectacular case, the Greek Catholic Church was granted an injunction to recover its Cathedral of the Transfiguration in Cluj. The court official refused to enforce the verdict, however, and in 1998 "[y]oung seminarians of both sides fought pitched battles inside the church, in the altar and, finally, on top of the holy table."[36]

Where the Democratic Convention failed most conspicuously was in the one area it had seen as its strongpoint: cleaning out corruption. It started out well, appointing human rights activist Valerian Stan to head the Department of Control and Anticorruption, which monitored public officials and members of the Chamber of Deputies. Within a few months, however, after Stan had been too zealous in naming not only ex-Communists but also government supporters who were paying only nominal rent for state-owned villas, the prime minister fired his top watchdog.[37] A series of bank and pyramid crashes, some involving criminal charges, was topped by the arrest of a colonel in President Constantinescu's security unit for allegedly smuggling 30 million cigarettes into the Bucharest airport. And in 1999 the collapse of Bancorex, the largest bank, and the Banca Agricola swallowed up $2.3 billion from the state budget in bailouts.[38] Moreover, ministers who gave their sons automobiles valued at ten times their own annual salaries—and channeled state assets into private wealth—offended impoverished voters.

Constantinescu himself was not suspected of wrongdoing. But as the 2000 election approached, the demoralized president had such low ratings that he announced that he would not run again for office. The governing coalition self-destructed in a cloud of recrimination. Widespread disillusionment with democracy and politicians led to opinion surveys showing that 53 percent of the population thought that life had been best under Ceausescu, while only 6.5 percent thought it had been best since 1989. Other surveys showed that more than 74 percent had no trust in parliament and 70 percent held that it was impossible to get rich in Romania by honest means.[39] The way was clear for a large protest vote for Corneliu Vadim Tudor, an antimarket, anti-Hungarian, anti-Roma, antisemitic, and anti-United States (a "colony of Israel") ultranationalist.

"Vadim," as he was universally known, had been a court poet to Ceausescu, and he now gathered various unsavory old Securitate agents in his Greater Romania Party.[40] To the shock of city voters, who regarded him as something of a clown, he received the second-highest vote of 28 percent in the presidential nominations, and in the runoff they were confronted with a choice between him and, inevitably, Ion Iliescu. Iliescu's main appeal seemed to be his attacks on the corruption of a political class that voters did not trust and did not like. To many it looked as if democratic choice was a farce, with each new team of ministers stealing whatever had not been filched by the last gang.[41] The Greater Romania Party, which had skyrocketed from 4.5 percent in 1996 to 20 percent in 2000, took a third of the seats in the Chamber of Deputies to become the second-largest bloc next to the Social Democrats, with their plurality of 36.6 percent. Yet in the most important race, Vadim did not defeat Iliescu in the presidential runoff.

The Negative Consensus

When Ion Iliescu moved back into the presidential palace, he was seventy-one years old. He still had some close advisers, who at their worst opposed the Social Democrats' recent shift to endorse the concept of private property. At their best, noted one European diplomat, they intended to write their own indulgent terms for EU entry, because they thought that "the world needs Romania, and not that Romania needs the international community."[42] Some foreign observers thought that Iliescu had changed his political approach a good deal during his novel experience of four years in opposition.[43] Certainly in that period he had had the opportunity to see the swift growth of Poland as its "shock therapy" took hold (and the obverse misery in next-door Ukraine, where reforms were repeatedly postponed). He had heard the lament among would-be domestic reformers that Romania, unfortunately, had never had a real Bulgarian-type meltdown to jolt it into emergency action.[44] And he had witnessed the debacle of Milosevic's illiberal attempt to substitute an ugly national ideology for Western political and economic norms. "Iliescu knows that the future lies with the EU," concluded one Western diplomat at the time.[45] The public knew it too; for all of the disillusionment about life after communism, popular support for EU membership stayed consistently in the 70th and 80th percentiles—a higher level than in any of the other applicant countries—even though there were already signs that Romania and Bulgaria would be dropped from the first tranche of EU accession in the twenty-first century.

Iliescu's choice for prime minister in the coalition led by the Romanian Social Democratic Party (PDSR) was Adrian Nastase. Nastase, who also issued from the Communist *nomenklatura*, announced a program that differed sharply from the NSF/Social Democratic drift of the first six Iliescu years, one that was promarket and pro-EU in wanting to accelerate privatization and make it more transparent, attract foreign investment, and cut taxes to lure the 40 percent of the economy that was in the shadows into legitimacy. He also pledged, of course, to stop corruption.

Nastase's reform program was no empty promise, declared Dorel Sandor, contradicting the many skeptics as the Social Democrats again took the helm. Sandor, whose true believer Communist father had once coerced peasants into joining collective farms, had joined the reform ministry of the first post-Ceausescu government to help disband those same collectives and now headed the Center for Political Studies and Comparative Analysis. Nastase's program reflected a real commitment to the reforms needed to qualify for EU membership, Sandor asserted. When the Democratic Convention government signed on to the four-year EU Membership Action Plan in early 2000, "the main parties in parliament, including the PDSR, agreed to support a strategy of integration," he noted. "If you are going to go to Brussels, you have go by Vienna, not by Beijing or Bombay. . . . In this condition there is no choice."[46]

In a way, a negative operational consensus that there was no alternative to the EU had finally coalesced. Partly consciously, partly without grasping what it was getting into, the Romanian political class was now embarked on the task of transforming centuries-old peasant mentalities of stagnation and fate. In the tumultuous new world, observed another Romanian commentator who declined to be identified, Vadim represented that poor but familiar and stable past. People missed "the safety of the communist world, where if you kept your mouth shut you had a reasonable life. Now people understand democracy as chaos, unemployment, pensions that do not cover the cost of living. The vote for [Vadim] Tudor has been a vote of scared people" who for ten years "have lost from reform." Bogdan Chirieac, foreign editor of the newspaper *Adevarul*, described just how hard it would be to overcome the inertia: "If you put $1 million into Hungary, you expect to get something back; you have a normal reaction. If you punch [something with your fist], you feel the pain. In Romania, though, you can punch the economic body and nothing happens. It's in a profound coma."[47]

When he took office, Prime Minister Nastase had behind him a disciplined party and coalition of the sort that his revolving-door predecessors from the center-right could only envy. The Social Democrats did not have to resort to executive fiat and passed more legislation through the Chamber of Deputies in the first three quarters of 2001 than their predecessor government had passed in the previous three years. They restored parliamentary oversight of the military after four years of politicization and deprofessionalization of the senior officer corps.[48] In 2002, after the United States put Romania on its watch list for copyright piracy, the government managed to get the rate of video piracy down from an estimated 100 percent to 60 percent. It approved the opening of a new private Hungarian–language university in Transylvania, funded by the Hungarian state. It also led the passage in parliament of a new constitution in 2003 to replace the first post-Ceausescu constitution of 1991.[49] This revised basic document was more in line with EU requirements in defining the nation in civic rather than ethnic terms, protecting property rights, letting foreign businesses own land, guaranteeing legal redress for violations of minority rights, and limiting the legal immunity of members of parliament (MPs) to political opinions only (not shady commercial dealings). It endorsed the use of minority languages in public administration and the courts and bolstered judicial power. In the same year, parliament amended the penal code, decriminalized "insult," and ended prison sentences for "slander." In the next year, it adopted a set of laws on court organization, magistrates, and the Supreme Council of Magistrates, made running up tax arrears a criminal offense, and passed the country's first code of conduct for civil servants (though this did not cover conflict of interest on the part of elected or appointed officials).[50]

Not all of the constitutional and legal provisions advanced the cause of converting a politicized judiciary with low-paid jurists trained to serve a one-party state into dispensers of impartial justice. Certainly none of them addressed the urgent need to educate lawyers, and especially judges, in the complex commercial law that must underlie a modern market economy. Decreeing independence of the courts from executive interference and granting tenure to sitting judges was admirable in theory, but in practice doing so without vetting judges' legal competence or past willingness to bend the law in favor of the politically or financially powerful perpetuated incompetence and privilege (especially when the Social Democratic government appointed judges in a solo action just before conferring lifetime tenure on them), and it made independence the enemy of accountability.[51] Seven of the nine judges named to the High Court of Cassation (the equivalent of the U.S. Supreme Court) were either former Social Democratic parliamentary deputies or had other close ties to the party. And in mid-2004 someone who had never sat on the bench but had for years been a senior political adviser was made president of the High Court. Other impediments to justice included procedural rules that seemed designed to drag out restitution settlements over years and clog the National Anticorruption Court with such a heavy workload of minor cases that it was unable to try major cases of high-level corruption.[52]

In other domestic initiatives, the Nastase government improved conditions in orphanages, demilitarized the police and the prison system, and launched a drive to promote the education of Roma that was hailed by some West European activists as a model for their own more passive countries.[53] Belatedly, four years after lead and cyanide spills from two mines killed fish and poisoned hundreds of kilometers of the Tisza and Danube Rivers (and this while Romania was negotiating its environment chapter with the EU), the Chamber of Deputies also passed legislation, which took effect in mid-2004, imposing high fines and prison sentences of up to twenty years for polluters of air and water.

In the crucial area of the economy, Prime Minister Nastase turned his announced program into policy in accepting in 2001 the International Monetary Fund's conditions for a standby credit, which required faster privatization, reduction of subsidies to state enterprises, and trimming of budget deficits toward a 3 percent target in the name of macroeconomic stabilization and industrial restructuring. The government sold off Sidex, the largest steel mill, in 2001. More controversially, it also privatized the national oil firm, Petrom, in 2004, overriding the opposition of the Social Democrats' old clientele to sell the crown jewels to Austria's OMV Group; it sold off, as well, four electricity and gas distributors and raised electricity and heating fees to bring them closer to costs. In the wake of the earlier financial scandals, Romania bolstered bank supervision, and Austrian, Dutch, Greek, Hungarian, and other foreign banks began buying Romanian banks and bringing more stringent and transparent standards to the evaluation and tracking of loans. This stabilized the sector, even if financial intermediation remained low as a percentage of GDP—above that of Ukraine, but far below Hungary, Slovenia, Croatia, and Bulgaria.[54] Timken, the American ball-bearing leader that had bought a plant in Ploiesti in 1979 to manufacture its heavy ball bearings, praised Romania's treatment of investors—and reported that it never had to pay any bribes.[55]

By fall 2004 the European Commission finally certified that Romania had a "functioning market economy" and could proceed further along the path to EU membership. For all the progress, this certification was, the *Times* of London commented drily, "an act of wilful generosity."[56] The old Communist networks were digging in to preserve the old industrial dinosaurs through huge state subsidies—and they kept winning wage hikes that ran well ahead of productivity increases and kept the country uncompetitive against more agile rivals in Central Europe. State enterprises evaded taxes, with arrears reaching as high as 50 percent. For a potential market of 22 million people, Western investment stayed low—and the bulk of it went disproportionately to the northwest, given Transylvania's better infrastructure, somewhat greater transparency, and proximity to a booming Hungary. Some 40 percent of citizens remained below the World Bank's poverty line, autarchic peasant families still lived at subsistence level in rural "deep Romania," and the country was often described as part of the third world.

In foreign policy, the breakthrough in convincing the West of Romania's relevance came with the suicide attacks in New York and Washington on September 11, 2001. Bucharest seized the opportunity to be useful to Washington in the war on terror, immediately declared itself a "de facto NATO ally," and within weeks signed a status-of-forces agreement with the United States, making its bases available for the refueling of U.S. planes heading for Afghanistan, and later Iraq. It gladly contributed 400 troops to Operation Enduring Freedom in Afghanistan, and later 800 troops to the war in Iraq, with the help of enabling American financing. It further sided with Washington against the EU in 2002 in being the first country to sign a bilateral agreement ruling out the extradition of American personnel to the new UN International Criminal Court. By the banner EU year of 2004, Bucharest's efforts paid off in the West's military alliance as well. In March, in the company of Slovenia and the Baltic states, Romania graduated from NATO's Partnership for Peace to gain full membership in the alliance, after setting up a National Registry Office for the Protection of State Secrets to keep NATO secrets out of the hands of old Securitate agents.[57]

EU evaluators, while praising the large strides Romania had made in the previous half decade, still doubted whether Romania and Bulgaria would be ready to take on the responsibility of full membership by the target entry date of January 2007 and wrote into the Accession Treaties in April 2005 an escape clause allowing a one-year delay if remaining deficiencies were not corrected in time. In both cases concern focused primarily on systemic corruption, organized crime, the flawed judicial system, a weak bureaucracy that might collapse under the task of managing the increased EU financial aid and other programs that membership would bring, and haphazard implementation, at best, of the fine words in the flood of legislation harmonizing domestic statutes with the EU *acquis communautaire*.

Corruption, EU assessments noted discreetly, remained rampant. Some Romanian promoters even argued to potential investors that its pervasiveness was a competitive advantage, making business deals easier.[58] Romania placed a low eighty-seventh on Transparency International's ranking of perceived corruption, worse than Mongolia, Mali, Ghana, Bulgaria, Croatia, and Bosnia-Herzegovina, though better than Macedonia, Serbia and Montenegro, Albania, Moldova, and Ukraine.[59] The EU's Antifraud Office (OLAF) found more irregularities in Romanian programs than in any other of its country audits; this was a grave issue in a country that was receiving the second-highest EU assistance (after Poland) in all of "new Europe." A follow-up investigation into Romanian media reports revealed that more than a third of 150 active EU contracts in Romania broke conflict-of-interest legislation; the contracts had been awarded to close relatives of officials on the boards of these projects.[60] One survey, conducted in early 2004, found that 63 percent of Romanians did not believe that justice could be obtained through the courts. And a Transparency

International Global Corruption Barometer showed that Romanians judged political parties to be even more corrupt than the courts.[61]

In part, this perception arose from the high percentage of elected representatives who seemed to spend more time running their private businesses than fulfilling their civic duties. In part, the perception arose from the chronic cooption of parliamentary deputies and local mayors by the Social Democrats by less than transparent means; voters who elected, say, a Liberal member of parliament or a Democratic mayor could never be sure that their candidate would not end up in the Social Democratic camp anyway. In the run-up to the 2004 election the Romanian Coalition for a Clean Parliament, a nongovernmental organization (NGO), "documented 143 cases of candidates to Parliament from the ranks of the [Social Democratic] government party and its junior partner PUR [Humanist Party] who . . . made use of their public position for private gains for themselves or their party clientele; . . . amassed fortunes clearly out of line with their asset declarations; . . . [or] were connected with Ceausescu's Securitate."[62] The coalition sent each party "blacklists" of candidates who had "repeatedly shifted from one party to another in search of personal profit," had been "accused of corruption on the basis of published and verifiable evidence," had been "exposed as . . . agent[s] of the Securitate," owned private firms with "important tax arrears," could not "account for the discrepancy" between real and officially listed assets, or had turned "a profit from conflicts of interest involving . . . [their] public position." Mungiu-Pippidi, who spearheaded the effort, reported that ninety-eight candidates on the original blacklist lost their seats, either because they lost the vote or because their parties withdrew support, while 104 on the list won reelection. She also reported that the struggling Coalition for a Clean Parliament was "saddled with defending itself against four lawsuits for defamation, filed by two former heads of the secret service, a former minister of justice, and a former minister of defense."[63] After the election, eleven NGOs joined seven journalists at the Romanian public television station RTV in winning from the station's Ethics and Arbitration Commission an admission of censorship during the campaign in favor of the Social Democrats and their allied Humanists.[64]

For Mungiu-Pippidi's watchdog Romanian Academic Society (SAR), the most serious threat of corruption posed by the continuity of old cadres in positions of power in the new era was not so much one of appropriation of public assets for private gain. Instead, in Romania's "status society" (rather than an individualized or cash society), it was the threat of what Barrington Moore termed "'predatory elites,' who, in the process of generating prosperity for themselves, produce social poverty of a scale otherwise unwarranted in that society." In such a system, "politics remain confined to networks of clients and do not open to the entire society. Predators control their economies, not only taking the lion's share of resources but also, in the process of enriching themselves, generating massive poverty for the rest of society. There are appearances of democracy and market, but they are deceptive, remaining, for the most part, forms without content." Politics was cleaner in Bucharest and places like Sibiu, the SAR noted, but in the poorest rural areas, "practically all political parties are in the politico-economic network." As the general and presidential elections approached at the end of 2004, the SAR asked caustically if voters would help "free the Romanian state from capture," or whether Europe would "embrace its first fully-fledged predatory elite when Romania joins [the EU] in 2007."[65]

Provisional Denouement

By late 2004 voters who were warming to the notion of rotation in office responded to the familiar opposition charge of incumbents' corruption and unexpectedly ousted the Social Democrats both from the presidency and the government. Or at least they rejected Adrian Nastase as the successor to President Ion Iliescu. And once the presidential power tipped over to erstwhile Bucharest mayor Traian Basescu, the anticipated Social Democratic–led coalition melted away in the usual murky postelection shifts of allegiance among parliamentary parties and individual MPs. The Social Democrat–Humanist alliance could not parlay its 36.6 percent plurality into a majority in the Chamber of Deputies; instead, the center-right managed to leverage its 31.3 percent (double its vote in 2000) into the majority.

In this game the Liberals and Democrats, who had sublimated their previous quarrels to campaign together as the Justice and Truth Alliance, received some unintended assistance from the otherwise crafty Iliescu. In his last days as president he alienated many urban voters (and Westerners) by awarding the Star of Romania to Corneliu Vadim Tudor and pardoning the jailed Miron Cozma, the leader of the Jiu Valley miners who had been Iliescu's extralegal enforcers in the early 1990s. In reaction to the first blunder, Holocaust scribe Elie Wiesel returned his own medal, which he had received two years earlier from his native Romania. So did other Romanian emigrés. And outrage in Romanian cities at the amnesty for Cozma made the president retract the pardon within twenty-four hours. The Hungarian UDMR (with 6.2 percent of the vote) and even the Humanist Party then had a ready excuse to desert the Social Democrats and join the Justice and Truth coalition. The abandonment by the UDMR of its passive support for the Social Democrats raised fewer eyebrows than did the Humanists' severing of ties after the two parties had campaigned together, hand in glove, in two elections. The defection of the Humanists—who tended to be nouveaux riches businessmen who were keen to protect themselves against lawsuits—was seen as the sign of a new era. As a token of change, the Humanist Party adopted a new name, calling itself the Conservative Party.

Basescu, a scrappy former sea captain who made no more pretense of presidential neutrality toward his own Democratic Party than Iliescu had done toward the Social Democrats, branded inclusion of the Humanists/Conservatives in the governing coalition "immoral," but in the end did not call new elections over the move. The Greater Romania Party (with 12.9 percent, down from 19.5 percent in 2000) was not a player. Vadim, seeing diminishing returns from ultranationalism and antisemitism, had stopped being the *enfant terrible* and turned ostentatiously philosemitic. He had paid his respects at the Holocaust Museum, hired an Israeli adviser who himself later became a parliamentary deputy, and—inexplicably—erected a statue of Israeli Nobel prize-winner Shimon Peres in central Romania. After the political readjustments following the 2004 election, he again exerted control over his highly personalized party, expelling five parliamentary deputies who broke ranks and voted for the cabinet of the Justice and Truth Alliance.[66]

The new government took office with a flurry of activity. Prime minister and National Liberal Party chairman Calin Popescu-Tariceanu appointed a young, largely Western-educated cabinet.[67] His justice minister, Monica Macovei, was a former human rights activist, president of the Romanian Helsinki Committee, a lawyer for Romanians at the European Court of Human Rights in Strasbourg, and a student of comparative constitutional law with a master's degree from the Central European University in Budapest.

Popescu-Tariceanu announced that his government would bring "liberation from fiscal burdens" for companies and individuals; "liberation from state-dominance," by completing the process of privatization and "withdrawing the state from the economy"; "liberation from the political class," by abolishing political clientelism; "liberation from corruption"; and "liberation from bureaucracy." He further pledged to respect "the principles of a state based on the rule of law," with a free and professional judiciary, a free and independent media, a strong legislature, a strong civil society, and "a professional and moral corps of civil service." In addition, the government declared its intent to repeal legislation granting immunity from prosecution to former cabinet ministers who had not had their immunity exceptionally lifted by parliament. Adrian

Nastase, as the new speaker of the Chamber of Deputies, objected that this shift would open the door to "harassment" of former ministers with lawsuits.[68]

The government swiftly introduced 16 percent flat income and corporate taxes (which cost the government no more than a 1.5 percent drop in revenues in the first year) and annulled the write-off of debts to the state granted by the outgoing government to the Rafo Onesti refinery and Carom tire maker.[69] It amended the labor code to reduce the burden on would-be purchasers of existing enterprises—though the European Commission's 2005 economic report on candidate countries still deemed Romania's labor provisions too inflexible, especially in mandating countrywide wage settlements that made no allowance for widely divergent productivity in different parts of the country.[70] It resumed construction of a nuclear power station after a fifteen-year hiatus. It required a declaration of assets and interests by all senior government and judicial officials and civil servants (though there were no follow-up investigations of suspicious statements or cross-checking with tax returns). It, of course, stopped its predecessor's harassment of media critical of the Social Democrats, but in a move that elicited an objection from the Organization for Security and Cooperation in Europe it brought criminal charges against two journalists who had obtained (but did not publish) classified documents.[71] It took measures to strengthen local autonomy and decentralization. It amended laws for restitution that had become entangled in drawn-out legal challenges, speeding up restoration of property expropriated by the Communists to the original owners (including King Michael and also Dominic von Habsburg, who got back Dracula's 900-year-old castle), or else offering them financial compensation.[72] It passed new EU-vetted legislation to protect minorities. It introduced a code of ethics for police behavior and random assignment of cases to judges, and passed conflict-of-interest laws. It made Romania's Antifraud Department independent of the prime minister's office. It prolonged the life of the National Council for the Study of Securitate Files (CNSAS) for six years beyond its original deadline of December 2005 for vetting judicial and other officials, and by ordinance (rather than legislation) it made Securitate archives more available to citizens who wished to read their own dossiers.[73] It demilitarized both the foreign and domestic intelligence services.[74]

Prosecutors, under an emergency decree, opened or reopened major corruption cases against senior politicians, including former prime minister Nastase, and, from the governing coalition, Conservative Party multimillionaire and deputy prime minister George Copos and leading figures from Prime Minister Popescu-Tariceanu's Liberal Party and the Hungarian UDMR. Ironically, the most damning files had actually been drawn up (and then suppressed) under the ruling Social Democrats a few years earlier, when strong EU pressure on Bucharest to confront high-level corruption gave President Iliescu the leverage to appoint his own people to run intelligence investigations, over Prime Minister Nastase's objections.[75] Today the external pressure to get on with prosecutions is coming primarily from the United States and Britain, and secondarily from Brussels. For the EU, European Commissioner for Enlargement Olli Rehn, without commenting on the substance of the charges, noted approvingly, "In Romania there has been a sea change in the last 14 months thanks to the rigorous conditionality that the EU has applied and stubborn efforts . . . to pursue judicial reform and fight against corruption."[76] A backhanded tribute to Justice Minister Macovei's effectiveness also came from unknown persons who turned on all the gas taps in her apartment in her absence; fortunately, she smelled the gas and did not turn on any switches when she came home late that night.[77]

In an ongoing wrestling match with the Social Democratic bloc in both the lower and the upper houses of parliament (and with various MPs from parties within the ruling coalition as well), Macovei and prosecutors, despite strong backing from President Basescu, lost on shifting responsibility for the nomination of chief prosecutors from the Supreme Council of Magistrates to the justice minister and on preventing the Chamber of Deputies from barring the search of Nastase's apartment, as requested by prosecutors. They did win, with some weakening of the legislation, on extending the emergency powers accorded to the country's special Anticorruption Prosecutor's Office to investigate senior politicians and judges.[78] After some delay, they also won Nastase's resignation as speaker of the lower chamber; he was eased out by the new Social Democratic officials to limit damage to the party from the investigation.[79] Under pressure from the EU, the government reviewed two controversial contracts that had been signed without tender: one, a $2.5 billion deal with the U.S. firm Bechtel to construct Europe's biggest roadworks from Bucharest northwest to Western Europe; the other, a more modest €650 million deal with the Bavaria-based EADS for border surveillance and management along what will soon become the EU's southeastern boundary. The latter was renegotiated down to a cost of €524 million in late 2005; the former was negotiated down to a cost of $2.4 billion in early 2006.[80]

The rewards for these moves came in the EU's earmarking of up to €17 billion of aid (depending on Romania's absorptive capability) for regional development, social, and "cohesion" projects for the period 2007–13 under the PHARE, ISPA, and SAPARD programs.[81] This total would amount to more than 25 percent of overall investments in the Romanian national budget, and the infusion was expected to help draw more foreign direct investment.[82] FDI reached 7.4 percent of GDP in 2004, one of the highest proportions in the Balkans, and Bucharest is now trying to steer foreign investors beyond privatization to the opportunities arising from the country's basic competitive advantages. These include the sixth highest density of certified information technology specialists in the world (64,000), proportionally higher than in either the United States or Russia, and primary resources that make it the closest to energy self-sufficiency of any European country other than Russia. The hope was that enough investments would come in not only to accelerate economic development, but also to open up jobs for the educated and encourage the 4.9 percent of the population that emigrated in the decade between 1992 and 2002 to return to Romania.[83] The worry was that the increasingly public feud between President Basescu and Prime Minister Popescu-Tariceanu would revive the right's destructive habit of infighting and again incapacitate a center-right government.

In foreign affairs, the government formally signed the EU Accession Treaty in April 2005 and became an active observer in EU institutions, to the accompaniment of an 86 percent popular approval of the goal of EU membership. President Basescu took the occasion to laud Bucharest's close relations with Washington and London, and to rebuke Romania's one-time patron France for telling "new Europe" to "shut up" (President Jacques Chirac in 2003) and for complaining that Basescu did not have "a European reflex" (Foreign Minister Michel Barnier in 2005).[84] The government proudly continued its predecessor's close relations with the United States and in late 2005 became the first former Warsaw Pact country to host a long-term American military base, at the Mihail Kogalniceanu air base near the Black Sea. At the public inauguration of this "lilypad" jumping-off point for U.S. operations in the Mideast and Central Asia, Secretary of State Condoleezza Rice hailed Romania as one of Washington's "best allies." Romania reciprocally assured the United States that it would not withdraw its 860 troops from Iraq, and Foreign Minister Mihai-Razvan Ungureanu denied allegations that Romania had been letting the U.S. Central Intelligence Agency run secret prisons on its territory.[85] Within weeks, Romanians began hoping that America might also select their country as a site for missile defense installations.[86]

In relations with Soviet successor states to the east, Romania and Ukraine submitted their running border dispute over Snake Island and their Black Sea maritime boundaries to the International Court of Justice for adjudication. Romania also objected to Ukraine's reopening of a navigation canal from the

Danube border through Ukraine to the Black Sea, because of its impact on the ecology of the rich Danube delta. Bucharest was doing its best, however, to help extend Georgia's and Ukraine's Rose and Orange democratic revolutions, respectively, to ethnic Romanians in Moldova and dislodge Russian troops from Moldova's breakaway Transdnistria (or at least, secure Moldova's gas supplies from Russia).[87]

In relations with Hungary, at their first meeting Romanian prime minister Popescu-Tariceanu agreed with Hungarian prime minister Ferenc Gyurcsany that the two cabinets would come together annually to discuss political and environmental issues, and the Hungarians promised that ethnic Romanians as well as ethnic Hungarians from Romania would be eligible for long-term visas to enter Hungary. Gheorghe Funar, a one-time Hungarian-baiting mayor of Cluj, remained active in public life as a senator from that city, but ethnic tensions there had eased. Romanian fears that Hungary's "status law" establishing close relations between Budapest and Hungarians outside the country's borders might be the thin end of the wedge of an irredentist attempt to overturn the 1919 Treaty of Trianon and regain Transylvania had also eased, as Budapest modified the law, and the Rumanian election of 2004 had been the first in which there was no significant anti-Hungarian nationalist appeal.[88] In this taming of extremists on both sides, the European Union played no small part, making it clear that neither of the two countries could be admitted into membership as long as major bilateral disputes remained unresolved.

In retrospect, the Hungarian deputy ambassador in Bucharest, Sandor Mozes, saw bilateral reconciliation as following the pattern of French-German reconciliation after World War II. He elaborated: "Romania is the most important neighboring country now for us. It is in our national interest to help Romania become a member of the EU as soon as possible. . . . We can eliminate all the hatred and stereotypes inherited from the past. . . . In both countries you can still find people who try to do their utmost against this development—but they are losing their power."[89] Hungarian investment in Romania is now accelerating, he noted, especially in small and medium-sized business, and (Hungarian) MOL gas stations are common around the country.

Transmission

After the EU's Comprehensive Monitoring Report on Romania in October 2005 highlighted the familiar urgent needs, Minister for European Integration Anca Boagiu appeared in Strasbourg to tell a European Parliament committee why Romania should become a member of the EU in January 2007, despite all its remaining shortcomings. The exchange centered on corruption and border security, but it also addressed the environment, poverty, return of confiscated properties, and implementation of laws.[90] In its own report card, the European Parliament Committee on Foreign Affairs welcomed "the significant advances, particularly in the fields of freedom of expression, justice, the integration of minorities, the protection of children, [and] the restoration of property and competition policy," but called for "immediate action" to rectify flaws in reform of the judiciary and public administration, to prosecute high-level as well as low-level corruption, to combat trafficking of drugs and people, and to integrate the Roma.[91] In an interview with the Romanian press agency, Minister Boagiu acknowledged "the need to solve the problem of top-level political corruption, to speed up preparations for the management of the future European border, [and] to strengthen the capacity to absorb European funds."[92] Privately, even some European diplomats who had initially supported timely Romanian and Bulgarian accession were asking if they had made a mistake in locking themselves into automatic entry by 2008 at the latest, thereby losing the leverage of the preaccession period for change.[93]

In Romania the linkage of EU conditionality may not work quite the way planners in Brussels anticipated.[94] But it is working as a kind of yeast. Even though corruption is rife, even though there is little civil society to speak truth to power, even though political will is weak in the face of entrenched networks and dependent on a few crusaders, even though there is no visible spread of the more transparent government practices in Bucharest and Sibiu/Hermannstadt to the countryside, the body politic did manage to reject the xenophobic ultranationalism of Vadim, bring about reconciliation with Hungary, nudge the economy in a modern direction, and make a formal commitment to clean up graft. When asked what might be a realistic anticorruption target for Romania—the level of Italy, France, or Scandinavia, for example—one European diplomat promptly selected the Italian model for the short term. There is abundant corruption there, he said, but the system works despite the graft, in a way the still dysfunctional Romanian system does not. And part of the reason there is so much enthusiasm for Europe in both Italy and Romania, he added, is precisely citizens' mistrust of their own governments and a converse hope that Brussels will be a court of last resort to correct all the national inequities. Already, he noted, European embassies in Romania—for whatever reason, ambassadors seem to be regarded as more important in Bucharest than in any other European capital—are bombarded with letters from Romanians laying out heart-rending personal grievances in the hope that the European Union will redress what the Romanian bureaucracy has failed to. The perfect example of this faith was the demonstration in Bucharest in spring 2006 by hundreds of

peasants flourishing wooden hoes (symbols of poverty and of miserly government farm subsidies) with EU flags (symbols of the generous agricultural aid
from savior Brussels) tacked onto them.[95]

The diplomat believed that the greatest impact of Europeanization in
Romania comes not from the formal EU checklist of conditions, but rather
from "the increasing contact of the entire administration with their peers" in
other European countries. If the elites don't clean up their act, this will bring
the kind of pressure in which their counterparts say, "We can't work with you;
we don't trust you." The opinion of such international peers is crucial, since
Romania "is not like Russia or China. It's not an economy you have to invest
in if you want to go anywhere. Romania has to sell itself," and it won't succeed
"so long as foreign investors perceive it as an impossible place to work."

Domestically, the diplomat did not expect the political class to be an effective transmission belt for democratization and development. "The problem is
that in the political class, all are from the Communist Party. Romanians didn't
reject the party as in other countries or get fed up with the ex-Communists,
as in Bulgaria." No clear differentiation has developed between left and right
parties, nor is there any real alternative in elections beyond claiming that one's
own party would be better than its rivals at fighting corruption and winning
EU membership. The diplomat did think change would eventually come,
however, from awakening voters who dislike the constant petty bribes they
must pay to get a job or a bed in a hospital. "Corruption loses votes," he said
flatly and pointed to the substantial losses of the Social Democrats when they
were in power and were perceived to be corrupt.

Moreover, he continued, Romanians are open to Western influence because
they are outward looking. "They seek confirmation from external benchmarks. This is almost a national trait. They always looked to Western Europe,
and of course they have been waiting for the Americans—'the lord from outside'—since 1945. It's tied up with their sense of identity as being a Western
country." The drive for EU membership has therefore accelerated political and
social debates that would have come sometime anyway—and "this is perhaps
its greatest impact, because this external benchmark of the EU has provided a
whole set of benchmarks." The Romanians "want somebody to tell them what
to do."[96]

Nicolae Idu, head of the European Institute of Romania, agreed in essence
but focused on education as the key to transforming Romania. "If you try to
fight against [the culture of] corruption with only administrative and legal
measures, that's not enough if you don't touch the system profoundly. . . . You
have to start with the education system. It's a kind of behavior of the people

in this country that everywhere you go, you have to pay *baksheesh*. It's not always that the people who are doing a service for you request it, but you feel that if you pay more, you get better service, because everyone is badly treated, in health services, in education." Living standards must be improved, he acknowledged, but the thing that is needed above all is "to clean up a decadent society from the moral point of view. I think joining the EU gives us a chance to change the system, reduce the corruption, all the negative aspects of our society." In practical terms, he added, "joining the EU will bring a very strong monitoring system of financial deals and transparency about what happens with the budget . . . and all the companiess will have to pay taxes. . . . Don't forget that an important part of our budget will be used to cofinance projects with EU funds. . . . Even our national money will be more honestly used, because we will have rules in place, institutions. Civil servants will look to their future careers and not to [illicit] short-term gain. . . . When the EU is pushing you, you don't have a choice. You have to do what it requires."[97]

Political scientist (and former social psychologist) Alina Mungiu-Pippidi put it even more succinctly. Romania's peasants, she said, must become citizens.[98]

CHAPTER FOUR

Taming Kosovo

Kosovo, more than any other single spot in the Balkans, will challenge the ability of the postnational European Union to make others want the kind of democracy and peace it wants. Kosovo remains a bastion of nineteenth-century blood-and-soil loyalties, for both Albanians and Serbs. Historically, Kosovar Albanians have been unacquainted with any form of popular political participation; except for a few years under Tito, they never had the experience even of autocratic or semiautocratic self-government that Serbs and Croats and Bosniaks did—and among themselves, traditional authority has rested with clan patriarchs. Nor did they routinely intermarry with Serbs on the pattern of the Serbs, Muslims, and Croats in Bosnia. In addition, ruthless mafias are by now entrenched; close-knit ethnic Albanian gangs are, in fact, so successful throughout Europe that they have muscled the Russians out of Hamburg's St. Pauli and were the only nationality to warrant a special section in Europol's 2003 annual report and equal billing with Russian and Chinese gangs in its 2004 report.[1] Moreover, the listless economy offers few jobs for the average of 50 percent unemployed, or the 70 percent unemployed among the more than half of the population who are under the age of twenty-four—and few incentives for low-level traffickers to enter the legitimate market.[2] To the contrary, both the spending of the international community in the country and remittances from family members abroad are now dropping sharply, competing property claims deter even local investment, privatization has been a disaster, and exports cover only 4 percent of imports.

Furthermore, there is scant hope that a new generation will be more tolerant than its elders. Young Albanians and Serbs are, if anything, more closed to each other than older ones. Fewer of the young—including Serbs in Serbia—are studying or working abroad today and learning about other societies by osmosis. Far fewer than in their parents' generation speak the others' language—and those Albanians who do speak Serbian are careful not to do so on the open street. The 11,000 killed in the civil and then international war in Kosovo cast a long shadow.

All this makes the task of creating a self-sustaining peace and healing a war-torn society that much harder in what, institutionally, is one of today's purest tests of the capacity of outsiders to transform a static, paternalistic, agrarian society into a functioning new state. In Kabul, despite the presence of foreign troops in Afghanistan, Hamid Karzai is president and is the primary actor in balancing Afghan tribes and warlords. In Baghdad, Shia, Sunnis, and Kurds are also being compelled, ultimately, to strike their own political balance. In Bosnia-Herzegovina, High Representative Paddy Ashdown, however powerful he was, did not actually administer the country. In Kosovo alone in the Balkan region have international officials governed a protectorate operationally. The UN Interim Mission in Kosovo (UNMIK) gets blamed for everything that goes wrong—and so, increasingly, do the peacekeepers of the NATO-led Kosovo Force (KFOR), especially since they were commanded by an Italian general who cut ties with the Kosovars' own Kosovo Protection Corps and instead cultivated ties with Serb military and security authorities. For their part, the Kosovo Serbs have never come to see either UNMIK or KFOR as reliable protectors. And as the years have dragged on in legal limbo, Albanians have become more disenchanted with UNMIK and KFOR (if not with the United States), seeing them not as enablers but as barriers to Kosova's independence.

As the riots in March 2004 showed, the discontent of both Kosovar Albanians and Serbs has made the land a tinderbox that could once again set off fires in Macedonia, southern Serbia, Montenegro, and Albania, though by now probably not in Bosnia and certainly not in Croatia. It makes the outcome of the ongoing political struggle between the aggrieved Serbs in Serbia and the aggrieved Albanians in Connecticut-sized Kosovo a hard test of whether the Balkans can ever truly join Europe. In 2006 the prime venue for the test is the Serb-Kosovar negotiation on the "future status" of Kosovo.

Mitrovica, North

Anyone taking the eight-hour bus ride from Belgrade to Mitrovica passes first through the wide Morava Valley draining into the Danube, then climbs into the rocky, sparsely inhabited foothills of the Montenegro peaks before descending again, through the narrow Ibar Valley, to the last stop. The destination is a not untypical Serbian provincial town, with none of the glitter or sophistication of Belgrade. There is little to mark it as the center of Europe's largest lead and zinc mines and the world's third largest mining complex, which until the turmoil began in 1989 produced more than a million tons of ore and gave jobs to 23,000 people. Women hawk potatoes and carrots from street stalls. Open-air cafes under tarpaulins dispense espressos to mostly male customers. Clothes displayed in shop windows are rudimentary, rendered in basic reds, blues, and browns, with little aspiration to style. Years after Vojislav Seselj went to the Hague to face charges of war crimes, old posters of the Radical leader remain plastered defiantly on walls. An outsider does not feel overly welcome and walks by instinct rather than asking directions, especially if the address sought is in the pocket in north Mitrovica where Bosniaks live, or even worse, in south Mitrovica on the other side of the Ibar River, where the ethnic Albanians now live. A third of the remaining 80,000 Serbs of Kosovo live in north Mitrovica, after an equal number or more left Kosovo, out of discomfort, fear, or deliberate ethnic cleansing carried out under the noses of the international peacekeepers.[3]

A stroll down the hill to the bridge that periodically became the stage for rumbles between Serb and Albanian toughs in the early years after the 1999 war goes past the Dolce Vita café. There, for several years the "bridge watchers" sat in ancient overstuffed armchairs, spoiling for a chance to beat up their counterparts on the other side of the bridge. Both clearly felt cheated by being too young to have experienced their older brothers' joy in killing, respectively, Albanians or Serbs before and during the eleven-week war.

By rights, the wars of Yugoslav succession should have started in Kosovo. Certainly the U.S. Central Intelligence Agency expected as much when it warned of the high risk of Yugoslavia's dissolving in 1990.[4] This was the one place where animosities had erupted regularly over the previous century. To be sure, back in 1389, as both sides like to forget, Serbs and Albanians (along with Bosnians, Bulgarians, and Wallachians) actually fought on the same side against the Ottoman Turks at the fateful battle at Kosovo Polje—the site half an hour away from Mitrovica where Milosevic's chauvinism was born against the backdrop of the rampart-like stone monument of Blackbird Field.[5] In the late seventeenth century, as 30,000 Serbs migrated from Kosovo to Hungary to avoid conversion to Islam, Albanian ex-Catholics who had already converted took their place without recourse to warfare. And there were extended periods when Serbs and Albanians did live side by side in Kosovo without slaughtering each other.

As the Ottoman Empire began its final death throes in the late nineteenth and early twentieth centuries, however, Serbs, Montenegrins, Bulgarians, and Greeks all took the opportunity to appropriate their own slices of ethnic Albanian territory. Meanwhile, Albanian guerrillas strove to emulate their neighbors by founding, belatedly, their own national state, but by the time it was recognized in 1912 and its boundaries settled thereafter, half of the Albanians lived outside the Albanian state. The atrocities and revenge atrocities of the pre–World War I Balkan Wars are notorious, but nowhere were the beheadings and live immolations of whole villages of men, women, and children worse, as journalist Leon Trotsky informed his readers, than in the path of the Serbs' drive toward the Adriatic to try to seize the coveted port of Durres from the Albanians.[6] In the intervals of peace in predominantly Albanian areas, Albanians barred Serbs from building houses bigger than their own. During outbreaks of war, the much more powerful Serbs butchered Albanians, or just mutilated them; and when they got the chance, as when the remnants of the Serb army evacuated to the Adriatic over northern Albania in the face of the German-Austrian-Bulgarian winter offensive in Kosovo in 1915, the Albanians reciprocated.[7]

At the end of World War I, the Great Powers awarded Kosovo and its Albanians to Serbia; Serb settlers were accorded special privileges from 1913 to 1920 to encourage them to repopulate the province, where some 60,000 had been killed or vanished. In the next war, in a Greater Albania encompassing both Albania proper and Kosovo under Italian fascist rule from 1941 to 1943, Kosovar Albanians exacted retribution. And at the end of World War II the Serbs, dominant once again, settled old scores in return.[8] The repression may have been less lethal than before, but it was bad enough. The majority Albanians suffered arbitrary police brutality and severe discrimination at the hands of the minority Serbs, led by the feared Alexandar Rankovic, Yugoslav interior minister and chief of Tito's secret police. Not until Rankovic opposed Tito's reforms in the mid-1960s did Tito set the (largely Croat-staffed) military intelligence against his secret police tsar and fire him, and give Kosovo and Vojvodina autonomy in the new 1974 constitution. The Kosovars, who had been 90 percent illiterate in 1940, for the first time got a university of their own; and, most important, they were allowed to join the League of Communists in large numbers and take over party leadership positions in their own province from the Serbs.[9]

The experimental relaxation did not last long. After Tito's death in 1980 a student demonstration in Pristina in 1981 was harshly repressed; riots spread throughout the province. The Yugoslav People's Army (JNA) enforced emergency law More than 2,000 Albanians were arrested. Incidents of harassment of Kosovo Serbs by the majority Albanians—some legitimate, some invented— were reported in ever shriller tones in the Belgrade media. Leading Serb intellectuals made these grievances the centerpiece of their Serb revitalization movement and the corollary campaign to reinstate the Serbs' predestined leading role in Yugoslavia. In 1986 more than 200 writers, academicians, and generals signed a memorandum written by the Serbian Academy of Sciences and Arts (SANU) demanding redress for the persecution of Serbs outside Serbia, in general, and in particular, accusing the Yugoslav Communists of conspiring for half a century to keep Serbia weak and in the 1980s to surrender Kosovo to Albania.[10] Thus the last twentieth-century battle for Kosovo began, even if it would take a dozen more years before words escalated to bullets. The popular Serb view became (and remains today) that yet again, as so often in the past, Serbia was defending an ungrateful West against an Islamic incursion.

That ethnic war in fact broke out in Croatia and Bosnia almost a decade before it did in Kosovo perhaps owed something to the rank military imbalance between the basically unarmed majority Kosovar Albanians and the very well-equipped Yugoslav Army, Serbian Security Special Forces, and Serbian Ministry of Internal Affairs police in the province.[11] The Kosovars, who clandestinely elected Ibrahim Rugova as their president on his platform of passive resistance—modeled on the Polish Solidarity—and supported the underground assembly's declaration of independence in the early 1990s, made a rational choice if they did not want a bloodbath.[12] They also, simultaneously, made the unprecedentedly rational choice of suspending their internecine blood feuds to join forces against their common Serb enemy in response to a campaign arguing that there are times when "forgiving blood" is brave.[13]

For his part, Milosevic, too, was rational in not trying to solve his Kosovo problem with military force while his troops were still overstretched in Croatia and Bosnia. But as the West did not provide the hoped-for economic aid or relax sanctions on rump Yugoslavia after the Dayton Accord (primarily because Milosevic made none of the conciliatory moves in Kosovo that he had informally promised at Dayton), he began a brutal new military and police operation to suppress the infant revolt in Kosovo.[14] And young Kosovars, disappointed by the silence of the Dayton agreement on independence for Kosovo, seized the opportunity to turn militant. To their ears, it sounded like sophistry when the West refused to recognize the underground assembly's early vote for independence as it had recognized the votes of the Croatian and Bosnian parliaments and referendums, on the grounds that, as republics, the latter had the right to secede under the Yugoslav constitution, whereas the Serbian province of Kosovo did not. Impatient with the failure of either diplomacy or Rugova's nonviolence to advance Kosovo's independence, they began joining the new Kosova Liberation Army (KLA) that was starting to conduct what James Gow called "terrorist actions."

The first major Serb operation against the Albanian insurgency was directed at the Jashari clan, which, along with diaspora Albanians in Switzerland and Germany, was recruiting for the KLA. In February 1998 Serbian Interior Ministry police killed more than fifty Jasharis, with little regard for sex or age, in the village of Prekaz. In response, village militias of the KLA carved out exclusionary zones in central Kosovo that they administered and policed (in between sweeps by Serb forces) and set up blockades on major roads.[15]

In spring and summer Yugoslav security forces struck back in force. With tank and artillery backup from the army, Serb Interior Ministry special police units killed thousands of the perhaps 7,000 poorly armed KLA foot soldiers—and also, in Gow's analysis, went well beyond the suppression of domestic insurrection permissible under international law, using the operation as the pretext for a new wave of ethnic cleansing that had been in preparation for a year. The mass murder of civilians, including women and children, and the looting and burning of homes and strewing of land mines across the area drove some 300,000 Kosovars to flight as refugees and displaced persons.[16] In early 1999 came the massacre in Racak that drew the attention of Louise Arbour, prosecutor for the International Criminal Tribunal for the Former Yugoslavia (ICTY), and prompted the following description from a grim William Walker, head of the Organization for Security and Cooperation in Europe's (OSCE) monitoring team in Kosovo: "A village that had one KLA member would be subject to being surrounded by artillery, being surrounded by the army, being surrounded by the police, being bombarded for hours; the police units would then go in, separate the men and the boys, take them off and essentially pillage and loot and burn in the village."[17] NATO issued several warnings to Milosevic that if he did not desist from violating humanitarian law and draw down the Serbian security forces in Kosovo to their levels before July 1998 he would be compelled to do so by alliance airstrikes. The Serb leader ignored them, or at least assumed that he was tougher than public opinion in NATO member countries and could ride out what he once mockingly called "polite bombing."[18]

Had it not been for the memory of Srebrenica, even the new surge in Serb violence would hardly have triggered Western intervention at this point, especially given the off-putting incidents of Albanian violence against Serbs and Roma, and Milosevic's fine-tuned calibration in keeping operations below the threshold that might trigger a Western reaction. The reengaged United States, now with a secretary of state who spoke Serbo-Croatian and had lived through the Soviet takeover of her native Czechoslovakia, decided that enough was enough—and that the credibility of the NATO alliance that Milosevic was defying with apparent impunity was at stake. Madeleine Albright won out over those in the administration and Congress who thought that events in a far-off land of which Americans knew nothing should be left to take their own course. And, after some alliance maneuvering that included abortive negotiations between Serbs and Kosovar Albanians at Rambouillet, she also persuaded the European allies, if with varying degree of enthusiasm, to write contingency plans for what would become NATO's first-ever hot war.[19]

Under these circumstances, Milosevic crossed the threshold on March 20, 1999. Some 50,000 Army of Yugoslavia (VJ) and Ministry of Internal Affairs (MUP) troops under General Nebojsa Pavkovic of the Third Army, supplemented by Arkan's Tigers (who had an old training camp outside Mitrovica), began the Serbs' most audacious ethnic cleansing to date—against Kosovo's more than 80 percent majority of Albanians.[20] On March 24 NATO responded by bombing a supposedly top-secret list of Serbian and Kosovo targets that turned out to be no secret to Milosevic, thanks to a French officer at NATO headquarters.[21]

For the allies, the nadir of the war came within a week, as it became clear that the expectation that Milosevic would buckle in a few days was wrong. The formidable Yugoslav army and police were dug in in Kosovo, and were even accelerating their wholesale ethnic cleansing. Shock units raped, tortured, and murdered civilians. Special police separated Albanian men from their families and took them away to be shot by Red Berets. There were Hieronymous Bosch scenes of columns of bloodied survivors and refugees in horsecarts, on tractors, or on foot, streaming toward the Macedonian, Montenegrin, and Albanian borders. The Clinton administration and the U.S. Congress were flatly forbidding the deployment of ground troops to Kosovo. The danger was palpable that Milosevic would win his gamble by holding out until after it was too late to get what quickly became more than a million external and internal refugees back to Kosovo with roofs over their heads before winter set in; that Serb refugees from Bosnia and Croatia would resettle in the Albanians' houses in the meantime; and that the Kosovars would never be able to return to their homes without first evicting squatters by force and starting the whole cycle of revenge and counterrevenge anew.

Yet whatever the strategic and tactical quarrels among the allies, the sea change in European attitudes at this point was measured by the comments of Germany's top professional diplomat, Wolfgang Ischinger, in an interview on March 31. "In this day and age we cannot let this kind of atrocity happen in Europe," he asserted.[22] The unspoken assumption was just the opposite of the European premise in the early 1990s, before the shock of Srebrenica. Earlier, the stock phrase was: "We cannot allow this kind of atrocity to come *into* Europe." The Balkans were outside; the aim was to erect a firewall that would prevent Balkan barbarity from spilling over into civilized heartland Europe. Now, suddenly, the European conviction was that the Balkans could no longer be regarded as outside Europe—and that, willy-nilly, the EU would have to assume responsibility for their decent governance.

In early June, Milosevic finally gave up and agreed to pull all his security forces out of Kosovo, let NATO-led international Kosovo Force peacekeepers go in, and let the UN take over administration of the province. A few days before he did so, Louise Arbour, fearing that the West might sacrifice justice to peace and grant Milosevic legal immunity in order to achieve Serbian withdrawal, rushed to put on public record his indictment by the Hague Tribunal for individual and superior responsibility for crimes against humanity and grave breaches of the Geneva Conventions in Croatia, Bosnia—and Kosovo.[23] By then 10,000–11,000 Albanians had been killed in Kosovo; 600 towns and villages (most of them "militarily inactive," according to Gow) had been razed;[24] and 1.4 million people—an astonishing 60-plus percent of the Albanian population—had been expelled from their homes, with 863,000 registered as refugees abroad, primarily in Albania and Macedonia, and an estimated 590,000 remaining as displaced persons in Kosovo.[25] In apparent tacit acknowledgment that crimes had been committed and had to be concealed, the Serb security forces in the last few weeks of war removed bodies en masse, dumping truckloads of corpses into the Danube near Belgrade and incinerating others in an aluminum blast furnace in southern Serbia.[26] For their part, Albanians, holding the Roma to have been collaborators with and spies for the Serb secret police, torched and jackhammered the apartments of 4,000 to 7,000 Roma in south Mitrovica in one action alone.[27]

The UN Interim Mission in Kosovo took over the governance of Kosovo, which remained formally a province of Serbia but became in fact an international protectorate; KFOR assumed responsibility for its external and domestic security.[28] Without waiting even for land mines to be cleared, the refugees streamed back to reclaim what was left of their homes. A Kosovo Police Service was set up, and—whenever its international leadership was savvy enough to protect its Albanian (and a proportional number of Serb) recruits from mafia and clan pressure—began to restore order, at least in nonpolitical cases. A Kosovo Protection Corps (KPC) was also founded to absorb a core of old KLA guerrillas, under the command of General Agim Ceku, who had led two battalions of ethnic Albanians within the Croatian army during the Croatian war in 1991 and participated in Operation Storm.[29] Kosovars regarded the

KPC as the nucleus of their future army and never did slim it down from its oversubscribed 5,000; the internationals insisted in vain that the KPC was a service to render disaster relief and should not exceed 3,000—but did manage to ensure that Serbs were recruited into its ranks. Provisional district and central government administrations were established to exercise the less important competences that UNMIK did not reserve for itself. KLA veterans' organizations retained their networks.

In the interregnum of well over a year before international UNMIK officials and police were recruited and prepared for their positions, Kosovar mafias, like their counterparts in Serbia, murdered and coerced not only rival nationals but also their own countrymen, as they liquidated suspected informers and factional rivals, expropriated choice properties, and extracted protection money from restaurateurs and retailers below the radar of KFOR peacemakers. For many months, the only suspects the internationals would dare to extradite to the Hague or try before international judges in Kosovo would be Albanians who had killed other Albanians, not Albanians who had killed Serbs.[30]

Mitrovica, South

Under the new regime, Bajram Rexhepi, a respected doctor who had tended KLA fighters in the field and thus had a good reputation among the many post-KLA politicians—but was also free of any suspicion of war crimes—became mayor of Mitrovica as Kosovo started the twenty-first century. In practice, this meant he was the mayor of the Albanians' south Mitrovica, cooperating closely with UNMIK's regional office in the semi-high-rise just around the corner from his own office, overlooking the bridge to the north. The city government's powers were modest. They did not include taxation, policing (except in concert with the international forces), or the utterly alien idea of zoning to prevent the do-it-yourself buildings that were springing up helter-skelter.

By contrast to the north, the new south Mitrovica that Rexhepi tended was vibrant, packed with far too much automobile traffic for its streets, and full of pedestrian hustle and bustle. Within months of the end of the 1999 war, south Mitrovica exploded not just with restaurants and brothels catering to the incoming international officials, but with shops displaying a cornucopia of the everyday cooking pots, hammers and saws, Chinese shoes, Indian shawls, VW spare parts, battery toys, and Walkmans craved by the returning Kosovar Albanian refugees. They immediately erected house frames and ground floors with their own hands, then put up small forests of trees on the second floor to support construction of the third floor; cast curved cement balustrades for balconies; imported Italian tiles to sell to insatiable customers; set up car wash stands; opened myriad gas stations to launder money; revived and extended clan warfare to eliminate or incorporate rival smuggling rings; and learned to drink macchiatos. Why the cityscape of the south should look so much more prosperous than that of the north is something of a mystery, since the subsidies the north gets from Belgrade over and above those that both halves of the city get from Pristina make per capita income in the north more than double that of the south. Even so, given the collapse of the mines and the loss of jobs in the 1990s, both subsidies are miserly, at some €102 per month in the north.[31]

After north-south brawls in early 2000 that left nine dead and prompted 900 Albanians to flee their homes in the north, KFOR finally managed to secure the bridge connecting the two sectors of the city over the Ibar ravine, at the cost of reducing fraternization to an absolute minimum. KFOR patroled north Mitrovica, UNMIK introduced multiethnic police and courts there, and a few Albanian villages remained in the more rural parts north of the Ibar, but otherwise north Mitrovica, including its two contiguous districts, was de facto ceded to the Serbs to run as their own, in limited coordination with Belgrade. Only official vehicles recognized by UNMIK could cross the bridge. All pedestrians were screened. Serb gladiators were barred from charging south; Albanian gladiators, from charging north. Albanians found it prudent not to visit the Albanian cemetery in the north; Serbs found it prudent not to visit the Orthodox cemetery in the south. The Albanians who thought it safer to desert their homes in the north had no way to get their property back and did not receive rent from the Serb refugees from the rest of Kosovo who occupied their houses. There was segregation, except for the famous few, like Rexhepi, who took a leap of faith in rebuilding his damaged house in the north near the hospital he had served in before the 1990s Serbianization; and the Albanian judge who lived in Vushtrri and commuted north to the court every day under the protection of an army convoy. And even Rexhepi, when he appeared in north Mitrovica as Kosovo's prime minister with a World Bank delegation in late 2003, set off Serb demonstrations that destroyed or damaged a half dozen UNMIK and private vehicles.

In Mitrovica, as later in Pristina, Rexhepi's sparring partner in the quest for a modus vivendi was Oliver Ivanovic, chairman of the hastily founded Serb National Council of Kosovska Mitrovica. Ivanovic straddled the two worlds of the Kosovo Serbs. By far the more real world for the Mitrovcani of north Mitrovica—the one viable Serb community that was not an isolated enclave in the new Kosovo—was the lifeline to Milosevic's Belgrade. Buses traveled only to Kragujevac and Belgrade, not to Pristina and Prizren. Customers used dinars, not euros, in shops. Only Serb ID cards were recognized. And only the parallel institutions of pensions, schools, and health and social services that were funded and run by Belgrade mattered politically. In any Serb election—Kosovo's elections were irrelevant—Seselj's Radicals could count on a large majority among the Mitrovcani. For these voters, the Serbs had not lost Kosovo-Metohija, but only suffered a temporary setback that would surely be rectified.

The other world, that which UNMIK and Rexhepi were trying to entice the Serbs in north Mitrovica and elsewhere to join, was the abstract one in which their minority was guaranteed a generous number of reserved seats in the new Kosovo Assembly, they could complain about any discrimination or threat to the UN ombudsman, and those Serbs who were cooped up in urban ghettos elsewhere would be protected against Albanian taunts and Molotov cocktails by KFOR and barbed wire. In this unfamiliar world individual civic identity was supposed to replace collective national identity and patriarchal authority. Indeed, plural individual identities—Serb, Kosovo citizen, European—were to replace the monolithic identity of Serb. Real but fair aggregate interests were to replace favoritist criminal interests and to be reconciled in give and take without guns; the rhetorical clash of rational alternative policies was to replace lethal factional power struggles. Resources were to be allocated justly and transparently. The gray zones between business and crime, and between the public and the private purse, were to be cleared up. Cutthroat zero-sum competition among poverty-striken rivals for a miserly pie was to turn into postmodern win-win cooperation to expand the pie so that everyone might prosper. Like it or not, society was to become multiethnic. The game of the Kosovo Serbs was supposed to shift from constant seeking to recapture the province for Belgrade to participation in its civic life as equal citizens who happened to be Serbs. Individual human rights were supposed to supplant collective minority rights; their practice would be held on compass by individual moral intelligence and responsibility.[32]

Oliver Ivanovic—described as a "sphinx" or a "chameleon" by one European diplomat—gradually joined the second world in 2000–01 as anti-Milosevic reformers won the election in Belgrade and shipped Milosevic off to the Hague. A trained karate instructor, Ivanovic had in the early days organized some of his former students to protect Serbs against Albanian toughs, and more ambiguously, to become bridge watcher vigilantes with their walkie-talkies and (later) cell phones. Eventually he chose to participate in Kosovo politics in the 2001 election, founded the Serb List for the Kosovo and Metohija quasi-party, and became one of the most serious Serb deputies in the National Assembly. Life as a high-profile politician was not as dangerous as it would become after the murder of Prime Minister Zoran Djindjic, but Ivanovic came under sufficient threat from both Albanian and Serb extremists to require bodyguards; his car would be blown up in North Mitrovica. As with other Serb politicians, it was hard to know if he represented any real consituency at all. (Given fierce clan loyalty, Albanian politicians' constituencies were more obvious.) The other Serb members of the assembly often acted less like the lobby for the general well-being of Kosovo Serbs that the UNMIK democratizers kept hoping for and more like a permanent in-house protest—or out-of-house protest, when members of parliament repeatedly boycotted the assembly until just short of the deadline at which their paychecks would get cut off. On the face of it, the thesis that real representational and institutional accountability would evolve through its formal exercise seemed like a fairytale.

Yet there was some dialogue. Only days before the March 2004 riots, Rexhepi and Ivanovic sat down together once again to discuss how the Mitrovcani might better be brought into Kosovar institutions.

Vushtrri Municipality

On a typical working Sunday, UN municipal administrator C. Dennison Lane popped into his rabbit warren of an office, a twenty-minute ride south of Mitrovica, long enough to pick up a forgotten item before setting off in his four-wheel drive. He found what he was looking for among the flotsam of a *New Yorker* desk diary, a hookah presented to him by the United Arab Emirates' civic affairs unit in his area, and a Chinese scroll that allegedly said "Keep smiling," then ushered visitors to his vehicle. In his short time in Vushtrri he had already posted welcoming signs on the approach highway in Latin, drained "Lake Vushtrri" of sewage overflow at the bus stop in the nether part of town, and run a competition to design a municipal flag, which could then be flown in lieu of the ubiquitous black-on-red double-headed eagle that hinted at Greater Albanian dreams. In addition, he had successfully charged rent from the mafioso restaurant that had camped in the UN-donated park and, in what became a highly popular festivity, had married or remarried hundreds of Muslim couples to the strains of Mendelssohn and the solemn words of the *Book of Common Prayer*.

On this Sunday Denny was, first of all, relieved that his fire chief could finally leave his house after Denny had helped negotiate a *besa* (truce) so he would not be shot the instant he ventured out onto the open street. The problem was that under the medieval Albanian *kanun* of Prince Lek, the family of a man who was found dead after a conversation with the fire chief's brother sought to kill the fire chief in revenge. (Retaliatory killing is authorized only outside, never inside, the target's home.)[33] There were political overtones to the vendetta as well. Under the increasingly brutal Serb hegemony in the 1990s, the KLA's followers had blackballed the followers of President Rugova for having worked in Serb-led fire crews in Vushtrri District. Rugova's followers—the present fire chief among them—had maintained that since 95 percent of the local dwellings were Albanian, it benefited Albanians more than Serbs to have Albanian firefighters, no matter who gave the orders. The feud continued in the new regime, as adherents of Hasim Thaci's Democratic Party of Kosova (PDK) bitterly contested the 2001 election with adherents of Rugova's Democratic League of Kosova (LDK)—generally with more lethal results for the LDK than for the PDK. Whatever the mix of motivations, with the *besa* in place, Vushtrri's fire chief could now get back to extinguishing conflagrations.

Denny's main task now was to dissuade a farmer from Grace, one of the few Serb villages in Vushtrri District, from selling his house to an ethnic Albanian for triple the price he would get from a Serb. Although his title was municipal administrator, Denny actually administered the whole Vushtrri urban and rural district, which sprawls midway between Mitrovica and the capital, Pristina. Before the war, Vushtrri had been populated by an even higher percentage of ethnic Albanians than Kosovo as a whole, some 95 percent. In the ethnic cleansing and war, 485 of Vushtrri's Albanians were killed; 82 disappeared. Some 5,000–6,000 homes were destroyed; between 13,000 and 14,000 head of livestock were slaughtered. The prewar Serb population of 8,500, living in a half dozen Serb villages, dwindled after the war to 4,500 living in four Serb and two mixed villages; the rest had either emigrated to nearby Serbia or died. Grace's population dropped steeply after the war to 58, but is now back up to 350. Denny wished to dissuade the farmer from selling his land to an Albanian out of concern that this might trigger an exodus of the remaining Serbs.

Like most of those working on the ground, Denny cared little about grand U.S. or European foreign policy. What counted was the nitty-gritty of extracting funds for his urgent projects from any donor who might be tapped, whether USAID, CARDS (the EU's Community Assistance for Reconstruction, Development and Stabilization program), or some nongovernmental organization (NGO). En route to Grace, Denny pointed out the passing landmarks. The house with a roof but no walls near the highway had been constructed illegally; now that negotiations with the builder had failed—and KFOR had refused to get involved—the municipality was going to have to take on the task of tearing down the building, a disciplinary operation doomed to failure in the face of the bigger and bigger mansions that were mushrooming at random across the fields. The new school off a dirt road was a success; some of the locals were even suggesting that under the regular half-day system, it could perhaps be used for Albanian pupils in the morning and Serb pupils in the afternoon. Not far from it, the new bridge for which villagers had petitioned the UN office, to avoid a several-kilometer detour to get to their fields, was largely unused for reasons that were not obvious. The new hospital (for both Albanian and Serb patients) had been built by the United Arab Emirate forces. In addition, the UAE contingent was constructing twenty-nine small mosques in villages and was planning on putting up a grand central mosque in Vushtrri city as well. At the Greek KFOR checkpoint to protect the village of Grace, Denny ascertained that there had been no further Albanian harassment of Serbs after the Greeks had caught and identified schoolboys from a neighboring village who had recently thrown rocks at a Serb house. The warning to the boys' parents by the Vushtrri Administration that the parents would be held responsible if there were any further incidents seemed to have worked. A bit farther on, Denny asked directions to the farm at a house with white UN vans parked outside it. Noting the presence of rather more young women than is customary in a single family, he jotted down the license numbers of the vans, along with a reminder to himself to issue general instructions the next day that the UN's international police officers must not visit bordellos in officially marked vehicles, and should in any case preferably choose venues outside Vushtrri District.

When Denny arrived at the conspicuously empty house for sale, the seller's brother—the farmer himself had moved to Serbia—materialized from the yard next door and invited Denny and his guests to come in for *raki* and strong coffee. His wife, elderly father, and daughters were also present, but let Mr. Pajovic do the talking. He appreciated that everyone should live together, he began, in oblique reference to his brother's absence, but everybody needed to wait for a better situation. Denny replied bluntly: "I can't forbid the sale— but I can make it very difficult for you by requiring papers you don't have." This was an altogether credible threat since the marauding Serb militias of 1998–99 had destroyed or removed land records wholesale. Well, Pajovic countered, he would like to buy his brother's house himself, but he did not have enough money to buy the fields too. His wages as a bus driver for the Danish Refugee Council were too low.

"You're a bus driver?" Denny interjected happily. Spain had just donated four buses to transport Serbs between their enclaves, and Denny was looking for drivers and security now that the KFOR forces had stopped their bus escort. Turning to the women, Denny asked where they would like to go if he could get this bus service going? To Vushtrri center for shopping, they agreed, if they would be safe from attacks by Albanians. One was so eager to get out of the confines of Grace that she announced she would go to Vushtrri center, even if she got stoned.

Emboldened, Pajovic raised the stakes. "We need a bridge to the other half of Grace," he declared; the hills of north and south Grace had been split by the Pristina-Mitrovica highway. Denny explained that he was already working the system of NGO bids to get an international donor for a footbridge. "And I need a cow," Pajovic continued. His cow had vanished some time ago, along with other village cows. There were conflicting theories about this phenomenon. One school held that Albanians had stolen the cows; the other school suspected that the Serbs themselves had eaten the cows and disposed of the remains in hopes that the UN would replace them with the much better milk cows the Swiss government had been donating after the wanton Serb destruction of Albanian livestock in 1998–99. Denny gave Pajovic his cell phone number to call in case there was any trouble, and promised to return for a further talk at 11 a.m. on Thursday.

Pajovic concluded aloud that he did not have any problem in waiting to sell his brother's house. Maybe this wasn't the best time anyway. People couldn't decide yet whether to stay where they were or to go home to Serbia. Denny, who had been in Serbia the day before, trying to arrange for the return of Ashkali ("Egyptian" Gypsy) families to Vushtrri, suggested, "There's probably not much in Serbia to go 'back' to."

"We must go forward," commented Pajovic noncommitally. On the drive back to Vushtrri center, Denny grumbled about UNMIK's irresponsible passivity in not trying hard to get Serbs who had fled to return to Kosovo.

That took care of the morning. In the afternoon Denny would try to pick up the pieces of an interethnic distaff group after the most respected of the Serb women at the first meeting had suddenly died of a heart attack. He took some encouragement from his modest success with discreet biethnic dinners of community leaders (discreet, he noted, apart from being surrounded by security cars, with their flashing blue lights). He had weathered the weekly market day demonstrations organized by veterans' organizations against the international authorities' arrest of three former KLA heroes earlier in the year on charges of murdering Albanians. And he had helped dissuade the Serbs of Gorbulja from burning down the new police station in their village and had even induced them to volunteer the name of a Serb candidate for the new police school that the UN had set up in Vushtrri. He hoped shortly to escalate his dinners to host a joint sheep barbecue for prominent local Serbs and Albanians. His to-do list further included wheedling funding from somewhere for a sports center and a cinema and procuring raw materials from Macedonia without prohibitive tariffs so that the Llamkos Steel Mill could reopen and provide jobs for seventy Albanians and thirty Serbs. In addition, he was trying to prevent the proliferation of reconciliation-chilling monuments to KLA martyrs—some of whom, he pointed out, had not even died yet.

This was the stuff of nation building.

Pristina

As mayor of Mitrovica, Bajram Rexhepi's main task—one for which he was well suited—was to attempt some sort of reconciliation with Serbs. He did so as a member of the Democratic Party of Kosova founded by Hashim Thaci, the young political leader of the KLA in the 1990s. Rexhepi was a much more conciliatory type than Thaci and was not burdened with associations that invited questions. When the PDK came in second to President Rugova's Democratic League of Kosova in the 2001 elections, then, and UNMIK barred Thaci from becoming prime minister, Rexhepi was the natural alternative choice.

As head of the awkwardly named Provisional Insitutions of Self-Government (PISG), Bajram Rexhepi found his writ limited. UNMIK kept for itself "reserved" powers dealing with security, the economy and customs, trials of war crimes and organized crime (with panels of international judges seconded to Kosovo), and any other sensitive areas. Albanian politicians constantly agitated for a settled "final status," which in their lexicon meant one thing only: independence. UNMIK, however, talked of both "standards" and "status," and said that while more powers would be granted to the PISG as it demonstrated its ability to respect the human rights of Serbs and Roma and to handle more of the reserved competences responsibly, "final status" negotiations could begin only after the Kosovo government had proved its ability to enforce the observance of minority rights and fulfilled 120 pages of other "standards" that would have been ambitious even for many West European states.[34] In this limbo Albanians became increasingly restive, especially after young Serb reformers ousted Milosevic in the elections in late 2000 and the West was treading carefully in Kosovo in order not to destabilize the new government in Belgrade. But UNMIK, instead of proactively shaping a political evolution, just kept hoping that some solution would turn up. At this stage, in contrast to the early 1990s, any Western differences in policy preferences for Kosovo arose less from transatlantic splits than from the divergent instincts of practitioners on the ground and their bosses back home.[35] Those working at the grass roots wanted UNMIK to take more initiative, explained one European diplomat, while "our capitals" wanted passively to "avoid anything that would give us the smell of an occupation power. We were so proud that no stones were thrown at KFOR!" But by keeping all its reserved powers and not delegating more competences to the frustrated PISG, UNMIK helped generate the very opposition it hoped to avoid. The veteran moderate, pro-West publisher Veton Surroi began writing about "empire lite," the diplomat continued, and about how the international officials were "treating them [the Kosovars] like little kids."[36]

This gently-gently approach was shattered on March 17, 2004. A sudden eruption of violence by 50,000 Albanian rioters left twenty dead and more than 900 injured. Thirty-six Serb churches and monasteries were desecrated, and some 4,100 Serbs, Roma, and other minorities were expelled from their homes—a greater number than the 3,664 who had returned over the entire previous year.[37] The outburst began spontaneously; Albanians surged over the bridge to vent their anger after reports that Mitrovcani north of the Ibar had chased two Albanian boys into the river, where they drowned. Rexhepi sped in person to scenes of confrontation to try to cool tempers. Some Albanians in the Kosovo Police Service also tried to protect Serbs, but others joined the mobs.

On the second day the protests became more organized; various leaders, working primarily through the associations of KLA veterans, invalids, and families of martyrs, mobilized more crowds to intimidate Serbs. For UN officials a particularly disturbing feature was the new animus toward the international overseers. Over the previous year—ever since the unique court of international prosecutors and judges in Kosovo had for the first time convicted some KLA figures, in late 2002—there had been small protests outside UNMIK headquarters in downtown Pristina, led primarily by the militant Pristina University Students Union. The protesters demanded instant independence for Kosovo and blamed UNMIK for not granting it—and also denounced the UN administration for persecuting KLA war heroes. But in the March unrest the rioters went well beyond civil protest and deliberately attacked some UNMIK vehicles and buildings. To restore order, international police and peacekeepers for the first time shot and killed some local Albanian ringleaders.

The violence demonstrated just how sharply the international officials and the Albanians diverged in their perceptions of the role of the KLA in the 1999 war and its consequent claims on postwar society. To the former, the KLA was a fledgling army that was decimated by the Serbian juggernaut but was nonetheless helpful in 1999 in spotting and flushing out hidden Serb units for the crosshairs of NATO planes. To the latter—and especially to the KLA daughter associations—the KLA warriors were the heirs of Scanderbeg who had finally expelled the Serbs from Kosovo, with some assistance from NATO, and especially the United States. To the former, KLA veterans had now returned to normal life and were no different from any other civilians—and when evidence indicated that they had committed wartime atrocities, they, too, had to be held legally accountable. To the latter, these paragons deserved reverence and should not be persecuted just for having paid the Serbs back in kind. As one of Hashim Thaci's entourage put it in a passionate outburst during a hair-raising campaign swing in Drenica, at 100 miles an hour after dark over unlit potholed roads, "What would you say if George Washington had been hauled into court after winning the American revolution?!"[38]

On the third day the spasm stopped, after the KFOR commander told both Thaci and AAK party leader Ramush Haradinaj to consider where their political credibility lay and to call off the militants. To many outsiders it seemed as if the politicians felt they could now stop the rampage because they had proved they could push the internationals around—especially since UNMIK disciplined no senior Albanians afterwards.[39] Or as if the drug-running gangs that were hard to distinguish from parties' enforcement squads had finished slipping the latest consignment of heroin over the northern border and no longer needed the cover of social bedlam. Clearly, the earlier blanket Albanian adulation of the international saviors had waned, though a popular expectation lingered on that ultimately the powerful Americans, if not the Europeans, would give the Kosovars their independence. The surprise was all the greater when Washington as well as Brussels condemned the Kosovars' paroxysm of violence. "I think this was a very good lesson for Thaci and Rugova," commented one European diplomat dryly.[40]

In the aftermath of the convulsion, UN Secretary General Kofi Annan commissioned Norwegian diplomat Kai Eide to draw up a post mortem. His report faulted the lack of preparedness and inaction of UNMIK and, by implication, of the steering Contact Group of the United States, the United Kingdom, Germany, France, Italy, and Russia.[41] The internationals concluded that they must diminish the volatility of the situation by accelerating the resolution of Kosovo's status, and accordingly modified their requirement that the PISG meet all the very detailed democratic and institutional UN standards before talks on the future status of Kosovo could even start—"standards before status"—and before the UN administration could transfer more competences to the provisional government. Under the more relaxed slogan of "standards *and* status," they also commissioned Kai Eide to write a progress report on Kosovo for delivery in autumn 2005, which, it was hoped, would show that real negotiations could start shortly thereafter to pin down Kosovo's eventual status somewhere on the theoretical scale from full independence to a return to Serbian rule. UNMIK also, for the first time, turned over the post of director of the Office of Public Safety in the PISG prime minister's office to a Kosovar—Enver Orucaj, an ex-KLA brigade commander from the Drenica region. It further invited a British Security Sector Development Advisory Team to help plan a reform and development strategy for the security sector in Kosovo. And it set out more realistic criteria for Kosovar compliance with "standards" in a new Kosovo Standards Implementation Plan, which also accorded priority to passing a law to regularize the vague legal status of the Kosovo Police Service.[42]

In the regular parliamentary elections half a year after the riots, the vote seemed initially to do no more than confirm stagnation. The list system that UNMIK had unfortunately approved perpetuated the iron grip of leaders on restive young assembly deputies in what were still only proto-parties. Rugova's LDK (autocratically run like a "Soviet-style party," one European diplomat noted) slipped somewhat from its position in the 2001 vote but retained a plurality of 45 percent. Thaci's PDK kept second place, with 29 percent; and the small Alliance for the Future of Kosova (AAK) led by a former senior KLA commander in Dukagjini, Ramush Haradinaj, again came in third, with 8 percent. The new, moderate, pro-Western Ora Party led by Veton Surroi trailed at 6 percent. Moreover, the election seemed to mark the end of efforts to reach any ethnic modus vivendi. Under strong pressure from Belgrade and Patriarch Pavle of the Serbian Orthodox Church, even most of those local Serbs who had previously run for the reserved minority seats in the Kosovo assembly boycotted the vote.[43]

After the election, the aloof Rugova again chose to stay on as president rather than mix into the hurly-burly of politics as prime minister. His LDK secured a parliamentary majority by forming a coalition with the AAK and offering Haradinaj the more active post of head of the provisional government. The choice raised eyebrows, both because it was widely expected that Haradinaj would shortly be indicted at the ICTY and because his own brother had earlier been convicted and sentenced to five years' imprisonment in connection with the 1999 murders of members of the armed wing of Rugova's party (in a trial in which key witnesses tended to meet premature death). But Haradinaj, his international admirers said, was something new on the political scene.[44] After the war, he had taught himself English, he had attended day-long EU seminars that no other politician bothered with, and he had studied law at Pristina University. He was the one party leader who was trying to modernize his organization away from a top-down patronage nexus and introduce significant grass-roots participation. And he and his brother Daut had taken their chance in the unfamiliar Kosovo state courts in the murder trial that convicted Daut, rather than relying on the *kanun* rules of vigilante clan justice. In Ramush's life as a KLA commander "something happened that he regretted," commented one European diplomat who worked closely with Haradinaj (but never learned what the something was), "and he had a Saul/Paul moment that was important to him." In postwar Pristina politics "Ramush was the one who would mediate. He was a force for deliberation. He tried to be not too radical."[45]

As prime minister, Haradinaj brought a younger, more pragmatic leadership to Kosovo. In his short three months in office before the Hague Tribunal did charge him with command responsibility for the abduction, torture, and murder of dozens of Serbs, Roma, and Albanians in Dukagjini during Milosevic's 1998 crackdown, he grasped the importance of decentralization, implemented it energetically, and took unprecedented local ownership of this and other policies.

When he was indicted in March 2005, Haradinaj promptly resigned his post and, in an unprecedented step for a Kosovar indictee, went to the Hague voluntarily, averring his innocence.[46] This time, apparently in part at Haradinaj's request, the demonstrations against the indictment of yet another Albanian were brief and ceased after a day or two. Within weeks the ex-commander and ex-prime minister, on furlough from his Dutch jail, paid a tragic return visit to bury a second brother, who had suddenly been gunned down, apparently in the continuing blood feud between the Haradinaj and Musaj clans. In his funeral oration, Ramush Haradinaj counseled calm and declared that ensuring protection of the "lives of every citizen of Kosovo . . . is the best way to support the state-building process that is going on in Kosovo."[47] No one personified more clearly the wrenching conflict between the durable system of clan justice that had been functional and even progressive when it was adopted by shepherd societies in medieval times and the impersonal Western system in which the family of a murdered man is denied the honor of revenge and is expected to be satisfied with seeing the murderer accused and put in jail (or sometimes even acquitted and set free). The Hague Tribunal allowed Haradinaj to await his trial at liberty in Kosovo with UNMIK as a kind of parole officer, and he was even allowed a discreet role in politics.[48]

Standards and Status

Throughout 2005 the West tried to bring movement to the twin issues of standards and status. Domestically, it promoted serious decentralization, both as a way to break the grip of top-down patriarchates and bring governance closer to citizens' daily lives in general, and to let Serb communities in particular take more control of their own fates. In this area the younger AAK assembly deputy who became prime minister after Haradinaj resigned, Bajram Kosumi, continued his mentor's engagement. He went personally to Grace (where Denny had tried to persuade Pajovic not to sell his brother's house), to appeal to its Serb farmers to "look toward the future and not remain hostage to the past" and to urge their brothers and cousins who had fled to Serbia to come back.[49]

As everyone waited for Kai Eide's evaluation of Kosovo, the West further began tentatively giving more powers to Albanians, even in the most sensitive realm of security and justice.[50] UNMIK officials began talking about a plan to transfer limited police and judicial responsibilities to the PISG, though UNMIK would retain supervisory powers and the right to intervene at any point. In June it turned over policing of the Mitrovica bridge to the Kosovo Police Service, while simultaneously opening it to civilian cars. Initially, at least, the experiment was not a success. The first Albanian auto to venture north was pelted with stones by Serb protesters. This reception deterred others from following—and the bridge watchers, back at their post, and apparently reinforced by Serbian security agents, demanded ID cards of all pedestrians from the south, letting only some through their cordon.[51] In August UNMIK's chief of police and justice affairs, Jean Dussourd, told the *Zeri* daily of UNMIK's intent to set up "an official intelligence organization" (and, implicitly, to dismantle the partisan intelligence networks of the old KLA factions and proto-parties).[52] In October Kai Eide presented his follow-up appraisal of the situation and, despite strong criticism of Kosovar failure to implement the requisite standards, recommended that status talks proceed.[53] In December UNMIK established Justice and Interior Ministries in the PISG government—and specified that both would be held to "vigorous accountability" and that UNMIK would have the right to intervene at any time. Serbian spokesmen called the move "reckless and dangerous."[54]

Devolving some security competences from UNMIK to the PISG and some municipal competences from Pristina to local communities—in effect, setting up totally new institutions and networks of resource distribution in this infant polity—would have been hard in the best of circumstances. And it was further hampered both by organized crime gangs that resisted any dilution of their own power and by the very effective expansion of Belgrade's competing parallel structures. Despite Albanian fears of a Serbian fifth column in Kosovo, Belgrade's sponsorship of social services there is not intrinsically harmful; some NGOs have even proposed ways to welcome Belgrade as a "strategic donor" and channel some of the financing to the gravely underfunded villages of subsistence farmers in which so many Serbs south of the Ibar live. Just such a proposal was the topic of the Rexhepi-Ivanovic meeting on the eve of the March 2004 violence.[55]

The problem, however, is twofold. First, the system of parallel structures has been used to rebuild the network of Serbian secret service agents inside Kosovo; in early 2004 Momir Stojanovic, now the head of Serbian military intelligence and chief of its operations in Kosovo in the mid-1990s, boasted that his agency had already rebuilt its Kosovo nexus.[56] Second, the Coordination Center for Kosovo and Metohija in Belgrade that runs Serbia's Kosovo policy deliberately conditioned use of these services by Kosovo Serbs on rejection of the jurisdiction of UNMIK and the PISG. This conditionality was a powerful tool in enforcing the boycott of the 2004 Kosovo elections demanded by Prime Minister Vojislav Kostunica. It was a deterrent to multiethnicity in society, and it could have been seen as preparation for the kind of decentralization that Belgrade was asking for as part of its vision of final status—a cantonization reminiscent of the no-go zone the Serbs carved out in Croatia's Krajina in 1990.

The parallel structures started in north Mitrovica. The Mitrovcani founded a university there in 2001 to cater exclusively to Serbs. Belgrade appointed the administration; in 2004, in a particular affront to the Kosovar Albanians, it installed as rector Radivoje Papovic: a man who during his tenure as rector of Pristina University in the 1990s had "Serbianized" that institution, firing almost 800 Albanian professors and lecturers; a man who branded Milosevic a traitor for having concluded an education agreement with Rugova in the 1990s. In an even greater affront, after the Pristina court decamped to Nis in Serbia in 1999, its Milosevic-era judge issued an arrest warrant for Commander Ceku of the Kosovo Protection Corps and managed to have him detained twice at European airports before UNMIK intervened to get him released.[57]

Then in late 2002 and mid-2003, Kosovo Polje and the town just south of Pristina around the Gracanica Orthodox monastery both turned their health centers into totally Serbian-run operations—with no protest from UNMIK. At the same time, the Coordination Center for Kosovo and Metohija established branches in Serb communities in the Pristina and Gnjilane areas. It increased its functions to form a virtual shadow government in Gracanica, and offered Serbs who had worked for UNMIK higher salaries to join this shadow administration and cut their ties with UNMIK and the PISG.

In an effort to end international drift and actively shape a "final status" for Kosovo, the Contact Group—or the Quint, as the Western caucus minus the Russians is termed—in spring 2005 set out a clear framework for any settlement by laying out "four nos": no return of Kosovo to Serbian rule; no immediate full sovereignty for Kosovo; no partition; and no mergers, for example, of Kosovo and Albania.[58] By fall it was clear that the only status the West would approve would be some version of conditional independence, with international overseers holding significant powers of defense, justice, policing, and the protection of minority Serbs for years to come. As the talks opened in early 2006, the Quint's position was described as three rather than four nos; the taboo on instant independence remained, but was couched in more positive terms of a status like that of West Germany before unification in 1990. The term "final status" was also downgraded to a more fluid "future status." Final status, it was stressed, would be full integration as a member of the European Union.

The most explicit articulation of what Kosovo's future status might look like was presented in the study that the blue ribbon International Commission on the Balkans issued in April 2005. This envisaged an initial "independence without full sovereignty" for Kosovo, followed by "guided sovereignty," and then the ultimate "shared sovereignty" that every EU member agrees to.[59] The vocabulary conspicuously avoided the red flag of calling such independence "limited" or "conditional" and emphasized the voluntary "pooling" of sovereignty that all present EU members have accepted on joining this unique hybrid between a confederation and a federation. No practitioner of the delicate diplomacy required to get even a Western consensus on this minimal course in 2005 dared be so blunt about the goals the Serbs and Kosovars were supposed to arrive at of their own free will, while at the same time being able to argue to their domestic constituents that the internationals had forced them into such a deal. But the similarity to the three (or four) nos was clear.[60]

As negotiations opened in 2006, Serbs and Kosovar Albanians had been adamant for seven years that, respectively, Kosovo must forever remain a province of Serbia and that Kosova must have instant independence. They appeared to be in total confrontation. Domestic politics on both sides argued powerfully against making any concessions that might give victory to extremists waiting in the wings—in Serbia, in the form of Seselj's Radicals; in Kosovo, in the form of a new generation of radicals. Creative diplomacy—and the leverage of the goal of eventual membership in the European Union—was at a premium.

CHAPTER FIVE

RECLAIMING HAPSBURG CROATIA

LIKE SERBS, CROATS feel aggrieved by their image in Western Europe, for some of the same reasons and for some different reasons. But today's 4.5 million Croats, far more swiftly than Serbs, are exorcising the ultranationalist demons that drove the two peoples to torture and kill each other in World War II and again in the early 1990s. The proof of conversion came with the arrest in December 2005 of Ante Gotovina, the most wanted Croat indicted for war crimes, after the Zagreb government finally cracked down on his support network in the Croatian security services. With General Gotovina in the dock, the country was well on its way to becoming the second Yugoslav successor state, after Slovenia, to reach the holy grail of membership in the European Union.

Corroboration of the ongoing metamorphosis came in the low turnout for protests against Gotovina's arrest in an indifferent Zagreb on the day after his detention and in the political survival of Prime Minister Ivo Sanader, despite what many in his own party deemed his betrayal of a larger-than-life Croat hero. Proof of the remaining resistance to change, however, came in the tens of thousands mobilized from around the country by veterans' associations to demonstrate in the accused's Dalmatian homeland four days after his arrest— and in a serious death threat to a Split journalist who has for years publicized Croat atrocities against Serb civilians.[1]

In a way, this liberation from its history was President Franjo Tudjman's final gift to the nation he led to independent statehood for the first time in a millennium. Had he lived long enough, he too would have had to appear at the Hague, and the swell of patriotic support for Croatia's modern founding father would have at the least postponed remorse for crimes committed so recently in the name of Croatia.² Tudjman could claim credit for the 1995 tour de force of Operation Storm, in which an army that had not existed four years earlier expelled, within forty-eight hours, the Serb armies that had seized a third of Croatian territory and held it for three years.³ Yet he was equally responsible for the high moral cost of that victory, as some 200,000 Serb refugees fled or were driven from their ancestral homes, and many of the elderly, who could not flee, were massacred; the total number of Serbs in Croatia's population dropped from 600,000 (12 percent) before the war to 200,000 (4.5 percent) afterward.⁴ General Gotovina commanded the southern theater in Operation Storm, where the worst atrocities were committed, but Tudjman, himself a former general, was the commander in chief. When the president died in December 1999, before he could be indicted, he spared his country; he did not become an albatross for Croats, but freed them from the past to look to the future. In this way, Croatia became something of a poster child for the transformative power of the EU magnet.

Dubrovnik

Any tourist coming to this fairytale city knows instantly that Croats are Europeans. There is no ambivalence. The tile roofs, the Italianate palaces, the cathedral and cloisters, and Europe's best-preserved medieval fortifications (now repaired after the Serb shelling a decade and a half ago) all testify to the provenance of this UNESCO-protected site and watering hole of the world's glitterati. The city-state that the Romans knew as Ragusa was once the leading port and intellectual center on the Dalmatian coast, rivaling Venice. And when the Ottoman Empire finally extended its rule to Ragusa, the town flourished under the Turks' low and uniform duties, which replaced the much higher levies imposed under Venetian and Hungarian suzerainty.

From the end of the Middle Ages Dubrovnik was the center of Croatian culture, and although it maintained its links with the Slavic east, its civilization "ultimately developed within the West European (Catholic Mediterranean and Central European) zone."⁵ Over the centuries Dubrovnik embraced everything that was alien to the anti-Western strains in Balkan culture and the Orthodox Church: the Renaissance and Enlightenment, "the exaltation of reason in place of dogma, the turn to Greek antiquity, and the preference for Plato rather than Aristotle." Its civilization was "secular, sophisticated, individualistic." Its literature "consisted of epic poetry, lyrics, and drama, comparable to the literature of Italy at this time."⁶ It was the cradle that nurtured the country's most famous poets, artists, mathematicians, and physicists. Dubrovnik can claim Europe's oldest (fourteenth century) apothecary and communal theater, both still functioning; just outside the city is the continent's first (fifteenth century) arboretum. In the eighteenth century Dubrovnik was the first state to recognize the United States of America. In the early nineteenth century it was freed from the Turks by Napoleon, then ceded to the Hapsburgs for the hundred years until formation of the first Yugoslavia.

Dubrovnik was always special, but it was not unrepresentative of inland Croatia as a whole. Croatia, like Serbia, had a glorious medieval kingdom—one that already included the Dalmatian coast. In the eleventh century, when King Zvonimir died without an heir, the Croatian nobles invited Hungarian king Ladislaus I to rule over them. In return, the Hungarians left in place indigenous nobles and bishops who commanded the vast feudal estates of the Roman Catholic Church. This dispensation ended when the Turks finally overran most of Hungary and Croatia in the sixteenth century and the nobles chose to support the Hapsburgs, only to lose their lands and status in the next two centuries of Ottoman rule. In this period, as the borderland military district between the two empires, Croatia's Krajina, in the mountains behind Dubrovnik (which would become one of the first venues of the 1990s wars), suffered depopulation and devastation. Croats, glossing over the fact that at least as many Serbs as Croats were recruited by the Hapsburgs for service in the borderland, recall this as a period in which they were the holy defenders of Catholicism and the West—militarily against the Turks, culturally against the Orthodox Serbs.

Yet when the Hapsburgs finally repulsed the Turks in the eighteenth century, the recovered estates were not returned to Croats, but were awarded primarily to Austrian and Hungarian nobles. Croats were governed "by a predominantly foreign nobility and by the princes of the church," while the "overwhelming mass of the Croatian people remained in servitude."[7] There were periodic serf revolts; several appealed in vain to the emperor in Vienna as the supposed protector of the peasants against the feudal lords. But after crushing the Magyar revolution in 1849, with the help of Croat baron Josip Jelevic, the Hapsburgs suppressed budding Croatian nationalism just as thoroughly. And when the Hapsburgs again turned Croatia over to Hungarian rule, many Croats, rather than striving for a particularist Croatian state, sought to rally their nationally more defined Serb brothers to join forces and strive for a common liberation from their respective empires in an independent "Yugoslav" (South Slav) state.

Up until World War I it was Croats rather than Serbs who were the most ardent champions of Balkan unification. As early as the sixteenth century the Dominican Vinko Pribojevic preached pan-Slavism, and in the nineteenth century a Croat "Illyrianism" romantically cast all Slavs as descendants of the pre-Roman inhabitants of the Balkans, rather than of fourth-century late-comers. Even if this quest ran counter to the nineteenth century zeitgeist of particularist nationalism in Europe, it made sense for a people who were far smaller in number than the Serbs and had little chance on their own of going beyond the considerable autonomy they already exercised to gain full inde-pendence from their Austro-Hungarian rulers. The first, short-lived attempt at South Slav solidarity was the Balkan League of the 1860s, assembled by Ser-bian prince Michael Obrenovic under the banner of expelling the Turks and restoring the ancient Serbian kingdom. After its failure, Serb mistrust of any Yugoslav amalgamation grew.

Echoing the "Great Idea" of uniting all Greeks, regardless of existing national borders, Serb intellectuals wanted to bring all Serbs within the Serb kingdom, whether they lived in Croatia, Bosnia, Herzegovina, Montenegro, or Macedonia. Serb writers suspected that Croat "Illyrianists" wanted to block and "denationalize" the Serbs by diluting them in some amorphous greater identity. As the nineteenth century rolled on and the desired Greater Serbia looked unattainable, some did concede that a South Slav state might be acceptable, but only if the Serbs became the "Piedmont" leaders they deserved to be as the largest South Slav population and the warriors who already in 1830 had won a pioneering autonomy within the Ottoman Empire and in 1878, independence.[8]

The Second Balkan League was formed in spring 1912, after Vienna had upset the thirty-year Austrian-Russian balance in the Near East by formally annexing Bosnia-Herzegovina in 1908. The Serbs, backed by the Russians (and secondarily by France and Britain), protested vehemently against the incorporation of these Slavic provinces into the Hapsburg empire—but quickly turned their full attention to ousting the Turks from their remaining Balkan garrisons in the First Balkan War. Within six weeks, to the surprise of the great European powers, the united Bulgarian, Greek, Serb, and Montene-grin armies—no army of Hapsburg-controlled Croatia joined in—did expel the Turks from all but a small corner of the peninsula. The victorious league immediately dissolved into fratricide and land grabs in the Second Balkan War, which lasted a short but bloody four weeks and expanded Serbia's pop-ulation overnight from 2.9 to 4.4 million.[9] Serbia occupied Albania. Bulgaria attacked Serbia and Greece. Montenegro, Romania, and Turkey attacked Bul-garia. Macedonia, with its strategic central location and claims on its territory by Serbia, Bulgaria, Greece, and Romania, and with its discrete mix of Bulgars, Greeks, Turks, Albanians, Serbs, Vlachs, Jews, and Gypsies, became the most ravaged battlefield of all. In the two Balkan wars 200,000 combatants and many more civilians were killed. The atrocities of bayoneted babies, gouged-out eyes, and live immolations in village after village shocked Europe.[10]

The Treaty of London of May 1913 and the Treaty of Bucharest of August 1913 ended the Balkan slaughter, for the time being. But after a year's respite, the assassination in Sarajevo in June 1914 of Archduke Franz Ferdinand, heir to the Austrian throne, triggered Europe's wider slaughter. By the time the armistice was declared in 1918, the *ancien régime*, four empires, and an unprecedented 10 million soldiers were dead. And still sporadic fighting erupted in the Balkans and Asia Minor over the next seven years, between Austrians and Slovenes; Italians and Croats; Romanians, Russians, and Ukrainians; and most monumentally, between Greeks and Turks. The Bolshevik Revolution in St. Petersburg was far away. The revolt of the Young Turks against the decaying Ottoman dynasty was already irrelevant. The one outside event that impinged on the South Slavs' thinking, perhaps, was U.S. president Woodrow Wilson's "Fourteen Points," promising self-determination to the peoples of Austria-Hungary in particular.

In the wake of all the mutual killing, the old ideal of South Slav unity looked illusory. The Croats held onto it the longest. Their pan-Slavism contained a strong core of admiration of Serbs. In the early twentieth century, Belgrade had been a lodestar for young Croatian artists; Croat Serbophilia reached its apogee during the Balkan Wars of 1912–14. Many in the Croat Progressive Youth movement had even embraced the concept of the superiority of the "kinetic" Serbs over the more passive Croats, following the Croats' debilitating exposure to the "decaying West."[11]

The degeneration of Croat enthusiasm for a "Serbcroat" people into mutual Serb-Croat butchery, for the first time in history, during World War II followed strife over the centralization that the Serbs carried out in the first Yugoslavia. The Croats' concept of a new South Slav state was basically federal, one that would preserve their accustomed autonomy and not subordinate them to the Serbs. In the new Kingdom of the Serbs, Croats, and Slovenes (and Montenegrins) that was formed on December 1, 1918, this expectation soon clashed with the contrary assumption by the Serbs that they were the natural leaders in a South Slav constellation. The monarch was Serb. Serb parliamentarians rammed through the centralized "Vidovdan constitution" in 1921, which snuffed out Croat and Slovene autonomy. All prime ministers in the decade of constitutional democracy were Serb. All but 2 or 3 percent of Yugoslav generals were Serbs.[12] Nor were the Serbs timid about enforcing their dominance; they were habituated to violence in politics from successive revolts against the Turks and from the bitter struggle between the Karadjord-jic and Obrenovic dynasties. The triumphant Serb army—and even more the undisciplined Serb paramilitaries—appropriated land and livestock, beat up or murdered those who resisted, and made life especially miserable for Muslim villagers in Bosnia-Herzegovina, Kosovo, and Macedonia. For a decade of parliamentary politics, the beloved leader of the Peasant Party, Stjepan Radic, led Croat resistance to centralization (sometimes from a jail cell). But in 1928 Radic was assassinated on the floor of the National Assemby by a Great Serbian Radical deputy. Within six months King Aleksandar suspended the constitution, dissolved the assembly, and banned political parties. He then ruled as an autocrat until he himself was assassinated, by a Macedonian backed by Italian and Hungarian authorities, in 1934.

The Croats came to see Svetozar Pribicevic, the fiery nationalist political leader of Serbs living in Croatia-Slavonia, "as the evil genius of 1918 unification and the chief force behind centralism, who destroyed Croat statehood . . . brought the crowns of Croatia, Dalmatia, and Slavonia to the House of Karadjordjevic, and used strong-arm methods in the persecution" of the Croatian Peasant Party. Curiously, in a volte-face in the late 1920s, Pribicevic wrote a book indicting with equal ferocity the *Dictatorship of King Alexander*, who "amputated" Croatia rather than tolerating federalism.[13]

As Europe was swept into its second inferno in 1939 and the Wehrmacht occupied the Balkan Peninsula, Serbs and Croats plunged into a mortal three-way struggle between Croat Ustashe, Serb Chetniks, and Tito's partisans. The subterranean and then raging conflict between liberalism and nationalism that plagued all of Europe in the nineteenth and first part of the twentieth centuries had been won decisively by nationalism in Croatia. Fascist Ustashe—ultranationalist terrorists who had lived in exile in the 1920s and 1930s—collaborated with Hitler's Germany in a puppet regime that incorporated most of Bosnia-Herzegovina. Ustasha leader Ante Pavelic boasted that his aim was to kill a third of Serbs in Croatia, expel a third, and convert a third to Catholicism. He was even more brutal with Jews, shipping them off to Germany for extermination. The regime's death squads, concentration camps, and corraling of Serbs into Orthodox village churches to be burned alive were infamous. So were the massacres of Jews and of Serb Chetnik guerrillas.[14]

By 1945, after years of internecine butchery, the winner was clearly Tito, a Slovene-Croat ethnically and a Yugoslav unifier politically—so long as that unified Yugoslavia was Communist. He worked to inculcate a sense of Yugoslav nationhood to supersede narrowly ethnic nationalisms, and he succeeded to the extent that a fair number of people identified their nationality as "Yugoslav" in censuses. During his own thirty-five-year rule, however, he never built an economic or political whole—or any pluralist system—that could continue on its own momentum once he was gone. Instead, he kept the federation together by the threat of coercion and by playing the smaller ethnicities—especially Croats and Albanians—against Serbs. Serbs felt deprived of their just reward for having provided the bulk of the partisans' foot soldiers in the war, and felt especially disadvantaged once Tito purged his secret service chief, Alexandar Rankovic, along with Rankovic's Serb entourage, in 1966. They felt further humiliated by Tito's award of autonomous status to the two Serbian provinces of Kosovo and Vojvodina in the 1974 constitution; this shift visibly helped to revive not only Serb, but also Croat and Albanian nationalism. Both Serbs and Croats resented Tito's suppression of their respective national revivals in the early 1970s, and the Croats resented the continuing preponderance of Serb (and Montenegrin) generals in the army.[15]

The upshot was that ethnic nationalism, far from having been overcome as Tito's spokesmen proclaimed, was only suppressed.[16] In the 1990s Franjo Tudjman came into his own with a groundswell of popular support, as he dropped his Communist atheist persona altogether and embraced the fascist Ustasha regime and the Catholic Church as preservers of Croat identity. Both rallying symbols were problematic. The resurrection of Ustasha leaders who had butchered tens of thousands of Serbs, Roma, and Jews repelled non-Croats. And the Roman Catholic Church, perceiving itself in fact as a catholic, universal religion, did not lend itself to nationalist particularism as readily as did the autocephalous Orthodox churches.

In an interview, Ivo Banac—Yale historian, author of the seminal *The National Question in Yugoslavia,* and fledgling politician as a member of the Croatian parliament from the new Croatian Social-Liberal Party—recalled with a twinkle how Tudjman and other Communist leaders suddenly began attending mass, sitting in the front row, while assiduously avoiding taking communion. "Nominally, Croatia is a country with a Catholic majority, but we have never had a Catholic political party," he noted. "The Croatian Peasant Party [formed in the early twentieth century], which was the national party, was anticlerical. . . . For Bosnia-Herzegovina the traditions are different; the church is a purely national Catholic church. Through the Ottoman and Austrian Empires it was the only native church. That means the Franciscan order." After World War II the Yugoslav (and Croat) Communists first executed priests and persecuted the church, but in the 1960s they liberalized in general and gave the Catholic Church possibilities that Christians in other Communist countries could only dream of. This dispensation ended when the national, liberal wing of the Communist Party was suppressed in 1971. Thereafter, the only place where "anything that smacked of Croat nationalism" could be expressed was in church. When Franjo Tudjman ran in the first multiparty elections in 1990 "it was clear that the church supported Tudjman." And when Croat forces began committing atrocities against Serbs and Bosniaks, while some in the Catholic hierarchy in Croatia quietly criticized the barbarity, "the Franciscans played a very bad role. They have not dissociated themselves from the worst of Tudjman's policies."[17]

The exclusivist Croat nationalism of the Franciscan monasteries in Herzegovina, honed by centuries of competion with their Serbian Orthodox rivals for Christian souls, was clear. But the popular charge in French and British media that the Vatican was manipulating Balkan politics in the 1990s on behalf of the national Croat agenda—or in the hope that Croat Catholics would now supply the surplus of priests for global missions that the Poles no longer did—was at best dubious. Pope John Paul II visited Croatia three times toward the end of his reign, in 1994, 1998, and 2003, but he did not endorse its partisan politics. And in the postwar period the role of the Christian Democratic parties in Germany and Austria, according to Banac, has been to counsel Croatian Catholics to mend relations with minority Serbs and fulfill all the requirements for EU membership.

Zagreb in the Aftermath

The Croatia that emerged victorious as its army became an effective fighting force in 1995 did not endear itself to its neighbors. For some years after Dayton it continued to covet Herzegovina and maneuvered to annex out of Bosnia-Herzegovina what local Croats had proclaimed the para-state of "Herceg-Bosna." The Croatian Community of Herceg-Bosna, with Mostar as its capital, was born as Croatian forces were recapturing the western part of Mostar from Serb troops in summer 1992. Its founders saw their ultimate goal as a Greater Croatia, whose boundaries would approximate those of Ustashi Croatia and, as much as possible, medieval Croatia; Tudjman planned to move Croats there to reinforce demographic claims to the territory.[18] At that point the Croats blocked the transport of weapons to Bosniaks, their supposed allies against the beseiging Serbs, and began expelling Bosniaks from some of the villages in the region. By spring 1993 the Croats, by now in tacit alliance with the Serbs, were battling openly with Bosniaks and, in the areas they controlled, conducting the same kind of systematic ethnic cleansing as Serbs had perfected in Croat and Bosniak villages. They herded Bosniaks into concentration camps where they were beaten and starved. They shelled and destroyed the graceful sixteenth-century Mostar bridge built by Suleiman the Magnificent, just because it was a Bosniak symbol.[19]

Zagreb's original "Homeland War" of defense of Croatian territory against Serb attacks in 1991 thus became a war of conquest in Bosnia in 1993, then turned into a defensive counterattack to push Serb forces (and Serb civilians) out of Croatia proper in 1995.[20] As the Croatian and Bosnian wars ended in 1995, fewer than half of the 600,000 Serbs who had lived in Croatia before the war remained there.[21] With barely concealed disgust, reporters Laura Silber and Allan Little concluded shortly after the Dayton Accord that Franjo Tudjman was the "big winner" of the war and that the West would overlook his "complicity in atrocities" in order to secure peace.[22] For his part, as late as April 1999 President Tudjman derisively told one of his ministers in private, "There is no serious man who does not claim that Bosnia will fall apart."[23]

In the midst of the war fever, Zagreb's Cardinal Franjo Kuharic was a notable dissenter. Much of the Catholic hierarchy in Herzegovina and in Croatia itself applauded the drive to help dismember Bosnia, but Cardinal Kuharic, and even Herzegovina's Cardinal Vinko Puljic—concerned about the possible consequences for scattered Croat Catholics outside Herzegovina— did not. The two cardinals publicly opposed Tudjman's Bosnia policy (as did the Vatican behind the scenes, even if Tudjman spun Pope John Paul II's visit to Croatia in 1994 as a personal endorsement). Cardinal Kuharic could be faulted for not protesting Tudjman's policies more vigorously and for not curbing the chauvinists in the Catholic clergy, but his personal position was clear. He fully backed the fight to free the homeland from Serb occupation, but he openly condemned both the Croatian takeover of Herzegovina and the murder of elderly Serbs as Croatian forces retook Krajina in 1995.[24]

As late as 2001, well after Tudjman's death, the congress of the Croatian Democratic Union (HDZ) in Mostar—which still ruled Herzegovina as its barony, regardless of what the new government in Zagreb was saying— declared its intent to set up a "self-governing council" in Bosnia, in contra-vention of the Dayton Accord.[25] And when the international high representa-tive in Bosnia-Herzegovina ordered a raid on the Hercegovacka Banka in Mostar in April 2001, well-organized mobs led by Croat plainclothes police-men and the canton interior minister beat up officials of the international authorities and the Bosnia-Herzegovina Federation, torched international vehicles, and forced the return of some confiscated documents by threatening to execute hostages. International auditors were not surprised to find direct links between the bank, the HDZ, and criminal mafias.[26]

Change came faster in Croatia proper than in Herzegovina. Within weeks of Tudjman's death, nationalism's stranglehold on liberalism weakened; suddenly, chauvinist passions were no longer all-consuming. In the parliamentary elections on January 3, 2000, voters, fed up with the self-enrichment and corruption of HDZ politicians and high unemployment, voted out the party that had ruled in authoritarian fashion for a decade. Social Democrat Ivica Racan—a man who was born in a Nazi forced labor camp in Germany, almost died in a car crash in the 1970s, and thereafter had to relearn how to walk, read, and write—won the vote decisively with a non-nationalist coalition. In an equally surprising upset, Stipe Mesic was elected president immediately thereafter over the HDZ candidate, served as a nonparty president of all Croats, and thereafter actively supported the institutional shrinkage of his own presidential power and enhancement of parliamentary power.[27]

Mesic was well known. Like Tudjman, he had been imprisoned in the early 1970s for "counterrevolutionary intrigues"—that is, for promoting the "Croatian Spring," a mix of literary nationalism, liberal oppostion to Belgrade's centralism, and agitation to send less of the hard-currency tourist revenues from the Adriatic coast to other parts of Yugoslavia.[28] After Mesic got out of jail, he nonetheless rose in Communist politics and by 1991 became the last rotating president of Yugoslavia before the country disintegrated. He joined Tudjman in declaring Croatian independence, and was a close adviser of the president. This fairly typical résumé for an old apparatchik gave little hint that Mesic would be a convinced democratic reformer—except for one major anomaly: when the Croatian army turned against the Bosniaks and began conquering Herzegovina through force and ethnic cleansing, he broke with Tudjman. It was thus in character when Mesic, on his inauguration day in February 2000, called for letting Hague Tribunal investigators inspect a mass grave thought to contain the bodies of Serbs murdered by Croats.

The new president and prime minister opened the country to the West, brought Croatia into NATO's Partnership for Peace within months, halted the worst harassment of journalists, cut support for Croat separatists in Herzegovina, promised to cooperate with the Hague Tribunal, launched economic reforms, and got tourism revenues to rise again. By autumn they had begun talks with the EU on a Stabilization and Association Agreement, the Western Balkan precursor of membership negotiations. And once Milosevic was ousted from office and sent to the Hague, the Croatian and Serb governments began probing a reconciliation that by September of 2003 would lead to cautious mutual apologies.

It was an astonishing turnaround—or at least it was a turnaround in the areas the prime minister and president could control. As in most of the Balkan states, the most important institutions that eluded control were the security services, which acted autonomously in what soon became a fierce controversy over the handling of those charged by the Hague Tribunal's prosecutors. Initially, as long as Serbs were the main indictees, ordinary Croats welcomed the tribunal's justice. And even when the ICTY indicted the first Croats, popular outrage was restrained, since the early charges dealt with events in Bosnia-Herzegovina rather than in Croatia proper. Disquiet grew as the tribunal moved up the chain of responsibility from the lower ranks that physically executed atrocities to senior commanders in the Bosnia-Herzegovina and then the Croatian theaters.

In August 2000 Milan Levar, a Croat who had testified at the Hague Tribunal in 1997 about mass executions of Serbs by Croats in his home town, was murdered. In response, the government arrested sixty-two people, including the suspected assassins, some military officers, and more war crimes suspects. Unrest mounted, and in 2001, when the ICTY began indicting some of the heroes of the Homeland War, veterans' associations and HDZ factions led a storm of public demonstrations. To many Croats, the new indictments constituted "criminalization" of their war of survival and was manifestly unfair in equating the helpless victims with the aggressors.[29] When a Rijeka court issued an arrest warrant for ex-general Mirko Norac in February 2001, 100,000 to 150,000 demonstrators turned out in the Split region to protest for several days against the arrest and the Croatian government. A Croat witness to the central atrocity in the case had already been blown up by a bomb in front of his house; that killer was never found.[30] President Mesic, whose competences covered foreign and security policy, fired seven Tudjman-era generals who led demonstrations (though he let them receive their pensions) and forbade army officers from expressing political views. He was obeyed only grudgingly, but he was obeyed.

When General Ante Gotovina was indicted four months later—just as Croats were glued to their TV sets watching Goran Ivanisevic win the Wimbledon tennis crown—hagiographic posters of Gotovina went up overnight around the country, the Adriatic city of Zadar made its famous son an honorary citizen, and prominent personalities accused the Hague Tribunal of plotting to block Croatia's entry into the EU. Gotovina had started his military career as a teenager in the French Foreign Legion and had served time in a French jail for jewelry theft. He returned to Croatia when his skills as a killer were especially needed, while he was under investigation in France for an abduction. He rose swiftly in the new army to the rank of general, with over-all operations command for part of Operation Storm in 1995. The ICTY indictment charged him with "murder of at least 150 Krajina Serbs" in that operation, along with "persecutions, murder, forced displacement, plunder of public or private property, wanton destruction of cities, towns or villages," arson, killing of livestock, and spoiling of wells. "The effect of these violent and intimidating acts was a deportation and/or displacement of tens of thousands of Krajina Serbs to Bosnia and Herzegovina and Serbia," the prosecution charged.[31] As a professional courtesy, the Hague Tribunal confidentially informed the Zagreb government a few days beforehand that it would indict Gotovina; that advance warning gave the Croat security services enough time to whisk him away and arrange a luxury globe-trotting lifestyle for their war hero for the next four years, while he evaded capture.[32] In July 2001 the Racan government narrowly survived a vote of confidence on the issue of its declared intent to deliver Gotovina to the Hague, should it find him. In response to the prodding of Western officials, the government protested that Gotovina was not in Croatia, and with his French passport, could be anywhere in the world.

By fall 2001, when the government persuaded a second indicted general to surrender to the tribunal, the wave of popular indignation seemed to have crested. Only 20,000 instead of the planned 100,000 rode to Zagreb from Herzegovina and other ultranationalist strongholds on free buses to demonstrate "in defense of the honor of the Homeland War."[33] But the controversy boiled up again with every new indictment. Each time, Mesic would contend, passionately, that "extreme political circles" must not stir up "anti-European and anti-democratic" emotions, "isolate" Croatia, and block its road to the EU. Repeatedly, the government made the same argument to counter political resistance to the economic liberalization that gored many an ox.[34] Yet under the constant pressure, Prime Minister Racan grew timid. He delayed the extradition of indicted former army chief of staff Janko Bobetko until he was found to be too ill to stand trial and died. He froze privatization and guaranteed the debts of several bankrupt companies, moves that placed a severe drag on the budget. He hesitated to bring back the hundreds of thousands of Serb refugees who had been driven out of Croatia during the war. And he held back from cleaning out the politicized and unqualified judges who had been hastily put on the bench when Croatia became independent.[35]

In February 2003, Croatia, having concluded its apprentice Stabilization and Association Agreement, made its formal application to become a candidate for proper EU membership. In the abstract, this move was uncontroversial, since all the parliamentary parties took it for granted that Croats were European and should join European institutions; in Croatia there was no equivalent of the suspicion by the Polish Catholic peasant Self-Defense or Serb Radical movements that the EU would dilute their national identity. Some 80 percent of Croats at large also favored EU membership. The rub came not in any ideological hostility to or fear of "Europe," but in the refusal to pay the price of cooperation with the ICTY. Because of Zagreb's failure to send Gotovina to stand trial, the British and Dutch were refusing to ratify even the Stabilization and Association Agreement, and it was clear that they would not let the Croats proceed far on the track toward full membership until they sacrificed their most famous war hero to the Hague. On this issue, pressure worked both ways. Because the Croats were united in seeing themselves as Europeans, the EU had greater leverage over them than over ambivalent Serbs, and could insist on the high price of extradition of indictees without fearing that this tough love might sabotage pro-European politicians and strengthen anti-European and antidemocratic forces in Croatia. On the other hand, Zagreb could and did argue to Brussels that if the EU did not admit Croats, who stood at the front of the line and desired membership, it would discourage less well prepared and less determined Western Balkan countries and invite a political backlash against Europe and its democratic and market standards. Specifically, under the quadripartite Adriatic Charter that was brokered and joined by the United States in May 2003, Croatia accepted the role of a model for the much poorer and less stable Macedonia and Albania in seeking to join both the EU and NATO; if the EU shut the door on Zagreb just because of Gotovina's truancy, Zagreb contended, then Skopje and Tirana could easily get disillusioned and stop their reforms altogether.

In this standoff, new elections were set for November 2003. Four years after the 2000 vote, the party roles were reversed. This time it was the Social Democrats who were worn out from the strains of office and were blamed by voters for all the hardships of transition. The HDZ was the fresh face—and it comfortably defeated the Racan coalition. The new party leader was Ivo Sanader, fifty years old, with a doctorate in comparative literature from the University of Innsbruck, who had been Tudjman's chief of staff in the mid-1990s. For several years, Sanader had been quietly sidelining the party's most rabid ultranationalists, especially those in the chauvinist hotbed of Herzegovina, who would have been more than willing to forfeit Croatia's future in the EU to maintain Croat purity. These hard-liners mattered, since Croats in Bosnia held dual citizenship at the time and voted in Croatian elections. His aims on becoming prime minister, Sanader said, were to turn the HDZ into a normal European Christian Democratic party, to bring his country into NATO (and possibly even get an American base in Croatia), and to catch up with Bulgaria and Romania to enter the EU as a full member by 2007. He did not stress publicly that this could happen only if the fugitive Gotovina went to the Hague, but this prerequisite "cash" payment (the meaning of the nickname *Gotovina*) was clearly understood.

Within his own party and parliamentary caucus, then, Sanader still had to contend with ideological nationalists who lionized Gotovina. After the election he won an important victory at a HDZ party convention that confirmed his moderate course—and he set a conciliatory marker by inviting a small Serb party to join his coalition and fill one cabinet slot.[36] Initially, he did not, however, try to root out the old boy network in the security services.

In foreign policy, Sanader stressed again and again that Croats share "European values." He opened up the country's security archives to some extent for Western inspection, in order to convince critics that Gotovina was not in Croatia. He satisfied Western governments sufficiently to win the status of official candidacy for EU membership in June 2004, with negotiations scheduled to begin in March of 2005—if, it was implied, Gotovina were extradited in the meantime.[37] When Gotovina still had not surfaced by March, the EU refused to proceed with the talks.[38] Carla Del Ponte—the formidable chief prosecutor at the Hague Tribunal, who had to spend as much time badgering Serbia and Croatia to produce indictees as she did preparing her legal briefs—charged publicly that Croatian "state structures" were helping Gotovina evade arrest. Prime Minister Sanader denied the accusation and demanded that she produce proof of her assertion.[39] For its part, Belgrade—which after long stonewalling had suddenly sent more than a dozen indictees to the Hague in the half year from the end of 2004 to spring of 2005—also failed to deliver either of the most wanted Serb indictees, Radovan Karadzic and Ratko Mladic. For the same reason of noncooperation with the tribunal, then, the EU held both in limbo: Zagreb, on the brink of membership negotiations; Belgrade, on the brink of a Feasibility Study to prepare for the entry-level Stabilization and Association Agreement.[40]

The government also had to deal with issues other than Gotovina's whereabouts, of course. Even though Croatia was richer than other Western Balkan countries, now that tourist spending had resumed on the Adriatic coast, it was undergoing all the usual agonies both of postconflict reconstruction and of the fundamental modernization that would have been necessary even if there had been no war.[41] Its economy was some years away from recovering even prewar production. The Western tourist trade, while welcome, was pushing prices in Zagreb up to something approaching Paris or Berlin levels. Unemployment was high; privatization lagged; industrial dinosaurs could not be disposed of properly because of political quarrels; and foreign direct investment preferred to go elsewhere, as long as Zagreb's future in the EU was not assured. Deficits had to be brought down from 6.3 percent in 2003 to 4.9 percent in 2004 and 4 percent in 2005 in order to qualify for standby support from the International Monetary Fund.[42] The army had to be downsized and retrained to become more professional and compatible with NATO. And the government had to cope with the usual charges of corruption; one foreign minister resigned over allegations of graft.

In addition, the country had bilateral disputes with neighbors, including the bad blood left between it and Serbia and a long-standing border dispute with Slovenia.[43] Sanader would not pay the first postwar visit by a Croatian prime minister to Belgrade (and agree on mutual protecton of minorities while there) until November 2004, nine years after the end of the war.[44] Croat businessmen in Vukovar, site of the 1991 war's first big atrocity, would not begin to meet regularly with Serb counterparts from across the Danube to plot the cross-border region's economic future until 2005.[45] Croatia would not begin to let Serb refugees return to Krajina in significant numbers—or to let potential returnees know in advance if they were on secret Croatian wanted lists—until after President Mesic visited Serbia and Montenegro in July 2005, talked with Krajina refugees there, and negotiated an agreement that, in principle, those who had committed war crimes should be held accountable for them, but whole nations should not be tarred by collective guilt.[46] Vojislav Kostunica would not pay the first postwar visit by a Serbian prime minister to Zagreb until November 2005, to discuss missing persons, return of property, and mutual trade and investment—and to get Sanader's promise to facilitate the return of Serb refugees to Croatia by the end of 2006.[47]

In the space where domestic and foreign policy overlapped, Sanader had to walk a fine line, allaying northern European misgivings about Croatia's democratic credentials because of lingering glorification of the Ustasha movement—while at the same time not alienating important factions in his HDZ. As the campaign for the next presidential election, in January 2005, heated up, clashes between Sanader and right-wing nationalists took the form of the competitive construction and dismantling of monuments to Ustasha leaders—and the continued poster wars over Gotovina and Ustasha chief Ante Pavelic. In late 2004 the government ordered the removal of statues of Ustasha heroes Jure Francetic and Mile Budak in central Croatia and had the police surreptitiously rip down (in the middle of the night) posters of Gotovina that had remained on walls in the center of Zadar since the 2001 protests. In December, however, when the election campaign was at its most intense, it did let World War II veterans march through Zadar with placards of Ante Pavelic. (In the same month, after a journalist let it be known that counterintelligence agents had tried to intimidate her into spying on Mesic's private life, Mesic fired the young Herzegovinan whom Sanader had appointed as head of counterintelligence.)[48] In January 2005 in the outskirts of Split, unknown persons erected overnight a memorial to Francetic and Budak—to show the extreme right's anger at Sanader's betrayal of the Ustasha cause and the prime minister's cooperation with the ICTY, in the view of Croatian commentator Davor Gjenero.[49] Right-wingers accused President Mesic of being a "spy" for the ICTY because he testified as a witness for the prosecution at the Hague.[50] More playfully, the radical right pressed its cause by naming a new Zadar wine after Gotovina.[51]

Whatever the other issues, though, Gotovina increasingly became the central point of EU conditionality (as delivery of Karadzic and Mladic to the Hague became the central point of conditionality for Serbia). To solve its economic and social problems, Croatia had to get into the EU, not only to gain access to greater financial aid, but also to master the skills needed in a globalized, postmodern world. And as the Hague Tribunal became far more significant than its reluctant founders would have dreamed possible, Gotovina had to be arrested if Zagreb were to get inside the EU gates. Some hard-liners who understood this stark choice began to oppose EU membership explicitly. Their numbers were far fewer, though, than would have been the case had Croats not already deemed themselves to be full Europeans. In the presidential election in January 2005, anti-European and anti-ICTY candidates Ivic Pasalic, Ljubo Cesic Rojs, and Tomislav Petrak together won less than 6 percent of the ballots. Stipe Mesic, just turned seventy, was reelected with a resounding two-thirds of the vote. He and Sanader together (and sometimes in conflict) had managed, gradually, to unbundle the strands of Croat pride and angst from the nastier strands of chauvinism, bloodlust, and the sense of special victimization that justifies any means.

Denouement

In spring 2005 both Croatia's and Serbia's relations with the European Union became entangled with the EU's own identity crisis. French and Dutch voters, angry over globalization and immigrants, vetoed the draft EU constitutional treaty that was, among other things, supposed to lay the foundation for the further accession of new members. EU planning ground to a halt; a consensus began forming that final entry talks should go ahead as planned with Bulgaria and Romania, and with Turkey too, but that other countries' negotiations would have to wait.[52] In Croatia 57 percent of the public turned against the EU membership that seemed to be slipping out of its grasp.[53]

For Zagreb the deus ex machina arrived in the form of Austria, which threatened to veto opening of the long-planned accession negotiations with Ankara on October 3 unless talks also began with its old Hapsburg protégé, Croatia. At the thirteenth hour (literally), in the peculiar working style of EU summits, the twenty-four other EU members conceded the point in order to avert yet another rebuff to Turkey in its forty-year quest to joint the EC/EU. Carla Del Ponte—who less than two weeks earlier had accused Zagreb and the Vatican of hiding Gotovina in one of the many secluded Franciscan monasteries in Croatia and Herzegovina—was hastily recruited to certify that Zagreb was now cooperating sufficiently with the ICTY to justify opening membership negotiations.[54] Choosing her words carefully, she confirmed that "Croatia's cooperation in the transmission of requested documents is indeed currently the best of all the countries in the region"—but she added that Gotovina still needed to appear at the tribunal.[55]

Zagreb was, in fact, cooperating. Behind the scenes, Western governments had decided to let Sanader prove his bona fides and had given him enough of their own intelligence on the top ten or so people in Gotovina's support network in Croatian security structures to enable the prime minister to crack down on them, if he had the political will to do so.[56] In a clear change of atmosphere, in September 2005 a Zagreb court convicted five former Interior Ministry reservists of torturing and killing Serb civilians in 1991; and the Split War Crimes Tribunal, on the orders of the Croatian Supreme Court, opened a retrial of eight former special police who had been acquitted in 2002 of torturing and killing Serbs a decade earlier. In the original trial of these eight, the first indictment of Croats for war crimes to come before Croatian courts after the Croat-Serb war (at the instigation of a Croat human rights NGO), witnesses had felt too intimidated to appear or to give detailed testimony. At the retrial, however, enough evidence was provided to convict them all; in March 2006 they were sentenced to jail terms ranging from six to eight years. There were no major public protests.[57]

The European Union duly began negotiations with both Turkey and Croatia on October 3 (with a bit of clock-stopping). To treat Zagreb and Belgrade equally, the EU also started talks with Serbia and Montenegro on its Feasibility Study. And in order not to leave Bosnia-Herzegovina isolated, the EU also began Stabilization and Association negotiations with Sarajevo, as soon as the

Republika Srpska stopped stonewalling and acquiesced in the formation of national Bosnian police under European supervision.[58] Subsequently, even though Gotovina was still at large, the tribunal gave a fresh vote of confidence in Zagreb by transferring the trials of two indicted Croatian general officers to Croatian courts for the first time. Notably, one of these was Mirko Norac, whose arrest had set off mass protests in 2001; he had subsequently been convicted by the ICTY on an earlier indictment and was serving a twelve-year jail sentence in Croatia.[59]

The Gotovina denouement came in December 2005. On tips provided by Western intelligence and augmented by new information from the Croatian security forces, Spanish police arrested Ante Gotovina in the restaurant of a luxury hotel in Tenerife. He was unarmed and put up no resistance. He was flown to the Hague in a Spanish military plane and pleaded not guilty to the charges of murder, arson, and intimidation. Prime Minister Sanader quickly met with senior officials of the Catholic Church and also publicly called for calm. Significantly, no prominent politician took part in the biggest pro-Gotovina demonstration, in Split; and in all the protests around the country, the main, moderate demand was simply that the government help provide for Gotovina's legal defense and support his family. The government immediately unfroze his pension account, which it had blocked the previous March under international pressure.

As Gotovina appeared at the Hague, the Croatian interior minister fired Zagreb's chief of police, and prosecutor Carla Del Ponte announced that she would reopen the case against Tihomir Blaskic, a Croat army colonel (later general) who had been sentenced by the ICTY to forty-five years in prison for the massacre of Bosniak civilians in the Herceg-Bosna para-state, but was freed on appeal. There was no official confirmation, but the retrial seemed to have been occasioned by incriminating new information winkled out of the Croatian security archives.[60] After an early period in which Croats viewed the ICTY "as a direct threat to Croatia's newly-realised independent statehood, the growing security of its situation worked together with the sustained pressure of international agents to promote a fairly general acceptance of the importance of the work of the Tribunal—especially among its political elite," concluded John B. Allcock in the Purdue Scholars' Initiative report on the court.[61]

Gotovina's years as a fugitive ended, then, when mainstream Croat conservative thinking evolved to favor the practical benefits of joining the EU over the romantic satisfaction of harboring a war hero/criminal—and when the man on the street no longer idealized wanton killing in the name of the Croatian nation. The tipping point came when a critical mass of ordinary and elite Croats defined their national identity less in monoethnicity than in modern European democracy.

With Gotovina in custody, six indicted fugitives remained at large, all Serbs: Radovan Karadzic and Ratko Mladic, the former political and military leaders of the Bosnian Serbs; Zdravko Tolimir, a former Bosnian Serb general; Goran Hadzic, the former president of the Krajina Serbian Republic in Croatia; Stojan Zupljanin, the former commander of the Bosnian Serb police; and Vlastimir Djordjevic, the former Serbian police general. In the wake of Gotovina's arrest, Serbian President Boris Tadic was emboldened to accuse Prime Minister Vojislav Kostunica of isolating Serbia internationally by refusing to send these men to the Hague.[62] Western diplomats nourished the hope that the Croat elites' evolution away from an exclusive ethnic to a more expansive European identity, with its approaching reward of early EU membership, might prove to be an example for the Serbian elites.

CHAPTER SIX

REVISING DAYTON'S BOSNIA

No spot in the Balkans illustrates the fundamental conundrum of institution, state, and especially democracy building by outsiders in a failed state more vividly than Bosnia-Herzegovina. Like Kosovo, it was clearly set up after the fighting ended as an international protectorate (though neither is formally so labeled); foreign administrators were made responsible, directly or ultimately, not only for foreign policy and security but also for domestic governance. Unlike Kosovo, however, Bosnia-Herzegovina was internationally recognized as a state from the beginning, and had no need to clarify its legal status. This has made it a somewhat more transparent test of state building than the anomalous Kosovo.

The patron of the Bosnian protectorate is the "international community"—de jure, still the Dayton signatories, operating as the Peace Implementation Council (PIC); de facto, the West (including Japan), which finances 85 percent of its civilian budget and still holds ultimate authority, though it now wields its power with more restraint than in the recent past.[1] The European Union, which already pays 53 percent of Bosnia's budget and in late 2004 succeeded NATO in command of peacekeeping forces (under the "Berlin-plus" arrangements that let the EU borrow NATO assets), will soon have full operative responsibility for Bosnia. But in practice it will cooperate closely with the United States, which maintains a small contingent of forces under an independent NATO headquarters that both the EU and Bosnians want to preserve as security insurance.[2]

Basically, the conundrum arises from the fact that outsiders can induce self-sustaining democratic change only by persuading local actors to want such change and then empowering them to effect it in a resistant environment, by blocking criminals or bullies and helping to introduce more open politics, rule of law, and increasingly responsive institutions. Yet the evisceration of society in civil war often confronts foreign would-be enablers with a range of unpleasant choices, from passively accepting stagnation and crime to enacting change by fiat over the heads of local players. The more fiat there is, the more local actors are disempowered. But the more interveners incline to patience in identifying and nurturing local leaders, the greater the risk of forfeiting momentum. Furthermore, as virtually all Western postmortems of the Bosnian experience point out, if elections and other democratic forms are brought in too early, they can serve to polarize a conflicted society rather than move it toward urgently needed commonality, tolerance, and compromise.

In this context, the case for a positive gloss on the international community's performance in Bosnia is this: despite the Rube Goldberg institutional construction of the 1995 Dayton Accord—a single state of Bosnia-Herzegovina containing two "entities," the Republika Srpska (RS, or Serb Republic) and the (Muslim-Croat) Federation of Bosnia and Herzegovina; and within the Federation, ten cantons to reflect ethnic distribution of Bosniaks and Croats—the nominally sovereign state of Bosnia-Herzegovina has survived.[3] It has remained at peace for a decade, and has even managed to overcome many of the convoluted administrative layers that Dayton established as the price of a cease-fire. The international overseers have progressively cajoled or coerced Bosnian politicians to accept single license plates (so a Bosniak who is driving his car into the RS does not immediately announce his ethnicity and invite hostility); a single currency and passport system; a single customs system, with Bosniak, Serb, and Croat officials assigned to border crossings irrespective of the majority ethnicity of the neighboring district; a single army command; a single criminal intelligence agency; the breakup of the old Yugoslav defense industry in the Bosnian mountains, which had been shipping weapons clandestinely to Saddam Hussein and other unsavory customers; and the return of more than a million refugees. Moreover, in the RS they have effected a managed transition from the de facto rule of a still-triumphant Radovan Karadzic in 1996 to his ouster; and in 2004, the first public apology by the RS government for the Srebrenica massacre, and its delivery to prosecutors in 2005 of a list of 17,000 Serb perpetrators and abettors.

At the end of 2004 security duties passed without incident from the NATO-led Stabilization Forces (SFOR) to a European Union Force (EUFOR) contingent (and the small residual NATO unit under U.S. command). In 2005 the Bosnian Serbs finally agreed, on paper at least, to a unified national police force.[4] In 2006 Bosnia collected a nationwide value added tax for the first time and opened Stabilization and Association talks with the EU. Bosnia's seven largest parties also agreed tentatively on the framework for a new constitution, with strengthened state-level institutions that the EU requires as a precondition for signing a Stabilization and Association Agreement.[5] Finally, by now, RS politics has basically been separated from Belgrade politics.

The case for a negative gloss is this: the achievements won by such huge international efforts and the outlay of $4.5 billion for the 4.5 million Bosnians in the first two postwar years alone amount to only the bare minimum of what is needed to prevent its spiral back down into a failing or failed state.[6] The internationals had to expend enormous energy just to correct the congenital institutional defects of Dayton; they did not rise above that to build either a genuine state with a sense of common citizenship or a self-sustaining process. Worse, the Dayton Accord and its follow-on international stewardship in a sense legitimated the ruthless ethnic cleansing of 1992–95, leaving today, after extensive refugee returns, only an estimated 15 to 20 percent of non-Serbs in the Republika Srpska and Serbs in the Federation.[7] Many refugees have in any case "returned" only to sell their houses, not to live in them. The police have never been vetted thoroughly enough to destroy systemic links with traffickers of weapons, drugs, and women.[8] Crime is still rampant.

The positive attainments of the internationals have been produced by fiat—including High Representative Paddy Ashdown's wholesale dismissal of fifty-nine government officials and nine senior security and police officials of the Republika Srpska as late as 2004. And the successes may not survive, once Western voters tire of the high costs and end their Balkan engagement. Bosnia and the Western Balkans as a whole remain plagued, in the words of Francois Heisbourg, head of the Foundation for Strategic Research in Paris, with "unmitigated levels of ethnic hatred, the highest unemployment in Europe, the poorest education system in Europe, smuggling, human trafficking, the arms trade—all things that affect Western Europe."[9] Moreover, successes were won at the heavy price of denying policy ownership to local politicians and giving the latter an alibi for not wrestling out political compromises among themselves. Lord Ashdown, in particular, taught not democracy but only subservience to the mighty internationals, this critique runs.[10]

Brcko District

"Nothing of this could have been accomplished if there had been no international supervisor," declared Brcko mayor Branko Damjanac.[11] He checked off the things that had been put right in a few short years in the war-ravaged Bosnian northeast: refugees have returned, repossessing their properties; a multiethnic police force has been established that is trusted by the populace;

a multiethnic judiciary has been set up that is widely seen as fair; Bosniak, Serb, and Croat children are educated in the same classes—uniquely in Bosnia-Herzegovina—with an ethnic mix of teachers; customs are collected, with a reputation for greater efficiency and less corruption than elsewhere in Bosnia-Herzegovina, and providing enough revenues to fund the local government and pay twice or four times as much per capita as any other part of the country to the national government; and the initial apartheid ethnic sectors of the district have been melded into one. "I maintain that if there were no supervisor and international community present here, nothing of this could have been accomplished, and we would probably still live in two divided sectors."

Damjanac, a Serb married to a Muslim, stayed in Brcko throughout the war, even when many others fled. "My wife keeps telling me when things get tough that even in the most difficult times I had a clear and sober head, and said that one day things would be all right, and all this cruelty would be part of the past. To be completely honest, there were moments when I did get discouraged. A lot of ugly things happened between the citizens of our town during the war. Hate was created. I can't describe in words how people actually behaved then. But somehow, I knew we would manage to live together again. You can't change nature. You can't make some kind of stall and divide it into small compartments and close them off from each other. After the war we divided the electricity, the railroad, the rivers, the roads—everything, for heaven's sake!"

It's like a marriage, he continued. "I have been married to my wife—I exaggerate—a hundred years. And it's normal that there have been moments when we were angry with each other and didn't understand each other. In such situations I always used to say to my wife: when you are mad at me over something, or when I make some mistake, try not to lose your temper, and I will try not to lose my temper, because tomorrow morning we have to get up together again, sit at the table together, and think about our children and what is going to happen in our lives. And if we have said things to hurt each other, it will be hard to overcome those words.

"Even during the war people did try to help each other, to rescue each other, without regard for nationality.[12] They visited each other and sent packages of aid, without paying attention to nationality. They did not forget that we were born together, spent our childhoods together, and created many wonderful things together. But when the war started here, there were people who thought they could just erase the old world they had lived in and create a new world.

"I'll tell you a story. My wife is a Bosniak. And during the war for a while my children attended school in Subotica, in Serbia. One weekend my wife and I went to visit them. We came to the Bijeljina border, and they didn't want to let any Muslims through. So I said, 'What do you propose I do? Throw her into the Sava River?! I've been married to my wife for twenty years. I have two children by her. And I'll tell you something. They don't want to see me; they want to see her!'" The soldiers let them both pass.

Other citizens of Brcko were less fortunate.

The Serb military preparation for the Bosnian incursion began well before the fighting broke out in Bosnia, before the EU recognized Slovenia and Croatia as new sovereign states, and before the Bosnian referendum on and declaration of independence. Even as fighting progressed in Croatia in 1991, the Yugoslav People's Army (JNA) followed its earlier pattern in Croatia, separating Bosnian Territorial Defense Forces (TOs) into Serb and non-Serb units; it transfered weapons from its own arsenals to the all-Serb TOs and to Serb paramilitaries and trained them intensively, while stripping the non-Serb units of rifles, artillery, and antitank rockets. In Brcko, as elsewhere, Muslim officials actually abetted the disarming of non-Serbs. Complying with the Bosnian government's policy, they attempted to confiscate weapons from all civilians equally, in order to avoid provoking the Serbs. In practice, however, Bosnian Serbs refused to give up their guns. Thus both the unannounced Serb actions and the official Bosnian operation disproportionately disarmed Bosnian Muslims and Croats, even as militant Serbs acquired more and more weapons. Hardly seeking to disguise its steering hand in Bosnia at this point, the JNA stationed soldiers at strategic spots and in Serb neighborhoods in Brcko, and compelled the city police to let its personnel accompany them on patrols.[13]

The parallel political preparation for the war can be traced back to April 1991, when Bosnian Serb leaders began forming "associations of municipalities" that were initially legal under the republic's laws, but soon began operating illegally as para-governments. By September, the associations were upgraded to "Serbian Autonomous Regions" that requested protection by the JNA over the head of the government in Sarajevo. In November, Bosnian Serbs approved the formation of the Serbian Autonomous Regions in a referendum.[14] On December 19, 1991, the leadership of the Bosnian branch of the Serbian Democratic Party (SDS) under Radovan Karadzic—"almost certainly under the tutelage of the Serbian Security Service"—laid out confidential, detailed plans for well-prepared shadow governments ("crisis headquarters") to take control of the Bosnian localities earmarked for Serb takeover.[15]

With this softening up, after a staged provocation on April 2, 1992, Arkan and Seselj's feared paramilitaries stormed into Bijeljina wearing black balaclavas and jackboots and firing machine guns, routed the makeshift Muslim militia, searched house to house for young or educated or well-to-do Muslims, shot them in the head, and left their bodies in the streets. The JNA, which had ringed the city with artillery, shelled non-Serb neighborhoods to rubble. On April 30 the exercise was repeated in Brcko; non-Serb political, academic, and military leaders were killed or expelled as the Serb forces secured Bosnia's peripheries en route to conquering two-thirds of Bosnian territory.[16] Arkan's thugs, in coordination with the JNA, restricted the movement of or evicted non-Serbs, dismissed them from their jobs, and turned over the local police, radio and television, and civil administration to the local Serb-only crisis headquarters. The Serb forces looted non-Serb neighborhoods in an organized fashion, destroyed mosques and Roman Catholic churches, resettled Serbs in those non-Serb houses that had not been bulldozed, and had an administration in place almost immediately, with official letterhead, documents, and stamps, to process expulsions.[17] Non-Serbs were intimidated into leaving. If they did not, they risked psychopathic orgies of murder, with many of the corpses (and possibly even still-living bodies) casually dumped into a local animal feed plant.[18] An unknown number of persons were killed or driven out of Brcko; families were severed. Fifteen thousand out of the town's 25,000 housing units were destroyed or severely damaged.[19] Its community was shattered.

After the JNA formally became the totally Serb-run Army of Yugoslavia (VJ), thousands of VJ troops with more than a hundred tanks were openly involved in securing the Posavina Corridor at Brcko in early 1993. This corridor was especially important to the Serbs. It was the hinge that would connect an ethnically cleansed Drina Valley in southeastern Bosnia (once Srebrenica, Zepa, and Gorazde were mopped up) with the ethnically cleansed northwest around Banja Luka and Prijedor, and connect Serbia proper with the new Serb strongholds in Krajina and other noncontiguous parts of Croatia. At Brcko the corridor was at times only five kilometers wide and thus "the Serb state's Achilles heel," the "sine qua non of the Serbian project."[20]

This was the legacy that faced the negotiators at the Dayton talks in 1995, as Milosevic insisted that the Serbs must be awarded the Brcko corridor in the final apportionment of territory between Serbs, Bosniaks, and Croats, and Bosnian president Alija Izetbegovic insisted equally vehemently that the Bosnians must get back the city that had been stolen from them. After three weeks of wrestling had resolved all other disputes at Dayton, Brcko was the last unresolved issue. It would have torpedoed the talks altogether had not Milosevic, just before the American "drop-dead time limit," abruptly agreed to a binding future arbitration on the status of Brcko.[21]

The arbitration took a long time. Not until 1997 did an interim award provide for a Brcko government, under an international supervisor operating under the Office of the High Representative (OHR) in Sarajevo. Not until 1998 did the presiding arbitrator, Roberts Owen, citing lack of cooperation by the Bosnian Serbs, give the supervisor the same sweeping powers as the high representative for Bosnia, under a supplemental award; and not until 2000 would the final award be completed under the General Framework Agreement for Peace in Bosnia and Herzegovina.

If Bosnia was one of the purest tests of attempted democratization by foreigners, Brcko was the most pure of the many local tests within Bosnia. In trying to avoid the dangerous polarization that early elections wrought in the rest of the country, the first supervisor of Brcko, Robert Farrand, delayed any citywide popular vote. Under the precept of establishing the rule of law before holding elections, he exercised his considerable powers by appointing the first assembly, choosing a representative spectrum of Bosniaks, Serbs, and Croats, but excluding the most hate-filled.

Under the circumstances, no one would have wagered that this would be the one spot in ex-Yugoslavia where enthusiasm for Western intervention in its most concentrated form would long survive the first flush of gratitude for rescue from murder, or that international guardianship would come to be seen as empowering rather than colonizing. Few would have predicted that Brcko would soon be the most successful municipality in Bosnia in beginning a recovery from the nightmare. Yet unlike most Bosnian towns, Brcko's ethnic mix is not lopsidedly different from its prewar proportions. Today's population of 85,000, of which some 40 percent are Bosniaks, 40 percent are Serbs (reflecting an influx of refugees, especially from the war's last exodus from Sarajevo), and 20 percent are Croats is roughly comparable to the prewar population (from the 1991 census) of 88,000, composed of 44 percent Muslims, 21 percent Serbs, and 25 percent Croats. The swiftness of reconstruction in Brcko District, by contrast with other communities destroyed in the Yugoslav wars—the sad present-day ghost of Srebrenica comes to mind—is striking.

The first, appointed assembly argued a lot, but it passed thirty needed laws and amendments depoliticizing the police, allowing choice of citizenship, regularizing illegal buildings and above all, restoring property to refugees and settling conflicting claims to housing. Under property laws quickly worked out by the Organization for Security and Cooperation in Europe (OSCE) and the Council of Europe, all of the 10,889 real estate claims registered in Brcko through 2003 were resolved administratively (rather than in lengthy court proceedings) by the end of that year; thereafter, new requests were settled as they came in. More than 5,700 houses were reconstructed for occupancy by refugees and returnees by the end of 2004, with some 2,500 houses still waiting to be rebuilt.[22] The controversial statue of Chetnik leader Draza Mihailovic erected by triumphant Serbs in the center of town was removed, under new legislation on national monuments, to the private grounds of the Orthodox church, where it could still be visited by Serbs but no longer affronted Bosniaks and Croats. Small-scale investors began to come to Brcko because of its congenial business climate and reputation for administrative honesty. The notorious "Arizona Market," a hotbed of stolen cars, drugs, and prostitution, was cleaned up and turned into a legitimate bazaar of licensed vendors.[23] Brcko's share of Bosnia's 3.7 million unexploded land mines were defused.

Brcko also led Bosnia-Herzegovina in the nationwide vetting and retraining of the judiciary under new standards of competence, nonpartisan adherence to the rule of law, and resistance to bribery or political influence; the Brcko District Judicial Commission that oversaw the legal reform was able to disband by the end of 2003. This screening was essential, given the politicization of the legal profession under Milosevic. The thoroughness of the program was unique to Bosnia in the Western Balkans; compliance with judicial standards was the first of the sixteen requirements to be checked off on the EU's 2003 Feasibility Study of changes needed to qualify Bosnia for a Stabilization and Association Agreement with the EU. As Nada Majinovic, president of the Brcko commission and a lawyer herself, explained it, the reform aimed to protect the judiciary from pressure by the executive or legislative branches, to professionalize judges and prosecutors, to ascertain that judges were neither engaged in criminal activity nor squatting in refugees' apartments, to ensure that local laws complied with the European Convention on Human Rights, to guarantee fair procedures in both civil and criminal trials, and to take investigative powers away from judges and give them instead to prosecutors.[24] Judges and prosecutors who were appointed or reappointed— 80 percent of the former judges passed nationwide, and all but two in Brcko, though only 20 percent of the higher ranks of chief prosecutors and court presidents passed—attended seminars to help them learn European legal and ethical guidelines and were given a one-year test term in office. During this period the judicial commission continued its monitoring and encouraged members of the public who had complaints to file them. The new criminal law practices did not differ greatly from the old Yugoslav system, apart from removing investigative powers from judges and introducing transparent, court-supervised plea bargaining, which helped clear the huge backlog of cases on the docket.[25] "In the past three years we have very gradually understood the essence of the new laws and implementation of them," Majinovic said, "but in the entities even today they cannot accept the changes and have major problems."

Countering false rumors elsewhere in Bosnia-Herzegovina, she stressed that Brcko judges are not paid more than those in other parts of the country. "Brcko is some kind of a thorn in the eyes of others," and for this reason, too, she found the support and pressure of the the internationals indispensable. "My theory is that outsiders, the international community, cannot impose a new positive system" on Bosnia, but what they can do is help make a more level playing field for those who do want to reform the system. "Without them the changes would not have happened. By ourselves we could have changed some things, but there would have been other things that dragged us back—people, traditions. You have to see the mentality of the people, their history, their habits, how ready they are to accept change. In the old system the executive and legislative power was always stronger than the judicial. So we have to make a major change in the heads of people so they see that the judiciary has to be independent. Even today when I meet with some Assembly members from the old system, they do not understand that they cannot influence court decisions. They think they can impose things and influence the courts the way they used to. . . . The judiciary of Brcko District was the first to start with all the major reforms; and the reelection of judges and prosecutors was the cause of much discussion and conflict between political factions, because some unknown agitators arrived. If we had not been supported by the OHR, especially the office for legal reform, I can assure you that we would not have been strong enough to resist the pressure of the legislature and the executive or to show them that we must be an independent and equal branch."

The first municipalitywide election in Brcko District, in October 2004, drew a respectable 62 percent turnout that basically opted for continuity in moderation, even if the precise coalition took a few months to form. Supervisor Susan Johnson praised the turnout as showing "strong democratic legitimacy, greater than anywhere else in Bosnia and Herzegovina."

The local pride that is developing even among the many townspeople who are new to Brcko is palpable. So is the positive view of international administrators as local boosters who can lobby for Brcko's interests in Sarajevo and help mobilize Western funding. The International Sava River Commission, which began operating in 2006, with headquarters in Zagreb, to help investors export their products more easily to European customers, is a case in point. In few other localities in ex-Yugoslavia would a mother, spotting the international supervisor on the street during the gala spring *corso* of high school graduates, spontaneously present her with the rose she was carrying. In few others, confides one young Serb, do drivers actually stop at pedestrian crossings—or the police enforce seat-belt laws, other than as an excuse to pocket bribes. In few other places would a local middle-class entrepreneur like Ilija Studen feel confident enough of the parceled region's future to found a cooking-oil firm with offices in Brcko, Vienna, Croatia, and Slovenia and promote the long-term planting of sunflowers and rapeseed throughout the sun-blessed Sava River valleys, heedless of new national borders.[26]

To illustrate the dynamics, Mayor Damjanac contrasted Brcko's recovery with the continuing ethnic animosity in Mostar. There, once the Bosniaks and Croats together had repulsed the Serb attackers, they turned their guns on each other. Croat forces gratuitously blew up the sixteenth-century bridge of Suleiman the Magnificent, which had survived all previous wars and was a UNESCO protected site.[27] "Both in Mostar and the Brcko District the population was mixed; all three peoples lived in those towns. And the war that lasted for four years here also lasted in Mostar for quite a while. Of course people started to hate each other, to have problems with each other, both on the front line and behind the lines. But during the war and especially after the war ended, people started making contacts again in Brcko. The population here is a bit softer, readier to talk with each other than in Mostar and more tolerant. Regardless of what happened to a person during the war—and very bad things happened—and regardless of their nationality, somehow people managed to get back to living with each other. They did not forget what happened, but they are working with each other, cooperating with each other, and even making new [mixed] marriages. They have accepted our need for cooperation and have built new institutions and a new life here. . . . Bosniaks again visit Serb friends on St. Sava Day. Serbs visit Bosniak friends during Ramadan. Both even attend each other's funerals. We have our problems today, but the role of Supervisor Farrand and all that followed is huge."

In Mostar "such cooperation is still not possible, even though Mostar, too, had a supervisor and the help of the international community. If you go to Mostar today, you will see from the first moment which part of the city is Bosniak, which is Croat. If you go to the Bosniak district and ask for a hotel in the Croat district, they don't even want to tell you where it is, and vice versa." Even the dead are divided, he might have added; after violent clashes between Bosniak mourners and Croat police at the Liska Street cemetery in 1997,

Bosnian Serbs and Croats exhumed their corpses from the common burial ground and moved them to segregated graveyards.[28]

An enormous amount remains to be done in Bosnia, Damjanac continued. "We always have a habit of asking how come this or that is happening in the West [when it doesn't happen here]. We forget that the West did not accomplish all this overnight. Our men here do not respect traffic signs or environmental signs; they throw garbage everywhere. When they go to the West, they respect traffic signs and environmental signs. They don't throw papers on the street, because of the mental climate—and also, the punishment is huge—so the state is functioning. So if we do the same, we have a hope of developing a democratic and uncorrupt society. We are a nation that hasn't had lots of experience. We lived in a one-party system for fifty years. And to a certain extent we are a bit primitive or uneducated. All of that has to be overcome in order to become like what Europe is today. And unfortunately, there was no generation here that lived a life without war. One generation created something, and the next generation devastated everything that was created. Now I hope we will be better at it."

Like many other Bosnians, he placed his hopes in eventually winning EU membership.

Sarajevo

The Bosnian government that took office in Sarajevo after the war ended needed to create a state and modern institutions from scratch. It had the good fortune, however, not to have to create an identity from scratch. Sarajevo, above all, has long been a rich melting pot of Islamic, Orthodox, Catholic, and Jewish culture. In Bosnian towns, intermarriage between Orthodox and Muslim Serbs and even Croat Catholics was common, as was daily tolerance of or indifference to the often syncretic religious practices. But this multicultural essence existed in what was always a province of some larger polity, whether Ottoman, Hapsburg, or Belgrade-centered Yugoslav. Bosnians participated in governance by adapting to the regnant hierarchy, as Nobel prizewinner Ivo Andric showed readers around the world in *The Bridge on the Drina*, but they were always the objects, not the subjects, of their history. They did not set the rules of their own engagement. In the Communist era they played no leading role in the successive disputes among Serbs, Croats, and Slovenes. In the post-Communist era they never developed the kind of world-class market economists that Serbia did. To this day, the Serb elites in Belgrade still tend to view Bosnians as exotic, wild country cousins—an attitude that made it easy for Milosevic to drop Karadzic as his Serbian project ran into the ground in 1995. And on top of the ingrained habits of political dependency, the 100,000 war deaths—combined with emigration from a war zone—bled Bosnia of a generation of leaders. Across the land, communities were wrenched apart as the brutal ethnic cleansing reduced the non-Serb population in what is now the Republika Srpska from its prewar level of 46 percent to 3 percent, and reduced the Serbs in what is now the Federation from 17 percent to 3 percent.[29] Color-coded maps of before and after ethnic distribution graphically illustrate the phenomenon, shifting from a Jackson Pollock splattering in 1991 to Rorschach blobs in 1995.

When the internationals took over Bosnia-Herzegovina as a quasi protectorate in 1996, they had little concrete concept of what they wanted to achieve or how to proceed. The whole aim of the Dayton Accord had been to end the fighting; anything that would have imperiled that already Herculean task, like planning a functioning day-after civil administration, was left to the future improvisation of the Europeans who were tasked with running the fledgling state. Carl Bildt, the first high representative in Sarajevo of the nebulous international community, arrived with no office space, no assured appropriations, and a mandate that, because of national disagreements, said only that he was the final authority on whatever he was reseponsible for (whatever that was). He had to bring, personally, 300,000 deutsche marks in small denominations in order to rent a windowless, unheated office, with no telephone and no running water. Initially he had to sleep on a sofa in the Swedish ambassador's small apartment, use the ambassador's Land Rover to get around the country, and borrow a plane from French president Jacques Chirac to get in and out of the country.[30] He had an array of autonomous institutions to cajole and coordinate: the United Nations International Police Task Force, the Organization for Security and Cooperation in Europe, the EU Customs and Fiscal Assistance Office, the UN High Commission for Refugees, the UN Development Program, and, outside his writ, the NATO-led Implementation Force (IFOR, soon to be renamed SFOR) peacekeepers. And he had surly Bosniak, Croat, and Serb politicians, organized and solo criminals, and other gunslingers to keep from murdering each other. Tongue in cheek, filmmakers among the intellectuals who had not deserted Sarajevo soon produced a spoof of the chaos: Bosniak villagers, awaiting a visit by the U.S. president, rehearse "The House of the Rising Sun" in English to greet the guest and make a deal with RS guards just over the supposedly nonexistent internal Bosnian border to rent back some reluctant Serb peasants for the afternoon (with partial payment in Pampers) to prove their multiethnicity to the visitors.[31]

Bildt strove valiantly to increase the authority of the high representative and finally persuaded the supervisory nations and the UN to assign to the office extended "Bonn powers" of summary dismissal of Bosnian officials just as Bildt's own tenure ended, in 1997. His successor, former Spanish foreign minister Carlos Westendorp, began exercising the new powers and also presided over one of the most important turning points in Bosnia—the Sarajevo Declaration of February 1998.[32]

Until then, hardly any of the 2 million Bosnian refugees and displaced persons had returned to their former homes. Sarajevo was one of the most conspicuous offenders. Most vacant apartments, rather than going to ordinary returnees, were being snatched up by high officials and cronies. Before the 1992 war—even though Sarajevo never recovered the Jewish fourth of its pre–World War II population lost to the Holocaust—half of the city's population consisted of minorities. After the war the non-Muslim figure was down to 13 percent, and more Bosniaks from elsewhere were pouring in every day. The last ethnic cleansing of the war occurred when Serb districts in Greater Sarajevo were turned over to Bosniak jurisdiction under the Dayton Accord in March 1996; 100,000 Serbs fled the city.[33] This was the dismal legacy that the Sarajevo Declaration sought to remedy, thereby setting a signal for Bosnia as a whole.[34]

Under a threat by international donors to cut financial assistance if vigorous steps were not taken to restore multiethnicity, the agreement was signed by representatives of the state of Bosnia and Herzegovina, the Federation of Bosnia and Herzegovina, Sarajevo Canton, and the international community. It called for the return of 20,000 members of minorities to Sarajevo during the year, employment of more Serbs and other minorities on the police force, protection of human rights, amendment of discriminatory housing and property legislation, teaching of tolerance in the schools, "reform [of] the business and employment tax structure to facilitate the development of a market-based economy," and restoration of the capital's position "as a model of coexistence and tolerance for the rest of the country."[35] Implementation was sluggish, but under constant international prodding the first refugees began to trickle back. "Without that success, there would have been far fewer returns," commented Mirza Hajric, the young aide to Izetbegovic who acted as the Bosniak coordinator for the Sarajevo Declaration.[36] The largely peaceful return of a million refugees throughout the country followed the Sarajevo agreement, and brought minority representation up to today's estimated 15 to 20 percent of non-Serbs in the Republika Srpska and Serbs in the Federation.[37]

Westendorp was succeeded in 1999 by the Austrian and EU diplomat Wolf-gang Petritsch, then in 2002 by Paddy Ashdown, the first high representative to be selected by the EU's General Affairs Council. A former member of the British parliament and leader of the Liberal Democrats, and a former Royal Marines officer in Borneo and Belfast, Ashdown was no newcomer to Sara-jevo. During the siege he was a leading advocate of international intervention and visited the city many times to publicize its plight. "He had a passion for the country. He had convictions. He had a flair for this place," commented Hajric. "And one important job he had to do (and did) was to streamline the international community. They were fighting among themselves; they were in disarray." Lord Ashdown had no qualms about using the Bonn powers. His own definition of his task was threefold: to defeat the two "monsters" of the "dysfunctional" institutions of the Dayton Accord and the hopelessness of that half of the population living below the poverty line—and to make faith in a European future stronger than Balkan blood-and-soil "myths." All of this had to be done swiftly, before EU publics lost patience with enlargement and with the Balkans.[38]

By the time Ashdown took office, his civilian and military predecessors (and the Americans) had leaned on Izetbegovic to expel Iranians and mujahideen from Bosnia; suppressed residual paramilitary terrorism; impounded heavy weapons in guarded depots (without otherwise disarming the three ethnic armies); enforced the right of the Hague Tribunal's forensic teams to inspect mass graves in areas that were now Serb; cleared roads and rebuilt bridges; halted the most virulent arson and attacks on Muslim refugees trying to return to Banja Luka and Muslim candidates who opposed the rul-ing Bosniak nationalist SDA (Party of Democratic Action) in the Federa-tion—and in 1997 rescued the fledgling OHR team in Brcko from rent-a-mob hard-line Serbs.[39] The annual Sarajevo Film Festival, which had been launched as an open-air act of defiance while the city was still under siege, had begun making its own contribution to reconciliation by busing in Serb, Croat, and Bosniak schoolchildren to see free showings of, inevitably, *101 Dalmatians.* The NATO-led peacekeepers had been reduced from 60,000 to 20,000 and no longer needed to patrol the countryside obtrusively. The level of education at Sarajevo University had deteriorated sharply as many professors emigrated or drifted off to new public or private universities, and young people escaped to the better opportunities in Western Europe as fast as they could.

The first general election, called less than a year after Dayton in the hope that democratic choice would reveal and legitimize more moderate leaders,

had instead legitimized the war-hardened Serb, Croat, and Bosniak nationalist parties.[40] So had the adamant refusal of the American IFOR commander,
Admiral Leighton Smith, to risk his troops in trying to arrest Radovan
Karadzic.[41] The internationals had, however, managed to exclude Karadzic
from public office in the RS.[42]

The 2000 general election had worked better in terms of democratic evolution, still perpetuating the regional near-monopolies of the Serbs' ultranationalist SDS and the Croats' ultranationalist HDZ (Democratic Union) in
their respective ethnic areas, but according a full half of Muslim votes to a
multiethnic challenger to the Bosniak SDA and leading to an Alliance for
Change coalition that pledged to carry out reforms.[43] Herceg-Bosna, which
with the full backing of Tudjman (and contrary to the Dayton provisions) had
continued to proclaim itself a sovereign ministate, had finally acquiesced to
the authority of the Federation. Mutinous Croat soldiers had finally been persuaded to join the ranks of the single Bosniak-Croat Federation army after all.
The Bosnia-Herzegovina Constitutional Court of mixed international and
Bosnian judges had compelled the two entities to amend their constitutions to
guarantee government participation by Bosnia's three "constituent peoples"
proportionally to their far more mixed population distribution of the prewar
1991 census.[44] The OHR, with only half-hearted protection by SFOR peacekeepers, had raided the HDZ-run Hercegovacka Bank in Mostar to block illegal financing of separatist operations.[45] The OSCE had handed over management of the 2002 elections to a Bosnian Election Commission of four
Bosnians and three internationals. Mostar's municipal elections, however, had
aggravated Bosniak-Croat divisions in that city.

In Banja Luka, a mob of a thousand Serbs had burned prayer rugs, thrown
stones and firecrackers, and blocked the groundbreaking ceremony for
rebuilding the sixteenth-century Ferhadija mosque, which the Serbs had
destroyed during the war as they expelled the 40 percent of the population
that was Muslim. The cornerstone had subsequently been laid without violence, but the fenced-off, weedy lot remained vacant for years. In Banja Luka
too, editor Zjelko Kopanja had survived the bomb attack on his car after his
Nezavisne Novine published details about ongoing large-scale corruption and
about a massacre of 200 Muslims by Serb police in the Bosnian war—but he
had lost both legs and now walked with prostheses.

When Ashdown became the high representative, and simultaneously the EU
special representative, hopes were still high that democratic trends in neighboring Croatia and Serbia might form a synergy with growing pragmatism in

Bosnia. Moderate president Stipe Mesic and the reform-minded Social Democrats had opened Croatia's borders with Bosnia and were expediting identity checks for Serbs who wished to resume vacationing in Dalmatia. The Democratic Oppostion of Serbia (DOS) had toppled Milosevic and extradited him to the Hague. Three months thereafter the RS National Assembly, however reluctantly, had passed legislation on cooperating with the tribunal. The Bosnian Serb SDS had expelled its founder, Karadzic, and all ICTY indictees; and even hard-liners at the party congress had talked of the need to get rid of the republic's "burden as an apartheid state." Biljana Plavsic, who had succeeded Karadzic as president of the Republika Srpska and moved the Serbs toward less fanatical and more realistic politics, had gone to the Hague Tribunal as its only woman indictee, though she had yet to plead guilty to crimes against humanity and serve her sentence in a Swedish jail. Banja Luka's streets were once again reasonably safe for Bosniaks to walk in (though they still avoided calling out each other's typically Muslim given names in the marketplace).

At the Bosnian state level the Alliance for Change government was proclaiming "partnership" with the OHR, and the OHR and the U.S. Embassy were quietly writing programs for the government, which the latter then presented and either legislated or dithered over for months. The OHR got to advance its desired reform agenda, while the politicians managed to escape public ire over painful changes by diverting popular wrath to the internationals. The game worked well tactically, but strategically it reinforced popular perceptions that reform was something alien imposed by foreigners, rather than an essential, organic modernization of Bosnian society.[46]

Ashdown's explicit intent was to empower local democrats and write himself out of a job, and for half a year he abstained from ruling by decree.[47] But as the general election of 2002 reversed the liberal hopes of 2000 and returned the nationalist SDA to a central role in Bosniak regions, the proconsul increasingly resorted to his Bonn powers to overcome inertia, impose laws, and dismiss corrupt or uncooperative officials, above all in the RS.[48] His predecessors had already decreed laws, which had long been stalled in the legislature, on such matters as fighting corruption; setting up an Independent Judicial Commission; requiring all judges and prosecutors to resign and then prove that they were clean and proficient enough to be reappointed; sacking or suspending more than a hundred elected officials, including a deputy minister of justice and the elected Serb mayor of Drvar; and standardizing weights and measures. Westendorp had used his powers of imposition on average once a week, according to the highly critical European Stability Initiative, while

Petritsch and eventually Ashdown ratcheted this up to an average three times a week.[49]

In one of his first dramatic successes, Ashdown used a scandal over the revelation of illicit sales of weapons, explosives, and airplane parts to Saddam Hussein's Iraq in 2002 to halt such clandestine exports from the ORAO plant in the RS. Following his old partisan instincts, Tito had prepared for guerrilla war against any attackers in part by locating weapons production in the Bosnian mountains, and these factories had continued producing their wares long after the Yugoslav breakup. Precisely which politicians in the RS and Serbia proper were getting cuts from the embargo running was never very clear to outsiders, but a former RS president of the Bosnia-Herzegovina triple presidency, Mirko Sarovic, was forced to resign, while a dozen of the more immediate conspirators in the ORAO management and the Bosnian customs service were sentenced, lightly, to up to two years in prison. More important, in an operation planned jointly by the clutch of international organizations in Bosnia, teams of auditors supplemented military raids on the ORAO plant, traced financial links, and wielded the information gleaned to not only close down ORAO but also begin herding the three ethnic militaries into one state-level armed force.[50]

During his incumbency, the Peace Implementation Council granted Ashdown expanded powers to veto nominations for many posts in ministries and agencies and authorized the EU Police Mission, which replaced the UN International Police Task Force, to recommend dismissals to the OHR.[51] The removal of the most obstructionist old-regime power holders and their lieutenants in the political food chain to make way for less tainted newcomers is a crucial task in any democratization, but it was exceedingly difficult in this case. The OHR had no intelligence capabilities of its own, and to uncover corruption or incitement to violence or abetment in hiding fugitive war crimes indictees it had to rely on the police or on whatever intelligence it could prise bilaterally out of national surveillance operations (primarily, but not exclusively, those of the United States).[52] The failure of the UN police advisory unit—which, because of disputes among sponsoring nations, was kept in an unarmed, nonoperational role—and its follow-on EU Police Mission to screen out policemen who were getting cuts from trafficking gangs was long an open secret.[53] In addition, outsiders predictably found it difficult to penetrate the kind of obfuscation that Bosnians of all ethnicities had perfected over centuries. "We know only 20 percent of what's going on here," mused OSCE head Robert Beecroft.

"It's our country, and we know only 25 percent of what's going on here!" lamented one Bosnian graduate student in response.[54]

Banja Luka

"To start our cooperation, we had to accept that Bosnia-Herzegovina is our common state," explained Zhivko Radisic, the first Serb to head the collective three-member presidency of Bosnia-Herzegovina, from 1998 to 2002. "The extreme nationalists considered me a national traitor, a heretic who had turned Muslim, a slave of the international community." Looking back, he saw some changes: "That was the beginning of creating the presumption of one normal state. Now peace is not in question any more. Bosnia-Herzegovina is not in question. That is the first change since my presidency.

"Unfortunately, in the meantime some other things happened, and that is the second change. I think Bosnia-Herzegovina has still not taken its own fate into its own hands. I think that the intervention, the politicization, by the international community is too large." In particular, Bosnia's "position and status is defined mainly by our relations with the international tribunal. That's not good." Paddy Ashdown, he thought further, was too intrusive, and some RS officials were too intent on keeping their positions by doing just what the OHR wanted. "The Republika Srpska and the Serb people, one of the constituent peoples of Bosnia, are hostages to circumstance and to obligations to the Hague Tribunal.

"There were crimes here by all three sides [during the war]. In 1992 more than 1,300 innocent Serbs were killed in Srebrenica and its environs. That's why [Serb indictees] are now being prosecuted in the court," because they were righting the wrongs done to Serbs. "Of course, those responsible for killing Bosniaks in 1995 should be held responsible. But [Naser] Oric [commander of the Army of Bosnia and Herzegovina in the Srebrenica area, who had been in custody at the Hague Tribunal for two years at the time of this conversation], Izetbegovic [who had been dead for a year], and all the others should be held responsible too. And the international community cannot be absolved either. I personally think the international community made the greatest mistake in recognizing Bosnia-Herzegovina as an independent state in April 1992, because one of the constituent peoples didn't stand behind that state. It was created by representatives of the Bosniak and Croat people only, and later confirmed by Dayton."

Radisic's sense that Serbs had been unfairly victimized was emphasized even more by others in interviews in Banja Luka. Branko Neskovic, chief of staff to then RS prime minister Dragan Mikerevic, also stoutly defended the RS's failure to deliver Mladic, asking rhetorically, if NATO's 30,000 troops had not been able to find Mladic, how could the international community expect the RS to find him? "Then you are equally guilty. Don't blame us if you can't find him." Neskovic also thought that Ashdown was heavy handed in firing Serb officials, and that he favored the Muslims unduly. All Serbs wanted was respect for soldiers who had simply defended their families—and for the media to stop harping on the past war and saying the Serbs were guilty.

Neskovic further dismissed the example of Brcko as any model for other parts of Bosnia and saw its success as another instance of international favoritism. Brcko was prospering only because outsiders had poured so much money into it. "Brcko District has a budget of 200 million. Is this dirty money? Is this black money? Or is it clean money? Brcko is only a third of the size of Banja Luka, and Banja Luka has only a hundred million."

Milos Solaja, the head of Banja Luka's press center and Center for International Relations, detailed Serbs' resentment of high-paid internationals who were looking for ways to perpetuate their jobs and now impose 76 percent— "some say 90 percent"—of the country's policies on Bosnia. He also observed that the judicial reforms, far from eradicating bribes, had simply made them more expensive. "Petritsch decided to give enormous salaries to upright prosecutors and judges. They are well paid now, and so you have to give them more money."

By contrast, editor Zjelko Kopanja mourned the loss of Serbia's reforming prime minister Zoran Djindjic, murdered in 2003, and the gambling away of the good chances that Yugoslavia had in the 1980s to effect modernization and a successful transition to the post-Communist world. Milosevic and Tudjman killed these chances with their nationalist passions, he said. They and Karadzic "became the icons." The adulation made people "easy to manipulate." Unfortunately, "the Serbs won't have another leader like Djindjic for 200 years. He was the hope and the opportunity." But he was killed by "the anti-Hague lobby, those people who work for different security structures, mafia structures, conservative political structures." Yet he detected some shifts: "People do not want to be hostages of Karadzic and Mladic any more. . . . Everyone, all EU politicians, know that the war criminals are in Serbia. In my opinion the RS is a kind of hostage of the government of [Serbian prime minister] Kostunica." Nevertheless, Kopanja was no fan of Ashdown and thought he should not exercise his powers like a "maharajah."[55]

Just why Lord Ashdown acted like a maharajah was explained by one international official in Bosnia: Republika Srpska officials "want a strong RS monoethnicity. The war criminals have networks that are extremely powerful and take all the money from sectors that can hardly stand on their feet. Public companies are deprived of their poor assets. The networks supporting Karadzic are like an octopus. The mafia organization is really corrupting all society. Clearly, the police have been protecting them. That explains the failure of privatization. The police are corrupt; customs are a problem. Nobody is satisfied with us, and not just the extreme nationalists, but also people who should be on board with us. We are, in a way, stuck. We want things to go forward, but time and money are running out. People are exhausted ten years after the war. Should we spend our time negotiating" and watering down every single reform that is needed to get institutions with the authority to act for the state as a whole, "and then end up with what are not really reforms? Or should we go on and say, 'Listen, guys, [the haggling] was fun, but now we have to go ahead and do it' with police reform, tax and customs and defense reform, where basically the RS has lost competences that went up to the Bosnia-Herzegovina level. There is no way they can get into the EU if they have three different interlocutors [with Brussels] with three different views. But Serbs see themselves in a sort of fortress attacked by the international community.

"SDS, the core political party, does not really have a specific strategy. It's just: they don't want this, they don't want that. We negotiate and we give them things at the edges; the new VAT (value added tax) administration will have its headquarters in Banja Luka, and will provide 250 local jobs. But they say, 'We fought for the Republika Srpska. We had friends dying for the project. Our own families were killed.' They still perceive that they were the victims of the war, who just reacted to the threats of Muslims; just as in the Ottoman Empire, when Serbs revolted against an unjust government. What is scary is that this is not just the speech of the ultranationalists. Also in the younger generation there is a very strong nationalist feeling." Indeed, more than 60 percent of Bosnian Serbs strongly supported Karadzic in an opinion poll in April 2005. Moreover, Bosnian Serbs in their late teens and early twenties considered Karadzic a hero, just above the World War II Chetnik Draza Mihailovic and just behind, curiously, Tito.[56]

Yet there were also contrary signs. Some international officials in Bosnia questioned the real salience of such opinion surveys and thought the problem with young Bosnian Serbs was less ultranationalism than political passivity. And Mirza Hajric, aide to Izetbegovic in the late 1990s, sensed that "RS political interests are now different from Belgrade's. I think politicians there want [their turf] to be the Republika Srpska within Bosnia," rather than a province of Serbia that Belgraders look down on. "I think they realize that Greater Serbia is not going to happen. And frankly, they are big bosses in Bosnia. In Belgrade they would be little provincial cousins nobody loves. So I think realistically and emotionally" they now see their future in Bosnia. Moreover, Hajric suggested, Serbs can now live better in Banja Luka than in Belgrade. "For the first time in history, students from Belgrade come to Banja Luka to be bartenders. Belgrade professors come to Banja Luka to get more money teaching. So why would these guys wish to change things?" Overall, popular acceptance of the state of Bosnia has increased, Hajric observed, from perhaps 51 percent in 1995 to 60 percent today. "Why? Because in 1996 [Serbs] going from Trebinje [a Serb nationalist stronghold in southwest Bosnia] to Banja Luka [in the RS] for a health checkup took twenty hours to get there. Now they can travel in less than three hours to Mostar [in the Bosniak-Croat Federation], as they always did in the past. Maybe if you asked them what the ideal situation would be, they would say it's to be part of Serbia, but they understand that's not realistic. As pragmatists, they say, 'Let's take the benefit of being Serbs in Bosnia.' And the Serbs have more than enough political power in the [Bosnian] institutions to continue being Serbs."[57]

Showdown

In his last year and a half in Sarajevo, Paddy Ashdown stepped up the pressure to achieve his goals of fixing the dysfunctional Dayton institutions, giving hope to the poverty-stricken half of the population, displacing Balkan myths with an operational faith in a European future, and getting the top Bosnian Serb indictees to the Hague. In summer of 2004 he fired fifty-nine RS officials—including the SDS leader and speaker of the Bosnian Serb National Assembly, Dragan Kalinic, and the RS interior minister, Zoran Djeric—for corruption and obstructing justice at the Hague Tribunal.[58] In July the painstakingly reconstructed Mostar arch was opened and local daredevils again leaped the thirty-two meters from its span into the green Neretva River in the gorge below.[59] In October an official RS commission admitted for the first time that Serbs had massacred thousands of Muslims in Srebrenica and the RS handed over 600 war-related documents to the Hague Tribunal; in November RS authorities apologized for the first time for the massacre and gave prosecutors a list of 17,000 Serbs who took part in the massacre.[60] By then technically qualified Bosniak job hunters were finally getting hired again by Serb businesses in Banja Luka. But 16,600 Bosnians were still missing, the Red Cross reported.[61] The 117-year-old Bosnian Regional Museum, which with international donations had briefly opened a wing to display Sarajevo's magnificent fourteenth-century Haggadah, was again closed. Officially, the reason was lack of funding from entity budgets. The underlying problem, however, according to Jacob Finci, the head of the Bosnian Civil Service Commission and the most prominent member of the Jewish community, was disagreement over which ethnic group should be presented as having been the largest in the region in Roman times—a particularly difficult issue to resolve, since all standard histories of the Balkans record that no Slavs at all had yet arrived in the area.[62]

In early December EUFOR replaced SFOR—remarkably, the NATO-led forces had not suffered a single service fatality in their nine-year mission—and broadened its mandate to include fighting weapons trafficking and extremist religious groups, bolstering border security, and apprehending war criminals.[63] Under pressure, the RS sent to the Hague 1,500 kilograms of documents that the tribunal had long been requesting. In mid-December Paddy Ashdown sacked nine "obstructionist" RS officials and froze the bank accounts of six—prompting RS president Dragan Cavic to call a referendum on the status of the RS, Serbian president Kostunica to warn that this could destroy the Dayton agreement and destabilize the whole region, and the synod of the Serbian Orthodox Church to admonish that people in the RS might "lose every trust in democratic processes" in Bosnia.[64] Bosnian Serbs had been sheltering Mladic, Ashdown told reporters. The general had been seen several months earlier on a military base an hour out of Sarajevo, and the Bosnian Serb army had even kept Mladic on its payroll until very recently. All of the twenty war crimes suspects arrested on RS territory had been picked up by peacekeeping troops; not one had been detained by the RS army. "The whole of the country," he stated, was "being held to ransom by the failure of the RS" and could not move toward either the EU or NATO's Partnership for Peace (PfP) until this obstructionism ceased.[65] EUFOR commander David Leakey promptly announced that the Han Pijesak military complex, where Mladic had been sighted, would be closed, along with all other underground bases unless they had a legitimate use. The United States froze all SDS assets in its jurisdiction, banned Americans from conducting any financial transactions with the party, and barred party leaders from visiting America.[66]

On January 1, 2005, the bloated entity police intelligence agencies were formally consolidated and downsized into a single State Investigation and Protection Agency (SIPA) charged with "[f]ighting drug traffickers, exposing money launderers, tackling corruption, investigating war crimes, tracking down terrorists and protecting witnesses."[67] Within a year the agency—which employed only 703 personnel, or about half of the number in the old Federation and RS units combined—issued an early report pegging money laundering in Bosnia-Herzegovina in 2005 at nearly $70 million.[68] Trade between entities was liberalized, and customs, excise, and all indirect taxes were for the first time consolidated and channeled into the Bosnia-Herzegovina budget for further distribution, rather than flowing into the entities in a murkier process that invited embezzlement. This reform, required under the EU Feasibility Study, also made financial obligations more predictable for potential investors.[69]

In mid-January the Hague Tribunal convicted Colonel Vidoje Blagojevic of complicity to commit genocide and convicted Dragan Jokic, chief of engineering in the First Zvornik Brigade, of extermination, a crime against humanity, at Srebrenica.[70] In mid-March Bosnia inaugurated the War Crimes Chamber of the Court of Bosnia-Herzegovina, the first judicial panel in ex-Yugoslavia that would be entrusted by the Hague Tribunal with trying war crimes suspects.[71]

In late March Paddy Ashdown suspended the lucrative privatization by Bosnian officials of military real estate made redundant by the army unification, until such time as the oversight Commission for State Property could be fully functional.[72] In the same month, he dismissed the Croat member of the tripartite presidency of Bosnia-Herzegovina, Dragan Covic, while he faced corruption charges in court; the HDZ defiantly elected Covic head of the party and refused to name a replacement to the joint presidency for two months of government crisis.[73] In April Serb recruits refused to pledge allegiance to the state of Bosnia-Herzegovina or sing the Bosnian national anthem, and instead took an oath to the RS and sang its anthem.[74] But by late April 2005, as the half-year spurt of arrivals of Serb and Bosnian Serb indictees at the Hague came to an end, the tribunal had a dozen more suspects in custody.[75]

In May the ad hoc UN War Crimes Tribunal, beginning its own phase-out, delegated its first case to the Bosnian War Crimes Chamber for trial, while Radovan Stankovic was accused of eight counts of war crimes and crimes against humanity in the rape of up to nine Muslim women and girls in Foca.[76] In June, sensationally, a previously secret two-hour video was aired on TV, showing uniformed "Scorpion" special police of the Serbian Interior Ministry torturing and then killing four Bosniak boys and two Bosniak men from Srebrenica in 1995.[77]

In July, on the tenth anniversary of the massacre at Srebrenica, Serbian president Boris Tadic for the first time laid a wreath at the commemoration.[78] Only a few hundred Serbs held a counter commemoration and chanted "Long live Karadzic" in a town that has now shrunk from 37,000 to 6,000–7,000 and has become overwhelmingly Serb.[79] In early August RS president Dragan Cavic declared in Banja Luka that Karadzic must surrender to the Hague Tribunal in the interests of the Republika Srpska, or else "he must be arrested. . . . There is no third way." This necessity "is painful; many believe it's not fair; many say it is politically influenced but it is completely clear that without this we have a serious political problem that will escalate and prompt a new, much sharper political course of big powers toward Republika Srpska and its institutions."[80] This was not the way Westerners would have phrased the obligation, but they welcomed the changed tone after earlier RS adulation of these men—and they welcomed Cavic's shepherding of laws forming a single Bosnian army command through the RS legislature. In late August the reluctant National Assembly passed legislation finally abolishing the separate RS military command, budget, and general staff, and approving a single nationwide army of all three ethnicities, under a single Serb defense minister in the maiden incumbency.[81]

This still left two major barriers to be overcome before Bosnia could proceed further on its desired path toward joining the two prime Euroatlantic institutions of the EU and NATO, the latter in the initial form of the Partnership for Peace. Bosnia could not go beyond the Feasibility Study of 2003 to conclude a Stabilization and Association Agreement with the European Union until it combined all key institutions, including the police, in a way that would let the government of Bosnia-Herzegovina speak with one voice—and, of course, until it was making its own decisions without depending on the high representative's decrees. And it could not sign such an SAA agreement with the EU or join NATO's PfP—to the chagrin of their generals, Bosnia-Herzegovina and Serbia-Montenegro were by 2005 the only two Western Balkan countries still blackballed by NATO—until it delivered Mladic and Karadzic to the ICTY. Despite all the tantalizing hints to the contrary in 2005 and early 2006, it was clear by summer 2006 that neither Banja Luka nor Belgrade was ready to give up Mladic or Karadzic. The stream of Serb suspects to the Hague dried up on the April day in 2005 when Serbia won its quid pro quo Feasibility Study for sending the third most wanted Serb indictee to the tribunal.[82]

Paddy Ashdown's last major showdown—apart from firing RS education minister Milovan Pecelj in October 2005 because he failed to carry out Ashdown's 2004 decree to dismiss Radomir Lubic, the extreme nationalist dean of the law faculty at the East Sarajevo university,[83]—was a confrontation with the RS over transferring police command authority from the entities to the state level and redrawing police districts to cut across RS-Federation borders.[84] Surrendering control of the police to Bosnia-Herzegovina seemed more threatening to those Serbs in security-criminal networks than surrendering control of the army, since policemen often formed their operational core. Special police like the Scorpions and the paramilitary forces of Arkan and other criminals had in any case been the shock troops for both the Serbian and the Bosnian Serb armies during the 1990s wars. As the International Crisis Group's report on the long deadlock over the police talks bluntly stated, "Police throughout the country have remained highly politicized, acting at the behest of politicians to obstruct implementation of the Dayton Peace Accords, in particular refugee return, and heavily involved in organised crime. The RS force is filled with war criminals and actively supports persons indicted by the International Criminal Tribunal for the Former Yugoslavia in The Hague. . . . The leading RS party—the Serbian Democratic Party (SDS)—openly blocks all efforts at reform and receives active encouragement from the Serbian government, the Serbian Orthodox Church and Serbia's security structures, which desire to annex RS as part of a Kosovo final status settlement." The RS police force, the report continued, consumes 10 percent of the Bosnian budget (double EU members' average proportional spending on police) and is the "worst police force in Bosnia." Its "structures" are "founded on violence and ethnic cleansing." In a "criminalized political system it is more important to control the police than the army."[85]

In fall 2005, after almost a year of rejecting the EU's precondition of police reform for starting talks on a Stabilization and Association Agreement, the RS suddenly gave in, after one of the more artful sequences of diplomacy. Austria withheld its veto on opening scheduled talks on Turkish accession only after it won the trade-off of a start to EU membership talks with Croatia.[86] The EU, having earlier postponed the opening of Croatian negotiations because of Zagreb's failure to deliver Ante Gotovina to the Hague Tribunal, noted intramurally that Croatia had been cooperative in recent months in tracking down the top ten names on a list of Gotovina's support network in Croatia, which EU countries had given to Zagreb officials.[87] EU officials then persuaded ICTY prosecutor Carla Del Ponte to modify her open criticism of Zagreb and her own Roman Catholic Church a few weeks earlier for allegedly hiding Gotovina in a monastery in Croatia or Herzegovina.[88] She willingly certified—while pointedly noting the continued absence of Gotovina from the Hague—that "Croatia's co-operation in the transmission of requested documents is indeed currently the best of all the countries in the region."[89]

Once the EU began talks with Croatia, of course, the need to balance Serbia and Croatia prompted the EU to open long-postponed talks with Belgrade too on a Stabilization and Association Agreement, despite Serbia's failure to send Karadzic and Mladic to the Hague. And when it looked as if the Bosnian

Serbs' stubbornness would isolate Bosnia-Herzegovina as the only country in the Western Balkans lacking negotiations with the EU—and with no prospect of eventual visa-free travel for Bosnian citizens in the EU—Banja Luka buckled. Within a few days of the start of the Turkish-EU talks on October 3, both houses of the RS legislature approved the police reform that Ashdown had been seeking. Once they made this concession, the EU immediately invited Bosnia-Herzegovina to begin negotiating its own Stabilization and Association Agreement.[90]

The Bosnian talks opened in January 2006. In February the RS National Assembly voted out the old government as ultranationalist SDS deputies walked out, and moderate Milorad Dodik of the Alliance of Independent Social Democrats (SNSD) again took the office of prime minister that he had held from 1998 to 2001. The top priority of the RS government would be economic development, he said, and pledged full cooperation with the Hague Tribunal. He immediately cut the pay of government officials and managers of state firms, opened investigations into suspected insider privatizations, fired all the SDS loyalist deputy ministers and state secretaries he had inherited, and halted SDS kickbacks. He was backed by a coalition of parties—the Social Democratic Party, the Bosniak SDA, and the Party for Bosnia-Herzegovina— that wanted a strong state-level government. Within days the RS National Assembly voted to freeze the funds of fugitive indicted war criminals and the accomplices who helped hide them.[91] Simultaneously, the Banja Luka district court handed down the longest sentence for war crimes meted out to an ethnic Serb by any RS court: twenty years for killing five Muslim civilians in 1992.[92] In 2006 the War Crimes Chamber gave its first verdict in a case transferred by the Hague Tribunal, sentencing a Bosnian Serb to thirteen years in jail for abetting persecution, rape, and torture near Foca in 1992.[93] Further, RS police chief Dragomir Andan finally resigned, in response to Carla Del Ponte's long-standing charge that he was helping to hide war criminals (and possibly in response to repeated newspaper allegations that he was running parallel police structures that abetted mafia smuggling). Notably, for the first time, a Bosniak became the acting RS police chief.[94] And in a lighter vein, the new youth group Dosta ("Enough") staged a concert by twenty bands to call for moving beyond the fixation on ethnic clashes to the real issue of jobs.[95]

With these shifts, the main resistance to a U.S.-sponsored attempt to write an amended constitution that might overcome Dayton in a less piecemeal and more coherent way and turn Bosnia-Herzegovina into a more functional single state shifted from the Serbs, who constitute a third of the population, to the Croats, who constitute a fifth and constantly fear that their identity is under threat. A majority of Croat legislators in the Bosnian parliament split from the HDZ to reject the constitutional draft that had been approved by leaders of the seven main parties, including their own. They were joined by some Bosniak members of parliament who thought, conversely, that the constitution should go further and dissolve the entities altogether in favor of a more unitary state that the Bosniaks, with half the population, could expect to lead. Together, the dissenters defeated the draft, which fell two votes short of the two-thirds majority required for passage. Bosnia-Herzegovina's frustrated (Serb) foreign minister, Mladen Ivanic, objected in vain that this failure would bar Bosnia'a entry into the EU.[96]

In fact, negotiations on Bosnia's Stabilization and Association Agreement proceeded despite rejection of the constitutional draft—and despite the accelerated politicking in the runup to fall elections—in the expectation that patchwork institutional adjustments could keep things moving in the right direction even without formal constitutional resolution. By summer 2006 the unflappable Bosnian vice minister and director of European integration, Osman Topcagic, was expecting the Stabilization and Association Agreement to be initialed toward the end of the year and to be signed by Bosnia as a full sovereign state in summer 2007. By that time, announced Paddy Ashdown's successor as high representative, Christian Schwarz-Schilling, the OHR would cease to exist and he himself would stay on in Sarajevo only in the reduced role of EU special representative (EUSR). Asked to evaluate Ashdown's reign retrospectively in this context, Topcagic declared, "When he came here, there were thirty ministries and agencies at state [rather than entity] level. Now there are sixty" out of the 100 needed for EU membership. "I think he succeeded."[97]

A year before his departure, Ashdown had declared himself "deeply impatient about the pace of change."[98] The incoming Schwarz-Schilling, for his part, felt that the pace of change had at least advanced sufficiently for him to reduce overt intervention to a minimum. He relaxed the blanket ban on political activity by various politicians who had been dismissed by his predecessors (as long as they had not sheltered or abetted war crimes suspects). He quickly set the date for terminating the OHR. He focused less on politics than on the economic development that Ashdown had deliberately eschewed at an earlier stage.

As anticipation built up about Bosnia'a forthcoming march down the road to EU membership, it looked at last as if the attraction of the European Union had trumped violent Serb nationalism after all. The dream—or nightmare— of a Greater Serbia at the expense of Bosnia had dissipated, as had the vision of a Greater Croatia that might wrench Herzegovina out of the Bosnian state.

A number of politicians in Banja Luka were coming to perceive more advantages in being masters of their own future than in submitting to sometimes condescending leadership from Belgrade. A growing number, suggested one Austrian with decades of experience in the region, were starting to consider whether they should aspire not only to the premiership of the small Republika Srpska, but also to the premiership of the larger Bosnia-Herzegovina—especially when Bosnia was suddenly outperforming all other Balkan lands in economic growth, and when average net wages in the RS were projected to rise to Federation levels as early as 2007.[99] Younger politicians—but also some of those who had risen high in the old mafia structures in the RS—were coming to see their best chances for the future in complying with tough EU standards in order to win European financial aid and help in building administrative and institutional capabilities fast. The feeling of new dynamism arose not just from the healthy supplanting of belligerent identity politics by the more negotiable politics of economic interest. It represented the first green shoots of what the old Austrian Balkan hand described as the maturing of the political class out of the dependency that characterized so much of Balkan history. "None of these people had to make decisions before," he observed. "They just waited until somebody else decided which way to go, and then followed. They looked to the Ottoman rulers or to Vienna or Budapest, or, in Tito's time, to Belgrade. Until now only the political classes in Slovenia and Croatia have broken out of this mold to take initiatives of their own." By implication, he raised the question of whether the Bosnians might now become the third people in the region to dare to take more initiative.

Without directly addressing this question, Paddy Ashdown, in one of his early valedictories, qualified his own impatience with the slowness of transformation thus: "[I]f you look at this in comparison to any other peacekeeping operation I cannot think of a single one in the whole of history, except for East Timor, where we have moved so far from war to peace. Far from getting nowhere in nine years—nine brief years after one of the worst wars, post–second world war," in which 100,000 were killed and 2 million, or half the population, were made homeless, "this place is a miracle."[100]

CHAPTER SEVEN

RESCUING MACEDONIA

IF MACEDONIA, THAT borderland of borderlands, has now lost its reputation as a tinderbox, it owes its escape both to the inattention of history and to
the intensive attention of the European Union. By its fifteenth birthday, the
new state of 2 million had survived an almost successful assassination attempt
on its first president; the overnight influx of more than 300,000 refugees from
Kosovo, equal to 15 percent of the country's population; armed ethnic clashes
that looked like the start of a fifth war of the Yugoslav succession; and the
death of its second president in an airplane crash.[1] In addition, its interior
minister had been indicted for the murder of seven Asian economic migrants
under the pretense that the victims were Islamist terrorists—apparently so the
minister could curry favor with Washington. Throughout the period Macedonia repeatedly appeared to be lurching into civil war. Yet each time, in
perils-of-Pauline episodes, it stepped back from the brink, and by 2006 it was
the improbable third in line among the ex-Yugoslav states for future EU membership, after much richer and politically more stable Slovenia and Croatia.
The story of how Macedonia managed this prestidigitation is also the story of
how the European Union came to conduct its first-ever solo military operation and how the odd triple of Croatia, Macedonia, and Albania arose in
regional cooperation.

Macedonia was the main object of the 1878 Treaty of San Stefano, which
was hastily revised in the 1878 Treaty of Berlin. Bulgaria, suddenly freed from
the Turkish yoke after five centuries by the Russo-Turkish war, emerged from
San Stefano in March of that year as the largest state in the Balkans, ruling over
the Macedonians, whom it viewed as a sub-branch of the Bulgarian tribe. Four
months later, under Bismarck's orchestration of the Treaty of Berlin, Macedo-

nia was snatched back from Sofia and returned to Ottoman administration; Bulgaria lost a third of its San Stefano territory and its access to the Aegean Sea as well. Berlin's profligate redistribution of lands, wrote historian L. S. Stavrianos, left "every one of the Balkan peoples . . . thoroughly dissatisfied. The Bulgarians were embittered by the partition of their country, the Serbians by the advance of Austria into Bosnia-Herzegovina, the Rumanians by the loss of southern Bessarabia, and the Greeks by their failure to obtain any territorial compensation. . . . The direct and logical outcome of the Berlin settlement was the Serbian-Bulgarian War of 1885, the Bosnian crisis of 1908, the two Balkan wars of 1912–1913, and the murder of Archduke Francis Ferdinand in 1914."[2] The bloodiest venue of the very bloody Balkan wars that presaged World War I was Macedonia.

When Macedonia became a republic in Tito's Yugoslavia in 1945, its ethnicities remained as mixed as the coinage of the word *macédoine* for a fruit cocktail implied. Slavic Macedonians, Turks, Bulgars, and Serbs, along with non-Slavic Albanians, Greeks, Vlachs, Jews, and Gypsies inhabited the land.[3] The "Macedonian question" of 1870—bluntly, how to split up the amorphous territory among its Serb, Greek, and Bulgarian neighbors—continued to roil relations among Yugoslavia, Greece, and Bulgaria throughout the 1940s. But with time that dusty, poor republic came to be seen as provincial and uninteresting by the Serbs, Croats, and Slovenes to the Yugoslav north, and once Tito broke with Stalin, an iron curtain separated Macedonia from Bulgaria for half a century. Apart from eliciting global sympathy after the devastating Skopje earthquake of 1963, Macedonia was forgotten by the rest of the world.

When Yugoslavia broke up in the early 1990s, Macedonia, too, became independent, as a kind of afterthought. Its elites had not sought independence, nor were they prepared for it. Even more than in Croatia, Bosnia, and Kosovo, the default mode of the residue of the Communist bureaucracy was not only everyday corruption, but also an aversion to making any decisions. In November 1990, in common with other Yugoslav republics, Macedonia held its first multiparty elections. The VMRO-DPMNE, resuscitating the name of the Internal Macedonian Revolutionary Organization that constituted a virtual state within a state between World Wars I and II, won a majority over the Communists.[4] The parliament, following a referendum in which 97 percent of ethnic Macedonians voted for independence (and which ethnic Albanians boycotted), reserved for itself the right to independence accorded republics in the Yugoslav constitution, and in September 1991, after the war in Croatia had already begun, it activated this right.

Milosevic cared little for the 40,000 Serbs in Macedonia and did not oppose the move, even if the Serbian Orthodox Church tended to classify Macedonians as "south Serbs" and fiercely protested the Macedonian Orthodox Church's claim to autocephaly. To its west, Albania actively welcomed the new state "as a counterweight to Serbia and an irritant to Greece."[5] Irritated Greece indeed opposed the advent, or at least the name, of the new country, which it said implied illicit claims on the Greek-held portion of the old geographic Macedonia. Athens vetoed EC/EU recognition of the new state for two years, until a compromise formula was invented to recognize the "Former Yugoslav Republic of Macedonia." Under this provisional name, FYROM was admitted to the UN in 1993, and pledged to enforce the UN's Yugoslav blockade on its border with Serbia, despite the considerable economic loss to the state (and gain to its many smugglers). Two years thereafter, Skopje and Athens, sidestepping the issue of nomenclature, normalized bilateral relations.[6] Greece lifted the trade blockade it had imposed on its northern neighbor, and within a few years Greeks became the largest investors in Macedonia.[7] This normalization cleared the way for Macedonia to join NATO's Partnership for Peace—the second Western Balkan state to do so, after Slovenia—and also the Organization for Security and Cooperation in Europe (OSCE), and to receive the democratic certificate of membership in the Council of Europe. From 1992 Macedonia received financial assistance from Brussels, in increasing amount as the EU applied the PHARE program to the Western Balkans in 1996, for the development of democracy and a free-market system.[8]

In 1995 competing political claims between the dominant 65 percent Macedonians and the 21 to 40 percent ethnic Albanians (depending on which nationality's statistics one credits) erupted in violence as Skopje blocked the opening of an Albanian-language university in Tetovo, in the ethnically Albanian west on the Kosovo border.[9] One student died and eighteen were injured in clashes between police and demonstrators. Albanian grievances increased as Belgrade implemented new regulations requiring passports to cross the Macedonian border into Serbia. In the half century of Tito's Yugoslavia, Albanians with extended families on all three sides of the purely administrative borders between Serbia, Macedonia, and Kosovo had moved freely back and forth; they found the new restriction unnatural. Also in 1995, once the Dayton negotiations had excluded the cause of Kosovo's independence, the Kosovar Albanians became increasingly radicalized, and their cousins and friends in Macedonia willingly helped the new crusade by slipping weapons into Kosovo for the nascent Kosova Liberation Army (KLA). The trafficking was easy. No matter what Serb checkpoints were set up, no matter how much official Belgrade and Skopje might denounce contraband running, the Albanians easily traversed the uninhabited mountain paths with their laden donkeys, and modest bribes to Serbian border guards sufficed to let passenger buses do a profitable side business transporting rifles and ammunition.[10] In an ethnic division of labor, while Albanians smuggled arms into Kosovo, Macedonians smuggled oil into Serbia—and both smuggled cigarettes, drugs, and human beings. In 1998 and 1999, as the Serbian security forces in Kosovo wiped out fifty of the Jashari clan and the KLA stepped up its raids on Serbs, Albanians from Macedonia flocked to join the uprising, with scant regard for formal boundaries. The UN and NATO forces that had been present in Macedonia in various configurations as deterrent peacekeepers since 1992 were increased.

As tensions mounted in Kosovo in February 1999, Macedonian president Kiro Gligorov offered amnesties to the ethnic Albanian mayors of Tetovo and Gostivar, who had been imprisoned on charges of "antistate crimes." In the same month Macedonians and Bulgarians signed a reconciliation after eight decades of their own mini–cold war. Hundreds of Kosovar refugees who were being driven out of their homes by Serbian security forces surged over the border seeking safety and were welcomed into the homes of Tetovo Albanians, who opened their hearts and purses to their poorer compatriots, paying generously for their food and clothes.[11] In late March and April, as NATO bombarded Kosovo and Serbia and the Serbs accelerated their ruthless ethnic cleansing of Kosovars, the flow to Macedonia swelled to more than 300,000 refugees. Skopje, fearing destabilization, at first tried to bar them from entering its territory, but as CNN day after day broadcast clips of wailing babies and ten-kilometer-long lines of hungry, cold Albanians in tractors and carts, Macedonia finally yielded to international pressure. NATO engineers built four camps for the UN High Commission for Refugees, which reluctantly accepted military help in this emergency situation.[12] One muddy Macedonian camp at Cegrane housed 43,000 on the site of a rubbish dump.[13]

Abruptly, Milosevic conceded defeat in June, just under the deadline for getting the refugees back to their Kosovar villages in time to put roofs over their heads before cold winter set in. Virtually overnight—even before NATO ground troops could finish deploying into Kosovo and clearing land mines in the fields—the camps emptied out, and the migratory columns of carts and tractors vanished as swiftly as they had come.

Throughout 2000 the West had a generally favorable view of ethnic relations in Macedonia; some even called it the best record in the region—which, given the competition, it may have been. In that year the government finally granted Albanians permission to proceed with establishing the South East

European University in Tetovo. Critics, however, charged that the West had too rosy a view and was misreading the relative peace as social harmony, whereas the calm reflected only an unstable truce of parallel lives in which Macedonian police did not venture into the Albanian sector of western Macedonia, while Albanians did not venture into Macedonian sectors in the east.[14]

Whatever the truth, Macedonia became the first Western Balkan nation to sign on to the EU's Stabilization and Association Process, which had been set up "to bridge the gap between post-conflict management and longer-term political and economic development" in the Western Balkans.[15] This experiment had two aims. It could help Macedonia gain confidence by defining interim goals that Skopje could feasibly attain, winning public praise and encouragement from Brussels at each incremental step on the long road to EU membership. And it could begin to shift the dynamics away from improvisatory short-term crisis management to long-term reliance on the incentive of EU membership to discipline the country's political and economic development. The West shrank from adding a third full protectorate to its commitments in Bosnia and Kosovo, and in Macedonia confined its tutelage to a kind of "protectorate lite." The Skopje government held sovereignty in a way that the Bosnian government and the Kosovo provisional government did not, but the EU (joined by the OSCE) kept a stronger overseer role in Macedonia than in any other sovereign state in the Balkans.

Ohrid

In early 2001 Macedonia faced its own military crisis. Violence flared up as the KLA look-alike Liberation Army of Presevo, Bujanovac, and Medvedja began ambushing policemen and soldiers in Serbia's heavily Albanian Presevo Valley on the Serbia-Kosovo-Macedonia triborder. The international Contact Group agreed to let Serbian forces—pro-European Serbian prime minister Zoran Djindjic had not yet been assassinated—reoccupy the buffer zone on the Serbian side and push out the Albanian rebels. Some of these insurgents, rather than fleeing to Kosovo, took their struggle to Macedonia under the banner of another KLA look-alike calling itself the National Liberation Army (NLA). There they attacked police and army posts, championed the cause of Albanian equality and rights more vehemently than the two Albanian political parties of Macedonia were doing—and increasingly attracted local Albanians to join their mixed bag of KLA veterans, pan-Albanian romantics, opportunists, and criminals. The first clash was in Tanucevci, an Albanian town that had been in Kosovo but had been awarded to Macedonia and cut off from Kosovo in Serbian-Macedonian border adjustments.[16] The small, ill-trained Macedonian security force responded clumsily, with a combination of irresolution and a brute force that destroyed whole sections of Albanian villages. Macedonia looked very much like a failing state. Civil war loomed, should the country's Albanian population join the rebels. The government seemed to be hostage to both Albanian and Macedonian hard-liners, who could in an instant shatter any painstakingly built ethnic accommodation with some new murder or torching. Certainly the weapons for a war were abundantly available in the region, including an estimated 280,000 Kalashnikovs, 1 million antitank missiles, 3 million hand grenades, and 1 billion rounds of ammunition.[17]

During the crisis the OSCE's Spillover Monitor Mission did its best at least to track cross-border movements, and EU High Representative for Common Foreign and Security Policy Javier Solana, EU Commissioner for External Affairs Chris Patten, and NATO Secretary General George Robertson shuttled in and out of Skopje, counseling the Macedonians, above all, to be more responsive to Albanian demands for equal treatment. In an attempt to conjure up a united front, the internationals pressured the two main Macedonian and two main Albanian parties (plus four minor parties) to pull together in an omnibus coalition that then squabbled for seven weeks before settling down to govern.

Conditions did not look at all propitious for arresting the escalation. As the International Crisis Group put it, for three months Macedonia "stared into the abyss of inter-ethnic conflict, pulled away from the precipice, squandered opportunities for a political settlement, then returned as if sleepwalking to the brink of civil war." Toward the end of these three months, the chances for reconciliation looked especially remote when, in a TV interview on June 3, VMRO-DPMNE prime minister Ljupko Georgievski took a much tougher line than he had previously adopted. He implicitly endorsed ethnic partition and complained that the Albanians were breeding so fast they would soon outnumber Macedonians. Parliamentary speaker Stojan Andov further objected to the constant international interventions: "Macedonians thought they were doing everything right in terms of inter-ethnic relations. They were told that their country was the only multiethnic success story in the region, and were duly rewarded for their good behaviour. Then, after the fighting in Tetovo, Macedonians suddenly became the pariah and were told that they were doing everything wrong and had to give the Albanians everything the terrorists demanded."[18]

Interior Minister Ljube Boskovski was even harsher than his colleagues in his criticism of the internationals' softness on Albanian "terrorists." He advocated an all-out military offensive against the insurgents; to spearhead it, he formed a 1,400-strong special "Lions" police unit (named after the hotel he owned in Croatia and his own brand of wine there). With his tough approach, "Brother Ljube" (as he was universally known) quickly became one of the most popular politicians among Macedonians. Alienation fed further alienation, and by mid-June there were severe strains between Macedonians and Albanians in the coalition government. Macedonian demagogues branded cooperation with the internationals' demands as cowardice or betrayal; with unusual bluntness British historian Timothy Garton Ash described the Slav Macedonian politicians at the time as more "pig-headed" and "shortsighted" than any other elite he had ever encountered.[19] Albanian extremists looked outside the political system for leadership and turned to the rebels' political director, Macedonia-born Ali Ahmeti, a veteran of the 1981 Pristina student protests and subsequent incarceration and a participant in the KLA drive for Kosovo's independence.[20]

The obdurate Macedonians and the high-stakes Albanians thus looked like unpromising material for the reconciliation the internationals importunately sought to broker. Albanians saw themselves as perennial victims of discrimination and pogroms at the hands of the majority Macedonians. Macedonians, who had acquired a titular polity very late, feared losing this identity if the ethnic Macedonia defined by the 1991 constitution were turned into a civic state. Ethnic hostility and fear were at a high pitch. When brothers and sons are getting killed and refueling rage and revenge every day, momentum tends toward war rather than peace. And criminals from all the regional ethnicities had their own interests in prolonging the instability and lawlessness that favor trafficking and profits.[21] Yet just as the clashes grew worse in June 2001—there were several nasty incidents of torture and killing as the NLA overran a town outside Skopje—the government and the rebels abruptly accepted a proposal for a political solution that was mediated by the Americans and the Europeans and put forward by the VMRO-DPMNE's Boris Trajkovski, Gligorov's successor as president. Trajkovski was an anomaly in the region in coming from a devout Protestant family rather than from the Serbian Orthodox or rival Macedonian Orthodox Church; in the Communist era he had been banned to the countryside, where, as a lay pastor he had shepherded, unusually, a Roma congregation. He was more flexible than prime minister Georgievski in talks, but he, too, tended to see the negotiations "as a zero sum game in which any compromise was likely to lead to an ethnic partition of the country."[22]

Under heavy pressure from the United States and the European Union, a framework agreement was finally reached by August—with these two as guarantors of the pact. What seemed impossible in the overheated politics of

Skopje was accomplished in the placid lakeside resort of Ohrid, near the Albanian border. "In 2001 the outbreak of conflict sparked an intense effort by the international community, feeling that this time we must act strongly and early on," commented one international civil servant in Skopje. "It was the first time there was more or less timely and adequate intervention by the international community. If not, the fighting would have continued," concurred a second European. "Having had the humiliation of failure in Bosnia," and then "having invested rather much prestige" in stanching any subsequent bloodshed in the region, added a third European, the international community "for once stopped a war from going large-scale. . . . After [EU High Representative Javier] Solana visited Macedonia thirteen times, I stopped counting."[23]

The Ohrid Agreement was comparatively simple. The insurgents renounced violence, accepted an immediate cease-fire, and consented to surrender their weapons in exchange for amnesty or safe exit from Macedonia. Albanians did not acquire the rank of a "constituent people" of the country as they desired, but they did win the right to have Albanian recognized as the second official language in any locality in which the minority exceeded 20 percent—and to get municipalities redistricted to increase the number of such consolidated Albanian areas, even in the capital. The Macedonians pledged to hire more Albanians in the administration and police; to give Albanians better access to higher education; to amend the constitution to describe the country as a nation of all its citizens and not just of ethnic Macedonians; and to hand over all cases of conflict-related crime to the Hague Tribunal.[24] Furthermore, Skopje undertook a commitment to decentralize and devolve control of the very sensitive area of education, along with health, environment, and urban planning, to municipalities.[25] Adequate funding was to be provided by a mix of transfers from Skopje, 1 percent of VAT, and new local taxes.[26] Some 27,000 jobs would shift from central to local control in the process.[27]

There was little expectation that the peace would endure.[28] Indeed, within three months of the signing of the Ohrid accord, just before the Macedonian assembly was to pass the first agreed constitutional amendments, Boskovski's Lions defied the warnings of the international community and provocatively took control of mass graves in the Tetovo area. Albanians ambushed and killed three of the Lions. The Lions again put on shows of force in Albanian areas in January 2002 and during the election campaign in September 2002.[29]

Yet somehow these actions failed to escalate the constant low-level violence into a resumption of villagewide battles. The two sides persevered in carrying out the Ohrid bargain. Arben Xhaferi, leader of the Democratic Party of Albanians (DPA) in the government coalition, was instrumental in bringing the suspicious Albanians along. The NLA insurgents surrendered a symbolic 3,875 arms (mostly rifles) to NATO forces in Macedonia in the month-long Operation Essential Harvest, whose objective was less to remove as many arms as possible than to introduce a cooling-off period in which to begin building tentative confidence between the adversaries.[30] And even if the region remained awash in weapons, that main objective was accomplished. NATO's Operation Amber Fox smoothly succeeded Essential Harvest from September 2001 to December 2002.[31]

In 2003, under UN Security Council Resolution 1371 and with full American backing, the EU took over the peacekeeping task from NATO and deployed its first (modest) solo military operation of 400 peacekeepers, from thirteen member and fourteen nonmember nations. Notably, in this Operation Concordia the European Union used NATO assets for the first time, under terms worked out between the two organizations in half a decade of wrangling.[32] And over the border, NATO-led Kosovo Force (KFOR) peacekeepers, though they could not prevent all militants from slipping over the mountainous Kosovo-Macedonian boundary, did improve their interception rate and begin countering the rumor coursing among Serbs, Macedonians, and Albanians alike that a pro-Albanian United States had deliberately been turning a blind eye to the cross-border incursions.

For its part, the government majority in the assembly in Skopje specified that Macedonia was a unitary and multiethnic state of all its citizens; went beyond the earlier formal decentralization of 1990 to pass a law on the principles of local self-government and "decentralization-plus" in early 2002; and on one of the most sensitive issues, began redistricting in Skopje, where almost a third of the population lives. The 160,000 refugees from the fighting began to get resettled. The percentage of Albanians in the civil service jumped within a few years from 4 to 11 percent.

"The main achievement [of the Ohrid Agreement] was to break the myth that Macedonians and Albanians don't turn in weapons . . . without the use of force or coercive measures," explained one European diplomat involved in monitoring its implementation, in retrospect. Several thousand "weapons were in fact turned in voluntarily. Theoretically, we had a campaign promoting weapons collection, but practically we used weapons collection to promote the campaign." That campaign "to ensure long-term stability and development" continues today. "There is no other way. That is the road. There are no shortcuts. . . . Three things now have to be done to pave the way for economic progress: [instilling] trust that stability is sustainable," even as international forces are drawn down; implementing the peace agreement fully, including decentralization; and carrying out "the important structural reforms in the labor market and public sector."[33]

Skopje

Astonishingly, given the visceral ethnic distrust, the Ohrid Agreement succeeded even in its primary goal of offering Albanians a stake in the Macedonian political system. None other than the insurgent political director, Ali Ahmeti, put rebellion behind him, founded a new party called the Democratic Union for Integration (DUI)—and even managed, eventually, to get his name removed from Washington's blacklist of undesirables who are denied entry to the United States. Although it was only a year old, the DUI won 6 percent of the vote in the September 2002 election, joined a coalition government with the relatively pragmatic Social Democrats—and cemented Macedonia's unique institutionalization of minority representation in having two (and sometimes three) Albanian parties that form shifting alliances with the two main Macedonian parties.[34] In contrast to Bulgaria and Romania, where the Turks and the Hungarians, respectively, have formed a single party to champion their community's (or at least their leaders') interests by joining with whichever ethnic Bulgarian or Romanian party wins an election, the Macedonian system thus provides some choice of the minority as well as of the majority partner in government. As Musa Xhaferi, the DUI deputy prime minister, explained it, the benefit to Albanians from participating in the political process comes especially from the joint quest for EU membership, which would "make Albanians feel more certain that they [the Macedonian Slavs] would not revert to discrimination, and they would have more free rein for economic development. . . . Then we would be in the system; the values would be standardized."[35]

Similarly, Foreign Minister Ilinka Mitreva sketched in the benefit to her West Macedonia voters of the Ohrid accord's ending of hostilities and Macedonia's acceptance as a candidate for EU membership: "Now when I visit my constituency and have a beer with voters, they are talking about football, not stability. The main question is a normal question in a normal state: the economy. They tell me, 'We need jobs!' I am pleased to be criticized in this way. . . . In 2002–03 it was not easy for children to go to school, or for women to get water. And in only two years the main issues have become economic ones about employment and the standard of living."[36]

In the new ruling coalition formed after the 2002 election, Ahmeti found compatible partners in Prime Minister Branko Crvenkovski, a graduate of Skopje University in the field of information technology, and Interior Minister

Hari Kostov, a convinced reformer. Ahmeti appealed to his fellow former insurgents to cooperate with the police who had so recently been their bitter enemies, and Kostov managed to defuse various confrontations by eschewing displays of force and instead sitting down to talk out problems with local Albanian leaders. As trust was built up, more local Albanian officials began to seek the help of police to counter intimidation by criminals—especially as the number of Albanian police officers and biethnic patrols increased in ethnic Albanian areas.[37]

The Social Democratic–DUI government continued the Ohrid reforms.[38] It gave final legal approval to the university in Tetovo. It hired interpreters to make it possible to use the Albanian language in the assembly, administration, and courts. It put up Albanian street signs alongside Macedonian signs in Albanian areas. It recruited more Albanians for the army, even if it did not meet the target of 14 percent Albanian representation by 2003.

The reforms came at a political cost to both parties in the new coalition. Once he was out of power, former prime minister Georgievski turned even more nationalist. He criticized the concessions that his successor was making to the Albanians, and he eventually split off from the VMRO-DPMNE to form a more strident People's VMRO faction. His successor as head of the parent party, Nikola Gruevski, steered the VMRO-DPMNE back toward the center, though it would side with the would-be Ohrid spoilers in the referendum showdown in 2004. On the Albanian side, once Ali Ahmeti chose coalition with the Social Democrats and began pressing erstwhile rebels to seek power politically rather than militarily, the DPA's Arben Xhaferi also turned against the Ohrid compromise—despite his role as a facilitator of Ohrid in the Georgievski government—and sought to outflank Ahmeti, whom he branded a "lackey" of Prime Minister Crvenkovski. Among the internationals, opinions of Ahmeti varied. Some saw him as "a man of almost Gandhian restraint," one "faithful to the social contract"; they found plausible his strategy of waging enough of a war to get the West's attention, while imposing enough constraints to induce Westerners to intervene to restore stability in a way that would aid the Albanian cause.[39] Others were less impressed.

In 2003 two EU initiatives in particular affected Macedonia. The first was the reaffirmation at the Thessaloniki summit that the Balkan states, too, had a "European perspective." While the lack of any explicit time frame for EU membership disappointed many in the Western Balkans, the European promise was at least repeated and extended, instead of stopping at the border with Southeast Europe. The second initiative, establishing an EU Police Mission in Skopje, elicited mixed reactions among Macedonian officials. They welcomed assistance that would produce a more governable country and thwart challenges to their authority. Many were wary, however, of giving "criminals" (as they regarded the Albanians) a greater share in the system—and especially in the police—as the internationals clearly wanted to do in depoliticizing and professionalizing security forces.

At this point policing was a hot new topic in the West's postconflict policy, especially as the disaster of the security vacuum in Baghdad after U.S.-led forces occupied the city in spring 2003 became clearer. The Western alliance had already commissioned many studies of the military suppression of insurgency or civil war, and many studies of civilian institution building and even democracy building thereafter. There was a gap, however, in conceptualization of strategies for how, in the the crucial transition between the two, to ensure the kind of community security that is viewed positively by local populations, while still maintaining "escalation control" through graduated use of force by well-armed police backed up by military troops. Neither armies nor humanitarian nongovernmental organizations (NGOs) were suited to urban riot control or the suppression of organized crime. The Italian carabinieri and French gendarmerie came the closest to the kind of robust police force that was needed. The U.S. Justice Department had provided some police training in Macedonia several years earlier, and had then turned the assignment over to the OSCE—which was supposed to have some operational authority in policing but chose to interpret its mandate narrowly and focus on training alone.

In fulfilling that task, the OSCE made a major contribution to increasing minority representation in the police, graduating 1,000 cadets from the police academy at Idrizovo. In the opening years of the new millennium the share of Albanians among the 300-strong police force in Tetovo, the scene of firefights in 2001, shot up from 8 to 25 percent. Since the academy had to compensate for the grossly disadvantaged education of many Albanian cadets, the quality of the newcomers was not always as high as might have been hoped. Interior Minister Kostov admitted to one International Crisis Group interviewer that "incompetence, intimidation and periodic cooperation with criminal elements has undercut effectiveness."[40] But this was offset by the pacifying effect of fielding mixed police teams in tense situations. The international advisory programs were far less effective, however, in increasing minority representation in the special or secret police. Despite Kostov's efforts, these remained the preserve of Boskovski's Lions and other nationalist hard-liners, who could not legally be fired.

The EU Police (EUPOL) Mission Proxima that the European Union ran in Macedonia from the end of 2003 to the end of 2005, with an initial 200 persons, was modeled in part on the EU Police Mission in Bosnia.[41] Like the OSCE program, it focused on training rather than hands-on operations, on encouraging implementation of reform in the Interior Ministry, building a border service, and monitoring and supporting the essential biethnic police patrols. It further taught skills for combating organized crime and the kind of forensic investigation that does not depend on confessions, voluntary or involuntary.[42] And willy-nilly, in the case of Khaled el Masri, a German citizen of Lebanese origins, the Proxima mission demonstrated the irrelevance of the EU and its sanitized rules once American power comes into play.

Masri, according to the *Washington Post* account that was obliquely confirmed by Secretary of State Condoleezza Rice on her visit to Europe in December 2005, had been taken off a bus bound for Skopje and detained by Macedonian police at the Serbian border on New Year's Eve 2003, on the strength of an American list of terrorist suspects. He was held for twenty-three days, he said later, then turned over to what he inferred were masked CIA agents, who hooded him, drugged him, and whisked him out of the Skopje airport to what seemed to be a secret American prison in Afghanistan, where he was beaten. Five months later, when evaluators ascertained that Masri was not the suspect they were seeking, he was flown to Albania and released.[43] It is highly unlikely that the Proxima police mission knew anything about the incident at the time. One former member of the Macedonian secret service commented to the *Neue Zürcher Zeitung,* "It's easy to circumvent the Europeans. Our partners are the Americans." And a senior Macedonian diplomat told the newspaper that the Americans hold all the trump cards in security issues: "They keep the Albanians in Kosovo in check; they are key to our getting into NATO, which will finally secure our borders. The EU is our future. But when it's a question of our present security, it's the Americans who count."[44]

By the end of its tour in 2005, the Proxima team had hopes that the Macedonian Interior Ministry might reach European standards in another four or five years.[45] "European standards" was a flexible concept. A West European who worked with Macedonian security forces described an episode in which one Albanian shot and killed a fellow Albanian in front of two Albanian policemen; the policemen looked the other way, neither arresting the murderer nor asking his name. "You can't expect a man who gets €200 a month and has to feed his family not to get drawn into other structures" that pay more, the West European commented, alluding to recruitment of policemen by criminal gangs. And he added that the follow-on police advisory team, from the German state of Brandenburg under an EU "twinning" arrangement, was to be reduced to thirty personnel at the request of the Macedonians, in order to thin out foreigners who gave unwelcome counsel.[46]

There were numerous other proofs of the difficulty of transforming Macedonia's police into a multiethnic, nonpartisan force, including unsolved kidnappings, intimidation of witnesses by criminals, escapes from prison, violent disputes over education, and the continued presence of known criminals in the special police. One of the most notorious incidents was the police killing of seven Asians in March 2002, half a year after the Ohrid Agreement. Though facts remain murky, the six Pakistanis and one other South Asian victim, apparently migrants who were on their way to Greece to look for jobs, were killed in a police set-up. Interior Minister Boskovski initially described the dead men as Islamist infiltrators who had planned to attack foreign embassies in Skopje and portrayed the Macedonian action as a contribution to America's war on terror—a claim that both American and Western European diplomats in Skopje quickly rejected. Three policemen and one businessman were charged with the murders, but were acquitted by the Skopje district court in 2005, for lack of evidence. After Boskovski himself was indicted for the murders in 2004, he fled to Croatia, where he holds dual citizenship; he was subsequently arrested there and sent to the Hague on unrelated charges of war crimes.[47]

The Long Road to Europe

In May 2003, under U.S. patronage, the Crvenkovski government took a step toward Euroatlantic integration in joining with the United States and the utterly unlike Croatia and Albania in an Adriatic Charter. The main aim was to champion the NATO candidacy of these three countries on the peripheries of the Western Balkans' hottest danger zones, and to help them assert civilian control over their militaries in order to qualify for accession at the alliance's next summit.[48] A secondary aim was to encourage regional cooperation, both bilaterally and multilaterally, and to generate mutual support for reforms in governance, especially in the judicial branch. Croatia was vastly better prepared for a globalized, postnational world than its two Balkan partners. It had inherited more developed institutions in the breakup of Yugoslavia; it had already begun to shed ultranationalism after Tudjman's death, by electing the democratically minded Stipe Mesic as president and then electing a Social Democratic government to replace the HDZ that had been in power since independence. Ivo Sanader, Tudjman's successor as leader of the HDZ, had further started to marginalize some of the party's most adamant hard-liners and was on his way to winning the December 2003 election and becoming prime minister. Within a year, Zagreb would be invited to upgrade its association with Brussels and join Bulgaria and Romania as full candidates for membership.[49] By contrast, Macedonia was at best fragile. Albania, too, was fragile, but had at least rebuilt a functioning government after the pyramid collapse and anarchy of 1997.[50]

In February 2004 Macedonian president Trajkovski was killed in an airplane crash. Two weeks later, riots erupted in Kosovo.[51] Slav Macedonians, Albanian officials, and the internationals alike crossed their fingers and deemed it a triumph that the unrest in Kosovo did not reignite armed clashes in Macedonia. A week thereafter, Skopje filed its formal application to join the European Union. One month after that, the country held a presidential vote in which, significantly, no candidate openly opposed the Ohrid Agreement. Branko Crvenkovski, elected third president of Macedonia with majority support from both Macedonians and Albanians, duly resigned as head of the Social Democratic Party, as required by the constitution. The reform-minded Hari Kostov moved up to take his place as prime minister. But parties, with their internal squabbles, remained, in the analysis of the International Crisis Group, "more mechanisms for distribution of patronage and running election campaigns than real engines of democratic inclusion."[52]

The government now faced two huge tasks. The first was to carry out the final, controversial Ohrid provision on decentralization by cutting the number of municipalities from 123 to 85; redistricting, in a kind of positive gerrymandering, to give Albanians more of a voice in Skopje and in Struga and Kicevo to the southwest, in particular; and turning those 27,000 jobs and the corresponding funding over to local control. The second essential task—entrusted to rising young technocrats—was to translate the EU's priority demands into legislation and implemention fast enough to advance Macedonia toward EU candidacy, while also completing the EU's exhaustive questionnaire about the country's readiness to become a full candidate handed to Skopje on October 1, 2004. The aspiring eurocrats—in the words of Gerald Knaus, "institutional islands within a highly fragmented administration"—had to respond to questions no one in Skopje had ever asked before, about everything from prison management to organigrams of food safety departments.[53]

The first mission, implementing decentralization, was complicated by a Macedonian backlash against the growing political role of Albanians, as manifested in a write-in demand for a referendum against the government's devolution program. As early as August 2003, the old coalition allies, former prime minister Georgievski of the VMRO-DPMNE and Arben Xhaferi of the DPA, had branded the Ohrid Agreement "dead" and once again called for partition of the country. Now they began a real drive to void the Ohrid Agreement in the referendum in November 2004. Arben Xhaferi, reversing his own role as Ohrid facilitator in 2001, now outbid the pragmatic, horse-trading Ahmeti in calling for greater concessions to the Albanians. Xhaferi's deputy, Menduh Thaci, went so far as to threaten that if the demands of the DPA were not met, it would resort to "the 'ultimate solution' of the Albanian issue"—that is, partition and a drive for a Greater Albania.[54]

So belligerent was the mood among Macedonian activists that the government did not even try to persuade a majority of the virtues of its program. It simply argued, negatively and accurately, that fulfillment of Ohrid was a precondition for becoming a candidate for EU membership—and that a yes vote on the plebiscite would be a no vote for Europe. Therefore it counseled citizens to boycott the referendum altogether, so that the turnout would fall short of the 50 percent required for the vote to be valid. This was not the most daring approach, but it worked.

The proreferendum, antidecentralization campaign—stoked by strident propaganda from the Macedonian diaspora—dominated the run-up to the ballot on November 7, 2004. But playing an unexpected trump card three days before the Macedonian vote—and two days after the U.S. presidential vote, so as not to prejudice support for Bush among disgruntled Greek Americans— the United States suddenly recognized the Republic of Macedonia by its chosen name, thus rewarding Skopje for its calculated participation in America's coalition of the willing in the Iraq war and coalition of the unwilling against the International Criminal Court. The referendum turnout, a weak 26 percent, revealed no newfound love for multiethnicity. But it did suggest that a majority of Macedonians were becoming resigned to the Ohrid compromises as the price they must pay to get into the EU and NATO.[55] The public had been socialized into becoming pro-EU—however fuzzy its understanding of what the EU was—and making political trade-offs on the basis of this preference.

The Skopje rollercoaster did not stop with this victory by default, however. A week after the failed plebiscite, the exasperated Kostov resigned as prime minister, saying that squabbling within the government was blocking reforms. Social Democratic Party leader Vlado Buckovski, a forty-one-year-old lawyer who had written his Skopje University doctoral dissertation on comparative Roman and contemporary law, moved up from defense minister to become the new prime minister. He proceeded with decentralization, and when an armed group of Albanians occupied Kondovo, on the edge of Skopje, for several weeks, he remained calm and gave the leaders of the two main ethnic

Albanian parties time to persuade the rebels to lay down their weapons. For this restraint, he reaped the wrath of hard-liner Macedonians, who condemned his "betrayal" of "patriotism" and threatened to "bypass" the government and internationals and revive the Macedonian paramilitaries of 2001 as "neighborhood defense groups."[56] In connection with the incident, the EU subsequently blacklisted a former commander of the Lions, the driver and bodyguard of Ahmeti, a DPA member of the assembly, and several other Albanians for undermining peace and security.[57]

The new government persisted with reforms. It drew up a detailed plan for decentralization and passed laws in 2004–05 to let the Albanian flag fly alongside the Macedonian flag in areas where Albanians constituted more than 50 percent of the population.[58] It accelerated reforms to make the army compatible with NATO and completed the transfer of border control from the army to the police. And it hammered out compromises with the opposition People's VMRO on the nomination of prosecutors and judges, finally overriding the no votes of the main opposition VMRO-DPMNE to pass ten constitutional amendments ending the parliamentary appointment of judges and curtailing parliament's political influence on the judiciary.[59]

Confirmation of the government's victory in the referendum—or at least, confirmation of the splintering of the opposition parties—came in the next local elections, in March 2005. The Social Democrats won in fifty-one of the eighty-five communities. In Tetovo, Ahmeti's DUI won as the DPA boycotted the election; and Hazbi Lika, former chief of intelligence for the National Liberation Army, became mayor. Rich businessman Trifun Kostovski became the senior mayor of Skopje; an independent Roma became mayor of the Roma district of Suto Orizari, on the outskirts of Skopje, but could not assume office because of his 2003 court conviction for large-scale theft. Some observers had second thoughts about the virtues of decentralization in practice and wondered whether elected officials would simply become minions of village bosses and "commanders."[60] One skeptical European diplomat in Skopje stated flatly that "municipalities do nothing much other than collect garbage. They are nests of corruption." Within the Islamic community—which kept its distance from the Albanian political parties—feuding factions took to branding their rivals "Wahhabi" as an omnibus insult, in much the same way that every political party accused political rivals of being corrupt.[61]

Through all the upheavals, the technocrats kept to a grueling schedule to answer the European Commission's questions within four-and-a-half months. In mid-February 2005 Deputy Prime Minister for European Integration Radmila Sekerinska presented Macedonia's 14,000-page response to Brussels, noting pointedly that the EU's "last enlargement round [in 2004] brought those [newcomers] democracy and economic development," and arguing that the admission of Macedonia by 2010 should similarly bolster Balkan stability, democracy, and economic growth. Making a virtue of necessity, she maintained that "answering the questionnaire amid the turmoil provoked by the resignation of the Prime Minister, Hari Kostov, the election of a new government and a hotly debated referendum on the controversial issue of decentralization, all show that Macedonia's institutions can work—and achieve results—in extraordinary circumstances."[62] In reward for its strenuous efforts, Skopje received asymmetric trade rules that gave Macedonia unlimited duty-free access to the EU market for virtually all its products and, on acceptance of its candidacy for accession, increased EU assistance under the Instrument for Structural Policies for Pre-Accession (ISPA), above and beyond the €728 million that Macedonia received from the EU from 1992 to 2004 and the planned €79 million for 2005–06.[63]

By the end of 2005 the European Council summit had accepted Macedonia's candidacy for membership, but it postponed concrete negotiations with Skopje indefinitely, pending the "full discussion" of further enlargement among present EU members that the French insisted on.[64] As planned, the EU dropped its special overseer role in the form of the EU special representative, who had been double-hatted with the European Commission's representative (effectively, the EU ambassador) in Skopje. Popular enthusiasm for EU membership remained high, at 90 percent according to one survey.[65] One hundred thousand Macedonian citizens with some claim to Bulgarian ancestry had already voted with their passports, applying for the Bulgarian citizenship that lets them travel freely in EU countries today—and will let them continue to travel freely in Bulgaria after it joins the EU and must require visas of its non-EU neighbors.

The final EU report cards on Macedonia's candidacy for membership in November 2005 agreed in their evaluation. They commended Skopje for its progress, which by then included a rise in the number of Albanian policemen and army officers from 150 and 60, respectively, in 2001 to more than 1,800 and 1,100—and also an impressive wireless broadband coverage of 95 percent of the population, with comprehensive information technology training in schools.[66] They then went on to stress, though, how much still remained to be done, especially in "implementation of the police reform, . . . firm commitment to eliminating external influences over the judiciary," and combating corruption and its "threat to the stability of democratic institutions and the rule of law."[67] Specifically, Western observers had grave doubts about Macedonia's capacity to try four war crimes cases that the Hague Tribunal wanted to send back to Skopje and feared that contentious trials might undermine the delicate amnesty deal in the Ohrid Agreement.[68]

In its own follow-up report, "Macedonia: Wobbling toward Europe," the International Crisis Group was blunter than the European Commission. "The judicial system remains unreformed and dysfunctional. A country of two million citizens has a backlog of some 1.2 million cases. The crippled system, which is still subject to excessive executive branch influence and corruption, suits entrenched political interests," it asserted. "Macedonia is still an immature democracy, vulnerable to spoilers seeking to hijack or exploit an imperfect reform process." It urgently needs to "purge corrupt and non-performing judges" and "establish a permanent judicial and prosecutorial training academy." And the EU needs to set up a successor police mission to Proxima and place advisers in the Justice and Interior Ministries, as well as in the prime minister's office. Three-quarters of the judges should be swept off the bench, it said further, to make way for younger and more modern successors.[69]

On the other looming issue that could have a major, and potentially destabilizing, impact on Macedonia, the Kosovo status talks, Macedonian officials seemed to be less nervous in 2006 than they were a few years earlier. They wanted to complete border demarcation with the UN Interim Mission in Kosovo (UNMIK) before any change of status rather than wait until afterward, as the Kosovar Albanians insisted, but they were not agitated.[70] DPA leader Arben Xhaferi, out of government from 2002 until 2006, said that the land next door should no longer be known by the Slavic name of Kosovo (or even Kosova), but should go by the old Illyrian name of Dardania and merge with Albania. But as of this writing, officials in Tirana, while publicly supporting Kosovar independence, are unambiguous in also supporting present borders, including Macedonia's borders, and are not putting at risk their hard-won normalization with both Skopje and Belgrade.[71]

As Macedonia took its place in line for EU membership, the ICG clearly saw no reason to reverse its earlier judgment of 2003 that the West must "revise substantially the conventional assessment that Macedonia is the foremost political 'success story' in the Balkans. It is instead an underperforming post-conflict country still very much at risk, unable to tackle—operationally or politically—its security challenges without upsetting an uncertain ethnic balance." This constellation, it contended, is "driving unrest, from criminality and weak policing to an equally weak economy and corruption."[72]

By contrast with the ICG, the blue-ribbon Amato Commission on the Balkans viewed the glass as marvelously half full as Macedonia achieved full EU candidate status. "Although in theory, Macedonia should not exist, it is actually a modest but significant success story," it argued. "The country illustrates our thesis that a final and clear constitutional arrangement and the institutionalization of European perspectives are the two institutions that can work apparent miracles in the Balkans" and overcome crises.[73]

CHAPTER EIGHT

INVENTING ALBANIA

THE BURLY YOUNG man on the Austrian Air flight with the ripped-off sleeves that displayed the tatoos on his upper arms—one of the Albanian flag, the other of Scanderbeg—was indisputably Albanian. When he noticed that the mother sitting in front of him was uncertain about airplane protocol, he kindly leaned forward to explain in Albanian that she must be sure to buckle up herself and her toddler. Yet when the stewardess came down the aisle, he spoke to her in Cockney. He was, it turned out, exercising his new freedom by studying sports therapy in England. He was astounded to be asked if he might have been with the Kosova Liberation Army, but he was pleased that an American recognized the fifteenth-century Albanian hero on his right bicep. After some pleasantries, he recounted the latest joke.

An Albanian road engineer visited his Italian counterpart and found him living in a lovely lakeside villa. "How did you manage this?" the Albanian asked admiringly.

"Oh, that's simple," came the reply. "When I lay out autostradas, instead of putting down eight centimeters of foundation, I put down seven centimeters. And with the other centimeter, I built this house."

Two years later, when the Italian paid a return visit and discovered that his Albanian friend was the proud owner of a four-story hotel on the Adriatic coast, he naturally asked the same question. "Oh, that's simple," the Albanian replied. "I did exactly what you said, only instead of laying a seven-centimeter foundation, I put down one centimeter."

It was as good an introduction as any to Albanian potholes, the symbiosis between the two sides of the Adriatic, and Albanians' fast learning curve once they emerged out of their time warp in 1991. It was supplemented by a conversation in Tirana with a young English-, Italian- and Greek-speaking man who tried to help a foreigner understand the difference between blood feuds on the southern plains and those in the northern mountains. "In the north, if a member of your clan kills a member in my clan, I must kill someone—any male—in your clan," he explained. "But in the south, if a member of your clan kills a member of my clan, then I'm not allowed to kill anyone except the man who actually shot him—just like in America." A brief discussion of rule of law in the United States did nothing to dispel his conception of American justice, formed from all those Hollywood whodunits that convey around the globe the essence of American values.

In fact, not only differences, but also political tension between the Geg clans in the north and the Tosk clans in the south was taken by Western analysts for decades as the key to understanding politics during the half century when Communist Albania sealed itself hermetically from the world. Party and state chief Enver Hoxha and the majority of his Communist cadres came from the south. And despite Albanian protests at this oversimplification, outsiders still believed that the Geg-Tosk dichotomy cast light on Albanian politics after student demonstrations prodded Hoxha's successor to allow the first multiparty elections in 1991. Fatos Nano, the sort-of reform Communist who became the maiden prime minister in the new era, today is a member of parliament representing Saranda, as far south as one can go without crossing into Greece. His government was distinguished by closeness to "expanding Greek Orthodoxy" and "Greek business interests," according to James Pettifer, a specialist on Albania at the U.K. Defence Academy's Conflict Studies Research Center. By contrast, Sali Berisha, the cardiologist (and therefore, by definition, intellectual) who was Nano's nemesis and alternated with him as Albania's leader over two decades, came from Tropoja, as far north as one can go without crossing into Kosovo. In his government, Pettifer saw a closeness to Kosovar Albanians.[1] John R. Lampe of the University of Maryland also noted Berisha's charges in the mid-1990s "that the small Greek minority and, by religious association, the Orthodox Albanians of the far Tosk south were seeking autonomy as a prelude to secession."[2] Such regional identification must be put in perspective, however. Nano has also represented other constituencies in parliament in the past decade, including one in Tirana. For his part, Berisha rarely set foot in his native Tropoja during the whole post-Communist era, and since 1991 has been elected to parliament from Kavaja, a small city just south of Tirana. A number of insiders think that the two politicians, despite their conspicuous enmity, really operated, and still operate today, in tacit collaboration.

The two rivals led the two main parties that emerged from the Communist Party in the 1990s. After his election, Nano renamed the Communists "Socialists." Berisha, although he had been as much a part of the old system as his adversary, championed anticommunism, the right to private property, and free elections. For several years he and his Democratic Party were lionized especially by American Republicans, European Christian Democrats, and the British Foreign Office, until word got out about the persecution of political opponents and maltreatment of prisoners under his government—and until the pyramid scams collapsed in 1997.

Shkodra/Scutari

The strongest impression a first-time visitor gets of the regional capital of northern Albania, unfortunately, is one of garbage—in the streets, covering the grass and bushes in city parks, everywhere, like some kind of parasitical kudzu. Nature may have absorbed all the shoes and wooden plows that villagers tossed into the void fifteen years ago, but the earth simply cannot absorb the unrecyclable urban debris it has been plagued with since Albania joined the modern world. Throughout the Balkans, trees alongside streambeds are festooned with plastic bags deposited once upon a time by higher waters, but surely nowhere is there a greater concentration of open trash than in Shkodra.

The surface appearance belies the city's historical preeminence. That heritage can be seen in ruins of Ottoman buildings and in the citadel towering above the city on limestone cliffs. The castle walls enclose twenty-two acres of underbrush, deep cisterns, secret passageways down to the river, and the remains of the Italianate fourteenth-century St. Stephen's Cathedral turned fifteenth-century mosque. The stones testify to serial battles from the second century B.C. up to World War I. In the most famous of them, in the 1470s, the Albanians held out against the besieging Turks, at a terrible cost; it was left to the vultures to clean up the 60,000 corpses. The site's very first human sacrifice, according to the grandfather of the many "immurement" and betrayal legends in the Balkans, was the wife of the youngest of the three brothers who built the fortification. As she was being cemented into the masonry, she asked that one breast be left free to feed her baby, and it is said that a rock in the wall with the shape of a breast still emits a trickle of milky water today.[3]

The legend traces back to the Illyrian heritage that makes today's Albanians the oldest people in the Balkans, predating the Hellenic arrivals by several centuries, the Slav newcomers by a millennium, and Ottoman rule by a millennium and a half.[4] In the third century B.C. the conquered Illyrians undermined the victory of the conquering King Pyrrhus. From the third century B.C. until after the Roman conquest of Illyria in 168 B.C., the Ardiaeans, operating out of their capital at the southern tip of Lake Shkodra, were renowned raiders of Greek ships along the Peloponnesian coast. In later centuries Scutari, as the city was then known, was Roman, Byzantine, Slav, and Venetian before it became Turkish.

When the final Turkish conquest threatened in the fifteenth century, Gjergj Kastrioti (Scanderbeg), as every Albanian schoolchild knows, brought his fellow chieftains together—a feat as remarkable as his military prowess—to postpone for twenty years, by hit-and-run guerrilla tactics, the subjugation of the last sliver of the Balkans. After the great war leader died in 1468 and Venice surrendered its last Albanian outposts to the Turks in 1479, many Albanians converted to Islam, and they soon provided some of the Ottoman Empire's best troops against European foes. (Indeed, Scanderbeg had himself converted to Islam and become a famous Ottoman general before he returned to his birthplace to defend his father's lands against seizure by the Turks.) Muslim Albanians had full access to careers in the Ottoman bureaucracy and rose so fast in the ranks that of the forty-two grand viziers in the Ottoman apogee between 1453 and 1623, eleven were Albanian, while only five were Turkish.[5] During this period Shkodra remained the largest town in Ottoman Albania and the center of one of the largest administrative *sanjaks* in the Balkans.

The Albanians' success in the Ottoman system came at a price, however. Since they did not feel exploited by Constantinople—and since, uniquely in Albania, the Porte forbade any schools or any publications in the local language—the cultural and national awakening that inspired a corollary political awakening among Greeks, Serbs, Montenegrins, and Bulgarians in the nineteenth century passed the Albanians by. (The Greek patriarch, who feared the spread of the vernacular as much as Constantinople did, reinforced the Ottoman ban by threatening to excommunicate Orthodox Albanians who read or wrote in their native language.) There was no consistent Albanian orthography until 1879, and the large bulk of Albanians were illiterate. If they wished to send letters, they had to hire scribes to write their messages phonetically in either the Greek or the Arabic script, the working language for documents in the Ottoman Empire. The drive for a common Albanian language and literature for both north and south thus came primarily from Albanian settlers abroad, where the prohibition on Albanian publications and schools did not apply, especially in Sicily, Calabria, Constantinople itself, Romania, Bulgaria, Egypt, and, by the early twentieth century, the United States. It was in Brussels that Faik Konitza resurrected Scanderbeg as a folk hero. "If the Albanian language is not written, in a short time there will be no Albania on the surface of the earth nor will the name Albania appear on the map of the world," lamented Konstandin Kristoforidhi, who himself translated the Bible into Albanian toward the end of the nineteenth century.[6]

In the Albanian heartland, it was not until 1878, when the Treaty of San Stefano provoked alarm over the parceling out of Albanian-populated territories to Slavic states, that the first overt political assembly of nationalists was formed as the Prizren League. And even then, the three hundred delegates, who came mostly from Kosovo or western Macedonia, initially demanded not an independent Albania, but simply a halt to "encroachment by foreign powers on Albanian national lands."[7]

One main reason for their lag behind other Balkan peoples in developing a national consciousness, noted the nineteenth-century poet Naim Frasheri, was that no common religion united the Albanians. The Greeks had their Greek Orthodox Church, the Serbs their Serbian Orthodox Church, the Croats their Catholic Church, and the Bulgarians their Bulgarian Exarchate. Different Albanian tribes, by contrast, had embraced Catholicism, Orthodoxy, and Islam, in both Sunni and Bektashi forms. To be sure, there was a good deal of syncretism, especially among Muslim Albanians in Montenegro, who joined the Orthodox in looking to the relics of St. Vasili Ostroski in the Niksic Monastery to work miracles. And the most distinctive Albanian Islamic denomination, the Bektashi sect, was itself highly syncretic; deriving from a fourteenth-century Persian sect, it melded Zoroastrianism, Buddhism, and animism, and revered Christ as one carrier of the divine spirit. Toward the end of the nineteenth century, the *tekke* houses of worship of the Bektashi religion did adopt a nationalist tone, becoming centers of Albanian book smuggling and some armed bands. The number of *tekkes* doubled between 1878 and 1912. Yet adherents of Bektashi Islam remained a minority of perhaps 15 percent, larger than the 10 percent of Catholics, who were concentrated in the northern mountains, but smaller than the 20 percent of Orthodox, who were dominant in the south, and the 55 percent of Sunni adherents, located above all in central Albania.[8]

More generally, some contemporary historians attribute the drive for an Albanian national state, when it finally came, less to the usual Balkan dynamics of a cultural awakening than to the decay of the Ottoman system. When Constantinople could no longer protect the Muslims on its peripheries, the once preferred Albanian Muslims turned to nationalism from weakness, rather than from strength and growing self-confidence.[9]

The Albanian Question

Their late development of a sense of belonging to a nation meant that they were the last in line to acquire a state of their own in the Balkans, and the territory inhabited by half of their fellow Albanian speakers had already been incorporated into Greece, Serbia, and Montenegro. Indeed, it was only because of the great powers' desire to block Serbian (and vicariously, Russian) access to the sea that Albanians got a state at all at the London Conference of 1913 during the Balkan Wars. This new state, the smallest in the region at about the size of Massachusetts, did not even get fixed borders until 1924. At the time of its creation the Albanians were hardly prepared for self-government, and the German prince who was selected to rule them, Wilhelm of Wied, proved to have less talent for the job than some of the other German princes enthroned in the new Balkan states. He fled the country after only six months, in September 1914, as the Great War engulfed all of Europe.

In Wilhelm's stead after World War I came an ambitious Muslim bey named Ahmet Zog, who arranged to have himself appointed president of Albania in 1925 and monarch in 1928. He paved streets in the small town of Tirana, which had become the capital in 1920, and commissioned Italian architects to construct a palace and imposing public buildings on the expansive Piazza Scanderbeg. He reduced banditry by bringing in a tough British inspector-general of the gendarmerie. He began draining the malarial swamps near Shkodra. And he required all Zog families except his own to change their surnames. While campaigning against hereditary blood feuds, the suspicious King Zog also killed so many putative rivals that he greatly increased the number of vendettas; he alone was personally involved in an estimated 600 feuds and survived some fifty-five assassination attempts. In 1939, as Benito Mussolini turned from occupying Ethiopia to invade Albania in order to dominate the Balkans, King Zog fled his country.[10]

In the interwar years the more cosmopolitan Shkodra was, by all accounts, a pleasant city. The educated class enjoyed Mozart and Beethoven, and traveled to Rome, Vienna, and Budapest and spoke the corresponding languages. The townhouses of its doctors and lawyers were furnished with Biedermeier chairs, and with oil portraits of their fathers or grandfathers painted by French artists. The Catholic villagers in the mountains that swept up from the coast to the northeast toward Kosovo might still wear their beribboned white shepherds' outfits and conduct blood feuds under the elaborate rules of the medieval *kanun* (law) of Lek Dukagjini, which could confine the men of a clan to their inviolate homes for years or decades to escape revenge murder. But such practices were increasingly seen as old-fashioned by intellectuals, who felt more at home in Paris and Rome than in their homeland's northern crags. Ismail Kadare, Albania's first novelist of note and winner of the inaugural British Man Booker International Prize in 2005, expressed the ambivalence in his 1970s novel *Broken April*, written from the point of view of Gjorg, the reluctant young avenger in a vendetta, who knows that his own life will be doomed as soon as his thirty-day grace period is over.[11]

Everything changed as World War II shredded the old social and political fabric. The Yugoslav Communists appointed schoolteacher Enver Hoxha as party secretary of the tiny cadre of Albanian Communists—about 150 at the beginning of the war—and Yugoslav organizers helped the Albanians expand their cells by promising land to the peasants, along with liberation from their Italian occupiers.[12] The Kosovars were far more suspicious of Tito and of the Serbs' intentions than were the Albanians in the new state of Albania; the former viewed communism as a Slav ideology and certainly deemed the Serbs worse oppressors than the Italians or (after Italy dropped out of the war) the Germans. Moreover, while Tito dismissed as a quisling creation the Greater Albanian puppet state set up by Mussolini in wartime Albania, Kosovo, and western Macedonia, the Kosovars saw in it the realization at last of their aspiration to unite Albanians in the region in a single state.

As Tito emerged victorious in 1945, he, Stalin, and Hoxha all took it for granted that Albania would be a Yugoslav satellite. Tito appeased the Serbs he was otherwise easing out of their old preeminence in Yugoslavia by giving Kosovo back to them and further planned to expand his own power on the peninsula by establishing a grand, Yugoslav-run Balkan Federation that would include Bulgaria and Greece. His ambitions were checked, however, when the Communists lost the Greek civil war, the Soviet Union claimed Bulgaria as its own satellite, and Tito's humiliations of Hoxha pushed the Albanian leader into an alliance with Stalin against him and into a bizarre North Korea–like personal dictatorship in Europe's most isolated and most draconian Communist regime.[13]

From 1948 until 1961 Hoxha sealed his country off from all its neighbors and depended for his own survival on the patronage of Moscow. When Kremlin revisionists abandoned the true Stalinist path, Hoxha abandoned the Soviet Union and in 1961 shifted his allegiance to Beijing. Thereafter, some collective farms in northern Albania had to cultivate silkworms, Hoxha ran a copycat Cultural Revolution in Albania, and a generation of curious students who yearned to see the wider world had to learn Mandarin and go to Beijing.

In this period Hoxha declared Albania the world's "first atheist state" in 1967, closed all churches and mosques, and persecuted the Catholics in the north especially ruthlessly. He turned the Shkodra Cathedral into a sports palace, complete with swimming pool. He converted other churches to apartments and warehouses. He withdrew from the Warsaw Pact in 1968 and built hundreds of thousands of shallow, two-man bunkers around the country to defend against any attack from the Soviet bloc (or Yugoslavia or NATO). When Chairman Mao died in 1976 and China, too, relaxed a bit, Hoxha cut off even that connection, and Albania became a hermit state. Throughout his four decades in power he maintained control by means of the ubiquitous Sigurimi secret police.[14]

The propulsion from Ottoman feudalism into twentieth-century totalitarianism was so much more compressed in Albania than elsewhere in the Balkans that the transformation there must be examined in more detail than its Serb, Croatian, or Bosnian equivalents. To begin with, the Albanian peasants who formed the partisan shock troops in World War II discovered that they endured the hardships of forest living better than the more effete city dwellers, and that the urban folk needed the peasants' grain more than the peasants needed manufactured goods. They therefore lost their awe of the old beys and other elites and followed revolutionaries like Hoxha. After the war, peasant Communist apparatchiks reveled in dispossessing the Shkodra bourgeoisie, expropriating their houses and furniture, and trashing their pianos.[15]

In some respects Hoxha did modernize Albanians, force-feeding them into literacy at night schools so all could read Marxist-Leninist tracts, introducing schools and compulsory education through the eighth grade, and giving Albania, until then the only European country without a university, a university in Tirana in 1957. By 1963 illiteracy had essentially been eradicated. Hoxha also set up clinics to provide free medical treatment; life expectancy jumped from fifty-four years in 1959 to sixty-seven years in 1970.

In other respects Hoxha turned the clock back. Private cars were forbidden; Albanians traveled in crammed free buses, trains, oxcarts, and—after Hoxha's break with Beijing stopped the import of spare parts—in broken-down Chinese trucks pulled by horses. Over four decades, Western journalists who managed to sneak into the country in the occasional package tours could ferret out little to write about other than the mushrooming of the militarily useless minibunkers and the eerie bucolic silence of Tirana's Scanderbeg Square, the center of a city of more than 100,000. Ordinary Kosovars who idealized Albania for its independence (if not the young Kosovo intelligentsia who encountered Tirana University in the 1970s) were shocked by the poverty they found once they actually visited the country—Hoxha did allow Kosovar Albanians in, expecting that they would naturally become his supporters—and went home murmuring that Tirana's streets were so clean because Albanians had nothing to throw away.[16] "Albania has come out of one of the most outrageous dictatorships in Europe, and this dictatorship lasted for forty-five years," explained Albanian president Alfred Moisiu in an interview. "In other Communist countries one could detect some elements of democracy, however small, but in Albania these elements were not even at zero level, but at a minus level." This dearth is responsible for "our long and difficult period of transition."[17]

After Hoxha died in 1985, the Communists again tolerated religious worship and authorized the first legal Catholic mass in Shkodra in a quarter century.[18] They also loosened Hoxha's harsh controls a bit—but when European communism collapsed in 1989–91, they could no longer keep pace with rising expectations. Students demonstrated in Tirana and Shkodra, gaining some pluralism and the renaming of the Enver Hoxha University as Tirana University. Thousands of young men with no hope of finding jobs at home fled to Greece; 200,000 paid to get onto rubber speedboats or commandeered boats in Durres and Vlore to sail the hundred miles across the Adriatic to Italy.[19] Others occupied Western embassies in Tirana to demand asylum. Adventurers and criminals in league with old Sigurimi agents easily stole arms from unprotected army and police depots; the country was awash with weapons.

Eventually the unrest forced Hoxha's successors to declare the first multiparty elections in sixty years, in 1991. Their old (Communist) Party of Labor won, primarily on the votes of peasants who feared that farmland would be given back to the old feudal owners. But growing anarchy and hunger—despite substantial EC food aid—forced the government to declare new general elections in March 1992. This time Sali Berisha claimed victory; the Democratic Party he had founded with financial assistance from Ibrahim Rugova's Democratic League of Kosova (LDK) in Kosovo and Albanian emigrés in the United States won a landslide. President Ramiz Alia, who had once been Hoxha's deputy, resigned voluntarily, and the parliament voted Berisha in as president, with the strengthened constitutional role that he had insisted on.

After the election Berisha focused, as he had promised, on instituting market economics. Domestic growth and remittances from Albanians working abroad helped him out, rising appreciably between 1994 and 1996. So did a favorable Trade and Economic Cooperation Agreement with the European Union and the first inflow of PHARE assistance.[20] Integration into European structures in the 1990s was slow, however. The Albanian desire to proceed faster was "seriously undermined by [the] very low socio-economic starting point, . . . severe socio-economic crises, weak state institutions, a particularly difficult regional situation, a fragile democracy, and a conflict-ridden internal political scene," the European Commission found in a 2001 assessment.[21]

In Europe's poorest country, abutting a war zone, development was grossly uneven. There were no oligarchs and rent-seekers on the Russian and Ukrainian pattern, but professional smugglers of cigarettes, drugs, and weapons made fortunes in the early 1990s by breaking UN sanctions on Yugoslavia and running fuel into Serbia—and in the late 1990s, by sneaking Albanians posing as Kosovar refugees into Western Europe.[22] And money manipulators spun pyramid scams paying back 8 percent of principal per month to inexperienced investors who mistrusted the state bank and had as yet no alternative for depositing their meager savings. A number of the pyramid operators boasted to customers that they were close to President Berisha and senior Democratic politicians. "The nominal value of pyramid schemes liabilities peaked at almost half of the country's GDP towards the end of 1996, involving more than 2 million people, almost two thirds of the overall population" of 4.5 million, the EU's 2004 economic report on the Balkans estimated.[23]

By the early 1990s, "Albania was already under the control of numerous armed gangs, which were acting in an increasingly organized manner. Extortion and racketeering, prostitution, drug trafficking, looting and robberies enabled the accumulation of substantial capital and facilitated the transformation of anarchic criminal gangs into highly organized and clearly hierarchical criminal clans, known as *fares*, resembling the Sicilian Mafia," the Center for the Study of Democracy in Sofia reported.[24] Brigands throughout the dirt-poor Ottoman Balkans always had a certain Robin Hood aura and in the nineteenth century they became the spearhead of national uprisings. The *fares,* however, were vicious in a way that no Robin Hood legend would tolerate. Even today, the *fares* owe their takeover of St. Pauli and other profitable venues in Western Europe at least in part to their readiness to deliver the corpses of rival bosses to their gangs in small pieces. The other secret of their success is the tightness of their clans and the code of honor, family, and absolute loyalty to hierarchy as laid down in the *kanun.*

Even as most other Balkan gangs have gone multiethnic, Albanian gangs recruit only within their clan—apart from outsourcing for specific purposes— making them all but impossible for undercover agents to infiltrate. The numerous Albanian criminals operating in Italian mafias in the 1980s saw how Italian investigators cracked these gangs open, attributed their breakup to the laxity of younger bosses in enforcing the total *omerta* secrecy pledge, and were careful not to be so negligent themselves. As Albania's borders became porous in the early

1990s, home-grown criminals established links with those in the Kosovar diaspora, in particular, who had already become major dealers in the European heroin trade. The Albanian diaspora in Italy, Turkey, Greece, Switzerland, Germany, Canada, and the United States, then, was key to the swift induction of neophyte Albanian criminals into global criminal organizations. In a very specialized kind of privatization, these traffickers quickly bought up hundreds of Albanian state businesses cheaply, stored weapons and drugs on their premises, and laundered money through them. Soon the Italian mafias were buying arms and explosives from the Albanians, and the two groups were cooperating in transporting drugs and illegal immigrants across the Adriatic to Italy.[25]

As Berisha settled into his presidency, he dismissed wholesale the Sigurimi personnel who had continued largely unchanged in the new National Intelligence Service, or SHIK, and replaced them to a large extent with his own loyalists. In a land in which pashas, king, and Communists had always regarded the security services as their personal agents and suppressors of dissent, few expected security services suddenly to become enforcers of a more depersonalized, abstract law. A fair number of the 7,000 or 8,000 security service agents who were sacked clearly found new employment in organized crime, as revealed in the 1990s tradecraft of "military-style operations" by criminal groups in Albania, as well as in Western Europe, the United States, and Australia.[26]

In 1996 Berisha was reelected, in an election that monitors from the Organization for Security and Cooperation in Europe (OSCE) said was marred by double voting and fraud, and Amnesty International said was preceded by arrests and beatings of opposition politicians and critical journalists.[27] Both the United States and the EU demanded a rerun, and were ignored. Outsiders increasingly concluded that neither Berisha nor Nano was maturing out of the old Communist authoritarianism, and that the only difference in the new "democratic" politics was the lack of an accepted mechanism to resolve the bitter conflict between the two factions as each sought to establish one-party rule. There was no discernible mellowing of political strife into a grumpy search for compromise, as in Croatia or Bulgaria or even Serbia. Fatos Nano was by then in jail, having been convicted in April 1994 of misuse of state funds (but he remained a political player). Albanians at large assumed that while Nano probably did have his hand in the till, so did all the top politicians, and that the singling out of Nano for punishment was highly political.

In late 1996 and early 1997 the pyramid rackets collapsed. If they endured much longer than most Ponzi schemes, they owed their longevity only to the millions of dollars being poured into them to be laundered. Once the new money leveled off, the funds could no longer keep up the exorbitant payments. Alert criminal gangs pulled their own investments out in time and moved them to Italy. The 2 million poor Albanians who had put their life savings into the pyramids did not; altogether, two-thirds of the country's population lost more than $1 million. The little investors who had been duped poured onto the streets and vented their anger and despair on the government. In March 1997 Berisha, trying to hang on to power, proclaimed a state of emergency, merged the SHIK with the police under a single commander who reported only to him, and ordered troops to surround the Socialist Party headquarters in Tirana.[28] "SHIK agents arrested a large number of opposition figures, journalists and other government critics, many of whom were taken away in the middle of the night without arrest warrants, and were severely beaten and tortured," the Center for the Study of Democracy recounted.[29] They also organized groups of criminals and prison inmates to attack antigovernment demonstrators with sticks and crowbars—and sometimes issued to thugs shields and helmets used by riot police.

In the south firefights broke out between the supporters of Berisha and Nano. Residents of Vlore and of Hoxha's (and Lord Byron's) Gjirokastra in the south were among the first to seize control of their towns and expel Democratic Party municipal officials. The army—in which the previous officers had also been sacked by Berisha to make way for his own supporters—disintegrated. As discipline broke down and conscripts were not even given rations, Tirana conscripts who had been stationed in the south deserted, threw away their weapons, and walked or hitchhiked the hundred miles home.[30] Riots and anarchy reigned. More than 2,000 people were killed in the chaos, though the vast majority of them seemed to be less victims of political clashes than of robberies, gang turf wars, or personal vendettas.[31]

Within days of the pyramids' collapse, Kosovars fresh from Switzerland, where they had been gathering money and organizing the beginnings of the Kosova Liberation Army from afar, arrived to buy up as many of the estimated 600,000 AK-47s from looted army and police arsenals as they could stash into their pick-up trucks, and then deliver them to depots in Macedonia for further transport into Kosovo. Criminal gangs did the same. As the anarchy and potential insurrection spread north to the outskirts of Tirana, Berisha pardoned and freed all prisoners, including Fatos Nano. In the name of the EU and under a UN mandate, the Italian army led an eight-nation force of 5,000 that deployed to Albania for four months to distribute food and humanitarian aid to needy Albanians and restore a modicum of order. A unit of Italian police was also assigned to curb Adriatic smuggling, and a 100-member Multinational Advisory Police Element (MAPE), under the auspices of the Western European Union, was stationed in Tirana in coordination with American and other advisers to teach courses in fighting organized crime, community relations, and "democratic policing"—and to get heating, electricity, and running water into police cadet barracks.

In one oddity amid all the turmoil, after parliament declared the sweeping state of emergency, the very new constitutional court approved this measure in a ruling on a legal challenge to prior censorship. To Western observers this might have looked like an example of the kind of unfortunate executive coercion to be expected in the successor to one of Europe's severest dictatorships—but ironically, the court's judgment also reflected the hazards of well-intentioned European advice. Albania, on applying for membership in the Council of Europe in 1992, had consulted with European lawyers about how to meet the associated human rights requirements; in response, the lawyers had tacked onto the draft Albanian constitution the limitations included in article 10 of the European Convention on Human Rights. These allowed prepublication censorship during a state of emergency under certain conditions (and were highly controversial in Western Europe). The original Albanian draft, however, in accord with democratic theory, flatly banned any such restraints. As a result, articles 2 and 41 of the constitution were totally contradictory. It was left up to judges who had plunged in a decade from authoritarian rule to utterly unfamiliar constitutional jurisprudence to sort out the mess. In a further irony, by the time the constitutional court issued its 5-to-3 ruling three months later, Berisha's power had disintegrated in the anarchy and the prior censorship had already been rescinded.[32]

In the early parliamentary elections in June 1997, the Socialists trounced the discredited Berisha and purged his appointees in the security services. Senior Berisha officials, including his interior minister, chief of police, and head of the presidential guard, fled to Italy or Greece.[33] Berisha finally resigned. And in 1998, "[n]otwithstanding the assassination of an opposition leader, an attempted coup d'état, and the resignation of Prime Minister Fatos Nano, all in the space of less than three weeks," the new parliament passed a broadcast media law that was better than most in the region at protecting the freedom of the press.[34]

At that point security outside the cities was close to nil; bandits ambushed cars at will on country roads, especially those winding through the northern mountains to Kosovo. Organized crime was on the rise; there were on average fifteen murders a month connected with the hard drugs trade. On a more mundane level, Albania was quickly becoming the biggest supplier of cannabis to Italy and the rest of Europe as peasants resumed cultivating the plant after the end of Communist rule. Poorly paid, poorly equipped, and demoralized police who were mistrusted by the public were no match for well-paid, well-equipped, and swaggering criminals who were feared by the public. An estimated 40 percent of Albanian men between the ages of nineteen and forty emigrated in the late 1990s. Some 30,000 Albanian women were working in brothels in Western Europe. Northeast Albania was coming increasingly under KLA control, with the collaboration of the villagers.[35] American electronics experts began appearing in the sector to install sensors, in preparation for possible future interventions.[36]

When NATO intervened in Kosovo in March 1999, the Serbs accelerated their ethnic cleansing there. As a consequence, some 450,000 homeless Kosovars—a number well over 10 percent of Albania's own population—poured into northern Albania.[37] Those who could do so moved in with relatives; others found shelter with total strangers. Some of these hosts charged rent from guests who were clearly richer than themselves (or had been richer, before they lost everything). Others, in accord with the traditional hospitality required by the *kanun*, opened their homes with no expectation of reimbursement, even though they had little to eat themselves. As the weeks dragged on, though, some city dwellers in Tirana and elsewhere tired of refugees' gripes about primitive living conditions. They considered their cousins ungrateful and pushy, and became even less enthusiastic about the century-old dream of a single Albanian state that might subject them to the more assertive Kosovars.[38]

Through all the turmoil, organized crime exploited the weakness or absence of state institutions and expanded its power in Tirana and in the main ports of Vlore and Durres.[39] Berisha and Nano continued snarling at each other and at rivals within their own parties. The International Crisis Group recommended that Albania find better judges, perhaps by including international representation in selection panels; that the mandate of the West's police advisers be expanded to allow them to act operationally and that international donors establish conflict resolution centers in northern Albania, to reduce blood feuds.[40]

In 2000 the EU proposed a new Stabilization and Association Process (SAP) for Western Balkan countries, granted Tirana extended duty-free trade privileges, and helped Albania join the World Trade Organization. Soon thereafter, it launched the supplemental Community Assistance for Reconstruction, Development, and Stabilization (CARDS) program for SAP countries. This program, while not as generous as the EU assistance set aside for the Central European states that were already candidates for full member-ship, fitted the more primitive absorptive capacity of the Western Balkans in general, and of Albania's very weak institutions in particular. The EU and the European Investment Bank allocated Albania some €1 billion to aid its mod-ernization through judicial reforms; helped design plans for a census, major constitutional reform, market liberalization, land mapping, and veterinary control; started rehabilitating the prison system; funded hundreds of projects at the community level, including upgrading roads to remote areas; and sup-ported nongovernmental organizations (NGOs) working in the areas of democracy and human rights, civil society, the teaching of tolerance, and the reintegration of victims of trafficking.[41]

Whatever the periodic misfits between the Albanians' own perception of needs and EU programs that were basically designed for very different, Cen-tral European conditions, the twin goals of membership in the EU and in NATO were uncontroversial in Albania. After seeing the glittering lights on tel-evision, young villagers were less and less attracted to subsistence farming or even the boredom of living in Tirana slums with no jobs and no money, and dreamed instead of escaping to Switzerland visa-free, to work for real pay. A slowly reemerging middle class saw the EU and NATO as the only hopes for modernizing the country. And those segments of the elite that were profitably involved in criminal networking welcomed the inflow of EU money and assumed they could keep unwelcome kibbitzing by EU advisers at a manage-able minimum.

Local elections in October 2000, under a new and fairer electoral code, "took place in a tense but remarkably peaceful atomosphere; with only a few isolated incidents of violence," OSCE monitors reported. It was "the most peaceful campaign in Albania since 1991. For the first time, a broad spectrum of media offered voters a wide range of information. The public broadcaster provided free airtime to all election contestants in accordance with the law, and increasingly fair coverage as the campaign progressed." The observers found some irregularities, but none that would have changed the outcome. The Socialists won in three-quarters of the municipalities. "However, the Albanian political scene remain[ed] highly polarized."[42]

Tirana

The new mayor who took over Tirana in 2000 shook up Nano's and Berisha's feuding establishments. Like the other two politicians, Edi Rama was a scion of the Communist nomenklatura, but his weapon of choice was neither vitu-peration nor the old Sigurimi. It was paint. He is an artist, the son of a sculptor honored in Hoxha's era. He flirted briefly with Berisha's Democratic Party in the early 1990s, then became disillusioned and took off instead for the artist's obligatory bohemian years on the Parisian Left Bank. He kept an interest in domestic politics, however, and wrote irreverent columns skewering the new Socialists, and especially the new Democrats, for a Tirana newspaper. When he returned to Albania in his early thirties in 1998 he was drafted by Fatos Nano, who was again prime minister, to become minister of culture. And when the mayoral election came up in 2000, Rama ran as an independent candidate with Socialist backing. He won, with a 54 percent majority, and began by painting the town peach pink and violet as his way of enlivening the facades of the dreary, Communist-era, cement apartment blocks in the center of town. This became his trademark; photos of the buildings with his geometric color contrasts, swirls, and checkerboard trompes l'œil adorn his savvy website, and were even featured on the cover of the geographically flexible magazine *Art in America*. This playfulness caught the eye of outsiders and won him the UN Poverty Eradication Award in 2002 and the title of World Mayor in 2004, conferred by a London-based NGO.

Far more striking to anyone who has seen the depressing garbage of Shkodra, however, is Rama's unique triumph over trash. He put some of the capital's high number of unemployed to work scooping up all the old plastic bags, newspapers, bottles, tin cans, and other detritus that made banks of the Lana River look like the city dump and planting flowers and bushes instead. His workers removed 90,000 tons of garbage, along with 123,000 tons of concrete. He planted 4,000 new trees around the city, and cleaned up and seeded 36 acres of parks. He fixed the streetlights, only 78 of which worked when he took office. He opened movie theaters showing popular foreign films. He began the Sisyphean task of filling potholes and paving roads for the city's impressive number of S-class and less-class Mercedes of doubtful provenance. He constructed schools and playgrounds. He removed 2,000 wildcat kiosks and shanties in the center of the city. He encouraged the opening up of Tirana's old quarter, once off bounds to all but the top Communist echelon, and its transformation into a district of popular bars and discos. He brought in Argentinian architect Jorge Mario Jauregui to give lectures on how the slums in São Paulo and Rio de Janeiro had been legalized and regenerated, with due attention to breaking up drug sellers' hangouts, while preserving the cohesiveness of low-crime quarters. He has not by any means managed to stop all the illegal building in a city whose population has almost tripled from 250,000 in 1990 to 700,000 today. Nor has he vanquished the residues of Ottoman bureaucracy. But he has started to extend water and electricity lines to the new slums ringing the city. He has humanized the vast expanse of Scanderbeg Square outside the mayor's windows, by bringing children's pedal cars and balloon vendors into a traffic island in the middle of it. And he has mobilized a young staff to work long hours for inadequate pay in the feeling that they are accomplishing something.

For Rama, that initial cleanup of junk was an essential, and not just some cosmetic, step in the modernization of Tirana. In an interview in which he gave perfunctory answers to the first dozen questions, he suddenly turned eloquent on the subject of educating citizens out of casually throwing their garbage onto the street, and on the wider ramifications of such a revolution. "It's a matter of tradition, of redesigning a society where people live together and have a sense of living together. Because we have passed from a very brutal collectivist system to a very brutal individualist system, a total atomization of society. We need to think about public space and get a sense of belonging." In theory, political parties should help with this shift of mind-set, "but practically, they cannot. It's a matter of a political generation that has been educated and prepared for another system. Now they have to manage democracy and a free market. They are not prepared for it; they are not educated for it."

More broadly, Rama expressed optimism about overcoming resistance to reforms at Albania's niveau of social development. "We are at a level where every reform brings better quality [of life]. We are not at the level of a very developed country, where reforms [are perceived as harming] masses of the population and where [positive] results need years to be seen. The kind of reforms we need will touch the lives of people [immediately], for the better. Because people here can't have a worse standard of living in the future. I would say that everybody here is [already] living better than yesterday. Even the poor are living better than yesterday, and not only because they are free." Statistics confirm the mayor's observation. While 60 percent of Albanians remain below the World Bank's poverty line, per capita income has tripled in the decade since the mid-1990s, with remittances from the diaspora, in particular, accounting for up to a third of family income.

"We are still in a very naive phase, where heroes are not yet replaced by managers. But heroes cannot manage things in a time of peace," Rama continued. He praised the "incredible energy" of the Albanian population, while acknowledging that "this energy sometimes gets transformed into destructive energy." He blamed such deformation on a "lack of engineering that would transform the power [positively]. This river needs to be channeled, and these energies need to be synchronized with a vision, a political project with a national or city program" that inspires citizens.[43]

Not everyone likes the mayor, of course. One dark night in 1997, thugs whom he is persuaded were working for Berisha beat him senseless with lead pipes. Later a would-be assassin fired several shots into his apartment window, inducing him to move to a less exposed building. During his campaign for reelection as mayor in 2003, Berisha accused him of trafficking, laundering money, and associating with mafiosi, drug runners, and terrorists. Yet despite his having evicted so many squatters, enough Tiranans liked him well enough to increase his majority to 59 percent. A new generation of politicians was emerging.

Nano Wins

As ethnic Albanian militants began their armed raids in southern Serbia and in next-door Macedonia in early 2001, the Albanian Socialist government had to tread a fine line. It needed to show sympathy for fellow Albanians, yet at the same time convince the international gatekeepers of the EU and NATO clubs that Tirana was not secretly striving for a Greater Albania.[44] The Socialists, like the Democrats before them, stressed that they did not support the insurgency and wanted the territorial integrity of Macedonia preserved; accordingly, they asked NATO to help them secure the Albania-Macedonia border. "Ironically, Albania of all Macedonia's neighbours, has shown the greatest support for its sovereignty and security, including by cracking down on some prominent 'greater Albania' extremists," observed the International Crisis Group.[45] This restraint was all the more notable in that the preamble to the 1998 Albanian constitution specifically endorses the "centuries-old aspiration of the Albanian people for national identity and unity."[46]

In quick succession, Prime Minister Ilir Meta visited Pristina to promote economic and cultural links with Kosovo, and the government reopened diplomatic ties with the new Serbian leadership that had just ousted Slobodan Milosevic. Many Kosovars viewed Tirana's willingness to restore civil relations even with Serb democrats as a betrayal of the "national question."[47] The International Crisis Group argued, however, that militancy and agitiation for a Greater Kosovo are not popular, and that support for the National Liberation Army in Macedonia grew only when the NLA turned away from pan-Albanian insurgency to defend the everyday rights of Albanians peacefully in the Macedonian elections.[48]

Inside Albania, political turmoil had calmed down sufficiently by 2001 for the general elections that year to be uneventful. For the first time, the campaign revolved around issues other than the personalities of Berisha and Nano, though the familiar mutual accusations of corruption continued. OSCE monitors regretted the persistence of "a polarized political culture with deep antagonisms between political forces grouped around the dominant Socialist and Democratic Parties," but they welcomed the fact that this time, unlike after previous elections, "political parties sought legal redress to their grievances" (rather than resorting to violence, was the unstated implication). They found fewer incidents of ballot stuffing, premarked ballots, police interference, and court bias in favor of the ruling party than in previous elections.[49] When the vote again gave the ruling Socialists a decisive victory, Berisha appealed through the courts for a revote in thirty districts, but lost. For almost a year his Democratic Party boycotted parliament and paralyzed the government.[50] Eventually the parties worked out a modus vivendi, the Democrats took their seats in parliament, and the return to stability helped consolidate the economic recovery, after a drop in GDP during the anarchy.

In 2003 Albania became the fourth member of the U.S.-sponsored Adriatic Charter linking Zagreb, Skopje, and Tirana with Washington in a joint effort to promote the military and political reforms needed for the three Balkan states to join NATO.[51] In 2003 Albania also opened negotiations with the European Union on a Stabilization and Association Agreement. The EU goal was less controversial in Albania than in Brussels. Tirana was so far from qualifying for membership that the possibility stayed in a remote haze for most Albanians and basically meant the unimaginable opportunity to travel freely in Western Europe. Brussels, however, had to wrestle anew with the vexed issue of "standards" versus "politics." Those in favor of beginning the talks contended that allowances had to be made; since Albania, still emerging from Hoxha's isolation, was so far behind the rest of the Balkans, it needed the encouragement of seeing progress on the Stablization and Association road. Strict standards thus had to be relaxed in favor of a more political decision that could avert despair and backsliding. Critics who did not want to lower the standards that the Central Europeans had been roughly held to accused the EU of acting tactically, opening negotiations on a Stabilization and Association Agreement with Prime Minister Meta in a vain effort to strengthen him against the rather lazy Nano. Such a short-term approach would encourage sloughing off, they thought. It certainly did not block a comeback by Nano, who shortly became prime minister for the third time.

To the critics, the single most disturbing aspect of political decisionmaking has been the implicit signal that Tirana might get into the EU without ever having stemmed organized crime. Most analysts of the Balkans hold that Albania, like Macedonia, has escaped becoming a failed state by the skin of its teeth. At least two studies contend, however, that in Albania organized crime bosses in fact captured the failing state in the 1990s, "entrenched themselves in government, and essentially usurped government authority" and "took control over the whole country" in a way that, for all their power in the region, criminals never succeeded in doing elsewhere in the Balkans.[52] And despite attempts by a series of police advisory teams—Italy's Interforza since the early 1990s; the U.S. International Criminal Investigative Training and Assistance Program (ICITAP) and Office of Overseas Prosecutorial Development, Assistance, and Training (OPDAT) since the late 1990s; and the EU's MAPE, from May 1997 to May 2001, the European Commission Police Assistance (ECPA), funded under PHARE, from October 2001 to August 2002, and the Police Assistance Mission of the European Commission to Albania (PAMECA), funded under CARDS, since 2002—few inroads have been made. The constant reshuffling of personnel in Albanian police units prevents international advisers from developing long-term relationships with their counterparts. There is scant evidence that major police corruption is being rooted out. Organized crime is booming.[53]

Berisha Wins

By the next scheduled election in summer 2005, the 57 percent of voters who turned out, having discovered the sweet power of punishing incumbents for their misery, exercised it once again, and Berisha came back to office in an orderly process. OSCE monitors concluded that while the vote "complied, only in part, with OSCE commitments and other international standards for democratic elections," it did show "some progress in the conduct of elections in Albania." Minorities, "notably Roma, continued to be marginalized and were subjected to election intimidation and attempted 'vote buying.'" But there was only one fatal shooting, and election officials forgot less often than in previous elections that they were required to dip citizens' fingers into indelible ink to prevent multiple voting.[54] At the age of sixty-one, Sali Berisha became prime minister. Fatos Nano, after his defeat, resigned from the Socialist leadership to be replaced, in a close party vote, by forty-one-year-old Edi Rama.

Western European assessment of the election was cautiously optimistic in daring to hope that stability was finally being established in Albania—and that Berisha might begin to learn the gentler arts of moderation, compromise, and democracy. Some restraint seemed foreordained from the sheer fact that for the first time the winning party did not command a majority of its own, but had to depend on smaller coalition partners.[55] And a new generation of young, Western-educated ministers with a fresh style joined Berisha's cabinet.

This time around, noted Deutsche Welle's Balkans editor, Fabian Schmidt—"unlike in all the previous elections"—Berisha did not just make debating points with anti-Communist polemics against the ruling Socialists; he dealt with real issues. "He promised to fight corruption, to lower taxes, to attract investors to the land, and to create jobs"—and to accelerate the necessary reforms to get into the European Union. "People are gradually beginning to complain about the sluggish harmonization of Albania's legislation with European laws, the economic stagnation, and high unemployment."[56]

The jubilant Berisha was acutely aware of the EU conditionality and demands. "Albanians have voted for change by saying no to the corruption and organized crime that were blocking the reforms needed for integration into the EU," he stressed to reporters after his election.[57] "Our future is Europe and we must work to get there," a scarcely less ebullient Edi Rama told the *Financial Times* after he became the Socialist leader.[58]

Albania must do much more to implement its own reform legislation, promote freedom of the press, fight corruption, ensure the efficiency and independence of the judiciary, and protect property rights, the European Commission warned in its 2005 report card on the country.[59] It has initiated essential reforms in its customs and tax administration to bring in more revenue, but it must also strengthen the judicial system. And above all, it must fight organized crime and build up its administrative capabilities, admonished European Commission president Jose Manuel Barroso when Prime Minister Berisha made the pilgrimage to Brussels to press, successfully, Albania's desire to sign a Stabilization and Association Agreement by summer 2006.[60] A skeptical James Pettifer noted the conflict in continuing economic reform while at the same time clamping down on entrenched corruption.[61] And one young, American-educated Albanian expressed the wistful hope that the new ministers, instead of stuffing their pockets with two hands, would stuff their pockets with only one hand.

"Albania is a special country, in a good sense and a bad sense," commented an international adviser fondly. "Its peculiarities are partly its own fault—what has enabled it to survive has also kept it from flourishing. Look at the craziness of the isolation of the Enver Hoxha years, which has given most Albanians enormous blind spots. . . . Berisha himself is not different from what he was in 1992–97. . . . There is, however, one thing which is different in Albania from the mid-1990s: the rest of the Albanian people—even some politicians, although not many—have grown up over the last ten years. Many more have been educated abroad. If they can overcome their centuries-long tendency to keep their heads low and go along with things, there may be some dramatic and positive changes."[62]

A World Bank employee who has worked on development issues in both Albania and Africa put it another way. Albania's incomparable advantage, she declared, is proximity: it is in Europe.[63]

CHAPTER NINE

DEMYTHOLOGIZING SERBIA
AND MONTENEGRO

TWO SOULS, it would seem (to paraphrase Goethe), also lodge in Serbia's breast. The mythic, macho one revels in the kind of untamed violence that won Serbia its independence from the Ottoman Empire; in the politics by assassination of the century-and-a-half contest between the Karadjordjevic and Obrenovic dynasties; in the stubborn resistance to Nazi German conquest; and in the special Serb *inat,* or "malevolent, vengeful and obstinate defiance," as writer Aleksa Djilas defines it.[1] This spirit both is and is not anti-Western. It is not anti-Western in the sense of the late nineteenth- and early twentieth-century Germans and Russians, who saw themselves respectively as possessing a *kultur* superior to mere Anglo-Saxon civilization, and as purer and more virile than the decadent West in Aleksandr Blok's "Scythians, Yea, Asians, a slant-eyed greedy brood." The pride of Serbs in their role as the bulwark defending Christian Europe against the Islamic Turk is too strong for that. But the Serb soul is anti-Western in the Byzantine and Serbian Orthodox tradition of exclusivity and suspicion of the "Latin West."[2] Today this religious side of Serb identity is only reinforced by the common cause of the most traditionalist clergy and the "red" bishops appointed in the Communist era in blocking internal Serbian church reform and in championing war crimes indictees as national heroes (and perhaps even hiding some of them in monasteries).[3] Milosevic became expert at tapping this vein of Serb pride and its obverse sense of victimization, both among the intellectual theorists of the Serb revitalization movement, who expected to outsmart this latecomer to the nationalist cause, and among the Krajina and other rural Serbs untouched by modern urban ferment.

The second Serb soul is the cosmopolitan, skeptical, and ultimately Western one that produced a high incidence of draft dodging to escape conscription into Milosevic's wars, that elected independent mayors in Belgrade and a string of other cities in the mid-1990s, and that eventually toppled Milosevic in 2000.[4] This mind-set has also produced some of the Balkans' fiercest defenders of human rights. In Serbia the Western transforming magic of civil society and nongovernmental organizations—and the empowering of many NGOs by George Soros's gifts of computers to promising grass-roots leaders—has seemed more than justified by the defeat of Milosevic. True, the inflation, brutalization of war, embargo-running, and mass flight abroad of professionals during the 1990s robbed Serbia of the middle-class ballast that might have consolidated the gains of the democratic movement. But this failure was not for lack of activists' efforts. And today's contrarian human rights watchdogs, like the Helsinki Committee's Sonja Biserko and the Humanitarian Law Center's Natasa Kandic—and even the young activists who hang accusatory banners saying "guilty of crimes" on the walls of the Serbian Academy of Arts and Sciences (SANU) two decades after its chauvinists whipped up hatred against Albanians—are second to none in their zeal.[5]

"The country was always completely divided," notes Sonja Licht, president of the Belgrade Fund for Political Excellence. In the nineteenth and twentieth centuries "part of the intelligentsia would go to Moscow, part to Vienna and Paris."[6] Both the mythical and the skeptical souls continue to lodge in varying degree in today's elites, and in the man who succeeded Milosevic as president in 2000 and Zoran Djindjic as prime minister in 2004, Vojislav Kostunica.

In the view of Western outsiders, at least, the resolution of the conflicting claims of these two identities will determine whether Serbia's future lies in glorious exceptionalist defiance of the requirements of the EU and the Hague Tribunal or in the dull normality of the leveling European process. "In the end, the Serbs in Belgrade will have to choose between Brussels and Kosovo; it's as brutal as that," pronounced Richard Holbrooke in late 2005.[7] *Brussels* was his code word for the EU and what some Serb nationalists do call the Latin West; *Kosovo,* his shorthand for nursing the memory of the fourteenth-century Blackbird Field and refusing to accede to the international trial of Karadzic and Mladic and the loss of Kosovo.

Many Serb intellectuals—even those who opposed Milosevic and could themselves be classified as Western secularists—find this Western perception of a dichotomy, with its corollary fixation on bygone war crimes, insulting. They may personally consider Karadzic a boor. They may reject as overwrought the assertions by such contemporary Serb writers as Djordje Kadijević and Mihajlo Djuric that in the 1990s Serbs were fighting yet again in Bosnia and Kosovo (Croatia is more problematic) to defend an ungrateful West against the "Asiatic hordes," and their demands that the errant West return to its Greek and Balkan roots.[8] But many find it profoundly unfair that the West still punishes today's Serbian democracy for wars conducted by the autocratic Milosevic—who had, after all, been tacitly backed by the Americans in the 1990 Serbian presidential election and aggrandized by them in the Dayton negotiations, had been out of power since 2001, and had been dead since March 2006. They object that Americans and West Europeans never championed the 200,000 Serb refugees from brutal Croatian ethnic cleansing as they did Bosniak refugees in the mid-1990s, never demanded that Serb refugees be allowed to return to Croatia as importunately as they insisted that Croat and Bosniak refugees must return to the Republika Srpska. In their view, then, in 1999 "NATO was bombing a multiethnic democracy," Serbia, while cynically backing Serbia's adversary, a "Kosovo that was not multiethnic and not democratic. This fueled anti-Americanism," explained *NIN* magazine commentator Ljiljiana Smajlovic.[9] And after Milosevic was deposed, the West shunned the moderate nationalist Kostunica when Djindjic was sidelining him by legally questionable tactics; it should have bestowed greater rewards on democratic Serbia for having ousted Milosevic. Today's 10.8 million Serbs, the argument runs, should be allowed to get on with rebuilding their lives and their country in a new era, and not be constantly blackballed for what Milosevic did.

In exasperation, *NIN*'s editor-in-chief, Stevan Niksic, asks why the status of Karadzic and Mladic should be so much more important to Westerners than Serbia's democratic, social, and cultural development and economic recovery over the past five years. Why are outsiders not interested in exploring why American businesses are the leading foreign investors in Serbia these days, at higher levels than elsewhere in the Balkans? Why can't Serbia be portrayed in the round, and not just in the reductionist story of its foreign relations with the "international community" and the even more reductionist story of two fugitives? And why, he wants to know, didn't Croats, Bosnian Muslims, and Kosovar and other Albanians welcome the idea of a democratic Serbia?[10]

Aleksa Djilas, perhaps the most eloquent of the Belgrade intellectuals who reproach the West for one-sidedness, expanded on this same theme in his "Funeral Oratory for Yugoslavia: An Imaginary Dialogue with Western Friends":

> I could hear a chorus of Western voices rebuking me: Just remember what you Serbs did! You shelled Dubrovnik and laid Vukovar to waste; you surrounded Sarajevo with canons and snipers, and massacred several thousand Muslim men in and around Srebrenica; last but definitely

not least, you engaged in the repression and ultimately the expulsion of Kosovo Albanians. You have not apologized and are not forgiven. You must be punished and who is more expert and practised at death and destruction than yourselves? Have a taste of your own medicine. And have a nice day.

There was, of course, much truth in these accusations. But it was wrong to pass over the villainy of Croats, Bosnian Muslims and Kosovo Albanians with such insouciance. . . .

I had to retort: But, my Western friends, . . . [h]ad the Serbs not been punished enough? They were expelled from Croatia, from many parts of Bosnia and Herzegovina (including Sarajevo, much vaunted in the West for its multi-ethnic tolerance) and from the whole of Kosovo, except its most northerly part, making Serbia of all the states of former Yugoslavia the one with the largest number of refugees—800,000 at the last count. . . .

Forgive me for doubting your sincerity, my Western friends, but do you really not care for Yugoslavia?[11]

Cacak/Nis/Kragujevac

The story of the political victory of the heterogeneous Democratic Opposition of Serbia is well known in the West, at least the romanticized version in which the Americans slipped money to the DOS for office rent and other essentials, an American public relations firm helped coin the snappy slogan "*gotov je*" (He's a goner!) and persuade the various factions to back a single presidential candidate—and American-trained Serb "Otpor" (Resistance) activists then fanned out to reproduce the same kind of street protests and regime change in Georgia and Ukraine. The reality, of course, was somewhat more complex. As described by Ivan Vejvoda, an irenic and erudite stalwart of the democratic opposition throughout the 1990s and now executive director of the Balkan Trust for Democracy, the unseating of Milosevic in 2000 was no sudden reaction to street power, but "the result of ten long years of [nonviolent] struggle by Serbia's democratic opposition and civil society."[12]

To be sure, it was those last student-led protests against Milosevic's election fraud that finally tipped the scale, showing the risks an autocrat runs in staging even formal elections in an illiberal semidemocracy. But the DOS's crowning success in 2000 after a decade of ineffectual anti-Milosevic demonstrations in Belgrade resulted from the confluence of four other elements. The first was the shattering of the aura of invincibility of the strongman through his defeats in Croatia, Bosnia, and Kosovo.[13] The second was that agreement by the squabbling opposition factions to unite behind a single presidential candidate in the person of Vojislav Kostunica, the moderate but impeccably nationalist law professor and translator of the *Federalist Papers,* a man unsullied by past membership in the Communist Party, by support of Milosevic, or by any dabbling in politics whatever.

The third element was the deal between former Belgrade mayor and DOS organizer Zoran Djindjic and "Legija" (Milorad Lukovic-Ulemek), the head of the dread Special Operations Unit, or Red Berets, as well as cohead of the Zemun gang. Legija—the nickname comes from his time in the French Foreign Legion—promised to disobey Milosevic's orders to break up dissident marches on Belgrade and clearly understood that in return Djindjic would not crack down on the security-criminal nexus once he was in office.[14]

The fourth factor was the war fatigue in general, and fatigue with lost wars in particular, that spread in provincial cities as more local sons died and more penniless Serb refugees from Croatia, Bosnia, and Kosovo flooded into Serbia and strained municipal budgets and patience with their demands for food and shelter. (Security forces prudently kept the Serb refugees out of the capital.)[15] On October 5, 2000, it was a column of 10,000 protesters from Cacak, led by their mayor and augmented by tens of thousands more from Nis and Kragujevac and other southern towns, that spearheaded the assault of several hundred thousand on Milosevic's citadels in the capital. And when the Belgrade police were less accommodating than Legija, a construction worker from Cacak, Ljubislav Djokic, rammed a bulldozer first into the parliament building and then into the main entrance to Radio Television Serbia to break open the barricades for the crowd to storm through. Within a few hours the insurgents completed what the voters began in electing Kostunica president, and the army, too, refused to save Milosevic.[16] EU leaders immediately invited President Kostunica to join them in their summit at Biarritz, assuming that the Serbian black hole at the center of the Balkans would now be filled by a government speeding toward Europe and European standards and that this would help stabilize Belgrade's neighbors.

Improvement in relations between Serbia and Kosovo and between Serbia and the International Criminal Tribunal for the former Yugoslavia (ICTY) did follow quickly. Belgrade let Kosovo Serbs participate in the 2000 election in Kosovo without punishing them. Djindjic's government dismissed Legija as commander of the Red Berets in May 2001. Djindjic then delivered Milosevic to the Hague in June as the first Serb to be so extradited (and the first head of state ever to be thus hauled before an international court)—at the cost of a bitter split with Kostunica, who viewed the Hague Tribunal as politically biased against Serbs.[17] In the same month the international overseers in Kosovo cooperated with Belgrade to end the armed incursions into southern Serbia by Kosovar Albanians calling themselves the Liberation Army of Presevo, Medvedja, and Bujanovac; and with international blessing, Serbian security forces resumed patrols in the buffer zone on the Serbian side of the border for the first time since the Kosovo war. A Serbian military court for the first time convicted Serbian soldiers of war crimes against civilians in Kosovo, thus acknowledging "that crimes committed in Kosovo have not been random acts of violence by some renegades, as previously maintained, but rather part of the official plan to effect ethnic cleansing in Kosovo."[18]

Subsequently, Serbian courts issued international arrest warrants for Milosevic's wife, Mirjana Markovic, for incitement to abuse of power (she remained a member of parliament until February 2003 and then left Serbia to live in exile in Russia); and for their son Marko, for allegedly having threatened in 2000 to kill an Otpor activist with a chain saw and throw his body in pieces into the river. For its part, the West eased the terms of repayment of the huge foreign debts accrued by the forerunners of the new democratic government and made $1 billion available to Belgrade. With Milosevic gone, Tudjman dead, Izetbegovic dying, and Arkan murdered by a rival gangster, a new generation seemed ready to take command.

Despite having been elected mayor of Belgrade on the wave of anti-Milosevic victories in the 1997 municipal elections, the dynamic, abrasive Zoran Djindjic was never as popular a politician as Kostunica was in his heyday; yet as prime minister Djindjic acted as if he had a strong mandate. He had earned a doctorate in political philosophy in Germany under Jürgen Habermas; he bet on Western-style democracy as the route to modernization, even though "he was very skeptical of American democracy and cynical about America"; and he sold painful liberalizing reforms to his countrymen as the only way to win the empowering prize of membership in the European Union.[19] He counted on economic and political openness—and the support of the EU—to cure Serbia eventually of the compound ills of communism, ultranationalism, and the security-criminal chokehold on the economy and politics. "We must find a solution mainly by finding our place in Europe, not by seeking historical rights," he declared—if not to universal acclaim.[20]

Certainly he faced a formidable task. The hundreds of thousands of Serb refugees in the country needed homes, jobs, and some promise of permanence. Organized crime was bleeding the economy, public administration, and law enforcement. Serbia's neglected industrial plant lagged two decades behind EU equivalents; the nation's less tangible adaptations to accelerating globalization and the EU cosmos by now lagged a decade behind those of Slovenia, Romania, and Bulgaria. The dysfunctional 1990 constitution rammed through by Milosevic needed overhaul, and the institutions he destroyed in "politics, economy, society, education, the military, the judiciary and law enforcement agencies" had to be rebuilt, or built from scratch. "[V]irtually every aspect of the state and society had to undergo far-reaching reform at the same time, all within a context of scarcity of resources (both political and economic)," Vejvoda commented.[21] And while the peaceful revolution was admirable, it meant that Milosevic's henchmen could not be swept away wholesale but could only be dismissed one by one, in a laborious process that gave high officials ample time to destroy incriminating evidence.

Djindjic's government had its own share of power fights, especially over which parties would get which state companies as their fiefs. But the technocrats in the DOS government did a creditable job of putting the macroeconomy on a sounder footing and advancing privatization somewhat. Djindjic kickstarted reforms and got fifty major pieces of legislation through parliament to establish the framework of a market economy and a more welcoming atmosphere for crucial foreign investment. The economy grew in 2001 and 2002, and earned Yugoslavia the accolade of the European Bank for Reconstruction and Development as the best performer of the twenty-seven countries in which it operated.[22] Serbia and Montenegro joined the Stability Pact and other regional groupings and became a candidate for a Stabilization and Association Agreement with the EU.

Along the way, Djindjic broke eggs—not in the sense of lethal Leninist purges, but certainly in the sense of keeping politics confrontational. He was rough with political adversaries who got in his way. He aroused suspicion among some of his democratic allies that he might be building his own power for autocratic rather than democratic purposes.[23] He cut procedural corners—many of them left over from Milosevic's time, to be sure. He had no qualms about manipulating the required 50 percent electoral participation in order to void successive presidential votes from late 2001 through early 2003 and thus keep Kostunica from converting his presidency of Yugoslavia into the more powerful presidency of Serbia.

In setting priorities of urgency and feasibility, Djindjic had to postpone some of the most fundamental reforms. Removing the worst judges from the Milosevic era, tiptoeing into some kind of accommodation with the Kosovar Albanians, and most critically, cleaning out the security forces, were put on the agenda for 2003. In the meantime, government bureaucrats, Milosevic's

Socialist Party, and Vojislav Seselj's Radical Party in particular perpetuated the power of the old apparatchik types.

Links between the Communist security forces and criminal mafias were not unique to Serbia. Throughout the Balkans (as in Russia and Ukraine), the old secret police hierarchies—which may have enriched themselves in the Communist days but were limited in the size of their heists by the discipline of the monopoly party—spun free of political control in the 1990s just as maturing globalization and the Balkan wars opened wider opportunities to the unscrupulous. Serbia, however, presented "the most dramatic case" of this syndrome, in the judgment of the Bulgarian Center for the Study of Democracy. Since the top echelons of Tito's state security service (SDB) had been manned largely by Serbs until the mid-1960s—and returned to Serb domination in the 1980s after a Slovene interregnum—most of those agents who turned to personal crime in the 1990s were Serbs. Moreover, "Milosevic's government intentionally merged its law-enforcing institutions with organized crime to set up an extensive system of parallel gray and black economies to circumvent [international] sanctions. . . . In contrast to the other countries in transition, where personnel and structural reforms in the secret services were initiated, the Serbian State Security Service (SDB) was left almost intact through the 1990s. The main tasks of the SDB were not preservation of law and order and intelligence and counter-intelligence activities, as is the case with similar organizations around the world. The SDB's main responsibilities were linked with the preservation of Milosevic's rule. . . . [T]he SDB remained in its essence a typical authoritarian secret service."[24]

Milosevic's police force "also became one of the most corrupt state institutions and actively participated in transforming Serbia into a virtually lawless society. The Serbian police [were] transformed after 1991 into an exceptionally centralized organization." The army, counterintelligence, and customs service, too, were hotbeds of crime and corruption.[25] Their power waned somewhat after the war in Bosnia ended in 1995; "dozens" of the prominent criminals who had carried out the murders and smuggling for the security forces were deemed to know too much and themselves fell victim to professional assassins in the late 1990s. "None of these murders was ever resolved, nor were the perpetrators captured."[26] Nor, it might be added, were the private armies that Legija and others had built up disarmed and disbanded.

The organized crime and trafficking that plague the Balkans today arose (in varying combinations in each country) not only from degeneration of those old Communist security apparats, but also from the war economies and the international sanctions of Yugoslavia, which made the smuggling of fuel, weapons, excise goods, and drugs especially lucrative. In the 1970s and 1980s the Yugoslav SDB already had on its payroll some 150 convicted criminals— Arkan, king of the Serbian underworld, among them. And in the 1990s senior officials who had previously deployed murder squads to eliminate sixty emigré dissidents in Western Europe, smuggled in restricted technologies from the United States and Europe, smuggled out weapons to pariah countries against international embargoes, or simply played the black market to import normal goods and offset command-economy shortages lined their own pockets as well as waging Milosevic's wars.

Criminals did not actually hijack any of the weak emergent states in the region (apart from Albania in the 1990s), but such coups were usually not necessary. In Serbia, it almost seemed as if criminals eschewed capturing the state, as a potential distraction from their core business of amassing illicit profits. Sadists like Arkan found sufficient satisfaction in the early 1990s in forming paramilitary units to soften up Croatia and Bosnia, outfitted their militias handsomely with Serbian army tanks, helicopters, and heavy weapons—and remained outside the formal chain of command, thus blurring Milosevic's accountability for atrocities that could be blamed on freelancers. "[I]t can be argued that organized crime was a tool of Milosevic's government, and that it served his political, military and economic goals," the CSD's "Partners in Crime" concluded. "Somewhere between these two poles [of Albania and Serbia] are the other Southeast European countries, where corruption and common economic interests created a link between the respective security sectors and organized crime."[27]

As Djindjic finally moved to break criminal-security ties in Serbia in early 2003, he wielded both carrots and sticks. The carrots were inducements to some black marketeers to go legitimate—a shift that clearly alarmed those criminal entrepreneurs who were not so favored. The sticks, according to Ivan Vejvoda, who had just moved into the prime minister's office as a senior adviser to Djindjic, included the establishment of "institutions that would combat organised crime, corruption and the grey economy. Legislation had been prepared to introduce special courts to deal with organised crime and war crimes, and special prosecution procedures and witness-protection programmes were voted in by the Serbian Parliament. In January 2003 the heads of the Serbian secret service were changed in order to engage fully in the new struggle and ensure the country's movement forward. The final element of this reformed judicial and law enforcement architecture was supposed to be the federal . . . Minister for Defence. This last piece of the institutional structure—the first democratic Defence Minister—was supposed to be voted in on 13 March 2003. This would have put the military at last under full civilian democratic control."[28] Later that year he recalled, "It was the last piece of the reform puzzle, very important."[29]

Belgrade after Djindjic

The day before the Defense Ministry was to be taken over by Boris Tadic, a deputy in Djindjic's Democratic Party, the prime minister was assassinated. The official investigation—there has been no serious challenge to its conclusions—identified the three assassins as veteran Red Berets and named Legija as the ringleader.[30] The Red Berets were disbanded.[31] The acting Serbian president, Natasa Micic, declared a six-week state of emergency; the largest security sweep in the country's history, Operation Saber, broke up the Zemun gang and arrested more than 10,000 suspects, including Hague indictees Jovica Stanisic, head of the SDB under Milosevic, and General Nebojsa Pavkovic, former chief of staff of the Yugoslav Army (VJ).[32] Defense Minister Tadic announced army reform, full cooperation with the ICTY, and transfer of the military intelligence service from the General Staff to the Defense Ministry, and set the goal of joining NATO's Partnership for Peace. The parliament passed new laws that made it easier to fire judges; the government dismissed thirty-five of those appointed by Milosevic, including seven on the Supreme Court and also, critics maintained, some strong advocates of the new judicial independence. The Council of Europe promptly admitted to its ranks the new state that EU high representative Javier Solana had brokered, Serbia and Montenegro (*aka* "Solania"), and the Serbian legislature passed a new law on full and unconditional cooperation with the Hague Tribunal.

As of this writing, Legija was still awaiting trial for alleged complicity in Djindjic's assassination but he was already behind bars, having been convicted by Djindjic's special court for his part, on Milosevic's behalf, in the 2000 contract murder of Milosevic's mentor, Ivan Stambolic.[33] Incarceration did nothing to diminish the popularity of Legija. His maiden novel, *Iron Trench*, portrayed victimization of Serbs in Bosnia, drew rave reviews, and sold a record 70,000 copies in January 2005.[34]

The anticrime campaign after the murder of Djindjic "started well and ended fast," summarized one European diplomat in Belgrade. "It's very difficult to go much further without touching some balances which were at the core of power during the transition. The government made some mistakes in some areas by moving too fast, so it was not sustainable. . . . It didn't change the conditions of society. . . . Some of the measures were unfortunately selective. Like in ecology, you have problems when you selectively take out just one species. Very quickly there were complaints that the Bulgarian mafia had taken over [the Zemun gang's old criminal turf]. But this didn't change Serb society, which was made to survive from a long time ago through family connections, political connections, survival connections. Changing society is a very delicate matter, changing constitutions, changing the people who make the constitutions, changing the laws and their implementation. It's a matter of ten or twenty years."

Zoran Djindjic "was a man of very strong ability to change and move in a society which is not used to change. He was a visionary in a way. But reality was stronger, and he was without adequate protection from the system. He was a lonely man, I think, relying probably too much on foreign protection. With all his complex maneuverings, there was a good deal of childish naïveté to him. He was a sophisticated child who takes risks." A caricature by the Belgrade cartoonist Corax put it best, "showing Djindjic with a whip forcing a row of people with Serb hats to jump through the circus hoop of the EU and coming out on the other side dressed like Europeans."[35]

In Djindjic's stead Vojislav Kostunica became prime minister, forming a minority government only with the tolerance of Milosevic's Socialists, with Djindjic's Democratic Party (DS) in opposition. Kostunica faced mounting international pressure on two urgent interlinked issues: the extradition to the Hague Tribunal of those Serbs indicted for war crimes and the regularization of the status of a Kosovo that now looked as if it would never return to Serb rule. On the first issue, Kostunica was at best ambivalent; on the second, he was adamantly opposed to any change in Kosovo's de jure status as a Serbian province. The new prime minister came into office declaring that cooperation with the ICTY was not a priority. Later he did classify it as such, but only in terms of persuading indictees to go to the Hague voluntarily.[36] Throughout 2003 and most of 2004, however, the top indictees chose not to do so, and Serb security forces did not arrest them.

In this period Kostunica thus seemed to be immune to the whole dynamic that had galvanized reform and modernization in the Central European states and won them EU membership in 2004. The vision of eventual EU membership that powerfully motivated Prime Minister Ivo Sanader in Croatia—and had similarly motivated Djindjic—seemed absent. Kostunica did not campaign against the European Union but he firmly rejected EU conditionality, and he seemed quite willing to pay the price of forfeiting any claim to EU membership and its privileges. His relationship with ICTY prosecutor Carla Del Ponte was frosty; she had stormed out of a meeting with him in early 2001 after he reportedly told her that the ICTY was anti-Serb and was manipulated politically by the United States.[37] When he became prime minister in 2004, Kostunica held that "rushing to fulfill Ms. Carla Del Ponte's wishes is neither dignified nor patriotic," according to Sonja Biserko of the Helsinki Committee for Human Rights in Serbia, and he said publicly that Serbs would no longer "be transferred to The Hague . . . for command responsibility" (as distinct from the culpability of the lower ranks for actually pulling the trigger in obeying those commands). In May 2004 ICTY president Theodor Meron complained to the UN Security Council that Serbia was not cooperating with the Hague in extraditing the accused, in facilitating meetings with witnesses, or in providing crucial documents, to which one of Kostunica's advisers retorted that the tribunal was increasingly becoming a "one-sided, political institution."[38] When Del Ponte again traveled to Belgrade that October, she and other recent Western visitors to Belgrade won over most of Serbia's political elite—-but not Kostunica. Kostunica still argued instead that Serbia had the best record of cooperation with the ICTY, as more Serbs than indictees of any other nationality had gone to the Hague.[39]

In declining to deliver suspects to the Hague, Kostunica was fully in tune with Serb public opinion. From its first indictments in 1995 (which targeted Serbs especially heavily, since war crimes by the initially victorious Serbs preceded those of resurgent Croats and Bosniaks and were investigated first), Serbs saw the ICTY as prejudiced against them. One of the tribunal's intended functions—to lift collective guilt by establishing individual guilt—seemed not only to fail but to work in exactly the opposite direction. A hard core of some 20 to 30 percent of Serbs perceived the placing of individual Serbs in the dock—and charging them with the standard conspiracy to commit crime, in order to establish command responsibility—as the demonization of all Serbs, and a majority thought that the tribunal "did not offer justice."[40] In his own defense (he refused any counsel), Milosevic berated the tribunal as an illegitimate court and indeed treated his trial as a trial of all Serbs. The entrenched Communist-era party and security elites, who might well have felt threatened by any other approach, agreed.

In late 2004 Kostunica's attitude toward both the Tribunal and the EU suddenly seemed to soften.[41] Within a few months sixteen Serb indictees went to the Hague "voluntarily."[42] Reports quickly circulated that this burst of cooperation with the ICTY was greatly stimulated by state payments worth up to €100,000 in some cases and obverse threats of the withdrawal of pensions or even physical arrest in others.[43] The effective lever seemed to be the refusal of Brussels to allow Belgrade even the first step toward eventual EU membership, a Stabilization and Association Agreement—and NATO's refusal to let Serbia join the Partnership for Peace—until senior suspects appeared at the court.[44] The Bush administration, which until then had been suggesting, as an offshoot of its fierce opposition to the International Criminal Court, that all Serb generals other than Ratko Mladic could be tried in Serbia, also joined the chorus and in January 2005 suspended economic aid to Serbia until Belgrade cooperated with the ICTY. EU enlargement commissioner Olli Rehn further linked approval of the Feasibility Study to forthcoming status talks on Kosovo, as did the EU's high representative for common foreign and security policy, Javier Solana.[45] Prime Minister Kostunica, registering that the EU was being tough with Croatia as well as with Serbia, manifested his first public approbation of EU rewards, declaring, "We regard the EU as our common home."[46] President Boris Tadic became bolder in his public defense of compliance with the Hague as the indispensable precondition for "integration into international institutions, foreign investment, and improved living standards."[47] Western Europeans began stressing to Serbian officials that their country had the sophistication and the experienced personnel to proceed rapidly toward membership if they had the political will to meet the democratic and market requirements—and to extradite Mladic, who had been hidden for years by the Serbian and Republika Srpska army and military intelligence, sometimes in underground military facilities, sometimes in Belgrade apartments.[48]

Demonstrating that it was serious about demanding extradition of senior figures accused of war crimes before it would consent to any rapprochement with Serbia, Brussels delayed the release of its Feasibility Study for a Stabilization and Association Agreement with Serbia until some hours after Nebojsa Pavkovic, commander of the VJ Third Army in Kosovo, arrived at the Hague on April 25, 2005, as the last of the Serb indictees to show up at the tribunal through mid-2006. In parallel, three months later, Belgrade quietly signed an agreement with the Western alliance that had so recently bombed it, allowing NATO and UN Kosovo Force (KFOR) troops to transit Serbia when needed, for example, to protect Serbs in Kosovo.[49]

The domestic pressures that contributed to Kostunica's change of heart appeared to be the inroads being made on the prime minister's Democratic Party of Serbia (DSS) by ultranationalists and threats by the small G17 Plus technocratic party of economists to pull out of his coalition and force early elections if Kostunica did not send most-wanted indictees to the Hague in order to unblock international aid for Serbia. In summer 2004 the extreme nationalist Radicals shot up from their 9 percent in the 2000 parliamentary election to place second in the presidential runoff, winning 45 percent to the

53 percent for the pro-European, proreform Boris Tadic, who had assumed leadership of the DS after Djindjic's death. By late 2004 Kostunica's DSS was losing ground to Tadic's DS in opinion polls, but neither of these centrist parties managed to rise much over 20 percent in popularity ratings. The undisputed winners were the ultranationalist Radicals, who climbed to 32 percent approval by 2005 and to a rising 42 percent by mid-2006.[50]

At their most sanguine, Western diplomats hoped that the constellation might induce Kostunica to cut his losses by ending his flirtation with more radical nationalists and turning back toward more democratic allies. For two years, the most public difference between the prime minister, on the one side, and President Boris Tadic and foreign minister and leader of the Serbian Renewal Movement Vuk Draskovic, on the other, had been the issue of cooperation with the international court. For the latter, extradition of war crimes suspects was not only a requirement if Serbia were to move toward EU membership, but also a point of Serb honor. As Draskovic put it, "My stand is that cooperation is first of all our national obligation. Why? Because in the past in our history we had a lot of wars, but Serbs were never charged with war crimes. In the past my nation was the victim of ethnic cleansing, or genocide, as in the Second World War, but my nation never used revenge, and that was the reason we were very respected all over the world. . . . Slobodan Milosevic and his followers promoted an antihistorical movement and disgraced Serb history."[51] The two political camps remained at loggerheads; Western hopes for a reconciliation of the democratic center were dashed.

Long after Pavkovic became the last—and most senior—of the string of accused Serbs to appear at the Hague Tribunal, Serbian officials continued to hint that even the most-wanted Radovan Karadzic and Ratko Mladic might soon turn up there too after their decade on the run. Among other harbingers, Karadzic's wife, in what seemed to be a face-saving gesture, made public appeals to her husband to ease his family's plight by turning himself in.[52] And Amfilohije (Radovic), the Serbian Orthodox metropolitan of Montenegro and the Littoral—a man who is said to be the "spiritual father"of Karadzic and whose wife's sister is married to Kostunica—told Serb reporters in summer 2005 that he expected Karadzic to appear before the Hague Tribunal voluntarily; he also implied that he had previously suggested this course of action to some of those who had surrendered themselves.[53] Patriarch Pavle, though, expressed more concern about the persecution of innocent members of the Karadzic family who were "blackmailed, abused, and punished" by "powerful foreign actors whom I trust are also Christians."[54] Indeed, Amfilohije displayed similar sympathy for Karadzic's mother at her funeral, comparing her with the mothers of medieval Serb heroes.[55] This accolade contrasted sharply with his lukewarm eulogy at the funeral of Zoran Djindjic, which some read to imply that the assassinated prime minister got what he deserved for his infatuation with an alien Europe.[56]

The Politics of the Serbian Orthodox Church

It is hard for outsiders to pin down precisely either the balance of prevailing political opinions within the Serbian Orthodox Church (SPC) or the political impact of the church today. In past centuries it was much clearer. The church was the very heart of Serb identity; in the Middle Ages Serbs tended to think of their larger group as Orthodox rather than Serb (as Russians in that era identified themselves as Orthodox rather than Russian). The Serbian church became autocephalous in 1219, two centuries before the Russian Orthodox Church did. In 1345 or 1346 the Serbian bishop was elevated to become the patriarch of the Serbs and the Greeks. Some years after the battle of Blackbird Field, the seat of the Serbian archbishop was located in Kosovo, and the monasteries and churches there remained dear to Serbs long after their mass exodus from their ancestral Kosovo in the seventeenth century.[57]

In the eighteenth century, as Ottoman rule disintegrated in Serb regions, so did the authority of the corrupted Serbian church hierarchy; after intrigues within the church and between the Serbian church and the patriarch of Constantinople, the patriarch reassumed direct control over the Serbian dioceses and installed a predominantly Greek hierarchy. "The change was strongly disliked by the Serbs, and the church thus lost its position as the accepted and unchallenged representative of the nation," according to historian L. S. Stavrianos. At the same time, the church suffered from the inroads of the European Enlightenment; "the Serbian world was transformed from an essentially theocratic community to one motivated by secular considerations and guided by secular leaders." When Serb peasants subsequently wrested independence from the Turks in the nineteenth century for political and economic reasons, the Serbian church, in Stavrianos's reading, was not a major inspiration.[58]

The Serbian Orthodox Church recovered sufficiently to acquire the privileged status of a "state religion" in pre–World War I Serbia and Montenegro, but even as the Serbian patriarchate was restored in 1920 it lost this position. Instead, the 1921 "Vidovdan constitution" of the first Yugoslavia proclaimed the freedom and equality of all religions. During World War II, however, Croats' fierce identification with the Catholic Church and Serbs' fierce identification with the Orthodox Church exacerbated the enmity between the Ustashe and the Chetniks; in the war the SPC suffered the greatest human and material losses of any of Yugoslavia's three main religious communities. The Chetniks were closely (but discreetly) allied with the Serbian church and were especially sympathetic to Father Justin (Popovic), the second most important Serb theologian at the time, and to his vision of "St. Sava-ism," equating Serbdom, Orthodoxy, and Christ.[59]

The church, which had welcomed the first Yugoslavia as unifying Serbs scattered across different lands, disapproved of the second, Communist Yugoslavia after 1945 as an atheistic state that was trying to divide the Serb nation and its church. While Tito did not ban religion, he marginalized the Orthodox, Catholic, and Islamic faiths alike, infiltrated them with secret service agents—and encouraged the Macedonian Orthodox Church to break off from the Serbian Orthodox Church in the 1960s. As part of Tito's drive to smother both Serb and Croat nationalism, the authorities also barred Father Justin from teaching, and turned him into the best-known anti-Communist dissident in the country. The charismatic Justin's anti-Western sacralization of the Serb nation nonetheless grew in popularity, and he quietly attracted a few disciples, despite the ban. Three of these rose to prominence in the 1980s: the ultranationalist metropolitan Amfilohije in Montenegro; the archconservative bishop Atanasije (Jevtic) in Herzegovina; and Bishop Artemije (Radosavljevic), the senior cleric in Kosovo, who preached tolerance in the run-up to the Kosovo war but is now one of the leaders of the resistance to church reform.[60]

As the Communist grip loosened in the 1980s, there was "a resurgence of religious feelings among all Yugoslavs. . . . Orthodoxy, Catholicism and Islam became increasingly important for cultural and national distinctiveness of Serbs, Croats and Muslims. . . . The crisis in the mostly Albanian populated Serbian 'holy land' of Kosovo, which erupted in the early 1980s, provoked strong feelings within the SPC, which became a main pillar of modern Serbian nationalism. The Orthodox clergy increasingly spoke the nationalist language, clearly trying to play a more prominent role in Serbia, now under the control of the new Communist leadership led by Slobodan Milosevic," according to Radmila Radic of the Serbian Institute of Contemporary History.[61]

For his part, Milosevic, though he long took care to invite representatives of all three major congregations to his receptions, welcomed the revived Orthodox Church's championing of Serbdom as he shifted his own base of legitimacy from socialism to nationalism. In 1987 SPC prelates triumphally carried Lazar's bones in emotional processions from one monastery to another, and the church helped stage Milosevic's famous Kosovo Polje appearance in 1989.[62] The church remained suspicious of him as a Communist atheist, but it wholeheartedly approved of his drive to keep Serbs in one country and thus maintain the unity of the Serbian Orthodox Church, as well as his rejection of Western liberal norms. "Notions such as democracy, liberalism, the freedom of conscience, western culture—all part of a new discourse in Slovenia—were seen as alien and anti-Orthodox," observed Radic.[63]

In 1990, before the Serb offensive in Croatia began, and in 1991, as the military campaign was bringing more and more Croatian territory under Serb control, the SPC news organ, *Pravoslavlje*, "stoked the flames of nationalist resentment by publishing article after article on the allegedly Serbian heritage" of parts of Croatia then under siege, "and on the sufferings of the Serbian people (only) during World War Two. . . . The Church remained consistently pro-war throughout the campaign in Croatia," reported Sabrina Ramet, an American academic who has long written on Balkan politics and religion. Then, as the Serb offensive shifted to Bosnia in 1992, the church gave "full support to the expansionist plans being pursued by Karadzic's forces." Serb partisanship was clear, for example, in late 1992, when Orthodox prelates issued a statement denying categorically that Serbs had organized rapes of Muslim or other women, while asserting that Muslims and Croats had raped many Serb women.[64] During the wars in Croatia and Bosnia, the church "took extremist positions, turning a blind eye to ethnic cleansing and in some cases justifying it; it has never distanced itself from, let alone apologised for, its statements from that time," the International Crisis Group charged in 2005.[65] And in a characterically blunt drawing up of accounts, Helsinki Committee director Sonja Biserko linked the "major moral problem of the Serbian society" in its "[u]nreadiness to face the recent past, wars and war crimes figures" with the values of the Serbian Orthodox Church, "marked by archaism, collectivism, anti-Western stands and xenophobia. . . . Extreme intolerance to everything belonging to . . . Western culture" is the message the church sends to believers.[66]

In April 1993, when Karadzic defied Milosevic and rejected the Vance-Owen peace plan, wrote Ramet further, "Patriarch Pavle and Metropolitan Amfilohije declared their opposition to the . . . plan for the same reason that Karadzic did: they hoped to see even more lands annexed by the Serbian side." And the church denounced the Dayton settlement that gave "49% of Bosnian land to the Serbs, who had made up only 32% of the population of Bosnia in the 1991 census, . . . on the grounds that the plan was 'unfair' to Serbs." In addition, in the mid-1990s "Patriarch Pavle and Bishop Atanasije called on Belgrade to refuse to cooperate with the International War Crimes Tribunal."[67]

By contrast, Obrad Kesic, an activist in the anti-Milosevic democratic opposition in the 1990s and now senior partner of the Washington-based TSM Global Consultants, perceives the Orthodox hierarchy's role as much more nuanced. During the wars, he said, the patriarch always spoke for moderation and condemned atrocity. And while many soldiers killed others in the name of religion and some Orthodox clergymen participated in the fighting, some Orthodox bishops—especially those from Bosnia—met with imams and Catholic clergymen during the war in Bosnia and appealed jointly for peace.[68] This is true, but the appeals were all quite ineffectual, since the different sides had utterly incompatible notions about what would constitute an equitable peaceful solution. Patriarch Pavle presupposed the right of Serbs in Croatia and Bosnia to live together in a united Serbia that would keep the Orthodox flock from being split up. The Croat Catholics, by contrast, presupposed the right of Croatia to independence within the borders of the old Yugoslav Croat republic, including those districts populated primarily by Serbs. And the imams, with no possible congruence of religious and ethnic identity unless Bosnia was carved up, presupposed the right of Bosnians of all faiths to live within the borders of the old Bosnian republic.

From the beginning, the SPC backed both Milosevic's campaign to re-Serbianize Kosovo and Radovan Karadzic's and Vojislav Seselj's more extreme plans—years before Milosevic's mass ethnic cleansing in Kosovo—to expel from that province all the Albanians who supposedly moved there only after 1945. But as it became clear that the president was not going to grant the church the central role it wished to (re)claim in Serb society after its half century in the Communist wilderness, Orthodox disenchantment with the atheist Milosevic grew. Karadzic in Bosnia became instead the darling of the church. He was a nationalist, mystical poet who published in the popular *Svetigora* journal of Metropolitan Amfilohije's see. He eschewed the West's cold rationality and embraced the church; for him, Orthodoxy spoke to the inner heart of the collective Serb soul. The Bosnian Serb leader became a welcome guest at the metropolitan's residence in the Ostrog monastery (where he would make his last public appearance before going underground to escape capture and extradition to the Hague).

In the eyes of many prelates, Milosevic betrayed both Karadzic and the Bosnian Serbs at Dayton; they abandoned him accordingly.[69] In the late 1990s churchmen increasingly sided with the anti-Milosevic student demonstrators in Belgrade (and Amfilohije, who comes from an old Montenegrin family, sided with the prime minister of Montenegro, Milo Djukanovic, when he broke with his former mentor). Opposition to Milosevic did not by any means imply endorsement of the Hague Tribunal, which the church, too, regarded as an anti-Serb Western institution. In 1997 Patriarch Pavle joined other Serbian intellectuals in urging the annulment of the indictments against Karadzic and

Mladic. This appeal reflected the church's view that those Serb soldiers who were accused of having directly committed atrocities should go to the Hague to answer the charges, and be punished if they were guilty; but that senior commanders generally should not do so, since the just defensive war they were fighting on behalf of Serbs in Croatia, Bosnia, and Kosovo must not be impugned. (Croatia's Catholic clerics drew the same distinction among Croat indictees.)

As the Serb-Albanian confrontation heated up in Kosovo in 1997–98, Bishop Artemije became the most prominent church spokesman on the issue, and a voice for moderation—in part, international officials in Pristina thought in retrospect, because he sensed ultimate disaster for the minority Serbs in Milosevic's brutal crackdown on the overwhelming majority of Albanians. Notably, Artemije condemned the Serb security forces' failure to distinguish between armed rebels and civilians.[70] When the Kosovo war ended and the U.S. bombing stopped in June 1999, the Holy Synod (the church's permanent executive body) immediately called on Milosevic to step down: "In face of the tragic situation of our people and country and in the belief that final justice comes from the Lord but not from the instrumentalized court in The Hague, we charge that the current president of the country and his government step back, for the sake and salvation of the people."

At that point Patriarch Pavle "seemed to abandon the Greater Serbian project, telling his listeners, 'If the only way to create a greater Serbia is by crime, then I do not accept that, and let that Serbia disappear,'" noted Ramet.[71] Recalling his own stewardship in Kosovo from the late 1950s to the late 1980s as a time of continuous Albanian harassment of Serbs, the patriarch saw the appearance of General Vladimir Lazarevic, commander of the Pristina Corps in 1999, before the tribunal not as a test of his responsibility for war crimes, but rather as a defense of Serb honor before the world's improper accusations. Intriguingly, after elections and demonstrations toppled Milosevic, Bishop Artemije said publicly that Milosevic should go to the Hague to answer the charges against him. He refused to tell a BBC journalist what crimes Milosevic should be held accountable for, however—and some of Artemije's increasingly bitter rhetoric following the NATO bombing gave the impression that Milosevic's main crime was to have started a war that he could not win and that left the church and Serbs in Kosovo vulnerable.[72]

Even this much evidence of its attitudes does not measure the political salience of the Orthodox Church, of course. Prime Minister Kostunica may be very close to Metropolitan Amfilohije, and he may place unusual priority, for a politician, on making periodic visits to monasteries in Kosovo and on Mt.

Athos in Greece. Obrad Kesic described Kostunica's religious allegiance as personal rather than political, however, and pointed out that in Belgrade the prime minister attends a local church rather than the politically more impressive St. Sava's, the largest house of worship in the Balkans. He noted further that chaplains accompany armies the world over, and that Orthodox priests' blessing of Serb soldiers in the field fits in this context. Similarly *NIN* editor Niksic scoffed at the notion that the church wields strong power behind the scenes. "How many Belgraders do you know who go to church?!" he demanded rhetorically. He found the flirtation of Serb politicians with the SPC hierarchy no more indicative of power relations than the cultivation of clerical friends by politicians in the United States or other countries—and noted that Al Capone's generous donations to the Catholic Church did not implicate that church in his crimes. Milosevic's old security forces are much more influential in Serbia than the prelates, he suggested, as are the cigarette, telecommunications, and oil multinationals. By contrast, one Serb historian suggested that the church has a pervasive political influence, since its assumptions shape the public discourse in ways that are not always recognized—especially in its concept of the Serbs as Christian victims throughout history.

It does seem that there is something of a revival of interest in the church, as measured by the fair number of educated urban men now entering monasteries, for the first time in the past century and a half. Surveys also suggest that there is a strong church influence on public opinion. In mid-2003 some 68 percent said they trusted the Serbian church more than any other institution—a ranking that topped even the army's 61 percent.[73] Amfilohije's hints in 2005 that Karadzic might surrender after ten years as a fugitive—along with some startling comments by the young bishop Grigorije (Djuric) of Zahumlje-Herzegovina—therefore found some popular resonance.

Within the church, it was Bishop Grigorije—a man who conducts friendly dialogue with other denominations and regularly condemns attacks on mosques in Bosnia-Herzegovina—who in 2005 spearheaded the boldest new approaches to the interrelated issues of war crimes, the cause of a Greater Serbia, and the internal liberalization of the Serbian Orthodox Church. Grigorije's ecumenism and activism were all the more remarkable because his pastoral seat of Trebinje was one of the Serb nationalist strongholds both in World War II and in the 1992–95 Bosnia war. Significantly, the reconstruction of Trebinje's historic Osman Pasha mosque, one of ten razed by Serbs in the region at the apogee of the Republic of Serbian Krajina, was completed in summer 2005, despite initial opposition from a Serb mob, which Grigorije helped bring under control.[74]

In spring 2005 Grigorije shocked Serbs when he publicly urged indictees to surrender and go to the Hague, and spoke of the harm that Karadzic had done to Serbs. Thereafter, some other members of the Orthodox clergy in Serbia and Bosnia-Herzegovina made similar statements, apparently with the understanding of Metropolitan Amfilohije.[75] Nationalists rounded on Grigorije, calling him a traitor and an agent of NATO for calling for delivery of Hague inductees to the executioner instead of defending them against the treacherous Belgrade government, as bishops should do.[76]

Grigorije seemed to have won the support of his patron, Bishop Atanasije, despite their divergent political views, for efforts to unite the two warring wings of the Orthodox Church. Crucially, Metropolitan Amfilohije also seemed to back Grigorije, perhaps out of concern that the church was in danger of losing support among the key constituency of the Serb diaspora in the United States. And the American-born, ecumenical-minded Irinej (Dobrijevic)—a priest whom Patriarch Pavle had called to Belgrade as his "foreign minister," and was said to be the bête noire of the conservative old guard—seemed to have persuaded the patriarch, too, to tolerate calls for church reform.

By contrast, the conservative clergy, led today by Bishop Artemije and Bishop Filaret (Micevic) of Milesevo, adamantly oppose any liberalization and weakening of church traditions. Fierce internal disputes both about Hague indictees and about internal church reforms continue, with opposition to Grigorije's more open attitude coming from conservatives like Artemije out of fear that the church could thereby lose its soul and become "too Protestant," as one Serb phrased it. For the clergy who see the church as the one remaining Serb institution in Kosovo and the tacit ruler of Kosovo Serbs—and also for the "red clergy" who were put in place by Tito's secret services—any internal liberalization or formalization of Kosovo's breakaway from Serbia are anathema. The dominant view of the church was clear in the hierarchy's condemnation of President Tadic's call to Kosovo Serbs to participate in the 2004 Kosovo election and in Bishop Atanasije of Zahumlje-Herzegovina's Easter message admonishing Serbs to reject any deal that would sell out Kosovo for a fast track to membership in the European Union.[77] It was also clear in the highly unusual failure to renew Bishop Grigorije's tenure on the Holy Synod at the end of 2005. It would be surprising if the outcome of the Serbian Orthodox Church's internal battles over the Hague Tribunal, Kosovo's future, and church reform did not have a strong impact on public opinion in terms of Serb pride, European identity, and criminal accountability.[78]

Political Crisis

Even more sensational for the average Serb than Grigorije and Amfilohije's pronouncements on indictees was the surfacing in 2005 of a previously secret two-hour video of the torture and execution in 1995 of six Bosniaks from Srebrenica, four of them under the age of eighteen, by uniformed Serbian Interior Ministry paramilitary police called Scorpions. Twenty copies of the video, which was filmed by the Scorpions themselves—and opened with the police being blessed by an Orthodox priest declaring, "The Turks are rising again; they come to take our sacred places"—had been available in one video shop for loan exclusively to Scorpions. As word about the video seeped out after a decade of sworn silence, an order was given to destroy all the copies. One survived, however, and was ferreted out by Serbian human rights activist Natasa Kandic, who passed it on to the Hague Tribunal in May.[79] "Most Serbs till now either believed nothing happened [at Srebrenica] or that the people who did the atrocities were Bosnian Serbs, wild guys from the mountains, or even French special forces—but this is forcing Serbs as a whole to come to grips with what happened," commented businessman Kesic at the time.[80] Parts of the video were aired in Serbia, not only by the independent television station B92, but also by state television. Serbian authorities swiftly arrested eight of the Scorpions shown in the video. The Serbian Orthodox synod condemned "the cold-blooded killing of unarmed, defenseless civilians"—though only weeks later senior clergy attended a Radical Party rally on the tenth anniversary of the Srebrenica massacre to celebrate the Serb victory there and to commemorate the victimization of Serbs in the 1990s wars.[81]

As usual in the ambivalent Balkans, there were contrary signals. Personnel reshuffles in the Justice Ministry and police promoting old Milosevic appointees and sidelining reformers were troubling to Westerners, as was the abrupt withdrawal by Serbian courts of the international arrest warrant for Slobodan Milosevic's son in summer 2005.[82] The bland explanation for the abandonment of Marko Milosevic's indictment was that the Otpor activist who had originally pressed charges could no longer recall the details. The widespread assumption in Belgrade, however, was that this was the price demanded by Milosevic's Socialist Party for its passive support for Kostunica's minority government.[83]

These events coincided with a political crisis that left Kostunica's coalition government more dependent than ever on the parliamentary "tolerance" of Milosevic's Socialist Party and more at the mercy of the high-flying Radicals.[84]

Kostunica's fortunes were revived only temporarily by the deus ex machina of Austria's threat to veto the start of forty-years-delayed accession negotiations between the EU and Turkey unless the EU simultaneously opened the half-year-delayed accession negotiations with Croatia. ICTY prosecutor Carla Del Ponte duly certified that the need to suspend membership talks with Croatia had been voided by Zagreb's recent cooperation with the tribunal, and both sets of talks began in October 2005. Relaxation of the "no Gotovina, no talks" rule in the case of Croatia logically opened the way for relaxation of the "no Karadzic/Mladic, no talks" rule in the case of Serbia.[85] Belgrade responded by finally acting on the EU's eighteen-month request to freeze all assets of war crimes fugitives.[86] The EU was further encouraged when Serbian prosecutors investigating government corruption had police detain two senior judges and seven other officials and lawyers, in what Finance Minister Mladjan Dinkic called "the strongest blow to organized economic crime and corruption in Serbia" since the fall of Slobodan Milosevic.[87]

The opening of negotiations on a Stabilization and Association Agreement with the EU (and similar negotiations between the EU and Sarajevo, once the Bosnian politicians saw they would be the only ones left out if they did not adopt a more unifying constitution) did not make it any easier for Serbian politicians to yield to the inevitable and let go of Kosovo. But it did for the first time let Kostunica's DSS "portray itself as the leading pro-European force in Serbia." And by the end of October this had nudged the popular rating of the DSS up two points, from 12 to 14 percent, to surpass businessman Bogoljub Karic's Force Serbia party for the first time—at the cost of Tadic's DS (down from 24 to 20 percent) but not of the Radicals, who still led the pack with approval well above 30 percent.[88] Perhaps the EU magnet was working on Kostunica and the Serb electorate after all. Or perhaps Kostunica was just reaping temporary benefit from his defiance of reality both on Kosovo's independence and on Montenegro's secession—until such time as the Radicals would unseat him.

Podgorica/Cetinje

Before he was murdered in early 2003, Serbian prime minister Djindjic had by and large agreed with Montenegrin president Milo Djukanovic on the basis for a velvet divorce of the two lands, according to Kesic; Djindjic wished to repay Djukanovic for sheltering him in Montenegro during the Kosovo war and also viewed Montenegro as something of an economic burden for Serbia.[89] Djindjic's assassination scotched this understanding, however, and the EU feared that Montenegro's independence would destabilize Kosovo and impel a premature redefinition of the latter's formal status. Brussels also thought that the 650,000 Montenegrins (just under the population of the city of Baltimore) were too few to construct a viable state. In 2003 EU high representative Solana therefore pressed Podgorica and Belgrade into prolonging their eighty-five-year-old formal union for another three years before considering any breakup.[90] The United States, by contrast, held that it was folly to compel Serbia and Montenegro to stay united, and to waste the leverage of Western aid donors—who kept Montenegro afloat financially—on this side issue rather than using it to crack down on crime. In this case, however, Washington deferred to Brussels. In the event, even the Serbian-Montenegrin Constitutional Charter did elicit an angry resolution from the Kosovo Assembly declaring the preamble's reference to Kosovo as an autonomous province of Serbia invalid; in Pristina, the head of the UN Mission in Kosovo (UNMIK), Michael Steiner, overruled the resolution.

Whatever its impact on Kosovo, the cooling-off period seemed to work domestically; by May 2006, when the people of Montenegro approved independence by referendum by the 55 percent minimum set by the EU for recognition of the new state, it was no longer a burning issue in Belgrade.[91] As ethnic Montenegrins themselves split half-and-half in their attitudes—it was the Albanian minority that tipped the balance to independence in the referendum—many Serbs displayed the ennui of the Czechs in their relief at Slovak secession in 1993. In Belgrade the feeling grew that the much poorer Montenegro was free riding on Serbia. Exceptions to the Serb indifference were Metropolitan Amfilohije and segments of the Serbian army. In the run-up to the vote Amfilohije campaigned actively against independence. In a dramatic flourish in June 2005, he emphasized the Serbian Church's claim to preeminence in Montenegro by borrowing a Serbian army helicopter and, without government permission, hoisting a prefabricated chapel onto public land at the peak of Mt. Rumija, thereby offending Montenegrin Orthodox, Catholics, and Muslims, all of whom, like the Serbian Orthodox, hold the site sacred. Government officials ordered the chapel's removal, but neither Amfilohije nor the Serbian army complied, and the Montenegrin armed forces did not have a heavy-duty helicopter to do the job. Amfilohije charged that the officials in question were possessed by "a demonic spirit" and branded them "Turkish occupation forces."[92]

The even balance of the pro-Serb and pro-independence camps among Montenegrins was understandable to any observer proceeding not from the fierce duel between Djukanovic and Milosevic over the run-up to the Kosovo war beginning in 1997, but from the historical intertwining of Serbs and

Montenegrins. Over many centuries Montenegrins have seen themselves as the most passionate Serbs of all, the guardians of Serb freedom even in the darkest days of Ottoman rule. They were part of the medieval Serb empire, then developed separately after the Ottoman Turks conquered Serbia and the Montenegrin lowlands but never bothered to seize the sheep, goats, cattle, and 19,000 beehives in the peaks of central Montenegro. Like other alpine enclaves in northern Albania and elsewhere, Montenegro paid tribute to the Porte but exercised tribal autonomy. In the sixteenth century the monks of the Cetinje monastery elected a prince-bishop. In the seventeenth century the fierce mountaineers rebelled against paying even their head tax. In the eighteenth century they made the office of prince-bishop hereditary, and finally won full independence for Montenegro in 1799. Over the next eighty years they kept the dream of wider Serb independence alive and fought alongside their lowland brothers whenever revolts broke out. This Montenegrin romanticism quickly became part of the West's myth of the Yugoslav defiance of Stalin, as partisan Milovan Djilas split with Tito and had ample time in jail to write books about the flaws of the Communist faith and the virtues of his beloved native Montenegro.

During the wars of the early 1990s there was no clash of views between the Serbs and the Montenegrins. Serb military units were dispatched interchangeably from Serbia proper or from Montenegro to fight Croats and Bosniaks; Montenegrins gleefully joined in targeting the glitterati's yachts in Dubrovnik harbor.[93] Among some Montenegrins this solidarity continued for a decade thereafter; when NATO-led Stabilization Force (SFOR) troops got more serious about looking for Karadzic and he could no longer move freely in Bosnia, he was said to be slipping back and forth in the rugged forests that straddle southeastern Bosnia and Montenegro. The government in Podgorica—"Titograd" reverted to its old name as Yugoslavia broke up—dropped its official solidarity when Milo Djukanovic was elected Montenegrin president in 1997, however. He split with Milosevic over the latter's attempt to curtail Montenegrin autonomy (including control of smuggling, it was widely assumed), then sought and won the patronage of the United States, opposed the Serbian war in Kosovo, and gave Zoran Djindjic protection against bodily harm in Budva during that Kosovo war.

The assassination of Djindjic in March 2003 did not alter Serbian-Montenegrin relations. Paradoxically, however, it did advance rapprochement of Serbia and Montenegro with Europe, as worried policymakers in the European institutions tried to bolster democrats in the union by relaxing the stricter conditionality they had applied to the new Central European democracies. Serbia and Montenegro, which had previously been deemed unready for membership in the Council of Europe, the basic certifier of democratic practice in Europe, was now allowed to join it. And by 2004, in an effort to accelerate eventual EU membership, EU foreign ministers agreed on a "two-track" process that would let the economically very different Serbia and Montenegro negotiate separate Stabilization and Association Agreements with the EU.[94] This was a nightmare for EU lawyers, but in the Western Balkans it made sense not to treat the long path to EU accession as a rigid set of rewards for benchmarks achieved (and not to ostracize recalcitrants), but to shape the process into a more flexible political instrument, in the hope that faster integration into European structures would itself help Balkan states overcome the rampant smuggling, organized crime, trafficking, corruption, homicide, and politial warping of criminal justice.

Montenegro duly passed new laws liberalizing the economy to make it compatible with the EU, though implementation lagged. In contrast to Serbia, it apologized to Croatia for the Dubrovnik bombardment and tendered €375,000 in reparations.[95] Also in contrast to Serbia, Montenegro pledged cooperation with the Hague Tribunal (and repeatedly pointed this out to EU contacts to justify a faster track to Brussels for Podgorica than for Belgrade).

Montenegro has its flaws, of course. Police inspectors have a conspicuously high mortality rate; as of this writing, the murders of three senior inspectors remained unsolved.[96] In 2001 Montenegro cracked down on speedboat links with Italian mafias across the narrow Adriatic, an area of flagrant smuggling, but by 2002 this trade seemed to be flourishing again. British ambassador to Serbia and Montenegro Charles Crawford bluntly summed up the problem as a "dangerous combination of weak institutions and strong criminals."[97] Opposition politicians added the charge that the government had sold out the land to Russian oligarchs, including the choice sliver of Adriatic coast and the aluminum smelter and bauxite mines that produced half of Montenegro's GDP.[98]

Throughout the era of sanctions in the 1990s and beyond, Montenegrin smugglers specialized in cars (preferably Mercedes-Benz), cigarettes, and prostitutes. After years of heavy revenue losses from excise tax evasion on tobacco, the EU sued American cigarette manufacturers for alleged collusion in the smuggling (and named Djukanovic, who was now prime minister, as one participant in the illegal trade) and in 2004 won an out-of-court settlement from Philip Morris of more than a billion dollars.[99] As a corollary, Montenegro—probably second only to China in the ubiquity of smoking—also adjusted to the requirements of the World Trade Organization by passing domestic laws banning ads for cigarettes and forbidding smoking in closed public rooms.

In religious affairs, Montenegro distinguishes itself from Belgrade by nour-ishing (since 1993) the small autocephalous Montenegrin Orthodox Church, which periodically spats with the Serbian Orthodox hierarchy over Serbian and Montenegrin nationalism, ownership of Montenegro's 660 churches and monasteries, and possession of Filermosa's twelfth-century icon of the mother of God that is now in Cetinje, the old Montenegrin capital and new seat of the church. The Montenegrin church accuses the Serbian church of following a Greater Serbia agenda. The Serbian church mocks the Montenegrin church as a political rather than a spiritual organization, dependent on support from Montenegrin Roman Catholics and Muslims—and accuses its followers of altering protected Romanesque historical monuments to give them Byzantine features.[100] On occasion hostility between the two churches explodes into armed clashes.

Despite the enthusiasm of the Montenegrin hierarchy for independence, Djukanovic by no means favors the Montenegrin Orthodox breakaway over the mother church. He is grateful for the support he received from the Serbian Orthodox hierarchy in his successful bid for the presidency in 1997, and from Patriarch Pavle, who within days of the Kosovo cease-fire publicly called for more influence for Montenegro in the union with Serbia. Djukanovic may have annoyed the Serbian hierarchy when he prudently sent equal Easter greetings to both churches in 2000. But he seems to be comfortable with the Serbian Orthodox Church's occupation of the bulk of the vast ecclesiatical real estate holdings in Montenegro and with its expansion in the decade and a half since Amfilohije became metropolitan, increasing its priests threefold, to sixty, and its monks eightfold, to 160. In the unequal contest for the faith-ful, Amfilohije wins, outdrawing congregations even on the inauguration day of the Cetinje church's synod in 2002.[101]

Such issues—and not abstract reckoning with past Serb atrocities in Prije-dor, Srebrenica, or Drenica—are the stuff of politics in Montenegro today. Montenegro's political elite is not obsessed with Kosovo as the Serb political elite is, and the government maintains good relations with UNMIK and Kosovo. Although it was part and parcel of Milosevic's establishment during the Croatian and Bosnian wars, the Montenegrin political class separated from Belgrade during the Kosovo war and feels no compunction today to wal-low in that past. Nor does it share the Serb sense of victimization. "You think, do Serbs really believe that? Or are they just putting it on? But they really do," marveled one young Montenegrin official. "Everybody knows in their hearts that Kosovo is gone. Or they should know. . . . We have to realize that the mentality is different in Montenegro and Serbia. Anybody here under thirty thinks differently from the Serbs."[102]

Facing the Past

In Belgrade, for good or ill, the past is not so easily forgotten. The defeats of Milosevic in his three and a half wars for Serbian aggrandizement in the 1990s (in Croatia, Bosnia, and Kosovo and the sham war in Slovenia) and the subsequent misery and influx of Serb refugees to Serbia proper may have checked the most belligerent nationalist virus. But the disillusionment and sheer cussedness of life in the past decade and a half also discredited Djindjic's short flawed experiment with democracy, and poisoned politics. In elections the alternatives have gotten stuck in choices between moderate and surly nationalists, with the moderate variant constantly on the defensive. Successive hybrid coalitions remain vulnerable to shrill populists, and repeated early elections shuffle parties but maintain paralysis. Milosevic's Socialist Party has not evolved into a Social Democratic Party on the pattern of the Polish and Hungarian ex-Communists. Serb voters have not mastered the Croatian and Bulgarian art of resentfully voting out old governments over the pains of reform, only to have the new governments, whether from the right or from the left, continue the same indispensable reforms. This political and economic stagnation in a land that on its historical record should have been a leader in the Balkans in adapting to the modern, globalized world has cost the Serbs almost two decades of failed modernization since the Soviet and Communist collapse.

A small Western-oriented elite in Belgrade now argues explicitly that Serbs must first of all transform their imperial mind-set, just as the Germans did after 1945.[103] Yet, as one member of its core puts it, such humility born of shame was far easier for Germans, who lost completely, than for Serbs, who only partially lost their wars. Just as some Germans in the 1940s blamed all atrocities on Adolf Hitler to exonerate themselves, the temptation is strong today, even among Serbs who do not defiantly wear Mladic T-shirts, to blame all Serb brutality on Milosevic and ignore Serb voters' acquiescence or even pride in lethal chauvinism as long as it was victorious. And just as the postwar Germans in the end had to confess and repent of their will not to know about the barbarity committed in their name, so, too, only the Serbs can effect their own metamorphosis.

However, as the Radicals' popularity shows, the searing Germanic Protestant honesty in admitting broader culpability is rare among Serbs. Their widespread victimization complex is a hindrance. So is the exodus of liberal Serb intellectuals, middle-class professionals, and students in the 1990s, coupled with the rise of criminals and anti-urban peasants to riches and power in the decade of embargoes and smuggler barons. In the Balkan vortex that perpetuated revenge killings, Serb brutality is still widely excused by Serbs as no more than a response in kind to Croatian, Bosniak, and Kosovar brutality.

"Each of us should reconsider what has happened and assume responsibility," mused one Serb sociology professor, who saw himself as part of a tiny minority in comparing the Serb mass psychology with the same phenomenon in Hitler's Germany. "When they mobilized us, I hid myself, but my friends went to war," recalled an educated young Serb in similar vein in the wake of the Kosovo war. "I always thought that I knew them as well as I knew myself, and I could not believe that they had killed whole families, but this was a fact. Now I think that I deserted not because I had fears for myself, but because I was afraid of myself. I am terrified at the thought that if I had gone to the front, I would have turned into a killer too. I am not sure of myself anymore." A third person said, "I am ashamed to be a Serb; I'll call myself Montenegrin now; at any rate they live as free people."[104]

In this interior realm, constant hectoring by Western outsiders avails little. It tends to cause many in the Serb political class to pull together, defend their own, and perceive their countrymen's bygone conquest of 70 percent of Bosnia-Herzegovina with mortars, concentration camps, and systematic rape primarily as an attempt to protect Serb victims. Ironically, this view, as represented most coherently by the Radicals, may not reflect the majority Serb opinion. Sonja Licht of the Belgrade Fund for Political Excellence estimates that only some 15 percent of the population are real hard-liners, and polls in early 2006 indicated that more than half the Serbian population would have welcomed packing Mladic off to the Hague.[105] In any clear electoral confrontation between pro- and anti-European policies, defined as such, the perhaps 70 percent silent majority might well favor the prosperity that eventual membership in the EU would promise their children and grandchildren over the ultranationalists' defiance of what are perceived as unjust Western demands. The tragedy is that since Djindjic's murder, it has basically been the Radicals who have set the agenda, and the nation's political choices have not in fact been shaped in terms of Europe. The democratic moderates have done no more than survive, passively. Rather than taking initiatives of their own, Kostunica's minority government and Djindjic's Democratic Party, in opposition, have been in defensive mode, simply reacting to the accusations of the Radicals, over Montenegro's secession, the Hague Tribunal, and, above all, Kosovo. The civic enthusiasm of the 2000 election that overthrew Milosevic is gone. Fewer and fewer people bother to cast their ballots, and by now it is doubtful that many of the listless majority, disillusioned with politics, would vote at all. The aggrieved do vote, in order to protest their misery, and swell the representation of the Radicals; while increasing numbers of those who might once have been inspired by the vision of a modern, less inward-looking Serbia stay at home.

Under the circumstances, the most the internationals can do is to provide some external constraint on local bullies who would exploit the Serbs' schizophrenia and provide some reward for local democrats who would reconcile the two souls in the Serb breast. The problem is that the most effective sanction on the former—blocking the rewards of progress on the road to Europe—is the diametric opposite of the most effective reward for the latter—progress on the way to Europe. Calibration will be difficult.

CHAPTER TEN

Europeanizing the Balkans

In one offbeat dip into comparative political development, ebullient Bulgarian historian Ekaterina Nikova was invited to spend a year at the Slavic Research Center in Hokkaido just after the end of the eleven-week war in Kosovo. Inevitably, her fresh point of departure was Japan's nineteenth-century controlled modernization and westernization in the Meiji Restoration. In her valedictory in Hokkaido, not entirely tongue in cheek, she had a go at comparing apples and daikons, contrasting the present transition in the "turbulent, neurotic, bankrupt, desperate Balkans" with Japan's "serenity, calmness, silence, and feeling of safety" and the successful pretense in the Meiji transformation that all that was happening was a return to an ancient order. Throughout history the Balkans suffered from "alien, brutal reign, which, however, was easy to cheat and resist by cunning and corruption." While "[i]n Japanese tales, the authorities always punish the bad guys, Balkan folklore glorifies the hayduks/klephts [outlaws]. Obeying the law, the rules, is a virtue in Japan; in our lands cheating the authorities, from tax evasion to traffic regulation, is a national pastime." For the "talkative, hyperemotional, gesticulating, fiercely arguing, theatrical inhabitants" of the "socially amorphous, organically democratic Balkans," the only continuity has been "the continuity of discontinuity, each new stage beginning from zero."[1]

That discontinuity makes it as hard to compare apples and daikons within the Balkan region as between the Balkan and Meiji revolutions. Each land in Southeastern Europe has its own dynamic; every corner in each land differs even from every other corner in the same land. Sibiu to the north and Saranda to the south have precious little that unites them. The Balkans form no single politotope.

Yet in an age of globalization the Balkans are being compelled to come together to deal with huge common problems that they can no longer hope to solve by themselves. An Albania half the size of West Virginia cannot be autarkic economically and politically in the way Hoxha kept it in the twentieth century and still meet rising popular expectations. A Bosnia just under the size of West Virginia cannot stop trafficking in drugs and women unless those war-weary Bosnians who now want a "normal" life clean up their own police and cooperate with neighbors' cleaned-up police to fight organized crime. Tiny Kosovo and Macedonia cannot get off their dwindling intravenous feed of remittances from native sons working abroad unless they begin producing things they can sell to others and thereby offer their unemployed young men noncriminal jobs. This chapter therefore examines some regionwide issues and projects—not because the multifarious Balkans will ever move as a uni-fied bloc, but because its states and quasi states must work together if they want to solve their problems, and because the general atmosphere does affect the dynamics of each individual land.

Stability Pact and Economic Development

Ever since it gave some priority to the Western Balkans in the wake of the Kosovo war, the European Union has been preaching the credo of regional cooperation, both as an objective necessity and as insurance against recidivism to war. Just as Washington, in its seminal Marshall Plan after World War II, made joint agreement on projects among West European beneficiaries a pre-requisite for financial assistance, so the EU required agreement on common projects in the Western Balkans before it would release funds under the Sta-bility Pact for Southeastern Europe, the international coordinating body for civilian aid that the EU leads.

This regional dimension was an added prerequisite for EU membership for the Western Balkan countries, on top of the democratic and human rights conditions set down for Spain, Portugal, and Greece in the European Com-munity's Birkelbach report in the 1960s; the 1990 political prerequisite for loans from the European Bank for Reconstruction and Development; the 1992 inclusion of a "human rights clause" in EC/EU agreements with members of the Organization for Security and Cooperation in Europe (OSCE); and the 1993 democratic and free-market preconditions set down for the Central Europeans in the Copenhagen criteria.[2] Conditionality is no idle threat, even if it is exercised subjectively. The EU's PHARE aid was withheld from Roma-nia until early 1991 and Croatia was not allowed to join the Council of Europe until 1996, because the two countries did not meet the requirements of rule of law, respect for human rights, and economic liberalization, and in the case of Croatia, also cooperation with the Hague Tribunal.

To be sure, the Brussels-based Stability Pact, founded on a German initiative in 1999, is only a gentle enforcer of regional collaboration. It has no executive power and no money of its own to finance projects. It can only broker projects between donors and recipients. Moreover, the pact has deliberately limited its own powers by insisting on the co-ownership of programs through equal representation of donors and beneficiaries in the three decisionmaking "working tables" that deal with democracy, economics, and security—and on its own replacement in 2008 by local leadership of a more structured Regional Cooperation Council. Yet under its umbrella more than €25 billion has flowed into Southeastern Europe from some fifty donor countries.[3] And in one measure, constant badgering by the Stability Pact has already managed to nudge up pan-Balkan trade and inculcate a nascent habit of joint action in the region. Special coordinator Erhard Busek notes with satisfaction that "heads of governments [in the Balkans] call on each other nowadays just as naturally as elsewhere in Europe"—and this in a region where only a few years earlier "[s]ome governments bluntly explained that we could not expect them to design joint projects with neighbours they did not know or wish to know."[4]

To be funded, projects must involve two or more Balkan participants. Among those approved so far, the Sava River Commission in 2006 brought together Slovenia, Croatia, Bosnia-Herzegovina, and Serbia over water management.[5] New "euroregions" promote joint local development and solutions to environmental and other common problems across Serbian, Bulgarian, Macedonian, Albanian, and Greek borders and have necessarily introduced a modicum of fiscal decentralization. Two dozen bilateral free-trade agreements are intended to lead to a Balkan–Central European free-trade zone by early 2007; and indeed, between 2002 and 2004 alone Balkan cross-border trade grew by a third to reach €3.5 billion—a significant sum, even if it pales in comparison with annual EU-Balkan trade of €79 billion in 2005.[6] Security initiatives include the Stability Pact Police Forum, the Bucharest-based Regional Center for Combating Transborder Crime of the Southeast European Cooperative Initiative (SECI), and the Stability Pact Initiatives to Fight Organized Crime (SPOC) and Corruption (SPAI). A Council of Ministers of Culture of South East Europe has been formed. And a South East Europe Regional Energy Market has built pan-Balkan gas and electric grids, the latter linked since 2004 with the European grid, and has required liberalization of electricity and gas markets as a precondition for participation. Stability Pact officials estimate that the regional energy community will need further investments of $15 billion to make a real common electricity market for the Balkans' 55 million people, but they compare this beginning with the birth of today's European Union in the European Coal and Steel Community of 1951.[7]

These programs supplement the umbrella Southeast European Cooperation Process, a locally run series of regional meetings, and massive EU investment in such regional projects as new arteries of highways, railroads, and ports.[8] And they are paralleled by NATO's encouragement, under the alliance's Partnership for Peace, of regional initiatives like the Southeastern Europe Brigade that took over responsibility for peacekeeping in one sector in Afghanistan in 2006. "It is important to have successful reforms in every part of the region. Communicating vessels can have a positive influence, and this is what I expect," commented one Serb diplomat, referring both to pan-Balkan and Balkan-EU communicating.[9]

So far the billions of euros that have poured into the Balkans have not gone beyond recovery to produce sustainable economic development.[10] The internationals have had other priorities in suppressing bloodshed and establishing rudimentary political and administrative institutions—and as the prerequisite to development, rudimentary macroeconomic stabilization. Yet this precursor stabilization has been broadly successful. Slovenia restored its 1989 GDP by 1997, joined the EU in 2004, exceeded its prewar production by more than a third in 2005, qualified to join the eurozone in 2006, and now provides important investment throughout ex-Yugoslavia. Romania restored its 1989 GDP by 2004; Croatia did the same by 2005. Albania, starting from a much lower level, shot up to 148 percent of its (tiny) 1990 GDP by 2005. Macedonia, as of this writing, has not yet recovered its 1990 level, nor has Bulgaria equaled its 1989 prewar benchmark. And the still united Serbia and Montenegro remained a huge 36 percent below its prewar GDP. Bosnia-Herzegovina had no reliable statistics before war-torn 1994; by 2005 it was producing five times as much as in that year.[11] Inflation has been reduced to nondistorting levels (with the exception of Serbia's estimated 17 or 18 percent in 2005).[12] Budgets are more or less balanced in Bulgaria, Macedonia, Bosnia-Herzegovina, and Serbia, and deficits have declined in Albania, Montenegro, and Romania; Croatia and Serbia are the odd men out, with Zagreb building up the highest budget deficits, and overall indebtedness of €25.5 billion, or some 85 percent of GDP.[13] Regional growth rates since 2000 have generally maintained a respectable 4 or 5 percent (with the exception of Macedonia and Kosovo). Solid investments are beginning to come in, especially in Bulgaria, Romania, and Croatia, even if the high volume of foreign direct investment that was the key to Central

Europe's reindustrialization and growth in the 1990s has eluded Southeast Europe.

However, foreign aid is now declining sharply, and the prime source of state revenues, customs duties, will dry up once the EU's goal of a Balkan free-trade zone is reached. Faster development is handicapped in varying degree by sheer poverty, the wars' destruction, chaos, and theft. Most of the countries import more than they export and are running up increasing deficits. Collusive lending, credit acceleration, and undisciplined financial intermediation still risk crisis, although Austrian and other foreign banks have bought up many local banks and are bringing their stabilizing experience into the region.[14] Unemployment ranges from 14 or 15 percent in Croatia and Albania to 20 percent in Serbia and over 25 percent in Montenegro to 30-plus percent in Bosnia-Herzegovina and Macedonia to more than 50 percent in Kosovo; as a consequence, there is a persistent exodus of young people from the region. Institutionalization of the market economy is weak in terms of corporate as well as public governance, labor market regulations, financial markets, competition policy (and competitiveness), and restructuring in general.

There is little prospect of generating the urgently needed investment domestically. Only Croatia has had any surplus to invest in infrastructure beyond straight reconstruction—as only on Croatia's Adriatic coast is real estate beginning to attract significant Western and Russian buyers. Per capita GDP is highest in Croatia (at €10,300 about 59 percent of Slovenia's €17,580 and 46 percent of the EU-25 average).[15] Romania and Bulgaria come next, at €7,070 and €6,660 respectively, or less than a third of EU-25 levels. In the rest of the Western Balkans Bosnia, surprisingly, takes the lead at €5,840 over Serbia at €5,700, Macedonia (€5,650), Montenegro (€5,469), Albania (€4,570), and Kosovo (€790).[16] Income levels in the Balkans are far lower than they were in Central Europe in the early 1990s. Official poverty runs as high as 40 percent in Romania and 37 percent in Kosovo, though poverty is shallow throughout the region and there is no threat of famine.

In its own evaluation of the readiness of the four current Western Balkan candidates for EU membership—Bulgaria, Romania, Croatia, and Macedonia—the European Commission awards potentially passing grades. All have been certified as having "functioning market economies." On the parallel requirement for accession—the capacity to withstand stiff competition in the single EU market—the commission characterizes Croatia's economy alone as "already well integrated with that of the EU." Romania, it warns, must "vigorously [implement] its structural reform programme" in order to be competitive by its planned accession date. Macedonia, the weakest of the four, "would not be able to cope with competitive pressure" in the medium term, and could do so in the longer term only if economic reforms are "vigorously pursued," it concludes. As for those that are still in the precandidate Stabilization and Association Process, the commission judges that both Albania and Serbia and Montenegro (which were still unified in the last assessment period) operate "to some degree within the framework of functioning market principles," that Bosnia-Herzegovina "operates only to a limited degree within the framework of functioning market principles," and that Kosovo has "serious shortcomings in competitiveness."[17]

The commission assesses overall regional performance as showing "relatively favourable economic development in most countries, characterised by fairly strong growth and increasing macroeconomic stability and further progress in economic transition and structural reform." But it warns that the gap between the four candidate countries and the others poses risks. The report identifies the "recurring challenges" in the region as "a weak institutional setting," only "patchy" adoption of legislation for a market economy, limited administrative capacity, and "a slow and inefficient judiciary [that] hampers contract enforcement," along with "malfunctioning" labor markets, capital and land markets that are "weak and uncompetitive," and "still relatively high state ownership and state interference in the business sector."[18]

Various critics in nongovernmental organizations (NGOs) like the European Stability Initiative, based in Berlin and Istanbul, fault international aid programs in the Balkans for having focused far too long on reconstruction rather than turning to development. Paddy Ashdown's retort to such criticism during his tenure as high representative in Sarajevo was sharp. Just after the September 2002 elections in Bosnia-Herzegovina, he told the UN Security Council, "My approach will be to distinguish ruthlessly between those things that are truly essential, and those that are simply desirable. The OHR [Office of High Representative], with the executive power it wields, should focus on the first. There are many other agencies to undertake the longer-term, developmental tasks once we have gone."[19] By 2006 Lord Ashdown was gone, and with post-Dayton institutions more or less in place and a pragmatic government finally in office in Banja Luka, the new high representative, Christian Schwarz-Schilling, did put his top priority on longer-term development and local ownership.[20] Significantly, he also decided that the time had come to allow those local officials who had been dismissed by his predecessors to return to politics—as long as they had not been implicated in sheltering war criminals.[21]

Security

"South-Eastern Europe is probably the most exciting laboratory of externally assisted security sector reform," begins an enthusiastic evaluation by the EU's Institute for Security Studies (ISS) of the regional prospects in this field. What the authors mean is not only that the Balkan lands are starting at such a low point on the scale that the only way they can go is up, but also that these lands have a strong incentive to move toward openness and accountability. "What all states in the region have in common, albeit to differing degrees, is the ambition to accede to, or at least closely associate themselves with, the key security providers and exporters in Europe: NATO and the EU," the study continues. "NATO and increasingly so the EU hold considerable leverage over the Western Balkans given their dominant presence in international peace-building missions in the region and, even more importantly, the 'carrot' of eventual membership which they both have to offer."[22]

The ISS Chaillot Paper describes a division of labor—at first implicit, then spelled out in 2003—in which NATO deals with military issues, while the EU deals with police reform and internal security in the Balkans.[23] NATO's instruments are the Partnership for Peace (PfP), begun in 1994, and individually tailored membership action plans since 1999. The PfP program, which started as a hedge for wannabe alliance members that NATO was not sure it wished to let into the club (and was not sure that Russia would let enter the West's security sphere), was transformed after the Kosovo war and the first NATO enlargement of 1999 into a school for alliance membership for a contiguous arc of Central European and Southeast European lands. Balkan political leaders tend to welcome NATO membership not only as security insurance, but also as a way station to the far more demanding EU membership and as a reassuring signal of stability to investors. Hard-strapped Balkan military hierarchies are eager to participate in the program because of the extra money it brings for modernization of forces or other purposes, the experience it provides in joint exercises with some of the world's most sophisticated armed forces, and the opportunity for study tours at Berchtesgaden and elsewhere in Western Europe.

The ISS study gives the highest grades in restructuring and establishing democratic control over the armed forces to Bulgaria and Romania, which in 2004 won NATO membership. In the Western Balkans, military reform is much more difficult, given the postconflict, as well as postauthoritarian "and to a certain degree even developmental," setting, and all the nonstate paramilitaries, guerrilla bands, and criminal militias, the study notes. Croatia has already modernized its armed forces to a considerable extent, though it has not established full civilian control over the military. With Gotovina now in dentention at the Hague Tribunal, and with the accelerated retirement of some of its more hard-line military and police officers, Zagreb is on track for NATO membership. And in the U.S.-sponsored Adriatic Charter it is pulling Albania and Macedonia along in its wake. Albania's military reforms outpace its political reforms; its army's yearning to join NATO is graphically illustrated in a book of photos of the Albanian armed forces throughout history, published by the Albanian Defense Ministry—starting before Scanderbeg, it devotes the last third of the volume to a section entitled "Towards NATO."[24] As for the others, Bosnia-Herzegovina—now that its constituent ethnicities have downsized their separate armies and put them under unified state command—is working toward NATO membership. Serbian military officers, despite NATO's airstrikes against their country a few years ago, want to join PfP, but Serbia will remain in the waiting room as long as much of Milosevic's old officer corps remains in place and Ratko Mladic remains at large.

Kosovo officially has no armed forces of its own, and the NATO-led Kosovo Force (KFOR) has impounded and keeps control of the heavy weapons of the former Kosova Liberation Army (KLA).[25] There is, however, a Kosovo Protection Corps, which Kosovar Albanians regard as their future army. There are as well shadowy party intelligence units—especially the Institute for Researching Public Opinion and Strategies (IHPSO) of the late Ibrahim Rugova's Democratic League of Kosova (LDK) and the Kosova–National Intelligence Service (K-SHIK) of Hashim Thaci's Democratic Party of Kosova (PDK), all of which are inimical to Western standards of accountability and government monopoly on the use of force. The main parties are "underpinned," in the words of the International Crisis Group, by "underworld and intelligence structures" that will not let themselves be easily tamed.[26] The international overseers of any conditional independence for Kosovo therefore will presumably have to wrestle with elementary military discipline for several years.

In the NATO-EU division of labor, police reform and border and internal security fall to the European Union. For the toughest jobs in bridging the crucial gap between the end of war and the restoration or establishment of community-based policing—the gap that allowed wholesale looting in Baghdad in 2003, the shakedown of Albanian shopowners by Albanian gangs in Kosovo in 1999–2000, and arguably the Kosovar riots of 2004—it has set up a European Gendarmerie Force. The five EU members that have long had paramilitary national police—France, Italy, Spain, Portugal, and the Netherlands—paved the way with the Italians' crisis intervention during the anarchy in Albania in 1997 and the Multinational Specialized Unit led by the Italian carabinieri in Bosnia-Herzegovina in 1998–99. The latter provided urgently needed security for returning refugees in hostile ethnic environments and began to chip away at organized crime. Other typical tasks, besides preventing looting, included riot control, defusing civil disturbances, conducting domestic surveillance, restoring basic services, and mounting joint patrols and liaison with local police. This niche security function was formalized in 2006 with inauguration of the headquarters of the European Gendarmerie Force in Vicenza, Italy; 800–900 police officers have been earmarked for rapid deployment, 2,300 for eventual longer term deployment on assignment for the EU, NATO, UN, OSCE, or ad hoc coalitions.[27] The United States, by choice, has not developed a corresponding dedicated constabulary force, choosing to depend instead for postconflict missions on general forces that can escalate quickly to high-intensity combat if necessary.[28]

As violence subsides in a postconflict environment, the militarily less demanding but still critical policing tasks are taken over by more lightly armed indigenous police and customs officials, with the help of European advisers. These key services are doubly sensitive; they are the essential enforcers of law and order, but for that very reason they also tend to be a lucrative recruiting ground for foot soldiers for predatory elites and organized crime. Outside advisers need to learn their local street smarts fast, to establish relations of trust with counterparts who will remain honest under intense pressure—and often enough, to beat down fierce resistance by local power holders to their efforts to professionalize and depersonalize allegiances in internal security services. The high representative in Bosnia-Herzegovina may have managed to send auditors into the ORAO firm and break up an illegal weapons-exporting clique of Bosnian and Belgrade Serbs. And fears over getting left behind in the race to join the EU may have, at the last minute, induced the Republika Srpska to sign on in principle to a unified police service in Bosnia-Herzegovina. But the old guard in Banja Luka (and Mostar) can be expected to obstruct police unification in its practical details. And Macedonian officials successfully insisted that the current follow-on to the Proxima police advisory team had to be smaller and less intrusive than Proxima, presumably to deter outsiders from penetrating the ambiguity about who controls whom within the security apparatus.

The EU's main instrument for prodding reforms in general in the Western Balkans is the long-term Stabilization and Association Process (SAP) that began in the wake of the Kosovo war, and in particular the CARDS (Community Assistance for Reconstruction, Development and Stabilization) program of aid that was made available under the SAP process beginning in 2001. Croatia and Macedonia have already signed Stabilization and Association Agreements, the first step on the way to eventual EU membership.

In the field of security, besides working on police restructuring and border management, European efforts focus on judicial reform; "justice and home affairs" partially became European Community competences (as distinct from solely national responsibilities) with the Nice Treaty of 2000, and thus became a legitimate subject for conditionality for candidates for EU membership. The major EU operations have been the EU Force's (EUFOR) peacekeeping initiative, Althea, and the EU Police Mission (EUPM) in Bosnia-Herzegovina; the Concordia peacekeeping and Proxima police missions in Macedonia; assistance to the Kosovo Police Force under the UN Mission in Kosovo (UNMIK); and the Multinational Advisory Police Element that began operating in Albania in 1997 and has been followed by two successor sets of advisers.

Since 2004 the EU has echoed NATO in making civilian control of the military a political condition in the Stablization and Association Process. In the Ohrid border process it has further joined with NATO, the OSCE, the Stability Pact, and the Western Balkan lands to begin setting up integrated border management systems throughout the region. This involves some improvement of infrastructure and transfer of equipment, along with police training and policy advice. EU projects have set up the State Border Service in Bosnia-Herzegovina, and are working on demilitarizing border control and transferring responsibility for it from the Defense to the Interior Ministry in Macedonia. Other EU projects are working on depoliticizing police, inculcating an ethos of community policing in protecting the rights of citizens, and training police to combat organized and transnational crime in Albania, Croatia, and Serbia and Montenegro.

More broadly, the Council of Europe urges member states to adopt its Code of Police Ethics, and the OSCE is helping to build the expertise of parliamentary defense committees in Bosnia-Herzegovina. The Stability Pact's Working Table 3 deals with such issues as improvement of the judiciary, defense conversion, and border security, and has initiated meetings of Balkan parliamentarians, prosecutors, ministers, border guards, customs officers, and police chiefs on such topics as capacity building; witness protection; the upgrading of the SECI Center in Bucharest; harmonization of legislation on organized crime; contacts with the European Parliament, the European Commission, and the Council of Europe; adoption of some police cooperation measures from Schengen practices; and regional ownership. The Stability Pact has further spawned the Regional Arms Control Verification and Implementation Assistance Center, the

South Eastern Europe Clearing House for the Control of Small Arms and Light Weapons, the Migration, Asylum, Refugees Regional Initiative, and the all-important Initiative against Organized Crime.[29]

With surprising speed, seven out-of-area EU security missions followed the pioneer Western Balkans security operations. The EU's first rule-of-law mission, EUJUST Themis, assisted the reform of Georgia's system of criminal justice, facilitated the country's participation in regional cooperation in this field, and supported development of the Georgian Border Service. On an appeal from the UN, the EU deployed military forces outside Europe for the first time in mid-2003, sending 2,000 peacekeeping troops from six member countries, South Africa, Brazil, and Canada to protect refugee camps in the Democratic Republic of Congo and help train 32,000 local police officers to maintain law and order during elections. The EU has extended more modest support for African Union peacekeepers in Darfur, Sudan, in stabilizing the situation and providing equipment, airlift, and police training. For its first mission in Asia, in 2005, the EU insisted on having the Association of Southeast Asian Nations (ASEAN) as a local partner; in tandem, the two have been monitoring the peace agreement between the government of Indonesia and the Free Aceh Movement (GAM), demobilizing GAM and destroying weapons, ammunition, and explosives, and helping soldiers to reintegrate into civilian life. In Iraq the EU gave support to the first democratic election in half a century, worked on restoring education, health care, sanitation and other public services, and undertook the training of judges, magistrates, police, and prison officials.[30]

Crime

The scourge of organized crime, of course, exists in every corner of the globe. Yet it is a particular curse in the Balkans, because of the huge proportion of the economy—and politics—that it controls or warps to its advantage. In the West, corruption preys on the system. But in some Balkan countries it not only exploits the system, it becomes the system, and in what amounts to state capture strangles legitimate economic and political development. Sofia's Center for the Study of Democracy puts Albania in the 1990s in this category. Even in other Balkan countries that are not failed states, the symbiosis between official security forces and organized criminals makes it very hard to reduce crime in the face of entrenched political power.

"Thus far, none of the reform attempts undertaken by the governments have been able to break this link" between organized crime and law enforcement institutions, the Center for the Study of Democracy concluded flatly in its 2004 study "Partners in Crime."[31] Very little has changed since then to revise this somber judgment. For every Zemun gang that is neutralized, plenty of rivals stand ready to take its place. Organized crime groups seem to have learned more quickly than legitimate authorities in the Balkans the lessons of globalization and the necessity of transethnic cooperation (apart from the Albanian gangs, which remain monoethnic except for outsourced operations, according to law enforcement studies).

The most comprehensive public report on crime in the Balkans to date, sponsored by the European Commission and the Council of Europe and issued by the CARDS Regional Police Project (CARPO) in 2005, called organized crime "a major threat to democracy, the rule of law, human rights and social and economic progress in Europe." Overall, the "Situation Report on Organised and Economic Crime in South-eastern Europe" registered a drop in smuggling of oil and cigarettes once the embargoes on Serbia were lifted and noted "considerably reduced" smuggling of excise goods (and murders in Serbia) once Milosevic was toppled in 2000.[32] It found extensive tax evasion and money laundering, however, with all the appurtenances of forged documents and fictitious companies; rising fraud related to privatization, public procurement, and the financial sector; and the expansion of Balkan drug trafficking into "a two-way road, with heroin [from Afghanistan] going to the EU and precursors, cocaine and synthetic drugs, . . . moving eastward."[33] Criminal investigations have increased, it said, but few have led to convictions. Corruption, it declared, "appears to be a main tool for influencing and penetrating political and commercial structures."

The report did not trace "the nexus between the security services and criminals" back to Communist practices, as "Partners in Crime" did. It stressed instead the growth of this "particularly volatile subculture" in the 1990s, as the Yugoslav wars, "international sanctions against Serbia, and the Albanian state collapse . . . offered unique opportunities for organised crime to infiltrate governance structures, primarily security services and agencies patrolling the borders."[34] It portrayed the 1990s as a period when illegal businesses were built. and the 2000s as a period in which organized criminals consolidated these businesses and diversified their investments into the legal economy, with "corruption appearing to be one of the main means being used."[35] The Situation Report explained: "Corruption breeds long-term relationships which are more sustainable and reliable than those based on violence and intimidation. . . . In some countries in transition corruption appears to have permeated most structures of public life, including law enforcement and criminal justice systems. Low salaries, unemployment, insecurity and poverty, and often the example set by senior officials, make public officials vulnerable targets and reliable partners of organised crime groups."[36] More colloquially, in the Balkans "businessmen say that up to 20 percent, it's baksheesh; over 20 percent, it's crime."[37]

One of the striking features of organized criminals in the Balkans is the swiftness of their response to fast-moving changes in the environment. Besides building multiethnic cooperation, they have been evolving away from violence, as human traffickers in Kosovo and Bosnia-Herzegovina have found that giving prostitutes modest pay and better living conditions attracts less unwanted attention from police. In addition, there has been an organizational shift that parallels the decentralization of the terrorist groups sponsored by al Qaeda in recent years; today there is "decentralization of previously highly hierarchical Cosa Nostra, and 'flattening' and 'networking-like' crime groups," along with reliance on small cells. In operations, when the cigarette smuggling corridor through Montenegro was closed down, this contraband was quickly diverted to new routes through Kosovo, Macedonia, Bulgaria, Romania, and Croatia.[38] Moreover, gang bosses are certainly better able than cash-strapped police departments to afford the latest high-tech surveillance and tracking gadgetry to keep them ahead in the game of electronic cat and mouse.

The most dramatic structural change has been growth in the multibillion-dollar business of human trafficking, which has recently become the third most profitable type of crime, after drug and weapons running. This increase has arisen in part from the high demand in Europe for prostitutes, primarily women and girls, but also boys; low-paid or even slave labor; children for begging rings, petty theft, or "organ harvest"; and babies for adoption; and from the high demand in the third world for an escape from poverty through emigration to rich Europe.[39] The shift in criminal focus has also arisen from the calculation that the risks of getting caught and the corresponding punishments are much lower in human than in drug or weapons smuggling. In earlier years the Balkans served primarily as a transit route, but recruitment of women in the region itself is now increasing; and the Balkans have also become an end destination, largely, it seems, to meet the local demand for prostitutes among the high numbers of international officials, police, and military peacekeepers stationed there without their families.[40]

In striving to outwit the chameleon-like metamorphoses of criminals, European law-enforcement agencies, in good FBI fashion, are now devoting as much attention to tracking laundered money flows as they are to infiltrating gangs (other than Albanian ones) and eavesdropping on constantly changed mobile phone chips. The task requires sharing of hard-to-come-by police intelligence across borders to match the criminals' collaboration across borders. As with all efforts at state and institution building in the Balkans, in the short term this depends crucially on identifying and protecting those local law enforcers who resist political pressure and threats and have the local knowledge that is indispensable for combating crime. And it depends in the long term on establishing the salary levels and stability that will let such officers make decisions on the basis of planning for lifelong civil service careers rather than on the basis of survival from one day to the next.[41]

These committed professionals welcome whatever aid they can get from the U.S. Federal Bureau of Investigation, Europol, the OSCE, and the various EU or "twinning" teams of police trainers and advisers in the region. Typically, it was these Balkan law enforcement officials who prodded the West European participants at the meeting of Balkan interior ministers in Brijuni, Croatia, in September 2005 to insist that their ministers sign a pledge to carry out a list of elementary measures to fight organized and economic crime.[42] This document then allowed the professionals to hold their ministers' feet to the fire on improving the "legal framework and institutional capacities in the area of . . . criminal intelligence"; protecting "witnesses, vulnerable victims and collaborators of justice prior, during and after criminal proceedings"; and seeking "additional allocation of budgetary funds" to support the anticrime efforts.[43] A longer (unsigned) document also adopted at the meeting called for developing appropriate statistics and expert knowledge of the operations of organized and economic crime, setting up financial intelligence units and confiscating the proceeds of crime, "promoting a 'task force' approach in investigating complex cases," and conducting surveillance without violating human rights, among other things.[44]

In assessing crime in individual countries, the CARPO "Situation Report" praised Croatia for having moved furthest in setting up a functioning law enforcement system with a centralized crime database, and for winning some convictions against organized criminals. It noted that Albanian and Bulgarian gangs are fighting to dominate the drug trade in Serbia, that organized crime in Albania grew stronger after the pyramid crash, and that some criminal groups "increasingly tend to control a full cycle of the drug business (producing, collecting, delivering, financing, transporting, and dealing)," with Albanian gangs "occupying the top of hierarchies."[45] The report did not itself make odious comparisons, but the conclusion was clear that, overall, economies in Southeast Europe are far more beholden to criminals than are economies in Western Europe. European police officials do not deduce from this that Balkan candidates should be barred from the EU club, however, but assert on the contrary that it will be easier to fight crime if Southeast Europe becomes part of the European Union's law enforcement space.[46]

Under the circumstances, the economic liberalization that the EU has insisted on in the Balkans has often worked in the short run to enrich those high-ranking thieves and rent seekers who already wielded enough power to appropriate state assets for themselves.[47] Whether or not these little Balkan oligarchs then decide in the long run that, in accord with Western evolutionary hopes, they can best protect and expand their wealth and political power by establishing rule of law, remains to be seen. The more modest EU hope is that increasingly transparent economic liberalization will itself eventually remedy the early abuse, by opening up competition and squeezing out those entrepreneurs who have no managerial talents beyond extortion. Such a dynamic seems to have worked in part in Bulgaria and Croatia. It seemed to fail in Serbia when Djindjic tried to encourage some black and gray operators to go legitimate and cracked down on others—and paid for his efforts with his life.

In the face of this Sisyphean task, commented one thirty-something Serbian law enforcement official, progress "seems very slow—maybe because I'm young. Sometimes I feel I don't get support in the country." The atmosphere grew palpably worse after the assassination of Djindjic, he acknowledged, but added, "I think you can't turn the wheel back now."[48]

The International Criminal Tribunal for the Former Yugoslavia

In the realm of the most heinous crimes of all, war atrocities, the doggedness of successive prosecutors and of human rights activists on the ground, along with EU conditionality, has managed to get all but six indictees to the International Criminal Tribunal for the Former Yugoslavia (ICTY) in the Hague. As the ad hoc tribunal now winds down, to complete all trials and appeals by its prescribed end date of 2010, its track record invites evaluation.

The common reproach that the ICTY has not deterred war crimes usually rests on the failure of the court's existence to avert the Srebrenica massacre in 1995 or the wholesale ethnic cleansing in Kosovo in 1998–99.[49] This rebuke is rather unfair, however, given that the nations that founded the tribunal initially starved it of funds, intelligence, and help in arresting indictees, thus delaying the recruitment of a chief prosecutor for more than a year and postponing the first conviction in a contested trial until 1997, two years after the Srebrenica bestiality. What is much more striking is the court's achievement. It ended the typical immunity of top political leaders from accountability for war crimes. It affixed individual guilt for gross violations of international laws of war and humanity. It and its sister Rwanda Tribunal set case law precedent in applying the Genocide Convention for the first time in half a century. It determined legal truth beyond a reasonable doubt about the worst atrocities in Europe since the Holocaust. It eased the most bloodthirsty bullies out of politics in ex-Yugoslavia. And, not least, it initiated a transformation of justice in the Balkans by preemption and benchmarking for local courts.

To be sure, his death of a heart attack cheated the court out of judging the guilt of Slobodan Milosevic, the first-ever head of state to be tried in an international court for war crimes committed in office. Yet the 5,000 exhibits in his case alone, and the 3,500 witnesses and millions of pages of documents and transcripts for all the trials combined established enough legal proof of barbarity in Brcko, Foca, Prijedor, Srebrenica, and elsewhere to discredit denials of this holocaust early on. Without the ICTY, the evidence of Srebrenica would have been (re)buried far more extensively than it was. In the immediate aftermath of the massacre, the Serbs, who then occupied the ethnically cleansed terrain, were threatening interlopers who were too curious about the incident, and Implementation Force/Stabilization Force (IFOR/SFOR) commanders were in no mood to let mission creep take their troops into the realm of forensic archaeology. That left it to investigators from the ICTY prosecution to personally exhume corpses before they were all bulldozed away—and to shame international peacekeeping troops into protecting them as they did so. Moreover, in a not trivial contribution to sustainable peace, the ICTY indictments helped remove the poisonous influence of Radovan Karadzic, Ratko Mladic, and finally Slobodan Milosevic from politics during the critical post-conflict transition.

In terms of legal precedent, the Hague Tribunal "in one decade [was] able to create and maintain the appearance, as well as the reality, of justice. This is not an inconsiderable achievement for the first international criminal tribunal since Nuremberg," concludes ICTY judge (1999–2001) Patricia M. Wald with some awe. Its "premier accomplishment" could be described as "the development of a corpus juris of international humanitarian law, the fleshing out of what had been, up to that time, relatively bare-boned definitions of war crimes, providing for the first time a coherent concept of crimes against humanity, integrating universal elements of criminal law such as general and specific intent and defences of duress and mental disability into the law of war, and elucidating the criteria for customary international law and its sources." The tribunal "applied Geneva Convention principles to ethnic cleansing, built on Nuremberg concepts of criminal enterprise and command responsibility to . . . hold leaders legitimately responsible for the actions of their subordinates."[50]

Concurring, Gabrielle Kirk McDonald, ICTY judge from November 1993 to November 1999 and its president from 1997 to 1999, declares, "The tribunal has contributed more to the jurisprudence of international humanitarian law in 10 years than had been developed in the entire half-century since the Nuremberg and Tokyo trials."[51] One element of that new jurisprudence was the specific addition of systematic rape to the standard list of crimes against humanity. Other rulings, as the ICTY website points out, "expanded upon the legal elements of the crime of grave breaches of the Geneva Conventions of 1949 by further defining the test of overall control, identifying the existence of an international armed conflict, and also the extended and exact definition of protected persons under the Conventions"; "identified a general prohibition of torture in international law which cannot be derogated from by a treaty, internal law or otherwise"; "specified the definitions of enslavement and persecution as parts of crimes against humanity, resulting in the first convictions after World War II for enslavement on the basis of a broadened definition"; "identified and applied the modern doctrine of criminal responsibility of superiors, so-called command responsibility, clarifying that a formal superior-subordinate relationship is not necessarily required for criminal responsibility"; "created an independent system of law, comprising . . . elements from adversarial and inquisitory criminal procedure traditions"; "developed and maintained an effective victims and witnesses programme"; and "established a unique legal aid system, and groomed a group of defence attorneys highly qualified to represent accused in war crimes proceedings."[52] In this regard the high number of acquittals—fifty, as against thirty-seven convictions as of this writing—should be seen as a strength, not a weakness. It may frustrate the desire of victims for symbolic justice, but it does attest to the court's fairness—as court officials keep pointing out to the Serbs— in allowing an exhaustive defense.

The ICTY further taught one major negative lesson that judges on the new, permanent International Criminal Court have already taken to heart: not to let the best become the enemy of the good in trying to prove not just a few representative instances of war crimes but the whole gamut, as elaborated in the sixty-six counts against Milosevic. This ambition, along with the tactical skill of the defendant and frequent recesses for his ill health, accounted for the four-year duration of his trial and its abrupt halt, when Milosevic died, fifty court hours short of a verdict.

Critics also overlook the day-to-day educational contribution of the tribunal. By exercising concurrent jurisdiction over war crimes with local courts over several years (and superior jurisdiction in the case of Bosnia and Macedonia), the ICTY shielded these weak courts against exploitation as theaters for propaganda and prolongation of mutually reinforcing cycles of hate. In Bosnia just after the Dayton Accord, the ban on local court indictments for war crimes without prior certification by the Hague Tribunal greatly reduced intimidation and arbitrary arrests of Bosniaks and Croats by Republika Srpska police in an effort to intimidate others into not entering RS territory at all. In Macedonia, at a time when adversarial local court trials would only have aggravated ethnic passions, indigenous (Macedonian) prosecutors were prohibited altogether, under the Ohrid Agreement, from indicting (Albanian) war crimes suspects; the amnesty could thus proceed relatively smoothly.[53]

Together, the body of ICTY verdicts, opinions, and practices, its tutoring of new and old Balkan courts to try cases of war crimes and organized crime, and the cooling-off period that its assumption of responsibility allowed have effected a sea change. Local judges have already tried and convicted defendants of their own ethnicity in a way that would have been inconceivable without the judgments and proofs built up by the ICTY. In September 2005 a Croatian court sentenced five former Croatian Interior Ministry reservists to prison terms ranging from two to ten years for killing Serb civilians in 1991. And in May 2006 the Croatian parliament finally lifted the immunity of member of parliament Branimir Glavas, a founder of the Croatian Democratic Union (HDZ) and the political baron of Slavonia, to allow his prosecution for the liquidation of Serb civilians in Osijek in the early 1990s.[54] In November 2005 a court in the Republika Srpska sentenced three former Bosnian Serb policemen to prison terms of up to twenty years for killing Muslim civilians in 1994 at the Prijedor concentration camp.[55] In April 2006 Serbian prosecutors for the first time indicted eight senior Serb police officers for the murder of ethnic Albanians in Kosovo as the war there was begining in March 1999.[56] In the same month the hybrid local-international War Crimes Chamber in Bosnia-Herzegovina also gave its first verdict in a case on transfer from the Hague Tribunal, sentencing Bosnian Serb Nedjo Samardzic to thirteen years in jail for aiding and abetting persecution, rape, and torture near Foca in 1992.[57] And in December 2005 and January 2006 the War Crimes Chamber of Belgrade's District Court, in its opening trials, convicted fifteen Serbs on the basis of documents provided by the Hague Tribunal and sentenced them to jail terms ranging from five to twenty years for abusing Croat prisoners at the Ovcara farm in Croatia in 1991, the first major atrocity of the Yugoslav wars.[58] ICTY chief prosecutor Carla Del Ponte praised the maiden trial of the special Belgrade panel as the "best example of reciprocal cooperation."[59]

Finally, the Hague Tribunal has changed the public perception of war crimes, maintains Bruno Vekaric, spokesman for the Serbian prosecution. "No one denies any more that the crimes took place. The public has been confronted with them and accepted that such crimes must be tried and the perpetrators punished," he asserts.[60] As of this writing, more than fifty war crimes cases had been heard in the Federation (entity) of Bosnia and Herzegovina, "including more than a dozen involving defendants from the dominant ethnic group in the location in question"; thirteen had been tried in Serbia and Montenegro, twelve of which involved Serb defendants; and "a large number of trials" had been conducted in Croatia, nine of which involved Croat defendants.[61]

These landmark decisions got little publicity, not only because of the regional media's inexperience in covering complex legal issues—a dearth that the Institute for War and Peace Reporting is now seeking to correct—but also because of the fortunate lack of popular outcry against them.[62] In Croatia, the 100,000 to 150,000 protesters who erupted onto the streets when General Mirko Norac was arrested in 2001 all but ignored the arrest of the much more famous general Ante Gotovina a short four years later. In Serbia, the evidence of Serb savagery that accumulated at the Hague prepared the ground even for the significant number who initially denied the Srebrenica massacre to admit finally—when confronted with the Scorpions' own video of the torture and murder of unarmed Bosniaks by special police in 2005—that Serbs had executed thousands of Bosniak civilians. This, commented one Serb observer, caused "the first real moral consternation here since the end of the war."[63] At the outset there was a wave of Serb solidarity with Milosevic and his early browbeating of prosecution witnesses at the Hague in 2001 and 2002, but popular interest waned as the trial dragged on and ordinary people tired of fighting fourteenth-century wars over and over.[64] By the time Milosevic's coffin was put on display in front of parliament in early 2006, the million ecstatic aggrieved Serbs who had cheered their new savior as he talked of war at Blackbird Field in 1989 had shrunk to only 60,000–80,000, despite the best efforts of the Socialist Party to bus mourners to the capital.[65]

The more fundamental issue of whether special courts serve or deter peace and reconciliation in postconflict situations is more controversial. Successive ICTY prosecutors made the conscious decision to subordinate peace to justice, at least in the short term, in racing to indict the principals in the Bosnia and Kosovo wars before Western diplomats might be tempted to grant them immunity in return for peace settlements. Serb centrists complained that Chief Prosecutor Carla Del Ponte's single-minded focus on justice led her to ignore political reality and sabotage moderate democrats by indicting four Serbian generals just before the Serbian presidential election in November 2003.[66] Advocates of truth and reconciliation processes on the South African model often contend that this more informal and personal approach fosters reconciliation far better than do adversarial court trials, which tend to polarize communities and reinforce enmity.

Haris Silajdzic, Bosnia's foreign minister during the war, maintains on the contrary that in the longer term the tribunal "helps a cathartic process in societies on all sides. The message is that there is responsibility. There is crime and punishment, so the message is that you cannot murder, kill, or dislocate people without punishment."[67] Judge McDonald agrees, arguing that the tribunal "removed a 'criminal element' from the region—political and military leaders, the rank and file, and common criminals—thereby beginning to lay the foundation for a lasting peace and, ultimately, reconciliation."[68] In a similar vein, Antonio Cassese, president of the tribunal in the mid-1990s, argues that "[j]ustice is an indispensable ingredient of the process of national reconciliation. It is essential to the restoration of peaceful and normal relations between people who have had to live under a reign of terror. It breaks the cycle of violence, hatred and extra-judicial retribution. Thus Peace and Justice go hand-in-hand."[69]

Representatives of Belgrade's Humanitarian Law Centre, Zagreb's Documenta office, and Sarajevo's Research and Documentation Centre would certainly endorse this line of reasoning. These NGOs are working together to establish historical facts about the post-Yugoslav conflagrations. Together, they are amassing the region's largest and most accurate war crimes database, ascertaining the crimes that were committed and recording witness statements and documentary evidence against suspects for use in future trials in Bosnia, Croatia, and Serbia. They are also training teams of cross-border monitors and supporting both witnesses who testify in neighboring countries and victims' families from abroad who come to see how justice is administered in their cases in local courts.[70] And Serb and Croat journalists have teamed up to track down witnesses and amateur videos taken during the months-long Serb siege of Croatian Vukovar and its hospital and have produced the grimly named documentary *Vukovar—Last Cut.*[71]

More unexpectedly, although most of those convicted by the ICTY remain unrepentant, a few of the perpetrators have themselves been moved to express remorse for their conduct. Dragan Obrenovic, a Bosnian Serb sentenced to seventeen years in jail for crimes against humanity in Srebrenica, told the tribunal: "In Bosnia, a neighbor means more than a relative. In Bosnia, having coffee with your neighbor is a ritual, and this is what we trampled on and forgot. We lost ourselves in hatred and brutality. And in this vortex of terrible misfortune and horror, the horror of Srebrenica happened. . . . I will be happy if my testimony helps the families of the victims, if I can spare them having to testify again and relive the horrors and the pain during their testimony. It is my wish that my testimony should help prevent this ever happening again, not just in Bosnia, but anywhere in the world."[72]

To be sure, a judicial process can never replace a political process in healing the scars of torture and war. But in the Balkans, it can be said after a decade of experience, the Hague Tribunal has helped shape discourse in a way that ultimately promotes political healing.[73]

Who Lost Montenegro and Kosovo?

The year 2006 offered nothing except foreboding to Prime Minister Vojislav Kostunica and President Boris Tadic, and nothing except anticipation to Serbia's Radical Party, which savored its plurality of 42 percent in opinion polls. Slobodan Milosevic's anticlimactic death by heart attack in March changed the equation not a whit.[74] Four years of inflammatory self-defense by "the Butcher of the Balkans" in the end wore thin on his own countrymen. Yet the leitmotif of Milosevic's court harangues about the victimization of Serbs throughout history still resonated sufficiently to swell the protest vote for the ultranationalist Radicals of Milosevic's creating. Faced with the unpalatable prospect of losing Montenegro and Kosovo, and potentially Mladic, all in the space of a few months—and of having to answer to Serb voters for this triple loss—both Kostunica and Tadic resorted to denial of reality, in different ways.

Taken singly, the Montenegrin referendum in favor of secession after eighty-eight years of union with Serbia would probably have been manageable politically. Serbian economists had long seen the alpine republic as an albatross, and ordinary Serbs seemed relatively indifferent to the outcome of the referendum in May 2006. When the EU set the bar high, requiring a 55 percent vote in favor of independence as a precondition for its recognition of the new state, the Montenegrin parliament immediately wrote this into the plebiscite law as its own standard—and when the 86 percent turnout indeed favored secession by slightly over that margin, Belgrade accepted the outcome, gracelessly. President Tadic did pay a prompt courtesy call on Montenegrin president Filip Vujanovic. But Prime Minister Kostunica sent no well wishes, rebuffed an EU offer to help facilitate the separation, and seemed stunned that fellow Serbs could have rejected Serb union.[75] Nor did the Serbian Orthodox Church look kindly on the swift demand of the Montenegrin Orthodox Church for recognition and the return of some of the country's 660 monasteries and churches to its ownership.[76] Mainstream Belgrade media speculated darkly about plots between Podgorica and Brussels to dismember Serbia and Montenegro, while, according to the International Crisis Group, "nationalist ideologues," including President Tadic's own father, wrote protest letters to the EU.[77]

In Montengro Prime Minister Milo Djukanovic announced that he would preserve his new country's open borders with Serbia, though few trusted his promise, since Podgorica immediately began striving to enter the EU fast, and if it preceded Belgrade the Montenegro-Serbia boundary would become an exterior border of the European Union, with tight security. In Bosnia the pragmatic Milorad Dodik, who was once again prime minister of the Republika Srpska and already campaigning for the fall elections, catered to Serb nationalists by calling for the RS to emulate its neighbor and hold its own referendum on independence from Bosnia. At the same time, however, he pledged full cooperation with the Hague Tribunal, and RS police arrested a Serb who had been indicted by a Sarajevo court in 2001 for war crimes and evaded capture ever since.[78] In Serbia the remnants of Milosevic's Socialist Party and the much larger Radical Party loudly blamed the government for the loss of Montenegro and waited for Kosovo, too, to slip out of Belgrade's grasp before forcing early elections that they were sure would reward them and punish both Kostunica and Tadic for their betrayal of the fatherland. Sonja Licht's estimate that real hard-liners constituted no more than 15 percent of the population may have been true. Yet after the murder of Zoran Djindjic, the centrist democrats never won over the perhaps 70 percent silent majority.[79] Instead, they seemed paralyzed, unable to take any political initiative. It was the ultranationalists—who had not held power since 2000 and therefore were not blamed by the public for the unemployment and economic misery that Milosevic left in his wake—who managed to attract a growing spectrum of protest votes against the moderate incumbents.

In early 2006 Kostunica gave increasing signs of having finally decided to surrender Ratko Mladic in order to meet the EU prerequisite of full Serbian cooperation with the ICTY for opening substantive Stabilization and Association negotiations. Tadic and Foreign Minister Vuk Draskovic had consistently urged such cooperation, and opinion surveys showed that more than half the Serbian population would have welcomed Mladic's extradition if this would set Serbia on the path to Europe.[80] It remained only for Kostunica to ratchet up the pressure on Mladic and negotiate the price that would persuade him to go there "voluntarily."

Instead of acting, however, Kostunica dithered. From January through April he implied to Brussels and the tribunal that it was just a matter of weeks before Mladic would show up. Radical member of parliament Natasa Jovanovic responded by taunting both prime minister and president, asserting that "Mladic is the pride of the Serbian nation and not those who have been in power." Serbian security forces did detain a number of their colleagues in the network that had helped Mladic elude capture for a decade. But there it ended. As deadline after EU deadline passed and Mladic remained at large, the EU finally suspended its Stabilization and Association talks with Serbia in May. With some heat, Kostunica accused the West of holding "the survival of an entire European democracy" hostage to "one single indictee"—and in effect rejected EU membership if that required letting Kosovo go.[81]

By contrast, Miroljub Labus—Serbian deputy prime minister, head of Serbia's EU negotiating team on Kosovo, and chairman of the small G17 Plus party—resigned his offices over this final sacrifice of Serbia's future prosperity to the empty satisfactions of pride and grandeur. "We have betrayed the most important interest of the country and citizens of Serbia," he declared in his resignation letter. The Serbian security services "searched for Mladic everywhere except where he was hiding," he added sarcastically to reporters.[82] "I fear there is a state within the state that can protect Mladic, so that it is not possible to arrest him without bloodshed," commented a senior West European diplomat. "But this would be a [political] death sentence among nationalists. Kostunica does not have the courage to do it."[83]

The resignation of Labus marked a defeat for Serb moderates. His failure to take the rest of his party with him out of the government and force early elections before the prospects for the centrists turned even worse postponed yet again the day when the Serbs might follow the lead of the Croats and Montenegrins and let the EU magnet pull them out of their past thralldom to war criminals as national champions. At worst, EU diplomats worried that hardliners might take an embittered Serb political class with them back to that antipodean pole of Moscow.[84] For Serb moderates the sword of Damocles was the negotiation about the "future status" of Kosovo that the internationals had imposed on Belgrade.[85] The West Europeans and Americans were orchestrating the talks to start "from the bottom up" and address less controversial, mundane aspects of decentralization first, before broaching the incendiary question of status. But they were pressing for conclusion of the talks by the end of 2006, and it became increasingly clear that the outcome was going to be the qualified independence for Kosovo, with international oversight, that the Contact Group saw as the only equitable and stable possibility.

Kostunica and even Tadic, however, were totally passive. Kosovo was easily as much of a burden on Serbia as was Montenegro, given its poverty and potential claims both to financial investment and to prominent Albanian political representation in any reintegration with Serbia. Yet its mystique as the cradle of the Serbs lingered on, in part because centrist Serbs after Djindjic never dared confront the romantic myth. Prime Minister Kostunica clung to the legalistic argument that since UN Security Council resolution 1244 formally held Kosovo to be a province of Serbia, this status could not be altered without Belgrade's consent. Obversely, he ignored the countervailing "responsibility to protect populations from genocide" that informed the NATO intervention in 1999 and was endorsed in the UN summit's sixtieth anniversary declaration in 2005, which limits claims of sovereignty by states that fail egregiously to protect their citizens.[86] In parallel, President Tadic—who was widely credited by Contact Group diplomats with realizing that Milosevic had forfeited the Serbs' claim to Kosovo by his barbarity and that all the Serbs could now salvage would be protection of minority Serbs there—resorted to pledging that he would never sign any document relinquishing sovereignty over Kosovo. EU diplomats understood this as a thinly veiled invitation to the Contact Group to impose Kosovar independence on Belgrade, so that democratic Serb politicians might avoid voters' wrath by arguing that they had never agreed to the loss.[87] This ruse, however, offered no way forward to Serb-Kosovar consensus.

In this vein, both prime minister and president endorsed the categorical rejection by the Serbian parliament of Kosovar secession. Both allowed defense lawyers for Serbia in the thirteen-year-old genocide suit filed by Bosnia—which also came to trial at the International Court of Justice in this awful year of reckoning—to contend disingenuously that Belgrade's Yugoslav People's Army left Bosnia in May 1992 and did not thereafter participate in the war.[88] Both feared that Serbia's democratic center would be crushed in the looming general election if their parties were blamed for surrender of the Kosovo patrimony. But the longer they stonewalled and did not gradually prepare Serbs for the inevitable in Kosovo or defend the interests of those Serbs remaining there, the more they inflated the blame that would ultimately be heaped upon them.

"Djindjic would have played it very differently," sighed one West European diplomat. "He would have been on the offensive, calling the shots." By contrast, today's centrist politicians "are totally passive, waiting until the Kosovars or the international community call the shots." In his analysis, the Serb electorate now accorded a far higher priority to getting on with joining Europe and creating jobs, and might well have been ready to abandon destructive chauvinism. But the politicians were not calling the Radicals' bluff by stating frankly that independence for Kosovo was now unavoidable, and then setting out a deal to protect Orthodox Church property, minority Serb rights, and open borders. If they did so, he continued, at the end of the negotiations "they could face their electorate and say, 'We have negotiated successfully 10 out of 12 points.' Otherwise, they will have a total loss on all scores and go to the electorate—and guess what happens?! In my opinion, people will elect the original," the ultranationalist Radicals, and not Kostunica's me-too nationalists.[89] Tomislav Nikolic, the Radicals' deputy leader—and acting leader, since Vojislav Seselj was still in an ICTY remand cell—clearly sharing this instinct, proclaimed his party's anti-NATO, anti-EU, pro-Russian stance and declared that Serbs would take up arms to retain Kosovo.[90] As a surrogate for the mute Serbs in the Kosovo negotiations, the Europeans began suggesting to the Kosovars that they might have to accept some continuing role for Belgrade in North Mitrovica after independence; and that they might have to forgo their cherished seat in the UN for a number of years, as the Germans did for more than two decades after World War II.

All told, it was a dreadful time for the Americans and the West Europeans to compel the Serbs to give up the pretense that they still ruled over Kosovo—but it would always be a dreadful time, and the internationals could no longer wait.[91] The United States, overstretched militarily, facing incipient civil war in Iraq, the disintegration of its dream of democratizing the Middle East, the prospect of open-ended pacification in Afghanistan, the nuclear defiance of Iran and North Korea, and oil at $70 a barrel, wanted to accelerate the negotiations, declare at least one victory, and pull troops out of Kosovo, and the sooner the better. Or at least Defense Secretary Donald Rumsfeld did.[92] The State Department tended to agree with the Europeans that withdrawing abruptly and coercing the Serbs into disgorging Kosovo in a 2006 Balkan summer of discontent could even risk turning the semisuccess in the Balkans into a rout of new fighting, and it wanted to postpone a change in status until the end of the year. The National Security Council fell somewhere in between the two. The Europeans negotiated with all three American institutions, with themselves, and with their Balkan partners, and kept urging Serb moderates, in vain, to seize the initiative. In exasperation the United States, citing Belgrade's failure to extradite Mladic over four months, froze $7 million in aid earmarked for the Serbian government, while pointedly continuing to disburse $62 million in aid to NGOs in Serbia.[93] At the same time, it became known that the UN had made contingency plans to deal with the potential flight of as many as 70,000 Kosovo Serb refugees to Serbia and Montenegro.[94] NATO finally played hardball with Kostunica and announced that it would reopen a base north of Mitrovica on the Serbian border. Serb leaders in the four northern Kosovo municipalities retaliated by declaring a state of emergency and threatening to hire "999 Serbian police officers." The West's message was clear that the alliance was preparing to enforce whatever conclusion emerged from the status negotiations.

As for the Kosovar Albanians, they went into the talks in 2006 without their father figure. Ibrahim Rugova died in January, deliberately leaving no obvious successor as president of Kosovo and head of the LDK. Across the political spectrum, the Kosovars pocketed the independence they were increasingly sure would be theirs and talked more often about some future pan-Albanian state for the second-largest Balkan ethnicity after the Serbs—not by force of arms and not immediately, of course, but eventually and naturally. Some Western diplomats dismissed such talk as an outflanking threat to strengthen the Kosovars' real, less extreme bid for independence for Kosovo within its present borders. Others took it at face value and were especially concerned about the demands of former student leader Albin Kurti, who asserted (as Rugova always had) that Kosovo already was independent and did not need to negotiate the terms of this sovereignty or compromise with anyone else. Kurti had some popular appeal, not only because of his radical rejection of either Serb or international limitations on independence, but also because of his criticism of the lavish lifestyles of Kosovar politicians at a time when poverty and even reversion to barter were growing in the countryside. Diplomats feared that competition for Rugova's succession, and perhaps the breakup of his authoritarian-run LDK into hostile factions, might trigger ever more extravagant positions, as rivals tried to outbid each other in patriotic fervor.

Surprisingly, however, within weeks of Rugova's death, the Kosovar dynamic began to favor moderation. Pragmatic LDK member Fatmir Sejdiu (rather than the polarizing speaker of the assembly, Nexhat Daci) was quickly named president. Kole Berisha, who had been acting LDK head in the months since Rugova's incapacitation, retained his role. PDK leader Hashim Thaci, hoping to end his year of political marginalization in the opposition by filling the vacuum in the center after Rugova's departure, displayed a statesmanlike willingness to compromise.

Most sensationally, as Agim Ceku, the most trusted public figure in the land, suddenly moved from the formally nonpolitical command of the Kosovo Protection Corps to become prime minister from the ranks of the Alliance for the Future of Kosova (AAK), the former KLA general addressed Kosovo Serbs in fluent Serbian—a tongue Rugova had refused to speak for years—and promised to protect them and their Orthodox sites.[95] Moreover, he endorsed the goal of "standards" that had long been rejected as insulting by the Kosovar Albanians. Not with that precise word, of course. But in language familiar to every other Central and Southeast European land aspiring to EU membership, as the holy grail of independence approached he told American hosts on a visit to Washington that what the Kosovars want is for Kosovo to become "a normal country."[96] *Normality* tacitly presumed rule of law, democracy, and protection of human and minority rights.

Throughout the political shuffles, Oliver Ivanovic, the North Mitrovcanin whose Serbian List for Kosovo and Metohija had won eight assembly seats in the 2004 election but never occupied them, maintained his contacts with all the Kosovar Albanian politicians. For his part, President Sejdiu rejected conditional independence and insisted on full sovereignty, but tended to define that happy state in negotiable terms, as Kosovar membership in "international organizations."[97] Veton Surroi, the veteran editor and publisher of the *Koha Ditore* newspaper, reinforcing the hint, made UN membership the centerpiece of his roman à clef about the negotiations.

As the once-a-month Serb-Kosovar talks ambled on, Kosovo remained the most volatile of any land in the region. Of all those who had been the subjects or the objects of the wars of the Yugoslav succession, only the Kosovars had not suffered enough deaths and destruction to view war, ultimately, as hell rather than heroism. Periodically, there would be some reminder of how close to the surface violence was, such as eruptions in the Presevo Valley or explosives planted outside the headquarters of a rival Kosovar party.[98] Prudently, NATO chose to put on shows of force, in the guise of regional reinforcement exercises that just happened to take place in Kosovo on successive anniversaries of the March 2004 riots. Yet post-Rugova politics remained a contest in moderation. Thaci, no longer blackballed by the Americans and the West Europeans, seemed to be aiming for a Rambouillet scenario, in which he would (under Contact Group pressure) drop maximalist demands and thus outmaneuver the intransigeant Serbs. Belgrade protested the appointment of Thaci as head of the Kosovar negotiating team—Serbian authorities had an arrest warrant out for him as well as for Ceku—but did not boycott the talks.

In this environment the international brokers tried to inculcate in the negotiators the lessons of the (West) Germans—and of the Hungarians, who, ever since the Trianon Treaty, have had more of their ethnic countrymen in neighboring countries than any other Central Europeans. To the Kosovars, the Quint presented as worthy models the Hungarian renunciation of irridentist resentment in the EU world of open, irrelevant borders and the West German contentment with the status of a semisovereign state from the late 1940s through 1990. To the Serbs, it stressed the Germans' evolution away from habits of hierarchical obedience to democratic skepticism of authority, renunciation of chauvinism, and atonement for the Holocaust in assuming a special responsibility for ethical state behavior today.

As Milosevic's chimera of a Greater Serbia shrank to an ever smaller fatherland that was falling behind its neighbors in the race to join the EU, few Serbs were in the mood to listen to the Quint's preaching.

Whose Song Is This?

By now there is some hope that old fatalistic, exclusivist ways of thinking in the Balkans—and the sharp divisions in outlook between city and countryside—are amenable to change. The deadweight of tradition, suspicion of the new, and rage over the wartime murder of family members still forms a barrier to fresh thinking, as does the narrowed field of vision of today's young Serbs, who cannot travel freely in Western Europe as their parents did in the Tito era. But local challengers are also vigorously confronting the inertia of received wisdom. One of the most ambitious initiatives is the groundbreaking Southeast European Joint History Project, in which four dozen leading scholars from all eleven countries in the broader region have come together to write a single collaborative textbook, with supplemental workbooks, about Balkan history for university and secondary school use. The aim of the undertaking is to supplant nineteenth-century stereotypes with detoxified, multiperspective teaching about the times and contexts of the battle at Blackbird Field, the Byzantine, Ottoman, and Hapsburg Empires, the Balkan Wars of the early twentieth century, World War II, and other controversial events in the region. Education with these textbooks should "raise awareness and reduce the likelihood of the misuse of history for political ends," its statement of purpose declares. Designed by Bulgarian American professor Maria Todorova (of *Imagining the Balkans*) and Costa Carras in 1998, the project has already made a critical examination of the particularist teaching of history in the region and completed the first master text in English of four projected volumes, with financing provided by the Stability Pact, the German Foreign Ministry, and the U.S. State Department.[99]

The umbrella NGO for the project, the Thessaloniki-based Center for Democracy and Reconciliation in Southeastern Europe (CDRSEE), is writing companion workbooks, collecting original source material from each of the participating countries, translating all material into ten languages, training teachers in this unfamiliar genre, engaging education ministries and teachers unions in spreading the books to rural as well as urban schools, and field testing the concepts. The whole enterprise might seem futile, especially given the brain drain of many of the most ambitious young people out of the region.

But if economic development begins to create decent white-collar jobs, such teaching in the schools should help encourage many of the best and brightest to return to their homelands, in the expectation that their children could put down roots while still receiving a more modern education. Already Sasha Bezuhanova, general manager of Hewlett-Packard Bulgaria, sees the beginning of a return trend among young emigrés.[100] And so far the experimental history text has met with a favorable reception among Bulgarian and Serb teachers, if not always among Croats (who want to be considered Central European rather than Balkan).[101]

Other NGOs in Bulgaria have wrestled with the competing Greek and Macedonian claims to be the heirs of Alexander the Great, the claims of both Hungarians and Romanians to be the heirs of Janos Hunyadi and his staunch resistance to the Ottoman invaders, and the claims of both Macedonians and Bulgarians to be the descendants of Sts. Cyril and Methodius. In the "missionary function of history," textbooks exist "to adjust the optical apparatus of the young person—not only and not so much with respect to the past, as with respect to the present and future," notes "The Image of the Other," an analysis published in 1998 in Sofia. "While the Bulgarians 'liberate' Edirne, the Greeks 'seize' Thessalonike; . . . while during the Balkan Wars and World Wars I and II the Bulgarian troops in Macedonia are 'liberators,' they are 'occupiers' for the Greek, Serbian, Macedonian and even the Romanian textbooks." The typical Balkan history book "is a classic example of a text designed to provide a necessary minimum of socio-cultural background," the study records with sociological distance. "After being covered by the individual, this minimum enables him to integrate himself within his national community and see his individual destiny as meaningful inasmuch as he belongs to his national collective body."[102] Similarly, Sofia University's Ivan Ilchev deconstructs disputes about the identity of the proto-Bulgarians, Thracian antiquity, the glorious medieval Bulgarian Empire, the Turkish yoke, the eighteenth- and nineteenth-century prelude to a "reborn Bulgarian state," and the disappearance of minorities from Bulgarian history texts after 1878.[103]

There are still huge barriers to the general acceptance of such projects, however. When the Helsinki Committee and the Center for Human Rights and Conflict Resolution in the Macedonian Institute for Sociological, Political, and Juridical Research brought twenty-five ethnic Albanian and Macedonian teachers together to write a pluralist account of the fighting in 2001, they sparked controversy. The teachers overcame their suspicion sufficiently to work together, but their compilation of the mutually exclusive nationalist narratives, and a third version that tried to make a synthesis of the other two, drew strong opposition from parents in schools that might otherwise have adopted the study in their curriculum.[104]

Less provocatively, Bulgarian filmmakers have taken a sly look at the monopolization of a common musical heritage in the melody that appears variously as a religious hymn, a revolutionary herald, a love song, and, improbably, a military march in Bulgaria, Macedonia, Greece, Turkey, Serbia, Montenegro, Albania, and Bosnia. "Whose song is this?" the documentary innocently asks different ethnic groups after playing the tune that in Bulgaria is known as "The Clear Moon Rises." The instant reply, sometimes condescending at the questioner's ignorance, sometimes belligerent at the implied challenge, is always: "It's ours, of course."

CHAPTER ELEVEN

REACHING CRITICAL MASS

IT'S EASY ENOUGH to check off the boxes. Vigorous civil society: A+ for Serbia and, more surprisingly in any historical context, Bulgaria. Judiciary with aspirations to ethics and sophistication: yes for Serbia, Croatia, and Bosnia; "tries hard" at last for Romania; "could try harder" for Bulgaria. Refusal to abet war crimes suspects in evading arrest: F for Serbia, as of this writing. Parties that are more than just patronage networks, or at least some recognizable polyarchy: D for Albania, Kosovo, and Macedonia; rising C– for the Republika Srpska.[1] Liberation from rule by the old nomenklatura/kleptocracy: Republika Srpska, knock on wood, rising C–. Return of refugees and restoration of their property: B+ for Bosnia; F for Croatia until 2005, C thereafter; for Kosovo, A+ in resettling Albanians and F in resettling Serbs. Entrepreneurial animal spirits disciplined by regulations that are not just invitations to baksheesh or legislatures that are more than just guarantees of parliamentary immunity for members' extracurricular wildcat capitalism: ask again in five years. Rejection of war as the default mode of resolving disputes in this once and recent powder keg of Europe: impressive almost everywhere. Learning curve: prodigious everywhere. Disentangling of interlinked government, business, and organized crime: bits of progress, but still a failing grade everywhere.

Low as many of the grades might seem, this report card is encouraging. The trends are up, even if improvements remain fragile. The Balkan lands are responding, asymmetrically, to the call of Brussels. Croatia yields explicitly to blunt ICTY and EU conditionality in turning Gotovina over to the Hague in order to win candidate status for EU membership. Bosnia is frog-marched into becoming a more open society by Royal Marines drillmaster Paddy Ashdown. Romania works more by osmosis. Some 100,000 Macedonians apply for Bulgarian passports to gain visa-free travel in Western Europe more quickly than they otherwise would. Preaccession Balkan observers at European Union summits, the European Parliament, and all the peripatetic committees in the EU universe absorb the union's arcane consensus culture long before their countries become full members.[2] Bulgarian students in Berlin pepper the visiting Bulgarian president with sharp questions they would have been far too deferential to pose if they had stayed at home. And for all the debate about whether new Balkan members will now enter the EU under the individual regatta or the bloc convoy system, it is clear that all the aspirants are affected by the general Europeanizing environment in the region, manifested most acutely in anxiety about getting left behind all the others.

Benchmarking competition is slowly augmenting, if not yet supplanting, that old negative political profiling against the enemy "other." Identity politics has begun to yield, slowly, to interest politics, which is less ideological and more amenable to trade-offs and compromise. The cumulative evidence now suggests that, against the odds, the Balkan lands have reached the critical mass to continue the momentum toward more transparent, democratic, and tolerant societies. The remaining dangers are palpable, but in the judgment of Ivan Vejvoda, executive director of the Balkan Trust for Democracy, the region is "closer to success than to failure."[3]

But if this is true, just how did the Balkans achieve critical mass? Theoreticians differ. In years to come, the Balkans will offer enough contradictory phenomena to ignite many an academic dispute. It would be beyond the scope of this book to evaluate the claims of the shifting hypotheses about nation, state, institution, capacity, and democracy building, along with diffusion, empowerment, and other constructs. A few observations can be made, however, about the light various theories cast on the case studies in this book.

At the most rudimentary level, nation and state building is still ongoing among the latecomers to the Balkans nineteenth-century awakening to national consciousness. But for Albania, Kosovo, and Macedonia (and in a different way Bosnia), it is now a question of accepting second best to the once sacrosanct gathering of one's whole tribe within a single border. Some Albanians in Kosovo, Macedonia, and southern Serbia may still dream of a Greater Albania (or a Greater Kosova), to be won, if necessary, by romantic wars of liberation. The Albanian government, however, places a much higher priority on security, stability, and economic development than on the old "Albanian question"; it will do whatever it takes to secure a Stabilization and Association Agreement with the EU, including supporting Macedonia's existing borders against Kosovar encroachment. The scattering of Albanians in five lands (including Montenegro and Greece) is not so bad, European diplomats keep telling the ethnic Albanians, if all are guaranteed the level of respect for minority rights that the EU has insisted on in Macedonia.

For their part, Macedonians—who never got even a titular state, as Albanians did by the early twentieth century, and whose nominal status as a republic in Yugoslavia never engendered a real sense of national solidarity comparable to that of Serbs or Croats—must now build their state on an unfamiliar civic rather than national identity. And Bosnian Serbs and Croats, who are slowly reorienting themselves to the reality of a Bosnian rather than a Greater Serbian or Greater Croatian state, will have to contribute, along with Bosniaks, to some reconstitution of the old multicultural spirit of Sarajevo.

In the early post-cold war years, at the beginning of what was called the transition paradigm, American policymakers and think tanks in particular tended to downplay the need for prior nation and state building—or indeed, any particular historical path—as a precondition for democratization in the Central European and Central Asian states that broke out of Moscow's empire. The fairly simple sequence of toppling Communist rule and instituting elections, it was thought, would free the peoples of both regions to seize the democracy that all must inherently want. Francis Fukuyama's aperçu of the "end of history" in Europe, as liberal regimes vanquished totalitarianism in the twentieth-century struggle with Hitler and Stalin's social engineering, was widely understood as some kind of automatism on a predetermined road to democracy.[4] Any "'preconditions for democracy' were enthusiastically banished in the heady early days of the third wave" of democratization in Latin America and elsewhere in the 1980s that was expected to continue in Central Europe in the 1990s, notes the Carnegie Endowment's democratization specialist Thomas Carothers.[5] The "contrary reality—the fact that various structural conditions clearly weigh heavily in shaping political outcomes"—was ignored (and continued to be scorned by Washington in 2004 in expecting the toppling of Saddam Hussein to trigger positive democratization throughout the "Broader Middle East").[6]

In the oft-cited bellwether examples of the German and Japanese transformations after 1945, Carothers further pointed out, state building was unnecessary, since strong bureaucratic states already existed, and all that needed to be done was to change the basis of political legitimation from authoritarianism to democracy. Where strong states do not exist, as in Albania and the southern tier of ex-Yugoslav states, however, state building is essential. It "has been a much larger and more problematic issue than originally envisaged in the transition paradigm. . . . In countries with existing but extremely weak states, the democracy-building efforts funded by donors usually neglected the issue of state building. With their frequent emphasis on diffusing power and weakening the relative power of the executive branch—by strengthening the legislative and judicial branches of government, encouraging decentralization, and building civil society—they were more about the redistribution of state power than about state building" or "bolstering state capacity."[7] They thus put the evolving political systems at risk of recapture by old predatory elites or their clones, with either consolidation of an elective but illiberal democracy that produces "feckless pluralism" (as in all of the Balkan lands, at different times) or pendulum swings into and out of democracy (as has happened with some regularity in Latin America).[8]

To construct an emerging state that is strong in the right ways but also weak in the right ways in turn requires effective institution building—of state administration, professional police, political parties, civil society, and media, among others.[9] Often enough in the Balkans it also requires building bureaucratic and analytic capacity from scratch.[10]

In this area external actors today are less likely to err in slighting the overall need for institution building than in leaping from one fad to another at the expense of incremental, balanced development—and in treating successive pet institutions as panaceas. The emblematic first craze centered on civil society, a cause adopted more generally after Central European dissidents resurrected the concept in the 1980s to mount oblique opposition to centralized domestic rule and Soviet hegemony. These dissidents spawned literary, jazz, philosophical, and other apolitical associations outside the Communist purview and (re)asserted a putative "Central European identity." They then combined their drive for civil society with native nationalisms that (unlike nationalisms in the Balkans) worked positively; their anti-Soviet allergy promoted more democratic and open systems at home in opposition to the hierarchical Kremlin, without igniting wars with Russia or other neighbors.[11] A strategy that worked well in the Central European setting, however, has encountered far more resistance in the Balkans (and in east Slav and Central Asian societies), where the political and institutional break with the past was more ambiguous and the continuity of old apparatchiks in post-Communist governing structures was much greater. Any proto-democratic institutions that existed were often too weak to democratize governance. Serbia, for example, had the most vigorous civil society (and as a corollary, the greatest draft evasion) of any Balkan country in the 1990s. Yet it also had the most ruthless leader, one who did not shrink from using violence to destroy Serbia's nascent pluralism and institutions and apparently did not mind the resulting exodus of "3,000 to 4,000 mainly young professionals from the country because they were looking for breathing space."[12] Elsewhere—most dramatically in Ukraine between 2004 and 2006—euphoric victories for civil society turned to ashes as institutional structures proved too feeble to sustain initial democratic breakthroughs.[13] As Claus Offe pointed out very early in the post–cold war transition, everything has to advance together simultaneously, in rough balance, to prevent the failure of fragile democratic transformation. This is fiendishly difficult.[14]

In the postconflict Balkans the conspicuous absence of such a balance hindered democracy building, the centerpiece of the European Union's engagement on behalf of peace and stability. Old Communist Party factions morphed and split into more autonomous social democratic (and even neoliberal) political parties that looked in their organizational charts like their namesakes in the West, but tended to remain patronage networks rather more than channels for the broader inclusion of citizens. Judges almost everywhere were poorly paid and susceptible to bribery and were the products of quite inappropriate Communist legal training. Many economic ministries persisted as fiefdoms of their ministers. And many senior ministry officials manipulated raging inflation to their own financial advantage before macroeconomic stabilization took hold, "privatizing" enterprises by selling them to themselves at nominal prices, stripping assets, bankrupting their new firms to the benefit of their personal bank accounts, and then extracting more subsidies from the government, allegedly on behalf of their workers. The nouveaux riches flocked to buy parliamentary seats to gain immunity from lawsuits challenging shady business practices. Old ruling cliques frequently converted their political clout in the old system into political or economic clout, or both, in the new system, as demonstrated by Milosevic, Iliescu, Nastase, Nano, Berisha, and almost all the thuggish security services. Even the brash Serbian prime minister Zoran Djindjic did not feel that he could begin to purge the Serbian security services until two years after his election—and that attempt invited an assassin's bullet. Old Serb military and police networks have hidden war crimes indictee Ratko Mladic for a decade, and have given strong signs of collusion in mafia smuggling and money laundering. The Balkan soil has hardly inspired hope that new, open systems might prevail.

In the Balkan setting institution building cannot be accomplished "merely by the 'import' of modern institutional mechanisms" into a vacuum, without "wholescale modernization" of entire "communities," warns Ognyan Minchev, executive director of the Institute for Regional and International Studies in Sofia. It requires "maximal mobilization of the existing institutional resources of Balkan societies individually and in collaboration." Lands like Kosovo and Bosnia-Herzegovina that have emerged out of interethnic war, mass ethnic cleansing, and the disintegration of the old administrative infrastructure need to be treated as protectorates to "create the necessary organizational background for a sensible peacekeeping, humanitarian and reconstruction and development program" and institute "a step by step development of [an] autonomous democratic process of political representation at municipal and national levels under international supervision."

Albania and Macedonia did not suffer full collapse of their old administrations as the war-ravaged lands did, Minchev continues, but "the ability of the government and the public administrative system to enforce law and order and to exercise the basic functions of a state are seriously reduced." They therefore require a "semi-protectorate" to "reproduce [a] normal environment in the fields of security, law and order, [and] welfare provision." Macedonia is better served than Albania in its public institutions, but it still needs "mass scale international assistance in the field of security and national defense," in "maintaining interethnic stability and in resisting the attempts of the present day Belgrade regime to de-stabilize and control the country."

Bulgaria, Romania, and Macedonia "(apart from its security dilemma)," Minchev notes, do "have the autonomous ability to implement their political decision making in a public administrative process. Nonetheless, the efficiency level of their public administrative systems is remarkably low compared to the standards of the developed world. A system of direct assistance and indirect stimuli should be developed to motivate these national governments to perform a large scale administrative reform, to reduce the skyrocketing levels of corruption, to promote a more effective system of public control over the executive and legal systems, to de-centralize the decision making process, and strengthen the municipal powers' authority."

At the heart of the Balkans, Serbia does have "a relatively well developed institutional system inherited from the former Yugoslav communist state." But it has other serious problems. After its military defeats, "the growing political unrest will start Yugoslavia on its process of uneasy political transformation from authoritarian rule to democracy." Yet this "process is very likely to be accompanied by weakening of public institutions, disintegration of the system of law and order, and decline of the state's ability to serve the basic needs of the community. This case represents the most difficult scenario, and a minimum of political and institutional transformation should be carried out by Yugoslav citizens before the international community" can even begin to provide help.[15]

The ubiquitous Western agents for change in the Balkans tend to make the same differentiations as Minchev. They take it for granted that democracy is a worthy aim and will promote reconciliation, and that democracy and its sister rule of law can be established even in a poor Southeast Europe with little historical preparation for either.[16] They disregard theories arguing that emerging democracies are more prone than nondemocracies to go to war; if they did not, they might well be trying to prolong stable authoritarianism rather than bolster unruly democracy in their host lands.[17] Instinctively, they side with Immanuel Kant's thesis that liberal—read "democratic"—states are more peaceful, and make a strong plea to put democratic development at the heart of development assistance.[18]

In interviews, some of the most dedicated local reformers and Western advisers repeatedly identify two elements as the keys to success in their endeavors: soft power, or the art of making others want what you want; and local ownership. European soft power is reflected in the Balkan yearning to partake of the EU's security, prosperity, and "normality."[19] This desire by no means always overrides inertia, entrenched interests, and violence, but what is striking is the number of times it has in fact functioned to induce Balkan governments to pay the high price of painful reforms. In the Balkans the EU operates only as a magnet, not as a hammer. No country is coerced into joining the club. On the contrary, many current EU member governments, facing "enlargement fatigue" among their own citizens—especially since French and Dutch voters rejected the EU constitutional treaty in spring 2005—want to close the doors. Yet the European Commission, noting that "[e]nlargement is one of the EU's most powerful policy tools" in promoting reform and peace in its neighborhood, is pressing members to continue admitting newcomers despite the defeat of the framework intended to keep the EU's own institutions functioning in a growing club.[20]

EU spats over the draft constitution make the Western Balkan countries worry that they might never get to join the club, and the polemics will surely continue to reverberate until some substitute framework can be negotiated after the French presidential elections in 2007. In the meantime, however, French prime minister Dominique Villepin and interior minister Nicolas Sarkozy have bluntly called for enlargement to be suspended, and in March 2006 Paris successfully insisted that European foreign ministers specify that future admissions must depend on the EU's dubious "absorption capacity."[21] The European Parliament, too, has explicitly warned what it regards as an overenthusiastic commission not to push expansion beyond this absorption capacity, and the phrase has become a code word in every subsequent EU communiqué that touches on widening.[22]

Nonetheless, the Stabilization and Association and candidacy processes continue; Germany and Austria, in particular, keep working away on enlargement as if the 2003 Thessaloniki promise of eventual EU membership for the Balkan lands still holds. By the time additional Balkan states have actually made themselves ready for accession in ten or fifteen or twenty years, Berlin and Vienna contend, the old union members will again realize the importance of enlargement for European stability. Ironically, this good cop–bad cop routine increases EU bargaining power by reminding applicants that they are the demandeurs, and that if they do not wish to meet the requirements, they are perfectly free to stay outside the euroatlantic haven of prosperity and security.[23]

The effectiveness of soft power rests crucially on the desire of indigenous actors to seize "local ownership" to emulate the EU's democracy and markets and make them work, even in an initially inhospitable environment. In this dynamic, outsiders can help motivate domestic reformers, widen their spectrum of policy choices, provide models and technical help, level the playing field somewhat against local bullies—and provide crucial educational opportunities abroad for the coming generation—but they cannot do the heavy political lifting. Only those who will be affected can mold proreform constituencies in any land, in an accelerated evolution that is just the opposite of social engineering from above. External financial assistance and tough conditionality can both be helpful in providing public goods in ways that give reformers political rewards, and in bringing outside donor pressure to bear (as in the pledge signed by the interior ministers in Brijuni). But for evolution to become self-sustaining, even in the case of an assertive proconsul like Paddy Ashdown, there must be, in the apt phrase of Wade Jacoby, "coalition" building between outsiders and insiders. In his analysis, those Westerners who wish to effect regime change in foreign countries have a choice of three means: inspiration, subsidization, or substitution. The most effective means for inducing durable democratization, Jacoby suggests, is a combination of the first two, inspiration and subsidization, in empowering and protecting indigenous reformers.[24]

The centrality of such local ownership is clear from a quick review of some of the actors who have in fact made democratic transformation their own cause and have been instrumental in moving their Balkan lands toward European normality—people like President Stipe Mesic and Prime Minister Ivo Sanader in Croatia; Prime Minister Zoran Djindjic and democratic activists Ivan Vejvoda, Sonja Licht, and Natasa Kandic in Serbia; Justice Minister Monica Macovei in Romania; businesswoman Sasha Bezuhanova in Bulgaria;

and any number of thirty-something civil servants in various Balkan foreign and European ministries. Even in the most extreme case of a Kosovo with little self-government that is ruled by a surrogate UN administration, ethnic Albanians who had been shut out of all official positions (and any Albanian-language education) for more than a decade had to be groomed fast to take over utterly unfamiliar public management, policy, and administration functions, under conditions of postconflict volatility, widespread extortion, and ethnic hatred. To fill the specific, abrupt vacancy of a customs service as Serb security forces evacuated Kosovo, the action-oriented United States and the internationally oriented UN wished to follow the pattern of the UN police, foreign policemen recruited worldwide for service in Kosovo. The EU refused, however, and insisted instead on building a domestic service under international leadership (with new young Kosovo Serb officers assigned to the border crossings with Serbia). As a result, the customs agency was the first service with sensitive security competences to be turned over to the Kosovo provisional government to run, and it now employs some 375 young Albanian and Serb Kosovars and only two dozen internationals. Kosovars today are proud of their professional, state-of-the-art service and do take ownership of it, commented one European Commission official who participated in the original decision.[25]

To be sure, some EU decisions are short-sighted, some advisers on the ground are unsuited to their role, and many of the bureaucratic rules and regulations in the obligatory 93,000 pages of the *acquis communautaire* prove too rigid and complex—or even just geared too much toward Central European conditions—when superimposed on very different Balkan societies. Yet in a postwar atmosphere, in a region of low political institutionalization and capacities, where there is no quick fix, the European Union is deliberately taking on a generations-long commitment with impressive dedication.

This, then, is clearly the third secret to Balkan success, beyond soft power and local ownership—the heavy Western investment of financial and human resources in Southeast Europe's democratization and modernization. The United States spent $22 billion in the Balkans between 1992 and 2003. The Europeans spent €33 billion in bilateral and multilateral aid in the region between 2001 and 2005 alone.[26] Aid to Bosnia per capita in that country's first two postwar years exceeded per capita aid to Germany or Japan in their first two years after World War II.[27] Transformation does not come on the cheap. The total Western outlay in the Balkans looks huge—until it is compared with the loss of life in the Iraq war since 2003 and its cost of between $540 billion and $670 billion.[28]

One European Commission staff member reviewed the accomplishments and the commitment of the internationals: "In Bosnia they ended the war very successfully. Then came crisis management, reconstruction, and humanitarian needs. Half the population was displaced. The infrastructure was destroyed. We completely rebuilt villages, bridges, schools, hospitals, to restore the basis for normal life. This was very successful, the first phase.

"Then came rule of law, judicial reform, laying the basis for refugee return and everything humanitarian, and construction, and raising the standards to make EU membership even feasible. Then the offer of membership, combined with reconstruction. Then we shifted to institution-building, JHA [Justice and Home Affairs], border management, refugee returns. It's true it was slow, but these are new countries; they weren't countries before.

"In Albania, capacities were a huge issue. And the market economy. In 2001 you still met people who thought that economic recovery meant revival of all those old steel factories. We got Albanians to pay for public services not in cash [which is easy to divert into private pockets], but through bank accounts. Albania was a cash economy. We were giving technical assistance to increase capabilities—customs, tax police. . . .

"Macedonia has been kept together. Civil war was prevented; decentralization was begun. Even in Croatia, where people have done things reluctantly, because they had to and not because of a drive that these are the right things to do, a lot has happened.

"We put in €2 billion of European money to bring Kosovo back to the situation it was in before the war. But even with that, we did not put Kosovo into the twenty-first century, but only into Communist times. The transition time there will last fifty years."[29]

On balance, any fair observer must conclude that the thousands of judges from Rome, gendarmes from Marseilles, bankers from Vienna, academics from Uppsala, party organizers from the Konrad Adenauer Foundation, and Greek diplomats with recent memories of their own country's Balkan metamorphosis are indeed transforming the region. Not least, increasing numbers of citizens are beginning to glimpse what a less exclusivist sense of identity might mean. In Serbia, President Boris Tadic's concept of Serbdom is far more broad minded than his father's. In Bosnia, the cosmopolitan Grand Mufti Dr. Mustafa ef. Ceric embraces the sense of multiple identities and declares, "We are, first, Muslim spiritually, second, Bosniaks ethnically, and third, Bosnians [citizens of Bosnia]. Our fourth identity is European. . . . There are Bosniaks and Muslims who would put these in a different order. But I think in these four identities there is no conflict. All day we are multi-identity personalities."[30] The Reis-ul-ulema sees this layered identity as a continuation of the historical experience of Bosnia-Herzegovina, which has always been part of a larger community, whether Roman, Ottoman, Austro-Hungarian, or Yugoslav. But the difficult reclaiming of the legacy of mixed cultures after their bloody clash depends greatly on the assurance of security and belonging offered by the broader European mixing of national cultures.

Throughout the Balkans, those who are seizing ownership of their transformations pay tribute to the working of the European Union leaven. In Romania, the drive for EU membership has accelerated political and social debates about modernization and offered European benchmarks to a land that craves to be considered European.

In Bulgaria, former president Zhelyu Zhelev declares, "For many, membership in the European Union is a guarantee for the future prosperity of Bulgaria. . . . I think the road we have taken to the EU and the market economy is a very stable process and irreversible. There is no other way."[31] Stefan Popov, chairman of the Open Society Institute in Sofia, elaborates: "The integration process in both NATO and especially the European Union is a sort of directive framework that makes us think with greater confidence that we can live without [the patronage of] Russia and reduce organized crime. We can live at the edge of Europe but still be out of reach of the dangers outside Europe—and at the same time govern ourselves. Without the EU and the integration track, I cannot imagine this could have happened. There are many big debates in Bulgaria now that would not have been possible without the integration process, in the sense that it brought us to ask new questions" about constitutional arrangements and the value of collective as against individual rights. "Without this, our whole public sphere would be immature."[32]

Hewlett-Packard's general manager in Bulgaria, Sasha Bezuhanova, confirming the importance of local initiative, perceives membership in the EU and NATO as a "catalyzer," but not "the real driver," which is instead "the objective need of this country to survive in the big competitive international game."[33] Nikolay Mladenov, member of parliament from the Union of Democratic Forces and deputy chairman of the European Integration Committee, noted (before he was defeated in the center-right debacle in the 2005 election) that "because it's a realistic prospect, politicians can attach their career to the agenda of EU membership. It will happen in our political lifetime, so it enables politicians to grasp and use it."[34] Most succinctly, J. D. Panitza, founder of the Free and Democratic Bulgaria Foundation and long-time Paris editor of the *Reader's Digest*, declared, "The only thing that counts today is the European Union, day and night, night and day."[35]

In Bosnia, the same singular focus has prevailed ever since the EU's Thessaloniki summit and the follow-up Feasibility Study launched the Bosnian Stabilization and Association Process in 2003. The study "definitely changed people's attitudes and opinions. Even as late as October [2002] in the elections all the talk of reforms and getting into Europe didn't cut the ice here. They took it just as rhetoric," observed a senior American diplomat. But now "they treat the Feasibility Study like the greatest thing."[36]

"The Feasibility Study was historic," agreed a senior European diplomat in Bosnia at the time. "When I first came here in 1996, there was some kind of fatigue; this was a devastated country. NATO took all the decisions. Even ten months after the war, the whole six kilometers from Sarajevo to the airport was still a moonscape. Here you had a complete division of the society itself. Here you had a war, divided families, divided societies, politicians mostly from the old times. . . . For several years there was no idea of a common country. Slowly, slowly the feeling grew that things could also work at the central [multiethnic] level. . . . I don't go to every small politician and push him. I say, 'I don't care about anything except the children who had nothing to do with the war. If the situation continues like this and there are no reforms, what will you do with your children? They'll all leave.' . . . I say, 'Maybe you are trying to defend interests that serve only the party or nation [ethnicity] you belong to. But in the medium and long term that's a lost cause. In the long and medium term it's complex, but I think you can see the light at the end of the tunnel. International aid is diminishing. You have a semiopen door; it's up to you to push it open and come in.' . . . I think there is a consensus here on the European perspective. Not always an absolute consensus about the speed and the intensity, but about the need for acting now."[37]

Certainly the Bosnian-Serbian normalization that began when Zoran Djindjic was still prime minister in Belgrade was continued after his assassination. "I do not think 'reconciliation' is too strong a word for it," commented one Serbian diplomat. "The future is the most important thing for both countries. . . . Fortunately, there is a group of Bosniaks who are thinking, 'the war is past. We are going to Europe, and on the way to Europe we have to pay the price. That price is to accept some painful truth, simply that the past [and revenge] cannot be our orientation. Europe is our orientation. And for this we have to forgive—not to forget, but to forgive.' These politicians are orientated not to their own [subjective] feeling, but to their strategic interest." Within a year of Bosnia's winning of a Feasibility Study, the Republika Srpska issued its first public apology for the Srebrenica massacre—and then went on to give prosecutors a list of 17,000 Serbs who were complicit in the massacre and to subordinate its "entity" army and finally even its police to the central command of multiethnic Bosnia. More pressure than the OHR and the EU would have wished to exert lay behind these words and acts, but the important thing was that they came, in order not to leave Bosnia behind in the Europeanization of the Balkans.

The same European drive and sense of enlightened self-interest prevails among other elites in the region. In Macedonia, State Counselor for EU Affairs Jovan Tegovski says, "In my personal opinion, all these reforms we are doing, we are doing first of all because of ourselves, not because NATO or the European Union is asking for them."[38] In Romania, embattled Justice Minister Monica Macovei says, "I believe it is no longer possible to turn everything back. The number of people driving this change is growing every day. The people stand behind us. We belong to Europe."[39] In Serbia, Foreign Minister Vuk Draskovic says, "I was born in Yugoslavia, the most wonderful country in Europe. It was like an America in the Balkans. Now I hope we will come together again in Brussels."[40]

At the end of the day, crisis management, including postconflict political development, is an art. All transformations, like all politics, are local. They depend on the harried internationals on the ground who have to make quick decisions on imperfect knowledge about which politicians and policemen they can trust—and on the reciprocal instinct of local reformers as to whom they can trust among their variegated advisers. Above all, metamorphosis depends on those mayors of Brcko and Hermannstadt, those Serb crime-busters, and those Balkan academics who are conspiring to write a common history textbook of Southeastern Europe that for the first time in two millennia will try to be fair to all.

The EU's commitment to revolutionary democratization in the Balkans is surprising, given Europe's conservative preference for stability over more radical American-style zeal for destabilizing entrenched regimes in order to trigger democratization. Certainly, without the provocation of the Srebrenica massacre the EU would never have been jolted into such open-ended engagement. Its hope now is that a sense of European identity will come to supplement and moderate exclusivist nationalisms, that borders will lose their old negative significance, and that synergy will replace hostile zero-sum thinking as Southeast Europeans, like their Central European forerunners, stop hoarding sovereignty and instead begin pooling it in the larger European Union.

To be sure, crime still thrives in the region. Albanian gangs—which pose much more of a threat than does Greater Albania zeal—will probably continue to expand their realm throughout Europe. Drug runners and money launderers and human traffickers, instead of simply warping politics and economics throughout the region, might actually capture one or two failing states. Kosovo/Dardania could blow up tomorrow. The ultranationalist Radicals could and probably will take over the government in Belgrade in early elections, and the Serbs' sense of unfair victimization will probably get worse before it gets better. The center-right coalition in Romania could implode the way the last one did. Croatia, despite its promises, could drag its feet on letting remaining Serb refugees return to their villages. Big gaps remain between elites and publics. Many of those who have had democracy (or at least elections) thrust upon them are disillusioned with the experiment, do not see that it has improved their lives, and do not bother to vote.

And yet, as of this writing, Croatian courts have begun convicting Croats for war crimes, and courts in Serbia and the Republika Srpska have begun convicting Serbs. Bulgaria and Romania, having finally broken out of political stagnation, are pushing on toward polyarchy and awaiting momentary accession to the EU. Croatia is next in the queue, even if it may be held in limbo for a few years while the European Union straightens out its own internal crisis after the constitutional debacle. Macedonia, too, is a formal EU candidate. Albania is on its way with its new Stabilization and Association Agreement. Serbia and Montenegro and Bosnia have started their Stabilization and Association negotiations. Kosova verges on conditional independence, while Kosovar Albanians are finally taking ownership of decentralization and some security services (and are being allowed to do so), and the country's prime minister has assured Kosovo Serbs, in Serbian, that their rights will be protected.

In Bosnia leading Republika Srpska politicians now see their future within Bosnia-Herzegovina rather than in a Greater Serbia. The mission impossible of restoring multiethnic society in Bosnia-Herzegovina that the internationals took on in 1995—against all the contrary counsel about the futility of such a quest—has at least progressed far enough that as of this writing, remarkably, a Bosniak was the acting RS police chief.[41]

Croatian businessmen from the once-besieged Vukovar are collaborating with Serb colleagues across the Danube border to enliven regional trade and commerce. Romania is for the first time seriously prosecuting high-level officials on corruption charges, and this example is putting pressure on Bulgaria to do the same. International peacekeepers in the region have been reduced to 23,000, with no combat deaths. The greatest eruption of Balkan violence in the past five years, in Kosovo in March 2004, has not been repeated. Serbia's human rights watchdogs are as formidable as ever.

Altogether, an expectation of European identity permeates the Balkans, and conformity to the qualifying European standards is gradually shaping up. The EU process of tutoring, hectoring, and funding candidates for membership has implanted hope in today's parents for the prospects of their children—and this in a transatlantic atmosphere of cooperation rather than strife. The Weberian politics of drilling through hard wood proceeds, millimeter by millimeter. Southeast Europe's transitional elites are paying the high price of extraditing compatriots to the Hague Tribunal, permitting greater transparency in governance, and investigating corruption in order to win their place in the EU constellation. Balkan peoples stumble often enough, but they are rushing through the political, economic, and social revolutions that it took Britain and France and the United States 200 years to get through—and this in one generation. In their attempt to escape from the nineteenth into the twenty-first century the Balkans are already light-years away from what the most optimistic observers foresaw in 1995 or 1999, or even 2004.

The novel exercise of soft power in this fundamental regime change may not yet have ensured the end of Hegelian history in Southeast Europe. But it is certainly better—and cheaper, in both blood and treasure—than any conceivable alternative. Anyone who doubts this need only look at Darfur. Or Afghanistan. Or Lebanon. Or Iraq.

NOTES

Notes to Introduction

1. James A. Baker 3rd, *The Politics of Diplomacy: Revolution, War, and Peace, 1989–1992* (New York: Putnam, 1995), p. 636; Richard Holbrooke, *To End a War* (New York: Random House, 1998), p. 29.

2. Robert Cooper, a senior British diplomat who is now the top policy adviser to the EU's "foreign minister," Javier Solana, defines the European Union, only partly tongue in cheek, as "a highly developed system for mutual interference in each other's domestic affairs, right down to beer and sausages." Robert Cooper, "The Post-Modern State and the World Order" (London: Demos, 1996): 23.

3. Guillermo O'Donnell, Philippe C. Schmitter, and Laurence Whitehead, *Transitions from Authoritarian Rule* (Johns Hopkins University Press, 1986); Juan J. Linz and Alfred Stepan, *Problems of Democratic Transition and Consolidation: Southern Europe, South America and Post-Communist Europe* (Johns Hopkins University Press, 1996).

4. Paul Johnson, "World War II and the Path to Peace," *Wall Street Journal Europe*, May 8, 1995, p. 6.

5. Leszek Balcerowicz, "Fallacies and Other Lessons," *Economic Policy* (December 1994): 47, and "The Interplay between Economic and Political Transition," *Polish Quarterly of International Affairs* (Summer/Autumn 1996): 9–28.

6. See, for example, Samuel P. Huntington, "Will More Countries Become Democratic?" *Political Science Quarterly* 99, no. 2 (1984): 193–218; Adam Przeworski, *Democracy and the Market: Political and Economic Reforms in Eastern Europe and Latin America* (Cambridge University Press, 1991); various essays in the periodical *Journal of Democracy* in the early and mid-1990s. For discussions of the content of democracy teaching, see Thomas Carothers, *Assessing Democracy Assistance: The Case of Romania* (Washington: Carnegie Endowment for International Peace, 1996); Thomas Carothers, *Critical Mission: Essays on Democracy Promotion* (Washington: Carnegie Endowment for International Peace, 2004); Martin Lipset and Jason Lakin, *The Democratic Century* (University of Oklahoma Press, 2004): Giuseppe Di Palma, *To Craft Democracies: An Essay on Democratic Transitions* (University of California Press, 1990). For a retrospective rebuttal of the pessimists by one of the Polish activists at the time, explaining why the transformation

worked, see Alexander Smolar, "Leadership and Postcommunist Transition," *Transatlantic Internationale Politik* 6, no. 3 (Fall 2005): 20–25. See also a specific contrast between Central Europe and Latin America in Alina Mungiu-Pippidi and Ivan Krastev, *Nationalism after Communism: Lessons Learned* (Budapest: Central European University Press, 2004), especially the last chapter; and the confessions of a reformed pessimist in Martin Krygier, "Traps for Young Players in Times of Transition," *East European Constitutional Review* 8, no. 4 (Fall 1999) (www.imf.org).

7. Polish economists drew the author's attention to this caution in interviews in the mid-1990s. See Elizabeth Pond, *The Rebirth of Europe*, rev. ed. (Brookings, 2002), especially pp. 105–34.

8. For an excellent discussion of the continuity of and contrasts between the EU's enlargement policy toward Central Europe and what became known as its Stabilization and Association Process (SAP) toward the Western Balkans, see Centre for European Policy Studies, "The Reluctant Debutante: The European Union as Promoter of Democracy in Its Neighbourhood," CEPS Working Documents 223 (Brussels: Centre for European Policy Studies, July 2005), especially pp. i–11 (http://shop.ceps.be).

9. To make this study manageable, I have, first, reduced the area covered to those Balkan lands that want to be but are not yet EU members. This excludes Greece and Slovenia, which are already in the club. I also exclude Turkey, simply because this giant candidate for membership is *sui generis*, and the disputes about its accession revolve around Islam and human rights, not about specifically Balkan issues. I therefore focus on Albania, Bulgaria, Romania, and Kosovo, along with the Yugoslav successor states of Serbia and Montenegro, Croatia, Bosnia, and Macedonia.

10. The term *ethnic* is a misnomer when applied to distinctions between Serbs and Bosniaks (the Bosnian Muslims), and even Croats, who come from the same Slavic stock and speak the same language, with regional dialects. It has become customary usage in the literature, however, and is therefore employed in this book for lack of a better term. Hereafter, *Serb* and *Croat* are used in the ethnic sense. *Serbian* and *Croatian* refer to the states or governments.

11. Author's interviews, Ukraine and the Balkans, 1990s.

12. For a decade the rule-of-thumb estimate of deaths in the war in Bosnia was 200,000 or 250,000. After painstaking compilation of name-by-name lists, however, the Sarajevo Research and Documentation Centre, a nongovernmental organization, concluded in 2005 that the more accurate figure was just under 100,000. Nidzara Ahmetasevic, "Serbia Faces Trial for Bosnia Genocide," Institute for War and Peace Reporting (IWPR), February 22, 2006 (www.birn.eu.com; http://iwpr.gn.apc.org).

13. Deutsche Welle, "Mehrheit der Kroaten ist gegen EU-Beitritt" (Majority of Croats is against EU accession), September 8, 2005 (www.dw-world.de); "Kroatiens 'europäische Werte'" (Croatia's "European values"), *Neue Zürcher Zeitung*, October 5, 2005 (www.nzz.ch).

14. The eight Central European states that joined with Malta and Cyprus in the "big bang" were Estonia, Latvia, Lithuania, Poland, the Czech Republic, Slovakia, Hungary, and Slovenia.

15. See, for example, European Commission, "2005 Enlargement Strategy Paper" (Brussels, November 2005) (http://europa.eu.int); Jack Ewing and others, "Rise of a Powerhouse," *Business Week*, December 12, 2005; Radmila Sekerinska, "Comment: Macedonia's Decisive Year on Road to NATO and EU," IWPR, January 27, 2005; "The Rise of Nearshoring," *Economist*, December 3, 2005, pp. 69–71; Stefan Wagstyl and Jan Cienski,

"Twin Perils: Poland's Nationalists May Turn Protectionist at Home and Awkward Abroad," *Financial Times*, November 21, 2005, p. 13; Daniel McLaughlin, "Accession States Defy Pessimists," *Irish Times*, May 2, 2005. For an examination of EU conditionality in this process, see Milada Anna Vachudova, *Europe Undivided: Democracy, Leverage, and Integration after Communism* (Oxford University Press, 2005); Frank Schimmelfennig and Ulrich Sedelmeier, eds., *The Europeanization of Central and Eastern Europe* (Cornell University Press, 2005); James Hughes, Gwendolyn Sasse, and Claire Gordon, "Conditionality and Compliance in the EU's Eastward Enlargement," *Journal of Common Market Studies* 42, no. 3 (September 2004): 523–51; and John P. Hardt, "European Union Accession, May 2004: A Mixed Blessing," *NewsNet* (American Association for the Advancement of Slavic Studies) 44, no. 5 (October 2004): 1–5. For generally positive evaluations of democratic transition in Central Europe, see Juan J. Linz and Alfred Stepan, *Problems of Democratic Transition and Consolidation: Southern Europe, South America, and Post-Communist Europe* (Johns Hopkins University Press, 1996); Jan Zielonka, ed., *Democratic Consolidation in Eastern Europe*, vol.1, *Institutional Engineering* (Oxford University Press, 2001); and Jan Zielonka and Alex Pravda, eds., *Democratic Consolidation in Eastern Europe*, vol. 2, *International and Transnational Factors* (Oxford University Press, 2001). For an early skeptical view of the results of EU tutoring, see Jon Elster, Claus Offe, and Ulrich K. Preuss, *Institutional Design in Post-Communist Societies: Rebuilding the Ship at Sea* (Cambridge University Press, 1997).

16. Jan Fidrmuc and Klarita Gerxhani, "Formation of Social Capital in Central and Eastern Europe," *Beyond Transition* (World Bank newsletter) 16, no. 3 (July–September 2005): 18–19.

17. European Commission, Directorate General for Economic and Financial Affairs, "Enlargement, Two Years After: An Economic Evaluation," Occasional Paper 24 (Brussels, May 2006) (http://europa.eu.int).

18. Radio Free Europe/Radio Liberty Newsline, August 30, 2004 (www.rferl.org).

19. For simplicity, the standard English-usage spelling of *Kosovo* is used in this book with no political overtones intended. The transliteration of the Albanian version, *Kosova*, is used only in proper names (Kosova Liberation Army) or in quotes. The Serb *Kosovo and Metohija* is used here only when a Serb point of view is being cited.

The definition of *ethnic cleansing* is "a purposeful policy designed by one ethnic or religious group to remove by violent and terror-inspiring means the civilian population of another ethnic or religious group from certain geographic areas," according to the study commissioned by the UN Security Council, "Final Report of the Commission of Experts Established Pursuant to SCR 780 (1992)," S/1994/674 (May 27, 1994), III. B., para. 2. As of this writing, the final report was not available on the UN website. It can be found at the Heller Information Services website, www.his.com.

20. For an account of the evolution of the Greens' and Social Democrats' position on this issue, see Brian C. Rathbun, *Partisan Interventions: European Party Politics and Peace Enforcement in the Balkans* (Cornell University Press, 2004), pp. 82–121.

21. In constant 2001 U.S. dollars. James F. Dobbins, "America's Role in Nation-Building: From Germany to Iraq," *Survival* 45, no. 4 (Winter 2003–04): 96.

Notes to Chapter One

1. Actually there were six nationalities, once Yugoslavia recognized Muslims as a separate ethnic *narodnost* in 1971, but the neat numerical summary was too clever for

Yugoslavs to forgo. Dejan Djokic, *Yugoslavism: Histories of a Failed Idea 1918–1982* (London: Hurst, 2003), p. 206.

2. Louis Sell, *Slobodan Milosevic and the Destruction of Yugoslavia* (Duke University Press, 2002), p. 4. With this, Sell explicitly debunks from the outset the widespread Western assumption that ancient hatreds inevitably bubbled to the surface once cold war constraints were removed—and also the assumption that great power meddling was to blame for the Yugoslav debacle. Sell argues further (pp. 34–35) that before the country's breakup there was a "definite sense of Yugoslav national identity" (rather than narrower ethnic loyalties), and not just among the seventh of the population who were in mixed marriages or the children of such marriages; moreover (p. 114), that relations were generally cooperative in ethnically mixed areas. I have relied on Sell as the most judicious and insightful English-language biographer of Milosevic. Warren Zimmermann, in his *Origins of a Catastrophe* (New York: Times Books, 1996), p. 209, makes the same argument against any assumed dynamic of ancient hatreds by pointing out that "Serbs and Croats, the most antagonistic of adversaries today, had never fought each other before the twentieth century."

3. The term *Bosniak* refers to Bosnians of Muslim descent, who up until the 1992–95 war identified themselves as *Muslims*. The term *Bosnians* refers to any citizen of Bosnia-Herzegovina, whether Muslim, Serb, or Croat.

4. Sabrina Ramet, "The Dissolution of Yugoslavia: Competing Narratives of Resentment and Blame (1986–1991)," Scholars' Initiative papers on Confronting the Yugoslav Controversies (hereafter, Scholar's Initiative papers), Team 2. The study was conducted between 2001 and 2005, a product of one of the excellent series of conferences on "Confronting the Yugoslav Controversies" organized by Pudue University for Serb, Croat, Bosniak, Kosovar, and American scholars, who subsequently wrote essays exploring their commonalities and differences of perception. As of this writing, reports from seven of the ten teams were available. In addition to the report cited above, these were Melissa Bokovoy and Momcilo Pavlovic, eds., "Kosovo under Autonomy (1974–1990)," Scholars' Initiative papers, Team 1; Drago Roksandić and Gale Stokes, eds., "Independence and the Fate of Minorities (1991–92)," Scholars' Initiative papers, Team 3; Dusan Janjic and Matjaz Klemencic, "International Community and the FRY/Belligerents (1989–95)," Scholars' Initiative papers, Team 5; Darko Gavrilovic and Charles Ingrao, eds., "The Safe Areas (1992–1995)," Scholars' Initiative papers, Team 6; James Gow and Miroslav Hadzic, eds., "US/NATO Intervention in Kosovo (1998-99)," Scholars' Initiative papers, Team 9; John B. Allcock and others, eds., "The International Criminal Tribunal for the Former Yugoslavia," Scholars' Initiative papers, Team 10. All of these papers were accessed at www.cla.purdue.edu; although they do not carry dates, they were written c. 2005-06. An earlier version of these papers is also available in the special Scholars' Initiative edition of *Nationalities Papers* (December 2005).

5. Sell, *Slobodan Milosevic*, p. 1. Laura Silber and Allan Little, in *Yugoslavia: Death of a Nation* (TV Books, 1995, 1996), p. 37, translate Milosevic's words as, "No one should dare to beat you." See also Sabrina Ramet, *Thinking about Yugoslavia: Scholarly Debates about the Yugoslav Breakup and the Wars in Bosnia and Kosovo* (Cambridge University Press, 2005).

6. Sell, *Slobodan Milosevic*, p. 89.

7. In 2003 James Gow published his analysis in narrative form for laymen in *The Serbian Project and Its Adversaries: A Strategy of War Crimes* (London: Hurst, 2003). While noting Serbs' protest at Gow's analysis on various issues, I take his basic account in this book as the legal truth as established in judges' verdicts at the Hague. See also the Scholars' Initiative report, Janjic and Klemencic, "International Community and the FRY/Belligerents."

8. See Zoran M. Markovic, "Die Nation: Opfer und Rache" (The nation: Victim and revenge), in Thomas Bremer, Nebojsa Popov, and Heinz-Günther Stobbe, eds., *Serbiens Weg in den Krieg: Kollektive Erinnerung, nationale Formierung und ideologische Aufrüstung* (Serbia's road to war: Collective memory, national formation and ideological rearmament) (Berlin: Berlin Verlag, 1998), pp. 319–37.

9. The Croats exited the Ottoman Empire by virtue of Hapsburg expansion, not by their own rebellion. The small community of Montenegrins in the high mountains maintained their autonomy even at the apogee of the Ottoman Empire and preceded the Serbs in winning full independence in 1799. For this book, historical facts and judgments are drawn primarily from L. S. Stavrianos, *The Balkans since 1453* (New York University Press, 2000); Ivo Banac, *The National Question in Yugoslavia: Origins, History, Politics* (Cornell University Press, 1984, 1994); Misha Glenny, *The Balkans 1804–1999: Nationalism, War and the Great Powers* (London: Granta, 1999); Dennison Rusinow, *The Yugoslav Experiment 1948–1974* (University of California Press, 1977); John R. Lampe, *Balkans into Southeastern Europe: A Century of War and Transition* (London: Palgrave Macmillan, 2006).

10. The size of the Serb minority is from the 1981 census.

11. Sell, *Slobodan Milosevic*, p. 270, citing the Mother Theresa organization.

12. On the likelihood of international assent, see ibid., p. 130.

13. According to Sell, the point at which Milosevic shifted to his fallback position was mid-1990; ibid., p. 123.

14. Ibid., pp. 113ff.

15. For the considerable effort Milosevic had to make to get Serbs in Croatia to murder their Croat neighbors, see Ivo Banac, "The Last Days of Bosnia?" interview, *Boston Review* (February–March 1994) (www.bostonreview.net).

16. Zimmermann, *Origins of a Catastrophe*, pp. ix, 95.

17. Lampe, *Balkans into Southeastern Europe*, p. 161.

18. Roksandić and Stokes, "Independence and the Fate of Minorities," p. 22. They footnote the Tudjman quote to Ejub Stitkovac, "Croatia: The First War," in Jasminka Udovicki and James Ridgeway, *Burn This House* (Duke University Press, 2000), p. 156.

19. Sell, *Slobodan Milosevic*, p. 118.

20. Ibid., pp. 115–17. See also Silber and Little, *Yugoslavia*, pp. 92–104.

21. The quote is from Gow, *The Serbian Project and Its Adversaries*, p. 79.

22. Center for the Study of Democracy, "Partners in Crime: The Risks of Symbiosis between the Security Sector and Organized Crime in Southeast Europe" (Sofia, 2004), pp. 42–44; Gow, *The Serbian Project and Its Adversaries*, pp. 79–84. Gow downplays the aim of disguising the involvement of the regular Serbian army in Milosevic's setting up of Arkan as a paramilitary commander at this point; unlike in Bosnia, the JNA did not attempt to hide its direct engagement in the Croatian fighting.

23. Gow, *The Serbian Project and Its Adversaries*, p. 148.

24. Sell, *Slobodan Milosevic*, pp. 114–15, 146; Tim Judah, *The Serbs* (Yale University Press, 1997), pp. 184–86; Janjic and Klemencic, "International Community and the FRY/Belligerents," p. 86; Silber and Little, *Yugoslavia*, pp. 131–32, 144, 212, 306–07. According to Susan L. Woodward, in *Balkan Tragedy: Chaos and Dissolution after the Cold War* (Brookings, 1995), p. 192, Tudjman and Milosevic had been talking about such a partition since early 1991; and Glenny, *The Balkans*, p. 633, takes it for granted that by March 1991 the two leaders had agreed on divvying up Bosnia-Herzegovina. During the war in Bosnia, Tudjman certainly claimed a third of Bosnia as Croatian territory. According to Sell, however (*Slobodan Milosevic*, p. 119), "Tudjman and Milosevic could never

consummate a deal on dividing Bosnia because they could not agree on what to do in Croatia."

25. Sell, *Slobodan Milosevic*, pp. 108–115.

26. For a sympathetic portrayal of Izetbegovic, see Noel Malcolm, *Bosnia: A Short History* (New York University Press, 1996), especially pp. 219–25.

27. The description is from Zimmermann, *Origins of a Catastrophe*, p. 119.

28. Sell, *Slobodan Milosevic*, pp. 5, 140–65.

29. Gow, *The Serbian Project and Its Adversaries*, p. 120. The summary of the wars in Croatia and Bosnia in this chapter draws primarily on Gow's book; Sell, *Slobodan Milosevic*; Silber and Little, *Yugoslavia*, especially pp. 169–264; David Rohde, *Endgame: The Betrayal and Fall of Srebrenica, Europe's Worst Massacre since World War II* (New York: Farrar, Straus and Giroux, 1997); John Hagan, *Justice in the Balkans* (University of Chicago Press, 2003); Zimmermann, *Origins of a Catastrophe*; the Purdue Scholars' Initiative papers. For accounts that are much more critical of the roles of the Slovenes, the Croats, the West, and the International Monetary Fund and more understanding of the Serbs, see Woodward, *Balkan Tragedy*, especially pp. 146–98; and more briefly, Glenny, *The Balkans*, especially pp. 636–52.

30. Gow, *The Serbian Project and Its Adversaries*, p. 159.

31. Sell, *Slobodan Milosevic*, p. 115.

32. For a concise account of Milosevic's Serbianization of the JNA, see Gow, *The Serbian Project and Its Adversaries*, pp. 51-89. See also Zimmermann, *Origins of a Catastrophe*, pp. 85–91.

33. Gow, *The Serbian Project and Its Adversaries*, pp. 226–28.

34. See Paul Hockenos, *Homeland Calling: Exile Patriotism and the Balkan Wars* (Cornell University Press, 2003).

35. Gow, *The Serbian Project and Its Adversaries*, p. 84; Sell, *Slobodan Milosevic*, p. 149; Hagan, *Justice in the Balkans*, pp. 41–42, 97–98; indictments by the International Criminal Tribunal for the Former Yugoslavia (ICTY) of Mile Mrksic, Miroslav Radic, and Veselin Sljivancanin, November 7, 1995, and November 15, 2004, on the website of the ICTY, www.un.org/icty. For this as the first war crimes case from the 1991–92 Serb occupation of parts of Croatia and Bosnia to be tried before a Serbian court, see also Goran Jungvirth, "Vukovar Three Trial Debated," Institute for War and Peace Reporting (IWPR), May 13, 2005 (www.iwpr.net). All subsequent information about ICTY indictments and verdicts comes from www.un.org/icty, where information is cumulative and continually updated.

36. Silber and Little, *Yugoslavia*, pp. 182-85. Gow, *The Serbian Project and Its Adversaries*, pp. 164–65, argues that the Serb forces had the real military objective of driving out the exclusively Croat population in order to control the northern flank of the one Serbian-Montenegrin port, Kotor.

37. Gow, *The Serbian Project and Its Adversaries*, pp. 102–13.

38. Author's interviews with American diplomats at the time. See also Hagan, *Justice in the Balkans*, p. 53. For an excoriation of "British complicity with the Milosevic regime and Serbia," French "collaboration with Serbian nationalism," and the "general pro-Serb inclination of the military culture in most EU armies," see James Pettifer, *Kosova Express* (University of Wisconsin Press, 2005), pp. 89, 231, 203; also Brendan Simms, *Unfinest Hour: Britain and the Destruction of Bosnia* (London: Penguin, 2001).

39. "The political and military leaders of the Bosnian Serbs bear the primary responsibility for the ethnic cleansing policy carried out there [in Croatia and Bosnia-Herzegovina]

in total disregard of their obligations. However, with the prolongation of the conflict more and more atrocities are being committed by the other parties," concluded UN special rapporteur Tadeusz Mazowiecki in February 1993 in his report on ethnic cleansing, summary executions, maltreatment of prisoners, rape, "the particular suffering of children," forced transfer of populations, attacks on nonmilitary targets, and the general "humanitarian crisis." Tadeusz Mazowiecki, *The Situation of Human Rights in the Territory of the Former Yugoslavia,* A48/92/S/25341 (New York: United Nations, February 26, 1993), para. 261, p. 57 (http://documents-dds-ny.un.org). The ICTY convicted the first Serb indictee, Dusko Tadic, in May 1997; the first Bosniaks, Zdravko Mucic, Hazim Delic, and Esad Lanzo, in November 1998; and Tihomir Blaskic, the first Croat (apart from Drazen Erdemovic, a Bosnian Croat who fought in the Bosnian Serb army at Srebrenica and immediately pleaded guilty), in March 2000.

40. See especially Gow, *The Serbian Project and Its Adversaries,* pp. 90–102, 183–84.

41. Genscher's campaign for recognition for Croatia came only after he had first tried to keep Yugoslavia together at an early stage by persuading Slovenia not to secede. On behalf of the Organization for Security and Cooperation in Europe—of which Germany was the rotating chairman in 1991—Genscher held talks on the issue in Belgrade and scheduled follow-on talks in Slovenia. The Serbs, however, rejecting OSCE meddling, refused to let his plane land in Ljubljana. Thereafter, he shifted German policy to press for recognition of the emerging new states as soon as possible. This information comes from an Austrian official who was involved in Balkan policy at the time; conversation with author, July 2006.

42. The view that German recognition precipitated war in Bosnia was conventional wisdom in Britain and France at the time. James Gow and Richard Caplan, however, offer strong evidence that Serb preparations for war in Bosnia preceded recognition, as did the resistance of non-Serb Yugoslav republics to "efforts by the Belgrade authorities to recentralise Yugoslavia." Gow, *The Serbian Project and Its Adversaries,* especially pp. 172–74; Richard Caplan, *Europe and the Recognition of New States in Yugoslavia* (Cambridge University Press, 2005), chap. 4 (quote from p. 97). The present chapter also reflects the author's conversations with Hans-Dietrich Genscher, Bonn, 1992; and Lothar Rühl, Michael Stürmer, and Michael Schäfer, Berlin, 2005. For a description of how strongly the Serbs propagated fear of a German "Fourth Reich," see Zimmermann, *Origins of a Catastrophe,* pp. 88, 89, 208. For more negative views of the role of Tudjman (and German deference to the Croatian lobby) in the descent into war, see Woodward, *Balkan Tragedy,* pp. 183–89. For a more positive view of German motivations, see Sell, *Slobodan Milosevic,* p. 138; Sabrina P. Ramet and Letty Coffin, "German Foreign Policy toward the Yugoslav Successor States," *Problems of Post-Communism* 48, no. 1 (January–February 2001): 48–64. For a German refutation of the French and British accusations, see Michael Libal, *Limits of Persuasion: Germany and the Yugoslav Crisis, 1991–1992* (Westport, Conn.: Praeger, 1997), and Michael Libal's critical review of Woodward's book, "The Balkan Dilemma," *Harvard International Review* 18, no. 2 (Spring 1996). For Secretary of State James Baker's disapproval of Bonn's recognition of Croatia (though without suspicion of its motives), see James A. Baker 3rd, with Thomas M. Defrank, *The Politics of Diplomacy: Revolution, War and Peace 1989–1992* (New York: Putnam's Sons, 1995), especially pp. 639–45. For summary discussions of the issues, see Beverly Crawford, "German Foreign Policy and European Political Cooperation: The Diplomatic Recognition of Croatia," *German Politics and Society* 13, no. 2 (Summer 1995); Franz-Lothar Altmann, "Die Balkanpolitik als Anstoß zur Europäisierung der deutschen Außenpolitik" (Balkan policy

as a spur to Europeanization of German foreign policy), in *Ausblick: Deutsche Außen-politik nach Christoph Bertram* (Outlook: German foreign policy after Christoph Bertram) (Berlin: German Institute for International and Security Affairs, September 2005), pp. 38–41.

43. For an exploration of the reaction to the Oslo Declaration by the "international community," see Janjic and Klemencic, "International Community and the FRY/Belligerents."

44. Radio Free Europe estimates, as given on the website of the Carnegie Endowment for International Peace, www.ceip.org.

45. Silber and Little, *Yugoslavia*, p. 198.

46. Maja Povrzanovic, "Ethnography of a War: Croatia 1991–92," *Anthropology of East Europe Review* 11, nos. 1–2 (Autumn 1993) (http://condor.depaul.edu).

47. The time sequence contradicts the Serb claim that the attack on Bosnia was only reactive, in response to the EC's sanctioning of the dissolution of Yugoslavia.

48. Gow, *The Serbian Project and Its Adversaries*, p. 172, quoting Veljko Kadijevic, *Moje Vidjenje Raspada* (Belgrade: Politika, 1993), p. 144.

49. Silber and Little, *Yugoslavia*, p. 224. Seselj's paramilitaries were proud to adopt the name of the World War II Chetniks. Vojislav Seselj, the founder of the new ultranationalist Radical Party, claimed not only ethnic Serb areas for Serbia, but all of old Yugoslavia except for its northernmost swath.

50. Silber and Little, *Yugoslavia*, pp. 222–23.

51. Mazowiecki, *The Situation of Human Rights*; Hagan, *Justice in the Balkans*, p. 13; Sell, *Slobodan Milosevic*, pp. 165-67.

52. ICTY Trial Chamber Judgment, May 7, 1997, and Appeals Chamber Judgment, January 26, 2000. See also Gow, *The Serbian Project and Its Adversaries*, pp. 134–38; Hagan, *Justice in the Balkans*, pp. 71–84; Sell, *Slobodan Milosevic*, pp. 166ff.

53. Hagan, *Justice in the Balkans*, pp. 176–203; ICTY conviction of Dragoljub Kunarac and Radomir Kovac, February 22, 2001. See also Deutsche Welle, "Serbien/Bosnien: Bricht ein Film Tabus?" (Serbia/Bosnia: Does a film break taboos?), March 8, 2006 (www.dw-world.de).

54. For wrestling over when violation of human rights and a "duty to protect" might override respect for national sovereignty and compel intervention, see Michael Walzer, *Arguing about War* (Yale University Press, 2004); Michael Walzer, "Human Rights in Global Society," *Transatlantic Internationale Politik* 6, no. 1 (Spring 2005): 4–13; Michael Ignatieff, *Virtual War: Kosovo and Beyond* (New York: Metropolitan, 2000); Oliver Richmond, *The Transformation of Peace* (Basingstoke, U.K.: Palgrave, 2005).

55. The ICTY was established by UN Security Council Resolution 808 (February 22, 1993); its predecessor, the Commission of Experts, was established by UN Security Council Resolution 780 (October 6, 1992).

56. For a description of the unprecedented "massiveness of population displacements and scale of international relief operations" in the Balkans from 1991 to 1999, see Sadako Ogata, *The Turbulent Decade* (New York: W. W. Norton, 2005), pp. 50–171.

57. See the print reportage of journalists and academics like Ed Vulliamy, *Seasons in Hell: Understanding Bosnia's War* (New York: St. Martin's Press, 1994); Roy Gutman, *A Witness to Genocide* (New York: Lisa Drew Books, 1993); Samantha Power, *"A Problem from Hell:" America and the Age of Genocide* (New York: Basic Books, 2002).

58. Cited in Mirko Klarin, "The Tribunal's Four Battles," *Journal of International Criminal Justice* 2, no. 2 (2004): 546. See also Hagan, *Justice in the Balkans*; Gow, *The Serbian Project and Its Adversaries*.

59. Sell, *Slobodan Milosevic*, p 168; Aurélien J. Colson, "The Logic of Peace and the Logic of Justice," *International Relations* 15, no. 1 (April 2000): 51–62.

60. See, for example, Hagan, *Justice in the Balkans*, in particular, pp. 112–13.

61. For discussion of the broader "political" nature of the court, in the sense that any special tribunal by definition chooses to enforce humanitarian law in some categories of cases, while excluding others, see Rachel Kerr, *The International Criminal Tribunal for the Former Yugoslavia: A Study in Law, Politics and Diplomacy* (Oxford University Press, 2004); Allcock and others, "The International Criminal Tribunal for the Former Yugoslavia."

62. Allcock and others, "The International Criminal Tribunal for the Former Yugoslavia," p. 45.

63. Minna Schrag, "Lessons Learned from ICTY Experience," *Journal of International Criminal Justice* 2, no. 2 (2004): 427–34, p. 432. See also Patrick L. Robinson, "Rough Edges in the Alignment of Legal Systems in the Proceedings at the ICTY," *Journal of International Criminal Justice* 3, no. 5 (2005): 1037–58.

64. Klarin, "The Tribunal's Four Battles," p. 549.

65. Ibid., p. 550.

66. See especially J. H. H. Weiler, "The Transformation of Europe," *Yale Law Journal* 100, no. 8 (1991): 2403–83.

67. See chapter 9. Until the end of 2004, Washington was hinting broadly to Belgrade that it would be acceptable for all indicted Serb generals other than the infamous Mladic and Karadzic to be tried in Serbian courts rather than in the Hague.

68. The other four safe areas were Bihac, Tuzla, Zepa, and Gorazde.

69. UN Security Council Resolutions 819 (April 16, 1993) and 824 (May 6, 1993).

70. See, for example, Tadeusz Mazowiecki, *The Situation of Human Rights*. Tuzla, uniquely, was not totally encircled but sealed off only on three sides.

71. The JNA became the VJ in November 1991. Sabrina Ramet, *Balkan Babel: The Disintegration of Yugoslavia from the Death of Tito to the War for Kosovo*, 3rd ed. (Boulder, Colo.: Westview, 1999), p. 69; Gow, *The Serbian Project and Its Adversaries*, pp. 51–89.

72. The best-known proponent of these theses was Robert Kaplan, *Balkan Ghosts: A Journey through History* (New York: St. Martin's, 1993).

73. Glenny, *The Balkans*.

74. Malcolm, *Bosnia*, pp. 51–69.

75. Gow, *The Serbian Project and Its Adversaries*, p. 6.

76. Malcolm, *Bosnia*, pp. 101–02.

77. Galic was sentenced to twenty years in prison on December 5, 2003, for individual and superior criminal responsibility for violations of the laws and customs of war and four counts of crimes against humanity. See also Daryl A. Mundis and Fergal Gaynor, "Current Developments at the Ad Hoc International Criminal Tribunals," *Journal of International Criminal Justice* 2, no. 2 (2004): 642-98, especially 643–46.

78. Gow, *The Serbian Project and Its Adversaries*, p. 184.

79. M. Cherif Bassiouni, chairman, "Final Report of the United Nations Commission of Experts Established Pursuant to Security Council Resolution 780 (1992)," S/1994/674/Add.2, vol. 2, annex 4, part 1, "Study of the Battle and Siege of Sarajevo" (New York: United Nations, May 27, 1994) (www.ess.uwe.ac.uk).

80. Bassiouni, "Final Report of the United Nations Commission of Experts"; Sell, *Slobodan Milosevic*, p. 29.

81. General Oric was indicted by the ICTY on March 28, 2003, for individual and superior criminal responsibility for violations of the laws or customs of war.

82. This account draws on Rohde, *Endgame*; Gow, *The Serbian Project and Its Adversaries*, pp. 187–89; General Sir Rupert Smith, *The Utility of Force: The Art of War in the Modern World* (London: Allen Lane, 2005), pp. 334–64.

83. Rohde, *Endgame*; Silber and Little, *Yugoslavia*, pp. 356–60; Gow, *The Serbian Project and Its Adversaries.*, pp. 187–88.

84. Rohde, *Endgame*; Gow, *The Serbian Project and Its Adversaries*, pp. 187–89; Smith, *The Utility of Force*, pp. 332–70; BBC, "Timeline: Siege of Srebrenica," June 10, 2005; author's interview with Nuhanovic, Sarajevo, November 2002; Emir Suljagic, *Postcards from the Grave* (London: Saqi, in association with the Bosnian Institute, 2005); Nederlands Instituut voor Oorlogsdocumentatie (NIOD, Netherlands Institute for War Documention), "Summary for the Press," of report requested by Netherlands government, "Srebrenica, a 'Safe' Area," April 10, 2002 (www.srebrenica.nl); "Klage gegen die Niederlande eingereicht" (Suit filed against the Netherlands), *Neue Zürcher Zeitung*, July 12, 2005 (www.nzz.ch).

85. Silber and Little, *Yugoslavia*, p. 201.

86. Quote from ibid., p. 159.

87. Sell, *Slobodan Milosevic*, p. 215. Italy joined the Contact Group in 1995.

88. Sell, *Slobodan Milosevic*, pp. 241–43. UN High Commissioner for Refugees Sadako Ogata gives the total number of Serb refugees from Croatia as half a million. Ogata, *The Turbulent Decade*, p. 134.

89. Gow, *The Serbian Project and Its Adversaries*, pp. 168–98, considered NATO's use of force as the turning point in Bosnia, both in disrupting Bosnian Serb communications and redeployments and in deterring any direct intervention by the JNA. The CIA, on the contrary, regarded air power as less decisive than the simultaneous ground advances by Bosniak and especially Croat forces in ending the war in Bosnia. Office of Russian and European Analysis, *Balkan Battlegrounds: A Military History of the Yugoslav Conflict, 1990–1995*, vol. 1 (Washington: U.S. Central Intelligence Agency, May 2002), pp. 394–96. Glenny, *The Balkans*, p. 651, tosses in a third view: that Milosevic consented to the airstrikes beforehand so that he could go ahead with his prearranged deal with Holbrooke at the forthcoming Dayton talks, while being "relieved of the responsibility of bringing the Bosnian Serbs into line." The most nuanced view of the dynamics is given by the commander of UN forces in Bosnia in 1995, General Sir Rupert Smith. He describes the "mental rather than physical battle" with General Mladic and his own objective of taking initiative and control away from Mladic. Smith, *The Utility of Force*, see the chapter on Bosnia, especially pp. 364–89. See also Roksandić and Stokes, "Independence and the Fate of Minorities"; Gavrilovic and Ingrao, "The Safe Areas."

90. Gow, *The Serbian Project and Its Adversaries*, pp. 188–89; Sell, *Slobodan Milosevic*, pp. 232–34, is more ambiguous on this point.

91. Francine Friedman, *Bosnia and Herzegovina: A Polity on the Brink* (London: Routledge: 2004), p. 78, cites 1996 estimates by the International Centre for Migration Policy Development that "540,000 Bosnian Serbs (39 percent), 490,000 Bosnian Croats (67 percent), and 1,270,000 Bosnian Muslims (63 percent) were dislocated by the war."

92. Milosevic's behavior is from author's interview with a Dayton participant.

93. Derek Chollet, *The Road to the Dayton Accords: A Study in American Statecraft* (New York: Palgrave Macmillan, 2005).

94. Derek Chollet, "Dayton at 10," *Transatlantic Internationale Politik* 6, no. 4 (Winter 2005): 18–23. See also Richard Holbrooke's own account, *To End a War* (New York: Random House, 1998).

95. Smith, *The Utility of Force*, p. 369.

96. See, for example, Carl Bildt, "Bosnia between 1995 and 2004," talk presented at the International Conference for Bosnia and Herzegovina, Geneva, October 20, 2005 (www.bildt.net).

97. Vladimir Gligorov, "Balkan Transition," *European Balkan Observer* (Belgrade Centre for European Integration and the Vienna Institute for International Economic Studies) 3, no. 2 (October 2005): 10–17 (www.wiiw.ac.at).

98. Author's interview with Ashdown, November 2003. See also chapter 6.

99. For an analysis of some of the earlier feuds and the development following Kosovo of a "mature collaborative relationship" in transatlantic relations in Balkan policy, see Lily Gardner Feldman, ed., *Cooperation or Competition? American, European Union and German Policies in the Balkans* (Washington: American Institute for Contemporary German Studies, 2001).

100. Charles Barry, "NATO's Combined Joint Task Forces in Theory and Practice," *Survival* 38, no. 1 (Spring 1996): 81–97; Philip H. Gordon, "Europe's Uncommon Foreign Policy," *International Security* 22, no. 3 (Winter 1997–98): 74–100; Crawford, "German Foreign Policy and European Political Cooperation."

101. The initial indictments were issued on July 24 and November 16, 1995, the latest amendments on May 31 and October 11, 2002. Chief Prosecutor Goldstone hurried to issue the public indictments before the United States might be tempted to offer Karadzic immunity in order to facilitate a peace agreement. A similar concern motivated Chief Prosecutor Louise Arbour's acceleration of the indictment of Milosevic in May 1999. See Hagan, *Justice in the Balkans*, pp. 119–26, 130–31.

102. Tihomir Blaskic, colonel in the Croatian Defense Council (HVO) and commander of the regional headquarters of the HVO Armed Forces in central Bosnia, was convicted in March 2000 of individual and superior criminal responsibility for grave breaches of the Geneva Conventions and other crimes and sentenced to forty-five years' imprisonment. An Appeals Chamber judgment reversed most of the convictions and reduced his sentence to nine years' imprisonment.

103. Louise Arbour, "Crimes against Humanity," *University of Toronto Bulletin*, January 11, 1999, p. 16, as cited in Hagan, *Justice in the Balkans*, p. 85.

104. ICTY; Hagan, *Justice in the Balkans*, pp. 132–51.

105. Hagan, *Justice in the Balkans*, p. 107.

106. Ibid., especially pp. 71–91, 83, 84. ICTY judge Gabrielle Kirk McDonald (1993–99) also flags the noncooperation of the states whose citizens were indicted by the court. Even by spring 1998, only six of the tribunal's 205 arrest warrants had been executed by these states. The "vast majority of indictees continue to remain free, seemingly enjoying absolute immunity," commented the tribunal's fourth annual report to the UN Security Council. Gabrielle Kirk McDonald, "Problems, Obstacles and Achievements of the ICTY," *Journal of International Criminal Justice* 2 (2004): 558–71.

107. Dokmanovic was the first person to be apprehended under a previously sealed indictment. His arrest precipitated the exodus from Croatian territory of other former Serb officials who were still trying to exercise authority in their communities. It also set a precedent—especially since it allayed the fears about Serb military retaliation that had deterred international peacekeepers from making arrests for the previous eighteen months—for the apprehension of other indictees two weeks later and subsequently in Bosnia. Dokmanovic managed to commit suicide in custody a year later and never came to trial. His fellow defendants in connection with the torture and murder of patients in

the Vukovar hospital were charged with individual and superior responsibility for crimes against humanity and violations of the laws or customs of war. As of this writing, their trial was still pending. See also note 35 above; David Sterling Jones and Paul J. McDowell, "Operation Little Flower: The United Nations' Apprehension of an Indicted War Criminal," *Military Intelligence* (April–June 1998): 46–51; "Press Statement by the Prosecutor, Justice Louise Arbour," June 30, 1997.

108. Hagan, *Justice in the Balkans*, pp. 101–14.

109. Gow, *The Serbian Project and Its Adversaries*, p. 205, says forty-six rather than forty-five.

110. The ICTY Appeals Chamber subsequently reduced the count to aiding and abetting genocide and cut his jail sentence from forty-six years to thirty-five years. For general appraisals of the concept of genocide, see Anson Rabinbach, "Raphael Lemkin's Concept of Genocide," *Transatlantic Internationale Politik* 6, no. 1 (Spring 2005): pp. 70–75; and William A. Schabas, *Genocide in International Law: The Crime of Crimes* (Cambridge University Press, 2000).

111. Hagan, *Justice in the Balkans*, pp. 176–203; U.K. Foreign and Commonwealth Office, "Challenges and Progress," annual report (2001?), p. 4 (accessed online). Before spring 1992 the majority of Foca's population was Muslim. By fall 1992 almost all of the Muslims had left or been killed, and the town was renamed Srbinje. For an account of an educational town hall meeting in Foca that was organized by the Helsinki Committee for Human Rights in Republika Srpska and the ICTY Outreach Program to present the court findings to the Serbs who now populate the town, see Bogdan Ivanisevic, "Foca Confronts Its Past," IWPR, October 15, 2004 (accessed at http://hrw.org).

112. Quoted from the documentary *Against the Odds*, by its author, Mirko Klarin, in "The Tribunal's Four Battles," p. 555.

Notes to Chapter Two

1. J. D. Panitza, founder of the Free and Democratic Bulgaria Foundation, disputes this statement, pointing out that Bulgaria is the oldest nation-state in Europe, with roots going back to 681 in the First Bulgarian Kingdom.

2. Author's interview, February 1999.

3. Ivan Krastev, "The Balkans: Democracy without Choices," *Journal of Democracy* 13, no. 3 (July 2002): 39–53.

4. This figure comes from Kyril Drezov, "Bulgaria and Macedonia: Voluntary Dependence on External Actors," in *Democratic Consolidation in Eastern Europe*, vol. 2, *International and Transnational Factors*, edited by Jan Zielonka and Alex Pravda (Oxford University Press, 2001), pp. 426–27. Drezov reports that by the end of 1989, 155,000 of those who had been expelled had returned, but that the exodus "directly pitted Turks and Bulgarians against each other in the mixed population districts."

5. Author's interview, February 1999.

6. Author's interviews with the first UDF prime minister, Philip Dimitrov, and other politicians, February and September 1999, March 2004.

7. For development of this line of analysis, see Milada Anna Vachudova, *Europe Undivided: Democracy, Leverage, and Integration after Communism* (Oxford University Press, 2005); Fareed Zakaria, "The Rise of Illiberal Democracy," *Foreign Affairs* 76, no. 6 (November/December 1997): 22–43. Philippe Schmitter, "Dangers and Dilemmas of

Democracy," *Journal of Democracy*, 5, no. 2 (1994): 57–74, terms this type of government "persistent unconsolidated democracies."

8. By contrast to the courts in Romania, Bulgaria's judiciary early displayed more independence from the ex-Communists who remained in power. Right after adoption in 1991 of the new constitution, which barred formation of any parties "on an ethnic basis" and was clearly aimed at ethnic Turks, some nationalist members of parliament connected with the Socialists appealed to the Constitutional Court to rule the party of ethnic Turks illegal. The court certified the party as constitutional, however, and paved the way for formation of two other Turkish and a dozen Roma and Macedonian parties. The court rulings thus guaranteed the inclusion of previously excluded minorities in the political process. The court also played an important role in resolving the 1996 crisis without bloodshed, by means of new elections. Venelin I. Ganev, "Bulgaria: The (Ir)Relevance of Post-Communist Constitutionalism," in *Democratic Consolidation in Eastern Europe*, vol. 1, *Institutional Engineering*, edited by Jan Zielonka (Oxford University Press, 2001), pp. 199–200.

9. Author's interview, Sofia, September 1999.

10. Author's interviews with George Prohasky, 1999. See also his "New Stability Factor in the Southeast of Europe," Paper presented at the NATO Economic Colloquium, Brussels, November 3–5, 1999.

11. Author's interview, February 1999.

12. Author's interviews, Sofia, February 1999.

13. Author's interviews, Sofia, February and September 1999.

14. Author's interview, February 1999.

15. Author's interview, February 1999.

16. Author's interview, Sofia, February 2004.

17. Author's interview, February 1999. Turkish and Pomak Muslims constitute some 12 percent of the total population. For information about the series of monographs issued by Zhelyazkova's International Center for Minority Studies and Intercultural Relations since 1995 about the problems of minorities in Bulgaria (as well as of Albanian and Serb refugees after the 1990s wars), see www.omda.bg/imir. For an analysis of the UDF proto-party's need for the political support of the Turkish-Pomak Movement for Rights and Freedoms in 1990–91, see Nadege Ragaru, "Islam in Post-Communist Bulgaria: An Aborted 'Clash of Civilizations'?" *Nationalities Papers* 29, no. 2 (2001): 293–324. In the author's interviews for this book, some Bulgarian sources dismissed fears of anti-Turk popular sentiment in the early 1990s as exaggerated. In retrospect, however, violent incidents at the time and the sudden explosion of voter support for the new xenophobic Ataka Party a decade later would seem to justify Zhelyazkova's concerns.

18. Author's interview, February 1999.

19. See also Institute for War and Peace Reporting (IWPR), "Macedonia: Bulgaria's Warm Embrace," January 21, 2005 (www.iwpr.net).

20. Author's interview, November 2005.

21. Author's interview, February 1999.

22. See also Center for the Study of Democracy (CSD), "The Role of Political Parties in Accession to the EU" (Sofia, 1999) (www.csd.bg).

23. Author's interview, September 2004.

24. PHARE stands for Poland Hungary: Aid for the Reconstruction of Economies, a pilot program begun in 1989, then turned into the preparation of Central European applicants for EU membership in the late 1990s.

25. CSD, "Preparing for EU Accession Negotiations" (Sofia, 1999), especially pp. 3, 6, 7, 9, 17, 18, 20; see also CSD, "Social Policy Aspects of Bulgaria's EU Accession" (Sofia, 1999). For a theoretical analysis of the effect of EU conditionality on the domestic politics of candidate countries, see Aneta Borislavova Spendzharova, "Bringing Europe In? The Impact of EU Conditionality on Bulgarian and Romanian Politics," *Southeast European Politics* 4, nos. 2–3 (November 2003), pp. 141–56.

26. Author's interview, February 2004.

27. Author's interviews in Sofia, March and September 2004. See also Deutsche Welle, "Die Transformationsleistungen" (The transformation accomplishments), January 18, 2005 (www.dw-world.de); Radio Free Europe/Radio Liberty Newsline, "Armenia Shares Bulgaria's Nuclear Problems with EU," July 15, 2004, End Note (www.rferl.org).

28. The precise legal status of the requirement of judicial reforms in candidate countries has been ambiguous since the French and Dutch rejected the draft EU constitutional treaty in spring 2005. "Judiciary and Fundamental Rights" constituted an additional "chapter" in membership negotiations with candidates after the 2004 enlargement, on the assumption that the draft treaty would be ratified and its Charter of Fundamental Rights would become binding for all members. The charter is held to codify preexisting provisions of the EU *acquis*, however, and it is in any case clear that judicial reforms are key *political* requirements, no matter how long the draft constitutional treaty remains in limbo. See Margarit Ganev, "Modernization of the Pre-Trial Phase of Criminal Proceedings," in CSD, "Judicial Reform: The Prosecution Office and Investigation Authorities in the Context of EU Membership" (Sofia, 2005–06), pp. 21–24.

29. Author's interview, 2004. See also Vassil Chobanov, Albena Shkodrova, and Svetlana Jovanovska, "Bulgaria: Powerful Investigators Resist Change," IWPR, June 27, 2005.

30. This was the unanimous view of Bulgarians and foreign diplomats interviewed by the author in Sofia.

31. Bartlomiej Kaminski and Francis Ng, "Bulgaria's Integration into the Pan-European Economy and Industrial Restructuring," Policy Research Working Paper 3863 (Washington: World Bank, March 2006), especially p. 4 (www.wds.worldbank.org).

32. For a comparative look at the problems of reformist center-right parties in Central Europe, see Svetoslav Malinov, "Rise, Fall and Disintegration: The Bulgarian Center-Right in Power and in Opposition (1997–2005)," in *Why We Lost: Explaining the Rise and Fall of the Center-Right Parties in Central Europe 1996–2002*, edited by Peter Ucen and Jan Erik Surotchak (Bratislava: International Republic Institute, 2005), pp. 13–30.

33. Project on Ethnic Relations, "The Bulgarian Ethnic Experience" (Princeton, N. J., 2002), report on the conference in Sofia, June 29–30 and December 18, 2001.

34. Krassen Stanchev, "Will Bulgaria Fall a Victim of Its Democracy?" *Economic Policy Review* (Institute for Market Economics, Sofia) 32 (May–June 2005) (www.ime.bg).

35. Deutsche Welle reported in July 2005 that out of $30 billion worth of assets privatized, only $3 billion went into government revenues. "Bulgarien: Enorme Wirtschaftsschäden durch organisiertes Verbrechen" (Bulgaria: Huge economic damage through organized crime), July 13, 2005.

36. www.transparency.org/surveys/index.html#barometer (accessed September 29, 2005); "Bertelsmann Transformation Index 2006," October 2005, www.bertelsmann-transformation-index.de; World Economic Forum press release, September 29, 2005 (distributed by e-mail); Bulgarian government cull of statistics from Bulgarian Finance Ministry, Bulgarian National Bank, National Statistical Institute, Bulgarian Foreign

Investment Agency, European Commission, Deutsche Bank, Eurostat, the OECD, and the IMF given to the author in Finance Ministry interview, September 2004.

37. Peter Baker, "U.S.-Russian Team Seizes Uranium at Bulgaria Plant," *Washington Post*, December 24, 2003, p. A19 (www.washingtonpost.com); Human Rights Watch, "World Report 2000," section on arms transfers (www.hrw.org); Peter Finn, "With Pain and Hope, Bulgaria Curbs Weapons Trade," *Washington Post*, July 8, 2001, p. A19; Human Rights Watch, "Reforming Bulgaria's Arms Trade: An Update," July 3, 2002; Human Rights Watch, "Bulgaria: Weapons Trade to Be Restrained: Joint Human Rights Watch and Bulgarian Helsinki Committee Statement," July 16, 2002; Human Rights Watch, "Bulgaria Approves Long Awaited Arms Trade Reforms," Monthly Email Update, September 2002; CSD, "Weapons under Scrutiny: Implementing Arms Export Controls and Combating Small Arms Proliferation in Bulgaria" (Sofia, 2004).

38. For a discussion of constitutional issues, see Venelin Ganev, "Bulgaria."

39. One opinion survey conducted by the Bulgarian Helsinki Committee also suggested that some 20 percent of Bulgarians would deny Turks and Roma the right to live in Bulgaria. Deutsche Welle, "Studie belegt interethnische Spannungen in Bulgarien" (Study documents inter-ethnic tensions in Bulgaria), July 21, 2005.

40. Novinite (Bulgarian electronic news service), "Nationalist MP Maverick Moves to Form New Party in Bulgaria," April 20, 2006 (www.novinite.com); Deutsche Welle, "Neue rechtsradikale Gruppierung in Bulgarien" (New radical right group in Bulgaria), February 21, 2006.

41. "Interview with Prime Minister Sergei Stanishev," *Sega*, September 26, 2005 (www.government.bg). See also Albena Shkodrova, "Bulgaria: Socialists Sound New Foreign Policy Note," IWPR, September 30, 2005.

42. Theodor Troev, "Bulgaria to Sack 900 Judicial Staff to Keep EU Entry on Schedule," *Financial Times*, October 4, 2005, p. 2; and Albena Shkodrova, "Bulgaria: Socialists Backtrack over Penal Reform," IWPR, October 21, 2005.

43. Reuters, "Bulgarian Prosecutor Says Faces Political Pressure," *Washington Post*, February 17, 2006.

44. Deutsche Welle, "Bulgarien: Sofias Bürgermeister als politischer Hoffnungsträger" (Bulgaria: Sofia's mayor as political hope), April 27, 2006.

45. Deutsche Welle, "Europäische Verkehrsplanung in der Kritik" (Criticism of European traffic planning), August 18, 2005.

46. Author's conversation in Bucharest; Albena Shkodrova and Marian Chiriac, "Europe Heals Old Divide between Bulgaria and Romania," IWPR, March 23, 2005.

47. The text of the energy treaty is available at www.stabilitypact.org.

48. On crime and justice in general, see also CSD, "Corruption Assessment Report 2003" (Sofia, 2004).

49. Statistics provided by Ognian Shentov, chairman, Center for the Study of Democracy, Sofia.

50. UN Office on Drugs and Crime, "Seventh United Nations Survey of Crime Trends and Operations of Criminal Justice Systems" (2001), covering the period 1998–2000, available at www.nationmaster.com; U.S. statistic provided by Ognian Shentov, CSD. For general crime statistics, see CSD, "Crime Trends in Bulgaria: Police Statistics and Victimization Surveys" (Sofia, 2005).

51. As of late 2005, the killer, the organizers, the intermediaries, and the person who ordered the fatal shooting of former prime minister Andrei Lukanov were serving life

sentences (upheld on appeal), while several dozen suspects were in prison on charges of performing contract killings. Information provided by Ognian Shentov, CSD.

52. Author's interview, Sofia, September 2004.

53. "Top Bulgarian Banker Murdered," *Sofia Echo*, October 31, 2005 (www.sofiaecho.com); Cristi Cretzan, "Crime May Delay Bulgaria EU bid," *Wall Street Journal*, October 28, 2005. Novinite, "Police Check White Audis over Doktora Murder," February 22, 2006.

54. Novinite, "Police Check White Audis over Doktora Murder," February 22, 2006.

55. CSD, "Partners in Crime: The Risks of Symbiosis between the Security Sector and Organized Crime in Southeast Europe" (Sofia, 2004). See also Deutsche Welle, "Bulgarien: Enorme Wirtschaftsschäden durch organisiertes Verbrechen." The CSD's very focused reports on links between criminal activity and the security services cite scattered sources. The center's own analysis is so much more coherent than any of the given sources, however, that I treat the CSD itself as the authoritative source in each case.

56. There is no precise statistical equivalent for the early twenty-first century. New statistics, however, indicate that the crime rate in Bulgaria decreased between 2000 and 2005 as the economy picked up, political stability was established, and institutional capacity increased. In 2004, according to the EU International Crime Survey, the prevalence rate for eleven categories of street crime among citizens older than fifteen years was 12.9 percent in Bulgaria, or better than the 15.6 percent EU average. CSD, "Crime Trends in Bulgaria 2000–2005" (Sofia, 2006).

57. See also CSD, "Smuggling in Southeast Europe" (Sofia, 2002).

58. CSD, "Partners in Crime," p. 41.

59. See also the World Bank's empirical analysis through foreign trade statistics of Bulgaria's structural change, Kaminski and Ng, "Bulgaria's Integration into the Pan-European Economy and Industrial Restructuring," especially pp. 49–50; World Bank, "Entering the Union: European Accession and Capacity-Building Priorities" (February 2006).

60. See Commission of the European Communities, "Comprehensive Monitoring Report on the State of Preparedness for EU Membership of Bulgaria and Romania" (October 25, 2005), especially pp. 3–9; European Commission, "Bulgaria 2005 Comprehensive Monitoring Report" (October 25, 2005), especially pp. 3–25 (both accessed at http://europa.eu.int). For concerns by the European Parliament, the International Monetary Fund, and others about Bulgaria and Romania, see Committee on Foreign Affairs, "European Parliament Resolution on the State of Preparedness for EU Membership of Bulgaria, 2005/2204(INI)," PE 364.917, Texts Adopted at the Sitting of Thursday, December 15, 2005, part 2 (www.europarl.eu.int); International Monetary Fund, "Bulgaria: Report on the Observance of Standards and Codes—Fiscal Transparency Module," Country Report 05/300 (August 2005), especially pp. 23–27 (www.imf.org); CSD, "Corruption and Tax Compliance. Policy and Administration Challenges" (Sofia, 2005); Deutsche Welle, "Bulgarien und Rumänien nehmen Kurs auf Europa" (Bulgaria and Romania set course on Europe), April 25, 2005; Deutsche Welle, "Bulgarien: Mit der Regierungsbildung 'leider viel Zeit vergeudet'" (Bulgaria: "Unfortunately much time squandered" in formation of the government), August 17, 2005.

61. CSD, "Development of the Second National Anti-Corruption Strategy for Bulgaria," Brief 7 (Sofia, January 2006). Other recommendations from Coalition 2000 on such issues as conflict of interest, integrity in public administration, and measures against economic corruption were not followed.

62. Maria Yordanova, "Judicial Reform—State of Play and Opportunities," in CSD, "Judicial Reform: The Prosecution Office and Investigation Authorities in the Context of EU Membership" (2005–06), p. 5; and Novinite, "Bulgaria's MPs Hold On to Limited Immunity" (March 2, 2006). See also the earlier CSD, "Development of the Second National Anti-Corruption Strategy for Bulgaria" (Sofia, 2005).

63. Yordanova, "Judicial Reform," p. 7.

64. For a discussion of how civil society and public-private partnerships can help combat corruption in Bulgaria, see CSD, "Anti-Corruption Reforms in Bulgaria" (Sofia, 2005), especially pp. 105–14.

Notes to Chapter Three

1. Maria Todorova, *Imagining the Balkans* (Oxford University Press, 1997), pp. 3–7, 122, citing the *Oxford English Dictionary* and Agatha Christie in *The Secret of Chimneys* (1925). In fairness to Agatha Christie, as reviewers have pointed out, her English manors also tend to be rather more prone to homicide than is justified by statistics.

2. In the sex trade, the Romanian specialty seems to be making boys available for homosexual encounters, as reflected in websites soliciting customers for sex tours to Bucharest. See Rebecca Surtees, "Second Annual Report on Victims of Trafficking in South-Eastern Europe" (Geneva: International Organization for Migration, 2005), p. 37 (www.iom.int).

3. Irish writer Bram Stoker's popular 1897 yarn about a ghoulish count was an update of the original fifteenth-century rumor mongering by Germans—complete with blood-curdling etchings—about the Wallachian voivode who was trying to tax them. I am indepted to Larry Watts for this point.

4. The Phanariotes and Greek Orthodox hierarchy were at their most powerful within the Ottoman Empire in the eighteenth century. Before 1711, the Romanian nobles in their heartland of the principalities of Moldavia and Wallachia had preserved their autonomy and the right to elect their own hospodars, or princes, by paying tribute to the sultan. After Peter the Great invaded Moldavia and the reigning hospodar defected to the Russians, however, the Porte installed loyal Greek Phanariotes as the hospodars there for the next one hundred years, until the Greek revolution of 1821. L. S. Stavrianos, *The Balkans since 1453* (New York University Press, 2000 [1965]), pp. 270–71.

5. Ibid., p. 346.

6. Author's interviews in Sibiu, September 2004.

7. Author's interview with Johannis, September 2004.

8. Author's interview with Thellman, September 2004.

9. The following summary of Transylvanian history derives from Stavrianos, *The Balkans since 1453*; Keith Hitchins, *The Identity of Romania* (Bucharest: Encyclopaedic Publishing House, 2003); Emil Sigerus and Beatrice Ungar, eds., *Chronik der Stadt Hermannstadt 1100–1929* (Chronicle of the city of Hermannstadt 1100–1929) (Hermannstadt: Honterus, 2000 [1930]); author's interview with Paul Philippi, September 2004; Paul Philippi, "Transylvania—Short History of the Region: The German and Hungarian Minority," *Accent: Community Colleges for Europe* 2 (2003): pp. 25–36 (www.acc.eu.org). Professor Philippi is a pastor, theologian, historian of his native Transylvania, and cofounder of the Democratic Forum of Germans in Romania. He was that organization's first chairman, from 1992 to 1998, and remains chairman emeritus. Toward the end of World War II, as a young Reichswehr soldier, he managed to get from the eastern

front to the western front in order to be captured by the Americans rather than the Russians. He then studied theology and Russian in West Germany in order to return to Romania as an ordained Protestant pastor, but was not allowed by Bucharest to do so until 1979.

10. Stavrianos, *The Balkans since 1453*, pp. 358–63.

11. Philippi, "Transylvania," p. 27.

12. Ibid., p. 31.

13. Hitchins, *The Identity of Romania*, pp. 62–76.

14. Stavrianos, *The Balkans since 1453*, p. 362, giving 1900 census figures. The Saxons numbered 233,000 at that point.

15. Ibid., p. 363.

16. Philippi, "Transylvania," pp. 32–34.

17. Some 200 Romanian soldiers were also killed in repulsing little-publicized attacks by still unidentified parties on arms depots and the Ministry of Defense. Larry L. Watts, "The Crisis in Romanian Civil-Military Relations," *Problems of Post-Communism* (July–August 2001): pp. 14–26, especially pp. 14, 24; Peter Siani-Davies, *The Romanian Revolution of December 1989* (Cornell University Press, 2005).

18. Tom Gallagher, *Theft of a Nation: Romania since Communism* (London: Hurst, 2005), pp. 75-76. See also his chapter, "Building Democracy in Romania: Internal Shortcomings and External Neglect," in *Democratic Consolidation in Eastern Europe*, vol. 2, *International and Transnational Factors*, edited by Jan Zielonka and Alex Pravda (Oxford University Press: 2001), pp. 383–412. For a summary of the coup, see Richard F. Staar, ed., *1990 Yearbook on International Communist Affairs* (Stanford: Hoover Institution Press, 1990), pp. 404–05.

19. Gallagher, *Theft of a Nation*, pp. 82ff.

20. Author's interview, Bucharest. February 2004.

21. Gallagher, *Theft of a Nation*, pp. 77–81.

22. Author's interview, Bucharest.

23. On Iliescu's new image, see J. F. Brown, *Hopes and Shadows: Eastern Europe after Communism* (Duke University Press), p. 96.

24. It was formally called the Party of Social Democracy in Romania (PDSR) from July 1993 until July 2001, and the Social Democratic Party (PSD) thereafter.

25. Gertrud R. Schrieder, Jürgen Munz, and Raimund Jehle, "Rural Regional Development in Transition Economics: The Case of Romania," *Europe-Asia Studies* 52, no. 7 (2000): 1213–235. By 2005 Anneli Gabanyi gave a lower figure for rural dwellers of 33 percent of the population in her "Rumänien vor dem EU-Beitritt" (Romania before EU accession), S 31 (Berlin: German Institute for International and Security Affairs, October 2005), p. 21. On rural underdevelopment, see also Zdenek Lukas and Josef Pöschl, "Landwirtschaft der MOEL im Zeichen des EU-Beitritts" (Agriculture of Central and East European lands in the context of EU entry), *Osteuropa Wirtschaft* 49, no. 3 (September 2004): 211–36.

26. Watts, "The Crisis in Romanian Civil-Military Relations."

27. "CIA Turncoat Sentenced to 23 Years in Prison," CNN, June 5, 1997 (www.cnn.com).

28. Thomas Carothers, *Assessing Democracy Assistance: The Case of Romania* (Washington: Carnegie Endowment for International Peace, 1996), p. 32.

29. Thomas Carothers, *Critical Mission: Essays on Democracy Promotion* (Washington: Carnegie Endowment for International Peace, 2004), pp. 172–73.

30. For this analysis, see Milada Anna Vachudova, *Europe Undivided: Democracy, Leverage, and Integration after Communism* (Oxford University Press, 2005).

31. Alina Mungiu, *Die Rumänen nach '89* (The Romanians after '89) (Bucharest: Inter-Graf, 1995), pp. 275–78.

32. For a comparative exploration of the problems of reformist center-right parties in Central Europe, see Sebastian Lazaroiu, "Have We Really Lost in Romania?" in *Why We Lost: Explaining the Rise and Fall of the Center-Right Parties in Central Europe 1996–2002*, edited by Peter Ucen and Jan Erik Surotchak (Bratislava: International Republic Institute, 2005), pp. 101–18.

33. Romanian Academic Society (SAR, an independent institute), "Tacitly from the Top, Local Governments Will Remain Weak," Policy Warning Report (Bucharest, June 2004) (www.sar.org.ro).

34. Lavinia Stan, "Spies, Files and Lies: Explaining the Failure of Access to Securitate Files," *Communist and Post-Communist Studies* 37 (2004), pp. 341–59. The center-right passed the appropriate legislation in 2000. By then there was ample evidence that many of the secret-police files had been tampered with in the years since 1989 to remove documents incriminating Securitate officials and collaborators and insert new notations implicating political adversaries. What killed the commission that was set up to administer the files, however, was the interest of all the new politicians of the 1990s, from left to right, in keeping their own Communist collaboration from coming to light.

35. See chapter 2.

36. Lavinia Stan and Lucian Turcescu, "The Romanian Orthodox Church and Post-Communist Democratisation," *Europe-Asia Studies* 52, no. 8 (2000): 1467–88, especially p. 1484.

37. Gallagher, *Theft of a Nation*, pp. 166–67.

38. Ibid., p. 173.

39. Polls conducted by the Romanian Academic Society. See also Gallagher, *Theft of a Nation*, pp. 245–46.

40. See Michaela Grün, "Rechtsradikale Massenmobilisierung und 'radikale Kontinuität' in Rumanien" (Mobilization of the radical right and 'radical continuity' in Romania), *Osteuropa* 3 (2002): pp. 293–305.

41. This, indeed, was the thesis of Gallagher's *Theft of a Nation*. Miklos Marschall, Transparency International's European regional director, calls Romania's corruption the worst of any EU member or current candidate. For one example of many newspaper articles about Romanian corruption, see Dan Bilefsky, "Taming Romania's Graft Woes," *Wall Street Journal*, February 2, 2005.

42. Elizabeth Pond, "Romania: Better Late than Never," *Washington Quarterly* 24, no. 2 (Spring 2001): 38.

43. Iliescu saw no such shift and viewed his approach during his two terms in the early 1990s and in the early 2000s as entirely consistent. Author's interview, February 2004. On this point, see Vladimir Tismaneanu, "Romania's First Post-Communist Decade: From Iliescu to Iliescu," *EES News* (Woodrow Wilson International Center for Scholars) (May–June 2001): 1ff; Vladimir Tismaneanu, *Reinventing Politics: Eastern Europe from Stalin to Havel* (New York: Simon and Schuster, 2001).

44. Author's interviews in Bucharest, 2000. See also Tony Judt, "Romania: Bottom of the Heap," *New York Review of Books*, November 1, 2001, pp. 41–45.

45. Author's interview, December 2000.

46. Author's interview, December 2000.

47. Author's interviews, December 2000.

48. Author's interviews; Watts, "The Crisis in Romanian Civil-Military Relations"; survey of Romania in the *Financial Times,* October 3, 2001.

49. For some of the constitutional issues, see Renate Weber, "Constitutionalism as a Vehicle for Democratic Consolidation in Romania," in *Democratic Consolidation in Eastern Europe,* vol. 1, *Institutional Engineering,* edited by Jan Zielonka (Oxford University Press, 2001), pp. 212–42.

50. Transparency International, "Country Report for Romania" (2005 [covering 2004]), pp. 196–99 (www.globalcorruptionreport.org).

51. For a general discussion of this problem in transition countries, where complicated judicial and other institutional reforms are typically addressed much later than simpler macroeconomic reforms, see James H. Anderson and Cheryl W. Gray, "Transforming Judicial Systems in Europe and Central Asia" (World Bank, January 2006), especially p. 11 (http://siteresources.worldbank.org); James H. Anderson, David Bernstein, and Cheryl W. Grey, "Judicial Systems in Transition Economies: Assessing the Past, Looking to the Future" (World Bank, 2005). For specific appraisals of judicial reforms in Romania, see the World Bank's "Project Appraisal Document on a Proposed Loan in the Amount of Euro 110.0 Million (US$130.0 Million Equivalent) to Romania for a Judicial Reform Project" (November 22, 2005) (www.worldbank.org); World Bank, "Romania—Judicial Reform Project" (2005) (www-wds.worldbank.org).

52. For Prime Minister Popescu-Tariceanu's reprimanding of courts for filling their time with low-level cases, see Rompres (Romanian press service), "PM Tariceanu: CSM Does Not Prove Able of Securing Smooth Functioning of Justice," January 10, 2006; Deutsche Welle, "Rumäniens Präsident fordert Justiz zu mehr Verantwortung auf" (Romania's president prods justice to more responsibility), October 26, 2006 (www.dw-world.de). For other discussions of judicial issues, see U.S. State Department, "Romania—Country Reports on Human Rights Practices, 2004" (www.state.gov); Amnesty International, "Bulgaria and Romania: Amnesty International's Human Rights Concerns in the EU Accession Countries" (October 2005) (www.amnesty-eu.org); Radio Romania International, "Controversy in the Romanian Judiciary," January 10, 2006; Romania 1 TV, "Constitutional Court Members' Links with Opposition," November 15, 2005, reported by BBC Monitoring European (accessed January 9, 2006); Mark Percival, "Judicial Reform: An Imperative for the New Government," *Vivid* (December 2004) (www.vivid.ro); BBC Monitoring European, "Romanian Judicial Watchdog Says Premier Did Not Influence Probe into Ally," December 2, 2005. For an analysis that views efforts by the present government to sack some judges more as interference with judicial independence—and its investigations of previous officeholders as a continuation of partisan wrestling—see Gabanyi, "Rumänien vor dem EU-Beitritt," p. 16.

53. Author's interviews.

54. Stefan Wagstyl and Phelim McAleer, "A Place in the Real Economy," *Financial Times,* October 3, 2001, special section on Romania, p. 2.

55. Author's conversation with Ambassador William R. Timken Jr., Berlin, September 2005. In Romania and elsewhere in the Balkans, not the least contribution to economic reform by large multinationals that reject bribes is that they have enough clout to refuse such graft and thus demonstrate that such a stand is possible.

56. "Road to West Remains Rocky, Even without Communists," *Times* (London), December 14, 2004.

57. Stan, "Spies, Files and Lies," p. 345. As a prerequisite for full membership in NATO, Romania also had to persuade U.S. lawmakers to ignore lobbying by U.S. adoption agencies against Bucharest's moratorium on foreign adoptions of orphans. The moratorium followed a report by the European Parliament that condemned as "child trafficking" the practice whereby domestic adoptions were priced out of the range of Romanians, who could not compete with the payment of up to $50,000 a child offered by Americans. See Phelim McAleer and Brendan Hightower, "Romania's Unwanted Babies Threaten Its NATO Bid," *Financial Times*, April 6, 2002; Alison Mutler, "U.S. Congressman to Seek Flexibility in Romanian Adoptions," Associated Press, January 10, 2006; Agence France-Presse, "US Repeats Demand for Romanian Child Adoptions," January 17, 2006.

58. "The Rise of Nearshoring," *Economist*, December 3, 2005, citing Stephen Bullas of eCODE.

59. 2004 rankings, as compiled in 2005. Transparency International, "2004 Corruption Perceptions Index" (www.globalcorruptionreport.org). See also Marian Chiriac, "New Impetus for Romanian War on Corruption," Institute for War and Peace Reporting (IWPR), August 25, 2005 (www.iwpr.net; www.birn.eu.com).

60. See also UN Office on Drugs and Crime, "Seventh United Nations Survey of Crime Trends and Operations of Criminal Justice Systems" (2001), covering the period 1998–2000 (accessed at www.nationmaster.com).

61. Transparency International, "Country Report for Romania," pp. 196–99.

62. SAR, "How to Understand Corruption in Romania," in "Policy Warning and Forecast Report, Elections 2004 Edition" (Bucharest, 2004), p. 1. See also Adrian Savin, "The Political Economy of Corruption in Transition and the Pressure of Globalization," *Romanian Journal of Political Science* 3, no. 1 (Spring 2003): 148–58.

63. Alina Mungiu-Pippidi, "The Coalition for a Clean Parliament," *Journal of Democracy* 16, no. 2 (April 2005): 154–55.

64. Peter Gross and Vladimir Tismaneanu, "The End of Postcommunism in Romania," *Journal of Democracy* 16, no. 2 (April 2005): 157.

65. SAR, "How to Understand Corruption in Romania," pp. 1, 6, 9.

66. Rompres, "Between Opportunity and Experiment," March 14, 2005; Rompres, "Greater Romania Party—2005 Roundup," December 30, 2005. A total of nineteen out of the party's original sixty-nine MPs had jumped ship by the beginning of 2006. See Rompres, "Greater Romania Party Has 19 MPs Less, Out of 69," January 13, 2006.

67. Sources gave the average age variously as forty-four or under forty.

68. Radio Free Europe/Radio Liberty (RFE/RL) Newsline, January 28, 2005 (www.rferl.org).

69. RFE/RL Newsline, January 28, 2005; Bilefsky, "Taming Romania's Graft Woes."

70. European Commission, Directorate General for Economic and Financial Affairs, "European Economy, Progress towards Meeting the Economic Criteria for Accession: 2005 Country Assessment" (Brussels, November 2005), p. 26 (http://europa.eu.int).

71. Agence France-Presse, "OSCE Calls on Romania to Drop Criminal Charges against Two Journalists," March 8, 2006. Basescu also made clear his unhappiness with a flood of media charges against the justice minister and denounced them as attempts to stop investigations of corruption by previous high officials. Deutsche Welle, "Basescu sagt 'Interessensgruppen' den Kampf an" (Basescu announces battle with 'interest groups'), February 2, 2006. For a critical report on restrictions on the media under the Nastase government, see Reporters sans Frontieres, "Caught between Old Habits and Democratic

Strides: Romanian Press at a Crossroads," April 2004; Paul Cristian Radu, Dan Badea, and Sorin Ozon, "The Muzzling of the Romanian Media," IWPR, October 29, 2002.

72. Christopher Condon, "Romania Brings Dracula Castle Saga to Close," *Financial Times*, April 7, 2006, p. 2.

73. Assciated Press, "Romania to Open Archives of Communist-Era Secret Police," February 22, 2006; Floriana Scanteie, "Romania Shines Torch on Communist Crimes," IWPR, January 19, 2006.

74. Deutsche Welle, "Rumänien: Diskussionen um geplante Reform der Geheimdienste" (Romania: Discussions about planned reform of the secret services), February 14, 2006.

75. Author's interviews, 2004, 2005, and 2006.

76. Daniel McLaughlin, "EU Hopefuls Gain in Corruption War," *Irish Times*, April 4, 2006; and Agence France-Presse, "Romanian Officials Charged in Corruption Cases," May 2, 2006; Transparency International Romania, "National Corruption Report" (April 2006) (www.transparency.org.ro).

77. Petra Pinzler, "'Ich will nicht freundlich sein'" ("I don't want to be friendly"), *Die Zeit*, May 11, 2006, p. 13.

78. Associated Press, "Europe's Justice Commissioner Says Lawmakers Risking Romania's EU Integration," March 13, 2006; Agence France-Presse, "Romania Passes Urgent Anti-Corruption Order," March 2, 2006; Christopher Condon, "Romanian Prosecutor Freed from His Political Leash," *Financial Times*, February 23, 2006, p. 2; Marian Chiriac, "EU Focus: Romania Shirks Anti-Graft Law," IWPR, February 16, 2006; Deutsche Welle, "Rückschlag für rumänische Regierung im Kampf gegen Korruption" (Blow for the Romanian government in battle against corruption), February 16, 2006.

79. Christopher Condon and Chris Smyth, "Ex-Romanian PM Quits Posts," *Financial Times*, March 16, 2006. The most embarrassing issue was the official investigation into the Nastase family's declared inheritance from a deceased Georgian aunt of $1 million—including three apartment houses in prime locations in Bucharest. "Ausmisten bei Rumäniens Sozialisten" (Cleaning the stables of Romania's Socialists), *Neue Zürcher Zeitung*, January 17, 2006 (www.nzz.ch); Associated Press, "Leading Romanian Lawmaker to Resign Following Corruption Allegations," March 15, 2006.

80. Rompres, "Romania Renegotiates Contract Concluded with EADS for Securing Borders," November 13, 2005; Rompres, "Contract for Building Transylvania Motorway to Be Published on Thursday," March 20, 2006.

81. For PHARE, see chapter 2, note 24. ISPA is the Instrument for Structural Policies for Pre-Accession; SAPARD, the Special Accession Program for Agriculture and Rural Development.

82. Rompres, "Romania to Benefit from Some 17 Billion Euros Worth of Structural Funds," April 3, 2006.

83. Economist Intelligence Unit, March 18, 2006.

84. George Parker, "Romania Hits Back at French 'Lecturing,'" *Financial Times*, April 19, 2005.

85. The allegations were repeated in June 2006 in a Council of Europe report and again denied by Romania. Council of Europe, Parliamentary Assembly, "Alleged Secret Detentions and Unlawful Inter-state Transfers Involving Council of Europe Member States" (June 7, 2006) (http://assembly.coe.int); BBC, "U.S. Secretary of State Condoleezza Rice Has Signed a Deal," December 6, 2005 (news.bbc.co.uk); Rompres, "Premier Says No Evidence of CIA Prisons, Stopovers in Romania," December 6, 2005; Christopher Condon,

"Romania Welcomes US Presence as a Guarantee of Its Security," *Financial Times*, December 8, 2005; Marian Chiriac, "Romania Investigates CIA Torture Claims," IWPR, December 8, 2005; Nicholas Wood, "No C.I.A. Traces Seen in Romania in Amiable Hunt on an Air Base," *New York Times*, December 9, 2005 (www.nytimes.com); Rompres, "Council of Europe Asks Romania for Info on Alleged CIA Interrogations," January 10, 2006.

Notwithstanding official denials that Romania hosted any CIA prison at the Mihail Kogalniceanu base, Ioan Mircea Pascu, Romania's defense minister 2001–04, told the Associated Press that parts of the base were "off-limits to Romanian authorities." Associated Press, "Former Romanian President Dismisses CIA Prison Allegations as 'Inventions,'" January 10, 2006. The Swiss *SonntagsBlick* of January 8, 2006, cited an Egyptian fax intercepted by Swiss intelligence as saying that the United States had held twenty-three Afghans and Iraqis at a prison in Romania, according to Doreen Carvajal, "Swiss Investigate Leak to Paper on C.I.A. Prisons in Eastern Europe," *International Herald Tribune*, January 12, 2006; and Deutsche Welle, "CIA-Affäre: Rumänisches Parlament Setzt Untersuchungsausschuss ein" (CIA affair: Romanian parliament establishes inquiry committee), January 13, 2006. The issue is a crucial one for Bucharest, since confirmation of the claims could lead to Romania's being barred from EU membership for human rights violations.

86. Radio Romania International, "Romania—A Possible Missile Defense Base?" January 10, 2006 (www.rri.ro).

87. See, for example, Nicholas Whyte, "Comment: In Search of a Solution," IWPR, November 3, 2004; RFE/RL Newsline, December 29, 2005; Mihai-Razvan Ungureanu, "Romania's Priorities in Foreign Policy," *Transatlantic Internationale Politik* 6, no. 2 (Summer 2005): 10–13; Neil Buckley and Sarah Laitner, "Moldova, Russia Fail to End Gas Dispute," *Financial Times*, January 13, 2006; Nicu Popescu, "The Revolutionary Evolution in Moldova," *CEPS Neighbourhood Watch*, no. 3 (April 2005).

88. For a look at the controversy over Budapest's status law, see "Ungarns Status-Gesetz in Kraft getreten" (Hungary's status law enters into force), *Neue Zürcher Zeitung*, January 4, 2002, p. 9.

89. Author's interview, December 2004.

90. Rompres, "Romania Submits to European Parliament an Action Plan to Be Carried Out by April 2006," November 15, 2005.

91. See Commission of the European Communities, "Comprehensive Monitoring Report on the State of Preparedness for EU Membership of Bulgaria and Romania" (October 25, 2005); and European Commission, "Romania 2005 Comprehensive Monitoring Report" (October 25, 2005) (both accessed at http://europa.eu.int). For the concerns of the European Parliament and others about Bulgaria and Romania, see Deutsche Welle, "Bulgarien und Rumänien nehmen Kurs auf Europa" (Bulgaria and Romania set course on Europe), April 25, 2005; European Parliament, "Resolution on the Extent of Romania's Readiness for Accession to the European Union,"2005/2205(INI), (2005), pp. 50–54 (www.europarl.eu.int).

92. Rompres, "We Are Entering the Last Lap of the Race," interview with Anca Boagiu, Minister for European Integration, November 2005.

93. Author's interviews, October 2005.

94. For one challenge to "the widespread belief that in post-Communist societies, once the democratic and market institutions are introduced, the emerging values and beliefs engendered by those very institutions will create the conditions for the consolidation and reproduction of democracy and market economy," see P. D. Aligica, "Operational Codes, Institutional Learning and the Optimistic Model of Post-Communist Social Change:

Conceptual Criticism and Empirical Challenges from a Romanian Case Study," *Communist and Post-Communist Studies* 36 (2003): 87–99.

95. Associated Press, "Hundreds of Agriculture Workers March through Romanian Capital to Demand More State Aid," April 4, 2006.

96. Author's interview, September 2004.

97. Author's interview, September 2004.

98. SAR, "How to Understand Corruption in Romania," pp. 4–10; Alina Mungiu-Pippidi, "Reinventing the Peasants: Local State Capture in Post-Communist Europe," *Romanian Journal of Political Science* 3, no. 2 (Winter 2003): 23–38 (www.sar.org.ro); Alina Mungiu-Pippidi, "Revisiting Fatalistic Political Cultures," *Romanian Journal of Political Science* 3, no. 1 (Spring 2003): 90–121.

Notes to Chapter Four

1. Europol, Annual Reports 2003 and 2004 (www.europol.eu.int). This implies no dearth of criminals of other ethnicities in the Balkans, but reflects the contrast between Albanian gangs, which tend to exclude other nationalities from their ranks, and other Balkan gangs, which are more multiethnic. See European Commission/Council of Europe, CARPO Regional Project, "Situation Report on Organised and Economic Crime in South-eastern Europe" (Strasbourg, August 2005), pp. 46, 53–55, 66, 67. For earlier situation reports, see www.coe.int.

2. Marie-Janine Calic, "Standards and Status," *Transatlantic Internationale Politik* 6, no. 1 (Spring 2005): 80–83.

3. The figure of 80,000 Serbs was given by UNMIK chief Soren Jessen-Petersen in 2006, according to the Public International Law and Policy Group's *Balkan Watch* 8, no. 5 (February 27, 2006) (www.pilpg.org). See also Human Rights Watch, "Federal Republic of Yugoslavia: Abuses against Serbs and Roma in the New Kosovo" (August 1999) (www.hrw.org); International Crisis Group (ICG), *Reality Demands: Documenting Violations of International Humanitarian Law in Kosovo 1999* (Brussels, 2000); Institute for War and Peace Reporting (IWPR), "Comment: Minority Rights Need Protecting," April 14, 2005 (www.iwpr.net). Few issues are more controversial in Kosovo than population figures. The last prewar census, taken in 1991, was boycotted by the Albanians and is deemed unreliable; postwar figures are further complicated by the fact that a majority of Serbs remaining in Kosovo are scattered subsistence farmers and thus likely to escape any count that is not systematic and comprehensive. The figures used in this chapter juggle the prewar population estimates of the Purdue-based Scholars' Initiative Team 1 (see notes to chapter 1); the postwar Serb population estimates of the Berlin-based European Stability Initiative (ESI), as extrapolated from registrations in Serb-language primary schools from the Kosovo Ministry of Education, according to average age distribution; and figures from the Independent International Commission on Kosovo. The Scholars' Initiative puts the total 1991 population at just under 2 million, of which 82 percent were Albanian (about 1.6 million) and 11 percent, Serbs and Montenegrins (about 215,000). In the 1920s the Serb percentage of the population was much higher, at 23 percent, according to Ivo Banac, *The National Question in Yugoslavia: Origins, History, Politics* (Cornell University Press, 1984, 1994), p. 166. The ESI estimates run as high as 130,000 Serbs in today's Kosovo. ESI estimates for Mitrovica's population also differ from the figures that have become conventional wisdom in finding that emigration by both Serbs and Albanians has made Mitrovica's total prewar population of 105,000 shrink to 82,000, with 13,000 Serbs

and Montenegrins (and 2,000 Albanians) in north Mitrovica; and 65,000 Albanians (and 300 Serbs) in south Mitrovica. Melissa Bokovoy and Momcilo Pavlovic, eds., "Kosovo under Autonomy (1974–1990)," Scholar's Initiative papers on Confronting the Yugoslav Controversies, Team 1 (no date, but c. 2005) (www.cla.purdue.edu); European Stability Initiative, "The Lausanne Principle: Multiethnicity, Territory and the Future of Kosovo's Serbs," June 7, 2004 (www.esiweb.org); Independent International Commission on Kosovo, *Kosovo Report* (Oxford University Press, 2000).

4. Walter Zimmermann, *Origins of a Catastrophe* (New York: Times Books, 1996), p. 84.

5. There were also Albanian and Bulgarian vassals who fought on the side of the victorious Sultan Murad I. L. S. Stavrianos, *The Balkans since 1453* (New York University Press, 2000), pp. 44–45.

6. See also Carnegie Endowment for International Peace, *Report of the International Commission to Inquire into the Causes and Conduct of the Balkan Wars* (Washington, 1914).

7. See Noel Malcolm, *Kosovo: A Short History* (New York: HarperCollins, 1999), pp. 253–60. For samples of Serb propaganda portraying Albanians as subhuman, see Banac, *The National Question in Yugoslavia*, pp. 293–97.

8. Miranda Vickers, *The Albanians: A Modern History* (London: I. B. Tauris, 1999), especially pp. 13–97.

9. Louis Sell, *Slobodan Milosevic and the Destruction of Yugoslavia* (Duke University Press, 2002), pp. 74–76; Malcolm, *Kosovo*, pp. 324–28; Misha Glenny, *The Balkans 1804–1999: Nationalism, War and the Great Powers* (London: Granta, 1999), pp. 579–80.

10. See especially the discussion of the Serbian revitalization project in Sabrina Ramet, "The Dissolution of Yugoslavia: Competing Narratives of Resentment and Blame (1986–1991)," Scholars' Initiative papers, Team 2 (no date, c. 2005) (wwww.cla. purdue.edu); Sell, *Slobodan Milosevic*, pp. 44–47; Christopher Cviic, "Kosovo 1945–2005," *International Affairs* 81, no. 4 (July 2005): 851–60; Jasna Dragovic-Soso, *"Saviours of the Nation": Serbia's Intellectual Opposition and the Revival of Nationalism* (London: Hurst, 2002); Bokovoy and Pavlovic, "Kosovo under Autonomy"; Olga Zirojevic, "Das Amselfeld im kollektiven Gedächtnis" (Blackbird Field in collective memory), Marina Blagojevic, "Der Exodus aus dem Kosovo. Ein serbisches Trauma im Propagandakrieg" (The exodus out of Kosovo: a Serb trauma in the propaganda war), and Latinka Perovic, "Flucht vor der Modernisierung" (Flight from modernization), in *Serbiens Weg in den Krieg: Kollektive Erinnerung, nationale Formierung und ideologische Aufrüstung* (Serbia's road to war: Collective memory, national formation, and ideological rearmament), edited by Thomas Bremer, Nebojsa Popov, and Heinz-Günther Stobbe (Berlin: Berlin Verlag, 1998), pp. 45–61, 75–91, and 479–89 respectively.

11. Gow, *The Serbian Project and Its Adversaries: A Strategy of War Crimes* (London: Hurst, 2003) pp. 200–01. The Albanians had only small arms.

12. See "Declaration of the Albanian Political Parties of Kosova," June 30, 1990; Assembly of Kosova, "Constitutional Declaration," July 2, 1990; "Resolution of the Assembly of Kosova," September 7, 1990; "Constitution of the Republic of Kosova," September 7, 1990; "Resolution of the Assembly of the Republic of Kosova on Independence," September 22, 1991; Central Board of Kosova for the Conduct of the Referendum, "Result," October 7, 1991; Coordination Council of Albanian Political Parties in Yugoslavia, "Political Declaration," October 12, 1991; and "Kosova Report: 24 May Multiparty Elections for Parliament and President of Kosova," June 15, 1992, in Marc Weller, ed., *The Crisis in Kosovo*

1989–1999, International Documents and Analysis, vol. 1 (Cambridge: Documents and Analysis Publishing, 1999).

13. Until this pact, the vendettas were killing an estimated 100 Kosovars annually and immobilizing up to 20,000, confined to their houses as their only sanctuary. In the campaign 2,000 families were reconciled. Independent International Commission, *Kosovo Report*, pp. 44–45; IPWR, "Comment: Time to End Destructive Kosovo Clan Warfare," April 20, 2005; Jeton Musliu and Bajram Lani, "Feuds Hold Kosovo Families in Thrall," IWPR, July 14, 2005; Jeta Xharra, Muhamet Hajrullahu, and Arben Salihu, "Investigation: Kosovo's Wild West," IWPR, February 18, 2005.

14. The exception to Western displeasure about Serb conduct in Kosovo was the EU's recognition of the new Federal Republic of Yugoslavia in early 1996 (implicitly acknowledging, according to critics, that Kosovo was part of Serbia)—a move that renewed both transatlantic strains and tensions between the EU and its high representative in Bosnia, Carl Bildt. Sell, *Slobodan Milosevic*, pp. 274–75.

15. Ibid., pp. 279, 284.

16. Gow, *The Serbian Project and Its Adversaries*, pp. 200–05, 258–62. Gow notes that he received confirmation of the earlier Serb military preparation of the ethnic cleansing initiative from "an officer in Belgrade" in October 1997. For the period preceding NATO intervention, see also James Gow and Miroslav Hadzic, eds., "US/NATO Intervention in Kosovo (1998-99)," Scholars' Initiative papers, Team 9 (no date, c. 2005) (www.cla. purdue.edu); Tim Judah, *Kosovo: War and Revenge* (Yale University Press, 2002), pp. 99–254; James Pettifer, *Kosova Express* (University of Wisconsin Press, 2005), pp. 85–240; ICG, *Reality Demands*, pp. 49–135. For UN and other international reports on human rights violations in Kosovo in this period, see Weller, *The Crisis in Kosovo*, pp. 185–238, 250–71.

17. BBC TV, *Fall of Milosevic* (2001), parts 1–3, as cited in Gow and Hadzic, "US/NATO Intervention," p. 15.

18. Sell, *Slobodan Milosevic*, p. 303.

19. For accounts of the diplomacy of the Kosovo war, see Ivo H. Daalder and Michael E. O'Hanlon, *Winning Ugly: NATO's War to Save Kosovo* (Brookings, 2000); John Norris, *Collision Course: NATO, Russia, and Kosovo* (Westport, Conn.: Praeger, 2005); Sell, *Slobodan Milosevic*, pp. 262–306. For documents from the Rambouillet conference and other prewar diplomacy, see Weller, *The Crisis in Kosovo*, pp. 272–495.

20. After a decade underground, Pavkovic appeared at the Hague on April 25, 2005, to face charges of crimes against humanity. In return for his extradition, the EU Council, approved a Feasibility Study putting Serbia on the track to EU membership. Deutsche Welle, "Der EU-Rat" (The EU council), broadcast in Bosnian, April 26, 2005 (www.dw-world.de).

21. Wesley K. Clark, *Waging Modern War* (New York: Public Affairs, 2001), pp. 175–76. For a study of the impact of the American bombing campaign in nudging Germans and other Europeans toward a common European Security and Defense Policy in order to gain more say in the conduct of future NATO interventions, see Günter Joetze, *Der letzte Krieg in Europa? Das Kosovo und die deutsche Politik* (The last war in Europe? Kosovo and German policy) (Munich: DVA, 2001).

22. Author's interview, March 1999.

23. For a broad discussion of the conflict between peace and justice, see Aurélien J. Colson, "The Logic of Peace and the Logic of Justice," *International Relations* 15, no. 1 (April 2000): pp. 51–62.

24. Gow, *The Serbian Project and Its Adversaries*, p. 210.

25. Independent International Commission, *Kosovo Report*, p. 304. The commission's calculation actually puts the percentage of refugees and displaced persons as high as 90 percent of the total Kosovar Albanian population.

26. IWPR, "Investigation: Serbia: More Mackatica Body Burning Revelations," April 20, 2005.

27. Marc Stegherr, "Kosovska Mitrovica—interethnischer Brennpunkt des Kosovo" (Kosovska Mitrovica—interethnic flashpoint of Kosovo), *Südosteuropa Mitteilungen* 45, no. 3 (2005): 72–81.

28. For a discussion of the difference between old "trusteeships" and today's "international administration," see Richard Caplan, *International Governance of War-Torn Territories: Rule and Reconstruction* (Oxford University Press, 2005), pp. 16–21. UNMIK brought together four coprincipals: the European Union, the Organization for Security and Cooperation in Europe (OSCE); the NATO-led Kosovo Force (KFOR), and the United Nations, in the form of its specialized agencies.

29. Gow, *The Serbian Project and Its Adversaries*, p. 260.

30. For an overview of UNMIK and of Albanian violence in this early period (1999–2000), see William G. O'Neill, *Kosovo: An Unfinished Peace* (Boulder, Colo.: Lynne Rienner, 2002). KFOR and the international police did succeed in lowering the rates of reported violent crime significantly from the last half of 1999 to the first half of 2000, from 454 to 146 murders; from 190 to 94 abductions; and from 1,327 to 362 incidents of arson. Independent International Commission, *Kosovo Report*, pp. 107–19. For a discussion of some of the lessons learned in Kosovo about the crucial importance of getting well-armed and well-trained international police into a postconflict zone quickly and coordinating their actions with international military peacekeepers, see Jock Covey, Michael J. Dziedzic, and Leonard R. Hawley, eds., *The Quest for Viable Peace: International Intervention and Strategies for Conflict Transformation* (Washington: U.S. Institute of Peace Press, 2005); Bathsheba Crocker, "Kosovo: Learning to Leverage 'Liberator' Status," *Winning the Peace: An American Strategy for Post-Conflict Reconstruction*, edited by Robert C. Orr (Washington: Center for Strategic and International Studies Press), pp. 193–209.

31. European Stability Iniative, "A Post-Industrial Future? Economy and Society in Mitrovica and Zvecan," Wilton Park Conference, January 30–February 1, 2004 (www.esiweb.org).

32. See, for example, the summary of the desiderata by OSCE High Commissioner on National Minorities Rolf Ekéus, "Establishing a Multi-ethnic Society in Kosovo," *Südosteuropa Mitteilungen* 45, no. 3 (2005): 50–54.

33. For a capsule description of the *kanun* law, see Malcolm, *Kosovo*, pp. 17–21.

34. "Many saw Kosovo as a laboratory to experiment with an ideal society," commented one EU official drily, referring to the 120 pages. Author's interview, April 2005.

35. At least this seemed to be the perception of European diplomats in Kosovo, as reflected in interviews. American diplomats tended to see more transatlantic strains, though their criticisms targeted primarily the status quo bias of laborious European decisionmaking processes rather than substantive policy.

36. Author's interviews in Pristina, February 2005.

37. "Report of the Secretary-General on the United Nations Interim Administration Mission in Kosovo," UNSC S/2004/348, April 30, 2004 (http://daccess-ods.un.org). The twentieth person died of injuries after this report was issued.

38. Exchange with the author in summer 2004. The reply that Washington should indeed have been summoned to court if he had murdered civilians met with incredulity,

especially at a time when revelations about American maltreatment of prisoners in the Abu Ghraib prison in Iraq were making headlines.

39. Author's interviews in Pristina, June and October 2004. See also the excellent ICG reports "Collapse in Kosovo," Europe Report 155 (April 22, 2005), and "Kosovo after Haradinaj," Europe Report 163 (May 26, 2005) (www.crisisgroup.org).

40. Author's interview, June 2005.

41. Kai Eide, "Report on the Situation in Kosovo," November 17, 2004 (http://daccessdds.un.org).

42. Edward Rees, "Public Security Management and Peace Operations. Kosovo and UNMIK: Never Land," in *After Intervention: Public Security Management in Post-Conflict Societies: From Intervention to Sustainable Local Ownership*, edited by Anja H. Ebnöther and Philipp Fluri (Geneva: Geneva Centre for the Democratic Control of Armed Forces, 2005), pp. 199–232 (www.dcaf.ch). Rees, a UN official who at the time was seconded as a security expert to the Kosovar prime minister, sharply criticizes the failure of UNMIK to give Kosovars more "ownership" of policy and institutions. Intriguingly, however, he lauds the high representative's strong hand in Bosnia and praises Paddy Ashdown's "limited foot print and robust executive powers" in Bosnia. This approach "not only provides political space for building 'local ownership' but it retains the powers necessary to remove public officials from office should they be deemed to be undermining the rule of law and thus healthy public security management. Colloquially, OHR [the Office of the High Representative] gives the spoiler 'the rope to hang himself' and the positive agent for change enough room to develop truly sustainable and representative public security management processes and structures" (p. 227).

43. The effectiveness of the boycott was shown on the author's visit to the main polling station in north Mitrovica at 5:00 p.m. on election day. A formidable Serb woman and her colleagues in an otherwise empty corridor pointed the way to a dusty schoolroom where no more than five ballots lay at the bottom of the plasticene ballot box.

44. See the laudations from UNMIK head Soren Jessen-Petersen and KFOR commander Yves de Kermabon on Haradinaj's resignation. Deutsche Welle, "Der ehemalige Kosovo-Premier" (The former Kosovo premier), March 10, 2005.

45. Author's interview, May 2005.

46. For Haradinaj's account of his activities during and after the war, see Bardh Hamzaj, *A Narrative about War and Freedom (Dialog with the commander Ramush Haradinaj)* (Pristina: Zeri, 2000).

47. Hajrullahu and Salihu, "Kosovo's Wild West"; Michael Farquhar, "A Chilling Charge Sheet," IWPR, March 11, 2005.

48. ICTY documents, 14 and 21 October, 2005 (www.un.org/icty); IWPR, "Haradinaj Defence Not Ready for Start of Trial," February 17, 2006; IWPR, "Haradinaj Gets Back into Politics," March 10, 2006. In the only verdict on accused Kosovar Albanians as of this writing, Haradin Balaj was convicted of having run an illegal KLA jail in which inmates were tortured and twenty-four Serbs and Albanians were killed in 1998–99. However, his superiors who stood trial with him, Fatmir Limaj and Isak Musliu, were acquitted for lack of evidence. The case is being appealed by the prosecution. See Michael Farquhar, "Tribunal Stages First Kosovar Trial," IPWR, November 14, 2004; ICTY, Limaj et al., IT-03-66 (www.un.org/icty); Deutsche Welle, "Freisprüche und ein Schuldspruch in Den Haag gegen Kosovo-Albaner" (Acquittals and one conviction in the Hague against Kosovo Albanians), November 30, 2005.

49. UNMIK Media Monitor, "PM Kosumi Visits Serbs in Grace near Vushtrri," August 11, 2005 (www.unmikonline.org).

50. Artan Mustafa, "Kosovars Concerned New Ministries May Be Politicised," IWPR, July 27, 2005.

51. Përparim Isufi, "Serbs Thwart Plan to Reopen Mitrovica Bridge," IWPR, June 30, 2005.

52. "*Zëri* interview with UNMIK Pillar I Head Jean Dussourd," UNMIK press summaries, August 11, 2005 (www.unmikonline).

53. Kai Eide, "A Comprehensive Review of the Situation in Kosovo," October 7, 2005 (http://daccessdds.un.org). For a skeptical academic evaluation of the results of the international community's pouring of twenty-five times more money and fifty times more troops per capita into Kosovo than into Afghanistan after 2002, see Paul E. Williams, "International Peacekeeping: The Challenges of State-building and Regionalization," *International Affairs* 81, no.1 (January 2005): 163–74.

54. Radio Free Europe/Radio Liberty Newsline, December 22, 2005, and February 28, 2006 (www.rferl.org). For the diplomatic fudges involved in the "parallel process" of setting up these ministries and entering status talks, see "UNMIK Press Briefing," June 15, 2005 (www.unmikonline.org). For concerns that the shadowy LDK or PDK intelligence structures might capture these ministries for their respective party's agendas, see Jeta Xharra, "Kosovo's Intelligence Services Come in from the Cold," IWPR, December 23, 2005.

55. European Stability Initiative, "The Lausanne Principle."

56. ICG, "UNMIK's Kosovo Albatross: Tackling Division in Mitrovica," Balkans Report 131 (June 3, 2002); ICG, "Kosovo after Haradinaj"; ICG, "Collapse in Kosovo."

57. "Neuer Chef der Übergangsregierung Kosovos" (New chief of the transitional government), *Neue Zürcher Zeitung*, March 11, 2006 (www.nzz.ch).

58. Author's interviews with German, U.S., and European Commission officials, Berlin, Washington, and Brussels, March, April, May, and June 2005. See also the more diplomatic codification of the "Guiding Principles of the Contact Group for a Settlement of the Status of Kosovo" (November 2005) (www.unosek.org); Dimitrij Rupel, "Completing Kosovo," *Wall Street Journal*, March 11, 2005; Deutsche Welle, "Herbst sollen Gespräche . . . " (Talks should start in fall), March 12, 2005; R. Nicholas Burns, Statement before the House Committee on International Relations, May 18, 2005 (www.state.gov); R. Nicholas Burns, "Ten Years after Dayton: Balkan Stability and the Kosovo Question," Remarks presented at the Woodrow Wilson International Center for Scholars, Washington, May 19, 2005; Michael Schäfer, "Kosovo 2005 aus deutscher Sicht" (Kosovo 2005 in the German view), *Südosteuropa Mitteilungen* 45, no. 3 (2005): 37–49 (received August 2005); Amelia Branczik and William L. Nash, "Forgotten Intervention? What the United States Needs to Do in the Western Balkans," Special Report 8 (Washington: Council on Foreign Relations, June 2005); Edward C. Meyer, chair, and William L. Nash, project director, "Balkans 2010," Report of an Independent Task Force (Council on Foreign Relations, November 2002).

59. Giuliano Amato and others, "The Balkans in Europe's Future" (Sofia, April 2005) (www.balkan-commission.org). See also ICG, "Kosovo: Toward Final Status," Policy Report 161 (January 24, 2005); European Council, "Declaration on Kosovo" in "Luxembourg Presidency Conclusions of the European Council—16–17 June 2005" (June 17, 2005), annex 3, pp. 33–35 (www.eu2005.lu). For a warning against taking any shortcuts

with the conditionality required in Kosovo's Stabilization and Association Process tracking mechanism, see Wim van Meurs, "Kosovo's Fifth Anniversary—On the Road to Nowhere?" CAP Working Paper (Munich: Center for Applied Political Research, March 2004) (www.cap.lmu.de).

60. For an exploration of the specific issue of Mitrovica, see ICG, "Bridging Kosovo's Mitrovica Divide," Europe Report 165 (September 13, 2005).

Notes to Chapter Five

1. Local media estimates of the protest in Split ranged between 40,000 and 100,000. Radio Free Europe/Radio Liberty (RFE/RL) Newsline put the figure at 70,000 (December 12, 2005, www.rferl.org). "Überraschungscoup des Haager Tribunals" (Surprise coup of the Hague tribunal), Neue Zürcher Zeitung, December 9, 2005 (www.nzz.ch); "Kroatien auf europäischem Kurs/Bis jetzt wenig Proteste nach der Verhaftung Gotovinas" (Croatia on European course/Until now few protests against the arrest of Gotovina), Neue Zürcher Zeitung, December 9, 2005; "Demonstrationen für Gotovina in Kroatien" (Demonstrations for Gotovina in Croatia), Neue Zürcher Zeitung, December 12, 2005; "Als Kriegsheld gefeiert, als Kriegsverbrecher gesucht" (Celebrated as war hero, wanted as war criminal), Frankfurter Allgemeine Zeitung, December 9, 2005 (www.faz.net); Marlise Simons, "War Crimes Case Revives Passions in a Torn Croatia," New York Times, December 12, 2005. For a summary article on the threat to Feral Tribune editor Drago Hedl after his reporting on torture and murder of Serb civilians by Croatian forces in Osijek in 1991 and on the continued atmosphere of fear and "lynch justice" there in 2005, see Deutsche Welle, "Morddrohungen gegen kroatischen Journalisten" (Death threats against Croat journalist), December 8, 2005 (www.dw-world.de). For Hedl's accusation that turning Gotovina over to the Hague let Croatia off the hook from pursuing other war criminals below the Hague Tribunal's radar, see Drago Hedl, "Comment: With Gotovina Arrested, Croatia's Soul-Searching Is Over," Institute for War and Peace Reporting (IWPR), December 16, 2005 (www.iwpr.net; http://iwpr.gn.apc.org; www.birn.eu.com).

2. Tudjman is explicitly named in Gotovina's indictment. International Criminal Tribunal for the Former Yugoslavia (ICTY), "Gotovina (IT-01-45) Case Information Sheet" (www.un.org/icty).

3. In particular, Tudjman could claim credit for the gamble that Milosevic's break with Radovan Karadzic—and desire for relief from Western sanctions—had finally gone so far that Milosevic would not send his Serb regulars into Krajina to back up the ethnic Serb territorial forces. See chapter 1; and James Gow, The Serbian Project and Its Adversaries: A Strategy of War Crimes (London: Hurst, 2003), pp. 168–71.

4. See chapter 1. The ICTY indictment refers to "large numbers" made homeless; Serb references generally give the figure as 250,000. The Croatian Helsinki Committee, in a scathing report on the miserable life of Serb refugees from Croatia who were living in temporary quarters in Serbia at the end of 2005 and were still barred from returning, gave the initial figure as 150,000. Deutsche Welle, "Flüchtlingsschicksale zehn Jahre nach Kriegsende in Kroatien" (Refugees' fates ten years after war's end in Croatia), August 3, 2005. The UN High Commission for Refugees estimated that 215,000 refugees from Croatia were still outside the country as of June 2005, according to the International Displacement Monitoring Center, Geneva (www.internal-displacement.org).

5. Ivo Banac, The National Question in Yugoslavia: Origins, History, Politics (Cornell University Press, 1994), p. 62.

6. L. S. Stavrianos, *The Balkans since 1453* (New York University Press, 2000), p. 103.

7. Ibid., p. 233.

8. Banac, *The National Question in Yugoslavia*, especially p. 79.

9. Barbara Jelavich, *History of the Balkans: Twentieth Century* (Cambridge University Press, 1983), p. 10.

10. For summaries of the Balkan Wars and the resulting shift of territories, see Misha Glenny, *The Balkans, 1804–1999: Nationalism, War and the Great Powers* (London: Granta, 1999), pp. 228–48; Stavrianos, *The Balkans since 1453*, pp. 517–43; Jelavich, *History of the Balkans*, pp. 89–105; and Banac, *The National Question in Yugoslavia*, pp. 70–115. For the first comprehensive report on the wars in the Anglo-Saxon world, see the Carnegie Endowment for International Peace, *Report of the International Commission to Inquire into the Causes and Conduct of the Balkan Wars* (Washington, 1914).

11. Banac, *The National Question in Yugoslavia*, pp. 101–02.

12. Jelavich, *History of the Balkans*, p. 152, citing Wayne S. Vucinich; Stavrianos, *The Balkans since 1453*, pp. 624–25.

13. Banac, *The National Question in Yugoslavia*, pp. 170–71.

14. Stavrianos, *The Balkans since 1453*, pp. 485-501; and Glenny, *The Balkans*, pp. 773–80.

15. Dennison Rusinow, *The Yugoslav Experiment 1948–1974* (University of California Press, 1977); Richard Crampton, *The Balkans since the Second World War* (New York: Longman, 2002).

16. Author's interviews; Louis Sell, *Slobodan Milosevic and the Destruction of Yugoslavia* (Duke University Press, 2002); Croatian Lt. Col. Marinko Gorec, paper on the Yugoslav breakup (no title or date) presented at the Hungarian Institute for Strategic Studies and given to the author in February 2005; Ivan Brcic, "Der Zerfall Jugoslawiens aus der Sicht des kroatisch-serbischen Historikerdialogs" (Yugoslavia's disintegration in the view of the Croat-Serb historians' dialogue), *Ost-West Gegeninformationen* 17, no. 4 (2005): pp. 40–43.

17. Author's interview with Ivo Banac, March 2004.

18. Ibid. Nationalist clergy in Mostar also laid architectural claims to their preeminence in that city by building a campanile that rose higher than the tallest municipal minaret and crowning the mountain that dominates Mostar with a gigantic cross.

19. Laura Silber and Alan Little, *Yugoslavia: Death of a Nation* (TV Books, 1995, 1996); Sumantra Bose, *Bosnia after Dayton: Nationalist Partition and International Intervention* (London: Hurst, 2002), pp. 95–148.

20. Gow, *The Serbian Project and Its Adversaries*, pp. 228–36; Silber and Little, *Yugoslavia*, pp. 293–302; Sell, *Slobodan Milosevic*, pp. 238–42; Warren Zimmermann, *Origins of a Catastrophe* (New York: Times Books, 1996), pp. 181–83. For criticism of the Western media's neglect of the Serb refugee tragedy by the British UNPROFOR commander in Bosnia at the time, see General Sir Rupert Smith, *The Utility of Force: The Art of War in the Modern World* (London: Allen Lane, 2005), p. 362.

21. According to Milorad Pupovac, the head of the Serbian National Council in Croatia, some 250,000 remained. Tim Judah, "Croatia Reborn," *New York Review of Books* 47, no 13 (August 2000): 22.

22. Silber and Little, *Yugoslavia*, p. 372.

23. From one of the 830 tapes and 17,000 transcripts that Tudjman made of his conversations in the president's office. The recordings were discovered after his death. Judah, "Croatia Reborn," p. 20.

24. Christopher Cviic, "Throne and Altar in Croatia," *The Tablet*, July 19, 1997 (www.thetablet.co.uk); author's interview with Auxiliary Bishop Pero Sudar, Sarajevo, May 2004.

25. High Representative for Bosnia-Herzegovina Wolfgang Petritsch immediately sacked the ringleader behind the declaration, Ante Jelavic, the Croat member of the federation's tripartite presidency. R. Jeffrey Smith, "Croat Hard-Liners Seek Separation in Bosnia," *Washington Post*, March 4, 2001; and "Schlag gegen die kroatischen Nationalisten in Bosnien" (Blow against Croat nationalists in Bosnia), *Neue Zürcher Zeitung*, March 8, 2001.

26. Interestingly, Croatian prime minister Ivica Racan quietly welcomed the raid and the information the OHR subsequently shared with him about where Croat ultranationalists and organized criminals were getting their money from; author's interview with a senior official in the Office of the High Representative, May 2006. See also International Crisis Group (ICG), "No Early Exit: NATO's Continuing Challenge in Bosnia" (May 22, 2001), pp. 3–7 (www.crisisgroup.org).

27. Sinisa Kusic, "Ende der Warteschleife: Kroatien nach Aufnahme der EU-Beitrittsverhandlungen" (End of the holding pattern: Croatia after the opening of EU accession negotiations), *Südosteuropa Mitteilungen* 46, no. 2 (2006): 34.

28. Sell, *Slobodan Milosevic*, p. 23.

29. "Kroatiens Mühen mit der Vergangenheit" (Croatia's struggles with the past), *Neue Zürcher Zeitung*, December 15, 2000; "Kriegsveteranen protestieren in Kroatien" (War veterans protest in Croatia), *Neue Zürcher Zeitung*, February 12, 2001; "Der kroatische Generalmajor Norac festgenommen" (Croatian major-general Norac arrested), *Neue Zürcher Zeitung*, February 22, 2001; John B. Allcock and others, eds., "The International Criminal Tribunal for the Former Yugoslavia," Scholars' Initiative papers, Team 10 (no date, but c. 2006), p. 78 (www.cla.purdue.edu).

30. Hedl, "With Gotovina Arrested."

31. ICTY, "Gotovina indictment case information sheet."

32. Author's interviews with Western European officials, 2005; see also note 1.

33. "Noch kein heisser Herbst in Kroatien (Not yet a hot fall in Croatia), *Neue Zürcher Zeitung*, October 22, 2001, p. 4.

34. "Mesic warnt vor Isolierung Kroatiens" (Mesic warns against isolating Croatia), *Neue Zürcher Zeitung*, September 27, 2002, p. 6; "Mit Reformdefiziten nach Europa aufbrechen" (Breakthrough to Europe with reform deficits), *Neue Zürcher Zeitung*, February 21, 2004, p. 5.

35. See, for example, Anna McTaggart and Drago Hedl, "Croatia: Work in Progress," IWPR, June 27, 2005; Massimo Moratti, "Comment: Croatian Serbs Await Return of Lost Homes," IWPR, August 4, 2005.

36. Author's interview, March 2004. For one description of the shifts in Croatian reactions to the ICTY's pressure to deliver Gotovina, see Vjeran Pavlakovic, "Heroes, War Criminals and EU Dreams," *EES News* (Woodrow Wilson International Center for Scholars) (March–April 2006): pp. 5–7.

37. "Europäische Dissonanzen wegen Kroatien" (European dissonances over Croatia), *Neue Zürcher Zeitung*, March 9, 2005; "Dämpfer für Kroatiens EU-Ambitionen" (Damper on Croatia's EU ambitions), *Neue Zürcher Zeitung*, March 17, 2005; European Commission, "Opinion on the Application of Croatia for Membership of the European Union" (April 20, 2004) (http://ec.europa.eu/comm).

38. Deutsche Welle, "EU-Beitrittsverhandlungen mit Kroatien liegen weiter auf Eis" (EU entry negotiations with Croatia remain on ice), April 27, 2005; Drago Hedl, "Sanader Isolated as EU Dream Crumbles," IWPR, March 16, 2005.

39. RFE/RL Newsline, November 29, 2004.

40. See chapter 9.

41. Croatia's purchasing power parity in 2004 was €10,290, below Slovenia's €17,580, but almost double Serbian and Bosnian levels and some €3,000 higher than Romanian and Bulgarian levels, according to data released by the Vienna Institute for International Economic Studies in December 2005 (www.wiiw.ac.at).

42. Deutsche Welle, "Ein Schock für Zagreb?" (A shock for Zagreb?), April 21, 2005; Deutsche Welle, "Gestoppte Beitrittsverhandlungen: Neue Chance für Kroatien" (Stopped entry negotiations: New chance for Croatia), March 24, 2005.

43. The dispute about the Adriatic Piran Bay was hot enough to raise fears in Zagreb that Slovenia might veto Croatian EU membership unless Zagreb acquiesced in Slovenian claims to the whole bay. See "Kroatisch-slowenischer Dauerstreit um Piran" (Ongoing Croatian-Slovenian dispute over Piran), *Neue Zürcher Zeitung*, January 10, 2006; "Neues Kapitel im Streit um die kroatisch-slowenische Grenze" (New chapter in fight over the Croatian-Slovenian border), *Neue Zürcher Zeitung*, June 21, 2006.

44. Drago Hedl, "EU Focus: Sanader's Belgrade Overture Aimed at Impressing Brussels," IWPR, November 19, 2004; "Belgrad und Zagreb für weitere Annäherung" (Belgrade and Zagreb for further rapprochement), *Neue Zürcher Zeitung*, July 8, 2005.

45. Deutsche Welle, "Kroatien und Serbien-Montenegro verstärken regionale Kooperation" (Croatia and Serbia-Montenegro strengthen regional cooperation), April 19, 2006.

46. "Belgrad und Zagreb für Weitere Annäherung."

47. Deutsche Welle, "Erster Besuch eines serbischen Ministerpräsidenten in Zagreb" (First visit of a Serbian prime minister in Zagreb), November 24, 2005; Moratti, "Comment: Croatian Serbs Await Return of Lost Homes."

48. RFE/RL Newsline, November 29, 2004; "Kroatiens allseits beliebte Kontrollinstanz" (Croatia's universally beloved court of appeal), *Neue Zürcher Zeitung*, January 16, 2005.

49. Author's interview, March 2004; Drago Hedl, "Croatia: Far Right 'Punishes' Sanader," IWPR, January 14, 2005.

50. This accusation was made by Antun Vrdoljak, a member of the International Olympics Committee, in refusing, should Croatia make it to the handball finals, to give the president a ticket to see them. Deutsche Welle, "Kroatisches IOC-Mitglied" (Croatia's IOC member), August 25, 2004.

51. RFE/RL Newsline, January 21, 2005.

52. See chapters 7 and 9.

53. Figures are from Zagreb's PULS institute. Deutsche Welle, "Mehrheit der Kroaten ist gegen EU-Beitritt" (A majority of Croats is against EU accession), September 8, 2005.

54. Patrick Moore, "Hague Prosecutor Says Vatican Is Shielding Top War Crimes Fugitive," RFE/RL Newsline, September 21, 2005; Deutsche Welle, "Kroatien weist Vorwürfe Del Pontes zurück" (Croatia rejects Del Ponte's reproaches), September 21, 2005.

55. "Kroatiens 'europäische Werte'" (Croatia's 'European values'"), *Neue Zürcher Zeitung*, October 5, 2005; "Hungarian Line on Croatia Riles EU Partners," IWPR, April 27, 2005; ICTY, "ICTY Prosecutor's Assessment of the Cooperation Provided by Croatia to the ICTY," Press Release JP/MO/1009e (October 3, 2005) (www.un.org/icty).

56. Author's interview with West European diplomat, October 2005.

57. RFE/RL Newsline, September 16, 2005; Deutsche Welle, "Kroatien: Kriegsverbrecherprozess erneut aufgerollt" (Croatia: war crimes trial rolled out anew), September 14, 2005; Deutsche Welle, "Urteil in umstrittenem Kriegsverbrecherprozess in Kroatien gefällt" (Verdict rendered in controversial war crimes trial in Croatia), March 3, 2006.

58. Deutsche Welle, "Ein Bonbon aus Brüssel zum Dayton-Jahrestag" (A bonbon from Brussels on the anniversary of Dayton), November 24, 2005; see also chapter 6.

59. ICTY, "Rahim Ademi and Mirko Norac Case Transferred to Croatia," Press Release (November 1, 2005) (www.un.org/icty).

60. The very well connected Neue Zürcher Zeitung concluded, for example: "According to our information, Croatia's authorities, under international pressure, made comprehensive documents available to the Hague Tribunal." "Demonstrationen für Gotovina in Kroatien" (Demonstrations for Gotovina in Croatia), Neue Zürcher Zeitung, December 11, 2005; see also "Gotovina an Den Haag ausgeliefert" (Gotovina extradited to the Hague), Neue Zürcher Zeitung, December 10, 2005.

61. Allcock and others, "The International Criminal Tribunal for the Former Yugoslavia."

62. dpa (German Press Agency), "Die sechs Flüchtigen" (The six fugitives), Frankfurter Allgemeine Zeitung, December 18, 2005.

Notes to Chapter Six

1. Statistics from the Office of the High Representative (OHR) give the percentages for the 2005 OHR budget of €16.9 million and the 2006 budget of €13.8 million as follows: EU 53 percent; United States 22 percent; Japan 10 percent; Russia 4 percent; Canada 3.03 percent; and other 8 percent. Office of the High Representative, "General Information" (Sarajevo, September 2005 and March 2006) (www.ohr.int).

2. Bosnians "trust the U.S. in a way they don't trust Europe. Unfairly!" explained Paddy Ashdown in an interview with the author in November 2003. See also International Crisis Group (ICG), "EUFOR: Changing Bosnia's Security Arrangements," Europe Briefing 31 (June 29, 2004) (www.crisisgroup.org). The senior U.S. commander in country is a one-star general, with a core of 250 U.S. forces in Sarajevo and Eagle Base in the north. The senior commander of the European Union Forces (EUFOR) is a two-star general.

3. Terminology in Bosnia is even more confusing than elsewhere in the Balkans. I generally use "Bosnia-Herzegovina" rather than the official name, Bosnia and Herzegovina, to refer to the state, in order to distinguish it from "Bosnia" and "Herzegovina" as two distinct geographical areas in the Federation. I use the even shorter form "Bosnia" for the whole country when the context makes it clear that Herzegovina and the Republika Srpska are included. In conformity with local usage, I generally use "Muslim" before the war, "Bosniak" after the war to identify those who consider themselves culturally Muslim in Bosnia. "Bosnian" refers to any citizen of Bosnia-Herzegovina, of whatever ethnicity. See also Introduction, note 10.

4. Radio Free Europe/Radio Liberty (RFE/RL) Newsline, February 28, 2005 (www.rferl.org); Nerma Jelacic, "Bosnian Court Issues Srebrenica 'Road of Death' Charges," Institute for War and Peace Reporting (IWPR) (www.iwpr.net; http://iwpr.gn.apc.org; www.birn.eu.com), December 23, 2005; Nidzara Ahmetasevic, "Lost in Translation," IWPR, March 31, 2006 (accessed at http://engl.bim.ba). For troubled parallel attempts to

form a nonjudicial "truth commission," see Nerma Jelacic and Nidzara Ahmetasevic, "Truth Commission Divides Bosnia," IWPR, March 31, 2006.

5. "Bosnier einig über Verfassungsreform" (Bosnians agree on constitutional reform), *Frankfurter Allgemeine Zeitung*, March 20, 2006, p. 6.

6. The $4.5 billion figure is from James F. Dobbins, "America's Role in Nation-Building: From Germany to Iraq," *Survival* 45, no. 4 (Winter 2003–04): 96. See also the longer original, James F. Dobbins and others, *America's Role in Nation-Building: From Germany to Iraq* (Santa Monica: RAND, 2003).

7. Estimates supplied by Mirza Hajric, as extrapolated from the UN High Commission for Refugees' statistics on returns and on voting registration; and for the Federation, based on the number of votes for the Serb nationalist SDS (Serbian Democratic Party), which only Serbs would vote for. There has been no census since the war. See also notes 29 and 32.

8. The UN International Police Task Force (IPTF) and its successor EU Police Mission (EUPM) were unarmed and had no law enforcement authority; their tasks included the key design of a single state-level police force, but they had no operational mandate and could only train, monitor, and to a certain extent vet the existing police forces in Bosnia. Because of the failure of the IPTF to carry out a sufficiently rigorous purge of local police who were taking bribes or acting as a network of support for war crimes indictees, the later mandate for the international police in Kosovo for the first time gave them full interim responsibility for law enforcement. See the ICG's scathing report, "Policing the Police in Bosnia: A Further Reform Agenda," May 10, 2002; Hugh Griffiths and Nerma Jelacic, "Investigation: Will Europe Take on Bosnia's Mafia?" Institute for War and Peace Reporting (IWPR), December 2, 2004; James Lyon, "EU's Bosnia Police Mission Is 'Laughing Stock,'" *European Voice*, July 25, 2006 (accessed at www.crisisgroup.org); Aida Sunje and Ilda Zornic, "Bosnia Sex Traffickers Corner New Markets," IWPR, July 22, 2005.

9. Quoted in Daniel Dombey, "Europe's Growing Pains," *Financial Times*, September 3, 2005, p. W2.

10. The most vocal critic in this vein has been the European Stability Initiative (ESI), a nongovernmental organization based in Berlin and Istanbul. See, for example, European Stability Initiative, "Post-Industrial Society and the Authoritarian Temptation" (October 11, 2004) (www.esiweb.org); ESI, "Waiting for a Miracle? The Politics of Constitutional Change in Bosnia and Herzegovina" (February 3, 2004); ESI, "After the Bonn Powers—Open Letter to Lord Ashdown" (July 16, 2003); Gerald Knaus and Felix Martin, "Lessons from Bosnia: Travails of the European Raj," *Journal of Democracy* 14, no. 3 (July 3, 2003). See also the debate between Gerald Knaus and Nicholas Whyte on "Does the International Presence in the Balkans Require Radical Restructuring?" *NATO Review* (Winter 2004) (www.nato.int); ICG, "Bosnia's Brcko: Getting In, Getting On and Getting Out" (June 2, 2003); and Nerma Jelacic, "Comment: Bosnia's Hollywood State," IWPR, December 21, 2005.

11. Author's interview, December 2004. For a concise list of accomplishments in Brcko, see also William Sommers, "Brcko District: Experiment to Experience," paper prepared for the tenth annual conference of the NISPAcee, Krakow, Poland, April 25–27, 2002 (http://unpan1.un.org).

12. The word *Damjanac* used in Serbo-Croatian, as he would probably still call the language, means literally nation or people and refers to the distinction between Serbs, Croats, and Bosniaks. When I quote Serbs, Bosniaks, or Croats, I use the terms they use. See also note 3 above.

13. James Gow, *The Serbian Project and Its Adversaries: A Strategy of War Crimes* (London: Hurst, 2003), pp. 123–25.

14. Ibid., pp. 148–151.

15. Ibid., p. 122. This document was a key exhibit of the prosecution in the trials of Dusan Tadic and Zejnil Delalic before the International Criminal Tribunal for the Former Yugoslavia (ICTY).

16. Chuck Sudetic, *Blood and Vengeance* (New York: Penguin, 1999), p. 96; Gow, *The Serbian Project and Its Adversaries*, pp. 128–31, 174.

17. Gow, *The Serbian Project and Its Adversaries*, pp. 130, 131, 174, 179.

18. Tim Judah, *The Serbs* (Yale University Press, 1997), p. 233.

19. Official statistics from the city of Brcko.

20. Laura Silber and Alan Little, *Yugoslavia: Death of a Nation* (TV Books, 1995, 1996), p. 256; Gow, *The Serbian Project and Its Adversaries*, p. 179.

21. Richard Holbrooke, *To End a War* (Random House, 1998), pp. 304–09.

22. Official statistics from the city of Brcko.

23. For one description of the Arizona Market in its seedier heyday, see Nidzara Ahmetasevic, "Thousands of Women Lured into Bosnian Brothels," IWPR, April 18, 2002.

24. Author's interviews, Brcko, May and December 2004. See also Brcko Law Revision Commission, "Chairman's Final Report," December 31, 2001 (accessed at www.esiweb.org).

25. The backlog was and is a serious problem in Bosnia, with delays in trials ranging from six months up to ten years. For an overview of the national program and some criticism of excessive micromanagement by internationals, see Aida Alic, Aida Sunje, and Hugh Griffiths, "Courting Controversy in Bosnia," IWPR, June 27, 2005. For criticism of plea bargaining, see Nerma Jelacic and Hugh Griffiths, "Bosnia: Mafia Prosecutors under Fire," IWPR, February 18, 2005.

26. Author's interview with Studen, May 2004.

27. The Croatian commander who ordered the bombardment (but denies having done so), Slobodan Praljak, was indicted by the ICTY, went to the Hague voluntarily, and was released pending trial. International Criminal Tribunal for the Former Yugoslavia, "Indictments and Proceedings" (www.un.org/icty); Gow, *The Serbian Project and Its Adversaries*, p. 69.

28. Emily Gunzburger Makas, "Representing Competing Entities in Postwar Mostar," *EES News* (Woodrow Wilson International Center for Scholars) (January–February 2006): 3.

29. ICG, "Implementing Equality: The 'Constituent Peoples' Decision in Bosnia and Herzegovina," Europe Report 128 (April 16, 2002). See also notes 7 and 32.

30. Carl Bildt, *Peace Journey: The Struggle for Peace in Bosnia* (London: Weidenfeld and Nicolson, 1998), pp. 172–74.

31. The film, directed by Pjer Žalica, in literal English translation *Fuse*, won prizes in Sarajevo, Zagreb, Marrakech, and Locarno in 2003.

32. See notes 7 and 29. Some statistics reported by the Helsinki Committee of Bosnia and Herzegovina, "Report on the Status of Human Rights in Bosnia and Herzegovina (Analysis for Period January–December 2004)," apparently issued in January 2005 (www.bh-hchr.org) seem to be unreliable. The report states that every municipality in the country except for Tuzla (near Brcko) now has a higher than 90 percent majority of one ethnicity, but this overlooks at least Brcko (40 percent Bosniak, 40 percent Serb, 20 percent Croat)

and Mostar (47 percent, 3 percent, 48 percent, respectively) and exaggerates the statistics for even largely monoethnic Sarajevo (77 percent, 12 percent, 8 percent, respectively).

33. Richard Holbrooke, and also Michael Dziedzic and Andrew Bair, maintained that *Serb* thugs terrorized their compatriots into leaving the city and burned their apartments, apparently out of anger that the RS was awarded only a tiny sliver of the capital. Carl Bildt, by contrast, blamed the Serb exodus much more on deliberately intimidating searches by Bosniak security forces as they took control of the ethnically Serb suburbs. Asked about the discrepancy, Bildt said, "I was there; Holbrooke was in Washington." He added that the Serb exodus followed from the "fear factor" following Bosniak intimidation in a few streets, and that in the later stages Serb enforcers did put pressure on Serbs to leave, perhaps out of "despair." Holbrooke, *To End a War*, pp. 335–37; Michael J. Dziedzic and Andrew Bair, "Bosnia and the International Police Task Force," in *Policing the New World Disorder: Peace Operations and Public Security*, edited by Robert B. Oakley, Michael J. Dziedzic, and Eliot M. Goldberg (Washington: National Defense University Press, 1998), pp. 253–314; Bildt, *Peace Journey*, pp. 193–97; and author's conversation with Bildt, Washington, May 23, 2006. Anecdotally, one lifelong Sarajevo Croat married to a Sarajevo Serb (both of whom remained in the city throughout the siege) backed Bildt's version.

34. ICG, "Too Little Too Late: Implementation of the Sarajevo Declaration," ICG, 9 (September 9, 1998); Holbrooke, *To End a War*, pp. 335–37.

35. OHR, Sarajevo, "Sarajevo Declaration," February 3, 1998 (www.ohr.int).

36. Author's interview, October 2005.

37. The other million refugees have largely resettled elsewhere, though some are still in refugee camps.

38. Author's interview with Ashdown, November 2003.

39. On the expulsion of Iranians and mujahideen, see Holbrooke, *To End a War*, pp. 319, 320, 334. For discussion of the information about the foreign fighters that came out at the Hague Tribunal, see Beth Kampschror, "Bosnia Charges Alleged Mujahedin," IWPR, September 17, 2004; Michael Farquhar, "Mujahedin 'Disrupted' Bosnian Military," 29 October 29, 2004; Michael Farquhar, "Bosnians' 'Tense' Dealings with Mujahedin," IWPR, November 5, 2004; ICG, "Bin Laden and the Balkans: The Politics of Anti-Terrorism" (November 9, 2001).

40. For the lack of the four essential freedoms—speech, movement, assembly, and media—in the 1996 election, see Noel Malcolm, "Observations on the Bosnian Elections (14 September 1996) and on the Post-Electoral Situation," no date but apparently late October 1996 (www.barnsdle.demon.co.uk).

41. See Richard Holbrooke, *To End a War*, especially pp. 327–29, 336–40. In later, informal comments Holbrooke was more biting in his portrayal of Smith, saying that Bill Clinton, after he left the White House, called Smith's conduct insubordination. At issue, according to Holbrooke, was Smith's conflation of his narrower specific orders and his broader authority, along with the military's exaggerated awe of Serb warriors, famous for tying down 300,000 Nazi German troops in World War II.

42. Here, too, the accounts of Holbrooke and Bildt diverge sharply. Holbrooke attributed Karadzic's departure from public life to Holbrooke's personal intervention with Milosevic. Bildt attributed it to his own previous two months of dogged maneuvering. See Holbrooke, *To End a War*, p. 342, 343; BBC, "'War Criminal' Karadzic Resigns," July 19, 1996 (news.bbc.co.uk); and Bildt, *Peace Journey*, pp. 209–39.

43. For a political evaluation of the RS in the period of hope for liberalization after the 2000 statewide elections, see ICG Balkans Report 118 (October 8, 2001).

44. ICG, "Implementing Equality"; Alic, Sunje, and Griffiths, "Courting Controversy in Bosnia"; and the English summary of the decision and opinions on the Constitutional Court's website, www.ccbh.ba, under Saturday, July 1, 2000.

45. For the relationship between the bank and the HDZ's challenge to the authority of Bosnia-Herzegovina, see ICG, "Turning Strife to Advantage: A Blueprint to Integrate the Croats in Bosnia and Herzegovina," Balkans Report 106, March 20, 2001.

46. See, for example, ICG, "Bosnia's Alliance for (Smallish) Change," Europe Report 132 (August 2, 2002).

47. Author's interviews in Sarajevo, November 2002, November 2003, May and December 2004.

48. For the wave of international pessimism that the 2002 election set off, see especially William Pfaff's recommendation to give up on multiethnicity and simply partition Bosnia in his "Time to Concede Defeat in Bosnia-Herzegovina," *International Herald Tribune*, October 10, 2002; and Paddy Ashdown's rebuttal in his "Peacemaking in Bosnia," *International Herald Tribune*, October 16, 2002.

49. See ESI, "After the Bonn Powers"; Knaus and Martin, "Lessons from Bosnia."

50. Author's interviews in Sarajevo, November 2002 and 2003. For a retrospective summary of the affair, see also Deutsche Welle, "Prozess um Verstoß gegen Waffenembargo wird neu verhandelt" (Trial on breaching of weapons embargo is being renegotiated" (www.dw-world.de).

51. See ESI, "After the Bonn Powers"; Knaus and Martin, "Lessons from Bosnia."

52. Author's interview with Michael J. Dziedzic, May 2005. For a general discussion of the common problem of civilian administrators' lack of access to intelligence in postwar international interventions, see Jock Covey, Michael J. Dziedzic, and Leonard R. Hawley, eds., *The Quest for Viable Peace* (Washington: U.S. Institute of Peace Press, 2005).

53. The international police in Bosnia-Herzegovina, unlike the international police in Kosovo, essentially had no executive authority of their own. Author's interviews in Sarajevo, Washington, and Berlin, 2002, 2003, and 2004. See also ICG, "Policing the Police in Bosnia"; Lyon, "EU's Bosnia Police Mission"; Richard Caplan, *International Governance of War-Torn Territories* (Oxford University Press, 2005), especially pp. 45–67; Covey, Dziedzic, and Hawley, *The Quest for Viable Peace,* p. 162; Griffiths and Jelacic, "Will Europe Take on Bosnia's Mafia?" For a more sympathetic assessment of accomplishments of the International Police Task Force and the EU Police Mission, see Dziedzic and Bair, "Bosnia and the International Police Task Force"; Dominique Wisler, "The Police Reform in Bosnia and Herzegovina," in *After Intervention: Public Security Management in Post-Conflict Societies: From Intervention to Sustainable Local Ownership,* edited by Anja H. Ebnöther and Philipp Fluri (Geneva: Geneva Centre for the Democratic Control of Armed Forces, 2005), pp. 139–60. For the EU Police Mission's own summary of its mandate, the first commissioned under the EU's common European Security and Defense Policy, see "Fact Sheet" at www.eupm.org (accessed December 4, 2005). A Multilateral Specialized Unit, consisting primarily of Italian carabinieri, also operated in Bosnia from August 1998 to January 1999 to facilitate refugee return and to counter organized crime and terrorism.

54. Author's interviews, Sarajevo, November 2003.

55. Author's interviews with Zhivko Radisic, Branko Neskovic, Milos Solaja, and Zjelko Kopanja in Banja Luka, December 2004.

56. Author's interview in Bosnia, December 2004 (poll results were given orally). See also BBC, "The Hunt for Mladic and Karadzic," July 25, 2006; Deutsche Welle, "Hoffnungen und Spekulationen nach Fernseh-Appell an Karadzic," (Hopes and speculation after TV appeal to Karadzic), August 1, 2005.

57. Author's interview, October 2005.

58. Gordana Katana, "Bosnia: Serbs Threaten Constitutional Crisis," IWPR, July 15, 2004; Nicholas Wood, "60 Bosnian Serbs Dismissed for Aid to War Crimes Figure," *New York Times*, July 1, 2004; "Harter Schlag gegen Karadzics Umfeld" (Hard blow against Karadzic's supporters), *Neue Zürcher Zeitung*, July 1, 2004 (www/nzz/ch).

59. In the official rhetoric, reconstruction of the bridge was portrayed as a symbol of ethnic reconciliation. More realistically, Emily Gunzburger Makas, a doctoral candidate in architectural history and urbanism at Cornell University, saw the bridge, as well as the huge cross on top of Hum Hill and the bell tower of the Franciscan Church in the center of town as confirmation of the divisions. See the summary of her presentation at the Woodrow Wilson International Center for Scholars in Washington on November 16, 2005, "Representing Competing Entities in Postwar Mostar," *EES News* (January–February 2006): 1–4. For other accounts, see Michael Ignatieff, "When a Bridge Is Not a Bridge," *New York Times*, October 27, 2002; Richard Bernstein, "Bridge Is Restored in Bosnia, and With It Hope of Peace," *New York Times*, July 24, 2004: Andrew Herscher, "Remembering and Rebuilding in Bosnia," *Transitions* 5, no. 3 (March 1998) (www.haverford.edu).

60. For the RS apology, see Nicholas Wood, "Bosnian Serbs Apologize for Srebrenica Massacre," *New York Times*, November 11, 2004. For the list of names, see "Licht auf Srebrenicas Schatten" (Light on Srebrenica's shadows), *Neue Zürcher Zeitung*, October 6, 2005. One European who closely followed the formation of the commission and the writing of the report explained that it was set up after the families of those killed at Srebrenica won a ruling from the Bosnia-Herzegovina Human Rights Court that they were entitled to be given information about their missing husbands and fathers—and after an earlier, official RS report turned out to have no investigation behind it, but to have been lifted wholesale from a pro-Milosevic Serb website in Canada. The RS stonewalled until the OHR threatened sanctions unless a commission was set up—and imposed the Bosniak academic commissioners, while vetoing politicians as the Serb participants. Initially, the Serb judges and prosecutors on the panel expected that their findings would show how victimized the Serbs had been; one of the judges argued at the beginning that this was a chance to show that not as many Bosniaks had died as the Bosniaks were claiming. The investigation proved otherwise, however. See also "Rätsel um Vollständigkeit des vom ICTY angeforderten Beweismaterials" (Puzzle about completeness of the evidence demanded by the ICTY), *Neue Zürcher Zeitung*, October 7, 2004; RFE/RL Newsline, October 15, 2004; Wood, "Bosnian Serbs Apologize for Srebrenica Massacre."

61. RFE/RL Newsline, November 30, 2004.

62. Author's interview with Jacob Finci, November 2003. See also RFE/RL Newsline, October 14, 2004.

63. See ICG, "EUFOR." On the question of the current risk of Islamist extremism, information is murky. The tenor of most of my interviews in Bosnia has been that Bosnia's tolerant Ottoman strain of Islam does not lend itself easily to extremism, and that the Reis-ul-ulema, Dr. Mustafa ef. Ceric, educated in Cairo and at the University of Chicago, has managed to curtail the influence of the new Saudi-built Wahhabi mosque in Sarajevo and of the few younger Bosniak imams who have studied in more radical madrassas abroad rather than in more traditional Cairo. EUFOR commander General David Leakey

has stated that there are no terrorist training camps in Bosnia; RFE/RL Newsline, August 24, 2005. See, however, reporting by Esad Hecimovic on terrorist infiltration in Zenica's weekly *Dani*; and Jaroslav Trofimov's interviews with several fundamentalists in *Faith at War: A Journey on the Frontlines of Islam* (New York: Henry Holt, 2005), pp. 271–96. Various Serb reports of a jihadi threat should perhaps be taken with some skepticism because of the Serb interest in tarring the Bosniaks with this brush; after the Madrid bombings in 2004, RS police chief Dragomir Andan announced that the explosives had been prepared in Bosnia, only to retract the charge when Western officials asked him for evidence. For skepticism about Serb claims, see ICG, "Bin Laden and the Balkans: The Politics of Anti-Terrorism," Balkans Report 119 (November 9, 2001). For greater concern about Bosnia's possible use as a safe haven for the preparation of Islamist bombings by Bosniaks radicalized in Muslim communities in Scandinavia or elsewhere in Western Europe, see Nicholas Wood, "Police Raid Raises Fears of Bosnia as Haven for Terrorists," *New York Times*, December 3, 2005. Moreover, despite Bosniak enthusiasm for Americans, some soccer fans—the foot soldiers of nationalism in the Balkans—have begun chanting "al Qaeda" and "bin Laden" along with "kill the Serb" as they physically assault visiting Serb teams; "Broke Coach's Nose, Cheered al Qaeda," *Podgorica Dan* (Montenegro), December 2, 2005.

64. ICG, "Bosnia's Stalled Police Reform: No Progress, No EU," Europe Report 164 (September 6, 2005), p. 8.

65. David Munk, "Ashdown Orders New Crackdown in Bosnia," *The Guardian*, December 17, 2004.

66. ICG, "Bosnia's Stalled Police Reform," p. 4.

67. According to the EU Police Mission's description of SIPA (www.eupm.org).

68. RFE/RL Newsline, January 4, 2005, and February 15, 2006.

69. Deutsche Welle, "Ein Etat statt drei" (One budget instead of three), January 9, 2005.

70. ICTY, "Key Figures" (www.un.org/icty).

71. See Deutsche Welle, "Sonder-Strafkammer für Kriegsverbrechen in Sarajewo" (Special chamber for war crimes in Sarajevo), March 2, 2005; Alison Freebairn and Nerma Jelacic, "Bringing War Crimes Justice Back Home," IWPR, November 27, 2004; IWPR, "Press Release: IWPR War Crimes Symposium," March 11, 2005; Nerma Jelacic and Hugh Griffiths, "Investigation: Justice Yet to Be Done," IWPR, March 11, 2005. The War Crimes Chamber had a hybrid local and international bench, with foreigners scheduled to phase out within a few years.

72. RFE/RL Newsline, March 22, 2005.

73. Deutsche Welle, "Korrupte Politiker im Visier der bosnischen Justiz" (Corrupt politician in the crosshairs of Bosnian justice), October 11, 2005; RFE/RL Newsline, June 6, 2005.

74. Deutsche Welle, "Auf dem Weg zur gemeinsamen Armee in Bosnien-Herzegowina," (On the way to a common army in Bosnia-Herzegovina), July 18, 2005.

75. See chapter 9. For a rather upbeat assessment of progress in Bosnia-Herzegovina at this point, see Roland Schönfeld, "Bosnien-Herzegowina zwischen Nachkrieg und Selbstverantwortung" (Bosnia-Herzegovina between postwar state and responsibility), *Südosteuropa Mitteilungen* 45, no. 1 (2005): 26–41.

76. ICTY, "Key Figures" and "Jankovic *et al.* (IT-96-23/2) 'Foca'" (www.un.org/icty)

77. See chapter 9.

78. See Nerma Jelacic, Stacy Sullivan, and Ed Vulliamy, "The Wall of Denial," IWPR, July 6, 2005.

79. RFE/RL Newsline, July 14, 2005; Deutsche Welle, "Eine Stadt in Lethargie: Srebrenica zehn Jahre danach" (A city in lethargy: Srebrenica ten years later), July 5, 2005; Nerma Jelacic and Mirna Mekic, "Serbs Subvert Srebrenica Commemoration," IWPR, June 30, 2005.

80. RFE/RL Newsline, August 2, 2005; Associated Press, August 1, 2005. For similar comments from others, see Gordana Katana, "Bosnian Serb Leaders Attack Mladic," IWPR, July 14, 2005.

81. The army of Bosnia-Herzegovina has three separate brigades and headquarters in Serbian, Bosniak, and Croatian regions. Each brigade has three ethnically based battalions, and each of these is connected with the other battalions of its compatriots in a regiment. As a kind of forerunner, a mathematically and politically correct unit of thirty-six demining specialists, with twenty-four soldiers from the Federation and twelve from the RS, went to Iraq for service in summer 2005. See Christian Haupt and Jeff Fitzgerald, "Negotiations on Defence Reform in Bosnia and Herzegovina," Eighth Workshop of the Study Group on Regional Stability in South East Europe (Vienna: National Defence Academy, May 2004), pp. 153–72; James R. Locher 3rd and Michael Donley, "Reforming Bosnia and Herzegovina's Defence Institutions," NATO Review (Winter 2004) (www. nato.int); RFE/RL Newsline, June 2, 2005, and August 30, 2005; Deutsche Welle, "Auf dem Weg zur Gemeinsamen Armee in Bosnien-Herzegowina"(On the road to a common army in Bosnia-Herzegovina); Deutsche Welle, "Schwierige Reformhaben in Bosnien-Herzegowina" (Difficult reforms in Bosnia-Herzegovina), July 26, 2005; Deutsche Welle, "Bosnische Serbenrepublik löst eigene Streitkräfte auf" (Bosnian Republika Srpska dissolves its own armed forces), August 31, 2005; Deutsche Welle, "Bosnische Reformen: Ein Schritt vor, einer zurück" (Bosnian reforms: One step forward, one step back), September 8, 2005; Gordana Katana, "Bosnian Serbs Surrender Their Own Army," IWPR, September 9, 2005.

82 Nebojsa Pavkovic, commander of the VJ Third Army in Kosovo arrived at the Hague on April 25; see chapter 9.

83. Deutsche Welle, "Internationaler Bosnien-Beauftragter greift erneut durch" (International Bosnia commissioner again intervenes), October 29, 2005.

84. A somewhat less problematic requirement for EU progress was reform of public broadcasting, but as the smallest of the constituent peoples, the Croats in Bosnia-Herzegovina were holding out for special rights in this area as long as the Serbs held out on unifying the police.

85. ICG, "Bosnia's Stalled Police Reform"; Deutsche Welle, "Polizei-Reform in Bosnien-Herzegowina gescheitert" (Police reform fails in Bosnia-Herzegovina), May 17, 2005; Deutsche Welle, "Internationaler Bosnien-Beauftragter forciert Polizeireform" (International Bosnia commissioner compels police reform), February 1, 2005; Deutsche Welle, "Grenzschutz und Polizei geraten in Banja Luka aneinander" (Border police and regular police fight in Banja Luka), January 26, 2005; Gordana Katana, "Bosnian Serbs Quash EU Plan for United Police," IWPR, May 25, 2005; Deutsche Welle, "Schwierige Reformhaben" (Difficult reforms); Deutsche Welle, "Wird Bosnien-Herzegowina erst im Oktober 2006 souverän?" (Will Bosnia-Herzegovina not become sovereign until 2006?), July 19, 2005.

86. Craig S. Smith, "European Union Formally Opens Talks on Turkey's Joining," New York Times, October 4, 2005.

87. Author's interviews with European diplomats, October 2005.

88. Deutsche Welle, "Kroatien weist Vorwürfe del Pontes zurück" (Croatia rejects Del Ponte's criticisms), September 21, 2005.

89. ICTY, "ICTY Prosecutor's Assessment of the Co-operation Provided by Croatia to the ICTY," Press Release JP/MO/1009e, October 3, 2005 (www.un.org/icty). See also chapter 5.

90. Deutsche Welle, "EU-Verhandlungen mit Bosnien in greifbarer Nähe" (EU negotiations with Bosnia in the forseeable future), October 19, 2005.

91. Deutsche Welle, "Neue Regierung für bosnische Serbenrepublik in Sicht " (New government for Republika Srpska in view), February 15, 2006; Deutsche Welle, "Neue Regierung in Banja Luka gewählt" (New government elected in Banja Luka), March 1, 2006 (http://newsletter.dw-world.de); Deutsche Welle, "Frischer Wind in Banja Luka" (Fresh wind in Banja Luka), March 8, 2006; Deutsche Welle, "Sarajewo legt Finanzquellen von mutmaßlichen Kriegsverbrechern still" (Sarajevo freezes financial sources of presumed war criminals), March 8, 2006.

92. RFE/RL Newsline, March 10, 2006.

93. RFE/RL Newsline, April 10, 2006.

94. Deutsche Welle, "Polizeichef der Serbenrepublik folgt Rücktrittsforderung" (Police chief of Republika Srpska responds to resignation demand), April 11, 2006 (http:// newsletter.dw-world.de).

95. Public International Law and Policy Group, *Balkan Watch,* June 5, 2006 (www.pilpg.org).

96. Author's interviews, April and May 2006; Deutsche Welle, "Bosnien-Herzegowina: Verfassungsreform im Parlament gescheitert" (Bosnia-Herzegovina: Constitutional reform defeated in parliament), April 27, 2006; "Bosnischer Außenminister: 'Weg in die EU ist das Wichtigste'" (Bosnian foreign minister, "The road to the EU is the most important thing"), April 27, 2006; Deutsche Welle, "Bosniens Politiker einigen sich auf Verfassungsreform" (Bosnian politicians agree on constitutional reform), March 20, 2006 (http://newsletter.dw-world.de); Deutsche Welle, "Bosnien-Herzegowina: Gespräche über Verfassungsänderungen gescheitert" (Bosnia-Herzegovina: Talks about constitutional changes break down), January 17, 2006; Nidzara Ahmetasevic, "Debate Follows Collapse of Bosnian Reform Drive," IWPR, February 9, 2006; Deutsche Welle, "Erneuter Anlauf zur Verfassungsreform in Bosnien-Herzegowina" (New attempt at constitutional reform in Bosnia-Herzegovina), February 21, 2006.

97. Conversation with author, Neum, Bosnia, June 25, 2006.

98. Munk, "Ashdown Orders New Crackdown in Bosnia"; Deutsche Welle, "Schwarz-Schilling wird Hoher Repräsentant in Bosnien" (Schwarz-Schilling becomes high representative in Bosnia), January 26, 2006. Ashdown drew the comparison with East Timor before violence broke out again there in 2006.

99. Conservative estimates give 2005 real growth of close to 6 percent; Alida Sofic, head of the Economic Policy Research Unit (EPRU) of the Bosnia and Herzegovina Council of Ministers; and EPRU, "Bosnia and Herzegovina Economic Trends: Annual Report 2005" (March 2006), pp. 7, 10, 21–23.

100. Munk, "Ashdown Orders New Crackdown in Bosnia."

Notes to Chapter Seven

1. The attempt on the life of President Kiro Gligorov in October 1995 was assumed by Balkan analysts in the Swiss Federal Office for Police to have been commissioned by Slobodan Milosevic's entourage because of Gligorov's announced intent to clamp down on narcotics and cigarette smuggling through Macedonia. See Thomas Köppel and Agnes

Szekely, "Transnational Organized Crime and Conflict in the Balkans," in *Transnational Organized Crime and International Security: Business as Usual?* edited by Mats Berdal and Monica Serrano (Boulder, Colo.: Lynne Rienner, 2002), p. 132.

2. L. S. Stavrianos, *The Balkans since 1453* (New York University Press, 2000), p. 412.

3. Following common usage, the term *Macedonians* is used in this book to designate the Slavs who call themselves Macedonians, with no implication that the Albanians and other minorities are not equal citizens of Macedonia. The term *Macedonia* is used as the name this country has adopted, as well as for the broader geographical area.

4. The full name of the VMRO-DPMNE in English is Internal Macedonian Revolutionary Organization–Democratic Party for Macedonian National Unity. In the interwar period it had three divergent wings: one pro-Bulgarian, one pro-Serb, and one pro-Macedonian.

5. James Pettifer, ed., *The New Macedonian Question* (London: Palgrave, 2001), p. 21. My summary history of Macedonia after the disintegration of Yugoslavia derives from this book. See also the Macedonian parts of James Pettifer, *Kosova Express: A Journey in Wartime* (University of Wisconsin Press, 2005).

6. Nikos Zaikos, "The Interim Accord: Prospects and Developments in Accordance with International Law," in *Athens-Skopje: An Uneasy Symbiosis (1995–2002)*, edited by Evangelos Kofos and Vlasis Vlasidis (Athens: ELIAMEP, 2005), pp. 21–54.

7. Some skeptics fear that the Greek money is less a vote of trust in the Macedonian economy than a conduit for Russian money laundering. International Crisis Group (ICG), "Macedonia: No Room for Complacency" (October 23, 2003), p. 14 (www.crisisgroup.org).

8. For PHARE, see chapter 2, note 24.

9. There are an additional 6 percent of Turkish and other Muslim minorities, 6 percent Gypsies, and 2 percent Serbs.

10. See Pettifer, *Kosova Express.*

11. Author's interviews in Prizren in summer 2000 with Kosovar Albanians who had fled to Tetovo and northern Albania.

12. Sadako Ogata, *The Turbulent Decade* (New York: W. W. Norton, 2005), pp. 147–56.

13. Pettifer, *Kosovo Express*, p. 249.

14. ICG, "Macedonia: The Last Chance for Peace" (June 20, 2001).

15. The Stabilization and Association Agreement was initialed in November 2000, signed in April 2001, and entered into force in April 2004. European Union, "Relations between the EU and the Former Yugoslav Republic of Macedonia" (no date, cumulative) and "The Declaration of the Zagreb Summit" (November 24, 2000) (both at http://europa.eu.int).

16. Camilla Algarheim, "Macedonia: Tanusevci Dying Slow Death," Institute for War and Peace Reporting (IWPR), January 14, 2005 (http://iwpr.gn.apc.org; www.iwpr.net; www.birn.eu.com).

17. ICG, "The Macedonian Question: Reform or Rebellion" (April 5, 2001), p. iv. The report also lists 24 million machine guns, but it seems implausible even in the excitable Balkans that the 8 million Albanian men, women, and children in Albania, Kosovo, and Macedonia would average three machine guns each. See also ICG, "The Albanian Question in Macedonia: Implications of the Kosovo Conflict for Inter-Ethnic Relations in Macedonia" (August 11, 1998); Tim Judah, "Greater Albania?" *New York Review of Books* 48, no. 8 (2001).

18. ICG, "Macedonia: The Last Chance for Peace," pp. ii, 13, 14, 19.

19. Timothy Garton Ash, "Is There a Good Terrorist?" *New York Review of Books* 48, no. 19 (2001) (www.nybooks.com).

20. James Pettifer, "Ali Ahmeti and the New Albanian Political Party in FYROM" (U.K. Defence Academy, Conflict Studies Research Centre, July 1, 2002) (www.da.mod.uk/CSRC).

21. See Philip Gounev, "Stabilizing Macedonia: Conflict Prevention, Development and Organized Crime," *Journal of International Affairs* (Columbia University) 57, no. 1 (Fall 2003), pp. 229–40.

22. ICG, "Macedonia: War on Hold" (August 15, 2001), p. 4. See also Ulf Brunnbauer, "The Consequences of Identity Politics: Security Dilemmas in the Republic of Macedonia," paper presented at the convention of the Association for the Study of Nationalities, April 11–13, 2002.

23. Author's interviews, Skopje, October 2004.

24. Especially controversial was the primacy of the Hague Tribunal in all cases that were excluded from the general amnesty for criminal cases arising from the conflict, since this meant not only that the ICTY could preempt cases in sovereign Macedonia's courts, but also that Macedonian prosecutors could not issue indictments for any conflict-related case unless the Hague Tribunal returned it to Skopje. This provision was even more restrictive than international limitations on the protectorate of Bosnia.

25. For conflicts that arose in education in the first few months of the decentralization, see Ivan Petrusevski and Maja Ivanovska, "EU Focus: Decentralisation Fuels Power Struggle in Macedonian Schools," IWPR, December 16, 2005.

26. Deutsche Welle, "Vier Jahre Ohrider Rahmenabkommen: Mazedonien zieht Bilanz" (Four years of the Ohrid framework agreement: Macedonia draws up the balance), August 13, 2005 (www.dw-world.de); ICG, "Macedonia: Make or Break" (August 3, 2004).

27. Radio Free Europe/Radio Liberty (RFE/RL) Newsline, April 27, 2005 (wwww.rferl.org).

28. See, for example, European Stability Initiative, "The Other Macedonian Conflict," Discussion Paper (February 20, 2002) (www.esiweb.org).

29. ICG, "Macedonia: No Room for Complacency."

30. NATO, "Press Briefing at NATO Press Centre, Skopje," September 27, 2001 (www.nato.int); author's interviews with European officials in Skopje, October 2004.

31. NATO, "Operation Amber Fox Background Information," updated February 12, 2003.

32. European Council, "EU Military Operation in Former Yugoslav Republic of Macedonia" (no date, cumulative) (http://ue.eu.int).

33. Author's interview, Skopje, October 2004.

34. For a discussion of election losses by the "center-right" in Macedonia, see Andrej A. Lepavcov, "Why We Lost—The Macedonian Case," in *Why We Lost: Explaining the Rise and Fall of the Center-Right Parties in Central Europe 1996–2002*, edited by Peter Ucen and Jan Erik Surotchak (Bratislava: International Republic Institute, 2005), pp. 71–86.

35. Author's interview, Skopje, October 2004.

36. Author's interview, Skopje, October 2004.

37. ICG, "Macedonia: No Room for Complacency."

38. For a detailed bipartisan account of the dynamic, and the turning point as voters in the 2002 election accepted the Ohrid Agreement, see IWPR, *Ohrid and Beyond: A*

Cross-Ethnic Investigation into the Macedonian Crisis (London, 2002). Serb, Turkish, Roma, and smaller Macedonian parties were also partners in the government coalition.

39. ICG, "Macedonia: No Room for Complacency," pp. 7, 28; Garton Ash, "Is There a Good Terrorist?"

40. ICG, "Macedonia: No Room for Complacency."

41. See Michael Sahlin, "Comment: NATO and EU Align Balkan Agendas," IWPR, April 20, 2005; and chapter 6.

42. Author's interviews, Skopje, October 25–28, 2004; ICG, "Macedonia: No Room for Complacency."

43. Dana Priest, "Wrongful Imprisonment: Anatomy of a CIA Mistake," *Washington Post*, December 4, 2005; Joel Brinkley, "Rice Is Challenged in Europe over Secret Prisons," *Washington Post*, December 4, 2005; Arno Luik, "'Zieh dich aus,' sagten sie zu mir" ("Strip," they said to me), *Stern*, December 15, 2005, p. 48.

44. "'Für die Amerikaner machen wir alles'" ("For the Americans, we'll do anything"), *Neue Zürcher Zeitung*, December 25, 2005 (www.nzz.ch).

45. Deutsche Welle, "Ende der EU-Polizeimission in Mazedonien" (End of the EU police mission in Macedonia), November 2, 2005.

46. Author's interview December 2005; Deutsche Welle, "Hilfe aus Brandenburg für mazedonische Polizei" (Help from Brandenburg for Macedonian police), July 7, 2005.

47. Ana Petruseva, "Rise and Fall of Macedonia's Nationalist Showman," IWPR, March 16, 2005; Mitko Jovanov, "Acquittal Dismays Macedonian Government," IWPR, April 29, 2005; Deutsche Welle, "Mazedonische Delegation besucht ICTY in Den Haag" (Macedonian delegation visits ICTY in the Hague), April 27, 2005; Ulrich Buechsenschuetz, "Verdicts over Migrant Killings Polarize Macedonia," RFE/RL Newsline, "End Note," May 4, 2005; Nevena Angelovska, "EU Funds for Macedonia in the Balance," IWPR, November 1, 2005.

48. RFE/FL Newsline, May 4, 2005; Andi Balla, "Albania Seeks Firm NATO Entry Date," IWPR, February 22, 2006.

49. See chapter 5.

50. See chapter 8.

51. See chapter 4.

52. ICG, "Macedonia: Make or Break" (August 3, 2004), p. 1.

53. European Stability Initiative, "Member State Building and the Helsinki Moment," January 13, 2005 (www.esiweb.org).

54. ICG, "Macedonia: No Room for Complacency." Also the following ICG reports: "The Albanian Question in Macedonia"; "Macedonia: Towards Destabilisation?" (May 21, 1999); "Macedonia's Ethnic Albanians: Bridging the Gulf" (August 2, 2000); "After Milosevic: A Practical Agenda for Lasting Balkans Peace" (April 2, 2001); "The Macedonian Question"; "Macedonia: The Last Chance For Peace"; "Macedonia: Still Sliding" (July 27, 2001); "Macedonia: War on Hold"; "Macedonia: Filling the Security Vacuum" (September 8, 2001); "Macedonia's Name: Why the Dispute Matters and How to Resolve It" (December 10, 2001); "Moving Macedonia toward Self-Sufficiency: A New Security Approach for NATO and the EU" (November 15, 2002); "Macedonia: Make or Break"; "Macedonia: Not out of the Woods Yet" (February 25, 2005).

55. Ana Petruseva, "Comment: Macedonians Turn Away from Ethnic Divisions," November 12, 2004. For the negative view that the whole exercise by the government and the internationals may have widened rather than narrowed Macedonian-Albanian divisions, see the

essay by former German ambassador to Skopje Klaus Schrameyer, "Makedonien: das neue Gesetz über die territoriale Organisation und das Referendum vom 7. November 2004" (Macedonia: The new law on territorial organization and the referendum of November 7, 2004), *Südosteuropa Mitteilungen* 45, no. 1 (2005): 12–24.

56. "Kondovo: If Government Won't Do It, Will Macedonia's People Defend Themselves?" Christopher Delio blog, December 9, 2004 (www.balkanalysis.com).

57. RFE/RL Newsline, February 2, 2005.

58. RFE/RL Newsline, "Macedonian Government Takes on the Flag Question," June 1, 2005, and "Macedonian Parliament Approves Key Law on National Symbols," July 18, 2005.

59. RFE/RL Newsline, August 30, 2005; Deutsche Welle, "Parlament in Mazedonien Billigt Verfassungsänderungen" (Parliament in Macedonia approves constitutional changes), December 7, 2005; Public International Law and Policy Group, *Balkan Watch* 7, no. 25 (December 2005).

60. "Wahlerfolg für Mazedoniens Regierung" (Election success for Macedonia's government), *Neue Zürcher Zeitung*, April 13, 2005; RFE/RL Newsline, April 19, 2005.

61. ICG, "Macedonia: Wobbling toward Europe" (January 12, 2006).

62. Radmila Sekerinska, "Comment: Macedonia's Decisive Year on Road to NATO and EU," IWPR, January 27, 2005; RFE/RL Newsline, August 30, 2005.

63. European Commission, "Proposal for a Council Decision on the Principles, Priorities and Conditions Contained in the European Partnership with the Former Yugoslav Republic of Macedonia," SEC (2005) 1425 (November 9, 2005), and EU, "Relations between the EU and the former Yugoslav Republic of Macedonia" (http://europa.eu.int). See also Deutsche Welle, "Mazedonien: Reformen vor EU-Kandidatur" (Macedonia: reforms before EU candidacy), February 16, 2005; Deutsche Welle, "Ein Berg von Aufgaben wartet auf Mazedonien" (A mountain of tasks awaits Macedonia), February 1, 2005; Tamara Causidis and Sase Dimovski, "Macedonia May Rue Hastiness," IWPR, June 27, 2005; Angelovska, "EU Funds for Macedonia in the Balance."

64. "EU über weiteren Ausbau uneinig" (EU at odds on further enlargement), *Neue Zürcher Zeitung*, December 12, 2005; Daniel Dombey and Sarah Laitner, "Talk of New Members on Hold until EU Frontiers Finalised," *Financial Times*, December 16, 2005, p. 2; Michael Sahlin, "Comment: The Credibility of the EU's Enlargement Process at Stake," IWPR, December 16, 2005. With the French and Dutch rejection of the EU's constitutional treaty in spring 2005, the operative EU regulations fell back on the provisions of the 2000 Nice Treaty; these allowed for the accession of applicants that were already as far advanced as Romania and Bulgaria, but not necessarily of later candidates like Macedonia, or even Croatia.

65. Deutsche Welle, "Parlament in Mazedonien billigt Verfassungsänderungen" (Parliament in Macedonia approves constitutional changes), December 7, 2005.

66. Deutsche Welle, "Ist das Ohrider Abkommen gescheitert?" (Has the Ohrid agreement failed?), June 28, 2006; Geoff Nairn, "Broadband Network Is Envy of the West," *Financial Times*, special section on Digital Business: Emerging Markets, March 29, 2006, p. 5.

67. European Commission, "Analytical Report for the Opinion on the Application from the Former Yugoslav Republic of Macedonia for EU membership" (November 9, 2005), p. 19. See also European Commission, "Opinion on the Application from the Former Yugoslav Republic of Macedonia for Membership of the European Union" (November 9, 2005), and "Proposal for a Council Decision on the Principles, Priorities and Con-

ditions Contained in the European Partnership with the Former Yugoslav Republic of Macedonia." All accessed at http://europa.eu.int.

68. ICG, "Macedonia: Wobbling toward Europe," pp. 2–4. In that other area of perennial weakness, lack of public administration capacity to manage EU-funded projects, see also Angelovska, "EU Funds for Macedonia in the Balance."

69. ICG, "Macedonia: Wobbling toward Europe," pp. 1, 6.

70. "Diplomatische Kosovo-Offensiven Skopjes" (Skopje's diplomatic Kosovo offensives), *Neue Zürcher Zeitung,* October 29, 2005.

71. Deutsche Welle, "Grenzgespräche zwischen Mazedonien und dem Kosovo" (Border talks between Macedonia and Kosovo), June 13, 2005; RFE/RL Newsline, May 16, 2005.

72. ICG, "Macedonia: No Room for Complacency."

73. Giuliano Amato and others, "The Balkans in Europe's Future" (Sofia, April 2005) (www.balkan-commission.org).

Notes to Chapter Eight

1. James Pettifer, "Albanian Election 2005—A New Ruling Elite?" (U.K. Defence Academy, Conflict Studies Research Centre, October 2005) (www.da.mod.uk/CSRC).

2. John R. Lampe, *Balkans into Southeastern Europe* (London: Palgrave Macmillan, 2006), p. 276.

3. This version of the citadel legend was recounted to Austrian anthropologists by villagers in the north Albanian mountains in the 1990s. Helmut Eberhart and Karl Kaser, eds., *Albanien: Stammesleben zwischen Tradition und Moderne* (Albania: Tribal life between the traditional and the modern) (Vienna: Böhlau, 1995), p. 188. The historical parts of this chapter, unless otherwise specified, are drawn from Miranda Vickers, *The Albanians* (London: I. B. Tauris, 1991); Miranda Vickers and James Pettifer, *Albania: From Anarchy to a Balkan Identity* (New York University Press, 1997); L. S. Stavrianos, *The Balkans since 1453* (New York University Press, 2000), pp. 496–512, 709–31; and James Pettifer, *Albania and Kosovo Blue Guide* (New York: W. W. Norton, 2001), pp. 65–111, 218–31.

4. This view is vehemently contested by Serb spokesmen, who hold that there is no continuity between the Illyrians and today's Albanians. See Rev. Irinej Dobrijevic (coordinator, Kosovo and Metohija Committee Office, Holy Assembly of Bishops of the Serbian Orthodox Church, Belgrade), "Kosovo: Current and Future Status," Testimony before the U.S. House of Representatives, Committee on Foreign Relations, May 18, 2005.

5. The others were usually Greek or Bosnian, and occasionally Georgian or Circassian. The first Albanian became grand vizier either in 1497 (on reasonably good historical evidence) or possibly 1477 (on little more than guesswork). Mass conversions to Islam (which occurred only in Albanian and Bosnian lands in the empire) took place only a century or two after the original Ottoman conquest, since the Turks did not proselytize as the Venetians or other early Christian hegemons did.

6. Cited in Vickers, *The Albanians,* p. 46.

7. Barbara Jelavich, *History of the Balkans: Twentieth Century* (Cambridge University Press, 1983), p. 84.

8. Karl Kaser, "Religionszugehörigkeit und Ethnizität der albanischen Bevölkerung im südöstlichen Europa: Verhandlungsspielräume und ihre Grenzen" (Religious affiliation and ethnicity of the Albanian population in Southeast Europe: Room for negotiation and

its limits) (no date, given to the author by Kaser on February 5, 2004). Other sources find all denominational estimates dubious and note that over the decades statistics have varied according to the political purpose of the compilers.

9. Peter Menzel, "Conclusion: *Millets*, States, and National Identities," *Nationalities Papers* 28, no. 1 (March 2000): 203.

10. Misha Glenny, *The Balkans, 1804–1999* (London: Granta, 1999), pp. 412–17; and author's interviews, including with one member of a family that is no longer called Zog, April and September 2004.

11. Ismail Kadare, *Broken April* (Lanham, Md.: New Amsterdam Books, 1990).

12. Vickers, *The Albanians*, p. 146.

13. See R. J. Crampton, *The Balkans since the Second World War* (London: Longman, 2002), pp. 38–49.

14. See Crampton, *The Balkans since the Second World War*, pp. 156–67.

15. See especially Vickers, *The Albanians*, pp. 146–61.

16. Ibid., p. 204.

17. Author's interview, April 2004.

18. Ibid., p. 214.

19. International Centre for Migration Policy Development, "Definition of a Blue Border Management System in Albania" (Vienna, May 2005), p. 35 (www.icmpd.org).

20. For PHARE, see chapter 2, note 24.

21. European Commission, External Relations Directorate General, "European Community CARDS Programme: Albania Country Strategy Paper 2002-2006" (November 30, 2001) (http://europa.eu.int).

22. Frank Cilluffo and George Salmoiraghi, "And the Winner Is . . . the Albanian Mafia," *Washington Quarterly* 22, no. 4 (Autumn 1999): 21–25.

23. European Commission, Directorate General for Economic and Financial Affairs, "The Western Balkans in Transition," Enlargement Papers 23 (December 2004), p. 24.

24. Center for the Study of Democracy (CSD), "Partners in Crime: The Risks of Symbiosis between the Security Sector and Organized Crime in Southeast Europe" (Sofia, 2004), p. 87 (www.csd.bg).

25. CSD, "Partners in Crime," p. 88, citing Xhudo Gus, "Men of Purpose: The Growth of Albanian Criminal Activity," *Transnational Organized Crime* 2, no. 1 (Spring 1996); Cilluffo and Salmoiraghi, "And the Winner Is."

26. CSD, "Partners in Crime," p. 91, citing Gus, "Men of Purpose."

27. Amnesty International, "Albania: Detention and Ill-Treatment of Government Opponents—The Elections of May 1996" (September 1996) (http://web.amnesty.org); Organization for Security and Cooperation in Europe (OSCE), Office for Democratic Institutitons and Human Rights (ODIHR), "Observation of the Parliamentary Elections Held in the Republic of Albania, May 26 and June 2, 1996" (June 1996) (www.osce.org).

28. Vickers, *The Albanians*, p. 246.

29. CSD, "Partners in Crime," p. 91.

30. Author's interviews, Tirana, April 2004.

31. Vickers, *The Albanians*, pp. 250–51. See also Crampton, *The Balkans since the Second World War*, pp. 300–07.

32. Kathleen Imholz, "States of Emergency as Pretexts for Gagging the Press," *East European Constitutional Review* (New York University) 6, no. 4 (Fall 1997) (www.law.nyu.edu).

33. Vickers, *The Albanians*, p. 250.

34. Kathleen Imholz, "Note on the Albanian Private Media Law," *Post-Soviet Media Law and Policy Newsletter,* no. 50 (November 1, 1998) (www.vii.org).

35. International Crisis Group (ICG), "The State of Albania" (January 6, 1999) (www.crisisgroup.org).

36. James Pettifer, *Kosova Express: A Journey in Wartime* (University of Wisconsin Press, 2005), p. 171.

37. ICG, "Albania: The State of the Nation" (March 1, 2000).

38. Author's interviews in Prizren, Pristina, and Tirana, July 2000 and April 2004.

39. ICG, "Albania: The State of the Nation" (2000).

40. Ibid. Under Albanian law, blood feuds are a punishable offense, and about 3,000 families, representing some 70 percent of live vendettas, are said to have been reconciled in recent years. The feuds persist, however, as described in Deutsche Welle interviews with a fifty-four-year-old who has been unable to leave his roofless house for nine years, and an activist who was promoting reconciliation, shortly before he was murdered in Shkodra. Deutsche Welle, Interviews with Pal Hila and Emin Spahija, August 18 and 9, 2004, respectively.

41. European Commission, "European Community CARDS Programme."

42. OSCE, ODIHR, "Republic of Albania Local Government Elections, 1 and 15 October 2000" (December 11, 2000) (www.osce.org).

43. The quotes here are from the author's interview with Rama, April 2004. See also the website of the City Mayors Network Platform, www.citymayors.com/mayors/tirana_mayor.html (accessed December 26, 2005); and Jane Kramer, "Painting the Town," *New Yorker,* June 27, 2005.

44. See chapter 7.

45. ICG, "Macedonia: No Room for Complacency" (October 23, 2003), p. 4. See also Elez Biberaj, "The Albanian National Question and Balkan Stability," *EES News* (Woodrow Wilson Center International Center for Scholars) (March–April 2003): 1.

46. Albanian Constitution in English, carried at Institute for Policy and Legal Studies, Tirana, www.ipls.org (accessed April 2, 2006).

47. ICG, "Albania: The State of the Nation" (May 25, 2001). On links between northeastern Albania and neighboring Kosovo, see also Deutsche Welle, "Kosovo und Albanien: Aufschwung durch grenzübergreifende regionale Projekte?" (Kosovo and Albania: Upswing through cross-border regional projects?), July 12, 2005 (www.dw-world.de/dw).

48. ICG, "Pan-Albanianism: How Big a Threat to Balkan Stability?" (February 25, 2004).

49. OSCE, ODIHR, "Republic of Albania Parliamentary Elections, 24 June–10 August 2001," Final Report (October 11, 2001) (www.osce.org).

50. ICG, "Albania's Parliamentary Elections 2001" (August 23, 2001).

51. See chapter 7; also Andi Balla, "Albania Seeks Firm NATO Entry Date," Institute for War and Peace Reporting (IWPR), February 22, 2006 (www.iwpr.net).

52. CSD, "Partners in Crime," p. 41; Cilluffo and Salmoiraghi, "And the Winner Is," p. 21.

53. Author's conversations, October 2005. See also Klaus Schmidt, "Strengthening Peace and Stability through Police Assistance in South East Europe: The Case of Albania" (no date, but apparently 2006) (www.bmlv.gv.at); U.S. Department of Justice, "Report to Congress from Attorney General Alberto R. Gonzales on U.S. Government Efforts to Combat Trafficking in Persons in Fiscal Year 2004" (July 2005) (www.usdoj.gov); Deutsche Welle, "Wirksame Hilfe im Kampf gegen die organisierte

Kriminalität in Albanien" (Effective help in the battle against organized crime in Albania), February 28, 2006.

54. OSCE, ODIHR, "Republic of Albania Parliamentary Elections, 3 July 2005," Election Observation Mission Report (November 7, 2005) (accessed at http://web.amnesty.org).

55. Deutsche Welle, "'Eine Chance zur Vertiefung der Reformen in Albanien'" (A chance to deepen reforms in Albania), September 13, 2005; Deutsche Welle, "Albanien: 'Reformen wären ein wichtiges Zeichen für Europa'" (Albania: "Reforms would be an important signal for Europe"), July 7, 2005; "Siegesfeiern der Opposition in Albanien" (Opposition celebrates victory in Albania), *Neue Zürcher Zeitung*, July 6, 2005 (www.nzz.ch); "Geregelter Machtwechsel in Albanien" (Orderly change of power in Albania), *Neue Zürcher Zeitung*, September 3, 2005; Deutsche Welle, "Albanien: Berishas Comeback" (Albania: Berisha's comeback), September 9, 2005.

56. Fabian Schmidt, "Eine zweite Chance für Berisha" (A second chance for Berisha), Deutsche Welle, July 6, 2005.

57. Suela Musta, "Dispute Delays Albanian Election Result," IWPR, July 14, 2005.

58. Kerin Hope, "Election Puts Albania at Crossroads on Europe," *Financial Times*, July 1, 2005.

59. Radio Free Europe/Radio Liberty (RFE/RL) Newsline, November 30, 2005 (www.rferl.org). For snapshots of the problems and of efforts to deal with them in the years since the 1997 anarchy, see the UNDP's "Albanian Human Development Report 2000" (www.al.undp.org); the EU's "Albania—Stabilisation and Association Report" (2002); and the EU's Stabilization and Association Process report, "Albania 2005 Progress Report" (November 9, 2005) (both available at http://europa.eu.int).

60. RFE/RL Newsline, November 10, 2005.

61. Pettifer, "Albanian Election 2005."

62. Author's conversation, May 2006.

63. Author's interview, Washington, October 2000.

Notes to Chapter Nine

1. Aleksa Djilas, "Funeral Oration for Yugoslavia: An Imaginary Dialogue with Western Friends," in *Yugoslavism: Histories of a Failed Idea, 1918-1992*, edited by Dejan Djokic (London: Hurst, 2003), pp. 317–33. On the broad issue of the role of historical myths in the Serb psyche, see Ivan Colovic, *The Politics of Symbol in Serbia: Essays in Political Anthropology* (London: Hurst, 2002). Politics by assassination took the lives of Milosevic's old mentor, Ivan Stambolic, Defense Minister Pavle Bulatovic, and numerous businessmen and journalists; the attempted murder of Vuk Draskovic, now foreign minister, failed.

2. In recent years the prominent Herzegovina bishop Atanasije (Jevtic), for example, "said that Europe came to the Balkans in tanks in 1914, 1941, and 1999, brought the world gas chambers and communism, and has been treating the Serbs like Kurds and Iraqis. Serbia, he said, fought for 200 years to free itself from Europe and looks to the east for its future." International Crisis Group (ICG), "Montenegro's Independence Drive" (December 7, 2005), p. 17 (www.crisisgroup.org). For a dissection of conflicted nineteenth- and twentieth-century Serb attitudes toward "the rotten West," see Colovic, *The Politics of Symbol in Serbia*, especially pp. 39–47, 89–111. See also L. S. Stavrianos, *The Balkans since 1453* (New York University Press, 2000), pp. 149–53.

3. For a description of the fiercely nationalist views of the Serbian Orthodox Church hierarchy, see Tanja Matic, "Church Wants Final Say on Any Deal," Institute for War and Peace Reporting (IWPR), May 18, 2005 (www.iwpr.net; iwpr.gn.apc.org).

4. On draft dodging, see especially Eric Gordy, *The Culture of Power in Serbia: Nationalism and the Destruction of Alternatives* (Pennsylvania State University Press, 1999).

5. See the websites of the Helsinki Committee for Human Rights in Serbia (www.helsinki.org.yu) and the Humanitarian Law Center (www.hlc.org.yu); Deutsche Welle, "Bilder des Schreckens aus Srebrenica" (Pictures of terror from Srebrenica), June 2, 2005 (www.dw-world.de); Deutsche Welle, "Serbische Jugendorganisation kritisiert Intellektuellenverband" (Serb youth organization criticizes intellectuals' club), August 16, 2005.

6. Author's interview, December 2004. Licht, the former director of the Open Society Institute in Belgrade, has been a pillar of the democratic movement in Serbia for the last two decades.

7. Agence France-Presse, November 8, 2005, cited in Public International Law and Policy Group, *Balkan Watch,* November 14, 2005 (www.pilpg.org).

8. Kadijević pinpointed the three most important attacks by Asia against Europe as the burning of the Alexandria library, the capture of Constantinople in 1453, and the "return to Europe of the Asiatic hydra" during the wars in Bosnia, Kosovo, and Macedonia. In all three cases, he wrote in Belgrade's *Politika* on October 27, 2001, "the same Asiatic hordes attacked European civilizations," while in the last two their success was "aided by the Latin West with its malicious refusal to help." Djurić wrote in *Politika* on February 24, 2001, that Europe thus lost once again the possibility of returning to itself and finding itself in the Serb cultural heritage. Both cited by Serb sociologist Ivan Colovic in "Culture, Nation and Territory," on the website of the Bosnia Institute (London), www.bosnia.org.uk (accessed November 14, 2005).

9. Author's interview, 2003.

10. Author's interviews, 2003 and 2004, and exchange of e-mails, 2005.

11. Djilas, "Funeral Oration for Yugoslavia," pp. 319, 320, 330. For an overall assessment of where Serbs stand today, see Judy Batt, "The Question of Serbia," Chaillot Paper 81 (Paris: EU Institute for Security Studies, August 2005) (www.iss-eu.org).

12. Author's interviews; Ivan Vejvoda, "Serbia after Four Years of Transition," in Judy Batt, ed., "The Western Balkans: Moving On," Chaillot Paper 70 (Paris: EU Institute for Security Studies, October 2004), p. 37 (www.iss-eu.org).

13. On this point the West and the Serbian anti-Milosevic opposition differed. The Western view was that Milosevic managed to distance himself from the Bosnian Serbs as they were routed by the Croatian army and NATO airpower in 1995, but that he was far too connected personally to the Kosovo war to pull off the same escape a second time in the eyes of Serb voters. The view of the Serbian opposition, by contrast, was that no sooner had Milosevic discredited himself in the wars in Croatia and Bosnia than he was rescued by the United States, when Washington made him its main interlocutor at the Dayton negotiations—and he was again rescued by the American bombing of Serbia in 1999, which rallied the Serbs behind Milosevic and let him reverse the concessions he had made to the opposition after his losses in the 1997 local elections.

14. Legija is usually identified as Djindjic's protector (and the organizer of Djindjic's assassination in 2003) in subsequent published accounts of the transition. The Sofia-based Center for the Study of Democracy (CSD), however, identifies Djindjic's real protector as the much higher ranking Jovica Stanisic, whose power as head of the Yugoslav/Serbian secret service (SDB/DB) was second only to that of Milosevic in the

president's heyday. Stanisic, whom the CSD calls the mastermind of ethnic cleansing, was indicted by the International Criminal Tribunal for the Former Yugoslavia (ICTY) in May 2003, appeared at the Hague in June 2003, and was provisionally released in December 2004. See Center for the Study of Democracy, "Partners in Crime: The Risks of Symbiosis between the Security Sector and Organized Crime in Southeast Europe" (Sofia, 2004), p. 45 (www.csd.bg).

15. For the refugees' plight, see, for example, Robert Vizi, "Ten Years On, Refugees Remain on the Outside," IWPR, July 31, 2005.

16. Louis Sell, *Slobodan Milosevic and the Destruction of Yugoslavia* (Duke University Press, 2002), pp. 344–52. For the protesters' own jubilant account of the October 5 demonstrations, see Dragan Bujosevic and Ivan Radavanovic, *October 5: A 24-Hour Coup*, 2nd ed. (Belgrade: Media Center, 2001).

17. Vejvoda, "Serbia after Four Years of Transition," p. 39.

18. Sonja Biserko, *Human Rights in the Shadow of Nationalism, Serbia 2002* (Belgrade: Helsinki Committee for Human Rights in Serbia, 2003), pp. 184–85; Beta (Serb news agency), June 13, 2003, carried in UNMIK news roundup of that date (www. unmikonline.org). Lieutenant Colonel Zlatan Mancic, Captain Rade Radojevic, and Corporals Danil Tesic and Misel Seregi were sentenced in October 2002 to prison terms of up to seven years each. On appeal, Serbia's Supreme Military Court in June 2003 doubled the sentences, with Mancic given the longest sentence of fourteen years.

19. The quote is from Obrad Kesic, an anti-Milosevic activist who later became a businessman in Washington. "It took us a long time to get [Djindjic] to seek American support; in some ways he was more difficult to get to work with America than Kostunica was," he explained. Initially, Djindjic thought that German support for the opposition would suffice. As a pragmatist, however, from 1998 he finally concluded that U.S. support was necessary. Author's interview with Kesic, February 2006.

20. Cited in Vejvoda, "Serbia after Four Years of Transition," p. 38.

21. Ibid., p. 38.

22. Ibid., pp. 37–51; Dusan Reljic, "Serbien kommt nicht zur Ruhe" (Serbia does not come to rest), *Linke Kommunalpolitik*, no. 137 (May–June 2004): 36–38; CSD, "Partners in Crime," p. 60.

23. Author's interview with Kesic, February 2006.

24. CSD, "Partners in Crime," p. 43.

25. Ibid., pp. 47, 52, 53; Boris Begovic and others, *Corruption at the Customs: Combating Corruption at the Customs Administration* (Belgrade: Center for Liberal-Democratic Studies, 2002) (http://unpan1.un.org).

26. CSD, "Partners in Crime," p. 57.

27. Ibid., p. 41.

28. Vejvoda, "Serbia after Four Years of Transition," p. 44.

29. Author's interview, November 2003.

30. The first comprehensive crime report on Southeastern Europe by the European Commission and the Council of Europe states flatly that Djindjic was killed because he tried to uncouple the "symbiotic" ties between Serbian security forces and organized crime. European Commission and Council of Europe, "Situation Report on Organised and Economic Crime in South-eastern Europe" (August 2005) (www.coe.int).

31. Bojan Dimitrijevic, "Serbia: Red Berets Disbanded," IWPR, March 27, 2003.

32. CSD, "Partners in Crime," p. 62.

33. Deutsche Welle, "Haftstrafen für Auftragsmörder von Milosevic" (Prison sentences for Milosevic's contract killers), July 19, 2005; Deutsche Welle, "Politischer Druck auf Justiz in Serbien" (Political pressure on justice in Serbia), March 1, 2005.

34. Nicholas Wood, "Raves for Authors with a Solid Grasp of Serb Atrocities," *New York Times*, January 21, 2005; "Wertvoller Romancier" (Valuable novelist), *Neue Zürcher Zeitung*, October 30, 2004 (www.nzz.ch).

35. Author's interview in Belgrade, November 2003.

36. Author's interviews in Belgrade, Berlin, and Washington, 2004 and 2005.

37. Zeljko Cvijanovic, "Hague Tribunal Prosecutor Carla Del Ponte Storms Out of Meeting with President Kostunica," Global Policy Forum (New York), January 24, 2001 (www.globalpolicy.org).

38. Author's interview with Biserko, June 2004; Sonja Biserko, "The Hague Coercion," Helsinki Committee for Human Rights in Serbia (no date, but apparently Spring 2005) (www.helsinki.org.yu).

39. IWPR, "Hague Tribunal" (no date, but apparently October 2004).

40. John B. Allcock and others, eds., "The International Criminal Tribunal for the Former Yugoslavia," Scholars' Initiative papers, Team 10 (no date, but c. 2006), pp. 27–28 (www.cla.purdue.edu), citing Serb sources.

41. Serb sources differ on this point. Some who have worked with Kostunica say he underwent a conversion that led to his new push for EU membership. Others contend that he had favored Serbian membership in the EU for many years. Certainly, Kostunica shifted on the price he was willing to pay at that point to get on the EU track.

42. Radio Free Europe/Radio Liberty (RFE/RL), September 30, 2005 (www.rferl.org); Human Rights Watch, "Real Progress in The Hague" (March 29, 2005) (http://hrw.org). In an interview with the author in December 2004, Kostunica stressed the voluntary nature of the indictees' presence at the tribunal.

43. ICG, "Serbia: Spinning Its Wheels," Update Briefing (May 23, 2005).

44. For a liberal Serb plea for Serbian admission to NATO's Partnership for Peace despite Belgrade's failure to send Radovan Karadzic and Ratko Mladic to the Hague, see Pavle Jankovic and Srdan Gligorijevic, "Burying the Hatchet," *NATO Review* (Summer 2004).

45. RFE/RL Newsline, April 18, 2005; interview of Javier Solana with author and *Internationale Politik* team, Brussels, April 2005. The text of this interview appeared as "'The EU—More Like a Molecule than an Atom,'" *Transatlantic Internationale Politik* 6, no. 2 (Spring 2005): 4–9.

46. RFE/RL Newsline, April 13, 2005.

47. RFE/RL Newsline, December 19, 2005.

48. Author's interviews with Western diplomats, 2005 and 2006. See also Daniel Williams and Rade Maroevic, "Serbs Admit That Officials Aided War Crimes Fugitive," *Washington Post*, March 28, 2006.

49. Deutsche Welle, "EU-Annäherung: Serbien-Montenegro einen Schritt weiter" (EU rapprochement: Serbia-Montenegro one step further), April 26, 2005; RFE/RL Newsline, July 22 and 27, 2005. Information about the 42 percent rating for the Radicals in 2006 came from Alexandar Fatic, director of the Belgrade Centre for Security Studies in June 2006.

50. Seselj and his party got their start in the 1990 Serbian presidential campaign, when Milosevic boosted the rabid nationalist intellectual as his foil, making himself look like

the moderate. See Warren Zimmermann, *Origins of a Catastrophe* (New York: Times Books, 1996), pp. 119, 152.

51. Author's interview, December 2004.

52. See RFE/RL Balkan Report, July 29 and August 12, 2005; RFE/RL Newsline, November 23, 2005.

53. RFE/RL Newsline, August 26, 2005. See also Matic, "Church Wants Final Say on Any Deal"; and for background, Thomas Bremer, Nebojsa Popov, and Radmila Radic, "Die Kirche und die 'serbische Frage'" (The church and the "Serbian question"), in *Serbiens Weg in den Krieg: Kollektive Erinnerung, nationale Formierung und ideologische Aufrüstung* (Serbia's road to war: Collective memory, national formation, and ideological rearmament), edited by Heinz-Günther Stobbe (Berlin: Berlin Verlag, 1998), pp. 196–207. Since Serbian Orthodox clergy adopt one of a limited number of names as their church names, initial references to them customarily give their last names in parentheses to avoid misunderstanding about which Amfilohije or Artemije is meant.

54. Deutsche Welle, "Hoffnungen und Spekulationen nach Fernseh-Appell an Karadzic" (Hopes and speculation after TV appeal to Karadzic), August 1, 2005.

55. ICG, "Montenegro's Independence Drive," p. 1.

56. Ibid., p. 17, citing *FoNet*, March 15, 2003; "Homily of His Eminence Metropolitan Amfilohije of Montenegro and the Littoral at the Funeral of Dr. Zoran Djindjic," Information Service of the Serbian Orthodox Church, March 15, 2003 (www.spc.yu).

57. Tim Judah, *The Serbs* (Yale University Press, 1997).

58. Stavrianos, *The Balkans since 1453*, pp. 240–68.

59. When the SPC opened a theological library in 1994–95 in Valjevo, forty miles east of Srebrenica on the Serbian side of the Drina, it was named after Justin. "As we have become alienated from Serbdom and St. Sava, we have become alienated from ourselves and from Christ, we are just idling about and are lost. The closer we are to ourselves, the more faithful we are to St. Sava, and the more faithful we are to St. Sava, the closer we are to Christ and Christianity," declared the main speaker at the dedication, the writer Matija Beckovic. See Klaus Buchenau, "Svetosavlje und Pravoslavlje" (St. Sava-ism and orthodoxy), no date, given to the author by Buchenau on February 3, 2004. The analysis in this section derives largely from Buchenau's insights.

60. Ibid.; author's interviews.

61. Radmila Radic, "Religion in a Multinational State: The Case of Yugoslavia," in *Yugoslavism: Histories of a Failed Idea, 1918–1992*, edited by Dejan Djokic (London: Hurst, 2003), p. 207.

62. Judah, *The Serbs*, p. 39; Sell, *Slobodan Milosevic*, pp. 2-4, 39; Laura Silber and Allan Little, *Yugoslavia: Death of a Nation* (TV Books, 1995, 1996), pp. 37–38.

63. Radic, "Religion in a Multinational State," p. 207.

64. Sabrina P. Ramet, "The Politics of the Serbian Orthodox Church," in *Religija i Politika u Centralnoj i Jugoistocnoj Evropi* (Religion and politics in central and southeast Europe), edited by Sabrina P. Ramet (Belgrade: Filip Visnjic, forthcoming).

65. ICG, "Montenegro's Independence Drive," p. 17.

66. Helsinki Committee for Human Rights in Serbia, *Human Rights and Accountability: Serbia 2003* (Belgrade: Zagorac, 2004), pp. 7–13.

67. Ramet, "The Politics of the Serbian Orthodox Church."

68. Author's interview with Kesic, February 2006. Kesic also said that the opposition of the patriarch and Amfilohije to the Vance-Owen plan was based on the desire not to separate the Orthodox Church, rather than on support for a Greater Serbia—and that

Karadzic was the first politician to realize "that if he wrapped himself in the church, he would separate himself from the others," including Milosevic.

69. Klaus Buchenau, "Divine Justice and the ICTY: An Orthodox and Catholic Perspective," draft paper given to the author by Buchenau on April 7, 2006.

70. Author's conversations with international officials and diplomats in Pristina, 2004.

71. Ramet, "The Politics of the Serbian Orthodox Church."

72. Buchenau, "Divine Justice and the ICTY."

73. Ramet, "The Politics of the Serbian Orthodox Church."

74. RFE/RL Newsline, July 14, 2005. The violence in Trebinje was even worse than in Banja Luka at the first attempts to rebuild the mosques; mobs set fire to cars and buses and trapped some 400 Bosniak pilgrims and officials inside the Islamic Community Center for hours. Richard Caplan, *International Governance of War-Torn Territories: Rule and Reconstruction* (Oxford University Press, 2005), p. 52.

75. Author's interview with a Serb source, June 2005; "Kopernikanski obrt" (Copernican rotation), *Vreme*, April 28, 2005 (www.vreme.com); Nachrichtendienst Östliche Kirchen (News Service of the Eastern Churches), "Bischof Grigorije: 'Kofi Annan begrüßt die Kooperationsbereitschaft der serbischen orthodoxen Kirche'" (Bishop Grigorije: "Kofi Annan welcomes the Serbian orthodox church's readiness to cooperate"), March 31, 2005 (www.kirchen-in-osteuropa.de).

76. "Hristos Vaskrese" (Christ is risen), on the chat site *freeserbs,* April 28, 2005, http://freeserbs.org (accessed April 8, 2006).

77. Matic, "Church Wants Final Say on Any Deal."

78. See especially Buchenau, "Svetosavlje und Pravoslavlje," and two other undated papers given to the author on February 3, 2004: "Was ist nur falsch gelaufen? Kritische Überlegungen zum Kirche-Staat-Verhältnis im sozialistischen Jugoslawien" (What went wrong? Reflections on the church-state relationship in socialist Yugoslavia), and "Die serbische orthodoxe Kirche seit 1996: Eine Chronik" (The Serbian orthodox church since 1996: A chronicle); also Matic, "Church Wants Final Say on Any Deal." Characteristically, Bishop Artemije's message for the Easter edition of the Belgrade daily *Danas* was: "The greatest tragedy for the Serb people would be for someone to accept Kosovo's independence."

79. "Founder of 'Scorpions' Free in Belgrade," *Blic Online,* June 6, 2005, www.blic.co.yu; "Srebrenica wird in Belgrad zum Thema" (Srebrenica becomes an issue in Belgrade), *Neue Zürcher Zeitung,* June 4, 2005; "Srebrenica-Video für Ausbildungszwecke" (Srebrenica video for training purposes), *Der Standard* (Austria), June 4, 2005 (http://derstandard.at).

80. Author's interview, May 2005.

81. Nicholas Wood, "Videotape of Serbian Police Killing 6 Muslims from Srebrenica Grips Balkans," *New York Times* online, June 12, 2004; RFE/RL Newsline, July 11, 2005. For continued Serb denials of a massacre at Srebrenica, see Nerma Jelacic, Stacy Sullivan, and Ed Vulliamy, "The Wall of Denial," IWPR, July 6, 2005; Courtney Angela Brkic, "The Wages of Denial," *New York Times,* July 11, 2005. According to Brkic, extremists "threatened to lynch Ms. Kandic at [one] law school debate on Srebrenica, and one of them spat in her face."

82. Moma Ilic, Daniel Sunter, and Pedja Obradovic, "Special Report: Police Torture Case Divides Serbia," IWPR, April 6, 2005; RFE/RL Newsline, June 1, 2005; Momir Ilic, "Serbian Prosecutors Accused of Serving Politicians," IWPR, August 25, 2005.

83. RFE/RL Newsline, "End Note," August 19, 2005.

84. Author's interviews and conversations, 2005.

85. See chapter 5.

86. Deutsche Welle, "Serbien-Montenegro: Vermögen von flüchtigen ICTY-Angeklagten blockiert" (Serbia-Montenegro: Property of fugitive ICTY indictees blocked), April 8, 2006 (http://newsletter.dw-world.de).

87. RFE/RL Newsline, April 13, 2006.

88. Beta, "Without a Strategy," November 10, 2005.

89. Author's interview, February 2006.

90. For snapshots of Montenegro before Solana's engagement, see ICG, "Montenegro: Settling for Independence?" Balkans Report 107 (March 28, 2001), and "Montenegro: Resolving the Independence Deadlock," Balkans Report 114 (August 1, 2001). In its report "Montenegro's Independence Drive," p. 5, the ICG argued that Solana's campaign had a negative impact on Belgrade, diverting Djindjic's attention from purging criminals in the Serbian security forces and thus leaving them in place to assassinate the prime minister in 2003. The sources I interviewed, however, did not think that preoccuption with the Montenegro negotiations was a significant factor in Djindjic's failure to clean out the security forces.

91. "Rückkehr zu alten Werten in Montenegro" (Return to old values in Montenegro), Neue Zürcher Zeitung, November 7, 2005; Deutsche Welle, "Ein Referendum in Montenegro nach EU-Vermittlung" (A referendum in Montenegro after EU mediation), March 2, 2006; and the series of broadcasts by Deutsche Welle, "Montenegro auf schnellem Weg nach Europa?" (Montenegro on the fast track to Europe?), May 22, 2006.

92. Christian Schmidt-Häuer, "Wie viele Divisionen hat der Patriarch?" (How many divisions does the patriarch have?), Die Zeit, September 22, 2005, p. 15; RFE/RL Newsline, August 8, 2005; ICG, "Montenegro's Independence Drive," p. 17.

93. Silber and Little, Yugoslavia, pp. 182–85.

94. RFE/RL Newsline, September 7, 2004; Deutsche Welle, "Assoziierung unter Vorbehalten" (Association with reservations), October 11, 2005.

95. ICG, "Montenegro's Independence Drive," p. 6.

96. Deutsche Welle, "Ranghoher Polizeibeamter in Montenegro ermordet" (Senior police official murdered in Montenegro), August 31, 2005; "Montenegro: Killing of Policeman Revives Organised Crime Fears," IWPR, September 9, 2005.

97. Quoted in ICG, "A Marriage of Inconvenience: Montenegro 2003," Balkans Report 142 (April 16, 2003). See also Nedjedjko Rudovic, Petar Komnenic, and Marijana Buljan, "Montenegro: Politicians Make Mockery of the Law," IWPR, June 27, 2005; Berislav Jelinic, Hugh Griffiths, and Gordana Igric, "Montenegro: Authorities Face Murder Cover-up Claims," IWPR, November 18, 2004; Deutsche Welle, "Belgrad: Verteidigungsminister zurückgetreten" (Belgrade: Defense minister resigns), September 14, 2005. For a more positive view of Montenegro's efforts to reduce crime, see ICG, "Montenegro's Independence Drive," p. 16.

98. "Rückkehr zu alten Werten in Montenegro," Neue Zürcher Zeitung; Deutsche Welle, "Montenegro: Russische Investoren erobern den Markt" (Russian investors conquer the market), June 13, 2006.

99. Philip Morris paid $1.25 billion and agreed to take measures to control smuggling in return for the EU's dropping of the case in July 2004. See Corporate Ethics and Governance report, "Company: Philip Morris," July 9, 2004 (www.icego.org).

100. ICG, "Montenegro's Independence Drive," p. 18, citing information from Montenegro's Ministry of Culture.

101. Buchenau, "Die Serbische Orthodoxe Kirche seit 1996." The Montenegrin Orthodox Church sees itself as the successor of the Cetinje metropolitanate of Ottoman times, which was dissolved when Yugoslavia was formed after World War I. At that point, all church property in Montenegro went to the Serbian Orthodox Church.

102. Conversation with author, October 2004.

103. This elite seems to be very small and is more apt to discuss such feelings with Western visitors than with Serb intellectuals, who bristle at any comparison between the mind-sets of post-Nazi Germans and post-Milosevic Serbs, descrediting such searchings by citing the Serb resistance to the Nazis in World War II.

104. All three quotes, recorded in May 2000, come from a study of the trauma and despair of the million Serb refugees who fled to Serbia proper in the decade to 2000 by a five-person Bulgarian team, including a sociologist, a specialist in Slavonic studies, a historian of the Balkans, a philosopher, and a historian/anthropologist. Antonina Zhelyazkova, "One Year after NATO Air Raids—The Frustration and Isolation of a European Nation" (May 2000), analyzes the team's "urgent anthropology" interviews with Serb and Roma refugees from Kosovo conducted in May 2000. The English version was given to the author by Zhelyazkova in July 2000; French versions of the team studies are available in *Ethnologie Francaise.*

105. Author's interview with Licht, June 2004; Deutsche Welle, "Zuckerbrot und Peitsche für Serbien (Carrot and stick for Serbia), February 23, 2006.

Notes to Chapter Ten

1. Ekaterina Nikova, "Comparing the Incomparable: Japan and the Balkans," *SRC English Newsletters,* Slavic Research Center (no date, Spring 2000) (http://src-h.slav.hokudai.ac.jp).

2. For discussions of conditionality, see James Hughes, Gwendolyn Sasse, and Claire Gordon, "Conditionality and Compliance in the EU's Eastward Enlargement," *Journal of Common Market Studies* 42, no. 3 (September 2004): 523–51: Karen E. Smith, "Western Actors and the Promotion of Democracy," Radovan Vukadinovic, "Former Yugoslavia: International Efforts to Link Peace, Stability, and Democracy," and Jan Zielonka, "Conclusions: Foreign Made Democracy," all in *Democratic Consolidation,* vol. 2, *International and Transnational Factors,* edited by Jan Zielonka and Alex Pravda (Oxford University Press, 2001), pp. 31–57, 437–54, 511–32, respectively.

3. Deutsche Welle, "Südosteuropa—Stabilitätspakt wird zum Rat für Zusammenarbeit" (Southeast European Stability pact becomes cooperation council), May 30, 2006 (www.dw-world.de).

4. Erhard Busek, "Five Years of Stability Pact for South Eastern Europe: Achievements and Challenges Ahead," Discussion Paper 70 (London School of Economics, Centre for the Study of Global Governance, March 2004) (www.lse.ac.uk). See also the Stability Pact's website, www.stabilitypact.org.

5. Deutsche Welle, "Südosteuropa: Gemeinsamer Einsatz für sauberes Wasser" (Southeastern Europe: Common operation for clean water), December 7, 2005.

6. Associated Press, "EU Backs Balkan Free Trade Pact," April 5, 2006. For a discussion of the potential role of EU enlargement in promoting Balkan regional trade liberalization, see Martin Dangerfield, "Subregional Integration and EU Enlargement: Where Next for CEFTA?" *Journal of Common Market Studies* 44, no. 2 (June 2006): 305–24.

7. Eric Jansson and Kerin Hope, "Using Trade Agreements to Help Bind the Balkans," *Financial Times*, January 30, 2006; Deutsche Welle, "EU schlägt Freihandelszone für den Westbalkan vor" (EU proposes free-trade zone for the west Balkans), January 31, 2006; Deutsche Welle, "Europäisches Stromnetz nach 13 Jahren wieder verbunden" (European electric grid reconnected after 13 years), October 11, 2004; Deutsche Welle, "Kosovo und Energie—Südosteuropäisches Außenministertreffen in Athen" (Kosovo and energy—Southeast European foreign ministers' meeting in Athens), January 25, 2006.

8. See European Commission Directorate-General for Energy and Transport, "Trans-European Transit Network: TEN-T Priority Axes and Projects, 2005" (http://europa.eu.int).

9. Author's interview, April 2004.

10. For a critical discussion of EU spending in the region, see European Stability Initiative, "Recommendations from Wilton Park Conference," June 10, 2004, updated September 12, 2005 (www.esiweb.org). Unless otherwise specified, statistics and judgments in this section are drawn from the EU's economic report card for the Balkans, issued by the European Commission Directorate General for Economic and Financial Affairs, "Progress towards Meeting the Economic Criteria for Accession: 2005 Country Assessment" (November 2005) (http://europa.eu.int); Vladimir Gligorov, "Balkan Transition," *European Balkan Observer* (Belgrade Centre for European Integration and the Vienna Institute for International Economic Studies [WIIW]) 3, no. 2 (October 2005): 10–18, 22–23 (www.wiiw.ac.at); WIIW, "Western Balkans Economic Development since Thessaloniki 2003" (March 7, 2006) (www.wiiw.ac.at).

11. GDP analysis provided by the Economic Analysis Division of the Austrian National Bank, May 26, 2006.

12. Mica Culibrk, "Serbian Inflation Soars," Insitute for War and Peace Reporting (IWPR), December 16, 2005 (www.iwpr.net; http://iwpr.gn.apc.org; www.birn.eu.com).

13. Deutsche Welle, "Kroaten in der Schuldenfalle" (Croats in the debt trap), March 6, 2006.

14. Christoph Duenwald, Nikolay Gueorguiev, and Andrea Schaechter, "Too Much of a Good Thing? Credit Booms in Bulgaria, Romania, and Ukraine," *Beyond Transition* (World Bank newsletter) 16, no. 3 (July–September 2005): pp. 21–23.

15. The purchasing power parity figures in this paragraph come from Gligorov, "Balkan Transition," pp. 10–18. EU-25 refers to the twenty-five present EU members, including the eight Central European newcomers. If Balkan living standards were measured againt the fifteen West European members before the 2004 "big bang" enlargement, the percentages would be significantly lower.

16. The figure for Kosovo comes from World Bank, "Kosovo Poverty Assessment," Report 32378-XK (June 16, 2005), pp. iii, 1 (www.worldbank.org), and refers to raw GDP per capita in 2003 rather than the equivalent purchasing power parity figure, which would be higher. This low GDP level reflects a drop of 50 percent in the early 1990s and a further 20 percent drop during 1998–99.

17. European Commission, Directorate General for Economic and Financial Affairs, "European Economy, Progress towards Meeting the Economic Criteria for Accession: 2005 Country Assessment," Enlargement Papers 26 (November 2005) (http://europa.eu.int).

18. Ibid.

19. "Speech by the High Representative for Bosnia and Herzegovina Paddy Ashdown to the United Nations Security Council," October 23, 2002 (www.esiweb.org).

20. Deutsche Welle, "Schwarz-Schilling wird Hoher Repräsentant in Bosnien" (Schwarz-Schilling becomes high representative in Bosnia), January 26, 2006; interview with Christian Schwarz-Schilling, "'Für Bosnien ist 2006 ein entscheidendes Jahr'" (For Bosnia 2006 is a year of decision), *Die Welt*, February 1, 2006 (www.welt.de); Christian Schwarz-Schilling, "Bosnia's Way Forward," *Transatlantic Internationale Politik* 7, no. 1 (Spring 2006): 84–86.

21. Radio Free Europe/Radio Liberty (RFE/RL) Newsline, March 22, 2006 (www. rferl.org); Deutsche Welle, "Bosniens abgesetzte Politiker dürfen wieder in die Politik" (Bosnia's dismissed politicians may return to political life), March 20, 2006.

22. Heiner Hänggi and Fred Tanner, "Promoting Security Sector Governance in the EU's Neighbourhood," Chaillot Paper 80 (Paris: EU Institute for Security Studies, July 2005), p. 43 (www.iss-eu-org).

23. North Atlantic Council, "Final Communiqué," June 12, 2003 (www.nato.int).

24. Etleva Bisha, ed., *Albanian Armed Forces in Photos: The History* (Tirana: Albanian Defense Ministry, no date, c. 2003).

25. Author's interviews, 2000 and 2006.

26. International Crisis Group (ICG), "Kosovo: The Challenge of Transition" (February 17, 2006), especially pp. 4, 6, 7 (www.crisisgroup.org).

27. Austrian Presidency of the European Union, "European Gendarmerie Force HQ Set Up at Vicenza, Italy," press release (January 23, 2006), (www.eu2006.at); David T. Armitage Jr. and Anne M. Moisan, "Constabulary Forces and Postconflict Transition: The Euro-Atlantic Dimension," *Strategic Forum* (Institute for National Strategic Studies, National Defense University), no. 218 (November 2005) (www.ndu.edu); Jock Covey, Michael J. Dziedzic, and Leonard R. Hawley, *The Quest for Viable Peace* (Washington: U.S. Institute of Peace Press, 2005), pp. 168–71, 186, 261–63; Robert B. Oakley, Michael J. Dziedzic, and Eliot M. Goldberg, eds., *Policing the New World Disorder: Peace Operations and Public Security* (Washington: National Defense University, 1997). See also Annika S. Hansen, "From Congo to Kosovo: Civilian Police in Peace Operations," Adelphi Paper 343 (London: International Institute for Strategic Studies, May 2002); Richard Caplan, *International Governance of War-Torn Territories: Rule and Reconstruction* (Oxford University Press, 2005), pp. 45–60; Michael Schmunk, "Die deutschen Provincial Reconstruction Teams: Ein neues Instrument zum Nation-Building" (The German Provincial Reconstruction Teams: A new instrument for nation-building), SWP-Studie 2005/S 33 (Berlin: German Institute for International and Security Affairs, November 2005).

28. See Samuel R. Berger and Brent Scowcroft, "In the Wake of War: Improving U.S. Post-Conflict Capabilities," Independent Task Force Report 55 (Council on Foreign Relations, September 6, 2005), pp. 16–17.

29. Hänggi and Tanner, "Promoting Security Sector Governance," pp. 43–54; Stability Pact for South Eastern Europe, Working Table 3: Security Initiative against Organised Crime, "Draft Programme and Priorities 2006" (October 20, 2005), and Working Table 3, "Progress Report of the Initiative to Fight Organised Crime by the Chairman of the SPOC Board," presented at the meeting of Working Table 3, Prague, November 15, 2005 (both available at www.stabilitypact.org); Deutsche Welle, "Polizei in Südosteuropa will besser zusammenarbeiten" (Police in Southeastern Europe want to cooperate better), June 18, 2005. See also the home page of the Council of Europe's Directorate General of Legal Affairs, www.coe.int/T/E/Legal_affairs; and Stability Pact, "Influence of Southeastern European Organised Crime on EU States," chart drawn from Europol, "2004 European Union Organised Crime Report" (December 2004) (www.stabilitypact.org).

30. Hänggi and Tanner, "Promoting Security Sector Governance"; Pierre-Antoine Braud and Giovanni Grevi, "The EU Mission in Aceh: Implementing Peace," Occasional Paper 61 (Paris: EU Institute for Security Studies, December 2005) (www.iss-eu.org).

31. Center for the Study of Democracy, "Partners in Crime: The Risks of Symbiosis between the Security Sector and Organized Crime in Southeast Europe" (Sofia, 2004), p. 41 (www.csd.bg).

32. CARDS Regional Police Project (CARPO), "Situation Report on Organised and Economic Crime in South-eastern Europe, 2005," p. 36 (www.coe.int/T/E/Legal_Affairs).

33. Ibid., p. 5. See also Deutsche Welle, "Organisierte Kriminalität: Bedrohung für Südosteuropa" (Organized criminality: threat for southeastern Europe), September 22, 2005.

34. CARPO, "Situation Report," pp. 12, 15.

35. Ibid., p. 12.

36. Ibid., pp. 47, 48. For an on-the-ground Balkan evaluation of the problem, see Martin Tisne and Daniel Smilov, *From the Ground Up: Assessing the Record of Anticorruption Assistance in Southeastern Europe: A Regional Initiative of the Soros Foundations Network in Southeastern Europe* (Budapest: Central European University, Center for Policy Studies, 2004) (www.ceu.hu).

37. Erhard Busek, special coordinator for the Stability Pact, at the Woodrow Wilson International Center for Scholars, Washington, February 2006.

38. CARPO, "Situation Report," pp. 36, 45, 46, 48.

39. Rebecca Surtees, "Second Annual Report on Victims of Trafficking in Southeastern Europe" (International Organization for Migration, 2005) (www.iom.int).

40. Ibid.; CARPO, "Situation Report," pp. 16, 25; Europol, "2004 European Union Organised Crime Report."

41. Author's conversation with a Serb law-enforcement officer, Berlin, October 2005.

42. Author's conversation with one of the West European participants at the meeting, October 2005. The identification of the signatories required diplomatic sleight of hand because of the old controversy about the official name of Macedonia. The solution was to omit the names of all countries and describe each signer only as an abstract "interior minister."

43. "Joint Declaration, High Level Meeting of Ministers of Interior and of Security and Senior Officials of Governments and Administrations from South-eastern Europe on the Regional Strategy on Tools against Organised and Economic Crime" (Brijuni, Croatia, September 23, 2005).

44. "Regional Strategy on Tools against Organised and Economic Crime with Project Area Specific Actions" (Brijuni, Croatia, September 23, 2005).

45. CARPO, "Situation Report," p. 54.

46. Presentations by and author's conversations with participants at a conference on fighting crime in the Balkans held at the German Academy for Security Policy, Berlin, October 21, 2005.

47 For a summary of one discussion of this general phenomenon, see John A. Gould, "Where Have All the Illiberal Democracies Gone? Privatization as a Catalyst to Regime Change in Postcommunist Europe," *EES News* (Woodrow Wilson International Center for Scholars), (November–December 2005).

48. Author's conversation, October 2005.

49. See Ruth Wedgwood, "The International Criminal Court: Reviewing the Case," *Berlin Journal*, no. 5 (Fall 2002): 4–12. James Gow argues exactly the opposite: that it was the ICTY's accelerated indictment of Milosevic in 1999 that induced the Serb leader to

capitulate in the Kosovo war on June 2, 1999. Gow maintains that the May 27 indictment had the "psychological impact" of convincing Milosevic that he "had lost control." See James Gow, *The Serbian Project and Its Adversaries: A Strategy of War Crimes* (London: Hurst, 2003), p. 296.

50. Patricia M. Wald, "ICTY Judicial Proceedings: An Appraisal from Within," *Journal of International Criminal Justice* 2 (2004): 466–73.

51. Gabrielle Kirk McDonald, "Problems, Obstacles and Achievements of the ICTY," *Journal of International Criminal Justice* 2 (2004): 558–71.

52. "The ICTY at a Glance," www.un.org/icty (accessed March 15, 2006).

53. For an overview of ethnic bias by judges, poor case preparation by prosecutors, poor police cooperation in investigations, and weak witness protection in local courts in the period before the ICTY began transferring war crimes cases to them in 2005, see Ulrich Garms and Katharina Peschke, "War Crimes Prosecution in Bosnia and Herzegovina (1992–2002): An Analysis through the Jurisprudence of the Human Rights Chamber," *Journal of International Criminal Justice* 4, no. 2 (May 2006): 258–82; "Justice at Risk," *Human Rights Watch* 16, no. 7(d) (October 2004) (http://hrw.org/). See also Human Rights Watch, "Balkans: Local Courts Currently Unprepared to Try War Crimes" (October 14, 2004); Human Rights Watch, "The Real State of War Crimes Prosecutions in Croatia, Response to an Article in *Vjesnik*" (October 30, 2004); Aida Alic, Aida Sunje, and Hugh Griffiths, "Courting Controversy in Bosnia," IWPR, June 27, 2005; Alison Freebairn and Nerma Jelacic, "Bringing War Crimes Justice Back Home," IWPR, November 26, 2004; Momir Ilic, "Serbian Prosecutors Accused of Serving Politicians," IWPR, August 25, 2005.

54. At the same time Croatia's new, activist chief prosecutor met with senior officials of the Interior Ministry, the police, and the secret service to initiate investigation of the most serious war crimes. Deutsche Welle, "Kroatien vor spektakulärem Kriegsverbrecher-Prozess?" (A spectacular war crimes trial coming in Croatia?), May 10, 2006 (http://newsletter.dw-world.de); Deutsche Welle, "Kroatische Justiz in der Kritik" (Croatian justice criticized), May 10, 2006.

55. RFE/RL Newsline, November 18, 2005.

56. RFE/RL Newsline, April 26, 2006.

57. RFE/RL Newsline, April 10, 2006; Human Rights Watch, "Bosnian Serb Republic Takes First Steps to Justice" (March 16, 2006); Human Rights Watch, "Memorandum on the Western Balkans Prepared for EU Foreign Ministers' Informal Meeting, Salzburg, March 10–11, 2006" (March 7, 2006); Human Rights Watch, "Looking for Justice: The War Crimes Chamber in Bosnia and Herzegovina" (February 2006). Within a few years the composition of the chamber will shift from its present majority of international judges and prosecutors to a majority of Bosnians.

58. RFE/RL Newsline, January 31, 2006; Deutsche Welle, "Erstes Urteil vor dem Belgrader Sondergericht für Kriegsverbrechen" (First verdict before the Belgrade special war crimes court), December 12, 2005; Deutsche Welle, "Serbische Ex-Offiziere wegen Massakers in Vukovar angeklagt" (Former Serb officers charged over Vukovar massacre), October 12, 2005.

59. Deutsche Welle, "Erstes Urteil."

60. Reuters, "Serbian Court Convicts 14 in Massacre of POWs in '91," *Washington Post*, December 13, 2005.

61. Human Rights Watch, "A Chance for Justice? War Crime Prosecutions in Bosnia's Serb Republic" (March 16, 2006), p. 1.

62. IWPR, "War Crimes Symposium," Press Release (Sarajevo, March 11, 2005).

63. Auhor's conversation, May 2005.

64. Ana Uzelac, "Serbs Tire of Epic Milosevic Trial," IWPR, February 17, 2006.

65. "Abschied von Milosevic" (Farewell to Milosevic), *Neue Zürcher Zeitung*, March 18, 2006 (www.nzz.ch).

66. Author's interviews, 2004. See also Tim Judah, "The Fog of Justice," *New York Review of Books* 51, no. 1 (January 2004): 23.

67. Judah, "The Fog of Justice," p. 25.

68. McDonald, "Problems, Obstacles and Achievements of the ICTY," pp. 568–69. For a much more negative reading arguing the failure of special tribunals to bring reconciliation, based primarily on African experience but also with reference to the ICTY, see Helena Cobban, "Think Again: International Courts," *Foreign Policy*, no. 153 (March–April 2006): 22–28. For an evaluation of the system of international prosecutors and judges for serious crimes in Kosovo, see Almut Schröder, "Der Beitrag internationaler Richter und Staatsanwälte zur Entwicklung der Rechtsstaatlichkeit im Kosovo" (The contribution of international judges and prosecutors to the development of rule of law in Kosovo), ZIF Analyse (Berlin: Center for International Peace Operations, August 2004) (www.zif-berlin.org).

69. "The ICTY at a Glance."

70. Aida Alic, Aida Sunje and Hugh Griffiths, "Balkan War Crimes Justice Breakthrough," IWPR, June 2, 2005.

71. Deutsche Welle, "Premiere: Serbisch-kroatischer Dokumentarfilm über Kriegsverbrechen" (Premiere: Serb-Croat documentary about war crimes), February 15, 2006.

72. Obrenovic, the court noted, went well beyond what was required under his plea agreement to reduce his charge from conspiracy in genocide, providing valuable insider military information about the Srebrenica massacre. "ICTY at a Glance"; "ICTY Cases and Judgements" (www.un.org/icty).

73. Author's conclusion from interviews with Serbs, 2005.

74. James Lyon, the International Crisis Group's analyst in Belgrade, takes the contrary view that Prime Minister Kostunica allowed Milosevic to have a state funeral in Belgrade in all but name and that this strengthened the Radicals and Socialists. These two ultranationalist parties could at any time force new parliamentary elections, which they would win. But so far they have wanted to let Kostunica stay in office long enough to lose Montenegro and Kosovo, and perhaps block the extradition of Mladic, Lyon says, and then win after blaming Kostunica and the West for Serbia's victimization yet again. See James Lyon, "Serbia's Stain Lingers," *Baltimore Sun*, April 10, 2006 (accessed at www.crisisgroup.org).

75. "Serbischer Präsident erkennt Unabhängigkeit Montenegros an" (Serbian president recognizes Montenegro's independence), *Neue Zürcher Zeitung*, May 23, 2006.

76. Deutsche Welle, "Montenegrinische Kirche fordert Autokephalie" (Montenegrin church demands autocephaly), May 29, 2006.

77. ICG, "Montenegro's Referendum," Update Briefing (May 30, 2006).

78. Deutsche Welle, "Premier der bosnischen Serbenrepublik schließt Referendum nicht aus" (Premier of the Bosnian Serb republic does not exclude referendum), June 6, 2006. High representative Schwarz-Schilling immediately contacted Dodik, who assured him that he was not going to make any rash moves.

79. Author's interview, June 2004. Licht faulted not only Serb politicians but also the EU for the disproportionate Radical lead. This reflected the party's ability to mobilize protest

voters—but also the failure of the EU to "make itself more magnetic and attractive," and not just act as a hard taskmaster who keeps setting new conditions for candidates.

80. Deutsche Welle, "Zuckerbrot und Peitsche für Serbien" (Carrot and stick for Serbia), February 23, 2006.

81. Agence France-Presse, February 23, 2006, cited in the Public International Law and Policy Group's *Balkan Watch* 8, no. 5 (February 27, 2006) (www.pilpg.org); RFE/RL Newsline, August 1, 2006.

82. RFE/RL Newsline, May 4, 2006.

83. Author's interview, May 2006.

84. Daniel Dombey and Neil MacDonald, "Tensions with Serbs Raise Fears about EU Links," *Financial Times*, June 19, 2006, p. 2.

85. See, for example, "Kosovo, Mladic und die Europäische Union" (Kosovo, Mladic, and the European Union), *Neue Zürcher Zeitung*, February 25, 2006.

86. "UN 2005 World Summit Outcome," final document (September 15, 2005) (www.un.org); Michael Walzer, "Human Rights in Global Society," *Transatlantic Internationale Politik* 6, no. 1 (Spring 2005): 4–13.

87. See, for example, "Kosovo, Mladic und die Europäische Union" (Kosovo, Mladic, and the European Union), *Neue Zürcher Zeitung*, February 25, 2006.

88. "War in BiH Was Not Aggression," *Blic*, March 11, 2006 (www.blic.co.yu); Nidzara Ahmetasevic, "Serbia Faces Trial for Bosnia Genocide," IWPR, February 22, 2006 (accessed at www.birn.eu.com); Deutsche Welle, "Bosnien-Herzegowina klagt gegen Serbien-Montenegro" (Bosnia-Herzegovina charges Serbia-Montenegro), February 28, 2006 (http://newsletter.dw-world.de).

89. Author's interview, February 2006. See also Dusan Reljic, "Kosovo—ein Prüfstein für die EU" (Kosovo—A test for the EU), SWP-Aktuell 14 (Berlin: German Institute for International and Security Affairs, March 2006), p. 6; Nicholas Wood, "The End of Greater Serbia," *New York Times*, March 17, 2006.

90. Reljic, "Kosovo," p. 6; RFE/RL Newsline, July 28, 2006.

91. For overviews of the negotiations on Kosovo's future status, see "Crunch Time for Kosovo : Imposing a Solution?" *Strategic Comments* (International Institute for Strategic Studies) 11, no. 3 (May 2005); William L. Nash, "Forgotten Intervention? What the United States Needs to Do in the Western Balkans," Special Report (Council on Foreign Relations, June 30, 2005); "The Future of the Balkans," *Strategic Comments* 11, no. 9 (November 2005); Nida Gelazis and Martin C. Sletzinger, "Kosovo: Mission Not Yet Accomplished," *Wilson Quarterly* 29, no. 4 (Autumn 2005): 35–41; Elizabeth Pond, "Kosovo and Serbia after the French Non," *Washington Quarterly* 28, no. 4 (Autumn 2005): 19–36; Tim Judah, "Defining Kosovo," ISN Security Watch, carried on Kosovareport blog, October 10, 2005 (http://kosovareport.blogspot.com); Charles A. Kupchan, "Independence for Kosovo," *Foreign Affairs* 84, no. 6 (November–December 2005) (www.foreignaffairs.org); Borut Grgic, "Endgame in the Balkans," *Transatlantic Internationale Politik* 6, no. 4 (Winter 2005): 11–17; Daniel Serwer, "Comment: How to Succeed in Kosovo," IWPR, December 2, 2005; Daniel Serwer, "Kosovo: Current and Future Status" (May 18, 2005) (www. usip.org); Wim van Meurs and Stefani Weiss, "Qualifying (for) Sovereignty: Kosovo's Post-Status Status and the Status of EU Conditionality," Discussion Paper (Bertelsmann Foundation, December 6, 2005) (www.cap-lmu.de); Steven Woehrel, "Kosovo's Future Status and U.S. Policy" (Congressional Research Service, January 9, 2006) (www.cfr.org); ICG, "Kosovo: The Challenge of Transition"; Reljic, "Kosovo—ein Prüfstein für die EU" (Kosovo—A touchstone for the EU). See also opinion surveys of Serbs and Kosovar Albanians on final status and other concerns,

in "Coming to Terms with the Problem of Kosovo: The People's Views from Kosovo and Serbia," KosovaLive (Pristina), Center for Democracy and Reconciliation in Southeast Europe (Thessaloniki), and Media Center Beta (Belgrade) (October 2005) (www.cdsee.org).

92. RFE/RL Newsline, February 23, 2006.

93. "Embassy Row," Washington Times, June 2, 2006.

94. RFE/RL Newsline, June 2, 2006.

95. Deutsche Welle, "General Ceku für Amt des Kosovo-Regierungschefs nominiert" (General Ceku nominated as Kosovo government chief), March 1, 2006 (http://newsletter.dw-world.de); Deutsche Welle, "Kosovo: Neue Regierung vor neuer Verhandlungsrunde" (Kosovo: New government faces new negotiating round), March 15, 2006; Tanja Matic, "Europe Softens Blow to Serbia over Mladic," IWPR, March 2, 2006; Zana Limani, "Kosovo Ditches Its Prime Minister," IWPR, March 3, 2006; "Neuer Chef der Übergangsregierung Kosovos" (New chief of Kosovo's provisional government), Neue Zürcher Zeitung, March 11, 2006.

96. RFE/RL Newsline, June 20, 2006.

97. Interview with Sejdiu, "'Für Belgrad herrscht noch immer Krieg um den Kosovo'" ("For Belgrad there is still a war over Kosovo"), Die Presse (Vienna), March 17, 2006 (www.diepresse.com).

98. RFE/RL Newsline, March 21, 2006; Nikola Lazic, "Partition Demand Fuels South Serbia Tensions," IWPR, February 16, 2006.

99. Southeast European Joint History Project, "Phase 4: History Teacher Training Project, Serbia and Montenegro" (www.see-jhp.org). See also the website of the Center for Democracy and Reconciliation in Southeastern Europe (CDRSEE), www.cdrsee.org. The eleven participating countries are Albania, Bosnia and Herzegovina, Bulgaria, Croatia, Cyprus, Greece, Macedonia, Romania, Serbia and Montenegro, Slovenia, and Turkey. See also Deutsche Welle, "Geschichtsbuch als Beitrag zur Versöhnung in Südosteuropa" (History book as contribution to reconciliation in southeast Europe), September 19, 2005.

100. Author's interview, September 2004.

101. Nor Turks, since their participating historian, Hali Berktai, is one of the few Turkish scholars who says publicly that the Armenian genocide of the early twentieth century actually occurred.

102. Balkan Colleges Foundation, "The Image of the Other: Analysis of the High-School Textbooks in History from the Balkan Countries" (Sofia, 1998), pp. 7, 10. This project was funded by George Soros's Open Society Institute and the EU's PHARE and TACIS programs. (TACIS was the EU program of Technical Assistance for the Commonwealth of [post-Soviet] Independent States that ended in 2006.)

103. Ivan Ilchev, "Minorities in Bulgaria According to History Textbooks Used in Bulgarian Schools," Südosteuropa Mitteilungen, no. 2 (2003): 67–77.

104. Ivan Blazevski, "Macedonia: Reworked History Lessons Cause Storm," IWPR, February 9, 2006; Violeta Petroska-Beska and Mirjana Najcevska, "Macedonia: Understanding History, Preventing Future Conflict," Special Report 115 (Washington: U.S. Institute of Peace, February 2004).

Notes to Chapter Eleven

1. Polyarchy includes free and fair elections, with representational politics and clear rules and financing, freedom of expression, and alternate sources of information. Robert Dahl, Polyarchy: Participation and Opposition (Yale University Press, 1971).

2. For the role of the European Parliament in vetting candidates for membership, see Hannes Swoboda, "Die Politik des Europäischen Parlaments zu Südosteuropa" (European parliament policy toward southeastern Europe), *Ost-West Gegen-Informationen* 17, no. 4 (2005): 8–12.

3. Ivan Vejvoda, "Bosnia-Herzegovina: Unfinished Business," Testimony before the U.S. House of Representatives, April 6, 2005 (www.gmfus.org).

4. Francis Fukuyama, *The End of History and the Last Man* (New York: Free Press, 1992).

5. Thomas Carothers, *Critical Mission: Essays on Democracy Promotion* (Washington: Carnegie Endowment for International Peace, 2004), p. 178. See also Samuel P. Huntington, *The Third Wave: Democratization in the Late Twentieth Century* (Oklahoma University Press, 1991); Larry Diamond, "Is the Third Wave Over?" *Journal of Democracy* 7, no. 3 (1996): 20–37. The "first wave" occurred in the century ending in the 1920s. The "second wave" refers to the democratization of Germany, Japan, and Italy after their defeat in World War II.

6. Carothers, *Critical Mission*; Thomas Carothers and Marina Ottaway, eds., *Uncharted Journey: Promoting Democracy in the Middle East* (Washington: Carnegie Endowment for International Peace, 2005), especially p. 7 for equation of the Balkan and Arab "antidemocratic forms of nationalism."

7. Carothers, *Critical Mission,* pp. 178–79.

8. Ibid., pp. 172–73.

9. Fukuyama, revisiting his own concepts of regime change after the intervening wars in the Balkans, Afghanistan, and Iraq—and before he broke with his fellow neoconservatives—chided them for having erred in making a virtue of small government across the board. The right kind of "stateness," Fukuyama contended, must be inculcated in new democracies. State "scope" should indeed be restricted to prevent excessive meddling in affairs best left to the decision of individuals or markets; but state "strength," while it should not be so powerful as to compel uniformity or strangle pluralism, must be powerful enough to enforce law, protect citizens, and maintain a monopoly on the use of force. Weak and failing states run all too great a risk of being hijacked by terrorists and criminals. Francis Fukuyama, *State-Building: Governance and World Order in the 21st Century* (Cornell University Press, 2004). For a reprise of his views on democratic development in general and his praise of the EU for avoiding many of the pitfalls, see Francis Fukuyama, *After the Neocons: America at the Crossroads* (London: Profile, 2006), pp. 114–80, especially p. 146. For his scolding of neoconservatives for failing to avoid the pitfalls in invading Iraq in 2003, see Francis Fukuyama, "After Neoconservatism," *New York Times Magazine,* February 19, 2006 (www.nytimes.com).

10. Klaus von Beyme, "Institutional Engineering and Transition to Democracy," in *Democratic Consolidation in Eastern Europe,* vol. 1, *Institutional Engineering,* edited by Jan Zielonka (Oxford University Press, 2001), pp. 3–24.

11. See Bronislaw Geremek, "Civil Society and the Present Age" (Triangle Park, N.C.: National Humanities Center, 1992) (www.nhc.rtp.nc.us); Thomas Carothers, "Civil Society: Think Again" (1999), reprinted in Carothers, *Critical Mission,* pp. 99–106.

12. Author's interview with Sonja Licht, November 2002.

13. For a prescient warning about the danger in Ukraine, see James Sherr, "Ukraine's Most Dangerous Hour," *Transatlantic Internationale Politik* 5, no. 1 (Spring 2005): pp. 65–69.

14. Claus Offe, "Das Dilemma der Gleichzeitigkeit. Demokratisierung und Marktwirtschaft in Osteuropa" (The dilemma of simultaneity: Democratization and market

economy in eastern Europe), *Merkur* 45, no. 4 (1991): 279–92. For a general review of democratization theory as applied to Europe's "periphery," including Bulgaria and Romania, see Sonia Alonso and José María Maravall, "Democratizations in the European Periphery," in *Governing Europe*, edited by Jack Hayward and Anand Menon (Oxford University Press, 2003), pp. 264–93.

15. These words on Serbia and Montenegro, written in 2004, look prescient in hindsight. Ognyan Minchev and others, "Security and Reconstruction of Southeastern Europe: A Policy Outlook from the Region" (Sofia: Institute for Regional and International Studies, Bulgaria, no date) (www.iris-bg.org, accessed August 27, 2004); author's interviews with Minchev, February 1999 and September 2004.

16. See Thomas Carothers, *Promoting Rule of Law Abroad: In Search of Knowledge* (Washington: Carnegie Endowment for International Peace, 2006).

17. See Edward D. Mansfield and Jack Snyder, *Electing to Fight: Why Emerging Democracies Go to War* (MIT Press, 2005).

18. For a recent restatement of this premise, see Morton H. Halperin, Joseph T. Siegle, and Michael M. Weinstein, *The Democratic Advantage: How Democracies Promote Prosperity and Peace* (New York: Council on Foreign Relations, 2005).

19. Joseph S. Nye Jr., *Soft Power: The Means to Success in World Politics* (New York: Public Affairs, 2004).

20. European Commission, "2005 Enlargement Strategy Paper" (November 9, 2005) (http://ec.europa.eu).

21. European Council, Western Balkans summit, "Salzburg EU/Western Balkans Joint Press Statement," March 11, 2006 (www.consilium.europa.eu).

22. European Parliament, "Resolution on the Commission's 2005 Enlargement Strategy Paper" (March 16, 2006) (www.europarl.europa.eu); Heinz-Jürgen Axt, Antonio Milososki, and Oliver Schwarz, "Das Europäische Parlament geht auf Distanz zur EU-Erweiterung" (The European parliament distances itself from EU enlargement), *Südosteuropa Mitteilungen* 46, no. 2 (2006): 15–27.

23. See Milada Anna Vachudova, *Europe Undivided: Democracy, Leverage, and Integration after Communism* (Oxford University Press, 2005), especially pp. 157–59; Michael Emerson and Gergana Noutcheva, "Europeanization as a Gravity Model of Democratisation," Working Document 214 (Brussels: Center for European Policy Studies, November 2004), p. 1 (http://shop.ceps.be).

24. Wade Jacoby, "External Influences on Postcommunist Transformations: A Review Essay," *World Politics* (forthcoming). The third category, substitution, ranges from relying on small teams of technocrats to legislate market reforms in the absence of any political constituency for these reforms, on the one hand, to the most extreme form of displacement of local politics through military occupation, on the other.

25. Author's interview, April 2005.

26. The two Balkan figures overlap; overall Balkan spending is hard to capture. The dollar figure comes from Paul Aaron, "The Anguish of Nation Building: A Report from Serbia," *World Policy Journal* 22, no. 3 (Fall 2005): 113–25; the euro figure, from the European Commission—World Bank Joint Office for South East Europe, "How Much Money Is Being Given?" (no date, cumulative) (www.seerecon.org, accessed April 2006).

27. James F. Dobbins, "America's Role in Nation-Building: From Germany to Iraq," *Survival* 45, no. 4 (Winter 2003–04): 96.

28. The Iraq war figures, defined as conservative estimates, come from the Congressional Research Service, as reported in Jonathan Weisman, "Projected Iraq War Costs

Soar," *Washington Post,* April 27, 2006, and Scott Walston and Katrina Kosec, "The Economic Costs of the War in Iraq," Working Paper 05-19 (Washington: American Enterprise Institute and Brookings, September 2005) (http://aei-brookings.org). See also Martin Wolf, "America Failed to Calculate the Enormous Costs of War," *Financial Times,* January 11, 2006, p. 15. For an estimate of ultimate costs running over $1 trillion, see Linda Bilmes and Joseph Stiglitz, "The Economic Costs of the Iraq War," Working Paper 12054 (Cambridge, Mass.: National Bureau of Economic Research, February 2006) (www.nber.org).

29. Author's interview, April 2005.

30. Author's interview, November 2003.

31. Author's interview, September 2004.

32. Author's interview, September 2004.

33. Author's interview, September 2004.

34. Author's interview, September 2004.

35. Author's telephone interview, November 2005.

36. Author's interview, November 2003.

37. Author's interview, November 2003.

38. Author's interview, October 2004.

39. Petra Pinzler, "'Ich will nicht freundlich sein'" ("I don't want to be friendly"), *Die Zeit,* May 11, 2006, p. 13.

40. Author's interview, December 2004. For a series of essays that express the rather different take of other Balkan analysts, see Denisa Kostovicova and Vesna Bojicic-Dzelilovic, eds., *Austrian Presidency of the EU: Regional Approaches to the Balkans* (Vienna: Center for the Study of Global Governance, Center for European Integration Strategies, and Renner Institute, 2006).

41. Deutsche Welle, "Polizeichef der Serbenrepublik folgt Rücktrittsforderung" (Serbian republic police chief resigns after demand), April 11, 2006 (www.dw-world.de).

REFERENCES

Sources for Articles, Transcripts, Reports, Files, or Listings

Agence France-Presse (www.afp.com)

Associated Press (www.ap.org)

Balkan Watch, Public International Law and Policy Group (www.pilpg.org/areas/poldev/balkanwatch)

BBC (http://news.bbc.co.uk)

Bertelsmann Transformation Index (www.bertelsmann-transformation-index.de)

Beta, Serb news agency (www.beta-press.com)

Beyond Transition, World Bank (www.worldbank.org/html/prddr/trans)

Blic Online, Serb newspaper (www.blic.co.yu)

Center for Democracy and Reconciliation in Southeast Europe (CDRSEE), Thessaloniki, (www.cdrsee.org)

Center for European Policy Studies (www.ceps.be)

Council of Europe Legal Affairs (www.coe.int/T/E/Legal_affairs)

Deutsche Welle (www.dw-world.de)

Economic Policy Review, Institute for Market Economics, Sofia (www.ime.bg)

The Economist

EES News, Woodrow Wilson International Center for Scholars, Washington

EU Police Mission (www.eupm.org)

Financial Times

Frankfurter Allgemeine Zeitung (www.faz.net)

Helsinki Committees for Human Rights in Bosnia, Bulgaria, Croatia, and Serbia

International Criminal Tribunal for the Former Yugoslavia (www.un.org/icty)

International Displacement Monitoring Center, Geneva (www.internal-displacement.org)

International Herald Tribune

Institute for War and Peace Reporting (www.iwpr.net; http://iwpr.gn.apc.org; www.birn.eu.com)

NATO (www.nato.int)

Neue Zürcher Zeitung (www.nzz.ch)

New York Times (www.nytimes.com)

Novinite, Bulgarian press agency (www.novinite.com)
Office of the High Representative, Sarajevo (www.ohr.int)
Project on Ethnic Relations, Princeton
Radio Free Europe/Radio Liberty Newsline (www.rferl.org/newsline)
Rompres, Romanian press agency (www.rompres.ro)
Stability Pact, Brussels (www.stabilitypact.org)
UNMIK (UN Mission in Kosovo) Media Monitor (www.unmikonline.org)
U.S. Congress, statements at hearings
Washington Post (www.washingtonpost.com)
Die Zeit

Books and Journal Articles

Aaron, Paul. "The Anguish of Nation Building: A Report from Serbia." *World Policy Journal* 22, no. 3 (Fall 2005): 113–25.

Acemoglu, Daron, and James A. Robinson. *Economic Origins of Dictatorship and Democracy*. Cambridge University Press, 2006.

Aligica, P. D. "Operational Codes, Institutional Learning and the Optimistic Model of Post-Communist Social Change: Conceptual Criticism and Empirical Challenges from a Romanian Case Study." *Communist and Post-Communist Studies*, no. 36 (2003): 87–99.

Alonso, Sonia, and José María Maravall. "Democratizations in the European Periphery." In *Governing Europe,* edited by Jack Hayward and Anand Menon, pp. 264–93. Oxford University Press, 2003.

Altmann, Franz-Lothar. "Die Balkanpolitik als Anstoß zur Europäisierung der deutschen Außenpolitik" (Balkan policy as a spur to Europeanization of German foreign policy). In *Ausblick: Deutsche Außenpolitik nach Christoph Bertram* (Outlook: German foreign policy after Christoph Bertram), pp. 38–41. Berlin: German Institute for International and Security Affairs (September).

Amato, Giuliano, and others. "The Balkans in Europe's Future." April 2005. www.balkan-commission.org.

Amnesty International. "Albania: Detention and Ill-Treatment of Government Opponents—the Elections of May 1996." September 1996. http://web.amnesty.org.

———. "Bulgaria and Romania: Amnesty International's Human Rights Concerns in the EU Accession Countries." October 2005. www.amnesty-eu.org.

Anderson, James, David Bernstein, and Cheryl Grey. "Judicial Systems in Transition Economies: Assessing the Past, Looking to the Future." Washington: World Bank, 2005. http://194.84.38.65/mdb/cmsitems/285/full_txt_eng.pdf.

Anderson, James H., and Cheryl W. Gray. "Transforming Judicial Systems in Europe and Central Asia." Washington: World Bank, January 2006. http://siteresources.worldbank.org.

Armitage, David T., Jr., and Anne M. Moisan. "Constabulary Forces and Postconflict Transition: The Euro-Atlantic Dimension." *Strategic Forum* (Institute for National Strategic Studies, National Defense University), no. 218 (November 2005). www.ndu.edu/inss.

Axt, Heinz-Jürgen, Antonio Milososki, and Oliver Schearz. "Das Europäische Parlament Geht auf Distanz zur EU-Erweiterung" (The European parliament distances itself from EU enlargement). *Südosteuropa Mitteilungen* 46, no. 2 (2006): 15–27.

Baker, James A., 3rd. *The Politics of Diplomacy: Revolution, War, and Peace, 1989–1992* New York: Putnam, 1995.

Balcerowicz, Leszek. "Fallacies and Other Lessons." *Economic Policy* (December 1994): 18–50.

———. "The Interplay between Economic and Political Transition." *Polish Quarterly of International Affairs* (Summer–Autumn 1996): 9–28.

Balkan Colleges Foundation. "The Image of the Other: Analysis of the High-School Textbooks in History from the Balkan Countries." Sofia, 1998.

Banac, Ivo. *The National Question in Yugoslavia: Origins, History, Politics.* Cornell University Press, 1984, 1994.

———. "The Last Days of Bosnia?" Interview. *Boston Review* (February–March 1994). www.bostonreview.net.

Barry, Charles. "NATO's Combined Joint Task Forces in Theory and Practice." *Survival* 38, no. 1 (Spring 1996): 81–97.

Bassiouni, M. Cherif, chairman. "Final Report of the United Nations Commission of Experts Established Pursuant to Security Council Resolution 780 (1992)." Annex 6— part 1, "Study of the Battle and Siege of Sarajevo." S/1994/674/Add.2, vol. 2. New York: United Nations, May 27, 1994. www.ess.uwe.ac.uk.

Batt, Judy. "The Question of Serbia." Chaillot Paper 81. Paris: EU Institute for Security Studies, August 2005. www.iss-eu.org/chaillot.

Begovic, Boris, and others. *Corruption at the Customs: Combating Corruption at the Customs Administration.* Belgrade: Center for Liberal-Democratic Studies, 2002. http://unpan1.un.org.

Berdal, Mats, and Monica Serrano, eds. *Transnational Organized Crime and International Security: Business as Usual?* Boulder, Colo.: Lynne Rienner, 2002.

Berger, Samuel R., and Brent Scowcroft, co-chairs. "In the Wake of War: Improving U.S. Post-Conflict Capabilities." Independent Task Force Report 55. Council on Foreign Relations, September 6, 2005.

von Beyme, Klaus. "Institutional Engineering and Transition to Democracy." In *Democratic Consolidation in Eastern Europe,* vol. 1, *Institutional Engineering,* edited by Jan Zielonka, pp. 3–24. Oxford University Press, 2001.

Bildt, Carl. *Peace Journey: The Struggle for Peace in Bosnia.* London: Weidenfeld and Nicolson, 1998.

Bilmes, Linda, and Joseph Stiglitz. "The Economic Costs of the Iraq War." Working Paper 12054. Cambridge, Mass.: National Bureau of Economic Research, February 2006. www.nber.org.

Biserko, Sonja. *Human Rights in the Shadow of Nationalism, Serbia 2002.* Belgrade: Helsinki Committee for Human Rights in Serbia, 2003.

———. "The Hague Coercion." Belgrade: Helsinki Committee for Human Rights in Serbia, no date (apparently Spring 2005). www.helsinki.org.yu.

Bisha, Etleva, ed.. *Albanian Armed Forces in Photos: The History.* Tirana: Albanian Defense Ministry, no date (c. 2003).

Bose, Sumantra. *Bosnia after Dayton: Nationalist Partition and International Intervention.* London: Hurst, 2002.

Branczik, Amelia, and William L. Nash. "Forgotten Intervention? What the United States Needs to Do in the Western Balkans." Special Report 8. Council on Foreign Relations, June 2005.

Braud, Pierre-Antoine, and Giovanni Grevi. "The EU Mission in Aceh: Implementing Peace." Occasional Paper 61. Paris: EU Institute for Security Studies, December 2005. www.iss-eu.org.

Brcic, Ivan. "Der Zerfall Jugoslawiens aus der Sicht des Kroatisch-Serbischen Historiker-dialogs" (Yugoslavia's disintegration in the view of the Croat-Serb historians' dialogue). *Ost-West Gegeninformationen* 17, no. 4 (2005): 40–43.

"Brcko Law Revision Commission, Chairman's Final Report." December 31, 2001. www.esiweb.org/bridges/bosnia/BLRC_ChairmansRep.pdf (September 12, 2005).

Brown, J. F. *Hopes and Shadows: Eastern Europe after Communism.* Duke University Press, 1994.

Brunnbauer, Ulf. "The Consequences of Identity Politics: Security Dilemmas in the Republic of Macedonia." Paper presented at the convention of the Association for the Study of Nationalities. April 11–13, 2002.

Buchenau, Klaus. "Die Serbische Orthodoxe Kirche seit 1996: Eine Chronik" (The Serbian orthodox church since 1996: A chronicle). No date (given to the author by Buchenau on February 3, 2004).

———. "Svetosavlje und Pravoslavlje." (St. Sava-ism and orthodoxy). No date (given to the author by Buchenau on February 3, 2004).

———. "Was ist nur falsch gelaufen? Kritische Überlegungen zum Kirche-Staat-Verhältnis im sozialistischen Jugoslawien" (What went wrong? Reflections on the church-state relationship in socialist Yugoslavia.) No date (given to the author by Buchenau on February 3, 2004).

———. "Divine Justice and the ICTY: An Orthodox and Catholic Perspective." Draft. No date (given to the author by Buchenau on April 7, 2006).

Bujosevic, Dragan, and Ivan Radavanovic. *October 5: A 24-Hour Coup.* 2nd ed. Belgrade: Media Center, 2001.

Burns, R. Nicholas. Statement before the House Committee on International Relations. May 18, 2005. www.state.gov/p/2005/46471.htm.

———. "Ten Years after Dayton: Balkan Stability and the Kosovo Question." Remarks presented at the Woodrow Wilson International Center for Scholars. Washington, May 19, 2005.

Busek, Erhard. "Five Years of Stability Pact for South Eastern Europe: Achievements and Challenges Ahead." Discussion Paper 70. London School of Economics, Centre for the Study of Global Governance, March 2004. www.lse.ac.uk.

Calic, Marie-Janine. "Standards and Status." *Transatlantic Internationale Politik* 6, no. 1 (Spring 2005): 80–83.

Caplan, Richard. *Europe and the Recognition of New States in Yugoslavia.* Cambridge University Press, 2005.

———. *International Governance of War-Torn Territories: Rule and Reconstruction.* Oxford University Press, 2005.

Carnegie Endowment for International Peace. *Report of the International Commission to Inquire into the Causes and Conduct of the Balkan Wars.* Washington, 1914.

Carothers, Thomas. *Assessing Democracy Assistance: The Case of Romania.* Washington: Carnegie Endowment for International Peace, 1996.

———. *Critical Mission: Essays on Democracy Promotion.* Washington: Carnegie Endowment for International Peace, 2004.

———. *Promoting Rule of Law Abroad: In Search of Knowledge.* Washington: Carnegie Endowment for International Peace, 2006.

Carothers, Thomas, and Marina Ottaway, eds. *Uncharted Journey: Promoting Democracy in the Middle East.* Washington: Carnegie Endowment for International Peace, 2005.

Center for the Study of Democracy. "Preparing for EU Accession Negotiations." Sofia, 1999. All CSD studies available at www.csd.bg.

———. "The Role of Political Parties in Accession to the EU." Sofia, 1999.

———. "Social Policy Aspects of Bulgaria's EU Accession." Sofia, 1999.

———. "Smuggling in Southeast Europe." Sofia, 2002.

———. "Corruption Assessment Report 2003." Sofia, 2004.

———. "Partners in Crime: The Risks of Symbiosis between the Security Sector and Organized Crime in Southeast Europe." Sofia, 2004.

———. "Weapons under Scrutiny: Implementing Arms Export Controls and Combating Small Arms Proliferation in Bulgaria." Sofia, 2004.

———. "Anti-Corruption Reforms in Bulgaria." Sofia, 2005.

———. "Corruption and Tax Compliance: Policy and Administration Challenges." Sofia, 2005.

———. "Crime Trends in Bulgaria: Police Statistics and Victimization Surveys." Sofia, 2005.

———. "Development of the Second National Anti-Corruption Strategy for Bulgaria." Sofia, 2005.

———. "Judicial Reform: The Prosecution Office and Investigation Authorities in the Context of EU Membership." Sofia, 2005/06.

———. "Crime Trends in Bulgaria 2000–2005." Sofia, 2006.

———. "Development of the Second National Anti-Corruption Strategy for Bulgaria." CSD Brief 7. Sofia, January 2006.

Center for European Policy Studies. "The Reluctant Debutante: The European Union as Promoter of Democracy in Its Neighbourhood." CEPS Working Documents 223. Brussels, July 2005. http://shop.ceps.be.

Chollet, Derek. *The Road to the Dayton Accords: A Study in American Statecraft.* New York: Palgrave Macmillan, 2005.

———. "Dayton at 10." *Transatlantic Internationale Politik* 6, no. 4 (Winter 2005): 18–23.

Cilluffo, Frank, and George Salmoiraghi. "And the Winner Is . . . the Albanian Mafia." *Washington Quarterly* 22, no. 4 (Autumn 1999): 21–25.

Clark, Wesley K. *Waging Modern War.* New York: Public Affairs, 2001.

Cobban, Helena. "Think Again: International Courts." *Foreign Policy,* no. 153 (March–April 2006): 22–28.

Colovic, Ivan. *The Politics of Symbol in Serbia: Essays in Political Anthropology.* London: Hurst, 2002.

———. "Culture, Nation and Territory." On the website of the Bosnia Institute, London. www.bosnia.org.uk.

Colson, Aurélien J. "The Logic of Peace and the Logic of Justice." *International Relations* 15, no. 1 (April 2000): 51–62.

Contact Group. "Guiding Principles of the Contact Group for a Settlement of the Status of Kosovo." November 2005. www.unosek.org.

Cooper, Robert. "The Post-Modern State and the World Order." London: Demos, 1996.

Covey, Jock, Michael J. Dziedzic, and Leonard R. Hawley, eds. *The Quest for Viable Peace: International Intervention and Strategies for Conflict Transformation.* Washington: U.S. Institute of Peace Press, 2005.

Crampton, R. J. *The Balkans since the Second World War.* New York: Longman, 2002.

Crawford, Beverly. "German Foreign Policy and European Political Cooperation: The Diplomatic Recognition of Croatia." *German Politics and Society* 13, no. 2 (Summer 1995).

Crocker, Bathsheba. "Kosovo: Learning to Leverage 'Liberator' Status." In *Winning the Peace: An American Strategy for Post-Conflict Reconstruction,* edited by Robert C. Orr, pp. 193–209. Washington: Center for Strategic and International Studies Press.

"Crunch Time for Kosovo: Imposing a Solution?" *Strategic Comments* (International Institute for Strategic Studies) 11, no. 3 (May 2005).

Cviic, Christopher. "Kosovo 1945–2005." *International Affairs* 81, no. 4 (July 2005): 851–60.

———. "Throne and Altar in Croatia." *The Tablet* (July 19, 1997). www.thetablet.co.uk.

Cvijanovic, Zeljko. "Hague Tribunal Prosecutor Carla Del Ponte Storms Out of Meeting with President Kostunica." New York: Global Policy Forum, January 24, 2001. www.globalpolicy.org.

Daalder, Ivo H., and Michael E. O'Hanlon. *Winning Ugly: NATO's War to Save Kosovo.* Brookings, 2000.

Dahl, Robert. *Polyarchy: Participation and Opposition.* Yale University Press, 1971.

Dawisha, Karen, and Bruce Parrott, eds. *Politics, Power and the Struggle for Democracy in South-East Europe.* Cambridge University Press, 1997.

Diamond, Larry. "Is the Third Wave Over?" *Journal of Democracy* 7, no. 3 (1996): 20–37.

Djilas, Aleksa. "Funeral Oration for Yugoslavia: An Imaginary Dialogue with Western Friends." In *Yugoslavism: Histories of a Failed Idea, 1918–1992,* edited by Dejan Djokic, pp. 317–33. London: Hurst, 2003.

Djokic, Dejan, ed. *Yugoslavism: Histories of a Failed Idea 1918–1992.* London: Hurst, 2003.

Dobbins, James F. "America's Role in Nation-Building: From Germany to Iraq." *Survival* 45, no. 4 (Winter 2003–04): 87–109.

———. *America's Role in Nation-Building: From Germany to Iraq.* Santa Monica, Calif.: RAND, 2003.

Dragovic-Soso, Jasna. *"Saviours of the Nation": Serbia's Intellectual Opposition and the Revival of Nationalism.* London: Hurst, 2002.

Duenwald, Christoph, Nikolay Gueorguiev, and Andrea Schaechter. "Too Much of a Good Thing? Credit Booms in Bulgaria, Romania, and Ukraine." *Beyond Transition* (World Bank) 16, no. 3 (July–September 2005).

Eberhart, Helmut, and Karl Kaser, eds. *Albanien: Stammesleben zwischen Tradition und Moderne* (Albania: tribal life between the traditional and the modern. Vienna: Böhlau, 1995.

Ebnöther, Anja H., and Philipp Fluri, eds. *After Intervention: Public Security Management in Post-Conflict Societies: From Intervention to Sustainable Local Ownership.* Geneva: Geneva Centre for the Democratic Control of Armed Forces, 2005. www.dcaf.ch.

Eide, Kai. "Report on the Situation in Kosovo." New York: United Nations, November 17, 2004. http://daccessdds.un.org.

———. "A Comprehensive Review of the Situation in Kosovo." New York: United Nations, October 7, 2005. http://daccessdds.un.org.

Ekéus, Rolf. "Establishing a Multi-ethnic Society in Kosovo." *Südosteuropa Mitteilungen* 45, no. 3 (2005): 50–54.

Elster, Jon, Claus Offe, and Ulrich K. Preuss. *Institutional Design in Post-Communist Societies: Rebuilding the Ship at Sea.* Cambridge University Press, 1997.

Emerson, Michael, and Gergana Noutcheva. "Europeanization as a Gravity Model of Democratisation." CEPS Working Document 214. Brussels: Center for European Policy Studies, November 2004. http://shop.ceps.be.

European Commission. "The Declaration of the Zagreb Summit." Brussels, November 24, 2000. All European Commission documents available at http://europa.eu.int.

———. "Albania—Stabilisation and Association Report." Brussels, 2002.

———. "Opinion on the Application of Croatia for Membership of the European Union." Brussels, April 20, 2004.

———. "Albania 2005 Progress Report." Brussels, November 9, 2005.

———. "Analytical Report for the Opinion on the Application from the Former Yugoslav Republic of Macedonia for EU Membership." Brussels, November 9, 2005.

———. "Bulgaria 2005 Comprehensive Monitoring Report." Brussels, October 25, 2005.

———. "Comprehensive Monitoring Report on the State of Preparedness for EU Membership of Bulgaria and Romania." Brussels, October 25, 2005.

———. "Opinion on the Application from the Former Yugoslav Republic of Macedonia for Membership of the European Union." Brussels, November 9, 2005.

———. "Proposal for a Council Decision on the Principles, Priorities and Conditions Contained in the European Partnership with the Former Yugoslav Republic of Macedonia." SEC (2005) 1425. Brussels, November 9, 2005.

———. "Romania 2005 Comprehensive Monitoring Report." Brussels, October 25, 2005.

———. "2005 Enlargement Strategy Paper." Brussels, November 9, 2005.

———. "Relations between the EU and the former Yugoslav Republic of Macedonia." Brussels, various dates (constantly updated).

European Commission, Directorate General for Economic and Financial Affairs. "The Western Balkans in Transition." Enlargement Papers 23. December 2004.

———. "European Economy, Progress towards Meeting the Economic Criteria for Accession: 2005 Country Assessment." Enlargement Papers 26. Brussels, November 2005.

———. "Enlargement, Two Years After: An Economic Evaluation." Occasional Paper 24. Brussels, May 2006.

European Commission, Directorate General for Energy and Transport. "Trans-European Transit Network: TEN-T Priority Axes and Projects." Brussels, various dates (constantly updated).

European Commission, Directorate General for External Relations. "CARDS Programme: Albania Country Strategy Paper 2002–2006." Brussels, November 30, 2001.

European Commission and Council of Europe. CARPO Regional Project, "Situation Report on Organised and Economic Crime in South-eastern Europe." Strasbourg, August 2005. Earlier Situation Reports at www.coe.int/T/E/Legal_Affairs.

European Commission—World Bank Joint Office for South East Europe. "How Much Money Is Being Given?" No date (apparently late 2005). www.seerecon.org.

European Council. "Declaration on Kosovo." In "Luxembourg Presidency Conclusions of the European Council—16–17 June 2005," annex 3, pp. 33–35. June 17, 2005. www.eu2005.lu.

———. "EU Military Operation in Former Yugoslav Republic of Macedonia." http://ue.eu.int (accessed January 14, 2006).

European Council, Western Balkans Summit. "Salzburg EU/Western Balkans Joint Press Statement." March 11, 2006.

European Parliament. "Resolution on the Extent of Romania's Readiness for Accession to the European Union (2005/2205(INI))." Text adopted at the sitting of December 15, 2005. www.europarl.eu.int.

———. "Resolution on the State of Preparedness for EU Membership of Bulgaria (2005/2204(INI))." Text adopted at the Sitting of December 15, 2005. www.europarl.eu.int.

———. "Resolution on the Commission's 2005 Enlargement Strategy Paper." March 16, 2006. www.europarl.europa.eu.

European Stability Iniative. "The Other Macedonian Conflict." Discussion Paper. Brussels, Berlin, and Istanbul, February 20, 2002. www.auswaertiges-amt.de; all other ESI reports available at www.esiweb.org.

———. "After the Bonn Powers—Open Letter to Lord Ashdown." Brussels, Berlin, and Istanbul, July 16, 2003.

———. "The Lausanne Principle: Multiethnicity, Territory and the Future of Kosovo's Serbs." Brussels, Berlin, and Istanbul, June 7, 2004.

———. "A Post-Industrial Future? Economy and Society in Mitrovica and Zvecan." Conference held at Wilton Park, U.K. January 30–1 February 1, 2004.

———. "Post-Industrial Society and the Authoritarian Temptation." Brussels, Berlin, and Istanbul, October 11, 2004.

———. "Recommendations from Wilton Park Conference." Brussels, Berlin, and Istanbul, June 10, 2004.

———. "Waiting for a Miracle? The Politics of Constitutional Change in Bosnia and Herzegovina." Brussels, Berlin, and Istanbul, February 3, 2004.

———. "Member State Building and the Helsinki Moment." January 13, 2005.

Europol. *Annual Report.* 2003 and 2004. www.europol.eu.int.

Feldman, Lily Gardner, ed. *Cooperation or Competition? American, European Union and German Policies in the Balkans.* Washington: American Institute for Contemporary German Studies, 2001.

Friedman, Francine. *Bosnia and Herzegovina: A Polity on the Brink.* London: Routledge, 2004.

Fukuyama, Francis. *The End of History and the Last Man.* New York: Free Press, 1992.

———. *State-Building: Governance and World Order in the 21st Century.* Cornell University Press, 2004.

———. "After Neoconservatism." *New York Times Magazine,* February 19, 2006. www.nytimes.com.

———. *After the Neocons: America at the Crossroads.* London: Profile, 2006.

"The Future of the Balkans." *Strategic Comments* (International Institute for Strategic Studies) 11, no. 9 (November 2005).

Gabanyi, Anneli. "Rumänien vor dem EU-Beitritt." (Romania before EU accession). Berlin: German Institute for International and Security Affairs, October 2005.

Gallagher, Tom. *Theft of a Nation: Romania since Communism.* London: Hurst, 2005.

Ganev, Venelin I. "Bulgaria: The (Ir)Relevance of Post-Communist Constitutionalism." In *Democratic Consolidation in Eastern Europe,* vol. 1, *Institutional Engineering,* edited by Jan Zielonka, pp. 186–211. Oxford University Press, 2001.

Garton Ash, Timothy. "Is There a Good Terrorist?" *New York Review of Books* 48, no. 19 (November 2001).

Gelazis, Nida, and Martin C. Sletzinger. "Kosovo: Mission Not Yet Accomplished." *Wilson Quarterly* 29, no. 4 (Autumn 2005): 35–41.

Geremek, Bronislaw. "Civil Society and the Present Age." Triangle Park, N.C.: National Humanities Center, 1992. www.nhc.rtp.nc.us.

Glenny, Misha. *The Balkans 1804–1999: Nationalism, War and the Great Powers.* London: Granta, 1999.

Gligorov, Vladimir. "Balkan Transition." *European Balkan Observer* (Belgrade Centre for European Integration and the Vienna Institute for International Economic Studies) 3, no. 2 (October 2005). www.wiiw.ac.at.

———. "Western Balkans Economic Development since Thessaloniki 2003." Vienna: Vienna Institute for International Economic Studies, March 7, 2006. www.wiiw.ac.at.

Gordon, Philip H. "Europe's Uncommon Foreign Policy." *International Security* 22, no. 3 (Winter 1997–98): 74–100.

Gordy, Eric. *The Culture of Power in Serbia: Nationalism and the Destruction of Alternatives.* Pennsylvania State University Press, 1999.

Gounev, Philip. "Stabilizing Macedonia: Conflict Prevention, Development and Organized Crime." *Journal of International Affairs* (Columbia University) 57, no. 1 (Fall 2003): 229–40.

Gow, James. *The Serbian Project and Its Adversaries: A Strategy of War Crimes.* London: Hurst: 2003.

Grgic, Borut. "Endgame in the Balkans." *Transatlantic Internationale Politik* 6, no. 4 (Winter 2005): 11–17.

Gross, Peter, and Vladimir Tismaneanu. "The End of Postcommunism in Romania." *Journal of Democracy* 16, no. 2 (April 2005).

Grün, Michaela. "Rechtsradikale Massenmobilisierung und 'radikale Kontinuität' in Rumanien" (Mobilization of right radicals and "radical continuity"). *Osteuropa,* no. 3 (2002): 293–305.

Gutman, Roy. *A Witness to Genocide.* New York: Lisa Drew Books, 1993.

Hänggi, Heiner, and Fred Tanner. "Promoting Security Sector Governance in the EU's Neighbourhood." Chaillot Paper 80. Paris: EU Institute for Security Studies, July 2005. www.iss-eu-org/chaillot.

Hagan, John. *Justice in the Balkans* (University of Chicago Press, 2003).

Halperin, Morton H., Joseph T. Siegle, and Michael M. Weinstein. *The Democratic Advantage: How Democracies Promote Prosperity and Peace.* New York: Council on Foreign Relations, 2005.

Hansen, Annika S. "From Congo to Kosovo: Civilian Police in Peace Operations." Adelphi Paper 343. London: International Institute fir Strategic Studies, May 2002.

Haradinaj, Ramush, with Bardh Hamzaj. *A Narrative about War and Freedom (Dialog with the Commander Ramush Haradinaj).* Pristina: Zeri, 2000.

Hardt, John P. "European Union Accession, May 2004: A Mixed Blessing" *NewsNet* (American Association for the Advancement of Slavic Studies) 44, no. 5 (October 2004).

Haupt, Christian, and Jeff Fitzgerald. "Negotiations on Defence Reform in Bosnia and Herzegovina." In *Eighth Workshop of the Study Group Regional Stability in South East Europe,* pp. 153–72. Vienna: National Defence Academy, 2004.

Helsinki Committee for Human Rights in Serbia. *Human Rights and Accountability: Serbia 2003.* Belgrade: Zagorac, 2004.

Helsinki Committee of Bosnia and Herzegovina. "Report on the Status of Human Rights in Bosnia and Herzegovina (Analysis for Period January–December 2004)." No date (apparently January 2005). www.bh-hchr.org.

Hitchins, Keith. *The Identity of Romania*. Bucharest: Encyclopaedic Publishing House, 2003.

Hockenos, Paul. *Homeland Calling: Exile Patriotism and the Balkan Wars*. Cornell University Press, 2003.

Holbrooke, Richard. *To End a War*. New York: Random House, 1998.

Hughes, James, Gwendolyn Sasse, and Claire Gordon. "Conditionality and Compliance in the EU's Eastward Enlargement." *Journal of Common Market Studies* 42, no. 3 (September 2004): 523–51.

Human Rights Watch. "Federal Republic of Yugoslavia: Abuses against Serbs and Roma in the New Kosovo." August 1999. All HRW reports available at www.hrw.org.

———. "World Report 2000." 2000.

———. "Bulgaria Approves Long-Awaited Arms Trade Reforms." *HRW Monthly Email Update* (September 2002).

———. "Bulgaria: Weapons Trade to Be Restrained: Joint Human Rights Watch and Bulgarian Helsinki Committee Statement." July 16, 2002.

———. "Reforming Bulgaria's Arms Trade: An Update." July 3, 2002.

———. "Balkans: Local Courts Currently Unprepared to Try War Crimes." October 14, 2004.

———. "Justice at Risk." *Human Rights Watch* 16, no. 7(d) (October 2004).

———. "The Real State of War Crimes Prosecutions in Croatia, Response to an Article in Vjesnik." October 30, 2004.

———. "Bosnian Serb Republic Takes First Steps to Justice." March 16, 2006.

———. "A Chance for Justice? War Crime Prosecutions in Bosnia's Serb Republic." March 16, 2006.

———. "Looking for Justice: The War Crimes Chamber in Bosnia and Herzegovina." February 2006.

———. "Memorandum on the Western Balkans Prepared for EU Foreign Ministers' Informal Meeting, Salzburg, March 10–11, 2006." March 7, 2006.

Huntington, Samuel P. "Will More Countries Become Democratic?" *Political Science Quarterly* 99, no. 2 (1984): 193–218.

———. *The Third Wave: Democratization in the Late Twentieth Century*. Oklahoma University Press, 1991.

Ignatieff, Michael. *Virtual War: Kosovo and Beyond*. New York: Metropolitan, 2000.

Ilchev, Ivan. "Minorities in Bulgaria According to History Textbooks Used in Bulgarian Schools." *Südosteuropa Mitteilungen*, no. 2 (2003): 67–77.

Imholz, Kathleen. "States of Emergency as Pretexts for Gagging the Press." *East European Constitutional Review* (New York University) 6, no. 4 (Fall 1997). www.law.nyu.edu.

———. "Note on the Albanian Private Media Law." *Post-Soviet Media Law and Policy Newsletter*, no. 50 (November 1, 1998). www.vii.org.

Independent International Commission on Kosovo. *Kosovo Report*. Oxford University Press, 2000.

Interior Ministers of Southeastern Europe. "Joint Declaration, High Level Meeting of Ministers of Interior and of Security and Senior Officials of Governments and Administrations from South-eastern Europe on the Regional Strategy on Tools against Organised and Economic Crime." Brijuni, Croatia, September 23, 2005.

———. "Regional Strategy on Tools against Organised and Economic Crime with Project Area Specific Actions." Brijuni, Croatia, September 23, 2005.

International Center for Migration Policy Development. "Definition of a Blue Border Management System in Albania." Vienna, Spring 2005. www.icmpd.org.

International Crisis Group. "The Albanian Question in Macedonia: Implications of the Kosovo Conflict for Inter-Ethnic Relations in Macedonia." Brussels, August 11, 1998. All ICG reports available at www.crisisgroup.org.

———. "Too Little Too Late: Implementation of the Sarajevo Declaration." September 9, 1998.

———. "Macedonia: Towards Destabilisation?" May 21, 1999.

———. "The State of Albania." January 6, 1999.

———. "Albania: State of the Nation." March 1, 2000.

———. "Macedonia's Ethnic Albanians: Bridging the Gulf." August 2, 2000.

———. *Reality Demands: Documenting Violations of International Humanitarian Law in Kosovo 1999.* 2000.

———. "After Milosevic: A Practical Agenda for Lasting Balkans Peace." April 2, 2001.

———. "Albania: The State of the Nation." May 25, 2001.

———. "Albania's Parliamentary Elections 2001." August 23, 2001.

———. "Bin Laden and the Balkans: The Politics of Anti-Terrorism." November 9, 2001.

———. "Macedonia: Filling the Security Vacuum." September 8, 2001.

———. "Macedonia: The Last Chance for Peace." June 20, 2001.

———. "Macedonia: Still Sliding." July 27, 2001.

———. "Macedonia: War on Hold." August 15, 2001.

———. "The Macedonian Question: Reform or Rebellion?" April 5, 2001.

———. "Macedonia's Name: Why the Dispute Matters and How to Resolve It." December 10, 2001.

———. "Montenegro: Resolving the Independence Deadlock." August 1, 2001.

———. "Montenegro: Settling for Independence?" March 28, 2001.

———. "No Early Exit: NATO's Continuing Challenge in Bosnia." May 22, 2001.

———. "Turning Strife to Advantage: A Blueprint to Integrate the Croats in Bosnia and Herzegovina." March 20, 2001.

———. "The Wages of Sin: Confronting Republika Srpska." October 8, 2001.

———. "Bosnia's Alliance for (Smallish) Change." August 2, 2002.

———. "Implementing Equality: The 'Constituent Peoples' Decision in Bosnia and Herzegovina." April 16, 2002.

———. "Moving Macedonia toward Self-Sufficiency: A New Security Approach for NATO and the EU." November 15, 2002.

———. "Policing the Police in Bosnia: A Further Reform Agenda." May 10, 2002.

———. "UNMIK's Kosovo Albatross: Tackling Division in Mitrovica." June 3, 2002.

———. "Bosnia's Brcko: Getting In, Getting On and Getting Out." June 2, 2003.

———. "Macedonia: No Room for Complacency." October 23, 2003.

———. "A Marriage of Inconvenience: Montenegro 2003." April 16, 2003.

———. "EUFOR: Changing Bosnia's Security Arrangements." June 29, 2004.

———. "Macedonia: Make or Break." August 3, 2004.

———. "Pan-Albanianism: How Big a Threat to Balkan Stability?" February 25, 2004.

———. "Bosnia's Stalled Police Reform: No Progress, No EU." September 2005.

———. "Bridging Kosovo's Mitrovica Divide." September 13, 2005.

———. "Collapse in Kosovo." April 22, 2005.

———. "Kosovo: Toward Final Status." January 24, 2005.

———. "Kosovo after Haradinaj." May 26, 2005.

———. "Macedonia: Not Out of the Woods Yet." February 25, 2005.

———. "Montenegro's Independence Drive." Brussels, December 7, 2005.

———. "Serbia: Spinning Its Wheels." May 23, 2005.

———. "Kosovo: The Challenge of Transition." February 17, 2006.

———. "Macedonia: Wobbling toward Europe." January 12, 2006.

———. "Montenegro's Referendum." Update Briefing. May 30, 2006.

International Monetary Fund. "Bulgaria: Report on the Observance of Standards and Codes—Fiscal Transparency Module." IMF Country Report 05/300. Washington: August 2005. www.imf.org.

Institute for War and Peace Reporting. *Ohrid and Beyond: A Cross-Ethnic Investigation into the Macedonian Crisis.* London, 2002.

Jacoby, Wade. *The Enlargement of the European Union and NATO: Ordering from the Menu in Central Europe.* Cambridge University Press, 2004.

———. "External Influences on Postcommunist Transformations: A Review Essay." *World Politics* (forthcoming).

Jelavich, Barbara. *History of the Balkans: Twentieth Century.* Cambridge University Press, 1983.

Joetze, Günter. *Der Letzte Krieg in Europa? Das Kosovo und die Deutsche Politik* (The last war in Europe? Kosovo and German policy). Munich: DVA, 2001.

Judah, Tim. *The Serbs.* Yale University Press, 1997.

———. "Croatia Reborn." *New York Review of Books* 47, no. 13 (August 2000).

———. "Greater Albania?" *New York Review of Books* 48, no. 8 (May 2001).

———. *Kosovo: War and Revenge.* Yale University Press, 2002.

———. "The Fog of Justice." *New York Review of Books* 51, no. 1 (January 2004).

———. "Defining Kosovo." ISN Security Watch. Carried on Kosovareport blog, October 10, 2005. http://kosovareport.blogspot.com.

Judt, Tony. "Romania: Bottom of the Heap." *New York Review of Books* 48, no. 17 (November 2001): 41–45.

Kadare, Ismail. *Broken April.* Lanham, Md.: New Amsterdam Books, 1990.

Kaminski, Bartlomiej, and Francis Ng. "Bulgaria's Integration into the Pan-European Economy and Industrial Restructuring." Policy Research Working Paper 3863. World Bank, March 2006. www-wds.worldbank.org.

Kaplan, Robert. *Balkan Ghosts: A Journey through History.* New York: St. Martin's, 1993.

Kaser, Karl. "Religionszugehörigkeit und Ethnizität der albanischen Bevölkerung im südöstlichen Europa: Verhandlungsspielräume und ihre Grenzen" (Religious affiliation and ethnicity of the Albanian population in southeast Europe: Room for negotiation and its limits). No date.

Kerr, Rachel. *The International Criminal Tribunal for the Former Yugoslavia: A Study in Law, Politics and Diplomacy.* Oxford University Press, 2004.

Klarin, Mirko. "The Tribunal's Four Battles." *Journal of International Criminal Justice* 2 (2004): 546–57.

Knaus, Gerald, and Felix Martin. "Lessons from Bosnia: Travails of the European Raj." *Journal of Democracy* 14, no. 3 (July 2003).

Knaus, Gerald, and Nicholas Whyte. "Debate: Does the International Presence in the Balkans Require Radical Restructuring?" *NATO Review* (Winter 2004). www.nato.int.

Kola, Paulin. *The Search for Greater Albania.* London: Hurst, 2003.

Kostovicova, Denisa, and Vesna Bojicic-Dzelilovic, eds. *Austrian Presidency of the EU: Regional Approaches to the Balkans.* Vienna: Center for the Study of Global Governance, Center for European Integration Strategies, and the Renner Institute, 2006.

Kramer, Jane. "Painting the Town." *New Yorker,* June 27, 2005.

Krastev, Ivan. "The Balkans: Democracy without Choices." *Journal of Democracy* 13, no. 3 (July 2002): 39–53.

Krygier, Martin. "Traps for Young Players in Times of Transition." *East European Constitutional Review* 8, no. 4 (Fall 1999). www.imf.org.

Kupchan, Charles A. "Independence for Kosovo." *Foreign Affairs* 84, no. 6 (November–December 2005).

Kusic, Sinisa. "Ende der Warteschleife: Kroatien nach Aufnahme der EU-Beitrittsverhandlungen" (End of the holding pattern: Croatia after the opening of EU accession negotiations). *Südosteuropa Mitteilungen* 46, no. 2 (2006): 28–41.

Lampe, John R. *Balkans into Southeastern Europe.* London: Palgrave Macmillan, 2006.

Libal, Michael. "The Balkan Dilemma." *Harvard International Review* 18, no. 2 (Spring 1996).

———. *Limits of Persuasion: Germany and the Yugoslav Crisis, 1991–1992.* Westport, Conn.: Praeger, 1997.

Linz, Juan J., and Alfred Stepan. *Problems of Democratic Transition and Consolidation: Southern Europe, South America and Post-Communist Europe.* Johns Hopkins University Press, 1996.

Lipset, Martin, and Jason Lakin. *The Democratic Century.* University of Oklahoma Press, 2004.

Locher, James R., 3rd, and Michael Donley. "Reforming Bosnia and Herzegovina's Defence Institutions." *NATO Review* (Winter 2004). www.nato.int.

Lukas, Zdenek, and Josef Pöschl. "Landwirtschaft der MOEL im Zeichen des EU-Beitritts" (Agriculture of central and east European lands). *Osteuropa Wirtschaft* 49, no. 3 (September 2004): 211–36.

Malcolm, Noel. *Bosnia: A Short History.* New York University Press, 1996.

Mansfield, Edward D., and Jack Snyder. *Electing to Fight: Why Emerging Democracies Go to War.* MIT Press, 2005.

Markovic, Zoran M. "Die Nation: Opfer und Rache" (The nation: Victim and revenge). In *Serbiens Weg in den Krieg: Kollektive Erinnerung, nationale Formierung und ideologische Aufrüstung* (Serbia's road to war: Collective memory, national formation and ideological rearmament), edited by Thomas Bremer, Nebojsa Popov, and Heinz-Günther Stobbe, pp. 319–37. Berlin: Berlin Verlag, 1998.

Mazowiecki, Tadeusz. *The Situation of Human Rights in the Territory of the Former Yugoslavia.* A48/92/S/25341. New York: United Nations, February 26, 1993. http://documents-dds-ny.un.org.

McDonald, Gabrielle Kirk. "Problems, Obstacles and Achievements of the ICTY." *Journal of International Criminal Justice* 2 (2004): 558–71.

Menzel, Peter. "Conclusion: *Millets,* States, and National Identities." *Nationalities Papers* 28, no. 1 (March 2000).

van Meurs, Wim. "Kosovo's Fifth Anniversary—On the Road to Nowhere?" CAP Working Paper. Munich: Center for Applied Political Research, March 2004. www.cap.lmu.de.

van Meurs, Wim, and Stefani Weiss. "Qualifying (for) Sovereignty: Kosovo's Post-Status Status and the Status of EU Conditionality." Discussion Paper. Gütersloh: Bertelsmann Foundation, December 6, 2005. www.cap-lmu.de.

Meyer, Edward C., and William L. Nash. "Balkans 2010." Report of an Independent Task Force. Council on Foreign Relations, November 2002.

Minchev, Ognyan, and others. "Security and Reconstruction of Southeastern Europe: A Policy Outlook from the Region." Sofia: Institute for Regional and International Studies, no date. www.iris-bg.org (accessed August 27, 2004).

Mundis, Daryl A., and Fergal Gaynor. "Current Developments at the Ad Hoc International Criminal Tribunals." *Journal of International Criminal Justice* 2 (2004): 642–98.

Mungiu, Alina. *Die Rumänen nach '89* (The Romanians after '89). Bucharest: InterGraf, 1995.

Mungiu-Pippidi, Alina. "Reinventing the Peasants: Local State Capture in Post-Communist Europe." *Romanian Journal of Political Science* 3, no.2 (Winter 2003): 23–38. www.sar.org.ro.

———. "Revisiting Fatalistic Political Cultures." *Romanian Journal of Political Science* 3, no. 1 (Spring 2003): 90–121.

———. "The Coalition for a Clean Parliament." *Journal of Democracy* 16, no. 2 (April 2005): 154–55.

Mungiu-Pippidi, Alina, and Ivan Krastev. *Nationalism after Communism: Lessons Learned.* Budapest, Central European University Press, 2004.

Nash, William L. *"Forgotten Intervention? What the United States Needs to Do in the Western Balkans."* Special Report. Council on Foreign Relations, June 30, 2005.

Nederlands Instituut voor Oorlogsdocumentatie (NIOD, Netherlands Institute for War Documention). "Summary for the Press of Report Requested by Netherlands Government, 'Srebrenica, a "safe" area.'" April 10, 2002. www.srebrenica.nl.

Nikova, Ekaterina. "Comparing the Incomparable: Japan and the Balkans." *SRC English Newsletters* (Slavic Research Center, Hokkaido), no date (but Spring 2000). http://src-h.slav.hokudai.ac.jp.

Norris, John. *Collision Course: NATO, Russia, and Kosovo.* Westport, Conn.: Praeger, 2005.

Nye, Joseph S., Jr. *Soft Power: The Means to Success in World Politics.* New York: Public Affairs, 2004.

Oakley, Robert B., Michael J. Dziedzic, and Eliot M. Goldberg, eds. *Policing the New World Disorder: Peace Operations and Public Security.* National Defense University Press, 1998. www.ndu.edu.

O'Donnell, Guillermo, Philippe C. Schmitter, and Laurence Whitehead. *Transitions from Authoritarian Rule.* Johns Hopkins University Press, 1986.

Offe, Claus. "Das Dilemma der Gleichzeitigkeit. Demokratisierung und Marktwirtschaft in Osteuropa" (The dilemma of simultaneity: Democratization and market economy in eastern Europe). *Merkur* 45, no. 4 (1991): 279–92.

Office of Russian and European Analysis. *Baltic Battlegrounds: A Military History of the Yugoslav Conflict, 1990–1995.* Vol. 1. U.S. Central Intelligence Agency, May 2002.

Ogata, Sadako. *The Turbulent Decade.* New York: W. W. Norton, 2005.

O'Neill, William G. *Kosovo: An Unfinished Peace.* Boulder, Colo.: Lynne Rienner, 2002.

Organization for Security and Cooperation in Europe, Office for Democratic Institutions and Human Rights. "Observation of the Parliamentary Elections Held in the Republic of Albania, May 26 and June 2, 1996." Warsaw, June 1996. www.osce.org.

———. "Republic of Albania Local Government Elections, 1 and 15 October 2000." Warsaw, December 11, 2000. www.osce.org.

———. "Republic of Albania Parliamentary Elections, 24 June–10 August 2001, Final Report." Warsaw, October 11, 2001. www.osce.org.

———. "Republic of Albania Parliamentary Elections, 3 July 2005, Election Observation Mission Report." Warsaw, November 7, 2005. http://web.amnesty.org.

Di Palma, Giuseppe. *To Craft Democracies: An Essay on Democratic Transitions.* University of California Press, 1990.

Percival, Mark. "Judicial Reform: An Imperative for the New Government." *Vivid* (December 2004). www.vivid.ro.

Petroska-Beska, Violeta, and Mirjana Najcevska. "Macedonia: Understanding History, Preventing Future Conflict." Special Report 115. Washington: U.S. Institute of Peace, February 2004.

Pettifer, James. *Albania and Kosovo Blue Guide.* New York: W. W. Norton, 2001.

———. "Albanian Election 2005—A New Ruling Elite?" U.K. Defence Academy, Conflict Studies Research Center, October 2005.

———. ed. *The New Macedonian Question.* London: Palgrave, 2001.

———. "Ali Ahmeti and the New Albanian Political Party in FYROM." U.K. Defence Academy, Conflict Studies Research Center, July 1, 2002. www.da.mod.uk/CSRC.

———. *Kosova Express.* University of Wisconsin Press, 2005.

Philippi, Paul. "Transylvania—Short History of the Region: The German and Hungarian Minority." *Accent: Community Colleges for Europe,* no. 2 (2003): 25–36. www.acc. eu.org.

Pond, Elizabeth. "Kosovo: Catalyst for Europe." *Washington Quarterly* 22, no. 4 (1999): 77–92.

———. "Reinventing Bulgaria." *Washington Quarterly* 22, no. 3 (1999): 39–53.

———. "Romania: Better Late than Never." *Washington Quarterly* 24, no. 2 (2001): 35–43.

———. "Nation-Building in the Balkans." Washington: American Institute for Contemporary German Studies, 2002.

———. *The Rebirth of Europe.* Rev. ed. Brookings, 2002.

———. "Kosovo and Serbia after the French Non." *Washington Quarterly* 28, no. 4 (Autumn 2005): 19–36.

Povrzanovic, Maja. "Ethnography of a War: Croatia 1991–92." *Anthropology of East Europe Review* 11, nos. 1–2 (Autumn 1993). http://condor.depaul.edu.

Power, Samantha. *"A Problem from Hell": America and the Age of Genocide.* New York: Basic Books, 2002.

Przeworski, Adam. *Democracy and the Market: Political and Economic Reforms in Eastern Europe and Latin America.* Cambridge University Press, 1991.

Przeworski, Adam, and Fernando Limongi. "Modernization: Theories and Facts." *World Politics* 49, no. 2 (January 1997): 155–83.

Purdue Scholars' Initiative. No dates, but all written c. 2005–06. Accessed at www. cla.purdue.edu/academic/history/facstaff/Ingrao/si/scholars.htm.

———. Allcock, John B., and others, eds. "The International Criminal Tribunal for the Former Yugoslavia." Team 10.

———. Bokovoy, Melissa, and Momcilo Pavlovic, eds. "Kosovo under Autonomy (1974–1990)." Team 1.

———. Gavrilovic, Darko, and Charles Ingrao, eds. "The Safe Areas (1992–1995)." Team 6.

———. Gow, James, and Miroslav Hadzic, eds. "US/NATO Intervention (1998–99)." Team 9.

———. Janjic, Dusan, and Matjaz Klemencic. "International Community and the FRY/Belligerents (1989–95)." Team 5.

————. Ramet, Sabrina, and Latinka Perovic, eds. "The Dissolution of Yugoslavia: Competing Narratives of Resentment and Blame (1986–1991)." Team 2.

————. Roksandić, Drago, and Gale Stokes, eds. "Independence and the Fate of Minorities (1991–92)." Team 3.

Rabinbach, Anson. "Raphael Lemkin's Concept of Genocide." *Transatlantic Internationale Politik* 6, no. 1 (Spring 2005): 70–75.

Radic, Radmila. "Religion in a Multinational State: The Case of Yugoslavia." In *Yugoslavism: Histories of a Failed Idea 1918–1992,* edited by Dejan Djokic, pp. 196–207. London: Hurst, 2003.

Ragaru, Nadege. "Islam in Post-Communist Bulgaria: An Aborted 'Clash of Civilizations'?" *Nationalities Papers* 29, no. 2 (2001): 293–324.

Ramet, Sabrina P. *Balkan Babel: The Disintegration of Yugoslavia from the Death of Tito to the War for Kosovo.* 3rd ed. Boulder, Colo.: Westview, 1999.

————. *Thinking about Yugoslavia: Scholarly Debates about the Yugoslav Breakup and the Wars in Bosnia and Kosovo.* Cambridge University Press, 2005.

————. "The Politics of the Serbian Orthodox Church." In *Religija i Politika u Centralnoj i Jugoistocnoj Evropi* (Religion and politics in central and southeast Europe), edited by Sabrina P. Ramet. Belgrade: Filip Visnjic, forthcoming.

Ramet, Sabrina P., and Letty Coffin. "German Foreign Policy toward the Yugoslav Successor States." *Problems of Post-Communism* 48, no. 1 (January–February 2001): 48–64.

Rathbun, Brian C. *Partisan Interventions: European Party Politics and Peace Enforcement in the Balkans.* Cornell University Press, 2004.

Reljic, Dusan. "Serbien Kommt Nicht zur Ruhe" (Serbia does not come to rest). *Linke Kommunalpolitik,* no. 137 (May–June 2004): 36–38.

————. "Kosovo—ein Prüfstein für die EU" (Kosovo—A test for the EU). SWP-Aktuell 14. Berlin: German Institute for International and Security Affairs, March 2006.

Richmond, Oliver. *The Transformation of Peace.* Basingstoke, U.K.: Palgrave, 2005.

Robinson, Patrick L. "Rough Edges in the Alignment of Legal Systems in the Proceedings at the ICTY." *Journal of International Criminal Justice* 3, no. 5 (2005): 1037–58.

Rohde, David. *Endgame: The Betrayal and Fall of Srebrenica, Europe's Worst Massacre since World War II.* New York: Farrar, Straus and Giroux, 1997.

Rusinow, Dennison. *The Yugoslav Experiment 1948–1974.* Berkeley: University of California Press, 1977.

SAR (Romanian Academic Society). "How to Understand Corruption in Romania." In "Policy Warning and Forecast Report, Elections 2004 Edition," pp. 4–10. Bucharest, 2004. www.sar.org.ro.

————. "Tacitly from the Top, Local Governments Will Remain Weak." Policy Warning Report. Bucharest, June 2004. www.sar.org.ro.

Savin, Adrian. "The Political Economy of Corruption in Transition and the Pressure of Globalization." *Romanian Journal of Political Science,* vol. 3, no. 1 (Spring 2003): 148–58.

Schabas, William A. *Genocide in International Law: The Crime of Crimes.* Cambridge University Press, 2000.

Schäfer, Michael. "Kosovo 2005 aus Deutscher Sicht" (Kosovo 2005 in the German view). *Südosteuropa Mitteilungen* 45, no. 3 (2005): 37–49.

Schimmelfennig, Frank, and Ulrich Sedelmeier, eds. *The Europeanization of Central and Eastern Europe.* Cornell University Press, 2005.

Schmidt, Klaus. "Strengthening Peace and Stability through Police Assistance in South East Europe: The Case of Albania." No date (apparently 2006). www.bmlv.gv.at.

Schmitter, Philippe. "Dangers and Dilemmas of Democracy." *Journal of Democracy* 5, no. 2 (1994): 57–74.

Schmunk, Michael. "Die Deutschen Provincial Reconstruction Teams: Ein neues Instrument zum Nation-Building" (The German provincial reconstruction teams: A new instrument for nation building). SWP-Studie 2005/S 33. Berlin: German Institute for International and Security Affairs, November 2005.

Schönfeld, Roland. "Bosnien-Herzegowina zwischen Nachkrieg und Selbstverantwortung" (Bosnia-Herzegovina between postwar state and responsibility). *Südosteuropa Mitteilungen* 45, no. 1 (2005): 26–41.

Schrag, Minna. "Lessons Learned from ICTY Experience." *Journal of International Criminal Justice* 2 (2004): pp. 427–34.

Schrameyer, Klaus. "Makedonien: das Neue Gesetz über die Territoriale Organisation und das Referendum vom 7. November 2004" (Macedonia: the new law on the territorial organization and the referendum of 7 November 2004). *Südosteuropa Mitteilungen* 45, no. 1 (2005): 12–24.

Schrieder, Gertrud R., Jürgen Munz, and Raimund Jehle. "Rural Regional Development in Transition Economics: The Case of Romania." *Europe-Asia Studies* 52, no. 7 (2000): 1213–35.

Schröder, Almut. "Der Beitrag internationaler Richter und Staatsanwälte zur Entwicklung der Rechtsstaatlichkeit im Kosovo" (The contribution of international judges and prosecutors to the development of rule of law in Kosovo). ZIF Analyse. Berlin: Center for International Peace Operations, August 2004. www.zif-berlin.org.

Schwarz-Schilling, Christian. "Bosnia's Way Forward." *Transatlantic Internationale Politik* 7, no. 1 (Spring 2006): 84–86.

Sell, Louis. *Slobodan Milosevic and the Destruction of Yugoslavia.* Duke University Press, 2002.

Serwer, Daniel. "Kosovo: Current and Future Status." Testimony before the U.S House of Representatives, Committee on International Relations. May 18, 2005. www.usip.org.

Sherr, James. "Ukraine's Most Dangerous Hour." *Transatlantic Internationale Politik* 5, no. 1 (Spring 2005): 65–69.

Siani-Davies, Peter. *The Romanian Revolution of December 1989.* Cornell University Press, 2005.

Sigerus, Emil, and Beatrice Ungar, eds. *Chronik der Stadt Hermannstadt 1100–1929* (Chronicle of the city Hermannstadt 1100–1929). Hermannstadt: Honterus, 2000 (1930).

Silber, Laura, and Allan Little. *Yugoslavia: Death of a Nation.* TV Books, 1995, 1996.

Simms, Brendan. *Unfinest Hour: Britain and the Destruction of Bosnia.* London: Penguin, 2001.

Smith, Rupert. *The Utility of Force: The Art of War in the Modern World.* London: Allen Lane, 2005.

Smolar, Alexander. "Leadership and Postcommunist Transition." *Transatlantic Internationale Politik* 6, no. 3 (Fall 2004): 20–25.

Solana, Javier. "The EU—More Like a Molecule than an Atom." Interview with author and *IP* team, Brussels, April 12, 2005. *Transatlantic Internationale Politik* 6, no. 2 (Spring 2005): 4–9.

Sommers, William. "Brcko District: Experiment to Experience." Paper prepared for the tenth annual conference of NISPAcee. Krakow, Poland, April 25–27, 2002. www.esiweb.org.

Southeast European Joint History Project. "Phase 4: History Teacher Training Project, Serbia and Montenegro." Thessaloniki, no date. www.see-jhp.org (accessed November 11, 2005).

Spendzharova, Aneta Borislavova. "Bringing Europe In? The Impact of EU Conditionality on Bulgarian and Romanian Politics." *Southeast European Politics* 4, nos. 2–3 (November 2003): 141–56.

Staar, Richard F., ed. *1990 Yearbook on International Communist Affairs.* Stanford, Calif.: Hoover Institution Press, 1990.

Stability Pact for South Eastern Europe, Working Table 3: Security Initiative against Organised Crime. "Draft Programme and Priorities 2006." October 20, 2005. www.stabilitypact.org.

———. "Progress Report of the Initiative to Fight Organised Crime by the Chairman of the SPOC Board." Presented at the meeting of Working Table 3, Prague. November 15, 2005. www.stabilitypact.org.

Stan, Lavinia. "Spies, Files and Lies: Explaining the Failure of Access to Securitate Files." *Communist and Post-Communist Studies* 37 (2004): 341–59.

Stan, Lavinia, and Lucian Turcescu. "The Romanian Orthodox Church and Post-Communist Democratisation." *Europe-Asia Studies* 52, no. 8 (2000): 1467–88.

Stavrianos, L. S. *The Balkans since 1453.* New York University Press, 2000.

Stegherr, Marc. "Kosovska Mitrovica—interethnischer Brennpunkt des Kosovo" (Kosovska Mitrovica—Interethnic focus of Kosovo). *Südosteuropa Mitteilungen* 45, no. 3 (2005): 72–81.

Stobbe, Heinz-Günther, ed. *Serbiens Weg in den Krieg, Kollektive Erinnerung, Nationale Formierung und Ideologische Aufrüstung* (Serbia's road to war: Collective memory, national formation, and ideological rearmament). Berlin: Berlin Verlag, 1998.

Sudetic, Chuck. *Blood and Vengeance.* New York: Penguin, 1999.

Suljagic, Emir. *Postcards from the Grave.* London: Saqi, in association with the Bosnian Institute, 2005.

Surtees, Rebecca. "Second Annual Report on Victims of Trafficking in South-eastern Europe." International Organization for Migration, 2005. www.iom.int.

Swoboda, Hannes. "Die Politik des Europäischen Parlaments zu Südosteuropa" (European parliament policy toward southeastern Europe). *Ost-West Gegeninformationen* 17, no. 4 (2005): 8–12.

Tismaneanu, Vladimir. *Reinventing Politics: Eastern Europe from Stalin to Havel.* New York: Simon and Schuster, 2001.

Tisne, Martin, and Daniel Smilov. *From the Ground Up: Assessing the Record of Anticorruption Assistance in Southeastern Europe: A Regional Initiative of the Soros Foundations Network in Southeastern Europe.* Budapest: Central European University, Center for Policy Studies, 2004. www.ceu.hu/cps.

Todorova, Maria. *Imagining the Balkans.* Oxford University Press, 1997.

Transparency International. "Country Report for Romania." Berlin, 2005. (Covering 2004.) www.globalcorruptionreport.org.

———. "Transparency International Corruption Perception Barometer." Berlin, 2004. www.transparency.org.

———. "Global Corruption Report." Berlin, 2005. www.globalcorruptionreport.org.

Trofimov, Jaroslav. *Faith at War: A Journey on the Frontlines of Islam.* New York: Henry Holt, 2005.

Ucen, Peter, and Jan Erik Surotchak, eds. *Why We Lost: Explaining the Rise and Fall of the Center-Right Parties in Central Europe 1996–2002.* Bratislava: International Republic Institute, 2005.

Ungureanu, Mihai-Razvan. "Romania's Priorities in Foreign Policy." *Transatlantic Internationale Politik* 6, no. 2 (Summer 2005): 10–13.

United Nations. "Final Report of the Commission of Experts Established Pursuant to SCR 780 (1992)." S/1994/674. New York, May 27, 1994. www.his.com.

———. "Report of the Secretary-General on the United Nations Interim Administration Mission in Kosovo." UNSC S/2004/348. New York, April 30, 2004. http://daccess-ods.un.org.

———. "UN 2005 World Summit Outcome." Final document. New York, September 15, 2005. www.un.org.

UN Development Program. "Albanian Human Development Report 2000." New York, 2000. www.al.undp.org.

UN Office on Drugs and Crime. "Seventh United Nations Survey of Crime Trends and Operations of Criminal Justice Systems." New York, 2001. (Covering 1998–2000.) www.nationmaster.com.

U.S. Department of Justice. "Report to Congress from Attorney General Alberto R. Gonzales on U.S. Government Efforts to Combat Trafficking in Persons in Fiscal Year 2004." July 2005. www.usdoj.gov.

U.S. Department of State. "Romania—Country Reports on Human Rights Practices." 2004. www.state.gov.

Vachudova, Milada Anna. *Europe Undivided: Democracy, Leverage, and Integration after Communism.* Oxford University Press, 2005.

Vejvoda, Ivan. "Bosnia-Herzegovina: Unfinished Business." Testimony before the U.S. House of Representatives. April 6, 2005. www.gmfus.org.

———. "Serbia after Four Years of Transition." In "The Western Balkans: Moving On," edited by Judy Batt, pp. 37–51. Chaillot Paper 70. Paris: EU Institute for Security Studies, October 2004. www.iss-eu.org/chaillot.

Vickers, Miranda. *The Albanians: A Modern History.* London: I. B. Tauris, 1999.

Vickers, Miranda, and James Pettifer. *Albania: From Anarchy to a Balkan Identity.* New York University Press, 1997.

Vienna Institute for International Economic Studies. "Economic Data SEE." Vienna, December 2005. www.wiiw.ac.at.

Vulliamy, Ed. *Seasons in Hell: Understanding Bosnia's War.* New York: St. Martin's, 1994.

Wald, Patricia M. "ICTY Judicial Proceedings: An Appraisal from Within." *Journal of International Criminal Justice* 2 (2004): 466–73.

Walston, Scott, and Katrina Kosec. "The Economic Costs of the War in Iraq." Working Paper 05-19. American Enterprise Institute and Brookings, September 2005. http://aei-brookings.org.

Walzer, Michael. *Arguing about War.* Yale University Press, 2004.

———. "Human Rights in Global Society." *Transatlantic Internationale Politik* 6, no. 1 (Spring 2005): 4–13.

Watts, Larry L. "The Crisis in Romanian Civil-Military Relations." *Problems of Post-Communism* (July–August 2001): 14–26.

Weiler, J. H. H. "The Transformation of Europe." *Yale Law Journal* 100, no. 8 (1991): 2403–83.

Weller, Marc. *The Crisis in Kosovo 1989–1999, International Documents and Analysis.* Vol. 1. Cambridge: Documents and Analysis Publishing, 1999.

Williams, Paul E. "International Peacekeeping: The Challenges of State-Building and Regionalization." *International Affairs* 81, no.1 (January 2005): 163–74.

Wisler, Dominique. "The Police Reform in Bosnia and Herzegovina." In *After Intervention: Public Security Management in Post-Conflict Societies: From Intervention to Sustainable Local Ownership,* edited by Anja H. Ebnöther and Philipp Fluri, pp. 139–60. Geneva: Geneva Centre for the Democratic Control of Armed Forces, 2005. www.dcaf.ch.

Woehrel, Steven. "Kosovo's Future Status and U.S. Policy." Congressional Research Service, January 9, 2006. www.cfr.org.

Woodward, Susan L. *Balkan Tragedy: Chaos and Dissolution after the Cold War.* Brookings, 1995.

World Bank. "Project Appraisal Document on a Proposed Loan in the Amount of Euro 110.0 Million (US$130.0 Million Equivalent) to Romania for a Judicial Reform Project." November 22, 2005. www-wds.worldbank.org.

———. "Romania—Judicial Reform Project." 2005. www-wds.worldbank.org.

———. "Entering the Union: European Accession and Capacity-Building Priorities." February 2006. www-wds.worldbank.org.

Zaikos, Nikos. "The Interim Accord: Prospects and Developments in Accordance with International Law." In *Athens-Skopje: An Uneasy Symbiosis (1995–2002),* edited by Evangelos Kofos and Vlasis Vlasidis, pp. 21–54. Athens: ELIAMEP, 2005.

Zakaria, Fareed. "The Rise of Illiberal Democracy." *Foreign Affairs* 76, no. 6 (November–December 1997): 22-43.

Zhelyazkova, Antonina. "One Year after NATO Air Raids—The Frustration and Isolation of a European Nation." May 2000.

Zielonka, Jan, ed. *Democratic Consolidation in Eastern Europe.* Vol. 1, *Institutional Engineering.* Oxford University Press, 2001.

Zielonka, Jan, and Alex Pravda, eds. *Democratic Consolidation in Eastern Europe.* Vol. 2, *International and Transnational Factors.* Oxford University Press, 2001.

Zimmermann, Warren. *Origins of a Catastrophe.* New York: Times Books, 1996.

Interviews

All interviews took place in person in the country listed, unless otherwise noted. Those interviewed who requested that their names not be made public are not included. Those interviewed in the 1960s and 1980s are also omitted.

Albania

Annen, Hans-Peter   German ambassador to Albania: April 15, 2004

Berisha, Sali   Leader of Democratic Party, former president and future prime minister, April 15, 2004

Bouthier, Rita   Project adviser, Goethe Institute, Tirana: April 15, 2004

Dervishi, Dashnor   Regional general director, Foreign Ministry: April 13, 2004

Gjatoja, Gen. Ruzhdie   Adviser to the president from the Defense Academy, April 14, 2004

Hoxha, Maj. Gen. Luan   Deputy chief of staff, Defense Ministry: April 13, 2004

Hroni, Sotiraq   Executive director, Institute for Democracy and Mediation: June 5, 2005 (Berlin)

Ibrahimi, Valter   Director, Department for European Integration: April 13, 2004

Imholz, Kathleen   Adviser to the Government of Albania (on legal issues): April 16, 2004

Jeffrey, James Franklin   U.S. ambassador: April 16, 2004

Kadare, Ismail   Novelist: April 14, 2004

Majko, Pandeli   Defense minister: April 13, 2004

Moisiu, Alfred   President: April 16, 2004

Rama, Edi   Mayor of Tirana: April 14, 2004

Thiel, Elke   Visiting professor of political science (from Germany), University of Tirana: April 17, 2004

Veliaj, Erion   Founder of Mjaft civic protest movement: April 15, 2004

Bosnia-Herzegovina (BiH)

Alagic, Fahid   Chief of police (Bosniak), Konjic: November 7, 2002

Alen X.   Student from Sandzak, Sarajevo University: November 6, 2002

Ashdown, Lord Paddy   High representative of the international community and of the EU: November 18, 2003

Azizuddin, Tariq   Pakistani ambassador: November 18, 2003

Banda, Izet   President of the Serbian Social Democratic Party (SDP), Brcko branch: May 28, 2004

Baydur, Sina   Turkish ambassador: November 17, 2003; May 25, 2004; December 7, 2004

Bazdar, Suad   Student, Sarajevo University: November 6, 2002

Beecroft, Robert   Chief of Organization for Security and Cooperation in Europe (OSCE) Mission: November 6, 2002; November 16, 2003; May 23, 2004; and October 12, 2005 (Washington)

Begtasevic, Sadeta   Education officer, OSCE Mostar Regional Center: November 20, 2003

Bond, Clifford   U.S. ambassador: November 8, 2002; November 19, 2003; October 11, 2004 (Washington)

Bozalo, Simo   Chief of staff of RS member of presidency: June 24, 2006

Ceric, Mustafa ef.   Reis-ul-ulema (grand mufti), Sarajevo: November 18, 2003

Covic, Dragan   Chairman and Croat member of the collective presidency, later sacked by Paddy Ashdown pending corruption trial: November 4, 2002; November 20, 2003

Damjanac, Branko   Mayor of Brcko, 2003–04: May 28, 2004; December 4, 2004

Dimitrijevic, Vedrana   Press spokesperson, OSCE, Banja Luka: December 9, 2004

Djapo, Mirsad   President, Brcko assembly 1997–2004 and mayor of Brcko 2005: May 28, 2004

Djurovic, Nedjo   Journalist, Radio BD, TV Hit, and Radio BH1, Brcko: May 29, 2004; December 4, 2004

Finci, Jakob   Member of the Jewish community, Sarajevo, and of the interfaith dialogue in BiH: November 8, 2002; November 17, 2003; May 26, 2004; December 6, 2004

Fraser, John   Director, National Democratic Institute, Banja Luka office: December 9, 2004

Frederiksen, Sven   Commissioner, EU Police Mission, Sarajevo: November 19, 2003

Fromentin-Kuljaninovic, Claire   EU representative, Banja Luka: December 10, 2004

Gobeljic, Mustafa   Imam of the Brcko Islamic Community: May 28, 2004

Gojic, Igor   Editor, *Novi Reporter,* Banja Luka: December 8, 2004

Hajric, Mirza   Chief of staff to Alija Izetbegovic, then director, Foreign Investment Promotion Agency, then adviser, Office of the Executive Director, World Bank: May 27, 2004; December 7, 2004; October 11, 2005 (Washington); February 16, 2006 (by telephone)

Humphreys, Michael B.   Chief of European Commission delegation: May 27, 2004; December 6, 2004

Ivanic, Mladen   Foreign minister: November 19, 2003; May 27, 2004; February 11, 2005 (Munich)

Jensen, Allan   Head of EU Customs and Fiscal Assistance Office (CAFAO), Sarajevo: November 8, 2002; November 19, 2003; May 26, 2004

Jez, Adem   Bosniak courier during the seige of Sarajevo, now owner of an upscale Sarajevo restaurant: November 20, 2003

Johnson, Susan   International supervisor, Brcko District: May 29 and December 4, 2004

Kisic, Sinisa   Mayor of Brcko 1997–2003: May 29 and 4 December 2004

von Kittlitz und Ottendorf, Arne   German ambassador: November 20, 2003; May 24, 2004

Klein, Jacques   Special representative of the secretary general, UN Mission: November 4 and 7, 2002

Kopanja, Zelko   Editor, *Nezavisne Novine*, Banja Luka: December 9, 2004

Koukakis, Mihail G.   Greek ambassador: November 18, 2003; May 25, 2004

Kremenovic, Tanja   Staff member, National Democratic Institute, Banja Luka office: December 9, 2004

Krezic, Zdravko   Deputy chief of police (Croat), Konjic: November 7, 2002

Ljubic, Mariofil   Chairman (Croat), House of Representatives: November 6, 2002

Llewellyn, Edward   Deputy to Lord Ashdown in the Office of the High Representative (OHR), Sarajevo: February 8, 2002 (Brussels); November 18, 2003; May 24, 2004; December 6, 2004

Malidzan, Vanja   Staff member, National Democratic Institute, Banja Luka office: December 9, 2004

Majinovic, Nada   President, Brcko District Judicial Commission: May 29, 2004; December 4, 2004

Maksimovic, Slavko   Serbian Orthodox priest, Brcko: May 29, 2004

Miljevic, Damir   Businessman, president of the Employers Confederation of the Republika Srpska (RS): December 8, 2004

Neskovic, Branko   Chief of staff to RS prime minister Dragan Mikerevic: December 8, 2004

Nuhanovic, Hasan   Interpreter for Dutch troops at Srebrenica, lost his parents and brother in the massacre: November 6, 2002

Osmic, Zerekijah   SDP official, Brcko: December 4, 2004

Ots, Richard P. T.   Senior business development adviser, OHR: November 20, 2003

Packett, (U.S.) Maj. Gen. Virgil, 2nd   Last non-EU commander of the Stabilization Force (SFOR): November 19, 2003; May 26, 2004

Peters, Hans Jochen   German ambassador: November 6, 2002

Potocnik, Mladen   Member of parliament, June 24, 2006

Prlic, Jadranko   President of Croat breakaway Herceg-Bosna before the Dayton Accord, later, director of the South East Institute for Strategic and International Studies, Sarajevo, and an indictee at the Hague Tribunal: November 19, 2003

Radisic, Zhivko   Serb member of the collective presidency 1998–2002: December 10, 2004

Ramljak, Vedad   Member of the "bulldozer" economic commission

Rodic, Rada   Staff member, National Democratic Institute, Banja Luka office: December 9, 2004

Serajdarian, Souren   Deputy special representative of the secretary general, UN Mission: November 7, 2002

Solaja, Milos   Head of the press center and Center for International Relations, Banja Luka: December 9, 2004

Stjepanovic, Ratko   Councilor, Brcko municipal assembly, and president, Serbian Democratic Party (SDS), Brcko branch: May 24, 2004; December 4, 2004

Studen, Ilija   Chief executive officer, Bimal, Brcko, and Seed Oil Holdings, Vienna: May 28, 2004

Sudar, Pero   Auxiliary Roman Catholic bishop, Sarajevo: May 25, 2004

Terzic, Adnan   Vice president, Party of Democratic Action (SDA): November 6, 2002

Topcagic, Osman   Vice minister and director of European integration: December 6, 2004; June 24, 2006

Vendors in markets Sarajevo

Vukicevic, Stanimir Ambassador of Serbia and Montenegro to Bosnia: November 18, 2003

Bulgaria

Atanassov, Vladimir Headmaster, The Balkan School: September 27, 1999

Bezlov, Tihomir Project coordinator (including drug study), Center for the Study of Democracy (CSD): September 14, 2004

Bezuhanova, Sasha General manager, Hewlett-Packard Bulgaria, Ltd., and vice president, Bulgarian International Business Association, Sofia: September 17, 2004

Bohlen, Avis U.S. ambassador: week of February 22, 1999

Boshkov, Alexander Deputy prime minister: week of February 22, 1999

Delia, Michael Deputy director, European Bank for Reconstruction and Development, Bulgaria: March 1, 2004

Dell, Christopher Deputy chief of mission, U.S. Embassy: September 23, 1999

Dimitrov, Konstantin Deputy foreign minister: week of February 22, 1999

Dimitrov, Philip Prime minister 1991–92, member of parliament 1991–97, later ambassador to UN, then to the United States, and director, Bulgarian Institute for Legal Development: March 3, 2004; September 13, 2004

Gounev, Philip Staff member, Center for the Study of Democracy: September 14, 2004

Gruber, Josef Director, Konrad Adenauer Foundation, Sofia office: week of February 22, 1999

Hadjihristov, Ivaylo First secretary, OSCE chairmanship: September 13, 2004

Harmandjiev, Philip Publisher, Kapital, and chief executive officer, Damianitza, Bulgaria: September 14, 2004

Ilchev, Ivan Professor and dean, Sofia University, Faculty of History: September 10, 2004 (Bonn)

Ilchev, Stanimir Chairman of the parliamentary group of the National Movement Simeon II: September 16, 2004

Ivanova, Krassimira Chief of the cabinet of the foreign minister: March 5, 2004

Kapitanova, Ginka Executive director, Foundation for Local Democratic Reforms: week of February 22, 1999

Kindermann, Harald German ambassador: March 2, 2004

Kostov, Ivan Prime minister 1997–2000, later member of parliament: week of February 22, 1999; September 15, 2004

Kourkoulas, Dimitris Ambassador and chief of European Commission delegation: March 2, 2004; September 15, 2004

Krastev, Ivan Chairman, Center for Liberal Strategies, Sofia: March 1, 2004; September 13, 2004

Lenkov, Lenko Executive director, Free and Democratic Bulgaria Foundation, Sofia: September 13, 2004

Levine, Jeffrey Deputy chief of mission, U.S. Embassy: September 14, 2004

Lingorski, Iliya First deputy minister, head of debt management and the Treasury, Finance Ministry: September 15, 2004

van Lynden, Aernout Journalist and professor, American University in Bulgaria: March 4, 2004 *van Lynden, Baroness Henriette* Dutch ambassador: March 2, 2004

Mancheva, Mila Project developer, International Organization for Migration: March 4, 2004

Miles, Richard U.S. ambassador: September 24, 1999

Minchev, Ognyan Executive director, Institute for Regional and International Studies: week of February 22, 1999; September 13, 2004

Mintchev, Emil Academic staff, Center for European Integration (ZEI), University of Bonn: September 14, 1999 (Bonn)

Mladenov, Nikolay Member of parliament for Union of Democratic Forces (UDF) and deputy chairman, European Integration Committee: September 16, 2004

Nikolova, Juliana European Institute, Sofia: March 5, 2004; September 17, 2004

Nikova, Ekaterina Professor of history, Institute of Balkan Studies, Bulgarian Academy of Sciences: March 1, 2004; September 16, 2004

Noev, Boyko Former defense minister and director, European Program, Center for the Study of Democracy: September 17, 2004

Panitza, J. D. Long-time Paris editor of the *Reader's Digest* and founder and chairman, the Free and Democratic Bulgaria Foundation, Sofia: November 8, 2005 (by telephone)

Pardew, James W. U.S. ambassador: March 1, 2004

Parvanov, Georgi Leader of the Bulgarian Socialist Party, later president: week of February 22, 1999

Passy, Solomon Vice president, Atlantic Treaty Association, later minister of foreign affairs: weeks of February 22 and September 20, 1999; March 5, 2004

Perkova, Sylvia Owner of the Two Sweetypies bakery: week of February 22, 1999

Philippov, Vladimir Foreign policy adviser to President Stoyanov: week of February 22, 1999

Popov, Stefan Chairman, Open Society Institute: September 15, 2004

Poptodorova, Elena Euroleft member of parliament, later Bulgarian ambassador to United States: week of February 22, 1999

Prohasky, George Economist and chief executive officer of Bulgarian Stock Exchange: week of February 22, 1999

Radojkovic, Cedomir Ambassador of Serbia and Montenegro: March 4, 2004; September 14, 2004

Roaf, James Resident representative, International Monetary Fund, Sofia: March 4, 2004

Shentov, Ognian Chairman, Center for the Study of Democracy, Sofia: September 14, 2004

Stanchev, Krassen Institute of Market Economics: February 29, 2004

Stanishev, Sergei Chairman of the Bulgarian Socialist Party Supreme Council and chairman of parliamentary group of the Coalition for Bulgaria, BSP, later prime minister: September 17, 2004

Stefanov, Ruslan Project coordinator, Economic Program, Center for the Study of Democracy, Sofia: September 14, 2004

Stock, Christof Second secretary, political affairs, European Commission delegation: March 2, 2004

Students at American University in Bulgaria September 22, 1999 (Blagoevgrad)

Tcherneva, Vessela Project director, International Commission on the Balkans (at Center for Liberal Strategies): March 1, 2004; September 13, 2004

Tsenkov, Emil Staff member, Center for the Study of Democracy: September 14, 2004

Tzvetanov, Valentin Deputy governor, Bulgarian National Bank: week of February 22, 1999

Vassilev, Boyko Journalist, *Panorama* program, Bulgarian National TV: September 14, 2004

Vassilev, Ilian Chairman, Agency for Foreign Investments: week of February 22, 1999

Veleva, Zinaida Director, Directorate of European Integration and Relations with International Financial Institutions, Council of Ministers: March 4, 2004

Wehmhörner, Arnold Regional representative, Friedrich Ebert Foundation: March 2, 2004

Zhelev, Zhelyu President 1990–97: September 16, 2004

Zhelyazkova, Antonina Director, International Center for Minority Studies and Intercultural Relations: weeks of February 22 and September 24, 1999; March 2, 2004; September 14, 2004

Zlatev, Ognian Head of Media Development Center: March 1, 2004

Croatia

Banac, Ivo Professor of history, Yale University, Croatian member of parliament, and president of the Liberal Party: March 29, 2004

Biskupic, Bozo Minister of Culture: March 30, 2004

Cvjetkovic-Kurelec, Vesna Croatian ambassador to Germany: March 22, 2004, January 28, 2005 (Berlin)

Dizdarevic, Zlatko Ambassador of Bosnia and Herzegovina: April 2, 2004

Fleck, Hans-Georg Head of Naumann Foundation, Zagreb office: April 2, 2004

Gjenero, Davor Journalist: March 28, 2004

Goldstein, Ivo Professor of history, Zagreb University: March 29, 2004

Grcic-Polic, Jelena Adviser to the Defense Ministry: October 29, 2004 (Sofia)

Grubisa, Damir Research fellow, Institute for International Relations, Zagreb: April 2, 2004

Hill, Nicholas Political counselor, U.S. Embassy: March 29, 2004

Klasan, Lt. Col. Vilko Defense attaché, Croatian Embassy in Berlin: January 28, 2005 (Berlin)

Konjhodzic, Indira World Bank country manager: April 1, 2004

Mesic, Stipe President: April 1, 2004

Milanovic, Zoran Foreign policy adviser to Ivica Racan, head of Social Democratic Party: March 29, 2004

Puhovski, Zarko Chairman, Helsinki Committee for Human Rights in Croatia: March 29, 2004

Pupovac, Milorad Member of parliament and vice president of the Independent Democratic Serbian Party: March 29, 2004

Pusic, Vesna Member of parliament, vice president of parliament, and president of Croatian People's Party: March 31, 2004

Rodin, Sinisa Professor of European law, Zagreb School of Law: April 1, 2004

Sanader, Ivo Prime minister: April 1, 2004

Semneby, Peter Head of OSCE Mission: April 1, 2004

Snider, Dennis Canadian ambassador: April 1, 2004

Stanicic, Mladen   Head of the Institute for International Relations, Zagreb: March 31, 2004

Weiss, Gebhardt   German ambassador: March 30, 2004

Kosovo

Arzoaallxhiu, Afrim   Deputy mayor of Prizren: July 2000

Bajrami, Agron   Editor, *Koha Ditore*: October 20 and 24, 2004

Bas Backer, Peter W. A.   Head of Netherlands Office, Pristina: June 11, 2004; October 21, 2004

Bearpack, Andrew   Deputy special representative of the UN secretary general at the UN Mission in Kosovo (UNMIK): March 6, 2002

Beqiri, Kenan   Project Coordinator, World Vision, Mitrovica: June 5, 2004

Bukoshi, Bujar   Underground Kosovar prime minister in the 1990s, later chairman of New Party of Kosova: December 2, 2003; June 10, 2004; October 24, 2004

Buchmüller, Klaus   German Federal Agency for Technical Relief, working on a project with prostitutes, Orahovac: July 2000

Fitt, James   Deputy to William Nash, Mitrovica, July 2000

Fleischer, Walter   Head of UNMIK/OSCE field office, Rahovac/Orahovac: July 2000

Gashi, Alush   Member of parliament and senior foreign policy adviser to President Rugova: December 1, 2003; June 7, 2004

Haliti, Xhavit   Member of parliament for the Democratic Party of Kosova (PDK) and member of the assembly presidency: December 1, 2003; June 9, 2004

Haradinaj, Ramush   President of Alliance for the Future of Kosova (AAK), later prime minister under the Provisional Instutitions of Self-Government in Kosovo (PISG) and an indictee at the Hague Tribunal: December 2, 2003; June 9, 2004

Haxhimusa, Rexhep   President of the Supreme Court: December 1, 2003

Haziri, Lutfi   Mayor of Gnjilane (Democratic League of Kosova, LDK) and chairman of the Association of Mayors, later minister for municipal self-government: June 10, 2004

Hecker, Lt. Col. Erich   Civil-military officer, Kosovo Force (KFOR), Prizren: July 2000

Hysa, Ylber   Executive director, Kosova Association for Civic Initiatives: December 1, 2003; June 7 and 11, 2004; October 20, 2004

Ivanovic, Oliver   Head of Serb National Council and one of the founders of the violence-prone bridge watchers in Mitrovica, later Serb member of parliament from North Mitrovica and member of the Kosovo assembly presidency: June 11, 2004

Jerliu, Naim   Member of parliament and vice president of the LDK: December 1, 2003; June 9, 2004; October 22, 2004

Jerliu, Florina   Association of Architects of Kosova: December 1, 2003

Kasapolli, Gezim   Student and interpreter for war crimes exhumations: March 7, 2002

Klasing, Hanns Christian   Press spokesman for OSCE in Mitrovica: July 2000

Königs, Tom   Deputy special representative of the UN secretary general at UNMIK: March 6, 2002

Kontovounisios, Christos   Head of Greek Liaison Office, Kosovo: June 8, 2004; October 21, 2004

von Korff, Brig. Gen. Fritz   Commander of Bundeswehr KFOR brigade: July 2000 (Prizren)

Korneck, Peter   International prosecutor, UNMIK: June 10, 2004

Krasniqi, Jakup   Minister of public services and head of PDK caucus in the assembly: December 5, 2003; June 10, 2004

Lambsdorff, Nikolaus   Deputy special representative of the UN secretary general: June 10, 2004

Lane, Dennison   District administrator, UNMIK, Vushtrri: July 2000; March 3, 2002

Ljubinko, Todorovic   Deputy ombudsperson (Serb), UNMIK: March 7, 2002

Lumezi, Nike   Deputy ombudsperson (Albanian): March 7, 2002

Lushta, Nesrin   Codirector, Kosovo Judicial Institute: March 6, 2002

McClellan, Michael   Public affairs officer, U.S. Mission to Kosovo: December 1, 2003; June 8, 2004

Menzies, John K.   Chief of U.S. Mission to Kosovo: March 5, 2002

Millotat, Maj. Gen. Christian   Commander, KFOR: March 6, 2002; also as director, Security Cooperation, Organization for Security and Cooperation in Europe in Bosnia-Herzegovina: June 23, 2006 (Bosnia)

Mulliqi, Luan   Director, Kosovo Art Gallery, Pristina: March 6, 2002

Novicki, Marek Antoni   Ombudsperson, UNMIK: December 5, 2003

Pfeiffer, Dale B.   Mission director, USAID, Kosovo: June 9, 2004

Pireva, Xhavit   Mobile telephone vendor, Pristina indoor bazaar: December 5, 2003

Polloshka, Arber   Owner of children's clothes shop, Prizren: July 2000

Radosavljevic, Nenad   Senior adviser on refugee returns to the special representative of the UN secretary general, UNMIK: December 2, 2003; June 9, 2004

Rexhepi, Bajram   Mayor of Mitrovica July 2000 and prime minister under the PISG 2002–04: December 2, 2003; June 11, 2004

Ries, Marcie   Chief of U.S. Mission to Kosovo: December 5, 2003

Roccatello, Myriam   Head of the Department of Judicial Affairs, Joint Interim Advisory Structures, UNMIK: June 10, 2004, October 22, 2004

Rondorf, Peter   Chief of German Liaison Mission: June 9, 2004; and as head of EU Enlargement and External Affairs section, German Foreign Ministry: February 9, 2005 (Berlin)

Rugova, Ibrahim   President of Kosovo and president of the LDK: December 4, 2003

Sakalis, Sophie   European Agency for Reconstruction, Operations Division, Local Government/Civil Society: June 11, 2004

Schmunk, Michael   Head of the German Liaison Office, Pristina: March 4, 2002; October 15, 2004; January 12, 2005; February 10, 2005; May 17, 2005; June 21, 2005 (2005 interviews in Berlin)

Shala, Blerim   Editor, *Zeri* newspaper: March 5, 2002; December 2, 2003; June 9, 2004

Shlapachenko, Dmitry   Political affairs officer, UNMIK: June 10, 2004; October 22, 2004

Steiner, Michael   Special representative of the UN secretary general, UNMIK: December 12, 2001 (Berlin); March 5, 2002

Surroi, Veton   Member of parliament, leader of Ora faction, and chairman, Koha Media Group: March 7, 2002; December 3, 2003; June 10, 2004; October 22, 2004

Sylva, Gjylnaze   Member of the assembly of Kosova and chairperson of the AAK parliamentary group: March 6, 2002

Tahiri, Edita   President of LDK breakaway Democratic Alternative for Kosova, which failed to win parliamentary seats in 2004 election: October 22, 2004

Thaci, Hashim   Head of PDK: December 3, 2003; June 9, 2004

Ugljaninn, Nedzat   Council for Peace and Tolerance, Mitrovica, a nongovernmental organization (NGO) promoting interethnic tolerance: June 5, 2004

Zylfiu, Albert Law student, Pristina University: March 6, 2002
Miscellaneous Serb teacher in the Serb enclave in Orahovac; grocery store manager; international officials and housebuilding and women's rights activists with NGOs in the Prizren region among others: July 2000

Macedonia

Butler, Lawrence U.S. ambassador: October 27, 2004
Cakioussis, Constantin Political adviser to Sahlin: October 29, 2004 (Sofia)
Gruevski, Nikola President of VMRO-DPMNE (Internal Macedonian Revolutionary Organization): October 26, 2004
von König, Florian Political adviser, EU Proxima police advisers: October 27, 2004
Levitin, Oleg Deputy head of UNMIK liaison office: October 27, 2004
Maragos, Vassilis Counselor, European Commission delegation: October 27, 2004
Marjanovic, Gorgi Professor of law (emeritus), Skopje University: October 25, 2004
Merseli, Nebi Correspondent, *Koha Ditore* (Pristina), Skopje: October 26, 2004
Mitreva, Ilinka Minister of foreign affairs: October 28, 2004
Nejkov, Kiril Counselor in the cabinet of the foreign minister: October 25 and 27, 2004
Nezirit, Jelal Correspondent, *Koha Ditore* (Pristina), Skopje: October 26, 2004
Sahlin, Michael Special representative of the EU, Skopje: October 26, 2004; October 29, 2004 (Sofia)
Sekerinska, Radmila Deputy prime minister for European integration: October 26, 2004
Tegovski, Jovan State counselor for EU affairs: October 25, 2004
Trajkovsky, Boris President: November 14, 2003 (Berlin)
Vakali, Heleni Deputy Greek ambassador: October 27, 2004
Xhaferi, Musa Deputy prime minister: October 26, 2004

Romania

Alexandru, Cosmin President of the Union for Reconstruction (URR), a political party of young entrepreneurs: week of December 7, 2000
Alexandrescu, Horia Editor-in-chief, *Independent*, Bucharest: February 26, 2004
Baier, Hannelore Correspondent, *ADZ* German-language newspaper, Sibiu: September 23, 2004
Blondini, Ana Cofounder of Civic Alliance NGO a month before Ceausescu was overthrown: week of December 7, 2000
Boc, Emil Member of parliament for the Democratic Party Group and later mayor of Cluj: February 24, 2004
Cakici, Yalcin Director, Regional Center for Combating Transborder Crime, Southeast European Cooperative Initiative: February 25, 2004
Chirieac, Bogdan Foreign affairs editor, *Adevarul*: week of December 7, 2000; March 14, 2002
Cioaba, Florin "King of the Gypsies," Sibiu: September 24, 2004
Cioaba, Luminatsia Author and poet, Sibiu: September 24, 2004
Ciobanu-Dordea, Aurel Law professor, lawyer, and preaccession adviser to the European Commission: February 25, 2002

Codita, Cornel Commentator and director, Institute of Strategic and International Studies, Bucharest: week of December 7, 2000; February 25, 2004

Constantinescu, Mihnea Foreign Ministry diplomat and one of the founders of the Southeast European Cooperative Initiative: March 14, 2002

Diaconescu, Christian Minister of justice: September 25, 2004

Dijmarescu, Eugen Adviser to the prime minister on economics: March 14, 2002

Fabini, Hermann Senator and designing architect of 2007 European cultural city of Sibiu (Hermannstadt): February 24, 2004

Farcas, Alexandru Minister of European integration: May 19, 2004 (Aachen); September 25, 2004 (Berlin)

Gant, Ovidiu Member of parliament and under secretary, Department for Interethnic Relations: February 24, 2004

Geoana, Mircea Foreign minister: February 24, 2004

Grasso, Vito Director, Italian Cultural Center: March 12, 2002

Gruber, Wilfried German ambassador: February 26, 2004

Habersack, Sabine Director, Konrad Adenauer Foundation, Bucharest: February 26, 2004

Henkel, Jürgen Pastor and director, Siebenbürgen Protestant Academy, Sibiu: September 23, 2004

Hiller, Armin German ambassador: March 11, 2002

Idu, Nicolae Secretary general of the European Institute of Romania: February 26, 2004; September 20, 2004; January 5, 2006 (by telephone)

Ijgyarto, Istvan Hungarian ambassador: March 11, 2002

Iliescu, Ion President: February 25, 2004

Johannis, Klaus Mayor of Sibiu since 2000: September 24, 2004

Johnson, Susan Deputy chief of mission, U.S. Embassy: March 11, 2002

Krauss, Mathias Chief executive officer, Mathias Krauss KG, Brauerei und Getränke (Munich and Grossau), Romania: September 24, 2004

Mitu, Octavian Social Democratic member of parliament: March 11, 2002

Morteanu, Madalin Programs coordinator, Romani CRISS (Roma Center for Social Intervention and Studies), Bucharest: September 20, 2004

Mozes, Sandor Deputy chief of mission in Hungarian Embassy: September 20, 2004

Orban, Leonard Deputy chief negotiator on EU accession, later chief negotiator: September 22, 2004

Petre, Zoe Vice president, Actiunea Populara, former adviser to President Constantinescu: March 11, 2002; February 25, 2004

Philippi, Paul Theologian and chairman emeritus of the Democratic Forum of Germans in Romania, Sibiu: September 23, 2004

Puscas, Vasile Chief negotiator on EU accession: February 24, 2004

Radu, Paul Freelance investigative journalist: February 22 and 23, 2004

Rauta, Emanuel Program officer, Romanian Academic Society (SAR): February 26, 2004

Rodica Paladi *magazine editors* February 25, 2004

Sabiel, Elke Head of the Friedrich Ebert Foundation, Romania: February 25, 2004

Sandor, Dorel Director, Center for Political Studies and Comparative Analysis: week of December 7, 2000; March 15, 2002; February 24, 2004; September 20, 2004

Scheele, Jonathan Chief of the Europeann Commission delegation: September 21, 2004

Serban, Liliana Security expert, Chamber of Deputies: week of December 7, 2000

Stuparu, Timotei   Member of parliament: week of December 7–13, 2000

Tanase, Stelian   Director, Civil Society Foundation, editor of the *Political Sphere*, and professor of political science: week of December 7, 2000; March 14, 2002

Thellmann, Daniel   Mayor of Mediasch, Sibiu District: September 23, 2004

Toma, Mircea   Columnist, *Academia Catavencu*: week of December 7, 2000; March 12, 2002

Ungar, Beatrice   Correspondent, *Hermannstädter Zeitung*, Sibiu: September 24, 2004

Ungureanu, Mihai Razvan   Foreign minister since December 2004: February 23, 2005 (Berlin)

Watts, Larry   Adviser to the Defense Ministry in the early 1990s: week of December 7, 2000; February 25, 2004

Serbia and Montenegro

Biserko, Sonja   Director, Helsinki Committee for Human Rights in Serbia: November 11, 2002; June 1, 2004

Barrett, Geoffrey   Chief of the European Commission delegation: June 3, 2004

Bleicker, Joachim   Deputy German ambassador: December 1, 2004

Braun, Bertram   Political counselor, U.S. Embassy: June 1, 2004

Carraciola di Vietri, Giovanni   Italian ambassador: November 23, 2003

Dacic, Ivica   President of the executive committee, Socialist Party: November 28, 2003; November 30, 2004

Dinkic, Mladjan   Former governor of Serbian central bank and a founder of G17 nongovernmental organization of economic technocrats, later finance minister: November 27, 2003

Djilas, Aleksa   Writer: November 12, 2002

Djulic, Dragana   Dean, Faculty of Civil Defense, University of Belgrade: November 11, 2002

Draskovic, Vuk   Foreign minister: December 3, 2004

Hellbach, Christian   German ambassador: November 12, 2002

Janjic, Dushan   Director, Forum for Ethnic Relations: November 11, 2002

Joksimovic, Alexandra   Assistant minister of foreign affairs: June 4, 2004

Jovanovic, Cedomir   One of the student leaders in 2000, Democratic Party (DS) vice president and deputy prime minister: November 30, 2004

Kostunica, Vojislav   President 2000–04, then prime minister, and head of Democratic Party of Serbia (DSS): December 1, 2004

Leonberger, Kurt   German ambassador: November 25, 2003; June 4, 2004

Licht, Sonja   Director, Open Society Institute, Belgrade office, then president, Belgrade Fund for Political Excellence: November 13, 2002; June 3, 2004; December 2, 2004

Lyon, James   Director, Serbia Project, International Crisis Group: December 1 and 2, 2004

Milenkovic, Alexandar   Adviser to the national coordinator of the Stability Pact for Southeast Europe, Belgrade: November 13, 2002

Milosevic, Milan   Columnist, *Vreme*: November 11, 2002

Misic, Milan   Editor-in-chief, *Politika* newspaper: November 11, 2002

Montgomery, William   U.S. ambassador: November 12, 2002; November 25, 2003

Mrgic, Susana   Deputy chief executive, G17 Plus: November 11, 2002

Niksic, Stevan   Editor, *NIN*: November 22, 2003; June 1, 2004; November 28, 2004

Polt, Michael U.S. ambassador: November 30, 2004

Presnall, Aaron Director of studies, Jefferson Institute, Belgrade: November 30, 2004

Pribicevic, Ognjen Deputy foreign minister: May 31, 2004; and as ambassador to Germany: May 19, 2005 (Berlin)

Radulovic, Dragana Department of Multilateral Relations, Foreign Ministry of Montenegro: October 29, 2004 (Sofia)

Samardzic, Slobodan Adviser on constitutional issues on President Kostunica's staff, later political adviser to Prime Minister Kostunica: November 12, 2002

Smajlovic, Ljiljana Columnist, NIN news magazine, later editor, Politika newspaper: November 24, 2003; June 1, November 29, 2004

Spasojevic, Dusan Foreign policy adviser to President Boris Tadic: December 2, 2004

Thimonier, Christian Political counselor, French Embassy, November 25, 2003; June 2, 2004

Tijanic, Aleksandr Director, RTS TV: November 27, 2003; May 31, 2004

Vejvoda, Ivan Director, Open Society Institute Belgrade office, then executive director, Balkan Trust for Democracy: November 13, 2002; November 24, 2003; June 4, 2004; November 29, 2004

Germany

Adam, Rudolf Vice president, Bundesnachrichtendienst (German intelligence agency), later president, Federal Academy for Security Policy: November 29, 2002; April 18, 2005

Altmann, Franz-Lothar Head of Western Balkan Research Group, German Institute for International and Security Affairs, Berlin, formerly deputy director of the East European Institute, Munich: August 29, 2002; March 19, 2004; November 24, 2004

Blomeyer-Bartenstein, Hans-Henning Deputy national security adviser to the German chancellor: April 30, 2003

Brey, Hansjörg Manager, Südosteuropa Gesellschaft (Southeast Europe Society): February 10, 2004 (Munich)

Cresswell, Jeremy Deputy head of mission, British Embassy: March 18, 2003; May 5, 2003; January 9, 2004

Deimel, Johanna Deputy manager, Südosteuropa Gesellschaft, Munich: February 10, 2004 (Munich)

Erler, Gernot Deputy parliamentary leader for the Social Democrat Party: May 22, 2003

Fleischer, Helge Diplomat, Romanian Embassy in Germany, later unsuccessful candidate in Romanian parliamentary elections: October 16, 2004

Gabanyi, Anneli Romanian analyst, German Institute for International and Security Affairs: February 3, 2004; September 10, 2004

Hockenos, Paul Author of Homeland Calling: Exile Patriotism and the Balkan Wars (2003): March 15, 2004

Kammerhof, Lt. Gen. Holger Commander, Bundeswehr Operations and commander of KFOR, 2002–03: March 15, 2004

Kastrup, Dieter National security adviser to Chancellor Gerhard Schröder: August 28, 2002

Lever, Paul British ambassador: May 14, 2003

Lleshaj, Col. Sander Albanian defense attaché: March 15, 2004; September 6, 2004

Mützelburg, Bernd Foreign policy and security adviser to Chancellor Schröder: March 23, 2005

Nikel, Rolf Deputy foreign policy and security adviser to Chancellor Angela Merkel: June 13, 2006

Petev, Petio Counselor, Bulgarian Embassy: February 17, 2004

Pleuger, Günter State secretary, Foreign Ministry, and ambassador to the UN: February 18, 2002; August 19, 2002; August 29, 2003; October 10, 2003 (New York)

Predescu, Brandusa Acting Romanian ambassador: March 7, 2006

Reljic, Dusan Balkan analyst, German Institute for International and Security Affairs, Berlin: May 17, 2005; November 10, 2005

Schäfer, Michael Political director, Foreign Ministry: May 8, 2003; February 16, 2004; January 24, 2005; February 28, 2005; September 14, 2005; October 27, 2005; March 1, 2006

Scharioth, Klaus State secretary, Foreign Ministry: February 6, 2003; March 24, 2003; June 2, 2003; October 7, 2003; November 4, 2003; March 19, 2004; November 24, 2004; January 5, 2005; August 24, 2005; November 4, 2005; January 18, 2006; May 24, 2006

Soos, Mario-Ingo Head of Stability Pact and Regional Cooperation in Southeastern Europe unit, Foreign Ministry: September 6, 2004

Struck, Peter Defense minister: April 10, 2003

Vierita, Adrian Romanian ambassador: February 10, 2004; September 8, 2004; December 20, 2004; June 21, 2005

United States

Ahrens, Geert German diplomat with experience in Albania, Macedonia, and Croatia, author of *Containing Ethnic Conflicts. A Mediator's Efforts in Yugoslavia 1991–96* (forthcoming), and fellow at Woodrow Wilson International Center for Scholars: April 28, 2004

Biberaj, Elez Head of Albanian section, Voice of America: 2000

Binder, David Former *New York Times* correspondent in the Balkans: April 29, 2004

Bohlen, Avis U.S. ambassador to Bulgaria, later undersecretary of state: April 25, 2002

Byrnes, Shaun Intelligence and Research, State Department: October 16, 2003; October 6, 2004

Carothers, Thomas Senior associate, Carnegie Endowment for International Peace: February 15, 2006

Dimitrov, Nikola Macedonian ambassador: October 7, 2004

Dobbins, James Director, International Security and Defense Policy Center, RAND; formerly assistant secretary of state for Europe and special adviser to the president and secretary of state for the Balkans: April 27, 2004

Dziedzic, Michael U.S. Institute of Peace: April 8, 2002; May 31, 2005

Evans, Charles Intelligence and Research, State Department: October 16, 2003

Fox, John Director, Open Society Institute, Washington office: April 24, 2002

Fried, Daniel Senior director for European and Eurasian Affairs, National Security Council: April 18, 2002; October 7, 2002; January 21, 2003; June 23, 2003; October 16, 2003; April 30, 2004

Gelbard, Robert Special representative of President Clinton for the Balkans, 1997–99: April 21, 2002; October 8, 2002 (both by telephone)

Grgic, Borut Director, Institute for Strategic Studies, Ljubljana: October 15, 2003

Haltzel, Michael Senior Staff, Senate Foreign Relations Committee: April 17, 2002 (by telephone)

Hays, Donald   U.S. Institute of Peace, formerly deputy to High Representative Ashdown in Bosnia: May 31, 2005
Holbrooke, Richard   Dayton Accords negotiator: July 11, 2006 (telephone)
Hunter, Robert   Senior adviser, RAND: October 10, 2002; April 2, 2003
Ischinger, Wolfgang   Political director, German Foreign Ministry, later German ambassador: March 31, 1999 (Germany); April 26, 2002 (Germany); April 3, 2003; September 12, 2003; October 13, 2003; April 26, 2004; October 7, 2004; May 31, 2005
Kesic, Obrad   Senior partner, TSM Global Consultants: October 7, 2004; May 31, 2005; June 5, 2005 (Germany); October 12, 2005
Markey, John   Southeast European Cooperative Initiative desk officer, State Department: April 28, 2004
Miller, Bowman   Head, Europe, Intelligence and Research, State Department: April 4, 2002; October 9, 2002; January 21, 2003; March 31, 2003; June 25, 2003; September 11, 2003; October 13, 2004; May 31, 2005; October 12, 2005
Miller, Laurel   U.S. Institute of Peace: June 1, 2005
Nash, Robert   Intelligence and Research, State Department: October 16, 2003; October 12, 2004
Nash, U.S. Maj. Gen. William (Ret.)   Successively commander of U.S. Army peacekeeping forces in Bosnia, regional UN administrator for Northern Kosovo, and General John W. Vessey Senior Fellow for Conflict Prevention and director of the Center for Preventive Action, Council on Foreign Relations: July 2000 (Mitrovica); April 5, 2002 (Washington); October 9, 2002 (Washington)
Norris, John   Special adviser to the president, International Crisis Group: May 30, 2005
O'Brien, James   Albright Group: October 14, 2002; May 31, 2005
Schulte, Gregory   Balkan desk, National Security Council: October 14, 2003
Serwer, Daniel   Director, Peace and Stability Operations and Balkans Initiative, U.S. Institute for Peace Balkan Program: October 9, 2002; October 17, 2003; April 28, 2004; October 13, 2004; June 1, 2005.
Sletzinger, Martin   Director, East European Studies, Woodrow Wilson International Center for Scholars: April 8, 2002; September 11, 2003; April 27, 2004; October 6, 2004; February 16, 2006

Other

Brolenius, Anette   Detached national expert, European Commission Directorate General for Enlargement: Brussels, April 12, 2005
Emerson, Michael   Center for European Policy Studies: Brussels, February 7, 2002
Emschermann, Rainer   Administrator for trade, econoomics, international financial institutions, European Commission Directorate General for Enlargement: Brussels, April 12, 2005
John Greenwald   Head of International Crisis Group, Brussels office: Brussels, February 5, 2002
Halki Balkan Conferences   Sponsored by the Greek Council on Foreign Relations (ELIAMEP): informal conversations with participants September 2002 and September 2003
Kursch, Donald   Deputy head of the Stability Pact: Brussels, February 8, 2002
Moran, Mary Teresa   Seconded from EU Balkans office as program officer, Office of the Coordinator of U.S. Assistance to Europe and Eurasia, U.S. State Department, then

policy officer, general coordination, European neighborhood policy coordination, European Commission Directorate General for External Relations: Washington, April 30, 2004; Brussels, April 12, 2005

Najman, Dragoljub Ambassador of Serbia and Montenegro to UNESCO: Paris, April 30, 2002

Pavret de la Rochefordiere, Christophe Deputy head of International Questions—Economic Affairs unit, European Commission Directorate General for Economic and Financial Affairs: Brussels, April 12, 2005

Petritsch, Wolfgang High representative in Sarajevo, 1999–2002: Vienna, May 11, 2006

Ruiz Calavera, Genoveva Deputy head of Serbia and Montenegro (including Kosovo) unit, European Commission Directorate General for External Relations: Brussels, April 12, 2005

Solana, Javier High representative for EU common foreign and security policy: Berlin, November 13, 2003; Brussels, April 12, 2005

Whyte, Nicholas Center for European Policy Studies: Brussels, February 7, 2002

INDEX